Theories of Psychopathology

MAN WAITING

by Sidney Goodman, (1961). Collection of the Museum of
Modern Art. Gift of Mr. and Mrs. Walter Bareiss.

Theories of Psychopathology

ESSAYS AND CRITIQUES

Edited and Introduced by

THEODORE MILLON, Ph. D.
Lehigh University

W. B. SAUNDERS COMPANY · Philadelphia and London

W. B. Saunders Company: West Washington Square
Philadelphia, Pa. 19105

12 Dyott Street
London WC1A   1DB

1835 Yonge Street
Toronto 7, Ontario

Theories of Psychopathology   SBN 0-7216-6381-8

Print No.:   4   5   6   7   8   9

Preface

Authors and editors feel called upon to present in the prefaces of their books well-reasoned justifications for their work; certainly there should be some sound rationale for contributing another volume to the surfeit of publications inundating the field. Typically, these rationales demonstrate the shortcomings of previous books and the clever manner in which the author has circumvented problems, brought matters up to date, and illuminated new directions for future work; the rationale for this present volume is no different. But it does have a less pretentious reason for its existence: no one has gathered the *diverse* viewpoints of the major theorists of psychopathology into one volume.

While researching the literature for another book, this writer was struck by the fact that no one text had been published dealing primarily with different schools of psychopathological thought. Excellent works had been written and edited contrasting *personality* theories, but none focused specifically on theories of personality *pathology*, or *abnormal* behavior. Useful volumes appeared discussing critical issues, case reports, and research methods in psychopathology, but these topics relate only peripherally to the systematic theories that generated them. In short, it seemed time to fill an important gap in our academic library, one that should have been filled years before.

The task of writing an original work in this field could not be undertaken by the editor because of prior writing commitments. The decision to bring together original papers by the major theorists should not be viewed, however, as a second-rate compromise. Original sources not only provide us with a theorist's clearest statement of his own position, but they also convey the special logic and subtlety of language that characterize the thought of the man himself. The intensity, flavor, and persuasiveness found in the writings of a primary exponent of a theory can rarely be matched by second-hand summaries.

There must be justifications for doing a book other than the fact that it had not been done before; many things that have not been done are best left undone since they accomplish no useful purpose. But as noted in the introduction, there is considerable confusion in psychopathological theory today. A dazzling array of doctrinaire concepts, propositions, and theories vie to catch the eye of the beginning student. They do not illuminate his pathway; rather, this profusion of disconnected and seemingly contradictory thought only confounds him. The impression the student comes away with is that the data and propositions of each theoretical school are inconsistent with those of other schools, that only one of these approaches is "right," and that his task is to learn which one possesses the "truth." Such an attitude can only lead him further from the truth.

It is the contention of this book that each of the major theoretical approaches makes a distinctive contribution to our understanding of that multidimensional complex of behaviors we call psychopathology. If these alternate theories can be organized in terms of their different and distinctive areas of focus, the student may learn that they are complementary and *not* contradictory approaches to the subject.

How can this intrinsically complementary character of theories be demonstrated?

The book's introductory essay asserts that diverse theorists can be grouped together in terms of the particular class of psychopathological data they emphasize. The complex phenomena included under the label of psychopathology can be, and has been, divided fruitfully into several categories of data; no single category, however, encompasses all of the multidimensional features of psychopathology. If properly divided, each of these classes of data will be complementary to the others in that together they will comprise the total body of psychopathological phenomena.

Four such classes of data have been specified; these data levels—*biophysical, intrapsychic, phenomenological,* and *behavioral*—serve as the basis for the four major categories of theoretical investigation organized in the text. Each of these theoretical levels displays a characteristic and internally consistent series of propositions regarding the *etiology and development,* the *pathological patterns,* and the *therapy* of mental disorders. Stated differently, none of these levels has failed to provide hypotheses regarding the acquisition, clinical structure, or treatment of psychopathology. These hypotheses are interconnected, not by secondary philosophical or methodological predilections, but by the kind of data they focus upon; different data result in different hypotheses. No one expects the propositions of a physicist to be the same as those of a chemist; nor should we expect those of a behaviorist to be the same as those of a phenomenologist.

It is possible for the student to read the text profitably in either of two ways, given the format within which the book has been organized. He can progress through each theoretical level as a unit and thereby obtain a unified picture of the way in which theorists utilizing that class of data approach etiology, pathological patterns, and therapy. Equally useful is a procedure in which each of the four theoretical levels is compared section by section on each of the three major topics. Thus, he may prefer to concentrate on etiology first, comparing the biophysical, intrapsychic, phenomenological, and behavioral approaches to that topic, before progressing to comparisons among theories on the pathological pattern and therapy sections.

In addition to the three topical areas of etiology, patterns, and therapy, each theoretical level is prefaced by two *orientation* papers describing the class of data and the basic philosophy guiding theorists of that persuasion. Since few theories have escaped the scrutiny of dissident investigators, a set of two papers devoted to a *critique* of each school of thought concludes each of the four theoretical sections; controversy and dissent not only enliven the literature but alert the student to the logical and methodological shortcomings of alternate theoretical approaches.

This book may serve only to whet the appetite of the serious student, since it offers but a small sample of the myriad theories that have been propounded; we have selected what we believe to be those views that have exerted a substantial influence upon investigators at work today. No doubt, new theoretical formulations will emerge in so vital and growing a field as psychopathology. We hope, however, that the basic format organized for this book, in which the data levels for theories are stressed, will remain a useful framework for appraising new work.

Many authors and publishers have permitted us to include their work; we thank them for their generosity and cooperativeness. Margaret Caffrey, medical librarian of the Allentown State Mental Hospital, was most helpful in suggesting and tracking down several difficult-to-locate references. Ann Zarinsky, departmental secretary at Lehigh University, provided me with her usual highly competent assistance. To Sally Perlis goes my appreciation not only for her expert handling of correspondence, but for her ever-present and radiant good cheer.

Theodore Millon

Contents

Introduction

    Theory in Psychopathology 1
    Theodore Millon

PART I BIOPHYSICAL THEORIES

Biophysical Theories: ORIENTATION

    Biochemistry, Genetics, and the Nature-Nurture Problem 10
    Bernice T. Eiduson, Samuel Eiduson and Edward Geller

    The Biological Approach to the Study of Personality 19
    Roger J. Williams

Biophysical Theories: ETIOLOGY AND DEVELOPMENT

    The Physiogenic and Psychogenic in Schizophrenia 32
    Eugen P. Bleuler

    The Genetics of Human Behavior 38
    Franz J. Kallmann

Biophysical Theories: PATHOLOGICAL PATTERNS

    Constitutional Psychiatry 43
    William H. Sheldon

    Schizotaxia, Schizotypy, Schizophrenia 59
    Paul E. Meehl

Biophysical Theories: THERAPY

Theories of Somatic Treatment 73
Lothar Kalinowsky and Paul Hoch

Psychopharmacologic Drugs 87
Harold E. Himwich

Biophysical Theories: CRITICAL EVALUATION

The Myth of Mental Illness 111
Thomas S. Szasz

Biochemical Theories of Schizophrenia 118
Seymour S. Kety

PART II   INTRAPSYCHIC THEORIES

Intrapsychic Theories: ORIENTATION

The Metapsychology of Instincts, Repression and
the Unconscious 140
Sigmund Freud

Psychoanalysis as a Scientific Theory 152
Heinz Hartmann

Intrapsychic Theories: ETIOLOGY AND DEVELOPMENT

On the Psychogenesis of Schizophrenia 165
Carl G. Jung

Growth and Crises 174
Erik H. Erikson

Intrapsychic Theories: PATHOLOGICAL PATTERNS

Culture and Neurosis 198
Karen Horney

Non-Productive Character Orientations 204
Erich Fromm

Intrapsychic Theories: THERAPY

Technique of Reconstructive Therapy 212
Lewis Wolberg

The Modified Psychoanalytic Treatment of Schizophrenia 217
Harry Stack Sullivan

Intrapsychic Theories: CRITICAL EVALUATION

Critique of Psychoanalytic Concepts and Theories 228
B. F. Skinner

Precision in Psychoanalysis 235
N. S. Lehrman

PART III PHENOMENOLOGICAL THEORIES

Phenomenological Theories: ORIENTATION

Existential Psychology 244
Rollo May

The Phenomenological Approach to the Problem of
Feelings and Emotions 254
F. J. J. Buytendijk

Phenomenological Theories: ETIOLOGY AND
DEVELOPMENT

A Theory of Personality 262
Carl R. Rogers

Defense and Growth 270
Abraham H. Maslow

Phenomenological Theories: PATHOLOGICAL PATTERNS

A Phenomenological Approach to Adjustment Theory 278
Arthur W. Combs

Ontological Insecurity 285
R. D. Laing

Phenomenological Theories: THERAPY

Existential Analysis and Psychotherapy 299
Ludwig Binswanger

"Daseinsanalysis" and Psychotherapy 303
Medard Boss

Phenomenological Theories: CRITICAL EVALUATION

The Phenomenological Approach in Personality
Theory: Some Critical Remarks 308
M. Brewster Smith

The Logic of the Romantic Point of View in Personology 315
Robert R. Holt

PART IV   BEHAVIORAL THEORIES

Behavioral Theories: ORIENTATION

What Is Psychotic Behavior? 324
B. F. Skinner

The Psychological Model 338
Leonard P. Ullmann and Leonard Krasner

Behavioral Theories: ETIOLOGY AND DEVELOPMENT

How Symptoms Are Learned 351
John Dollard and Neal E. Miller

Social Learning of Dependency Behavior 358
Albert Bandura and Richard H. Walters

Behavioral Theories: PATHOLOGICAL PATTERNS

Etiology of Human Neuroses 366
Joseph Wolpe

Behavioral Analysis: An Alternative to
Diagnostic Classification 375
Frederick H. Kanfer and George Saslow

Behavioral Theories: THERAPY

Learning Theory and Behaviour Therapy 388
H. J. Eysenck

Reinforcement and Punishment in the Control of
Human Behavior by Social Agencies 402
C. B. Ferster

Behavioral Theories: CRITICAL EVALUATION

A Critique of Dollard and Miller's "Personality
and Psychotherapy" 416
David Rapaport

Critique and Reformulation of "Learning-Theory"
Approaches to Psychotherapy and Neurosis 421
Louis Breger and James L. McGaugh

Introduction

Vincent Van Gogh—*Sorrow* (1882). (The Museum of Modern Art, New York.)

Theory in Psychopathology*

THEODORE MILLON

Nature was not made to suit our need for a tidy and well-ordered universe. The complexity and intricacy of the natural world make it difficult not only to establish clearcut relationships among phenomena, but to find simple ways in which these phenomena can be classified or grouped. In our desire to discover the essential order of nature we are forced to select only a few of the infinite number of elements which could be chosen; in this selection we narrow our choice only to those aspects of nature which we believe best enable us to answer the questions we pose. The elements we have chosen may be labeled, transformed, and reassembled in a variety of ways. But we must keep in mind that these labels and transformations are not "realities." The definitions, concepts, and theories scientists create are only optional tools to guide their observation and interpretation of the natural world; it is necessary to

recognize, therefore, that different concepts and theories may coexist as alternative approaches to the same basic problem. An illustration in the field of bridge design may serve to clarify this point (Hebb, 1958):

The engineer who designs a bridge must think at different levels of complexity as he works. His overall plan is in terms of spans, piers, abutments; but when he turns to the design of a particular span, he starts to think in terms of lower-order units such as the I-beam. This latter unit, however, is still quite molar; an engineer is firmly convinced that an I-beam is just a special arrangement of certain molecules, the molecule in turn being a special arrangement of electrons, protons and so forth. Now note: At a microscopic level of analysis, a bridge is nothing but a complex constellation of atomic particles; and a steel I-beam is no more than a convenient fiction, a concession to the limitations of thought and the dullness of human conception.

At another level of analysis, of course, the I-beam is an elementary unit obviously real and no fiction. At this level electrons have a purely theoretical existence, which suggests that "reality" is meaningful as designating, not some ultimate mode of being about which

*Abridged from Chapter 2 of *Modern Psychopathology*, to be published by W. B. Saunders Co.

1

there must be argument, but the mode of being which one takes for granted as the starting point of thought.

With this perspective in mind, let us look at the question, What is psychopathology? Clearly, mental disorders are expressed in a variety of ways; psychopathology is a complex phenomenon which can be approached at different levels and can be viewed from many angles. On a behavioral level, for example, disorders could be conceived of as a complicated pattern of responses to environmental stress. Phenomenologically, they could be seen as expressions of personal discomfort and anguish. Approached from a physiological viewpoint, they could be interpreted as sequences of complex neural and chemical activity. Intrapsychically, they could be organized into unconscious processes that defend against anxiety and conflict.

Given these diverse possibilities, we can readily understand why psychopathology may be approached and defined in terms of any of several levels we may wish to focus upon, and any of a variety of functions or processes we may wish to explain. Beyond this, each level or angle of approach lends itself to a number of specific theories and concepts, the usefulness of which must be gauged by their ability to help solve the particular problems and purposes for which they were created. That the subject matter of psychopathology is inherently diverse and complex is precisely the reason why we must not narrow our choice of approach to one level or one theory. Each has a legitimate and potentially fruitful contribution to make to our study. What should be clear, however, is that a theory is not "reality," that it is not an inevitable or predetermined representation of the objective world. Theories are merely optional instruments utilized in the early stages of knowledge. They serve to organize experience in a logical manner, and function as explanatory propositions by which experiences may be analyzed or inferences about them may be drawn. Their ultimate goal is the establishment of new empirical laws.

CRITERIA FOR EVALUATING THEORIES

Theories arise typically from the perceptive observations and imaginative speculations of a creative scientist. This innovator is usually quite aware of the limits and deficiencies of his "invention" and is disposed in the early stages of his speculation to modify it as he develops new observations and insights. Unfortunately, after its utility has been proven in a modest and limited way, the theory frequently acquires a specious stature. Having clarified certain ambiguities and survived initial criticisms, it begins to accumulate a coterie of disciples. These less creative thinkers tend to accept the theory wholeheartedly and espouse its superior explanatory powers and terminology throughout the scientific marketplace. They hold to its propositions tenaciously and defend it blindly and unequivocally against opposition. In time, it becomes a rigid and sacred dogma and, as a result, authority replaces the test of utility and empirical validity. Intelligent men become religious disciples; their theory is a doctrine of "truth," not a guide to the unknown.

Should we avoid theories knowing their frequent fate? The answer, of course, is no! Man will interpret his experience through either implicit or formal theories, regardless of the dangers and assumptions involved. Rather than dismissing theories as inevitable "religious doctrines," we should formulate criteria by which we can evaluate their genuine utility. There are several grounds upon which theories may be evaluated.

Simplicity and Parsimony. Many theories are shrouded in a dense cloak of words and concepts. Their structure is so opaque that assumptions may be concealed, principles may be difficult to extract, and consistent connections to the empirical world may be impossible to establish. In short, the structure of the theory is formulated more complexly than necessary.

The criteria of simplicity and parsimony require that a theory depend on a minimum number of assumptions and a minimum number of concepts. Alone, these criteria neither eliminate theoretical opaqueness nor verify the utility of a theory's propositions; they merely suggest that excess baggage be eliminated so that the central features of the theory can be seen more clearly. Theorists who prefer to formulate their ideas in a complex network of concepts and assumptions must carry the burden of proving the necessity of these components. Excess baggage invites only trouble and confusion.

Generality. Ideally, the number and extent of facts and data to which a theory may be generalized should not be limited. So comprehensive a system is, of course, neither feasible nor possible. However, many theories are constructed in their early stages to cover only the limited data from which they were generated; this first formulation often restricts its long-range or potential applicability. It is preferable, therefore, that the format and concepts of a theory be broad enough in scope to be extended to new data, should an elaboration be justified. Implicit in the criterion of generality, therefore, is the suggestion that the value of a theory may be gauged by its ability to generate new observations *after* its initial formulation. Despite the importance of this feature, it is wise to recognize that a disparity will exist between the *potential* range of a theory's applicability and its *actual* range of empirical support. Failure to keep this disparity in mind can lead only to erroneous generalizations.

Empirical Precision. The need to coordinate the concepts of a theory with observable data leads us to the criterion of empirical precision. The empirical criterion refers to the extent to which concepts can be anchored to assigned properties in the observable world; precision refers to the number of empirical phenomena to which each of these theoretical terms is connected. A problem arises when one attempts to balance the criterion of generality, already mentioned, with the criterion of empirical precision. How does one maintain empirical specificity, and thereby minimize ambiguity in language, while simultaneously freeing concepts to include a wide range of phenomena?

The frequent use of *intervening variables* in psychological theory results from the fact that each of these variables may be anchored to a variety of different empirical phenomena. By allowing a number of empirical events to be included in one concept, theorists may approach an ideal compromise between the criterion of generality, on the one hand, and explicitness, on the other.

Hypothetical constructs do not fulfill the empirical criterion; nevertheless, they often are necessary in the early stages of theory construction. Explanations of complex and unobservable processes may be either impossible or extremely cumbersome without them. Ultimately, hypothetical constructs should be coordinated to the empirical domain and transformed gradually into intervening variables. In general, then, theoretical concepts should be as precise and empirical as the current state of a field permits.

Derivable Consequences. Propositions or hypotheses may be derived by the systematic manipulation of several concepts in accordance with a series of correspondence rules. Unfortunately, these rules are either nonexistent or formulated imprecisely in most psychopathological theories. Because of this limitation, hypotheses derived from these theories must be evaluated carefully. After-the-fact "hypotheses" or "predictions" stated so imprecisely as to allow for different or even contradictory results must be avoided. When interrelationships among concepts are left ambiguous, the temptation arises to make "predictions" after the facts have been observed. The "prediction" is dressed up into an acceptable propositional form and then presented as a verification of the theory when, in fact, contradictory results could have also been "predicted" by the theory. The need for caution is clear: confidence in a theory's "predictions" must be restrained until the empirical hypotheses of a theory are unequivocal and genuinely predictive.

ORIENTATION OF THEORIES

Theories are designed as a guide to the discovery of empirical laws. Theories have a bias or *orientation* as to what kinds of laws should be sought, what empirical phenomenon should be observed, and what procedure should be used to observe these phenomena. This orientation consists, either implicitly or explicitly, of decisions made on such issues as whether to: (1) seek laws about the "unique" pattern of each individual's functioning *or* about commonalities among characteristics found in all individuals; (2) obtain data under rigorously controlled experimental procedures *or* in the settings within which events naturally occur; and (3) observe biophysical *or* intrapsychic *or* phenomenological *or* behavioral phenomena.

The data and laws produced by a theory will reflect decisions on each of these issues. Although each of the alternatives noted is a potentially fruitful approach in search of empirical laws, theorists engage in intense debates as to which of these approaches is best; the poor student wastes needless hours in trying to decide which "side" is correct. It is important to recognize at the outset that different theories ask different questions, use different procedures, and focus on different types of data. There is no "correct" choice; no rules exist in nature to tell us which methods are best or which laws are most important.

Unfortunately, the orientations of most theories are not explicit. As a result, the student is presented with a fantastic array of overlapping data and concepts which appear disconnected and contradictory and leave him dazzled and confused. Without differences in orientation clearly in mind, the student is like the young Talmudic scholar who, after immersing himself for weeks in ancient manuscripts, rose suddenly one morning, danced joyously in the streets, and shouted, "I have found the most wonderful answer; somebody please tell me the question!"

To make sense and give order to the data of his science, the student must know what kinds of laws each theory seeks to find. Only then can he construct meaning and coherence in his studies. With the goals of each theory clearly before him, he may separate them according to the laws they wish to find and compare them intelligently as to their success in answering the questions they pose in common. It should be obvious that theories seeking biochemical laws cannot be compared to theories seeking behavioral laws. And theories seeking causal sequences between past and present events should not be compared to theories seeking correlations among present events, and so on.

The student might ask at this point why different kinds of theories are needed. Cannot one theory encompass all that need be known in psychopathology? For the time being, at least, the answer must be no! At this stage of our knowledge, theories must serve as instruments to answer particular rather than universal questions. The clinician in the consulting room needs a different kind of theory to facilitate his understanding of verbal therapeutic interaction from that needed by the psychopharmacologist, who seeks to discover the effects of biochemical properties.

Recapitulating then, theories differ not only in their models, concepts, and derivation rules, but also in their orientation. This orientation is composed essentially of decisions made on three basic issues: the idiographic *or* the nomothetic approach; the experimental *or* the naturalistic approach; and different approaches in the level of data observed and conceptualized. We shall discuss next each of these three sets of alternatives.

Idiographic and Nomothetic Approaches. Some theorists seek generalizations which will hold for many individuals, whereas others are interested in the pattern with which characteristics combine within single individuals.

Typically, scientists study a specific class of phenomena until some regularity or uniformity is found which characterizes all phenomena of that class. This method, known as the *nomothetic* orientation, overlooks minor or individual variations in its search for laws common to a specific class of phenomena. Many kinds of *nomothetic* laws will be found, however, to characterize a complex organism such as man. These laws may themselves be combined in many ways; the number of combinations possible may, in fact, be infinite. The pattern with which nomothetic laws combine in particular individuals has been referred to as the *idiographic* orientation. In contrast to the nomothetic theorist, who searches for laws common to people in general, the idiographic theorist attempts to combine these laws into distinctive patterns which reflect the "uniqueness" of individuality. Both approaches ultimately are needed for scientific progress. Nevertheless, a vigorous debate has arisen in the literature as to which approach will be "most fruitful" to the study of psychopathology (Beck, 1953; Eysenck, 1954).

The issue of "fruitfulness" depends, of course, on one's personal predilections and the immediate goals one has in mind. In this regard, the nomothetic theorist usually is a basic laboratory scientist divorced from the pressing problems which the idiographic theorist faces in his typical activity of treating disturbed individuals. Away from the complexity of the whole person, the nomothetic theorist can pursue the search for basic general laws in a rigorous and systematic fashion. In contrast, the clinician, faced with the practical problems of distressed individuals, must find ways to "piece together" the unique set of experiences which have combined to create their problems. He cannot wait for the slow accumulation of group laws by nomothetic theorists because of his immediate needs and concerns. He must now discover laws which will enable him to make sense out of the pattern of experience of a particular individual.

Given the paucity of empirical laws in psychopathology, there need be no argument as to which approach is "most fruitful"; both are fully justified. What is unjustified are contentions that one approach alone is sufficient.

Experimental and Naturalistic Approaches. Scientists accept the principle of multiple determination, that is, that events do not result from random and isolated causes, but from an orderly and lawful sequence of complex influences. A problem facing the theorist concerns the settings and methods by which he will be able to trace the sequence and strands of these multiple determinants. Two solutions have been developed: (1) the classical experimental approach which stresses the manipulation and control of variables and seeks to establish the precise sequence of cause-effect relationships and (2) the naturalistic approach by which several variables are observed in their natural or real settings and then correlated in accord with their patterns of interaction.

In the experimental method, as borrowed from classical physics, the scientist selects certain variables which he considers basic and then manipulates them in a specially arranged setting that is less complex than the one in which they naturally function. This allows him to observe the precise consequences of one set of variables upon another. Its virtue is that the contaminating or obscuring effects of irrelevant variables are removed or under tight control. Hopefully, unequivocal conclusions may be drawn about causal effects or functional relationships.

Two objections have been raised against the experimental approach: controlled settings often are artificial, and the number and nature of variables which can be studied in this fashion are limited. These objections do not apply to the naturalistic approach. In this method the scientist analyzes a complex of naturally interacting variables without intervening controls or manipulations. Cronbach describes this approach in the following (1957):

The method, for its part, can study what man has not learned to control or can never hope to control. Nature has been experimenting since the beginning of time, with a boldness and complexity far beyond the resources of science. The . . . mission is to observe and organize the data from Nature's experiments.

Proponents of the naturalistic approach point out that experimentally oriented scientists often control or eliminate factors which should not be excluded or ignored. What does one do, they ask, when crucial variables which must be explored cannot be manipulated experimentally? To abandon an investigation because variables cannot be controlled in a classical experiment design seems foolish and may not be necessary if these variables operate in real life settings. The distinguished psychologist, Raymond Cattell, commented on this problem in this statement (1965):

The . . . laboratory method, with its isolation of the single process, has worked well in the older sciences, but where total organisms have to be studied, the theoretical possibility must be faced that one can sometimes hope to find a law only if the total organism is included in the observations and experiences—not just a bit of its behavior.
The fact that he can study behavior in its natural setting means that he can deal with emotionally important matters and real personality learning. Neither our ethics, nor the self-protectiveness of people themselves, will stand for psychologists giving subjects major emotional shocks or altering their whole personalities for a laboratory thesis.
An experimenter exactly following the classical experimental design, but who happened to be a moral imbecile, might with cold logic and force of habit set out to find the effect upon the personality of a mother of losing a child. Furthermore, he would need to "out-Herod Herod" by removing the child in half the cases, and continuing with the child in the other half of his 'controlled experiment.' Since life itself inevitably makes these tragic 'experiments,' a researcher . . . will simply compare mothers who have and have not suffered such bereavement and make his analysis of the result 'balancing' for things he cannot manipulate.

There are two methods which utilize the naturalistic approach: one is essentially intuitive and qualitative; the other is objective and quantitative. The first approach uses the data of case histories, clinical observations, and interviews; data obtained with these methods are subject to the pitfalls of memory and to the observa-

tional and inferential skills of the clinician. Although brilliant insights often have been derived in this fashion, they tend to be loosely formulated and invariably nonquantitative. More systematic and quantitative are methods which apply the technique of correlational statistics. These procedures have been referred to as multivariate methods by Cattell, who wrote (1965):

. . . the multivariate method is actually the same as in the clinical method, but it is quantitative and follows explicit calculations of laws and general conclusions. For the clinician appraises the total pattern by eye and tries to make generalizations from a good memory, whereas the multivariate experimenter actually measures all the variables and may then set an electronic computer to abstract the regularities which exist, instead of depending on human powers of memory and generalization.

In conclusion then, we may note that the experimental approach seeks to control contaminating influences and to establish precise causal connections between a limited number of variables. When complex interactions exist, or when crucial variables cannot be manipulated or controlled, the naturalistic approach may be fruitfully utilized. Both can contribute to the search for empirical laws in psychopathology.

Levels of Observation and Conceptualization. A major source of confusion for students stems from their difficulty in recognizing the existence of different levels of scientific observation and conceptualization.

As indicated earlier, the basic scientist approaches his subject somewhat differently than the practitioner. No conflict need arise. Psychopathology can be studied from many vantage points; it can be observed and conceptualized in legitimately different ways by behaviorists, phenomenologists, psychodynamicists, and biochemists. No point of observation or conceptualization alone is sufficient to encompass all of the complex and multidimensional features of psychopathology. Processes may be described in terms of conditioned habits, reaction formations, cognitive expectancies, or neurochemical dysfunctions. These levels of conceptualization cannot be arranged in a hierarchy, with one level viewed as reducible to another. Nor can they be compared in terms of some "objective truth value." These alternative levels of approach merely are different; they make possible the observation and conceptualization of different types of data and lead, therefore, to different theories and different empirical laws.

Theories are best differentiated according to the kinds of data they elect to conceptualize. These choices are purely pragmatic, and questions of comparative utility should be asked only of theories which deal with the same kinds of data. Data are the basic ingredients for concepts and for the theories which coordinate these concepts. Irrelevant controversies and confusions are avoided if the conceptual level or the kinds of data to which they refer are specified clearly. When this is done properly, the student and researcher can determine whether two concepts are comparable, whether the same conceptual label refers to different data, whether different theories apply to the same data, and so on.

There are many ways in which the subject matter of psychopathology can be differentiated according to "data levels." L'Abate (1964) has proposed levels of integration, interpretation, functioning, and development, whereas Ford and Urban (1963) have organized them in terms of degree of accessibility, order of abstraction, and hierarchical structure.

What classification scheme of levels will serve our purposes best?

The four major historical traditions in psychopathology suggest a particularly useful basis for us to follow, and one which corresponds closely to the major orientations in psychopathology today. These contemporary orientations not only reflect relatively distinct historical traditions, but, perhaps more importantly, also differ in the kinds of data they conceptualize. For example, followers in the tradition of psychiatric medicine focus upon the *biophysical* substrate of pathology; those within the psychodynamic tradition of psychiatry deal with unconscious *intrapsychic* processes; theorists within the clinical-personology tradition often are concerned with conscious *phenomenological* experience; and those in the academic-experimental tradition attend primarily to overt *behavioral* data. These four levels—biophysical, intrapsychic, phenomenological and behavioral—reflect, therefore, both different sources of data and the four major theoretical orientations in psychopathology.

Scientists who are preoccupied with only a small segment of the field often have little knowledge of the work of others. Intent on a narrow approach to the subject, they lose sight of perspective, and their respective contributions are scattered and disconnected. What is needed today is a syntheses in which divergent elements of knowledge are brought together to be seen as parts of an integrated whole. Until a psychological Newton or Einstein comes along, however, the student must do the next best thing: develop an attitude by which the various branches and levels of psychopathology are viewed as an interrelated, if not an integrated, unit. He must learn the language and orientation of each of the major approaches as if they were all parts of an indivisible piece. Until such time as a bridge is created to coordinate each theory and level of approach to the others, no one theory or approach should be viewed as all-embracing, or accepted to the exclusion of others. A multiplicity of viewpoints must prevail.

Any discussion of psychopathological theory should bring us to the question of defining psychopathology. It should be obvious from the foregoing that no single definition is possible. Psychopathology will be defined in terms of the theory one employs. An idiographically oriented theorist who emphasizes the importance of phenomenological experience will include uniqueness and self-discomfort in his definition of psychopathology; a biochemical theorist will formulate his definition in terms of biochemical dysfunctions, and so on. In brief, once a particular level and theory has been adopted, the definition of psychopathology follows logically and inevitably. Clearly, no single definition conveys the wide range of observations and orientations with which psychopathology may be explored.

Unfortunately, the observations, concepts, and propositions of the various theoretical approaches to psychopathology have not been collected within one cover. At present, no single journal covers all aspects of psychopathology either, nor is there a permanent professional organization which cuts across disciplinary lines on a regular basis. To fill this void is a monumental task and far beyond the scope of this book. At best, we hope to provide a brief panoramic view of these approaches and, hopefully, convey certain essential features.

In the following sections we will specify the four levels of theoretical analysis in greater detail. This will provide us with a picture of which data a theory has judged significant to its purposes and which it has de-emphasized. By arranging contemporary theories according to level of data observation and conceptualism, we shall be able to understand better the variety of definitions of psychopathology which have been developed. From this basis also, we should have a sound foundation for comparing the varied concepts and explanatory propositions which have been formulated regarding the development and modification of psychopathology.

References

Beck, S. J. The science of personality: nomothetic or idiographic? *Psychol. Rev.*, 1953, *60*, 353-359.

Cattell, R. B. *The Scientific Analysis of Personality*, Baltimore: Penguin Books, 1965.

Cronbach, L. J. The two disciplines of scientific psychology, *Amer. Psychol.*, 1957, *12*, 671-684.

Eysenck, H. J. The science of personality: nomothetic, *Psychol. Rev.*, 1954, *61*, 339-342.

Ford, D., and Urban, H. *Systems of Psychotherapy*, New York: Wiley, 1963.

Hebb, D. O. Alice in Wonderland, or psychology among the biological sciences. In Harlow, H., and Woolsey, C. (editors). *Biological and Biochemical Basis of Behavior*, Wisconsin: University of Wisconsin Press, 1958.

L'Abate, L. *Principles of Clinical Psychology*, New York: Grune and Stratton, 1964.

Part I

Biophysical
Theories

Jose Luis Cuevas—*Madman* (1954). (The Museum of Modern Art, New York, Inter-American Fund.)

INTRODUCTION

Theories at this level assume that biophysical defects and deficiencies in anatomy, physiology, and biochemistry are the primary determinants of psychopathology. According to this view, biophysical data should serve as the basis for the conceptualization of psychopathology, and biophysical methods should be the primary instruments for therapy.

Ample evidence from medical science exists to justify this biophysical "disease" model. It may be illustrated in physical medicine by infections, genetic errors, obstructions, inflammations, or other insults to normal functioning which manifest themselves overtly as fevers, fatigue, headaches, and so on. Certainly, significant prog-

ress was made in physical medicine when it shifted its focus from surface symptomatology to the biophysical disruptions which underlie them. Extending this model to psychopathology, one sees that these theorists believe that biophysical defects or deficiencies ultimately will be found for such "surface" symptoms as bizarre behavior, feelings of anguish, or maladaptive interpersonal relations. The major difference they see between psychological and biophysical disorders is that the former, affecting the central nervous system, manifests itself primarily in behavioral and social symptoms, whereas the latter, affecting other organ systems, manifests itself in physical symptoms.

9

Biophysical Theories:

ORIENTATION

The papers by Bernice Eiduson et al. and by Roger Williams outline the logic of the biophysical approach with clarity and persuasion. Eiduson presents an amply documented argument to the effect that a biochemical genetic model may prove extremely useful in organizing the data of pathology and its development; several interesting parallels are drawn between psychological and genetic dysfunctions, and she contends that a model that unifies these two conceptual spheres will avoid many of the theoretical difficulties which have plagued research in psychopathology. The distinguished biochemist Roger Williams persuasively argues the role played by each individual's biological make-up in shaping the course of his development. To Williams, the distinctive character of a man's morphology and chemistry is the most relevant factor in understanding his experience and behavior.

Biochemistry, Genetics, and the Nature-Nurture Problem

BERNICE T. EIDUSON, SAMUEL EIDUSON, and EDWARD GELLER

In a recent symposium on concepts in biology Spuhler said, "You hear very little now, outside of textbooks, about the heredity-environment controversy; the working people do not worry about this much anymore"(1). Psychologists arrived at a similar attitude 20 years ago. During the 1930's a large number of psychologists had been experimentally trying to parcel out the influence of heredity and environment in intelligence and other behavioral traits. Their results turned out to be equivocal; and this made most workers feel that research in this area was inevitably dogged by uncontrollable errors, statistical difficulties and questionable controls(2). Anderson, in summarizing the data,

From *Amer. J. Psychiat. 119*:342-350, 1962, by permission of the American Psychiatric Association and the authors.

suggested that nature-nurture was an unproductive area of research and advised psychologists to turn away from it, advice which most took.

In the intervening years, only a few papers have suggested its reconsideration. In these the trend has been to point out our need to conceptualize the heredity-environment problem differently, in ways that are more in line with some of the present theoretical formulations of biology, for example. If we followed these formulations, the question would no longer be simply how much heredity and how much environment, but rather the question would turn to their relevant contribution on each of the various levels or strata in terms of which the organism is conceived(3). Some psychologists(4) have suggested that perhaps behavioral data can contribute something to the mode or the mechanisms by which heredity and environment interact, for the fact of interaction is generally accepted, albeit more out of a feeling of helplessness at the complexity of the heredity-environment relationship than out of any real knowledge of the nature of the interplay.

Today some of the new experimental work in the biological sciences —embryology, genetics, biochemistry —is providing data about the nature-nurture factors and their interaction on the molecular level which elucidates the problem as it has been posed in regard to behavior. In the light of the new information, the assumptions generally held by psychologists about heredity turn out to be outdated, and even incorrect; and when the biological data about environment are considered along with the new findings in the behavioral sciences themselves even the conceptions about the nurture side demand revision. We had set out, in preparing this paper, to summarize the experimental data that we felt were beginning to detail the developmental processes, and that were already casting the heredity-environment issues in new light. However, this main intent turned out to have an intellectual by-product which began to interest us very much. Particularly as we reviewed the nature of the interaction between the nature-nurture factors, we became aware that many convergences and possible identities existed between phenomena and process on the biological level, and these on the psychological. In fact these turned up so regularly in the aspects we studied that we began to consider whether one model which had proved so useful on the molecular stratum could not be profitably transposed to the molar. We have taken the liberty of presenting our speculations about this at the end of this paper.

First a look at the new and enhanced concept of the heredity mechanisms to which biological scientists are directing our attention: until recently psychologists have been prone to consider biological or constitutional factors as constants, establishing the limits or boundaries of behavior, but reflecting none of its variance or uniqueness. They have looked to environmental contacts for providing the bulk of the organism's information content. Freud, for example, saw the infant as the passive recipient of stimuli from the outside world who learned his characteristic modes of thinking and reacting only when he began to take stock of the environment and perceived it through the processes of incorporation(5). Hebb has drawn attention to the same tendency among other psychological schools(6) to conceptualize motivation and drive in ways that are out of line with current physiological data. Elsasser suggests that this viewpoint stems from the strong influence of Darwinian notions on our scientific thinking(7). He, by contrast, feels that the bulk of the individual's information content is endogenous; and support for his position comes from the new genetic data which show that the hereditary mechanism itself can account for—at least has the potentiality for accounting for —all the vast differences that we see expressed in behavior(8). Biologists have now been able to show decisively that man has 23 pairs of chromosomes and they have been able, mathematically, to work out the possible combinations of chromosomes that can be transmitted by the parents to the child(9). It appears that the possibility for hereditary likenesses among children—even in the same family—is very small. The likelihood for 2 nonidentical siblings in one family to have exactly the same genetic characteristics is only one chance in 64 trillion; the probability that two unrelated individuals will share the same genotype turns out to be effectively zero(10). While identical twins have the same genotype by definition, in fraternal or siblings there is still no question that the possible genic combinations make, as some geneticists have said, this inheritance game the "greatest lottery of all."

Moreover, we have thought until recently that some variability in heredity resided in discrepancies in the number of genic components transmitted from parent to child. Recent experimental work has shown that there are certain pathological disturbances which are produced by too many or too few chromosomes. Mongolism is one such disorder, the result of one extra autosomal chromosome. Kleinfelder's and Turner's diseases which result in sexual aberration in boys and girls are the results of one extra sex chromosome and one too few sex chromosomes respectively—and Tarjan and his group at Pacific State Hospital in California are finding that mongolism and Kleinfelder's and Turner's diseases may actually be related to each other(11).

However, more pertinent a factor in normal and abnormal development is the composition of genic patterning, the sequential arrangement of the genetic components, and this turns out to be a highly intricate process, which is mosaic-like in its potential for variability. This has been most clearly elucidated in biochemical genetics which is concerned with genetically-determined enzymes and thereby with the control of certain aspects of metabolic reactions. The "one gene: one enzyme" hypothesis, that each gene is a coded template by means of which one specific enzyme (more generally, protein) is synthesized, was elaborated some time ago. This formulation proved to be a first wedge into the understanding of the mechanisms of certain intraorganismic functions, but this has been shown to be only part of the story. Subsequent investigation with specific metabolic systems has shown that many reactions are not exclusively determined by the presence or the absence of the appropriate enzymes(12).

Few geneticists today uphold the hypothesis of the autonomous gene. Mendel originally postulated the notion of dominance as a principle determining whether or not a trait would be manifest in the phenotype of an organism, but techniques were not available to demonstrate the actual mechanism. Technological advance has

resulted not only in a general investigation of this phenomenon, but in evidence indicating a host of other intragenetic relationships: suppressor genes and modifiers, which act as intensifiers, diluters, inhibitors; genes which exert their influences at early stages of development while the presence or identification of others can be recognized only when the organism reaches maturity; gene changes which may result in more than one observable change in the phenotype. For psychologists, it is particularly interesting to note that what changes are observed in this latter phenomenon—which is called pleitrophy—turns out to depend on the knowledge of the observer and the intensity with which the search was pursued(13)!

The now well known "inborn errors of metabolism" were the first inroads into the large area of pathological disturbance which we now accept as genetically determined(14). But with their exploration has come a host of syndromes which seem to be playing into a myriad of disorders in which classification of neither syndrome nor source is simple(15). Medical genetics has been able to elaborate many disturbances which are now recognized as genetically bound. As metabolic pathways are systematically mapped, their intricacies and circuities become apparent, and the possibilities for distortion of function and resultant pathology seem to multiply with the complexities of the intermediary processes. In studying mutant individuals with hemophilia, for example, it has been shown that at least 9 gene-controlled substances are required in the blood-clotting mechanism, and that each of the trace proteins involved may become dysfunctional through mutation(16).

Furthermore, medical genetics has shown that one cannot tell from the manifest behavior what has been the cause of the disturbance. In one individual an environmentally produced agent can lead to pathology; while in another, an equivalent syndrome can be caused by genetically induced substances. Hemolytic anemia, for example, can be induced by certain drugs which makes it look environmentally determined but yet it is a genetically bound disorder. To further complicate the picture, the overt disease picture may give no clues as to its genesis.

The wide range of individual differences found in this work has alerted biochemists to the biochemical differences among individuals. We have long been familiar with inter-individual physiological and anatomical differences, but until now attention has not been turned to how these differences in turn affect function, what intra-systemic differences exist, and how these make their appearance. Williams, in a systematic compilation of incidences of biochemical individuality, has shown, as one example, that the urinary amino acid profiles of individuals are considerably different(17). Interestingly enough, identical twins show patterns much more similar than do fraternal twins and siblings.

The recognition that one form of mental deficiency could be a concomitant of the inability to convert one substance to another to form the proper metabolic product in the now well-known phenylpyruvic oligophrenia disorder was an early encouragement to look for mental disturbances in genetic metabolic function. The subsequent search showed that this was only one of many ways in which interference with the necessary enzyme products can occur. Biochemists have found also partial lacks in enzymes; or overproduction of enzymes; that metabolites are shunted off in such ways that they do not quite do their proper duties at the right time or at the right place. As the number of physical and mental disorders that can be reduced to inborn metabolic errors is steadily increasing, investigations are developing increasingly sophisticated models of intra-organismic function, and while our conceptual framework permits us to speculate that phenomena which exist side by side are probably highly correlated with each other, there are many more phenomena which are still extremely diffuse and vague, and as yet indefinable.

As the genetic factors do not operate in a vacuum but in an environment, attention has simultaneously been drawn to nature of the host, its participation in the intra-organism processes, and in the resultant behavior. Here, researchers have been confronted with an active factor or set of factors, which condition not only what is genetically determined, but often whether a genetic characteristic will make its appearance, and when. The biological studies make it quite evident that environment can no longer be defined as something outside the organism which affects or becomes part of the organism by internalization; environment must include intra-organismic factors as well, for the nature-nurture interaction is so meshed and interdependent even on the prenatal level that it becomes impossible to determine what is heredity and what is environment. Study of prenatal development has shown that development is a long process of continuous changes, starting with a given genetic array acting in a given environment. The first interaction product then constitutes the background (or the environment) for the next step of interaction with the environment. In the case of a given cell, this includes the interaction product of other cells, and in this manner all future reactions then are codetermined by all preceding steps and hence also by genetic endowment.

Thus, at whatever point one arrests the sequential reactions for study, one can no longer—except arbitrarily—point to certain factors as genetic and others as environmental. As Weiss has said, there is no sharp dichotomy—even prenatally—between geneticists and environmentalists(18).

With the increasing knowledge of what goes on inside the organism, biologists have come to recognize the importance of the dimensions of time and space for even cellular phenomena. In the study of different metabolic needs of different cells, they have recognized that there are certain periods of sensitivity in cellular reactions— times at which things happen or interactions take place(19). Thus, even if all the structural components necessary for certain reactions to take place are in order, it is conceivable that these reactions just may not progress at the rate necessary to allow for a subsequent step to be instituted or systematically meshed with the first—or it is possible that certain reactions are physically separated by even so little as a fraction of a micron and that this may be enough to modify seriously a necessary and sequential relationship. Such dimensions are extremely significant in the elaborate system of regulatory relationships that exist in many metabolic processes. Feed-back mechanisms, as in the case of hormonal regulation of pituitary response to stress, are well known. It has been found, additionally, that in nervous tissue a chemical substance apparently may induce that enzyme which it subsequently needs for its proper action in transmitting electrical impulses across the synapse(20). Acetylcholine, for example, functions as a chemical mediator. Once it has so operated, however, it has to be destroyed (hydrolyzed) so that the proper termination of the membrane depolarization can take place. Acetylcholine has now been suggested as the embryonic determinant for the elaboration of acetylcholinesterase, the enzyme which hydrolyzes it. Therefore, one sees here not only a built-in feed-back system which permits proper functioning, but also a mechanism which appears to demand a more complex interpretation than simple feedback.

From the biologists we are also getting a picture of the kind of differential growth processes that are found prenatally. These are similar, we think, to the different capacities of the organism that have different maturational rates on the behavioral level. While in tissue growth there are presumably some metabolic requirements that are held in common for all tissues, the prenatal group processes do proceed differentially in certain tissues and cells, so that different tissues develop with different metabolic needs (19). Some growth agents seem to effect only specific partial processes; others have a generalized effect. Some agents effect certain growth processes only at times when certain metabolic needs can be interfered with and these same agents will be ineffective at other times. Thus, the "sensitivity periods" may be also described at times when the likelihood of throwing processes out of gear seems to be much more probable. We learn, too, that different tissues progressively develop different metabolic needs, which permits us to elaborate the notion of differential growth processes on the cellular level.

These "sensitivity periods" of the biologists are particularly interesting for they may be counterparts for the "critical periods" in development with which psychologists and ethologists are now becoming increasingly absorbed. Psychologists have found that there are specific times in ontogeny, or specific states, during which certain types of behavior normally first appear. If these times pass without the experiences having taken place, changes, and sometimes lags, in development occur which are never recoverable even though the "right" experiences are presented later. Lorenz's work on imprinting(21), and Thorpe's work(22) on bird songs have independently pointed to the importance of specific times for the occurrence of some kinds of species specific behavior which subsequently becomes indelibly stamped as part of the psychological armamentarium of the animal. Once the time for experiencing this behavior has passed, its learning subsequently never takes place.

It should be noted, however, that biochemical and biological maturation time may not be synonymous with chronological time, as one of us (S.E., 23) and others have pointed. S. Eiduson and E. Geller and their colleagues have been working with new-born chicks to see how various biochemicals and biochemical systems develop in the new-born chick brain. They have found that chicks differ with respect to the times at which certain biochemical substances make their appearance in the brain (unpublished data). Also,

Karki, Kuntzman, and Brodie(23) have found that new-born rats have low levels of brain noradrenaline and serotonin. In 2 weeks time the levels of these substances have reached 40% and 70% respectively of normal. In about 7 weeks after birth, the values are those of the mature animals. However, different chicks and different rats of the same age differ with respect to the concentrations of these substances in the brain. Therefore, if one were interested in those aspects of brain function which involved noradrenaline and/or serotonin, it would be erroneous to assume that chicks and rats of the same chronological age were all comparable with respect to noradrenaline and serotonin levels. Chronological age and biochemical or biological age may actually be different so that it might be much more nearly correct, in comparing the chicks and rats, to group those that had similar concentrations of these amines, rather than those that were the same number of days old.

Considerable behavioral work on very early learning has emerged as scientists have given up their long indulgence in "instinctive behavior," which seems to have cloaked certain early learned behaviors which were considered innate since they seemed to be species specific(24). When this "instinctive behavior" has been exposed to study, results have shown that even in those areas of behavior where the effective external influence may be practically nil, and where the behavior seems essentially unmodified by experience or unresponsive to environmental manifestation, the way that seemingly innate behavior is expressed or the conditions under which it is expressed depends upon experience(25). On whom the animal imprints, for example, is determined in some species by the environment, even if the fact of imprinting is not. The crucial importance of just this "environmental condition," or the person or thing imprinted, becomes evident as we see that this, and not the fact of imprinting by itself, determines in some species the character of adult sexual

behavior in later life(21). Portielje, the curator of the Amsterdam Zoo, a trained zoologist, raised and had a male South American bittern imprinted to him. The bittern was subsequently placed in a cage which was covered very carefully. A female bittern put in the cage was his constant and only companion. Although at first the male would have nothing to do with the female, he finally accepted her and for two years subsequently the pair lived together. They were not further exposed to any other animals or human beings, even being fed through the cage. The animals mated and hatched a number of broods together. Two years later the curator to whom the male bittern had been imprinted in infancy entered the cage and the male bittern saw him for the first time in these two years. When the keeper entered the cage the female bittern happened to be sitting on a nest of eggs, but as soon as the male bittern saw the curator he chased the female off the nest and proceeded to try to woo the curator and to inveigle him onto sitting on the nest of eggs. He showed all of the usual nest relief and social behavior toward the curator. Needless to say, that brood of eggs was never hatched(26)! This example illustrates that a behavior like imprinting that is thought to be genetically determined is very much dependent on the sequential development of the organism for the character of its expression. However, it illustrates as well that whether a genetically-bound behavior is expressed at all is similarly dependent on the experience to which the organism is exposed after birth. The absence of a necessary stimulus which serves as a releasing mechanism may make it appear as if the behavior trait were never transmitted genetically at all; or the absence of a later releasing stimulus may make what appeared to be an inevitably formative experience have no significance in adult life.

The cloak of ambiguity which "instinct" had thrown around early learning has had the further effect of drawing attention away from such factors as intra-uterine environmental conditions which influenced development. However, we today are becoming increasingly cognizant of the dependence of the phenotype on certain environmental conditions in the fetus such as nutrition and temperature. Ephrussi and Herold have shown that the phenotype expression of drosophila is temperature sensitive: W^{b1} flies have brown eyes at 30° and red-purple at 17° (27). Goldschmidt produced many phenocopies in wild types with temperature shocks (28). Thus, it is impossible to regard all intra-organismic phenomenon as genetically determined, and therefore not susceptible to environmental influence. This position has received support, too, from the recent attempts to show the effect of environmental influence during the gestational period. Ginsberg and Hovda transferred fertilized ova from the female of a strain of mice, inbred for susceptibility to audiogenic seizure, to the uterus of a female of a seizure resistant strain, and found that the resulting young showed an intermediate susceptibility (29). Thompson and Hochman changed the intra-uterine environment and found differences in the emotionality of rats which they speculated might be due to possible changes in fetal material in the blood stream (30). In a water maze learning situation, Thompson and Sontag showed that offspring of parent rats who were subjected to seizure were slowed in their response to this same task (31).

As the experimental data on the nurture side of the paradigm continue to support the biological work showing the early and inevitable interaction of nature and nurture, the definition of what is learned becomes more blurred than it once seemed. Previously, psychologists were very ready to label as learned those facets of behavior which were separate from central nervous system growth, responsive to experience and manipulation to change or extinction, characteristics which were distinguished by their variability and mutability, in contrast to hereditary mechanism which was more fixed and constant. This whole notion has been shown to be inappropriate in recent years. Sperry, the psychobiologist, tells us that in individual development the central nervous system must be sufficiently complex for coordinating any level of behavior when behavior begins, and this inevitably involves learning (32). Thus, learning is indistinguishable from CNS growth.

The definition of what is learned has also become less clear-cut as we have become aware of how much learning takes place without our being conscious of it. Experimental work, in discrimination and perception in both animal and human subjects, has suggested that the absence of normal amount of stimulation during developmental periods may result in an inability to respond effectively to sensory and perceptual cues when these cues become available. While much of the perceptual data is derived from studies of the visual modality, evidence demonstrates similar results with other sensory modes. The work on infant chimpanzees done by Nissen, Chow, and Semmes is in point (33): for when the chimp's normal tactual experiences on his own body and his environment were interrupted by placing mailing tubes over his hands and feet, no failure in development of primary sensory equipment of the skin was noted, but subsequently somesthetic learning and localization of the tactual stimuli were defective. This implied that more or less random tactual experience is necessary for the normal development of somatesthetic perception. The experiments on pecking behavior response in chicks raised in darkness with consequent deficiencies in motor and sensory development is similarly vivid, in that such chicks never learned to peck and so were unable to feed themselves in times of starvation although they stood in the midst of plenty (34). The deprived and enriched environment studies on dogs and monkeys not only show how much facilitation is affected by conditions of early learning, but also point to the crucial period in development—the age —at which the deprivation or enrichment takes place(35). With human subjects one gets additional evidence that seemingly irrelevant and peripheral stimuli are taken in as part of the perceptual process and become part of learning even though no direct learning experience seems to have promoted this. In the Poetzl experiments, for example, some parts of exposed stimuli were so unconsciously perceived that they were not subject to direct recall, even though it was apparent from dreams and subsequent conscious behavior that they had been part of the input(36). In summarizing the experimental work on effects of early experience upon the behavior of animals, Beach and Jaynes point out that with all its equivocality and undetermined reliability, the evidence suggests that habits formed in early life are persistent in adult behavior, that later perceptual capacities seem to be structured by early experiences, and that there seem to be certain stages in ontogeny during which certain types of behavior normally are molded and shaped for life(24).

Many years ago psychologists became aware that certain reactions like fear and rage, though admittedly unlearned, could not occur until the maturational development of the animal or infant had proceeded to a point where something in the environment could produce the innate response. Hebb has given the example of the infant chimp, who, though fearful of first strangers, only developed such fears after he had reached an age where he was able to recognize his usual caretakers (usually around 4 months)(37). Even the chimp reared in darkness to an age where fear is normally at its peak will not be disturbed by the first sight of a stranger until he has had the opportunity to learn to differentiate those who care for him daily.

Piaget's and Buhler's studies on the development of human thinking similarly have shown the importance of understanding the maturation of universal modes of thought for interpreting why a child handles experiences differently at different times in his

early life(38). The child, a few months old, will not be distressed when an object is removed from view; he behaves as if the toy ceased to exist. But a few months later he actively searches for the toy and tries to remove the obstacle which has taken it out of view. The child's response and his possible range of behaviors depends on his developmental level, and on the corresponding "mental structures" available to him. The child changes his behavior when the environment demands change; and yet the maturational level of the inherent "operatory structures" determines the nature of the response which will be made. The parallel to tissue differentiation seems cogent; for, as Weiss has described, during maturation, tissue increasingly differentiates and metabolic needs are correspondingly altered; but during this innately determined process, the nature of its differentiation is responsive to the local experience it meets, and to the environmental demands made on it(18).*

It becomes increasingly easy to draw such parallels with our extended knowledge—and increasingly provocative; and this has made us wonder if it would not be very profitable were such parallels systematically extended. We have been impressed that with new data, more and more convergencies appear. Pre- and post-natal growth processes seem to be analogous in many aspects; and also the nature of the interaction of genetic and environmental factors seems similar on both molecular and molar levels. Therefore, taking our clue from general systems theory, we wonder if formal identities do not actually exist between the biological molecular processes, and the behavioral(39). Rapaport's finding that there was comparability among diffusion of information (rumor) at the level of the social system, diffusion of

---

* While in this paper we have been primarily concerned with the local environmental changes and their effects on phenotypic expression of the genotype, there are as well many examples of extra-organismic (i.e., psychological or sociological) alterations of genotypic expression. One such example is the effect of sensory deprivation on visual acuity.

matter or energy (infectious agents) in a biological system, and diffusion of neural impulses in an organ (the central nervous system) shows the value of transposing a hypothetical model from one systemic level to another (39.)

We think that perhaps now we have the possibility of exploiting another model, that of biochemical genetics, for an exposition of the nature of the heredity-environment interaction on the behavioral strata. This would obviously be no simple job for psychology—for we would have to refine and recategorize some of our variables to make them suitable for the kind of differentiation that such a re-study would involve. Yet one gets the feeling that the time—and perhaps the means—are now ripe, for we have evidence that the interlocked relationships of the nature-nurture factors is in itself important, and can be differentially broken down into distinguishable reaction patterns.

The biochemical genetic model has enabled the biologist to trace a number of pathways by which certain metabolic reactions proceed. Investigators can indicate what substances are given genetically and then show to some degree how certain sequences are dependent on environmental agents normally, where these agents impinge, how they facilitate reactions or interfere with them. Once pathologies are set in motion subsequent metabolic reactions can be studied and eventually whole enzyme systems are, or in the future will be, mapped.

We are suggesting that such a model offers the potential for doing a similar job in psychology. Psychology has always assumed that development is sequential and reflects both heredity and environment, but it has seldom considered that from the first postnatal moments, it is already looking at an interaction product with all behavior subsequent to birth representing simultaneously modification of this product and the emergence of a new interaction phenomenon. To all intents and purposes the psychologists have assumed that heredity and environment factors were like dependent and independent variables with one albeit affecting the other, but with the results of these interacting effects not being taken into account as the changed stage on which a second subsequent behavioral segment is acted out.

To apply the biochemical genetic model in psychology, we would have to start with systematic observations on early development, draw our variables from these observations, and begin to trace their evolution. Clinical data have information which could be abstracted about interferences, distortions and pathologies in post-natal growth processes—how they set in, the kinds of sequences that follow once an original abnormality or disturbance has resulted, and their subsequent development. Thus could whole psychological reaction systems be tentatively mapped out. This seems to us to offer a possibility for plotting the ontogenetic sequences of psychological diseases—an important job that has long been overdue. The advantage of such a model for psychology is obvious; but additionally, if the convergencies between pre- and post-natal development continue to hold up, the psychological data based on post-natal observation and experimentation could conceivably offer to the biologist some clues about process in pre-natal development, and suggest to him some new avenues for research.

References

1. Spuhler, J. N.: Behav. Sci., 3: 95, 1958.
2. National Society for the Study of Education. 39th Yearbook, 2: Chicago, 1940.
3. Fuller, J. L.: Nature and Nurture: A Modern Synthesis. New York: Garden City Books, 1954.
4. Anastasi, A.: Psychol. Rev., 65: 197, 1958; Anastasi, A., and Foley, J. P., Jr.: Ibid., 55: 239, 1948.
5. Fenichel, O.: Psychoanalytic Theory of the Neuroses. New York: W. W. Norton, 1945.
6. Hebb, D. O.: Psychol. Rev., 62: 243, 1955.
7. Elsasser, W. M.: Physical Foundation of Biology. New York: Pergamon Press, 1958.
8. Muller, H. J.: Am. J. Psychiat., 113: 483, 1956.
9. Hsia, D. Y.: New Engl. J. Med., 262: 1172, 1960.

10. Hirsch, J.: Paper presented at AAAS Meetings. Chicago: Sept. 1959.
11. Tarjan, G.: *In* Kaplan, G. (Ed.): Prevention of Mental Disorders in Children. New York: Basic Books, 1959.
12. Snyder, L. H.: Science, *129*: 7, 1959.
13. Wagner, R. P., and Mitchell, H. K.: Genetics and Metabolism. New York: John Wiley & Sons, 1955.
14. Garrod, A. E.: Lancet, *2*: 142, 214, 1908.
15. Landing, B. H.: Metabolism, *9*: 198, 1960.
16. Graham, J. B.: Am. J. Hum. Genet., *8*: 63, 1956.
17. Williams, R. J.: Biochemical Individuality. New York: John Wiley & Sons, 1957,
18. Weiss, P.: *In* Mintz, B. (Ed.): Environmental Influences on Prenatal Development. Chicago: Univ. Chicago Press, 1958.
19. Mintz, B. (Ed.): Environmental Influences on Prenatal Development. Chicago: Univ. Chicago Press, 1958.
20. Koelle, G. B.: *In* Bass, A. D. (Ed.): Evolution of Nervous Control from Primitive Organisms to Man. AAAS, *52*: 87, 1959.
21. Lorenz, K. Z.: *In* Schiller, C. H.: Instinctive Behavior. New York: International Universities Press, 1957.
22. Thorpe, W. R.: Learning and Instinct in Animals. Cambridge, Mass.: Harvard Univ. Press, 1956.
23. Eiduson, S.: Am. J. Orthopsychiat., *30*: 1, 1960; Karki, N. T., Kuntzman, R., and Brodie, B. B.: Fed. Proc., *19*: 282, 1960.
24. Beach, F. A., and Jaynes, J.: Psychol. Bull., *15*: 239, 1954.
25. Simpson, A.: *In* Roe, A., and Simpson, C. (Eds.): Behavior and Evolution. New Haven, Conn.: Yale Univ. Press, 1958.
26. Beckwith, W. C.: Personal communication. 1961.
27. Ephrussi, B., and Herold, J. L.: Genetics, *30*: 62, 1945.
28. Goldschmidt, R.: Physiological Genetics. New York: McGraw-Hill, 1938.
29. Ginsberg, B. S., and Hovda, R. B.: Anat. Rec., *99*: 621, 1947.
30. Thompson, W. R., and Hockman, C. H.: Influence of Prenatal Maternal Anxiety on Emotional Behavior in Rats. Paper read at Proc. East. Psychol. Assoc., Atlantic City, Mar. 1956.
31. Thompson, W. R., and Sontag, L. W.: J. Comp. Physiol. Psychol., *49*: 454, 1956.
32. Sperry, R. J.: *In* Roe, A., and Simpson, G. (Eds.): Behavior and Evolution. New Haven, Conn.: Yale Univ. Press, 1958.
33. Nissen, H. W., Chow, K. L., and Semmes, J.: Am. J. Psychol., *64*: 485, 1951.
34. Padilla, S. G.: J. Comp. Physiol. Psychol., *20*: 413, 1935.
35. Harlow, H. F.: Psychol. Rev., *56*: 51, 1949; Scott, J. R., Fredericson, E., and Fuller, J. L.: Personality, *1*: 162, 1951; Scott, J. P., and Marston, M. V.: J. Genet. Psychol., *77*: 25, 1950.
36. Fisher, C.: J. Am. Psychoanal. Assoc., *4*: 5, 1956.
37. Hebb, D. O.: Brit. J. Anim. Behav., *1*: 43, 1953.
38. Piaget, J.: The Construction of Reality in the Child. New York: Basic Books, 1954; Buhler, C.: Kindheit und Jugend. Leipzig: Hirzel, 1931.
39. Miller, J. A.: Am. J. Psychiat., *113*: 776, 1956.

The Biological Approach to the Study of Personality

ROGER J. WILLIAMS

The study of personality logically involves trying to answer three questions: First, of what is personality composed; e.g., if two people have differing personalities, in what specific ways do they or may they differ? Second, how do distinctive personalities arise? Third, how can improvement or modification of personality be brought about?

The first question, of what is personality composed, is a difficult and complicated one, and the answers to the second and third questions hinge upon the answer to it. Our discussion in this paper will be a contribution toward the answering of all these questions. Our approach is in a sense not new but it is largely unexplored and, we believe, rich in potentialities. It has the advantage that it can be used to supplement all other approaches; it does not require the rejection of older insights regardless of their ori-

From paper presented at the Berkeley Conference on "Personality Development in Childhood," University of California, May 5, 1960, by permission of the author.

gin or how time-honored they may be.

Certainly one of the earliest attempts to account for personality differences was made by the astrologers who recognized that people differed one from another and sought to explain these differences on the basis of the influence of the heavenly bodies. The hypothesis of the astrologers has not stood up well in scientific circles, but there are numerous citizens who still believe in horoscopes and many magazines and newspapers that publish them. The tenacious belief rests, I believe, on a fundamental failure of real scientists to come up with other reasons and explanations which satisfy.

In the beginning of the nineteenth century, Gall and Spurzheim developed phrenology which was destined to be in public vogue for a number of decades. This purported to be a science essentially concerned with the relation between personality traits and the contours of people's heads. Partly because it lacked scientific validity and partly because its implications were fatalistic and deterministic, the fundamental idea has largely been discarded.

In the middle portion of the nineteenth century the possible importance of heredity as a factor in the production of personality differences was brought to the fore by the investigations and writings of Darwin and his nephew Galton. Galton, the founder of eugenics, had none of our modern information as to how complicated heredity is; his emphasis on "good" and "bad" heredity (his own, of course, was "good") was misleading and his ideas of improving the race not only flew in the face of religious teachings but were so over-simplified that they came to be regarded as unsound scientifically. The eugenic view also had the disadvantage from the standpoint of public acceptance of being impregnated with determinism.

Before the end of the nineteenth century, Freudianism came into being and has subsequently received such wide acceptance that it has dominated the field of psychiatry for several decades. Fundamentally, Freudianism is a system of surmises of such a nature that they have not and cannot be tested by controlled experiments. These surmises appear to some minds to be plausible to such a high degree that they demand acceptance. On the other hand, to some minds, some of the surmises appear so implausible as to demand rejection. Controlled experiments are quite outside the routine thoughts and discussions of adherents of the Freudian school.

The surmises which form the basis of the Freudian doctrine include the essential idea that personalities are built during the lifetime of the individual and that the prime factors which enter are the environmental happenings beginning on the day of birth—possibly even before—and the thoughts that are developed as a result of these happenings. Therapeutic psychoanalysis is based upon the idea that if an individual can come to understand how the events of his earlier life have developed his present unfortunate attitudes, his personality difficulties tend to evaporate. Inherent in this approach is the idea that minds are much more complex than they superficially appear to be; they are like icebergs in that there is much more "out of sight" than there is in open view.

That the Freudian approach to personality has elements of strength is so obvious as not to require argument. It leaves room for the unknown and unexpected in human behavior (which is needed), it emphasizes the dynamic aspects of personality, and strongly encourages the belief that human beings are not powerless to change and modify their personalities and that parents have tremendous potentialities in developing the lives of their children. The wide acceptance of Freudian ideas bears out the thought that the public, including the physicians, are first people and second, if at all, scientists. Certainly a cold-blooded scientific approach would never have developed and fostered the Freudian concepts.

Freudian doctrine tacitly assumes that at the beginning of their lives individuals are substantially duplicates of one another. This doctrine is almost, if not wholly, universalized; that is, its pronouncements apply to everyone alike. Freud himself wrote, "I always find it uncanny when I can't understand someone in terms of myself."

To be sure, people develop later in life very diverse personalities, but the observed differences are, according to the Freudian school, essentially environmentally induced and the laws of development are the same for all. Freud and his followers sometimes make references to tendencies which are inherited by the human race as a whole but it is the consistent practice to disregard or minimize individual differences in heredity as a potential source of personality differences. Certainly Freudians as such have not fostered research in this area.

The neglect of hereditary factors among those who are concerned with personality disorders is so pronounced that the veteran physician, Walter C. Alvarez, has recently complained "in most of the present day books on psychiatry, there is not even a short section on heredity. The book resembles a text on paleontology written for a fundamentalist college, with not one word on evolution!"[1] Of course, the dilemma of developing an environmentalist doctrine while paying some attention to heredity is a real one. If one begins to allow heredity to make inroads and demand attention, there is no telling where the process will end; the whole structure of environmentalistic Freudianism might come tumbling down.

On hard-nosed scientific ground one does not escape from determinism by adopting an environmentalist point of view, though many seem to think so. They resist considering the importance of heredity for this reason. Rigorous scientific thinking leads us to conclude that environmentalism is just as deterministic in its implications as is hereditarianism. People say, "If we don't like one environment we can move to another," but scientific reasoning if followed implicitly leads to the conclusion that we cannot move to a new environment unless there is some

stimulus in the old or the new environment which *makes us* move.

This subject is much too large to discuss in detail in this paper, but as a prelude to further discussions I will briefly state my position. In the first place I have not the slightest doubt that heredity has a great deal to do with personality development. I do not resist this idea. I do not believe this recognition leads inevitably to determinism. I do not know how or why intelligence originated on earth; I do not understand how or why free will originated or just how it works. But there are many other questions to which scientific reasoning gives me no answer. I do not even know why positive electricity attracts negative or why every particle of matter in the physical universe exerts an attractive force on every other particle. I do accept the idea of free choice, with limitations imposed by laws, as a fundamental premise. With the acceptance, as a background for my thinking, of the exercise of intelligence and free choice as prime factors in life, I do not resist the recognition of hereditary influences. Their recognition does not pin me down to determinism.

Behavioristic psychology which at its inception was *completely* environmentalistic has bolstered the environmental approach of Freudianism. This school of psychology has as a fundamental basis the facts discovered by Pavlov using dogs and commonly designated as conditioned reflexes. The development of personality thus becomes a pyramiding conditioning process whereby the developing infant is continuously modified in his responses by the stimuli he or she received.

What was not quoted by the behavioristic school were correlative findings by Pavlov which are highly pertinent. Pavlov found as a result of extensive study of many dogs that they often exhibited innate tendencies to react very differently to the same stimulus. He recognized in his dogs four basic types: (1) excitable, (2) inhibitory, (3) equilibrated, and (4) active, as well as intermediate, types.[2] He recognized enormous differences in dogs with respect to their condition-ability and was by no means inclined to focus his attention solely upon the behavior of "*the* dog." Scott and others have in more recent times found ample justification for Pavlov's concern over the fundamental differences between dogs of different breeds and between individual dogs within each breed. These differences, which can be studied under controlled conditions in dogs vastly easier than in human beings, are *not* the result of training.

It is beyond dispute, of course, that dogs, cats, rats, and monkeys, for example, show species differences with respect to their patterns of conditionability. Stimuli which are highly effective for one species may be of negligible importance for another. If hereditary factors make for inter-species differences, it is entirely reasonable to suppose that intra-species differences would exist for the same reason.

Before we proceed to the principal part of our discussion it should be pointed out that the pronouncements of men whose memories we may revere must be taken in their historical context. Freud, for example, developed most of his fundamental ideas before there was any knowledge of hormones, indeed before the term "hormone" was coined. He had at this time no knowledge of present day biochemistry; the chemical factors involved in nutrition were almost wholly unknown; and he certainly had no knowledge of the close ties which exist between biochemistry and genetics. It can safely be assumed that if the youthful Sigmund Freud were reincarnated today, he would include these vast developments in endocrinology, biochemistry, and genetics in his purview, and that his thinking would follow quite different paths from those which it followed about the turn of the century.

A parallel case has existed in the field of medicine with respect to the monumental work of Louis Pasteur. Pasteur's thrilling contribution may be summarized in a single sentence: "Disease is caused by micro-organisms." To convince his contemporaries of this fact Pasteur had to overcome terrific resistance. Once established, however, the next generation not only accepted the idea but was strongly inclined to go even further and assert that disease is caused *exclusively* by micro-organisms. After Pasteur's death substantial evidence began to accumulate that disease could be caused by malnutrition. This idea in turn met with terrific resistance, possibly because this was considered a slur on Pasteur's memory. Actually, however, if the youthful Pasteur could have been reincarnated about 1900 he probably would have been one of the first to recognize the importance of malnutrition—an importance which many physicians even today do not fully recognize or welcome with open arms.

The parallel between the two cases may be discerned if we summarize Freud's contribution thus: "Personality disorders result from infantile conditioning." It appears that many followers of Freud tend to insert the word exclusively and to say "Personality disorders result exclusively from infantile conditioning." It seems an extremely doubtful compliment to Freud's memory to follow slavishly doctrines which he—if he were alive and in possession of present day knowledge—would repudiate or radically modify.

A biological approach to personality should seek to bring from biology *everything* that can help to explain what personality is, how it originates and how it can be modified and improved. Biology has much to contribute, particularly in an area of biology which has received relatively little attention; namely, that involving anatomical, physiological, biochemical (and psychological) individuality.

It seems indefensible to assume that people are built in separate compartments, one anatomical, one physiological, one biochemical, one psychological, and that these compartments are unrelated or only distantly related to each other. Each human being possesses and exhibits unity. Certainly anatomy is basic to physiology and biochemistry, and it may logically be presumed that it is also basic to psychology.

Let us look therefore in the field of anatomy for facts which are pertinent to our problem.

Anatomists, partly for reasons of simplicity, have been prone in centuries past to concentrate on a single picture of the human body. Obvious concessions are made, when necessary, in considering the male and the female of the species, and always anatomists have been aware that within these two groups there are variations and anomalies. Only within the past decade,[3] however, has comprehensive information been published which indicates how great these inter-individual variations are and how widespread they are in the general population.

It makes no difference where we look, whether at the skeletal system, the digestive tract, the muscular system, the circulatory system, the respiratory system, the endocrine system, the nervous system, or even at the microscopic anatomy of the blood, we find tremendous morphological variations within the so-called normal range.

For example, normal stomachs vary greatly in shape and about six-fold in size. Transverse colons vary widely in the positions at which they cross over in the abdomen and pelvic colon patterns vary widely. Arising from the aortic arch are two, three, four, and sometimes five and six branch arteries; the aorta itself varies greatly in size and hearts differ morphologically and physiologically so that their pumping capacities in healthy young men vary widely. The size of arteries and the branching patterns are such that in each individual the various tissues and organs are supplied with blood unequally well, resulting in a distinctive pattern of blood supply for each.

Morphological differences in the respiratory systems of normal people are basic to the fact that each person exhibits a distinctive breathing pattern as shown in the spirograms of different individuals made under comparable conditions.

Each endocrine gland is subject to wide variation among "normal" individuals. Thyroid glands vary in weight about six-fold,[4a] and the protein-bound iodine of the blood which measures the hormonal output varies to about the same degree.[5] Parathyroid glands also vary about six-fold in total weight in so-called "normal" individuals, and the number of lobes varies from 2–12.[4b] The most prevalent number of lobes is 4, but some anatomists estimate that not over fifty per cent of the population have this number. The number of islets of Langerhans, which are responsible for insulin production, vary over a ten-fold range in diabetes-free individuals.[6] The thickness of the adrenal cortex, where the critical adrenal hormones arise, is said to vary from 0.5 mm to 5 mm (ten-fold).[7]

The morphology of the pituitary glands which produce about eight different hormones is so variable, when different healthy individuals are compared, as to allow for several-fold differences in the production of the individual hormones.[8,9,10] The male sex glands vary in weight from 10 to 45 grams[4c] in so-called "normal" males and much more than this if those with "sub-normal" sex development are included. The female sex glands vary in weight over a five-fold range and the number of primordial ova present at the birth of "normal" female infants varies over a thirteen-fold range.[4d] It is evident that all individuals possess distinctive endocrine systems and that the individual hormonal activities may vary over a several-fold range in individuals who have no recognized hormonal difficulty.

The nervous system is, of course, particularly interesting in connection with the personality problem, and the question arises whether substantial variations exist. The classification of the various kinds of sensory nerve endings, for example, is by no means complete nor satisfactory, and the precise functioning of many of the recognized types is unknown. Investigations involving "cold spots," "warm spots," and "pain spots" on the skin indicate that each individual exhibits a distinctive pattern of each. In a relatively recent study of pain spots in twenty-one healthy young adults, a high degree of variation was observed.[11] When subjected to carefully controlled test conditions the right hand of one young man "A" showed seven per cent of the area tested to be "highly sensitive," while in another, "B," the right hand showed one hundred per cent "highly sensitive" areas. On A's hand, forty-nine per cent of the area registered "no pain" under standard pain producing test conditions. On B's hand, however, there was no area which registered "no pain."

It is evident that there is room for wide variations with respect to the numbers and distributions of sensory nerve endings in different individuals. That such differences exist is indicated by the extreme diversity in the reactions of individuals to many stimuli such as those involving seeing, hearing, and tasting. An entire lecture could be devoted to this subject alone.

The branching of the trunk nerves is as distinctive as that of the blood vessels.[3] Anson, for example, shows eight patterns of the branching of the facial nerve, each type representing, on the basis of examination of one hundred facial halves, from 5 to 22 per cent of the specimens. About 15 per cent of people do not have a direct pyramidal nerve tract in the spinal column; an unknown percentage have three splanchnic nerves as compared with the usual two; recurrent laryngeal nerves may be wholly unbranched or may have as many as six branches;[12] the termination of the spinal cord varies in different individuals over a range of three full vertebrae.[3]

Variations in brain anatomy have received little attention. Thirteen years ago, however, Lashley in a review wrote:[13] "The brain is extremely variable in every character that has been subjected to measurement. Its diversities of structure within the species are of the same general character as are the differences between related species or even between orders of animals. . . . Even the limited evidence at hand, however, shows that individuals start

life with brains differing enormously in structure; unlike in number, size, and arrangement of neurons as well as in grosser features."

Unfortunately, partly due to the complexity of the problem, there is no information whatever available as to how these enormous anatomical differences are related to the equally striking personality differences which are commonplace. Recently there has been published, primarily for the use of surgeons, an extensive study of differences in brain anatomy.[14]

Up to the present in our discussion we have paid attention only to certain facts of biology—those in the field of anatomy. Before we consider other areas—physiology, biochemistry, and psychology—it seems appropriate to note whether we have made any progress in uncovering facts that have important implications for personality development.

Consider the fact (I do regard it a fact and not a theory) that every individual person is endowed with a distinctive gastrointestinal tract, a distinctive circulatory system, a distinctive respiratory system, a distinctive endocrine system, a distinctive nervous system, and a morphologically distinctive brain; furthermore that the differences involved in this distinctiveness are never trifling and often are enormous. Can it be that this fact is inconsequential in relation the problem of personality differences?

I am willing to take the position that this fact is of the *utmost* importance. The material in the area of anatomy alone is sufficient to convince anyone who comes upon the problem with an open mind that here is an obvious frontier which should yield many insights. Those who have accepted the Freudian idea that personality disorders arise from infantile conditioning will surely be led to see that, *in addition*, the distinctive bodily equipment of each individual infant is potentially important.

The failure of psychologists—and of biologists, too—to deal seriously with innate individual differences in connection with many problems probably has deep roots.

McGill has said, "Experimental psychologists . . . ignore individual differences almost as an item of faith."[15] The same statement holds, in the main, for physiological psychologists, physiologists, and biochemists. Anatomists have adopted in the past (and some do even at present) the same attitude. Generally speaking, individual differences are flies in the ointment which need to be removed and disregarded. Every subject becomes vastly simpler and more "scientific" when this is done.

If one is pursuing knowledge about personality, however, neglect of innate individual differences is fatal. All of biology and all of psychology have suffered, in my opinion, from at least a mild case of "universalitis," an overruling desire to generalize immediately—oftentimes long before sufficient facts are gathered to give the generalization validity. This desire to generalize is of itself laudable, but the willingness to do so without an adequate background of information is unscientific and has devastating effects in the area of personality study.

The most treacherous type of premature generalization is the one that is not stated, but is merely accepted as obvious or axiomatic. Such a generalization is hidden, for example, in the famous line of Alexander Pope "The proper study of mankind is man." This common saying *assumes* the existence of a meaningful prototype, *man*, a universalized human being—an object of our primary concern. From the standpoint of the serious realistic study of personality, I object to this implied generalization. If we were to alter Pope's line to read "The proper study of mankind is men," we would have detracted from its poetic excellence but we would have added immeasurably to its validity in the area of personality study.

"Universalitis" is probably born of fundamental egotism. If one can make sweeping generalizations, they are self-gratifying, they can be readily passed on to disciples, the atmosphere

seems to clear, life becomes simple, and we approach being gods. It is more pleasant often to retain one's conceit than it is to be realistically humble and admit ignorance. "Universalitis" is thus a sign of immaturity. When personality study has grown up it will recognize realistically the tremendous diversity in personalities, the classification of which is extremely difficult and must be based upon far more data than we now have.

With these ideas as additional background for our thinking let us consider some of the other aspects of biology. Physiologically and biochemically, distinctiveness in gastrointestinal tracts is just as marked as is the distinctiveness in anatomy. The gastric juices of 5,000 individuals free from gastric disease were found to contain from 0–4300 units of pepsin.[16] The range of hydrochloric acid in a smaller study of normal individuals was from 0.0 to 66.0 milliequivalents per liter.[17] No one can deny the probability that large variations also exist in the digestive juices which cannot be so readily investigated. Some "normal" hearts beat more than twice as fast as others,[18] some have pumping capacities at least three times as large as others,[19] and the blood of each individual is distinctive. The discovery of the existence of "blood groups" was just the beginning of our knowledge of the individuality of the blood. Enzyme levels in the blood, which are a reflection of fundamental biochemical differences, vary from one well individual to another over substantial ranges, sometimes ten-fold or even thirty-fold or more.[20]

Our neuromuscular systems are far from assembly line products as can easily be demonstrated by a study of motor skills and by a large number of physiological tests. Our senses are by no means identical, as has been made clear by taste tests for PTC and many other substances,[21] by tests involving sense of smell (verbenas,[22] hydrocyanic acid[23]), sense of sight (peripheral vision, foveal size, flicker fusion, and related phenomena, eighteen types of color "blindness"), sense of balance, pitch discriminations and hearing acuities at different frequencies, etc., etc. From the tremendous variation in the action of specific drugs and chemicals on different individuals, we gain further evidence of fundamental differences in physiology and biochemistry.[24]

Thurston's pioneering work on primary mental abilities called attention to the fact that human minds have different facets, and that some individuals may be relatively well endowed with respect to arithmetical facility, for example, while being relatively deficient in word familiarity or spatial imagery. Others may be strong in the area of word familiarity but weak in rote memory or arithmetic. Guilford has more recently suggested that there are at least forty facets to human minds, involving a group of memory factors, four groups of thinking factors, the latter involving abilities relating to discovering, evaluating, and generating ideas.[25] All of this leaves room for a multitude of mental patterns (patterns of conditionability) which it seems reasonable to suppose must be related to the enormous variation in the anatomy of human brains. People even when confronted with the same facts, do not think alike, and this appears to have a sound anatomical as well as psychological basis.

Those social anthropologists and other social scientists, who regard culture as the one factor which determines what an individual will be like, often say, or imply, that adult members of a society bear a very great resemblance to each other because of the similarities of their upbringing. In view of this common implication it may be well to ask whether inborn differentness and distinctiveness fades out as a result of the adjustment of the individuals to the culture to which they are exposed.

That this is not the case is indicated by the results of a game played anonymously with a group of 140 adults. They were given the following list of twenty desirable items, each of which was to be rated 0, 1, 2, 3, 4, or 5 depending on its satisfaction-giving

value for the individual making the anonymous rating.

1. Animals, pets of all kinds
2. Babies, enjoyment of
3. Bargaining, buying and selling
4. Beauty, as seen through the eyes
5. Conversation, all kinds
6. Creative work
7. Exploring, travel
8. Food, eating of all kinds
9. Gardening
10. Medical care
11. Music, all kinds
12. Nature, enjoyment of
13. Odors, perfumes, etc.
14. Ownership of property
15. Reading, all kinds
16. Religious worship
17. Routine activities
18. Self adornment
19. Sex
20. Shows, all kinds

The results showed clearly that every individual was distinct and different from every other individual. No two patterns were alike even with respect to a half dozen items; no pattern had a faint resemblance to the average for the group. Furthermore, the distinctiveness of each was not based upon minor differences in ratings; every item on the list was rated 0 by some individuals; every item was rated 5 by some individuals. In fact every item received, by members of this group, every possible rating from 0 to 5!

At the risk of being naive, it appears that the whole story we have been unfolding hangs together. Individual infants are endowed with far-reaching anatomical distinctiveness; each has a distinctive endocrine system, a highly distinctive nervous system, a highly distinctive brain. The same distinctiveness carries over into the sensory and biochemical realms, and into their individual psychologies. It is not surprising therefore that each individual upon reaching adulthood exhibits a distinctive pattern of likes and dislikes not only with respect to trivialities but also with respect to what may be regarded the most important things in life.

That culture has a profound influence on our lives no one should deny. The serious question arises, however, as to the relative position that different factors occupy in producing distinctive personalities. To me it seems probable that one's distinctive endocrine system and one's distinctive brain morphology are more important factors than the toilet training one receives as an infant.

We cannot state as a demonstrated fact that differences in brain morphology or in endocrine systems have much to do with personality differences. On the other hand we have no rigorous scientific proof that toilet training has any substantial effect on personality development. We can only surmise. In one sense, personality study is in its very early infancy.

Another pertinent question—simple but important—awaits a clear answer: Are patterns of brain morphology inherited? On the basis of what is known about the inheritance of other morphological features including fingerprints and the branching of blood vessels in the chest, etc., it may be *inferred* that specific morphological features in the brain are handed down by inheritance, but we do not have definite proof.

A fact which makes the study of the inheritance of such morphological features difficult is that expressed by geneticists David and Snyder.[26] "It has become more and more widely recognized that single-gene differences which produce readily distinguishable discontinuities in phenotype variation are completely non-representative of the bulk of genetic variability in any species." Multiple gene effects are extremely common and in many cases, because of the complexity of the inheritance process, it is impossible to trace them in families or to know when and where such effects may be expected to arise. This complication is not the only one which exists; there is also the possibility (and certainty in some species) of maternal influence (cytoplasmic) which does not follow the rules of gene-centered genetics, and can thus throw one's calculations off.[27]

The complications of broad genetic study are so great that closely inbred animals, which, according to the simpler concepts of genetics, should be nearly indentical in body make-up, are often relatively far from it. Even within relatively closely inbred groups of animals each has a distinctive pattern of organ weights, a distinctive excretion pattern, and at the same time a distinctive pattern of behavioral responses.

The technique of twin studies also has its pitfalls. Monozygotic twins have, according to the simpler concepts of Mendelian genetics, identical inheritance. Actually, however, because of cytoplasmic factors or other unknowns, they appear not to have. It is a common observation that so-called "identical" twins vary markedly in their resemblance to each other. Sometimes they have almost indistinguishable facial features and very similar temperaments. In other cases, however, they are readily distinguished one from another by facial features and/or by temperaments. Our study of excretion patterns suggests that these show in monozygotic twins a high degree of similarity but not an identity. Kallman states, "Discordance between them [monozygotic twins] is not, as is commonly assumed, a measure merely of postnatal or even prenatal development; it may also have a genetic component."[28]

Consideration of the available facts leads me to suppose, in the absence of completely definitive information, that differences in brain morphology, in endocrine patterns, in digestive, circulatory, muscular, and nervous systems, etc., have important roots in heredity. It is difficult to see how such differences as exist could arise independent of heredity. The exact mechanisms whereby all these differences are inherited will probably be obscure many decades hence.

The recognition of hereditary factors does not, by any means, exclude from consideration the dynamic aspects of personality development. Potentialities and conditionabilities are inherited, not fixed, characteristics.

The widespread idea that personalities are developed from early childhood is fully in accord with an appreciation of the hereditary factors. Conditioning still takes place but the recognition of innate biological differences calls attention to distinct make-up that each newborn baby possesses. Conditioning does not take place starting with assembly-line babies, each one, according to Watson, possessing exactly the same potentialities to develop into a "doctor, lawyer, artist, merchant, chief, and yes, even beggar-man and thief."

We have two choices in personality study: one is to neglect hereditary factors as we have done in the past decades, in which case progress will come to a full stop; the other is to recognize the numerous individual differences to be observed in the various areas of biology and study them intensively and ascertain their pertinence.

If we adopt the latter course this means the cultivation of spontaneity in research and perhaps a de-emphasis on theory until some valuable data are collected. Hebb has recently called attention to the weakness of the "design of experiment" approach.[29] "It assumes that the thinking is done in advance of experimentation, since it demands that the whole program be laid out in advance; it tends also, in its own Procrustean way, to confirm or deny the ideas with which one began the experiment, but its elaborate mathematical machinery is virtually certain to exclude the kind of unexpected result that gives one new ideas. . . . We must not let our epistemological preconceptions stand in the way of getting research done. We had much better be naive and productive than sophisticated, hypercritical and sterile."

To tackle in one giant undertaking the problem of understanding, characterizing, and cataloguing all personalities from the biological or any other point of view seems hopeless. A strategy which seems far from hopeless, however, involves studying one at a time various personality characteristics to ascertain what biological roots they may have. The personality characteristics to be chosen for investigation should, obviously, be as definite as possible. They might include not only matters of temperament or emotion but also the ability to perform specified types of mental processes, or they might include personality problems of numerous types.

Studying even one particular personality characteristic to ascertain its biological roots is a large undertaking and might involve making scores, possibly hundreds, of measurements on every individual subjected to study. If one has some rational basis for selecting wisely the measurements to be made, the number of desirable measurements might be reduced. This fact would constitute an argument for selecting as the "personality problem" to be investigated, one for which the type of biological roots *might be* successfully guessed in advance. Such might include hyper- or hyposexuality, homosexuality, obesity, depressions, alcoholism, insomnia, accident proneness, etc. When one after another of personality disorders have been studied from this standpoint, it seems very likely that the whole picture will begin to clear and that the study of specific personality characteristics and problems will become successively easier the farther it progresses. What I am considering is obviously a relatively long range proposal.

Such a type of study as I am suggesting is not in line with the vast amount of experimentation which is currently fashionable. It is very common, for example, to develop a measurement and then apply it to large numbers of people. It is almost or totally unheard of to apply a large series of measurements to a relatively few individuals to determine their individual distinctive patterns. This must be done if we are to find the biological roots of personality characteristics, and psychologists should be warned that the major part of the work must be done in the area of biology, and the biological scientists concerned cannot be looked upon as minor contributors.

Digressing for a moment, it has

been with this thought in mind that I have objected strenuously to the current widespread implication that "behavioral sciences" constitute a distinct group including psychology, sociology, and social anthropology and excluding the biological sciences. Hidden in this classification is the *assumption* that biological factors are of no importance in behavior and that conditioning is the whole story. It actually may well be, however, that anatomy, physiology, and biochemistry are, from the standpoint of the practical potentialities, the most important behavioral sciences at our disposal.

In connection with tracing the biological roots of personality characteristics or problems, a highly important part of the strategy is to recognize what I have elsewhere called "disconformities" in the various measurements that are made.[30] High or low values within the so-called "normal range," for example, are disconformities. Such values are abundant and may be highly meaningful, and more important (because of their wider occurrence) than "abnormalities," especially when, as is often the case, the adopted "norms" are selected arbitrarily and without any rational basis whatever.

One of the most encouraging aspects of this type of study is the potential application of high-speed computers to study biological disconformity patterns, and their pertinence to particular personality characteristics or personality problems. Techniques for studying patterns are in their infancy, but the possibilities are most alluring. It may spur our interest in these possibilities to know that, according to recent reports from the Soviet Medical Academy, an electronic diagnosing machine has been constructed. This utilizes, no doubt, some of the mathematical principles and techniques that would be useful in personality study.

Parenthetically, but very briefly, it may be stated that a study of disconformity patterns such as we have suggested is also urgent for reasons other than those involving personality study. These patterns constitute the basis for the complex patterns of innate susceptibilities which all individuals have for all types of diseases.

Space will not permit a discussion of the numerous ways in which my own discipline, biochemistry, impinges on personality problems.[31] The effects of various chemicals on personality behavior, the correlations between brain metabolism and behavior, the effects of various hormones on personality characteristics are all well recognized. What is not so well recognized is that each individual's body chemistry is distinctive and different, and that complex biochemical roots of personality characteristics are likely to be found when we look for them with due care and thoroughness.

Before I close this discussion, I want to stress a most important environmental factor which is capable of contributing enormously to healthy personality development.

The monumental work of Beadle and Tatum[32] demonstrated for the first time the vital connection between genes and enzymes, and, in effect, between heredity and biochemistry. Their work made clear the inevitable basis for individual body chemistry. As a direct consequence of this finding, it becomes inevitable that the nutritional needs of genetically distinctive individuals are quantitatively not the same. Carrying the idea still further it becomes inescapable that the brain cells of individual people do not have quantitatively identical nutritional needs.

It has been amply demonstrated that malnutrition of various kinds can induce personality disorders. This was observed in the starvation studies of Keys and associates,[33] in thiamin deficiency studies,[34] in amino acid deficiency studies,[35] and perhaps most notably in pellagra where unequivocal insanity may result from niacin deficiency and can be abolished promptly by administration of the missing vitamin. It has also been shown repeatedly that inadequacy of prenatal nutrition can cause all sorts of development difficulties and abnormalities in the growing fetus.

One of the most obvious environmental measures that can be taken to insure favorable personality development is to see, for example, that the nervous system of each distinctive individual, with his distinctive needs, receives prenatally and postnatally the best possible nourishment. Nourishment of brain cells like the nourishment of other cells throughout the body can be maintained at many levels of excellence, and of course achieving the best is no small order.

Serious attention to nutrition which must involve the utilization of substantial manpower and a great deal of human ingenuity and persistence can, I believe, make tremendous contributions to our knowledge of personality states and personality disorders, and to the alleviation and prevention of personality difficulties.

In conclusion I would emphasize that the biological approach to personality, outstandingly important as I believe it to be, is not a substitute for all other valid approaches. Whatever we may know or may be able to accomplish by other approaches, if valid, is not lost. Consideration of the biological approach expands our horizon and gives us a much broader view. In my opinion the insight we may gain from this approach will be most valuable and productive. I should reiterate also what I have said before, that personality study is in its early infancy.

References

1. Alvarez, Walter C., *Practical Leads to Puzzling Diagnoses*, J. B. Lippincott, Philadelphia, Pa., 1958, p. 181.
2. Maiorov, F. P., *History of Study on Conditioned Reflexes*, 2nd Rev. and Completed ed., U.S.S.R. Academy of Sciences, Moscow and Leningrad, 1954, p. 190. (In Russian.)
3. Anson, Barry J., *Atlas of Human Anatomy*, W. B. Saunders Co., Philadelphia, Pa. and London, England, 1951.
4(a). Grollman, Arthur, *Essentials of Endocrinology*, J. B. Lippincott Co., Philadelphia, Pa., 2nd ed., 1947, p. 155.
4(b). *Ibid.*, p. 247.
4(c). *Ibid.*, p. 460.
4(d). *Ibid.*, p. 497.
5. Williams, Roger J., *Biochemical Individuality*, John Wiley & Sons, New York, N. Y., 1956, p. 53.
6. Pincus, Gregory, and Thimann, Kenneth V., eds., *The Hormones*, Academic Press, Inc., New York, N. Y., 1948, Vol. 1, p. 303.
7. Goldzieher, Max A., *The Endocrine Glands*, D. Appleton-Century Co., New York, N. Y. and London, England, 1939, p. 589.
8. Rasmussen, A. T., *Am. J. Anat.*, 42, 1-27 (1928).
9. Rasmussen, A. T., *Endocrinology*, 12, 129-524 (1924).
10. Rasmussen, A. T., *Endocrinology*, 12, 129-150 (1928).
11. Tindall, George T., and Kunkle, E. Charles, *A.M.A. Archives of Neurology and Psychiatry*, 77, 605-610 (1957).
12. Rustad, William H., *Clin. Endocrinol. Metabolism*, 14, 87-96 (1954).
13. Lashley, K. S., *Psychological Reviews*, 54, 333-334 (1947).
14. Schattenbrand, Georges, and Bailey, Percival, *Introduction to Stereotaxis, with an Atlas of the Human Brain* (3 Vols.), Georg Thiene, Verlay, Stuttgart; Grune and Stratton, New York, N. Y., 1959.
15. McGill, W. J., *Amer. Psych. Ass'n. Symposium: Behavior Genetics and Differential Psychology*, New York, Sept. 4, 1957.
16. Osterberg, Arnold E., Vanzant, Frances R., Alvarez, Walter C., and Rivers, Andrew B., *Am. J. Digestive Diseases*, 3, 35-41 (1936).
17. Bernstein, Ralph E., *J. Lab. Clin. Med.*, 40, 707-717 (1952).
18. Heath, Clark W., et. al., *What People Are*, Harvard University Press, Cambridge, Mass., 1945, p. 126.
19. King, C. C., et al., *J. Applied Physiol.*, 5, 99-110 (1952).
20. Williams, Roger J., *Biochemical Individuality*, John Wiley & Sons, New York, N. Y., 1956, pp. 69-79.
21. *Ibid.*, pp. 127-130.
22. Blakeslee, A. F., *Proc. Natl. Acad. Sci.*, 48, 298-299 (1918); *J. of Heredity*, 23, 106 (1932).
23. Kirk, R. L., and Stenhouse, N. S., *Nature*, 171, 698-699 (1953).
24. Williams, Roger J., *Biochemical Individuality*, John Wiley & Sons, New York, 1956, pp. 106-118.
25. Guilford, J. P., *Science*, 122, 875 (1955).
26. David, P. R., and Snyder, L. H., *Social Psychology at the Crossroads*, Harper and Bros., New York, N. Y., 1951, pp. 61-62.
27. Williams, Roger J., *J. of Heredity*, 51, 91-98 (1960).
28. Kallmann, F. J., *Am. J. Human Genetics*, 6, 157-162 (1954).
29. Harlow, Harry F., and Woolsey, Clinton N., eds., *Biological and Biochemical Bases of Behavior*, The University of Wisconsin Press, Madison, Wisconsin, 1958, p. 464.
30. Williams, Roger J., *Texas Reports Biol. and Med.*, 18, 168-185 (1960).
31. Williams, Roger J., *Biochemical Individuality*, John Wiley & Sons, New York, N.Y., 1956, pp. 197-209.
32. Beadle, G. W., and Tatum, E. L., *Proc. Natl. Acad. Sci.*, 27, 499-506 (1941).

33. Keys, Ancel, "Experimental Induction of Neuropsychoses by Starvation," in *Biology of Mental Health and Disease*, Paul B. Hoeber, Inc., New York, N. Y., 1952, pp. 515-525.

34. Wilder, Russell M., "Experimental Induc-

tion of Psychoneuroses through Restriction of Intake of Thiamine," in *Biology of Mental Health and Disease*, Paul B. Hoeber, Inc., New York, N. Y., 1952, pp. 531-538.

35. Rose, W. C., personal communication.

Biophysical Theories:
ETIOLOGY AND DEVELOPMENT

Few theorists would deny that heredity plays a role in psychopathology, but most would insist that genetic factors can be modified substantially by learning and experience. This moderate view states that heredity operates not as a fixed constant, but as a disposition subject to the circumstances of an individuals's upbringing. Franz Kallmann, the most productive genetic researcher and theorist of contemporary psychiatry, takes a more inflexible position in his paper. He refers to a body of impressive data which implicates heredity in a variety of psychopathologies. Although he admits that variations in these disorders may be produced by environmental conditions, he is convinced that these are "superficial" influences which will not prevent the individual from succumbing to his hereditary defect. Eugen Bleuler, perhaps second only to Freud as the major theorist in psychopathology in the early years of this century, proposes in his article that the overt psychological features of "schizophrenia" are merely surface expressions of a physiological defect. He does not commit himself, as does Kallmann, to the view that schizophrenia is a hereditary disorder, but he opts unequivocally for a biophysical etiological explanation.

The Physiogenic and Psychogenic in Schizophrenia

EUGEN P. BLEULER

Since Jung and myself following in Freud's footsteps pointed out, that a great part of the symptomatology of schizophrenia is to be regarded as psychic reaction, and Adolf Meyer at the same time based his well-known theory of the disease on psychic causes, some of us are often inclined to overlook that these psychic mechanisms, as they are known at the present time, do not explain the whole disease. They are only possible, if there is a certain predisposition of the brain and this disposition in schizophrenia seems to be a processive disease.

According to our conception, we can distinguish in schizophrenia, primary and secondary signs. Most of the symptoms described by Kraepelin, such as autism, delusions, illusions of memory, a part of the hallucinations, negativism, stereotypies, mannerisms and most of the catatonic signs, are secondary signs. For the explanation of all these phenomena we have to utilize the mechanisms which are also true for the normal psychology, working on the

From *Amer. J. Psychiat.* 87:203-211, 1930, by permission of the American Psychiatric Association.

basis of the primary trouble. We consider as the main primary signs, both certain disorders in affectivity and in associations, which we have described upon other occasions. The disorder in the affectivity is the tendency of the feelings to work independently of each other, instead of working together, which becomes evident, for instance, in the ambivalence, in inadequate affective reactions, simultaneous crying and laughing, and many other observations which occur very frequently in schizophrenics. The associations, on the other hand, are no longer connected by a final aim and frequently deviate from the direction which is given in a normal person by the topic and by the aim of the central thoughts.

The purpose of this paper is to discuss for some forms and some signs in schizophrenia, what and how much can be explained by mere psychological considerations and, on the other hand, to show for what phenomena the psychological explanations are insufficient. There are even symptoms which seem to indicate that there must be physiological lesions.

The psychic mechanism is seen most clearly in paranoid forms. A working man, for instance, would like to earn more, and to be more than he actually is, but he does not get on. Even for a healthy person it is by no means pleasant to think that he himself is to blame for his failures. Everybody first looks elsewhere for the causes of his lack of success. The workman who makes impossible demands, must necessarily come into opposition or into actual conflict with his foreman and fellow-workers. This suggests to him, that these persons grudge him promotion or have given a post to one of their friends, which should have been given to him. Such a suspicion, it is true, can arise in the mind of a healthy person; but when there are primary lesions, when the affects exercise a greater influence on the process of thought than usual, the counter-concepts are suppressed and suspicion becomes more

easily conviction. Hence, delusions of persecution occur in many cases. The sick person finds direct fulfillment of his wishes in his delusions. According to the popular saying, even a healthy person believes in what he wishes; but the sick person knows it and actually *is* the founder of a religion.

Some delusions of grandeur ensue, when the thinking process has become so distintegrated or, in general, so illogical that the patient no longer notices the grossest contradictions to reality. This frequently occurs after long years of delusions of persecution. Then he is emperor, Pope, Christ, or even God himself; not only is he going to make inventions, but he actually *has* made them. Here, we can distinctly see how the psychic development of the delusions depends on the progress of the primary lesion.

Perhaps a patient will come to you and first complain of all sorts of paresthesias (neurasthenic state). After a year, possibly he may come again with the same sensations, but now, in spite of all the physician's proofs to the contrary, he draws the conclusion that he is suffering from some grave bodily disease, possibly syphilis, although he has never been infected (hypochondriacal stage). Again, after a long interval, the patient is seen to be in an excited state, inimically disposed towards his surroundings; he knows now that he has enemies who are causing him unpleasurable sensations, by all sorts of machinations; the paresthesias have become proprioceptive hallucinations. He is now in the paranoid stage and decidedly psychotic. The more seriously disturbed thinking-process has drawn quite impossible inferences from the unpleasurable sensations.

In a somewhat different way, the disturbances in thinking are manifested in the case of a woman disappointed in love, who suddenly eliminates the bitter reality, and, in her hallucinations *is* engaged, married, and not infrequently a child is born. Such dream states, in contrast with mere hysterical (mere psychogenic) ones, may last for months at a time. In principle, therefore, they would be a purely psychogenic syndrome. Its schizophrenic basis, however, is clearly shown in several peculiarities; on the basis of them, as a rule, diagnosis can be made rapidly. (Lack of connection and sequence in the patient's stream of talk and in his behavior, etc.)

Psychic reactions on the basis of a morbid disposition, which are at once comprehensible, are the exalted or anxious *excitations to unpleasant events,* and also autism, the withdrawal from the unsatisfying real world into an imaginary one, which offers more to the patient. The mechanism is, therefore, similar to that in neuroses but nearly all of these signify a direct "flight into illness," and this is rare in schizophrenic reactions; such reactions stray from the right path and their schizophrenic coloring is possible only if a morbid predisposition is present; and in schizophrenia this predisposition is very clearly seen in disturbances in thought and in feeling. It is not his "complexes" as such which *cause* schizophrenia, but they *shape* the morbid picture. The fundamental disturbances, those of the thinking process and those of affectivity, develop quite independently of disagreeable experiences, from which not one of us is spared. Thus all the difficulties of the European War did not cause any increase in the number of cases of schizophrenia.

For us the alteration of the thinking-process, or, elementarily expressed, of the association, is of special importance, and, as a matter of fact, nearly all the psychogenic symptoms can be derived from it. As far as we can recognize this alteration, it is a dynamic one. Thus, we also see something similar even in those cases in which the power of the train of thought is normally weakened, as in dreams and lack of attention, and in so called mind-wandering. In schizophrenia, it is the highest control which fails where it would be necessary to act, and this again must be referred

to a disturbance of the connections of all the individual functions; *for this highest control (Oberleitung) is not a special function of our soul, but the outcome, the integrated summarizing of all the individual functions.*

With this dismemberment of the connections, it is comprehensible that the logical function of thinking is disturbed by affective needs, as it is clearly evident in the example of manic forms.

Although similar association disturbances may also occur under normal circumstances, the schizophrenic thinking seems to be of direct physical origin: It shows itself in no way dependent on psychic influences, but solely on the seriousness of a fundamental process. When the disturbance is particularly severe, in acute mental aberration, catatonia and dyskinesis, it is accompanied as a rule by other symptoms, which we are rightly accustomed to regard as bodily: Raised or lowered temperature, albumen in urine, metabolic disturbances, gnashing of teeth, "Flockenlesen," fainting fits or cramps, not infrequently followed by temporary paresis of the limbs or the language, pupillary disturbances, greatly increased idiomuscular reactions, vasomotor disturbances, edema, somnolence, disturbances of the chemistry of the body, especially of the liver-functions, abnormal protein content in the spinal fluid. In many cases, too, the brain-trouble is demonstrated from the psychic side by the fact, that the confusions and delirium have absolutely the character of the "exogene" as Bonhoeffer designates it. Many cases of stupor, with their general prostraton of the elementary psychic functions, conception and train of thought, often point clearly to brain-pressure, and, on autopsy, tense edema of the pia or brain-swelling is found. In the various forms of such deliria, the fundamental similarity of certain symptoms or of the whole picture to other physiogenic conditions, intoxication, fever psychoses, epileptic absences, meningitis, encephalitis cannot be denied, and in all such cases, we also find in the autopsy histological alterations of the brain tissue, which show some uniformity. But in all chronic cases, too, decreases in the amount of ganglion cells and certain changes in the glia, furnish a proof that we are in presence of a brain lesion, of course not in the sense that the histological finding is the direct foundation of the primary psychic symptoms; it is merely an *indicator* of the existence of brain lesions, which, on the one hand, express themselves as psychic, and on the other hand as anatomical. Chronic histological findings always correspond with the clinical chronic picture, and acute changes, with acute ones. Organic symptoms are also the hyperkinesis and akinesis, which are likewise found in various diseases of the basal ganglia.

In contrast to encephalitis, affectivity in schizophrenia is not destroyed, but is, in some way, hampered in expression. Affective impulses which are in no way psychically perceptible, can be demonstrated in the psychogalvanic experiment, and the affects can again appear if a catatonic patient becomes senile, or if he is analyzed according to Freud's methods. Yet, we always obtain the impression that the affectivity is also primarily altered, but by no means in the sense of a simple destruction of all feelings as it was formerly believed.

In the case of hallucinations, we have already mentioned the excitatory states of the proprioceptive apparatus; but there are still other hallucinations which are to be attributed to a physiologic excitation of the nervous system; viz., the various kinds of a photopsia, the sensations of threads, the majority of animal visions, musical hallucinations. With respect to the latter category, it must be added that also purely psychogenic animal visions appear, but in every case, these are animals with sexual significance which are evolved from erotic complexes. Music is also heard in states of ecstasy which can be wholly, or in part, psychogenic and hysteriform.

Although we may register theoretically the majority of symptoms with great certitude, as physical or psychic, conditions in the clinical picture are often very complicated. There are catatonic spells of a purely physical, and others of a purely psychogenic nature, but when a certain psychogenic dulling of the consciousness is present, the spell may be brought about by something in connection with this disposition, which spell must then, naturally, have the commingled signs of both origins. Or a physiogenic spell increases the disintegration of the assocation so that the complex-tendencies, which are constantly present, can now manifest themselves by means of symptoms. The cause of the spell is physical, but the psychic symptomatology reveals the hidden complexes. Thus, it is the whole disease, and most distinctly with its acute exacerbations.

A girl is disappointed in love and has a catatonic episode. It is supposed that the disappointment is the cause of the episode, but it is only *one* of the causes; perhaps the girl has formerly experienced other equally great disappointments and has overcome them without any ill results. That the present disappointment has such results arises from the fact, that a physical process was already on the way, and when we are able to look more closely, we may find that the so-called falling in love was already a symptom and not the cause of the episode. We consequently see in these cases, too, a complete recovery, and in others, at least a disappearance of delirium, catalepsy or dyskinesis, *without any improvement in the situation.* The more serious the predisposing physical change, the less easily can the psychic causes produce an episode, or, better said, can make it manifest and vice versa. Hence, the physical and psychic symptoms and shades can mingle in all sorts of circumstances.

In *hallucinations,* we see yet other kinds of co-operation of both factors. The lack of control by the dissociation of the individual functions certainly causes the tendency to hear voices; the content, however, is determined by the complexes. Thus, in all states, the voices are the expression and confirmation of the delusions, whilst in acute delirium, it is true, they often follow in their own laws. We have seen above, how the paresthesias are transformed by the disturbance to logic and the need of justifying oneself, into bodily hallucinations, as a consequence of inimical machinations, but a fairly large portion of these same bodily hallucinations are psychogenic in later states.

In this way, the whole illness with its alterations, becomes intelligible. On the whole, schizophrenia seems to be a physical disease with a lingering *course*, which, however, can exacerbate irregularly from some reason unknown to us, into sudden episodes and then get better again. We then see the physiogenic catatonia and delirium of exogenous character. In principle, they are capable of involution, and, so to speak, all of them really do involute, but some almost to their previous state, whilst others leave behind a more or less pronounced schizophrenic condition, the "secondary dementia" of the older school of psychiatrists. The episodes, with their changing issue, can repeat themselves, and then their psychic residues are often summarized in time into the same grave picture as, in other cases, the first episode has caused, but the same picture can develop quite imperceptibly without an acute attack. Actual chronic states seldom improve to a recovery; chronic catatonic states never.

Theoretically, reactions have to be sharply separated from the episodes, although both forms of exacerbation are in practice not always easily distinguishable from each other, and are prone to mix, but if they are really only psychogenic, they can heal to the earlier state; real deterioration is in connection with the physiogenic process. The prognosis of the psychogenic-physiogenic mixing is dependent on it, however important each of the two components may be in the picture, and then on the unfortunately incalculable capacity for involution of the physiogenic part.

Other not infrequent exacerbations are caused by the manic and the melancholic affective states, which may have quite different significances: a considerable part of these, is a symptom of a manic-depressive psychosis, which mixes with the schizophrenia. Another, belongs to schizophrenia itself, and in addition, there must be other mood-swings whose genesis is not yet exactly known. The affective states, as such, heal. The prognosis, however, becomes less favorable if the physical process exacerbates with the manic or depressive state.

The manifest disease can remain at a standstill in every phase and everything that we can perhaps bring into relation with the acute cell-modifications can involute. I believe, however, that in most cases the standstill of the brain-process permits a considerable psychic recovery, because it is less a deficiency than an intoxication, or the continuance of the process which gives the symptoms their gravity. Such standstills and involutions are often practically identical to a recovery, and many formerly pronounced sick people, are considered to be well, although in such cases the psychiatrist, as a rule, can still discover traces of the illness on closer inspection. *Improvements up to what is practically a recovery do not, therefore, contradict the diagnosis of a schizophrenia.* More for doctrinaire than for real reasons an attempt has been made to include in schizophrenia merely incurable forms. This, however, is contrary to experience. All attempts to separate deteriorating forms from non-deteriorating ones have failed. With its symptoms, as at present known, it cannot be subdivided, although I myself expect that this will be done some day. Out of three apparently like cases, one can deteriorate in a few months; the second only after several years by a new episode; the third not at all.

In acute stages, as already hinted, the purely psychogenic ones pass away without causing any injury. The acute physiogenic episodes are indeed capable of involution, and all of them involute to a certain degree, but in the majority of cases, leave slight, or serious chronic defects behind them. On these, some are purely psychic residues: a patient, for instance, who has a suicidal tendency motivated by schizophrenic depression, although he is no longer depressed, and could easily come to terms with life, now continues to try to commit suicide with the same persistence, but for no reason. Or, if in an acutely delirious state, he tore and soiled his clothing, and cannot refrain from doing so afterwards, nobody knows why. A girl who mixed up various languages and ideas in an incomprehensible confusion, keeps up the tendency by mere force of habit, and for other reasons; e.g., because she is unconsciously afraid to take up life's task again. Other "secondary" states are more closely connected with the expired, but not quite involuted, physical process.

Although a certain number of patients become deteriorated with every treatment, and others improve even in apparently severe cases, the treatment will decide in more than one-third of schizophrenic cases whether they can become social men again or not. Hence, one hospital has many, another, only few cases of improvement. Proper treatment, however, is possible only if it is known, who is accessible to our measures and at what period. Hitherto, we have not been able to influence the physical process, however many alkaloids and gland extracts we give the patients. In acute cases, we shall, therefore, confine ourselves to expectant treatment, but we shall not trouble the patient with proceedings till the physical process takes a turn for the better; only then, shall we try to bring him back to reality. If he is left to himself, there is great danger that he will withdraw autistically into himself and lose touch with the world. Whether, in the course of a serious illness, an exacerbation occurs, is quite independent of our treatment, but the fact, that a certain patient breaks windows, soils and tears his clothes, cries, fights, *is not determined directly by the process of the disease; it belongs to the psychogenic superstructure, and it is a reaction of his complexes to inner, and particularly to outer experi-ences.* It is, therefore, possible to influence the patient in his symptoms. He should be made interested in some occupation, or, in grave cases, be so trained that, without his illness being improved, he gives up his bad manners and behaves better. A great deal can be accomplished with skill and patience. With many schizophrenics, not only negativistic ones, however, it is often impossible to get the necessary touch in the ordinary way; a semi-narcosis of 8 or 12 days, with somnifene or another narcotic, may bring about a complete change.

If, however, we do not wish to have all our trouble for nothing, and make the patient rebel against our measures, the right moment must be chosen for these. We must know, above all, when an acute process has so far improved that a good result is possible. Then it may happen that a patient who seemed to be quite deteriorated and was violent and noisy, can be given back to his parents, and behaves himself like a normal person from one minute to the other. We must notice when the patients have really needs to return home. Many patients have a secret animosity towards one or another members of the family; if, at this time, they are sent home, matters will go badly. Hence, we must wait till this attitude has been changed or dismiss them to another place. As the patients themselves are frequently unaware of such conditions, it is a great advantage for the physician to know all the signs that Freud has taught us to observe, which betray the concealed feelings of the patient with greater certainty than their words.

Ladies and gentlemen, no doubt a great many of the facts about which I have just spoken will be known to you: the more, therefore, may I hope for an understanding of those about which I was able only to hint. I hope, however, I have shown you how the exact knowledge of the connections of the symptoms can give us the proper directions for treating our patients and how theoretical science has also a practical utility in this matter.

The Genetics of Human Behavior

FRANZ J. KALLMANN

Experimental biologists are safely entrenched in the age-old esteem for progress through science and can well afford to withhold comments on the cultural and behavioral aspects of morphologic inequalities among people. It is only when such an investigator invades that particular province of psychiatry where belief in heredity in relation to personality development is equated with lack of empathy or a depraved social conscience that a sinister tinge accrues to him and his work (11, 19, 24).

In the face of such a 2-valued system of conceptualization and terminology, connoting either trust or distrust in man's perfectibility, even a truly liberal psychiatrist with genetic leanings finds it difficult to cast off the onus of being an unempathetic metascientist. To be sure, were he to feel called upon to express codified value judgments regarding the original goodness or sinfulness of mankind (22), he would be out of bounds. However, it is not his fault if his investigative data arouse so much disquietude that they need a de-emotionalized climate in which to be assimilated. Meanwhile, to balance the scales, there are zealous research workers everywhere who are ardent in their views, despite the fact that they have not had the benefit of genetic training.

In the search for the roots of human behavior, it would be well to stay clear of dichotomous absolutes. In particular, the interaction of heredity and environment is formulated as a meaningless antithesis as long as vague abstractions are used in describing the properties of an organism that is most certainly both active and reactive.

Man, to be sure, mirrors his culture and the social configuration of his

Abridged from *Amer. J. Psychiat. 113:*496-501, 1956, by permission of the American Psychiatric Association.

parental home. Yet he also forms an autonomous functional unit that perpetuates itself as the matrix of his hierarchically organized traits and self-assertive acts. The human infant, if normally endowed, is certain to possess those structural, functional, and behavioral potentialities that distinguish individuals of the human species from those of any other (15, 17). While the emergence of his individuality will depend in part on the nutritive capacities of his family group, the constructs of his mind are at no stage like a hollow shell or a *tabula rasa,* as Locke would have it (4).

In a more eclectic scheme of human personality development, the importance of genic elements in the organization of behavior patterns rests on the interdependence of organic structure and psychologic function throughout the life of the individual. There is no behavior without an organism, no organism without a genotype, and no physiologic adaptedness without continuous and integrated gene activity.

Environmental influences are vital, and after conception they gain coequality with those arising from heredity. However, only within the limits set by the genic constitution of the organism can external factors have an effect on the dynamics of physiologic functions and interactions. Beyond these limits, no power plant exists for generating behavioral potentials. Such basic phenomena as growth and maturation, homeostasis and adaptation, reflexive behavior and constitution remain chameleonic allegories without the solid foundations of genetic principles.

Man, in order to be able to maintain his present evolutionary level, must be both conditionable by culture and impressible by education. The ability to learn from others and to profit from experience is determined by the genotype, while cultural values and opportunities have to be acquired by each individual through communication with his group. Variations in basic traits are inherited to the extent that they are end-products of a chain reaction set in motion by genes.

The effect of a gene expresses itself through the control of a specific enzyme which spurs on the production of a unit difference in development or function. The outcome of this action is subject either to reinforcement or interference by nonallelic genes, that is, other genes which are not located at the same point of a chromosome.

Conversely, the occurrence of different mutants of the same gene at any one locus makes it possible for the given point to control various normal and abnormal versions of a trait. In fact the demonstration of specific pathologic changes producible by a mutant gene provides adequate proof of the existence of a normal allele. The action of the normal gene can be assumed to play an indispensable part in maintaining health and normal behavior, even if its biochemical equivalents have yet to be identified. Therefore, it is just as unfair to blame heredity for only the unpleasant events in life, as it is to hold the genes responsible for every unusual mode of behavior whose origin is still in the dark.

Broadly formulated, then, a person's phenotype may be defined as the visible expression of his moldability by environmental influences, while it is his genotype that determines his norm of reaction to the total range of possible environments during his lifetime. The implication here is that every gene-controlled mode of activity requires an operational area in which to unfold (9, 18, 23, 28, 31).

Since no part of this environmental area of operation is inert, in the sense of being ineffectual where the behavioral responses of the individual are concerned, appreciation of environmentally produced variations in the expression of gene-specific behavior components is clearly as essential to an understanding of heredity as is the knowledge of geometry to that of mathematics. Except for real instincts, which need not be learned, it is axiomatic that no type of behavior is controlled entirely by genic elements, nor is it ever the result of a single cause, genetic or nongenetic (5, 7, 33). Estimates of individual contributions are meaningful only when viewed against the backdrop of the total genetic and environmental variation observed in a population.

It has already been mentioned in this symposium that some traits occur more often in one population than in another, depending on the relative frequency of a gene in different populations. Also, noninstinctive responsiveness to conditioning influences varies in different stages of development, and from person to person at a comparable stage of development (7, 13). The aggregate of gene-specific personality constituents is so vast, and the number of interactive variables in the shaping of a behavior pattern so infinite, that every individual can count on being unique—identical twins excepted.

The gene-specific uniqueness of man's individuality is now recognized in all branches of the behavioral sciences, even if the parliamentary Bill of Acceptance has yet to be ratified by some. What differs most are the descriptive labels affixed to this uniqueness. For instance, the differentiation of early behavior patterns has been described as an "ordered sequence" that begins with the establishment of reflexive responses and gradually leads through progressive stages of maturing to the development of coordinated motor, perceptual, and intellectual functions (6) ; or as "hierarchical organization of traits," in the course of which the infant will in time develop a conscience and a sense of self (4) ; or as a process of "biosocial integration with the total family configuration" (1). Other genetic phenomena have been referred to as the result of an innate equipment "with specific power plants and tools" (25) and as a biologically determined trend toward security and homeostatic stability, identified with a striving for "survival with a minimum amount of expenditure"(2).

Despite these differences in terms used to describe the interaction of genetic and non-genetic components of behavior, there is interdisciplinary agreement on at least one general premise; namely, that those aspects of the environment which are potent in affecting the organism depend not only on the degree of maturity the organism has attained, but also on its ability to cope with extrinsic hazards. Another point of unanimity is the belief that many children are capable of working out fairly adequate ways of dealing with difficulties in their home milieu and interpersonal relationships. By the same token, the established interdependence of social aspirations and biologic needs would seem to impose certain limits on the diversity and reach of human motives and the sublimating endeavors taken up by self-determination.

Genetically, a chaotic lack of uniformity in human societies is prevented by various principles of selection, and by the fact that the cultural forces which mold, as well as the formative elements which secure moldability on the human level, are actually end-products of the same evolutionary process. Viewed in this light, they are like the 2 sides of a coin, defying analysis as independent variables(10, 12, 26). Hence, the inability to separate the 2 sets of determining factors can only in part be ascribed to the parental practice of rearing one's own children. It is more than likely, too, that this virtual inseparability will last as long as our knowledge of the constituents of the coin remains as limited as it is at present. A reflection of this state of affairs is seen in the fact that most test devices for measuring meaningful personality differences have proven refractory to standardization(8, 18, 21).

Apart from unavoidable limitations on the assessment of gene-specific personality components, the twin study method represents an excellent comparative procedure for demonstrating the significance of heredity in many behavior variations, both normal and abnormal. The effectiveness of the method is matched by its economy and versatility as a sampling procedure for investigating traits, which require vertical and longitudinal comparisons under controlled conditions, and personal contact with families from various population groups, including some whose private affairs might otherwise not be open to research. Procedurally, it is no real disadvantage that twins cannot be separated before they are born, or that they cannot be provided with 2 mothers of different age, personality, or health status.

The popular notion that the behavior patterns of 1-egg twins are alike chiefly because of unusual similarity in their early environments has yet to be substantiated. If confirmed, the argument would only strengthen, rather than weaken, any correctly formulated genetic theory. Psychodynamic concepts, too, are built on the premise that man is selective in respect to important aspects of his life experiences and so can be thought of as "creating his own environment"(2). Utilization of our "own potential formula of adjustment" evidently depends on what Sanford(27) calls the body's ability "to function at its own built-in best." Plainly, each of these elegant allegories conveys a genetic idea.

In the area of normal personality variations, gene-specific derivations have been shown by comparative twin data to range from physical, coordinative, physiognomic, and temperamental characteristics to intellectual abilities, affective regulations, and special talents(6, 14, 16, 29, 32, 34). In between are sex maturation patterns, variations in antibody production and neurohormonal alarm reactions, the capacity for longevity, and the ingredients for sustained tolerance of physiologic or psychologic stress, a highly essential prerequisite for a well-balanced personality(17, 20, 30). It is well known that each individual has his own threshold of adaptability to different types of stress, and his own pattern of stress symptom formation.

Consistent similarity in the composition of these personality components is not found in the absence of genotypic similarity. Two-egg twins of the same sex tend to differ as much in their personalities as do any siblings reared together or apart. In 1-egg twins, even pronounced differences in life experiences, however adverse, are rarely potent enough to erase basic similarities in appearance and general personality traits.

As to behavior disorders that are not sufficiently explained on a situational or experiential basis, the list of conditions for which complete twin sibship data are now available is headed by the schizophrenic and manic-depressive types of psychosis. Since these 2 disorders do not occur interchangeably in the same twin pairs, they are assumed to be genotypically specific. The potentialities for a cyclic psychosis are probably associated with a subtle disturbance in a neurohormonal control mechanism which ordinarily protects a person from having harmful extremes of emotional responses.

While the tendency to exceed the normal range of mood alterations apparently requires the mutative effect of a single dominant gene with incomplete penetrance, the metabolic deficiency in a potentially schizophrenic person is most likely the result of a recessive gene. The disordered behavior pattern produced by this specific vulnerability factor is not correlated with inadequacy of the parental home in a simple manner, but is subject to modification by mesodermal defense reactions. Psychodynamically, the pattern has been described as an integrative pleasure deficiency leading to adaptive incompetence (25).

Involutional melancholia and other non-periodic forms of depressive behavior in the involutional and senile periods have been shown by twin family data to be unrelated to the manic-depressive group of disorders. There is an indirect link with the schizophrenic genotype through certain forms of emotional instability characteristic of schizoid personality traits. Other symptoms of maladjustment in the senescent period may arise either from gene-specific metabolic dysfunctions peculiar to the senium, or from graded differences in general health and survival values.

Homosexual behavior in the adult male continues to yield a higher 1-egg concordance rate than any of the other conditions investigated. This finding points to a disarrangement in the balance between male and female maturation patterns, resulting in a shift toward an alternative minus variant in the integrative process of psychosexual maturation.

Another condition with a well-established monozygotic concordance rate of close to 100% is an entirely different defect of more obvious organicity, namely, mongolism (3). Since the corresponding rate for 2-egg co-twins does not exceed that of their later-born siblings (approximately 4%), the search for the etiologic factor in mongolism is narrowed down by twin data to a more or less permanent change in the mother's endocrine or reproductive system. Evidently, the noxious influence during a mongoloid pregnancy cannot be transient, but acts on a genetically predisposed embryo, or upon the ovum, or upon the embryo prior to the earliest stage when twinning occurs by division.

In regard to all these disorders, twin family studies are helping materially to focus attention on persisting obscurities in their etiology. Generally, the objective of genetic investigations in man is not only to demonstrate that gene-controlled phenomena play a role in the differentiation of normal and abnormal behavior patterns, but to determine how this action takes place.

In conclusion, it may be said with some measure of satisfaction that recent progress in genetics has been encouraging. Although exact studies of the subject only began at the turn of this century, advances in the cellular, structural and metabolic areas of personality organization have been remarkable. An immediate result has been the improvement of our knowledge regarding the interacting bipolarity of human life. Growing insight into this interaction will gradually unfold a better understanding of human behavior. Somewhere along this line it will be possible to explain variable behavior patterns in terms of physiochemical processes powered by genic elements.

Once this goal has been reached, psychiatrists and other workers in the behavioral sciences will no longer hesitate to welcome geneticists as allies in interdisciplinary studies of human frailties and capacities. Only then may modern man begin to recognize his potential ability to plan his own future, as well as that of the world around him. In consequence, he may learn to exercise his obligation of self-determination in this direction.

References

1. Ackerman, N. W., and Behrens, M. L. *In* Hoch, P. H., and Zubin, J., Eds. Psychopathology of Childhood. New York: Grune & Stratton, 1955.
2. Alexander, F. Am. J. Psychiat., *112*: 692, 1956.
3. Allen, G., and Baroff, G. S. *In* Testimonial Volume for Prof. Tage Kemp. Acta Genetica et Statistica Medica. Basel: S. Karger, 1956.
4. Allport, G. W. Becoming: Basic Considerations for a Psychology of Personality. New Haven: Yale University Press, 1955.
5. Anastasi, A. *In* Hooker, D., Ed. Genetics and The Inheritance of Integrated Neurological and Psychiatric Patterns, Vol. 33. Baltimore: Williams & Wilkins, 1954.
6. Bayley, N. *In* Hoch, P. H., and Zubin, J., Eds. Psychopathology of Childhood. New York: Grune & Stratton, 1955.
7. Beach, F. A. *In* Blake, R. R., and Ramsey, G. V. Perception, An Approach to Personality. New York: Ronald Press, 1951. *Also:* in Wilson, J., et al. Current Trends in Psychology and The Behavioral Sciences. Pittsburgh: University of Pittsburgh Press, 1954.
8. Cronbach, L. J. *In* Farnsworth, P. R., Ed. Annual Review of Psychology, Vol. 7. Stanford: Annual Reviews, 1956.
9. David, P. R., and Snyder, L. H. *In* Rohrer, J. H., and Sherif, M., Eds. Social Psychology at The Crossroads, New York: Harper, 1951.
10. Dobzhansky, T. Evolution, Genetics, and Man. New York: J. Wiley & Sons, 1955.
11. Dreikurs, R. Internat. J. Soc. Psychiat., *1*: 23, 1955.
12. Fuller, J. L. Nature and Nuture: A Modern Synthesis. New York: Doubleday, 1954.
13. Garn, S. M. Ann. N. Y. Acad. Sci., *63*: 537, 1955.
14. Glass, B. *In* Hooker, D., Ed. Genetics and The Inheritance of Integrated Neurological and Psychiatric Patterns, Vol. 33. Baltimore: Williams & Wilkins, 1954. *Also:* J. Hopkins Mag., *6*: 2, 1955.
15. Goldschmidt, R. B. Theoretical Genetics. Berkeley: University of California Press, 1955.
16. Grebe, H. A. Ge. Me. Ge., *4*: 275, 1955.
17. Kallmann, F. J. Heredity in Health and Mental Disorder. New York: W. W. Norton, 1953. *Also:* Am. J. Human Genet., *6*: 157, 1954.
18. Kallmann, F. J., and Baroff, G. S. Annual Review of Psychology, *6*: 297, 1955.
19. Karpman, B., Ed. Multiple Murders (Anon. Editorial). Arch. Crim. Psychodynamics, *1*: 713, 1955.
20. Lacey, J. I., and Van Lehn, R. Psychosomat. Med., *14*: 71, 1952.
21. McClelland, D. C. *In* Farnsworth, P. R., Ed. Annual Review of Psychology. Stanford: Annual Reviews, 1956.
22. Montagu, M. F. A. Am. J. Psychiat., *112*: 401, 1955.
23. Nissen, H. W. *In* Jones, M. R., Ed. Nebraska Symposium on Motivation. Lincoln: University Nebraska Press, 1954.
24. Pastore, N. The Nature-Nurture Controversy. New York: King's Crown Press, 1949.
25. Rado, S. Am. J. Psychiat., *110*: 406, 1953; J. Nerv. Ment. Dis., *121*: 389, 1955.
26. Riddle, O. The Unleashing of Evolutionary Thought. New York: Vantage Press, 1954.
27. Sanford, F. H. Am. Psychol., *10*: 829, 1955.
28. Schaffner, B., Ed. Group Processes. Madison: Madison, 1955.
29. Strandskov, H. H. Eugen. Quart., *2*: 152, 1955.
30. Sutton, H. E., and Vandenberg, S. G. Human Biol., *25*: 318, 1953.
31. Tanner, J. M., Ed. Prospects in Psychiatric Research. Oxford: Blackwell, 1953.
32. Thurstone, L. I., Thurstone, G. T., and Strandskov, H. H. A Psychological Study of Twins. I. Distribution of Absolute Twin Differences for Identical and Fraternal Twins. Report No. 4. The Psychometric Laboratory: University of North Carolina, 1953.
33. Tinbergen, N. The Study of Instinct. Oxford: Clarendon Press, 1951.
34. Vandenberg, S. G. A comparison of identical and fraternal twins on a battery of psychological tests: A preliminary report on the University of Michigan twin study. Paper presented at A.I.B.S. Meeting, East Lansing, Michigan, Sept. 5-9, 1955.

Biophysical Theories:

PATHOLOGICAL PATTERNS

How can the various forms of psychopathology best be classified? To the biophysical theorist, the answer lies in terms of these features of biological make-up which dispose individuals to pathology. Pathologic behavior patterns that are correlated consistently with measurable morphological characteristics offer a beginning toward a quantitative and stable psychiatric classification, according to William Sheldon. In his paper, Sheldon formulates an "operational" classification of psychiatric disorders based on his exhaustive studies of body build and temperament. In contrast to his forerunner, Ernst Kretschmer, Sheldon's theoretical speculations are founded on years of quantitative research. Paul Meehl's paper shows marked indebtedness to the fertile ideas of Eugen Bleuler. Meehl extends Bleuler's earlier notions by bringing together a wide range of current research; here he offers an intricate and ingenious biophysical hypothesis for the probable neurological substrate of "schizophrenia."

Constitutional Psychiatry

WILLIAM H. SHELDON

A. STRUCTURAL CONCEPTS

Constitution. The organizational or underlying pattern. Literally, the way a thing *stands together*. The whole aggregate of the relatively fixed and deep-seated structural and behavioral characteristics that collectively differentiate a personality. Perhaps the most satisfactory way to start an examination of the constitutional pattern of a human being is photographically, although this is only a beginning and offers but an anchorage or frame of reference for constitutional description. Behind the objective and

overt aspects of morphology lie individual differences first in those aspects of morphology which are not outwardly revealed, such as the structure, dysplasias, and *t* component of internal organs, of the nervous system, of the endocrine glands, and so on; and further, individual differences in physiology and chemistry. All of these differences contribute to and make up what is referred to as personality. The term *constitution* implies only a certain relatedness and orderliness or patterning with respect to the underlying aspects of personality. In so far as the student of constitution addresses his energies to the study of external morphology he is but trying to anchor (to something taxonomically describable) an approach to person-

Abridged from *Varieties of Delinquent Youth*, pages 14-62, 1949, by William H. Sheldon, E. M. Hartl, and Eugene McDermott. By permission of Professor Sheldon, copyright holder.

43

ality as a whole, in its physiological and immunological and psychological as well as morphological aspects.

The Somatotype. A quantification of the primary components determining the morphological structure of an individual. In practice the somatotype is a series of three numerals, each expressing the approximate strength of one of the primary components in a physique. The first numeral always refers to *endomorphy*, the second to *mesomorphy*, the third to *ectomorphy*. When a 7-point scale is used the somatotype 7-1-1 is the most extreme endomorph, the 1-7-1 is the most extreme mesomorph, and the 1-1-7 is the most extreme ectomorph. The somatotype 4-4-4 falls at the midpoint of the scale with respect to all three primary components.

Endomorphy, or the first component: Relative predominance in the bodily economy of structure associated with digestion and assimilation. Relatively great development of the digestive *viscera*. In embryonic life the endoderm, or inner embryonic layer, grows into what becomes the functional element in a long tube, stretched or coiled from mouth to anus with a number of appendages. This is the digestive tube. Together with its appendages it is sometimes called the vegetative system. Its organs make up the bulk of the viscera. Endomorphy means relative predominance of the vegetative system, with a consequent tendency to put on fat easily. Endomorphs have low specific gravity. They float easily in the water. When well nourished they tend toward softness and roundness throughout the body, but it should be remembered that in learning to gauge one of the components it is necessary to learn to gauge the other two at the same time.

Mesomorphy, or the second component: Relative predominance of the mesodermally derived tissues, which are chiefly bone, muscle, and connective tissue. These are the somatic structures, or the motor organ-systems. Mesomorphs tend toward massive strength and muscular development. When their endomorphy is low, so

that they remain lean, they retain a hard rectangularity of outline. If endomorphy is not low, mesomorphs tend to "fill out" heavily and to grow fat in middle life. However, because of the heavy underlying skeletal and muscular structure, they remain solid. When fat they are "hard-round," in contrast with the "soft-roundness" of endomorphy, and they continue in the general mold and in the proportions of athletic shapeliness. Endomorphs get roly-poly, globular, and pendulous. Mesomorphs just swell up in their generally athletic mold. Mesomorphs are of higher specific gravity than endomorphs. They are less buoyant in water but because of superior muscular power are nevertheless often good swimmers. The mesomorphic heart and blood vessels are large, and the skin seems relatively thick because of heavy reinforcement with underlying connective tissue.

Ectomorphy, or the third component: Relative predominance of the skin and its appendages, which include the nervous system. All of these tissues are derived from the ectodermal embryonic layer. In the ectomorph there is relatively little bodily mass and relatively great surface area —therefore greater sensory exposure to the outside world. Endomorphs and mesomorphs appear to be biological conservatives, the former investing faith in superior assimilative power or digestive ability, the latter in superior resistive substance and striking power. Ectomorphs seem to have departed from *both* of these essential biological insurances and to have embarked on an exteroceptive adventure. They have given up mass for surface, in a sense suppressing the primacy of both the digestive organ-system and the motor organ-system in favor of the sensory organ-system. The Italian School of Clinical Anthropology (Di Giovanni, Viola, Pende; *see* VHP, Chapter 2) calls them hyperevolutes, suggesting that in departing from the secure advantages of the coarser and heavier bodies of the endomorphs and mesomorphs (in favor of extending the sensorium externally), they tend

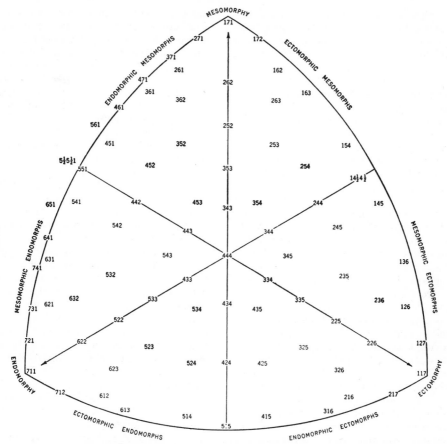

A SCHEMATIC TWO-DIMENSIONAL PROJECTION OF THE THEORETICAL SPATIAL RELATIONSHIPS AMONG THE KNOWN SOMATOTYPES

Figure 1.

to move out toward the end of an evolutionary limb whence it may be difficult to return. Morphologically, ectomorphy means flatness and fragility throughout the body, with a comparatively high height/weight index.

Mesomorphic endomorphs; endomorphic mesomorphs; ectomorphic mesomorphs; mesomorphic ectomorphs; endomorphic ectomorphs; ectomorphic endomorphs: These terms refer to physiques in which all three of the primary morphological components are of different strength. Figure 1 is a schematic two-dimensional presentation of the somatotypes in which these six various "families" are spatially delineated. An endomorphic mes-

omorph is an individual in whom mesomorphy predominates, with endomorphy second in order of strength, and ectomorphy third. Example: the somatotype 3–5–2.

B.   BEHAVIORAL CONCEPTS

Temperament.   According to Webster: (1) A mixing in due proportion; (2) The internal constitution with respect to balance or mixture of qualities or components; (3) The peculiar physical and mental character of an individual; (4) Frame of mind or type of mental reactions characteristic of an individual.

The original meaning of the Greek verb is to mix. As I use the term, temperament is simply some quantification of the mixture of components that a person presents. In this literal sense temperament at the morphological level is the somatotype. At a slightly more dynamic or behavioral level it is the pattern of the mixture of the three primary components *viscerotonia, somatotonia,* and *cerebrotonia.* At more complex and more culturally conditioned levels, temperament may be defined more elaborately and may embrace any schema for quantification of the manifest components of a personality that a psychologist can devise. In the academic exercise published in the second volume of this series (VT) it was shown that temperament can be measured at a level sufficiently basic to correlate about +.80 with the primary morphological components. It of course does not necessarily follow that the measurement of temperament at such a comparatively basic level is the most useful thing a psychologist can do with his time, especially if he should choose to stop at that level.

Temperament is the pattern at *all* levels. But as I use the term it is a little more specific than that. It is *the pattern quantitatively expressed, in terms of some schema of components which offers a frame of reference for an operational psychology.* The most difficult and most important task of the psychologist is that of making his choice of primary variables, or of getting down to primary components; that is to say, components which offer a basis for general quantitative comparison, and cannot be further factored. For elaboration of this exceedingly important point, see VHP, Chapter 5.

Viscerotonia: The first component of temperament, measured at the least-conditioned level of dynamic expression. Endomorphy is the same component measured at a purely structural or morphological level. Endomorphy is expressed by the morphological consequences of a predominance of the first component. Viscerotonia constitutes the primary or most general be-havioral expression of the same predominance; that is to say, predominance of the digestive-assimilative function—the gut function. A detailed ostensive definition of viscerotonia is presented in VT, pages 31–48. Twenty defining traits which when quantitatively scaled can be used to measure the first component at this level are those in the first column of Table 1.

In briefest summary viscerotonia is manifested by relaxation, conviviality, and gluttony for food, for company, and for affection or social support. When this component is predominant the primary motive in life seems to be assimilation and conservation of energy.

Somatotonia: The second component of temperament, measured at the least-conditioned level of dynamic expression. Mesomorphy is the same component measured at the morphological level. Somatotonia expresses the function of movement and predation—the somatic function. A detailed ostensive definition of somatotonia is presented in VT, pages 49–68. Twenty defining traits which can be used to measure this component at the "lowest dynamic level" are those in the second column of Table 1.

In briefest summary somatotonia is manifested by bodily assertiveness and by desire for muscular activity. When this component is predominant the primary motive of life seems to be the vigorous utilization or expenditure of energy. Somatotonics love action and power. Their motivational organization seems dominated by the soma.

Cerebrotonia: The third component of temperament, measured at the least-conditioned level of dynamic expression. Ectomorphy is the same component at the morphological level. Cerebrotonia appears to express the function of exteroception, which necessitates or involves cerebrally mediated inhibition of both of the other two primary functions. It also involves or leads to conscious attentionality and thereby to substitution of symbolic ideation for immediate overt response to stimulation. Attendant upon this latter phenomenon are the "cerebra

tragedies" of hesitation, disorientation, and confusion. These appear to
be by-products of overstimulation,
which is doubtless one consequence of

an overbalanced investment in exteroception. A detailed ostensive definition
of cerebrotonia is presented in VT,
pages 69–94. Twenty defining traits

Table 1. *The Scale for Temperament*

Name	Date	Photo No.	Scored by
I VISCEROTONIA....	**II** SOMATOTONIA....	**III** CEREBROTONIA....	
( ) 1. Relaxation in Posture and Movement	( ) 1. Assertiveness of Posture and Movement	( ) 1. Restraint in Posture and Movement, Tightness	
( ) 2. Love of Physical Comfort	( ) 2. Love of Physical Adventure	— 2. Physiological Over-response	
( ) 3. Slow Reaction	( ) 3. The Energetic Characteristic	( ) 3. Overly Fast Reactions	
— 4. Love of Eating	( ) 4. Need and Enjoyment of Exercise	( ) 4. Love of Privacy	
— 5. Socialization of Eating	— 5. Love of Dominating, Lust for Power	( ) 5. Mental Overintensity, Hyperattentionality, Apprehensiveness	
— 6. Pleasure in Digestion	( ) 6. Love of Risk and Chance	( ) 6. Secretiveness of Feeling, Emotional Restraint	
( ) 7. Love of Polite Ceremony	( ) 7. Bold Directness of Manner	( ) 7. Self-conscious Motility of the Eyes and Face	
( ) 8. Sociophilia	( ) 8. Physical Courage for Combat	( ) 8. Sociophobia	
— 9. Indiscriminate Amiability	( ) 9. Competitive Aggressiveness	( ) 9. Inhibited Social Address	
— 10. Greed for Affection and Approval	— 10. Psychological Callousness	— 10. Resistance to Habit, and Poor Routinizing	
— 11. Orientation to People	— 11. Claustrophobia	— 11. Agoraphobia	
( ) 12. Evenness of Emotional Flow	— 12. Ruthlessness, Freedom from Squeamishness	— 12. Unpredictability of Attitude	
( ) 13. Tolerance	( ) 13. The Unrestrained Voice	( ) 13. Vocal Restraint, and General Restraint of Noise	
( ) 14. Complacency	— 14. Spartan Indifference to Pain	— 14. Hypersensitivity to Pain	
— 15. Deep Sleep	— 15. General Noisiness	— 15. Poor Sleep Habits, Chronic Fatigue	
( ) 16. The Untempered Characteristic	( ) 16. Overmaturity of Appearance	( ) 16. Youthful Intentness of Manner and Appearance	
( ) 17. Smooth, Easy Communication of Feeling, Extraversion of Viscerotonia	— 17. Horizontal Mental Cleavage, Extraversion of Somatotonia	— 17. Vertical Mental Cleavage, Introversion	
— 18. Relaxation and Sociophilia under Alcohol	— 18. Assertiveness and Aggression under Alcohol	— 18. Resistance to Alcohol, and to other Depressant Drugs	
— 19. Need of People when Troubled	— 19. Need of Action when Troubled	— 19. Need of Solitude when Troubled	
— 20. Orientation toward Childhood and Family Relationships	— 20. Orientation toward Goals and Activities of Youth	— 20. Orientation toward the Later Periods of Life	

Note: The thirty traits with brackets constitute collectively the short form of the scale.

which can be used to measure cerebrotonia are those in the third column of Table 1.

In briefest summary cerebrotonia is manifested by (1) inhibition of both viscerotonic and somatotonic expression, (2) hyperattentionality or overconsciousness. When this component is predominant one of the principal desires of life seems to be avoidance of overstimulation—hence love of concealment and avoidance of attracting attention. While cerebrotonia seems to result from an evolutionary development in the direction of purchasing increased exteroception at the cost of *both* vegetative mass and motor strength, the *manifest traits* of cerebrotonia (in a crowded society) are associated largely with escaping the painful consequences of the increased exteroception thus attained. Yet cerebrotonia is probably in itself far from painful. There is a certain elemental ecstasy in the heightened attentionality just as there is a somatotonic ecstasy in vigorous muscular action and a viscerotonic ecstasy in first-rate digestive action.

The Suffix-otic. As in *viscerotic, somatorotic, cerebrotic;* also *viscerosis, somatorosis, cerebrosis.* This suffix signifies an abnormal or pathological overmanifestation of the primary component named. The extra syllable—*or* —is put in *somatorotic* for euphony and to maintain the syllabic parallel with *somatotonic.* Since the term *neurotic* is prepsychological in the sense that it came into use during an era before primary components had been defined, and when it was the custom to blame psychopathology vaguely on "nerves" or "glands," this term is not definitive. To call a person "neurotic" is about as meaningful as calling him "glandotic." If an individual is neurotic he is either viscerotic, somatorotic, cerebrotic, or a combination of any two or all three.

The Suffix-penic. As in *visceropenic, somatopenic, cerebropenic;* also *visceropenia, somatopenia, cerebropenia.* The suffix signifies *lack of,* or an abnormally low degree of the component named. Cf. *leukopenia,* lack of white corpuscles.

C. BABEL IN PSYCHIATRY

For anyone who has had firsthand contact with problems of delinquency the point will require no urging that the criminologist and the psychiatrist are fishing in the same pond. Both are dealing with temperamental pathology in its various manifestations, and in the last analysis a psychiatry or a criminology can be only about as good, or as true and useful, as the conception of temperament which it uses for its frame of reference.

One of the major hypotheses in Constitutional Psychology is that structure and function, or somatotype and temperament, are best viewed as a continuum. We are therefore not in this study primarily concerned with correlation between somatotype and temperament, for by hypothesis such a correlation is no source of new light but only a measure of the accuracy with which quantification has been accomplished at different levels of objectivity in the measurement of the same thing. In the second volume of the series, *Varieties of Temperament,* a crucial exercise on this correlational topic was presented. As the primary components of temperament were operationally defined and scaled in that study, the correlation between them and the primary components of the somatotype turned out to be of the order +.80. Here we are not concerned with a repetition of such an exercise but are after more elusive game than statistical correlation between stucture and function. That correlation is taken for granted. The problem now is to describe temperamental pathology, and if possible thereby to reflect a little light on the vast turmoil of verbality that psychiatric thinking and writing have created.

One of the things the human clan needs urgently is an operational psychiatry. It might turn out to be a keystone for the often prayed-for science of humanics. But to get an operational psychiatry it will first be necessary to establish the habit of systematically describing psychiatric behavior. Read cases 86 through 89 and I think it will be apparent enough, even if you have been exposed to some kind of psychiatric instruction, that what you have studied is confusion. Neither the Kraepelinian typology, which is still in almost universal use, nor the currently popular psychoanalytic slang* really brings order to the vagaries of human temperament any more than the crude morphological typologies of the Christian era, which could be called a biological age of shame, brought order to the study of human structure.

Observation of our series of 200 boys was not begun as a psychiatric exercise. The descriptions and notations on manifest temperament were routine to constitutional study. But they soon brought us squarely against the problem of psychiatric classification. Four-fifths of the youngsters had been "seen" by one or another kind of psychiatrist, and many were under constant psychiatric observation while at the Inn. As psychiatric diagnoses and recommendations piled up, the necessity for integrating two kinds of language—our operational structure-function language and the eclectic typologizing of the psychiatric fraternity—became increasingly urgent.

It was not uncommon to find that as many as a dozen different psychiatric diagnoses and interpretations

had been made on a youngster, and *sometimes the dozen would embrace the entire repertory of the Kraepelinian typology.* That is to say, the youth would at various times have been given diagnoses not only mutually contradictory and pointing in opposite directions therapeutically, but he would be taken entirely around the clock and would have *all* the possible diagnoses.

It grew clearer every day that a vocabulary problem of the most serious nature existed in the psychiatric field, that in fact the vocabulary the psychiatrists were trying to use was nonoperational. It didn't work. We held a series of seminars on the question, and invited several of our consulting psychiatrists to come and help thrash it out. One in particular, Dr. Bryant Moulton, spent many hours with us over this difficult and fascinating question.

For many years, in my attempts to correlate constitutional characteristics with psychiatric findings, I had been baffled by the lack of any quantifiable (operational) variables by which the psychiatric findings could be expressed. Patients were diagnosed as suffering from manic-depressive psychosis, *or* paranoid schizophrenia *or* hebephrenic schizophrenia, and so on. It was always a matter of either-or. Psychiatry had developed as a branch of clinical practice, where a patient either "had something" or didn't have it. If he had it, it was either measles *or* scarlet fever *or* perhaps a heat rash in Latin. In clinical medicine the either-or approach possesses a certain cogency, for there *are* disease entities which you can have or not have. But in psychology there is little use for such an approach. The constitutional psychologist tries to describe the behavior of a personality; that is to say, of an organic structure in action. His first job (I believe) is to describe the structure, in terms of the most primary or universal components of structure that he can measure. That done, the job is to describe the behavior in terms of similarly basic be-

---

* The term *psychoanalytic slang* is used not in disparagement of Freud or of his work, for I hold both in high regard. It is used as about the most descriptive way of referring to the garbled and careless use of Freudian concepts which during the past two decades has become popular in American psychiatry and social work. On reading the biographies it will be apparent that smatterings of Freudian "language" have seeped through to half or more of the youths of the series. These boys, and many of the social workers who have coached or have ridden herd on them, "talk Freud" with about as much insight and understanding as the average city urchin has of Christianity when he "talks Jesus." In this country psychoanalytic jargon has become a superficial and a vulgar fad —a form of slang. Priests of the Freudian church are partly responsible, for they have commercialized and prostituted Freud's teaching as possibly no religious preachment was ever prostituted before.

havioral components. Then the constitutional psychologist proceeds, or should proceed, to a consideration of the details of behavior in the light of the details of structure. In any event he deals mainly with components of structure and behavior, not with either-or phenomena.

We were confronted with the fact that psychiatry offered no handles that a psychologist could take hold of. It postulated no hierarchy of variables that were amenable to quantification or, therefore, to correlation. In short, psychiatry, with its either-or criteria, did not appear to present a psychologically true-to-life discipline. It seemed clear that if a psychologist were to hope to make progress in the interpretation and correlation of psychiatric phenomena, he must first translate these into a system of variables with which he could operate. Moreover this was something we had to do before the general subject of delinquency could be expected to make sense. It was clear enough that delinquent and psychopathic behavior overlapped like the shingles of a house, that to get at one was impossible without at the same time getting at the other.

In short, we found it necessary to formulate a new approach to psychiatric classification before we could integrate constitutional morphology and temperament with the vast wealth of specific information that was being accumulated through psychiatric study and referral.

D. FROM DISEASE ENTITIES TO COMPONENTS

Where, then, in terms of operational concepts or in terms of structure-function language could a beginning be made toward psychiatric classification? This was a problem on which much of the potential usefulness of a study of delinquency seemed to hinge.

It was evident that in psychiatric circles there had long been a tendency to rely on some variation of a three-pole typology for a diagnostic frame of reference. At the "psychotic" level, for example, it was common to hear that, in general, three kinds of psychotic personality (together with mixtures) were to be encountered: cases showing *affective exaggeration;* those showing *paranoid projection;* and those showing *hebephrenic regression.* Also at the "psychoneurotic" level a similar tripolar typology was usually assumed to exist, and was embraced within the concepts *hysterical, psychasthenic,* and *neurasthenic* psychoneurosis.

In the closing decade of the last century Kraepelin, by including both mania and melancholia under the general heading of *manic-depressive psychosis,* and by setting this new entity off against *dementia praecox,* had postulated a fundamental dichotomy in the field of the functional psychoses. But Bleuler's conception of *schizophrenia* as a group or pattern of psychotic *reactions* soon largely supplanted the disease-entity conception of dementia praecox and led to renewed activity in the direction of classifying or "naming kinds" of schizophrenia.

Among most present-day practicing psychiatrists quite a sharp distinction is made between schizophrenic patterns in which a hostile or harsh reaction *against* seems to be the predominant temperamental "set" of the patient, and patterns characterized by reaction *away from* (i.e., by apathy, withdrawal from social contact, refusal or failure to participate or to take an interest). The reaction against is often buttressed by more or less extensive and systematized delusions in support of the central fixed idea—delusions usually of persecution and of the subject's own importance. The subject distorts his world of actual experience to fit his primary attitude. Hence the term *paranoid.* The paranoid patient, even when psychotic (which is only to say, *seriously* deranged), is "in there fighting" against something. He has not given up, has not jettisoned his cargo. There is still a somatotonic drive and it is aimed against something.

The reaction away from is of an

entirely different nature, and the essential difference lies in the fact that the somatotonic drive is absent. It is as if the subject had lost, or had never had somatotonia. The drive to do things, to achieve, to dominate and triumph over others, to exercise and perfect the muscles, to compete and to fight—in short, somatotonia—is conspicuously absent. If any of this component ever was present it has been jettisoned, thrown overboard. The jettisoning may have been necessary to save the subject from further disastrous consequences of his ill-sustained and poorly executed efforts at normal or culturally expected somatotonic aggression. This is probably as plausible a "mechanism" as any to explain the pathological somatopenia; but the essential fact is the somatopenia, whatever its origin.

One conspicuous corollary of the jettisoned pattern of personality is what psychiatrists call regressive behavior. The subject seems to regress or fall back to what is in some respects an infantile level of behavior. He may lose all ability to take care of himself, even sphincter control. There is marked lack of energy and of motivation. He may fail to respond at all to social stimulation and to conversational contact. He may have to be fed, bathed, and dressed, and in general cared for as an infant. He is then said to have regressed to a *hebephrenic* (infant mind) state.

Objections can be well taken to the use of the term hebephrenic in this sense. It is only in some respects that the subject has become like an infant; that is to say, in his helplessness. Infants, on the other hand, are normally of vigorous motivation, are alertly somatotonic and within the limits of their repertory of muscular skills are inclined to be aggressively somatotonic and to "go after" what they want. Infants—normally vigorous ones—have not jettisoned anything. It is merely that their executive department has not yet caught up with their desires. To use the idea of infant-mind or infant-like as a descripton of the most extreme and helpless form of mental pathology, even if it is said in Greek, is not very good semantics. These patients have not "regressed"; you can't really go back in this life. They have reacted away from the problems and competitions of life. They have jettisoned their second component and they show a pathological somatopenia. A better term than hebephrenic might be *oneirophrenic* (dream mind). However, we need not further labor the terminological aspect of the problem at this point in the development of the theme.

The distinction between mental aberration in which the *against* reaction is predominant and that in which the *away from* reaction predominates is as sharp a distinction as is to be found in psychiatry. The psychiatrical-

Figure 2. *Illustrating the Kraepelinian Typology.*

Manic-Depressive Psychosis ⟷ Dementia Praecox

Manic-Depressive Psychosis (affective) ⟷ Paranoid Schizophrenia (projective)

Hebephrenic Schizophrenia (regressive)

ly conventional single-word symbols for the two reaction patterns are, respectively, *paranoid* and *hebephrenic*.

Thus one end point of the original Kraepelinian psychotic dichotomy has as it were grown apart into two end points. Figure 2 A has grown into Figure 2 B, and a tripolar orientation has replaced a bipolar one. One of the poles, that called hebephrenic, seems to make a degree of operational sense in terms of pathological somatopenia, a concept with biological meaning. What about the other two poles? Can any sense be made of these from a biological point of view?

The reaction patterns that psychiatrists conventionally label *manic-depressive* psychosis all have one essential characteristic in common. The subject always has a low threshold of reaction. There is also a low threshold of emotional expression. He is feebly inhibited. In the "manic" state, which may be chronic or intermittent, he expresses elation and euphoria on slight provocation or without any apparent provocation. In the "depressed" state, which also may be chronic or intermittent, he similarly expresses emotional sorrow, dejection, or self-deprecation without externally apparent justification. The emotion itself may range from extreme elation to extreme dejection; indeed, it may be any emotion. It is the uninhibitedly free expression of the emotion that is constant. Similarly with respect to action of all kinds, here too it is the lack of inhibition, the lack of the cerebrotonic function, that is constant.

During the phase called manic expansiveness, that is to say, when the subject is active, the constant feature is lack of normal constraint in both emotional and somatic expression. He is maladaptively hyperactive; he is responsive, like the proverbial dog in a forest of telephone poles. There may be euphorial emotionalism, motor overactivity, flight of ideas, press of speech, poor attentional focus, hypersuggestibility, uninhibited eroticism, bizarre exhibitionism; and with it all a forceful keyed-up vigor of physical expression far beyond that for which

the situation seems to call. All this is simply a description of somatotonia gone wild; pathological somatotonia, or somatorosis.

But in the phase called depression, or depressive melancholy, the dominant feature is not somatorosis but viscerosis—pathologically uncontrolled expression of viscerotonia, or lack of inhibition of affectivity. The subject is physically and mentally slowed up; overrelaxed, overly dependent, overly expressive of his now melancholy feelings. He has become untempered. In the viscerotic phase he is as uninhibitedly viscerotic as he is uninhibitedly somatorotic in the somatorotic phase.

The term manic-depressive psychosis does not then describe a disease entity, but a pattern of reaction in which the constant feature is pathological absence of inhibition. That is to say, the subject is cerebropenic. The result of the cerebropenia depends of course on the underlying temperamental endowment of the individual; that is what will determine his manner of expression. If he is mesomorphic and vigorous, strong and healthy, capable of sustained, violent exertion and of standing up well under it—if he is all this *and* cerebropenic—he will probably maintain a manic or hypomanic level of activity for long periods without recourse to rest. There are some who remain hypomanic all through life. These are athletes of a kind. One of them may exhaust a whole generation of contemporaries and two or three generations of wives or husbands, not to mention minor relatives; but they generally go out pleasantly enough in the end with a cerebral or cardiac "accident."

Such is the "pure manic," who is a comparative rarity. Similarly rare are cases of pure depression, or of "permanent aggressive melancholy." Far more common are the mixtures, and there are almost as many varieties of these as there are individuals. Typically there is some alternation between the somatorotic and the viscerotic cerebropenia, and there are cases where the individual seems to be caught in a regular rhythm or cycle of the two phases, as if he had to suspend the manic activity every so often to rest and recharge his battery. But I think that clear-cut examples of such a rhythmic cycle are less common than the term *cycloid psychosis,* which is often used instead of manic-depressive psychosis, would imply. What we find is not a disease entity but a more or less maladaptive reaction pattern characterized constantly by two things: (1) overly vigorous response, either visceral-emotional or somatic, or both; (2) feeble inhibition or lack of cerebrotonia.

We may then perhaps say that another of the poles in the tripolar schema of Figure 2 B seems to make some degree of operational sense. There may possibly be psychiatric meaning in the biological phenomenon of pathological cerebropenia. What about the third pole, which in the figure is labelled *paranoid?*

The reaction patterns that psychiatrists call paranoid, or paranoid projection—the reactions against—have as a constant characteristic a singular *lack of compassion.* The subject is without the bowels of mercy. According to his temperament and his strength he may look upon his world and his contemporaries as his persecutors or as legitimate objects of his own destructive fury. In either case his bond with his kind is one of hate, scorn, resentment, defiance; and all of this he "projects" against his environment. If he is weak the reaction pattern is more covert than overt. It then takes the form of involved delusional ideation centered particularly around the main idea of persecution. If he is strong—physically strong—overt aggression and an arrogant manner combine with opinionated superciliousness to produce quite a remarkably unpleasant personality. The strong paranoids are ugly customers, especially in a pulpit or a state legislature.

There are as many different kinds of the maladaptive paranoid-projection reaction as there are of the maladaptive affective or of the jettisoning reactions. Common to all paranoia is the lack of participant compassion. The affective psychotic on the other hand is one vast bowel of compassion. He tends to enfold his world in a cosmic Dionysian embrace, and he is so participant in *everything* that the focus of his energy is lost in ubiquity. He is at one with it all. The paranoid is unable to be at one with any of it. He cannot relax and accept; cannot accept comfort; cannot deliberately enjoy food, company, or the glories of digestion; he finds no joy in the social amenities, no "fulfillment" in knowing people and in knowing about them; he cannot express emotion smoothly; has neither tolerance nor complacency; cannot achieve mutual dependency with other people and so cannot invest hope outside himself, except abstractly. Alcohol has no good effect—it makes him not more viscerotonic but more paranoid. These are all traits of visceropenia. But this personality cannot jettison. Cut off from the main channels of viscerotonic expression (the reaction toward), yet constrained to carry on, there is only one direction that the reaction can take. The reaction is against. It may be against at a very high and idealistic level, as in the case of Prometheus against Zeus, and this may in the long run be a "good" reaction—good for both man and Zeus. It may somehow even be good for Prometheus, and may contribute to the working out of his destiny, but Prometheus remains blood brother to Paranoius.

Biologically, the paranoid reaction seems to stem from lack of, or from interference with, the normal expression of viscerotonia. The reaction against is a visceropenic reaction. This appears to be the constant in the formula, and if the appearance is not a misleading one, it would seem possible that all three of the poles in the tripolar schema of Figure 2 B may make biological sense. Figure 2 B might then be drawn a little differently to take the form of Figure 3. Up to the present point all this is of course speculative. We are following some of the steps in the formulation of what may be called a speculative hypothesis.

Figure 3. *A Tripolar Psychiatric Orientation.*

Hypothetically the three conventional poles for classification of the functional psychoses fall respectively *opposite* the three established poles for morphological and temperamental classification. The Dionysian-affective psychoses, in this hypothetical construct, are manifestations of something gone wrong either in the constitutional endowment or in the temperamental manifestations of the third component. Similarly for the paranoid-projective psychoses with respect to the first component; and for the hebephrenic-jettisoning psychoses with respect to the second component.

In the study of morphology and temperament we had made no progress beyond the types of Hippocrates until we emerged from the idea of typologies, or of dichotomies and trichot-

omies, and substituted for all that the conception of components capable of multidimensional distribution and therefore leading to a morphological and a temperamental taxonomy which the familiar biological distribution curves would fit—multidimensionally. The first two volumes of the Constitution series describe the steps leading to those two respective taxonomies. The question that now intruded itself was this: Could we take the same step in psychiatry, at last emerging from the Laocoön-like struggle to describe the mentally aberrant in terms of biologically unreal disease entities or types of reaction? Could we emerge from this and substitute for it a taxonomy psychologically operational and biologically true to life? In short, could mental aberrancy be described and diagnosed in terms of demonstrable, quantifiable components falling within a continuum with other biological phenomena? If it could, there would be a bridge between psychiatry and psychology, and the road might open to a biological humanics.

E. A HYPOTHETICAL PSYCHIATRIC INDEX

During the decade following 1935 I undertook exploratory constitutional studies on two groups of psychiatric patients at Worcester State Hospital, on a small group of 50 in the Army, and on 3,800 psychotic patients in the New York State mental hospitals. This latter group included all of the available male cases in the state who were under 30 and were at the time labeled dementia praecox (schizophrenia); also all available males under 45 who were labeled manic-depressive psychosis. Study of the psychiatric and diagnostic histories of these patients together with study of the physical constitution yielded a remarkable demonstration of the need for an operational frame of reference in diagnosis.

It is a common thing, not only in the New York mental hospitals but in every other mental hospital with which I am familiar, to find that the diagnosis of a psychotic case has been changed half a dozen or more times—usually about as many times as there have been changes of diagnosing officer. Yet even in this madness there is method. One observation first struck me forcibly at Worcester and later was borne out in the New York State study and in the Army. *It is the patients who fall in a particular range of somatotypes whose diagnoses get changed the most.* These are of two groups: (1) the midrange somatotypes; and (2) those falling near the morphological poles. *There is a clearly discernible tendency toward greater diagnostic agreement when the somatotype falls near any one of the three hypothetical psychiatric poles.*

A morphological 5–5–1, 4–5–1, or 5–4–1 who is psychotic has an excellent chance to be labeled manic or manic-depressive and to keep the label. A 1–4–5 or 1–5–4 is almost equally likely to continue through his diagnostic history as a paranoid; and a 4–1–5 or 5–1–4, or even a 4–2–5 or 5–2–4 seems to be almost certain to get and to keep the tag hebephrenic schizophrenia (or schizophrenia simplex).

That this tendency toward diagnostic agreement should disappear among the midrange somatotypes, such as the 4–4–3's and 3–4–4's, or even among the 3–5–3's and 4–5–3's might well be expected. But it also disappears, and just about as conspicuously, at the morphological poles. 7–2–1's and 6–2–1's, for example, are just about as likely to get labeled hebephrenic as manic-depressive, and in this somatotype area there is a remarkable tendency for hesitation and alternation between these two diagnoses.

Similarly the extreme mesomorphs, 2–7–1's, 1–7–1's, 1–6–2's, and so on perplex the psychiatrists. These mesomorphs get labeled both manic and paranoid, rarely hebephrenic (although not infrequently "catatonic," which seems to be a wastbasket category). One 2–7–1 in the first series I studied at Worcester had been diagnosed as a manic-depressive psychotic five times and paranoid schizophrenic six times—ten changes of diagnosis alternating between two diagnoses. He seemed to be balanced right in the middle, between those two diagnostic typologies, and I think that in fact he was so balanced. His biological position was almost perfectly centered between the two psychiatric poles.

The extreme ectomorphs, 1–1–7's, 1–2–7's, and even the far commoner 2–2–6's appear to defy diagnosis by the conventional Kraepelinian typology in about the same way. Many a dreary hour of psychiatric case conference drains off into the weighty business of deciding whether such a patient is *a* hebephrenic or *a* paranoid schizophrene; and then next month in deciding it back the other way again. The criteria on which such diagnostic decisions rest are more often derived from verbalistic hairsplitting than from inquiry into the biological nature of the patient.

For patients at all three morphological poles psychiatric diagnosis seems to run into conflict and tends to hesitate between *two* alternatives. In dealing with the midrange somatotypes the typological psychiatrist is confronted with a still more difficult diagnostic problem. The midrange people, with all three of the primary biological components more or less equally represented, tend naturally enough under varying circumstances to manifest more or less of all three of the primary psychiatric components. At times a psychotic with the somatotype 4–5–3 is very likely to behave like a manic-depressive, at times he will be singularly paranoid, at times he may be "hebephrenic as hell." Often he may be simply stuporous. His most common diagnosis is catatonic schizophrenia.

Now *catatonic* is one diagnostic term in common psychiatric use which has been defined in almost every way psychiatrically imaginable. Henderson and Gillespie* defined catatonia as "an alternating state characterized by a stage of depression, a stage of excitement and a stage of stupor." Many psychiatrists, particularly those of European training, follow Kraepelin in applying the term catatonic dementia praecox (schizophrenia) to virtually all cases of functional psychosis that show a mixture or alternation of *all three* primary psychiatric components.

In the original Kraepelinian typology there was first the primary dichotomy of manic-depressive psychosis and dementia praecox; second, a division of dementia praecox into the three types, paranoid, hebephrenic, and catatonic. The catatonic type, which Kraepelin considered the most common, has always been diagnosed in practice mainly by the fact of shifts between manic-like excitement, stuporous depressions, and both paranoid-like and hebephrenic-like reaction patterns—all or any of these mixed in various proportions, according to the temperament of the patient. Some of the patients with this mixed picture spend much of

their time in a cataleptic state, or state of sustained immobility. Many psychiatrists have adopted that characteristic as the critical or definitive one for the diagnosis of catatonic. Others, finding that catalepsy is by no means a constant feature, have considered it incidental. Still others, especially those not trained under the Kraepelinian tradition, have looked on "catatonic" as a mere wastebasket adjective more or less synonymous with "mixed" and so have not used the term diagnostically at all. In the mental hospitals of some states today as many as 70 per cent of the schizophrenic patients are labeled catatonic; in those of some other states the term catatonic rarely appears. The consequence of all this has been rather general confusion over the term catatonic and an increasing tendency to avoid use of it, except as a synonym for mixed.

Kraepelin later added a fourth "type" of dementia praecox—the *simplex* or simple type. The identifying characteristic is absence of any definite trend; simply a general falling away of interest and a general falling back or lack of effective adaptivity. Kraepelin described this as consisting of an "impoverishment . . . of the whole psychic life, which is accomplished quite imperceptibly." No particular manic tendency, excitement or depression, or paranoid reaction. There is general apathy or emotional dulling, and a sinking away from life. The individual is born and remains a weak nonentity. A more descriptive term than schizophrenia simplex might be, simply, mental asthenia. In short, schizophrenia simplex is a term commonly applied to a psychotic personality that seems to stay in the middle with respect to all three of the primary psychiatric components, and so never shows a pronounced tendency toward any of them. The catatonic also in the long run falls in the middle, but this is because, in the course of time, he reveals all the primary psychiatric components in some strength, and all this divergent psychiatric "strength" cancels itself out.

We have now considered all the

* *A Textbook of Psychiatry* (6th ed., New York, 1946), p. 316.

Figure 5. *Diagram for the Psychotic Reaction Patterns.*

main conventional categories in the Kraepelinian diagnostic schema, which remains in almost universal psychiatric use wherever the European languages predominate. We can see that Kraepelin covered the ground remarkably well, that he included in his typology just about all of the possible main directions of variation of pattern. His is a first-rate typology. First, there is a "type of reaction pattern" extending out into each of the primary dimensions of possible extension. These are the manic-depressive, the paranoid, and the hebephrenic reaction patterns. Second, there is a name for those personalities which, upon showing tendencies along all of these dimensions, nevertheless average out somewhere near the origin or center point. These are the catatonics. Finally, there is a name for those personalities that go nowhere at all, but *simply* stay at nothingness. These are the simplexes.

But typologies do not offer an operational frame of reference for social science. Even the best of typologies can offer no more than a preliminary scaffolding which may mark out the main lines along which an operational science is to develop. The question we now have to consider is that of whether or not the whole field of psychiatric description—and therefore perhaps of psychological description in general— is ready for translation from the current typological to an operational frame of reference.

The picture as we have reviewed it can be diagrammatically summarized as in Figure 5. Here all the Kraepelin psychotic types are written into a hypothetical three-dimensional structure. But along with these typological designations there is also the suggestion of a quantitative frame of reference. At what may be called the apex or pole of the region of manic-depressive psychosis is the symbol ψ 7–1–1.* A personality plotted at this point on the diagram would be visualized as overwhelmingly Dionysian (a 7 in that component), and as altogether lacking in any signs of either of the other two primary psychiatric components. Similarly the symbol ψ 1–7–1 marks the pole for the territory of paranoid psychosis, and ψ 1–1–7 marks the hebephrenic pole.

One other point of great psychiatric interest will perhaps have already occurred to anyone who in his thinking has begun to substitute the idea of a psychiatric index for the Kraepelinian typology. Psychotic personalities falling in the northwest sector of the distribution (see Figure 1, p. 16) are frequently referred to as "cycloid," or manic-depressive. At times they show manic euphorial aggression, at other times overt melancholic depression. Some individuals appear to present a rhythmic alternation between the two moods. For the northwest psychiatric territory the term cycloid has long been in common

use and is almost interchangeable with manic-depressive.

But anyone who will take the trouble to observe a group of psychiatric patients, while keeping in mind the structural frame of reference of Figure 1, will soon become aware of the same cycloid phenomenon in the northeast and south that is seen in the northwest. Among paranoid schizophrenes who present about the same strength in mesomorphy as in ectomorphy there is very much the same alternation between somatic aggression and ideational substitutive hostility as there is between euphorial and melancholic expression among the patients who are well balanced in mesomorphy and endomorphy. And the same cycloid phenomenon is seen at the south, among the hebephrenic patients who show about the same strength in endomorphy and ectomorphy. These patients often alternate between bizarre, irrelevant affect and bizarre, irrelevant ideation.

When psychiatric behavior is described against an operational frame of reference the alternational or cycloid phenomenon is seen to be general—not specific to the manic-depressive pattern. Moreover the alternation is not limited to a swinging back and forth across what I have called the psychiatric poles; that is to say, across the poles of cerebropenia, visceropenia, and somatopenia. The cycloid alternation is just about as conspicuous across the poles of the primary components as across the psychiatric poles. That is to say, the swing is also seen across the poles of viscerosis, somatorosis, and cerebrosis. Endomorphs frequently show a cycloid alternation between overt melancholic depression and bizarre, irrelevant affect. Mesomorphs are likely to swing between manic-euphorial aggression and somatic aggression, and ectomorphs between ideational-substitutive hostility and bizarre, irrelevant ideation.

Among psychiatric patients of midrange somatotype the alternations of mood and of behavior tend to become complex and some of these patients show, at different times, the

---

* The Greek ψ here stands for psychiatric, and this symbol placed in front of the three familiar numerals commonly used to define the somatotype indicates that we are now considering a *psychiatric*, not a morphological index.

The psychiatric index is expressed in the same way as the morphological index, or somatotype, but the poles for the psychiatric components fall opposite those used for the morphological components. This means that the three coordinates of the psychiatric system are rotated with respect to the coordinates of the morphological system. The rotation is about the center axis determined by the points 4–4–4, 3–3–3, 2–2–2, etc. Also in this center axis are the points 7–7–7 and 1–1–1.

What has actually happened in the change over from the somatotype designations to the psychiatric designations is simply a clockwise rotation of the poles through one-sixth of a complete turn, or through 60 degrees. The *psychiatric* 7–1–1 is just 60 degrees ahead of the somatotype 7–1–1, and the same is true of other corresponding numerals except those in the center axis, which remain fixed.

definitive criteria for *all* of the Krae-pelinian typological diagnoses. These are the people who get labeled cata-tonic. We cannot say whether or not there is usually some logical sequence, some "rhyme and reason," in their variations. There may be and some-body may find a good doctoral disserta-tion in the problem of working out relationships between overt constitu-tional factors and catatonic patterns.

In fairness to the psychiatric prac-titioners who have fallen into the con-ventional habit of applying the term cycloid only to the northwest sector, it should be pointed out that the alterna-tion phenomenon is in fact more dra-matic in that quarter than elsewhere. This is because all expressiveness reaches its maximal volume at the pole of the first psychiatric component. That is the area of pathological cere-bropenia, where inhibition of expres-siveness is at its physiological mini-mum and all reaction is therefore maximal. It was doubtless to be ex-pected that the phenomenon of swing-ing back and forth between two par-tially incompatible kinds of reaction would first be noticed in the sector where behavior is most overtly accen-tuated. To point out that the cycloid pattern is seen elsewhere as well as in the northwest does not detract from the usefulness of the concept or from the brilliance of Kretschmer's classic description of the cycloid—meaning manic-depressive—temperament.

Schizotaxia, Schizotypy, Schizophrenia

PAUL E. MEEHL

In the course of the last decade, while spending several thousand hours in the practice of intensive psycho-therapy, I have treated—sometimes unknowingly except in retrospect—a considerable number of schizoid and schizophrenic patients. Like all clini-cians, I have formed some theoretical opinions as a result of these experi-ences. While I have not until recently begun any systematic research efforts on this baffling disorder, I felt that to share with you some of my thoughts, based though they are upon clinical impressions in the context of selected research by others, might be an ac-ceptable use of this occasion.

Let me begin by putting a question which I find is almost never answered correctly by our clinical students on PhD orals, and the answer to which they seem to dislike when it is offered.

Suppose that you were required to write down a procedure for selecting an individual from the population who would be diagnosed as schizophrenic by a psychiatric staff; you have to wager $1,000 on being right; you may not include in your selection procedure any behavioral fact, such as a symp-tom or trait, manifested by the indi-vidual. What would you write down? So far as I have been able to ascertain, there is only one thing you could write down that would give you a better than even chance of winning such a bet—namely, "Find an individual X who has a schizophrenic identical twin." Admittedly, there are many other facts which would raise your odds somewhat above the low base rate of schizo-phrenia. You might, for example, iden-tify X by first finding mothers who have certain unhealthy child-rearing attitudes; you might enter a subpopula-tion defined jointly by such demo-graphic variables as age, size of com-munity, religion, ethnic background,

From the *Amer. Psychol. 17*:827-838, 1962, by permission of the American Psychological Associa-tion and the author.

or social class. But these would leave you with a pretty unfair wager, as would the rule, "Find an X who has a fraternal twin, of the same sex, diagnosed as schizophrenic" (Fuller & Thompson, 1960, pp. 272-283; Stern, 1960, pp. 581-584).

Now the twin studies leave a good deal to be desired methodologically (Rosenthal, in press); but there seems to be a kind of "double standard of methodological morals" in our profession, in that we place a good deal of faith in our knowledge of schizophrenic dynamics, and we make theoretical inferences about social learning factors from the establishment of group trends which may be statistically significant and replicable although of small or moderate size; but when we come to the genetic studies, our standards of rigor suddenly increase. I would argue that the concordance rates in the twin studies need not be accepted uncritically as highly precise parameter estimates in order for us to say that their magnitudes represent the most important piece of etiological information we possess about schizophrenia.

It is worthwhile, I think, to pause here over a question in the sociology of knowledge, namely, why do psychologists exhibit an aversive response to the twin data? I have no wish to argue *ad hominem* here—I raise this question in a constructive and irenic spirit, because I think that a substantive confusion often lies at the bottom of this resistance, and one which can be easily dispelled. Everybody readily assents to such vague dicta as "heredity and environment interact," "there need be no conflict between organic and functional concepts," "we always deal with the total organism," etc. But it almost seems that clinicians do not fully believe these principles in any concrete sense, because they show signs of thinking that *if* a genetic basis were found for schizophrenia, the psychodynamics of the disorder (especially in relation to intrafamilial social learnings) would be somehow negated or, at least, greatly demoted in importance. To what extent, if at all, is this true?

Here we run into some widespread misconceptions as to what is meant by *specific etiology* in nonpsychiatric medicine. By postulating a "specific etiology" one does *not* imply any of the following:

1. The etiological factor always, or even usually, produces clinical illness.
2. If illness occurs, the particular form and content of symptoms is derivable by reference to the specific etiology alone.
3. The course of the illness can be materially influenced only by procedures directed against the specific etiology.
4. All persons who share the specific etiology will have closely similar histories, symptoms, and course.
5. The largest single contributor to symptom variance is the specific etiology.

In medicine, not one of these is part of the concept of specific etiology, yet they are repeatedly invoked as arguments against a genetic interpretation of schizophrenia. I am not trying to impose the causal model of medicine by analogy; I merely wish to emphasize that *if* one postulates a genetic mutation as the specific etiology of schizophrenia, he is not thereby committed to any of the above as implications. Consequently such familiar objections as, "Schizophrenics differ widely from one another" or "Many schizophrenics can be helped by purely psychological methods" should not disturb one who opts for a genetic hypothesis. In medicine, the concept of specific etiology means the *sine qua non*—the causal condition which is necessary, but not sufficient, for the disorder to occur. A genetic theory of schizophrenia would, in this sense, be stronger than that of "one contributor to variance"; but weaker than that of "largest contributor to variance." In analysis of variance terms, it means an interaction effect such that no other variables can exert a main effect when the specific etiology is lacking.

Now it goes without saying that "clinical schizophrenia" as such cannot be inherited, because it has behavioral and phenomenal contents which are learned. As Bleuler says, in order to have a delusion involving Jesuits one must first have learned about Jesuits. It seems inappropriate to apply the geneticist's concept of "penetrance" to the crude statistics of formal diagnosis—if a specific genetic etiology exists, its phenotypic expression in *psychological* categories would be a quantitative aberration in some parameter of a behavioral acquisition function. What could possibly be a genetically determined functional parameter capable of generating such diverse behavioral outcomes, including the preservation of normal function in certain domains?

The theoretical puzzle is exaggerated when we fail to conceptualize at different levels of molarity. For instance, there is a tendency among organically minded theorists to analogize between catatonic phenomena and various neurological or chemically induced states in animals. But Bleuler's masterly *Theory of Schizophrenic Negativism* (1912) shows how the whole range of catatonic behavior, including diametrically opposite modes of relating to the interpersonal environment, can be satisfactorily explained as instrumental acts; thus even a convinced organicist, postulating a biochemical defect as specific etiology, should recognize that the causal linkage between this etiology and catatonia is indirect, requiring for the latter's derivation a lengthy chain of statements which are not even formulable except in molar psychological language.

What kind of behavioral fact about the patient leads us to diagnose schizophrenia? There are a number of traits and symptoms which get a high weight, and the weights differ among clinicians. But thought disorder continues to hold its own in spite of today's greater clinical interest in motivational (especially interpersonal) variables. If you are inclined to doubt this for yourself, consider the following indicators: Patient experiences intense ambivalence, readily reports conscious hatred of family figures, is pananxious, subjects therapist to a long series of testing operations, is withdrawn, and says, "Naturally, I am growing my father's hair."

While all of these are schizophrenic indicators, the last one is the diagnostic bell ringer. In this respect we are still Bleulerians, although we know a lot more about the schizophrenic's psychodynamics than Bleuler did. The significance of thought disorder, associative dyscontrol (or, as I prefer to call it so as to include the very mildest forms it may take, "cognitive slippage"), in schizophrenia has been somewhat de-emphasized in recent years. Partly this is due to the greater interest in interpersonal dynamics, but partly also to the realization that much of our earlier psychometric assessment of the thought disorder was mainly reflecting the schizophrenic's tendency to underperform because uninterested, preoccupied, resentful, or frightened. I suggest that this realization has been overgeneralized and led us to swing too far the other way, as if we had shown that there really *is* no cognitive slippage factor present. One rather common assumption seems to be that if one can demonstrate the potentiating effect of a motivational state upon cognitive slippage, light has thereby been shed upon the etiology of schizophrenia. Why are we entitled to think this? Clinically, we see a degree of cognitive slippage not found to a comparable degree among nonschizophrenic persons. Some patients (e.g., pseudoneurotics) are highly anxious and exhibit minimal slippage; others (e.g., burnt-out cases) are minimally anxious with marked slippage. The demonstration that we can intensify a particular patient's cognitive dysfunction by manipulating his affects is not really very illuminating. After all, even ordinary neurological diseases can often be tremendously influenced symptomatically via emotional stimuli; but if a psychologist demonstrates that the spasticity or tremor of a multiple sclerotic is affected by rage or fear, we would not thereby have learned anything about the etiology of multiple sclerosis.

Consequent upon our general assimilation of the insights given us by psychoanalysis, there is today a wide-spread and largely unquestioned assumption that when we can trace out the motivational forces linked to the content of aberrant behavior, then we understand why the person has fallen ill. There is no compelling reason to assume this, when the evidence is mainly our dynamic understanding of the patient, however valid that may be. The phrase "why the person has fallen ill" may, of course, be legitimately taken to include these things; an account of how and when he falls ill will certainly include them. But they may be quite inadequate to answer the question, "Why does X fall ill and not Y, granted that we can understand both of them?" I like the analogy of a color psychosis, which might be developed by certain individuals in a society entirely oriented around the making of fine color discriminations. Social, sexual, economic signals are color mediated; to misuse a color word is strictly taboo; compulsive mothers are horribly ashamed of a child who is retarded in color development, and so forth. Some color-blind individuals (not all, perhaps not most) develop a color psychosis in this culture; as adults, they are found on the couches of color therapists, where a great deal of *valid* understanding is achieved about color dynamics. Some of them make a social recovery. Nonetheless, if we ask, "What was basically the matter with these patients?" meaning, "What is the specific etiology of the color psychosis?" the answer is that mutated gene on the X chromosome. This is why my own therapeutic experience with schizophrenic patients has not yet convinced me of the schizophrenogenic mother as a specific etiology, even though the picture I get of my patients' mothers is pretty much in accord with the familiar one. There is no question here of accepting the patient's account; my point is that *given* the account, and taking it quite at face value, does not tell me why the patient is a patient and not just a fellow who had a bad mother.

Another theoretical lead is the one given greatest current emphasis, namely, *interpersonal aversiveness*. The schizophrene suffers a degree of social fear, distrust, expectation of rejection, and conviction of his own unlovability which cannot be matched in its depth, pervasity, and resistance to corrective experience by any other diagnostic group.

Then there is a quasi-pathognomonic sign, emphasized by Rado (1956; Rado & Daniels, 1956) but largely ignored in psychologists' diagnostic usage, namely, *anhedonia*—a marked, widespread, and refractory defect in pleasure capacity which, once you learn how to examine for it, is one of the most consistent and dramatic behavioral signs of the disease.

Finally, I include *ambivalence* from Bleuler's cardinal four (1950). His other two, "autism" and "dereism," I consider derivative from the combination of slippage, anhedonia, and aversiveness. Crudely put, if a person cannot think straight, gets little pleasure, and is afraid of everyone, he will of course learn to be autistic and dereistic.

If these clinical characterizations are correct, and we combine them with the hypothesis of a genetic specific etiology, do they give us any lead on theoretical possibilities?

Granting its initial vagueness as a construct, requiring to be filled in by neurophysiological research, I believe we should take seriously the old European notion of an "integrative neural defect" as the only direct phenotypic consequence produced by the genic mutation. This is an aberration in some parameter of single cell function, which may or may not be manifested in the functioning of more molar CNS systems, depending upon the organization of the mutual feedback controls and upon the stochastic parameters of the reinforcement regime. This neural integrative defect, which I shall christen *schizotaxia*, is all that can properly be spoken of as inherited. The imposition of a social learning history upon schizotaxic individuals results in a personality organization which I shall call, following Rado, the *schizotype.* The four core behavior traits are obviously not innate; but I postulate that they are universally learned by schizotaxic individuals, given any of the actually existing social reinforcement regimes, from the best to the worst. If the interpersonal regime is favorable, and the schizotaxic person also has the good fortune to inherit a low anxiety readiness, physical vigor, general resistance to stress and the like, he will remain a well-compensated "normal" schizotype, never manifesting symptoms of mental disease. He will be like the gout-prone male whose genes determine him to have an elevated blood uric acid titer, but who never develops clinical gout.

Only a subset of schizotypic personalities decompensate into clinical schizophrenia. It seems likely that the most important causal influence pushing the schizotype toward schizophrenic decompensation is the schizophrenogenic mother.

I hope it is clear that this view does not conflict with what has been established about the mother-child interaction. If this interaction were totally free of material ambivalence and aversive inputs to the schizotaxic child, even compensated schizotypy might be avoided; at most, we might expect to find only the faintest signs of cognitive slippage and other minimal neurological aberrations, possibly including body image and other proprioceptive deviations, but not the interpersonal aversiveness which is central to the clinical picture.

Nevertheless, while assuming the etiological importance of mother in determining the course of aversive social learnings, it is worthwhile to speculate about the modification our genetic equations might take on this hypothesis. Many schizophrenogenic mothers are themselves schizotypes in varying degrees of compensation. Their etiological contribution then consists jointly in their passing on the gene, *and* in the fact that being schizotypic, they provide the kind of ambivalent regime which potentiates the schizotypy of the child and raises the odds of his decompensating. Hence the incidence of the several parental genotypes among parent pairs of diagnosed proband cases is not calculable from the usual genetic formulas. For example, given a schizophrenic proband, the odds that mother is homozygous (or, if the gene were dominant, that it is mother who carries it) are different from those for father; since we have begun by selecting a decompensated case, and formal diagnosis as the phenotype involves a potentiating factor for mother which is psychodynamically greater than that for a schizotypic father. Another important influence would be the likelihood that the lower fertility of schizophrenics is also present, but to an unknown degree, among compensated schizotypes. Clinical experience suggests that in the semicompensated range, this lowering of fertility is greater among males, since many schizotypic women relate to men in an exploited or exploitive sexual way, whereas the male schizotype usually displays a marked deficit in heterosexual aggressiveness. Such a sex difference in fertility among decompensated cases has been reported by Meyers and Goldfarb (1962).

Since the extent of aversive learnings is a critical factor in decompensation, the inherited anxiety readiness is presumably greater among diagnosed cases. Since the more fertile mothers are likely to be compensated, hence themselves to be relatively low anxiety if schizotaxic, a frequent parent pattern should be a compensated schizotypic mother married to a neurotic father, the latter being the source of the proband's high-anxiety genes (plus providing a poor paternal model for identification in male patients, and a weak defender of the child against mother's schizotypic hostility).

These considerations make ordinary family concordance studies, based upon formal diagnosis, impossible to interpret. The most important research need here is development of high-validity indicators for compensated schizotypy. I see some evidence for these conceptions in the report of Lidz and co-workers, who in studying intensively the parents of 15 schizophrenic patients were surprised to find that "minimally, 9 of the 15 patients had at least one parent who could be called schizophrenic, or ambulatory schizophrenic, or clearly paranoid in behavior and attitudes" (Lidz, Cornelison, Terry, & Fleck, 1958, p. 308). As I read the brief personality sketches presented, I would judge that all but two of the probands had a clearly schizotypic parent. These authors, while favoring a "learned irrationality" interpretation of their data, also recognize the alternative genetic interpretation. Such facts do not permit a decision, obviously; my main point is the striking difference between the high incidence of parental schizotypes, mostly quite decompensated (some to the point of diagnosable psychosis), and the zero incidence which a conventional study would have yielded for this group.

Another line of evidence, based upon a very small sample but exciting because of its uniformity, is McConaghy's report (1959) that among nondiagnosed parent pairs of 10 schizophrenics, subclinical thought disorder was psychometrically detectable in at least one parent of every pair. Rosenthal (in press) reports that he can add five tallies to this parent-pair count, and suggests that such results might indicate that the specific heredity is dominant, and completely penetrant, rather than recessive. The attempt to replicate these findings, and other psychometric efforts to tap subclinical cognitive slippage in the "normal" relatives of schizophrenics, should receive top priority in our research efforts.

Summarizing, I hypothesize that the statistical relation between schizotaxia, schizotypy, and schizophrenia is class inclusion: All schizotaxics become, *on all actually existing social learning regimes,* schizotypic in personality organization; but most of these remain compensated. A minority, disadvantaged by other (largely polygenically determined) constitutional weaknesses, and put on a bad

regime by schizophrenogenic mothers (most of whom are themselves schizotypes) are thereby potentiated into clinical schizophrenia. What makes schizotaxia etiologically specific is its role as a *necessary* condition. I postulate that a nonschizotaxic individual, whatever his other genetic makeup and whatever his learning history, would at most develop a character disorder or a psychoneurosis; but he would not become a schizotype and therefore could never manifest its decompensated form, schizophrenia.

What sort of quantitative aberration in the structural or functional parameters of the nervous system can we conceive to be directly determined by a mutated gene, and to so alter initial dispositions that affected individuals will, in the course of their childhood learning history, develop the four schizotypal source traits: cognitive slippage, anhedonia, ambivalence, and interpersonal aversiveness? To me, the most baffling thing about the disorder is the phenotypic heterogeneity of this tetrad. If one sets himself to the task of doing a theoretical Vigotsky job on this list of psychological dispositions, he may manage part of it by invoking a sufficiently vague kind of descriptive unity between ambivalence and interpersonal aversiveness; and perhaps even anhedonia could be somehow subsumed. But the cognitive slippage presents a real roadblock. Since I consider cognitive slippage to be a core element in schizophrenia, any characterization of schizophrenic or schizotypic behavior which purports to abstract its essence but does not include the cognitive slippage must be deemed unsatisfactory. I believe that an adequate theoretical account will necessitate moving downward in the pyramid of the sciences to invoke explanatory constructs not found in social, psychodynamic, or even learning theory language, but instead at the neurophysiological level.

Perhaps we don't know enough about "how the brain works" to theorize profitably at that level; and I daresay that the more a psychologist knows about the latest research on brain function, the more reluctant he would be to engage in etiological speculation. Let me entreat my physiologically expert listeners to be charitable toward this clinician's premature speculations about how the schizotaxic brain might work. I feel partially justified in such speculating because there are some well-attested general truths about mammalian learned behavior which could almost have been set down from the armchair, in the way engineers draw block diagrams indicating what kinds of parts or subsystems a physical system *must* have, and what their interconnections *must* be, in order to function "appropriately." Brain research of the last decade provides a direct neurophysiological substrate for such cardinal behavior requirements as avoidance, escape, reward, drive differentiation, general and specific arousal or activation, and the like (see Delafresnaye, 1961; Ramey & O'Doherty, 1960). The discovery in the limbic system of specific positive reinforcement centers by Olds and Milner in 1954, and of aversive centers in the same year by Delgado, Roberts, and Miller (1954), seems to me to have an importance that can scarcely be exaggerated; and while the ensuing lines of research on the laws of intracranial stimulation as a mode of behavior control present some puzzles and paradoxes, what *has* been shown up to now may already suffice to provide a theoretical framework. As a general kind of brain model let us take a broadly Hebbian conception in combination with the findings on intracranial stimulation.

To avoid repetition I shall list some basic assumptions first but introduce others in context and only implicitly when the implication is obvious. I shall assume that:

When a presynaptic cell participates in firing a postsynaptic cell, the former gains an increment in firing control over the latter. Coactivation of anatomically connected cell assemblies or assembly systems therefore increases their stochastic control linkage, and the frequency of discharges by neurons of a system may be taken

as an intensity variable influencing the growth rate of intersystem control linkage as well as the momentary activity level induced in the other systems. (I shall dichotomize acquired cortical systems into "perceptualcognitive," including central representations of goal objects; and "instrumental," including overarching monitor systems which select and guide specific effector patterns.)

Most learning in mature organisms involves altering control linkages between systems which themselves have been consolidated by previous learnings, sometimes requiring thousands of activations and not necessarily related to the reinforcement operation to the extent that perceptual-to-instrumental linkage growth functions are.

Control linkage increments from coactivation depend heavily, if not entirely, upon a period of reverberatory activity facilitating consolidation.

Feedback from positive limbic centers is facilitative to concurrent perceptual-cognitive or instrumental sequences, whereas negative center feedback exerts an inhibitory influence. (These statements refer to initial features of the direct wiring diagram, not to all long-term results of learning.) Aversive input also has excitatory effects via the arousal system, which maintain activity permitting escape learning to occur because the organism is alerted and keeps doing things. But I postulate that this overall influence is working along with an opposite effect, quite clear from both molar and intracranial experiments, that a major biological function of aversive-center activation is to produce "stoppage" of whatever the organism is currently doing.

Perceptual-cognitive systems and limbic motivational control centers develop two-way mutual controls (e.g., discriminative stimuli acquire the reinforcing property; "thoughts" become pleasantly toned; drive-relevant perceptual components are "souped-up.")

What kind of heritable parametric aberration could underlie the schizotaxic's readiness to acquire the schizotypic tetrad? It would seem, first of all, that the defect is much more likely to reside in the neurone's synaptic control function than in its storage function. It is hard to conceive of a general defect in storage which would on the one hand permit so many perceptual-cognitive functions, such as tapped by intelligence tests, school learning, or the high order cognitive powers displayed by some schizotypes, and yet have the diffuse motivational and emotional effects found in these same individuals. I am not saying that a storage deficit is clearly excludable, but it hardly seems the best place to look. So we direct our attention to parameters of control.

One possibility is to take the anhedonia as fundamental. What is *phenomenologically* a radical pleasure deficiency may be roughly identified *behaviorally* with a quantitative deficit in the positive reinforcement growth constant, and each of these— the "inner" and "outer" aspects of the organism's appetitive control system— reflect a quantitative deficit in the limbic "positive" centers. The anhedonia would then be a direct consequence of the genetic defect in wiring. Ambivalence and interpersonal aversiveness would be quantitative deviations in the balance of appetitive-aversive controls. Most perceptual-cognitive and instrumental learnings occur under mixed positive and negative schedules, so the normal consequence is a collection of habits and expectancies varying widely in the intensity of their positive and negative components, but mostly "mixed" in character. Crudely put, everybody has *some* ambivalence about almost everything, and everybody has *some* capacity for "social fear." Now if the brain centers which mediate phenomenal pleasure and behavioral reward are numerically sparse or functionally feeble, the aversive centers meanwhile functioning normally, the long-term result would be a general shift toward the aversive end, appearing clinically as ambivalence and exaggerated interpersonal fear. If, as Brady believes, there is a wired-in reciprocal inhibiting relation between positive and negative centers, the long-term aversive drift would be further potentiated (i.e., what we see at the molar level as a sort of "softening" or "soothing" effect of feeding or petting upon anxiety elicitors would be reduced).

Cognitive slippage is not as easy to fit in, but if we assume that normal ego function is acquired by a combination of social reinforcements and the self-reinforcements which become available to the child via identification; then we might say roughly that "everybody has to learn *how* to think straight." Rationality is socially acquired; the secondary process and the reality principle are slowly and imperfectly learned, by even the most clear headed. Insofar as slippage is manifested in the social sphere, such an explanation has some plausibility. An overall aversive drift would account for the paradoxical schizotypic combination of interpersonal distortions and acute perceptiveness of others' unconscious, since the latter is really a hypersensitivity to aversive signals rather than an overall superiority in realistically discriminating social cues. On the output side, we might view the cognitive slippage of mildly schizoid speech as originating from poorly consolidated second-order "monitor" assembly systems which function in an editing role, their momentary regnancy constituting the "set to communicate." At this level, selection among competing verbal operants involves slight differences in appropriateness for which a washed-out social reinforcement history provides an insufficiently refined monitor system. However, if one is impressed with the presence of a pervasive and primary slippage, showing up in a diversity of tests (cf. Payne, 1961) and also on occasions when the patient is desperately trying to communicate, an explanation on the basis of deficient positive center activity is not too convincing.

This hypothesis has some other troubles which I shall merely indicate. Schizoid anhedonia is mainly interpersonal, i.e., schizotypes seem to derive adequate pleasure from esthetic and cognitive rewards. Secondly, some successful psychotherapeutic results include what appears to be a genuine normality of hedonic capacity. Thirdly, regressive electroshock sometimes has the same effect, and the animal evidence suggests that shock works by knocking out the aversive control system rather than by souping up appetitive centers. Finally, if the anhedonia is really general in extent, it is hard to conceive of any simple genetic basis for weakening the different positive centers, whose reactivity has been shown by Olds and others to be chemically drive specific.

A second neurological hypothesis takes the slippage factor as primary. Suppose that the immediate consequence of whatever biochemical aberration the gene directly controls were a specific alteration in the neurone's membrane stability, such that the distribution of optional transmission probabilities is more widely dispersed over the synaptic signal space than in normals. That is, presynaptic input signals whose spatio-temporal configuration locates them peripherally in the neurone's signal space yield transmission probabilities which are relatively closer to those at the maximum point, thereby producing a kind of dedifferentiation or flattening of the cell's selectivity. Under suitable parametric assumptions, this synaptic slippage would lead to a corresponding dedifferentiation of competing interassembly controls, because the elements in the less frequently or intensely coactivated control assembly would be accumulating control increments more rapidly than normal. Consider a perceptual-cognitive system whose regnancy is preponderantly associated with positive-center coactivation but sometimes with aversive. The cumulation of control increments will draw these apart; but if synaptic slippage exists, their difference, at least during intermediate stages of control development, will be attenuated. The intensity of aversive-center activation by a given level of perceptual-cogni-

tive system activity will be exaggerated relative to that induced in the positive centers. For a preponderantly aversive control this will be reversed. But now the different algebraic sign of the feedbacks introduces an important asymmetry. Exaggerated negative feedback will tend to lower activity level in the predominantly appetitive case, retarding the growth of the control linkage; whereas exaggerated positive feedback in the predominantly aversive case will tend to heighten activity levels, accelerating the linkage growth. The long-term tendency will be that movement in the negative direction which I call *aversive drift*. In addition to the asymmetry generated by the difference in feedback signs, certain other features in the mixed-regime setup contribute to aversive drift. One factor is the characteristic difference between positive and negative reinforcers in their role as strengtheners. It seems a fairly safe generalization to say that positive centers function only weakly as strengtheners when "on" continuously, and mainly when they are turned on as terminators of a cognitive or instrumental sequence; by contrast, negative centers work mainly as "off" signals, tending to inhibit elements while steadily "on." We may suppose that the former strengthen mainly by facilitating postactivity reverberation (and hence consolidation) in successful systems, the latter mainly by holding down such reverberation in unsuccessful ones. Now a slippage-heightened aversive steady state during predominantly appetitive control sequences reduces their activity level, leaves fewer recently active elements available for a subsequent Olds-plus "on" signal to consolidate. Whereas a slippage-heightened Olds-plus steady state during predominantly aversive control sequences (a) increases their negative control *during* the "on" period and (b) leaves relatively more of their elements recently active and hence further consolidated by the negative "off" signal when it occurs. Another factor is exaggerated competition by aversively controlled sequences, whereby the appetitive chains do not continue to the stage of receiving socially mediated positive reinforcement, because avoidant chains (e.g., phobic behavior, withdrawal, intellectualization) are getting in the way. It is worth mentioning that the schizophrenogenic mother's regime is presumably "mixed" not only in the sense of the frequent and unpredictable aversive inputs she provides in response to the child's need signals, but also in her greater tendency to present such aversive inputs *concurrently* with drive reducers — thereby facilitating the "scrambling" of appetitive-and-aversive controls so typical of schizophrenia.

The schizotype's dependency guilt and aversive overreaction to offers of help are here seen as residues of the early knitting together of his cortical representations of appetitive goals with punishment-expectancy assembly systems. Roughly speaking, he has learned that to want anything interpersonally provided is to be endangered.

The cognitive slippage is here conceived as a direct molar consequence of synaptic slippage, potentiated by the disruptive effects of aversive control and inadequate development of interpersonal communication sets. Cognitive and instrumental linkages based upon sufficiently massive and consistent regimes, such as reaching for a seen pencil, will coverge to asymptotes hardly distinguishable from the normal. But systems involving closely competing strengths and automatized selection among alternatives, especially when the main basis of acquisition and control is social reward, will exhibit evidences of malfunction.

My third speculative model revives a notion with a long history, namely, that the primary schizotaxic defect is a quantitative deficiency of inhibition. (In the light of Milner's revision of Hebb, in which the inhibitory action of Golgi Type II cells is crucial even for the formation of functionally differentiated cell assemblies, a defective inhibitory parameter could

be an alternative basis for a kind of slippage similar in its consequences to the one we have just finished discussing.) There are two things about this somewhat moth-eaten "defective inhibition" idea which I find appealing. First, it is the most direct and uncomplicated neurologizing of the schizoid cognitive slippage. Schizoid cognitive slippage is neither an incapacity to link, nor is it an unhealthy overcapacity to link; rather it seems to be a defective *control* over associations which are also accessible to the healthy (as in dreams, wit, psychoanalytic free association, and certain types of creative work) but are normally "edited out" or "automatically suppressed" by those super-ordinate monitoring assembly systems we lump together under the term "set." Secondly, in working with pseudoneurotic cases one sees a phenomenon to which insufficient theoretical attention has been paid: Namely, these patients cannot turn off painful thoughts. They suffer constantly and intensely from painful thoughts about themselves, about possible adverse outcomes, about the past, about the attitudes and intentions of others. The "weak ego" of schizophrenia means a number of things, one of which is failure of defense; the schizophrenic has too ready access to his own id, and is too perceptive of the unconscious of others. It is tempting to read "failure of defense" as "quantitatively deficient inhibitory feedback." As mentioned earlier, aversive signals (whether exteroceptive or internally originated) must exert both an exciting effect via the arousal system and a quick-stoppage effect upon cortical sequences which fail to terminate the ongoing aversive signal, leading the organism to shift to another. Suppose the gene resulted in an insufficient production (or too rapid inactivation) of the specific inhibitory transmitter substance, rendering all inhibitory neurones quantitatively weaker than normal. When aversively linked cognitive sequences activate negative limbic centers, these in turn soup up the arousal system normally but provide a subnormal inhibitory feedback, thereby permitting their elicitor to persist for a longer time and at higher intensity than normal. This further activates the negative control center, and so on, until an equilibrium level is reached which is above normal in intensity all around, and which meanwhile permits an excessive linkage growth in the aversive chain. (In this respect the semicompensated case would differ from the late-stage deteriorated schizophrenic, whose aversive drift has gradually proliferated so widely that almost any cognitive or instrumental chain elicits an overlearned defensive "stoppage," whereby even the inner life undergoes a profound and diffuse impoverishment.)

The mammalian brain is so wired that aversive signals tend to produce stoppage of regnant cognitive or instrumental sequences without the aversive signal having been specifically connected to their controlling cues or motivational systems. E.g., lever pressing under thirst or hunger can be inhibited by shock-associated buzzer, even though the latter has not been previously connected with hunger, paired with the discriminative stimulus, nor presented as punishment for the operant. A deficient capacity to inhibit concurrent activity of fringe elements (aversively connected to ambiguous social inputs from ambivalent mother) would accelerate the growth of linkages between them and appetitive systems not hitherto punished. Sequential effects are here especially important, and combine with the schizophrenogenic mother's tendency not to provide differential cues of high consistency as predictors of whether aversive or appetitive consequences will follow upon the child's indications of demand.

Consider two cortical systems having shared "fringe" subsystems (e.g., part percepts of mother's face). When exteroceptive inputs are the elicitors, negative feedback from aversive centers cannot usually produce stoppage; in the absence of such overdetermining external controls, the relative activity levels are determined by the balance of facilitative and inhibitory feedbacks. "Fringe" assemblies which have already acquired more aversive control, if they begin to be activated by regnant perceptual-cognitive sequences, will increase inhibitory feedback; and being "fringe" they can thereby be held down. The schizotaxic, whose aversive-feedback stoppage of fringe-element activity is weakened, accumulates excessive intertrial Hebbian increments toward the aversive side, the predominantly aversive fringe elements being more active and becoming more knit into the system than normally. On subsequent exteroceptively controlled trials, whenever the overdetermining stimulus input activates predominantly aversive perceptual-cognitive assemblies, their driving of the negative centers will be heightened. The resulting negative feedback may now be strong enough that, when imposed upon "fringe" assemblies weakly activated and toward the appetitive side, it can produce stoppage. On such occasions the more appetitive fringe elements will be retarded in their linkage growth, receiving fewer Hebbian increments. And those which do get over threshold will become further linked during such trials to the concurrent negative center activity. The result is twofold: a retarded growth of appetitive perceptual-cognitive linkages; and a progressive drawing of fringe elements into the aversive ambit.

"Ambiguous regimes," where the pairing of S+ and S− inputs occurs very unpredictably, will have a larger number of fringe elements. Also, if the external schedule is dependent upon regnant appetitive drive states as manifested in the child's instrumental social acts, so that these are often met with mixed S+ (drive-relevant) and S− (anxiety-eliciting) inputs, the appetitive and aversive assemblies will tend to become linked, and to activate positive and negative centers concurrently. The anhedonia and ambivalence would be consequences of this plus-minus "scrambling," especially if the positive and negative limbic centers are mutually inhibitory but here deficiently so. We would then expect schizotypic anhedonia to be basically interpersonal, and only derivatively present, if at all, in other contexts. This would in part explain the schizotype's preservation of relatively normal function in a large body of instrumental domains. For example, the acquisition of basic motor and cognitive skills would be relatively less geared to a mixed input, since "successful" mastery is both mechanically rewarded (e.g., how to open a door) and also interpersonally rewarded as "school success," etc. The hypercathexis of intellect, often found even among nonbright schizotypes, might arise from the fact that these performances are rewarded rather "impersonally" and make minimal demands on the reinforcing others. Also, the same cognitive and mechanical instrumental acts can often be employed both to turn on positive center feedback and to turn off negative, an equivalence much less true of purely social signals linked to interpersonal needs.

Having briefly sketched three neurological possibilities for the postulated schizotaxic aberration, let me emphasize that while each has sufficient merit to be worth pursuing, they are mainly meant to be illustrative of the vague concept "integrative neural defect." I shall myself not be surprised if all three are refuted, whereas I shall be astounded if future research shows no fundamental aberration in nerve-cell function in the schizotype. Postulating schizotaxia as an open concept seems at first to pose a search problem of needle-in-haystack proportions, but I suggest that the plausible alternatives are really somewhat limited. After all, what does a neuron do to another neuron? It excites, or it inhibits! The schizotypic preservation of relatively normal function in selected domains directs our search toward some minimal deviation in a synaptic control parameter, as opposed to, say, a gross defect in cell distribution or structure, or the kind of biochemical anomaly that yields mental deficiency. Anything which would give rise to defective storage, grossly impaired transmission, or sizable limitations on functional complexity can be pretty well

excluded on present evidence. What we are looking for is a quantitative aberration in synaptic control—a deviation in amount or patterning of excitatory or inhibitory action—capable of yielding cumulative departures from normal control linkages under mixed appetitive-aversive regimes; but slight enough to permit convergence to quasi-normal asymptotes under more consistent schedules (or when massive repetition with motive-incentive factors unimportant is the chief basis for consolidation). The defect must generate aversive drift on mixed social reinforcement regimes, and must yield a primary cognitive slippage which, however, may be extremely small in magnitude except as potentiated by the cumulative effects of aversive drift. Taken together these molar constraints limit our degrees of freedom considerably when it comes to filling in the neurophysiology of schizotaxia.

Leaving aside the specific nature of schizotaxia, we must now raise the familiar question whether such a basic neurological defect, however subtle and nonstructural it might be, should not have been demonstrated hitherto? In reply to this objection I shall content myself with pointing out that there are several lines of evidence which, while not strongly arguing *for* a neurological theory, are rebuttals of an argument presupposing clear and consistent *negative* findings. For example: Ignoring several early European reports with inadequate controls, the literature contains a half-dozen quantitative studies showing marked vestibular system dysfunction in schizophrenics (Angyal & Blackman, 1940, 1941; Angyal & Sherman, 1942; Colbert & Koegler, 1959; Freeman & Rodnick, 1942; Leach, 1960; Payne & Hewlett, 1960; Pollock & Krieger, 1958). Hoskins (1946) concluded that a neurological defect in the vestibular system was one of the few clear-cut biological findings in the Worcester studies. It is of prime importance to replicate these findings among compensated and pseudoneurotic cases, where the diffuse withdrawal and deactivation factor would not provide the explanation it does in the chronic, burnt-out case (cf. Collins, Crampton, & Posner, 1961). Another line of evidence is in the work of King (1954) on psychomotor deficit, noteworthy for its careful use of task simplicity, asymptote performance, concern for patient cooperation, and inclusion of an outpatient pseudoneurotic sample. King himself regards his data as indicative of a rather basic behavior defect, although he does not hold it to be schizophrenia-specific. Then we have such research as that of Barbara Fish (1961) indicating the occurrence of varying signs of perceptual-motor maldevelopment among infants and children who subsequently manifest clinical schizophrenia. The earlier work of Schilder and Bender along these lines is of course well known, and there has always been a strong minority report in clinical psychiatry that many schizophrenics provide subtle and fluctuating neurological signs of the "soft" variety, if one keeps alert to notice or elicit them. I have myself been struck by the frequent occurrence, even among pseudoneurotic patients, of transitory neurologic-like complaints (e.g., diplopia, localized weakness, one-sided tremor, temperature dyscontrol, dizziness, disorientation) which seem to lack dynamic meaning or secondary gain and whose main effect upon the patient is to produce bafflement and anxiety. I have seen preliminary findings by J. McVicker Hunt and his students in which a rather dramatic quantitative deficiency in spatial cognizing is detectable in schizophrenics of above-normal verbal intelligence. Research by Cleveland (1960; Cleveland, Fisher, Reitman, & Rothaus, 1962) and by Arnhoff and Damianopoulos (in press) on the clinically well-known body-image anomalies in schizophrenia suggests that this domain yields quantitative departures from the norm of such magnitude that with further instrumental and statistical refinement it might be used as a quasi-pathognomonic sign of the disease. It is interesting to note a certain thread of unity running through this evidence, which perhaps lends support to Rado's hypothesis that a kinesthetic integrative defect is even more characteristic of schizotypy than is the radical anhedonia.

All these kinds of data are capable of a psychodynamic interpretation. "Soft" neurological signs are admittedly ambiguous, especially when found in the severely decompensated case. The only point I wish to make here is that *since* they exist and are at present unclear in etiology, an otherwise plausible neurological view cannot be refuted on the ground that there is a *lack* of any sign of neurological dysfunction in schizophrenia; there is no such lack.

Time forces me to leave detailed research strategy for another place, but the main directions are obvious and may be stated briefly: The clinician's Mental Status ratings on anhedonia, ambivalence, and interpersonal aversiveness should be objectified and preferably replaced by psychometric measures. The research findings on cognitive slippage, psychomotor dyscontrol, vestibular malfunction, body image, and other spatial aberrations should be thoroughly replicated and extended into the pseudoneurotic and semicompensated ranges. If these efforts succeed, it will be possible to set up a multiple sign pattern, using optimal cuts on phenotypically diverse indicators, for identifying compensated schizotypes in the nonclinical population. Statistics used must be appropriate to the theoretical model of a dichotomous latent taxonomy reflecting itself in otherwise independent quantitative indicators. Finally concordance studies should then be run relating proband schizophrenia to schizotypy as identified by this multiple indicator pattern. Meanwhile we should carry on an active and varied search for more direct neurological signs of schizotaxia, concentrating our hunches on novel stimulus inputs (e.g., the stabilized retinal image situation) which may provide a better context for basic neural dysfunction to show up instead of being masked by learned compensations or imitated by psychopathology.

In closing, I should like to take

this unusual propaganda opportunity to play the prophet. It is my strong personal conviction that such a research strategy will enable psychologists to make a unique contribution in the near future, using psychological techniques to establish that schizophrenia, while its content is learned, is fundamentally a neurological disease of genetic origin.

References

Angyal, A., and Blackman, N. Vestibular reactivity in schizophrenia. *Arch. Neurol. Psychiat.*, 1940, *44*, 611-620.

Angyal, A., and Blackman, N. Paradoxical reactions in schizophrenia under the influence of alcohol, hyperpnea, and CO_2 inhalation. *Amer. J. Psychiat.*, 1941, *97*, 893-903.

Angyal, A., and Sherman, N. Postural reactions to vestibular stimulation in schizophrenic and normal subjects. *Amer. J. Psychiat.*, 1942, *98*, 857-862.

Arnhoff, F., and Damianopoulos, E. Self-body recognition and schizophrenia: An exploratory study. *J. abnorm. soc. Psychol.*, in press.

Bleuler, E. *Theory of schizophrenic negativism.* New York: Nervous and Mental Disease Publishing, 1912.

Bleuler, E. *Dementia praecox.* New York: International Universities Press, 1950.

Cleveland, S. E. Judgment of body size in a schizophrenic and a control group. *Psychol. Rep.*, 1960, *7*, 304.

Cleveland, S. E., Fisher, S., Reitman, E. E., and Rothaus, P. Perception of body size in schizophrenia. *Arch. gen. Psychiat.*, 1962, *7*, 277-285.

Colbert, G., and Koegler, R. Vestibular dysfunction in childhood schizophrenia. *AMA Arch. gen. Psychiat.*, 1959, *1*, 600-617.

Collins, W. E., Crampton, G. H., and Posner, J. B. The effect of mental set upon vestibular nystagmus and the EEG. *USA Med. Res. Lab. Rep.*, 1961, No. 439.

Delafresnaye, J. F. (Ed.) *Brain mechanisms and learning.* Springfield, Ill.: Charles C Thomas, 1961.

Delgado, J. M. R., Roberts, W. W., and Miller, N. E. Learning motivated by electrical stimulation of the brain. *Amer. J. Physiol.*, 1954, *179*, 587-593.

Fish, Barbara. The study of motor development in infancy and its relationship to psychological functioning. *Amer. J. Psychiat.*, 1961, *117*, 1113-1118.

Freeman, H., and Rodnick, E. H. Effect of rotation on postural steadiness in normal and schizophrenic subjects. *Arch. Neurol. Psychiat.*, 1942, *48*, 47-53.

Fuller, J. L., and Thompson, W. R. *Behavior genetics.* New York: Wiley, 1960. Pp. 272-283.

Hoskins, R. G. *The biology of schizophrenia.* New York: Norton, 1946.

King, H. E. *Psychomotor aspects of mental disease.* Cambridge: Harvard Univer. Press, 1954.

Leach, W. W. Nystagmus: An integrative neural deficit in schizophrenia. *J. abnorm. soc. Psychol.*, 1960, *60*, 305-309.

Lidz, T., Cornelison, A., Terry, D., and Fleck, S. Intrafamilial environment of the schizophrenic patient: VI. The transmission of irrationality. *AMA Arch. Neurol. Psychiat.*, 1958, *79*, 305-316.

McConaghy, N. The use of an object sorting test in elucidating the hereditary factor in schizophrenia. *J. Neurol. Neurosurg. Psychiat.*, 1959, *22*, 243-246.

Meyers, D., and Goldfarb, W. Psychiatric appraisals of parents and siblings of schizophrenic children. *Amer. J. Psychiat.*, 1962, *118*, 902-908.

Olds, J., and Milner, P. Positive reinforcement produced by electrical stimulation of septal area and other regions of rat brain. *J. comp. physiol. Psychol.*, 1954, *47*, 419-427.

Payne, R. W. Cognitive abnormalities. In H. J. Eysenck (Ed.), *Handbook of abnormal psychology.* New York: Basic Books, 1961. Pp. 248-250.

Payne, R. S., and Hewlett, J. H. G. Thought disorder in psychotic patients. In H. J. Eysenck (Ed.), *Experiments in personality.* Vol. 2. London: Routledge, Kegan, Paul, 1960. Pp. 3-106.

Pollack, M., and Krieger, H. P. Oculomotor and postural patterns in schizophrenic children. *AMA Arch. Neurol. Psychiat.*, 1958, *79*, 720-726.

Rado, S. *Psychoanalysis of behavior.* New York: Grune & Stratton, 1956.

Rado, S., and Daniels, G. *Changing concepts of psychoanalytic medicine.* New York: Grune & Stratton, 1956.

Ramey, E. R., and O'Doherty, D. S. (Ed.) *Electrical studies on the unanesthetized brain.* New York: Hoeber, 1960.

Rosenthal, D. Problems of sampling and diagnosis in the major twin studies of schizophrenia. *J. psychiat. Res.*, in press.

Stern, K. *Principles of human genetics.* San Francisco: Freeman, 1960. Pp. 581-584.

Biophysical Theories:

THERAPY

It should not be surprising that biophysical theorists prefer biophysical methods for treating psychopathology. According to them, the primary source of the difficulty exists in the biophysical make-up of the patient. It follows logically then that efforts should be made to remedy the defect directly. The fact that few of these "defects" have been specified or even localized has not deterred the development of biophysical therapies. The chapter by Lothar Kalinowsky and Paul Hoch summarizes the rather checkered history of theories of biophysical therapy, and offers incisive commentaries on their respective merits as theories and as therapies. In a different vein, Harold Himwich presents a detailed review of the biophysical substrate underlying the action of the new psychopharmacologic agents. Here he demonstrates the complex steps required to track down the varied and intricate neurophysiological reactions to these drugs.

Theories of Somatic Treatment

LOTHAR KALINOWSKY and PAUL HOCH

Psychiatry differs from other fields of medicine in a deplorable lack of facts on which all psychiatrists can agree. There is no generally accepted etiology of most mental diseases, and the entire foundation of the specialty of psychiatry is based on theories believed by some, and opposed by others. It is, therefore, not surprising that attempts to explain treatment procedures vary with the theoretical approach of the observer. This in itself leads to differences in explaining the mode of action of treatments. The matter is complicated by the fact that all psychiatric treatments were found empirically, and only later theories were developed to explain their action. Many

theories were offered for one individual method, and efforts to find a common denominator for several treatments with similar effects have also been made. None of these attempts was satisfactory. The following chapter tries to list the theories presented in the literature, and to scrutinize their validity.

PHARMACOTHERAPY

While in the field of the later discussed shock treatments, theories were primarily based on the individual belief of those who developed them, pharmacotherapy offered a more scientific basis of theoretical considerations. It must not be overlooked, however, that no theoretical concepts led to the intro-

From *Somatic Treatments in Psychiatry*, Chapter 7, Grune and Stratton, 1961, by Lothar B. Kalinowsky and Paul B. Hoch. By permission of the publisher and Dr. Kalinowsky.

duction of any of the new drugs into psychiatry. Even the hope that they would contribute to a better understanding of the pathophysiological manifestations underlying psychiatric disorders, was not fulfilled. The same hope had been expressed, when the shock treatments were introduced. Thus far, all forms of therapy were equally disappointing in this respect. In pharmacotherapy the interest of the basic sciences was greater than in previous somatic treatments, and it was justified to expect that this chemical approach would lead to better knowledge of the biochemical basis of psychopathological manifestations and their changes under the influence of known chemicals. Actually, the various theories presented for the action of the empirically found neuroleptics are still quite speculative. Some clearly defined theories on certain antidepressant drugs turned out to be inapplicable to other drugs with the same clinical effect. The following theoretical considerations are presented mainly as a starting point for further efforts.

The main basis for theory formation in pharmacotherapy is animal experimentation and observations in humans. Most pharmacological properties have already been described in the chapters on the various drugs or groups of drugs. Here, only some studies concentrating on theoretical implications will be added.

There is essential agreement on the regions of the brain on which the phenothiazines act. The regions of the brain that are affected are the thalamus, the hypothalamus, the reticular formation and the remainder of the extra-pyramidal system. Clinically one of the most prominent side-effects of this group of drugs are the extrapyramidal manifestations (parkinsonism, dystonia, and akathisia). Many of these symptoms have been compared to those occurring in encephalitis lethargica which affects similar areas of the brain. The potency of a phenothiazine appears to increase in association with the incidence of extrapyramidal effects. Stimulation of the

reticular formation alerting system produces characteristic low amplitude rapid waves in the EEG associated with arousal of the organism. In small doses chlorpromazine blocks this arousal pattern, but in large doses its action is reversed and the alerting system may be stimulated. Wase et al. have demonstrated the specificity of chlorpromazine for the recticular formation radiochemically.

The phenothiazines also have antiadrenergic activity. Dell and his group have shown experimentally that, after blockage of adrenergic intra-reticular mechanisms by chlorpromazine, the spontaneous activity of the reticular formation is diminished. There is no longer a reaction to adrenaline liberated through nociceptive stimulation, and the reticular formation becomes more sensitive to inhibiting influences. The animal receiving chlorpromazine has a reduced spontaneous activity, falls asleep readily, and, if it is awakened, the waking state is not maintained. Dell suggests that certain neurones of the reticular formation are adrenergic in nature and that consequently adrenaline or a related substance can have a central reticular action.

Phenothiazines have been found to block the central actions of norepinephrine analogs such as mescaline and amphetamine and of parenterally administered catechol amines. The substance used for the latter purpose is DOPA—dihydroxyphenylalanine—the amino acid precursor of the catechol amines which, when given intravenously to rabbits, produces typical sympathetic effects. Its breakdown product has a marked resemblance to norepinephrine. The excitement and increased psychomotor activity consequent upon the sympathetic stimulation are blocked by chlorpromazine. It has been suggested that chlorpromazine blocks the sympathetic activities by interfering with the action of norepinephrine in the brain. However, this does not account for all the actions of these drugs in psychiatric illness, such as on delusions and hallucinations, which are also alleviated together with the diminution of increased psychomotor activity.

Saunders has suggested the following hypothesis for the action of the phenothiazines, Raufwolfia alkaloids and iproniazid. He suggests that in schizophrenia transamination is excessive in the brain, while in depression it is oxidative deamination which is excessive. The transamination reaction is catalysed by ionic copper, with pyridoxine as the co-enzyme. Chlorpromazine and reserpine are able to form complexes and/or chelates with copper and to modify the action of copper—catalysed enzymes. They both increase copper plasma levels. Chlorpromazine and reserpine may, therefore, provide copper in the necessary physico-chemical state to control transaminase reactions at the proper rate.

Charatan has put forward the theory that chlorpromazine, as a tertiary ammonium compound, gives rise to free base in the central nervous system which has the property of entering nerve cells. It will achieve its maximum effects according to the density of the cell population. Thus selective concentration in the basal ganglia including the thalamus would lead to interference with corticothalamic circuits and a reduction in the pathologically increased psychomotor activity.

Gliedman and Horsley Gantt considered the greatest value of the tranquilizing drugs to be their ability to insulate organisms from stimuli to which they are subjected, but to which they do not have learned meanings. In acute excitement states, due to overwhelming stress, there might be a breakdown of learned reactions with a residue of heightened unlearned reactivity and consequent hyper-motor and hyper-autonomic activity. There might also be overactivity consequent upon a failure to have learned appropriate responses to stressful situations.

Pavlovian techniques, applied by Soviet psychiatrists, lead, according to J. Wortis, to the conclusion that chlorpromazine (aminazine) has a dual therapeutic role: The general inhibition of an animal exposed to overwhelming stimulation is relieved by the drug because of its dampening effect on over-stimulation. At the same time, the drug promotes a reorganization of the disordered conditioned responses.

Interesting attempts at distinguishing between the effects of phenothiazine on the cells and on the regulating centers of the two opposing parts of the vegetative nervous system were made by C. and H. Selbach. Few studies were made to investigate the effect of the neuroleptics on metabolism. An exception is the work by Consbrough and Faust who tried to correlate the treatment effect of phenothiazine and reserpine in various endogenous psychoses with changes of serum protein levels. They observed a characteristic lowering of serum albumen and rise of serum alpha-globulin in patients who responded to therapy. The changes of serum protein levels were only minimal, when therapeutic results were poor.

Himwich paid particular attention to the manner in which specific "tranquilizers" affect specific areas of the brain. Some of his conclusions are that the phenothiazines and also the barbiturates suppress the midbrain reticular formation, and that the rauwolfia derivatives stimulate it, and that meprobamate has no particular effect on this activating system. Serotonin is influenced by phenothiazines and rauwolfia derivatives but not by barbiturates and meprobamate. These last two drugs are also clinically very similar, but they differ in the depressive effect of barbiturates on the hypothalamus which meprobamate does not have. Aside from the midbrain reticular formation the activating system consists of diffused thalamo-cortical projections which may be influenced by the drugs in different ways. The second great system involved in emotion is the limbic system (rhinencephalon) or Papez circuit which is stimulated by the neuroleptic drugs but depressed by meprobamate and barbiturates. Similar attempts at stimulation of drug action on various parts of the brain were made by Kraines whose studies also include the psychoanaleptics.

The more clinically and psychopathologically oriented theories are mentioned in the clinical chapters. Freyhan's concept that the effect of neuroleptic drugs is dependent on hypomotility can be found under "central nervous system side-effects of chlorpromazine," where the question of the relationship between extrapyramidal manifestations and therapeutic effect will also be discussed.

The action of the various new drugs have also been explained in psychoanalytical terms. At the time this book goes to press Sarwer-Foner edited a volume with numerous contributions on "The Dynamics of Psychiatric Drug Therapy." We can only refer to this book which is not yet available to us with the exception of a contribution by Ostow. He infers that neuroleptics and antidepressants primarily affect a function which Freud hypothesized "psychic energy," which is ultimately derived at from instinctual impetus. Ostow stipulates that the phenothiazines decrease the amount of psychic energy available to the ego, while iproniazid increases it.

There are many psychoanalysts who reject pharmacotherapeutic support to patients on psychotherapy for theoretical reasons. It is difficult to see why, for instance, a patient should not be given relief by means of drugs because it has been claimed that this may diminish his efforts to work out his problems with the psychotherapist. A more valid objection to the use of the new drugs is that such symptoms as feelings of depersonalization might be produced by certain drugs, and, like other side-effects, interfere with the patient's cooperation in the analytical session. The question to what extent the new drugs really aid in psychotherapy is still open, and we agree with Sargant that in some cases older sedatives such as phenobarbital may be more helpful than the neuroleptics.

Concepts regarding the group of antidepressant drugs which found the greatest theoretical interest, were discussed in the section on monoamine oxidase inhibitors. Strangely enough, this rather hypothetical effect of iproniazid and similar drugs gave the name to this entire group of analeptics, and the term had to be explained together with their pharmacological properties prior to the discussion of the individual drugs.

INSULIN AND CONVULSIVE TREATMENTS

In the area of shock treatments, many theories have been presented, many of them without actual foundation in facts. Some overlap, and some express the same idea in different terms. This made it possible for Gordon to collect the surprising number of fifty different theories. We still agree with Nolan D. C. Lewis that "at the present time there is no theory as to the nature of the shock treatments sufficiently comprehensible to be taken very seriously."

The therapeutic action is explained by some authors on an organic basis, others believe that shock treatments effect essentially a psychogenic cure. The so-called somatic theories will be discussed first. The first explanation was advanced by Sakel concerning insulin treatment. The theory of insulin action was obviously evolved during or after the introduction of the treatment as an afterthought. Sakel himself realized that his theory was not too convincingly elaborated. He once wrote: "The mistakes in theory should not be counted against the treatment itself, which seems to be accomplishing more than the theory behind it."

Sakel believed that the nerve cell develops an exaggerated activity, becomes oversensitive to the normal stimuli of the outside world and elaborates these stimuli excessively. "To restore normal conditions again," he writes, "one has to either limit the supply of excitant material, or else diminish combustion in the cell by muffling it." He conceives the action of insulin as being due to neutralization of the excitant, which he believes to be a hormone, and to the vagotonic muffling of the cell. He further assumes that in schizophrenics, the phylogenetically youngest intracellular connections are injured, and the more ancient nerve pathways are activated. As the disease progresses, these normally obliterated pathways dominate the scene. The stronger the harmful influence of the disease, more and more deeply seated pathways are involved successively until phylogenetically ancient pathway patterns are reached which prove to be resistant to the toxic influences. Sakel also assumes a short-circuiting of the pathways between the nerve cells. Insulin shock treatment, according to him, reverses all these processes by blockading the cell through influence on the vegetative centers so that the injured or confused pathways are not exposed to further stimuli. By means of this artificial rest, the normal pathways recuperate and attain their former prominence. In schizophrenia, vegetative subcortical centers are assumed to be the site of the primary disturbance, of which the abnormal psychotic symptoms are secondary manifestations.

It is apparent that this hypothesis of Sakel's is far too vague and speculative to offer convincing evidence on the action of insulin shock. It leaves completely unresolved the questions as to how and where this overaction of the nervous system originates in schizophrenia, and, furthermore, what kind of physical-chemical process is responsible for the "blockade" of the cell or the short-circuiting of the pathways. Nor does this theory elucidate the etiology of schizophrenia which is a necessary shortcoming of all theories on treatments of this disease.

A similar theory centering on cell destruction was evolved more recently by Arnold. He assumes that insulin leads to an acute disorganization of carbohydrate metabolism of the ganglion cell which first interferes with cell function and ends in cell destruction. This effect of insulin is limited to those ganglion cells which for genetic reasons are predisposed to a disturbance in carbohydrate metabolism.

Meduna's introduction of the met-

razol treatment was based on premises which proved to be incorrect, but, as so often happens in science, an erroneous working hypothesis yielded an effective therapeutic weapon. We owe to it not only the pharmacological convulsive therapy but also the electric convulsive therapy for which no new theories have been developed by their inventors. Meduna's theoretical basis for the introduction of the convulsive treatment was the assumption that epilepsy and schizophrenia are antagonistic to each other. He found, in his clinical studies, that these two disorders very rarely occurred together. Moreover, his biochemical investigations supported this theory as determinations of uric acid, creatinine, nitrogen content, and blood sugar suggested that schizophrenics and epileptics had a different biochemistry. In addition, he made clinical observations which emphasized the beneficial effects of spontaneously occurring epileptic convulsions in schizophrenic patients.

Meduna's assumption that schizophrenia and epilepsy are antagonistic to each other has been refuted by a number of authors. The biochemistry of both disorders is so complicated and still so obscure, that no theory of similarity or antagonism regarding these two diseases can be formulated at the present time. Recently, in strong contrast to von Meduna's original concept of a biological antagonism between the two diseases, attempts have been made to establish a positive relationship between schizophrenia and epilepsy on the basis of electroencephalographic findings. This, however, was disproved by Hoch, who demonstrated in a genetic, electroencephalographic, and clinical study that the two disorders are neither related nor opposed to each other. The observation by Meduna that spontaneous epileptic attacks in schizophrenia influence favorably the clinical symptomatology is probably more valid. However, contrary to clinical evidence brought forward by other workers, Esser, on the basis of 10,000 patients surveyed in the literature, arrives at the conclusion that epileptic convulsions are not infrequent in catatonia and in many cases are not followed by improvement. But the main argument against von Meduna's theory is the fact that convulsive treatment is most effective in the manic-depressive psychoses. The great therapeutic value of convulsive therapy in the affective disorders was recognized, but not until several years after the theoretical foundation for the treatment of schizophrenia with convulsions had been developed. A theory of a biological antagonism, therefore, would have to be extended to cover the affective psychoses as well.

After Sakel and Meduna had given the first theoretical explanations for the treatments devised by them, other authors advanced theories which were partly elaborations of previous ones; again, others suggested some new mechanisms that might be responsible for the improvement, with more and more emphasis on the common denominators in view of the great similarity in the effectiveness of insulin and convulsive therapies. Georgi believes that alteration of the nerve cell membrane is responsible for the success of these therapies. Evidence of this membrane alteration is found in a reduction in the amount of sugar in the cell, which is produced slowly in the hypoglycemic coma and quickly with metrazol and electric shock. Demole and Freudenberg expressed similar ideas. Von Angyal believes that hypoglycemia affects the metabolism in the brain cells due to reduction of the sugar content followed by compensation and an increased metabolism stimulating the cells that are in a state of malfunction or degeneration. Similarly, Küppers thinks that metabolic exhaustion in the nerve cells due to insulin provokes a counteraction and finally restores the cells to normal functioning. An unknown toxic substance is assumed by Danziger to accumulate in the body. This substance might depress the rate of heat production by inhibiting one of the respiratory enzymes. Shock therapy is assumed to remove the postulated toxic material. This idea is similar to the assumption that in epilepsy the con-

vulsion eliminates toxic substances, and insulin, by way of sweating, does the same. Cerlettí formulated the theory that convulsions bring the organism to a state which is close to death, thereby arousing a reaction of extreme biologic defense in producing a substance he calls agonine, which exerts the therapeutic effect. Pappalardo explains the effect of shock as well as of fever therapies as means of modifying the defense mechanism of the organism via the reticuloendothelial system. Ewald believes that all shock treatments have a marked influence on the diencephalon whose regulatory mechanisms are intensely stimulated under any kind of shock treatment. He speaks of a "massage of the diencephalic centers" and states that changes in the vegetative regulation, expressing themselves, among other symptoms, by increased weight, are the important therapeutic factors. His theory follows logically his ideas on the origin of schizophrenia which he localized essentially in the diencephalon. In a paper on electric shock therapy, Ewald and Haddenbrock list various observations to support this theory.

A similar concept is Delay's and Mallet's, that the shock treatments exert a sedative effect on hyperthymias (manic states) and a stimulating effect on hypothymias (depressive states). The action of the treatment is explained as excitation of the diencephalon in the hyperthymias and as depression of the diencephalon in the hypothymias. Thus, it is postulated that the vegetative centers in the brain are influenced. Delmas-Marsalet's theory of dissolution and reconstruction of the mechanism of ECT is in many respects related. Delay and also Delmas-Marsalet expounded their theories in monographs on the subject.

Attempts were made to determine whether cerebral oxidation was the common denominator for the action of all shock treatments. High insulin doses prevent the utilization of carbohydrates by the central nervous system and indirectly reduce the oxidation of the brain, as demonstrated in human beings by Damashek and Myerson, and in animals by Himwich et al. Oxygen consumption of the brain drops during insulin treatment and the basal metabolism of the nervous system is reduced by about 60 per cent. The reduction in the metabolism of the brain is actually even greater if we consider that during hypoglycemia the circulation time of the blood in the brain is reduced by about 25 per cent. Serejski is of the opinion that it is not so much the reduction of oxygen as the inability to utilize oxygen that is important in this metabolic alteration. He finds relatively high oxygen content in the veins of the brain during insulin treatment. Convulsive treatments do not produce anoxemia for as long a period as does insulin, but anoxemia is present temporarily, during and shortly after the convulsion, due to the vasoconstriction which the convulsion produces. In electrically induced convulsions, Wortis et al. found interference with oxygen uptake. Due to the anoxia, a reduction in brain metabolism ensues, to be supplanted by a compensatory hyperactivity after the convulsion. In the light of experience with ECT under anesthesia during which the patient is not anoxic but rather oversaturated with oxygen, it is difficult to maintain the theory of anoxia as an important factor in this treatment.

Gellhorn believes that the sympathetic adrenal system dominates the vagoinsulin system in the normal person. In schizophrenia, however, clinical evidence exists pointing to a deficient sympathetic reactivity. The therapeutic effect of shock treatments in schizophrenia is due to the stimulation of the sympathetic adrenal system. This leads to a shift in the balance existing between the centers of the sympathetic adrenal and vagoinsulin systems. Prolonged excitation of the sympathetic centers by the shock treatments restores the disturbed autonomic balance and exerts far reaching effects on the cortex itself. According to Gellhorn, the fact that inhibited conditioned reflexes can be restored by subjecting the animal to insulin coma or to convulsions supports this interpretation. In insulin coma treatment and prolonged narcosis, the hypothalamic stimulation is a release phenomenon, the cortical control being abolished; in convulsive treatment, direct excitation of the hypothalamus takes place. Ivanov-Smolenskii also believes that the common therapeutic factor in shock treatments is the production of cortical decompression or inhibition coupled with subcortical release and vegetative mobilization. Abely et al. hold that the effect of ECT is determined by a short sympathetic stimulation followed by prolonged para-sympathetic excitation with stimulation of the anterior hypothalamus and the acidophile cells of the hypophysis. We repeatedly expressed the view that ECT exerts its influence on the diencephalon. This view based on clinical observations regarding sleep, weight, and menstrual changes, was supported by M. Roth in electro-encephalographical studies which also suggested the primary effect of ECT on the diencephalon.

There is no doubt that changes in the vegetative nervous system can be demonstrated experimentally and clinically during and following shock treatment. It is also apparent that vegetative regulations are changed, as evidenced by improvement in sleep, appetite, weight, digestion, and circulation. It is still uncertain, however, whether or not these changes are concomitant manifestations occurring with mental improvement rather than the basis of mental improvement. It has not been demonstrated conclusively that an alteration in vegetative regulations is the actual cause of schizophrenia; therefore, biochemical changes during successful treatment are not necessarily the cause of mental improvement. Moreover, these theories do not take into consideration the differences which exist between manic-depressive psychoses and schizophrenia and some other mental conditions in which shock treatments are generally effective in varying degrees. At present the most important point to recognize is that, as different forms of treatments may achieve the same results, none of them can be considered specific for a particular mental disease.

Of particular interest is the response to treatment of organic psychoses. The removal of psychotic syndromes in general paresis, of post-infectious psychoses and even psychotic syndromes in cases of pernicious anemia, led Fernandes and Polonio to the conclusion that the shock therapies and leucotomy have no bearing on the etiological causes of the psychoses. According to their concepts, psychotic symptoms arise from deviations of biopsychological functions caused by the noxious factors which, once in existence, may persist for a longer or shorter time. It seems doubtful, however, whether this must necessarily lead to the conclusion that we treat only symptoms or groups of symptoms, if we do not want to extend Bonhoeffer's concept of symptomatic psychoses to the symptoms of schizophrenia or manic-depressive psychosis, assuming that schizophrenia is a toxic disease acting secondarily on the brain.

On the basis of histopathological examinations, Stief formulated the theory that hypoglycemic coma and convulsive therapy produce spasms in the brain capillaries which eliminate diseased nerve cells, thereby bringing about the desired therapeutic results. That the vascular origin of cellular changes is disputed was discussed in the chapters on neuropathology. A more important objection to this theory is that there is no conclusive histopathological evidence that in schizophrenia diseased cortical cells are present in sufficient quantity to be responsible for the mental pathology. Stief's theory fits with the theories of the efficacy of frontal lobotomy. In the light of these concepts, shock treatment is considered a milder form of surgical procedure. While shock treatments may temporarily impair the function of cortical cells, in frontal lobotomy pathways are permanently cut between the cortical and subcortical centers. Both procedures supposedly lead to a reduction in cortical stimulation. LaValette assumes that the organic reaction in convulsive therapy produces a personality change on which the patient can reconstruct his personality.

Coma has also been credited as being the common therapeutic factor, whether caused by hypoglycemia or by convulsive therapy. Not only is coma brought about in hypoglycemia but the patient is in an equally comatose condition during and shortly after a convulsion as indicated by the term "electrocoma treatment" (Fettermann). Coma as the common denominator was suggested not only by those who consider therapeutically effective the pathophysiologic changes occurring in the brain during coma, but also by some who incline to psychologic explanations.

Quite recently, one of the few available experimental studies on clarifications of some of the main problems in ECT were published in a monograph by Ottosson. His questions concern the assumption of most clinicians that the convulsion rather than the electric current is responsible for a therapeutic effect, and, secondly, whether the memory impairment is a consequence of the seizure or a direct effect of the current as had been assumed by those who claimed diminished memory impairment with certain modifications of current. Ottosson uses the anticonvulsive effect of "lidocaine," a local anesthetic which abolishes electrically induced seizures and grand mal attacks in epileptics. He applied ECT to three groups, all of them receiving barbiturate and succinyl choline. The first two groups were given supraliminal and liminal electric stimuli, and it is shown that the electroencephalographic pattern is the same, characterized by an electric silence followed by delta waves. The lidocaine-modified seizures of the third group had hardly any electric silence and no delta activity. The clinical improvement is impaired, when lidocaine is given, and the conclusion can be drawn that the depression-relieving effect must be due to seizure activity and not to the current as such. The memory impairment, however, is only slightly less in ECT with lidocaine which permits the conclusion that a great part of the memory disturbance is accounted for by effects of the current other than the seizure. This most informative study on the action of ECT should be an important basis for any future research on the theory of ECT.

Soon after the first organic theories of the action of insulin coma and convulsive therapy appeared, other psychiatrists expressed a psychogenic point of view. These workers believe that the somatic part of the treatment is only incidental and that prolonged sleep, insulin, or convulsive therapies only prepare the soil for intensive psychotherapy. Meier was one of the first to advance the idea that the more intimate contact with physician and nurses produced by shock treatments exerts a marked psychotherapeutic effect on the patient. Somewhat similar views have been expressed by Schatner and O'Neill, who reason that with the patient helpless and dependent, the physician becomes a mother surrogate, the patient establishes a better transference and therefore becomes more psychotherapeutically approachable. This is true of insulin treatment, which requires a great deal of attention, but is less applicable to electric shock treatment, where the patient is returned to the general ward soon after the treatment or returns home soon after an office treatment. Furthermore, in many private institutions with large medical staffs, considerable attention was paid to the individual patient before the shock era; yet the results were not comparable to those with shock treatment. If rendering the patient helpless or unconscious were sufficient to produce recovery, many other forms of treatment, such as fever treatment, anesthesias, continuous sleep would be as effective as the shock treatments but such is not the case.

Another group of authors, emphasize the psychotherapeutic value of the psychic "shock." They assume that the treatments actually produce a shock in the patient. It is difficult to prove or disprove this idea. However, it is quite evident that the so-called shock treatments usually do not produce any mental shock. Also on the physical level, physiologists and pathologists object to the designation of these treatments as "shock" treatments because there are no phenomena observed similar to surgical shock which is a different and fairly well defined pathological condition. Some of these theories were evolved only because the patient was actually visualized as undergoing some form of mental shock. The patient is usually amnesic during insulin or convulsive treatment and is unable to report on his experiences or impressions during the state of unconsciousness. This naturally does not mean that there are no experiences in that condition, but since it is impossible to obtain any facts on these perceptions, it is pure assumption to say that the experience is that of mental shock. Jelliffe, and others believe that the patients undergo the experience of impending death followed by the feeling of rebirth, and the impetus of these sensations is so great that it breaks the autism of the patient and eliminates the regression and narcissism. We mentioned previously that these experiences of impending death are rather uncommon in insulin-treated patients and in those treated with electric convulsive therapy. Furthermore, there is the question of why it is that all the medieval tortures inflicted on the insane failed to produce impressive therapeutic results, especially when they were inflicted on a conscious person in whom the so-called emotional shock or death threat must have been much more intense. Millett and Moses found that in patients treated by electric shock the treatment is desired because it is felt to be a fitting punishment acceptable from the hands of a trusted and kind doctor-father who really wishes to do no injury but to temper retribution with mercy. Ideas of battering down the patient's defense mechanism, are based more on the impressions of the person who sees the treatment than on those of the patient himself. Some patients are concerned about the convulsion even before they receive the first treatment. This anticipatory fear produces associations of punishment, annihilation. But the fear *of* the treatment should always be differentiated from the fear *produced by* the treatment. Furthermore, many patients who display fear in connection with shock treatments do not improve, while many who display no fear do improve. In electric shock treatment it is a common experience that psychoneurotics express more fear of the treatment than any other group of patients and yet they show the poorest results.

Schilder tried to combine psychogenic and organic theories, stating that the victory over the death threat expressed in the epileptic fit and lingering in the perceptual and aphasic difficulty enables the individual to start life and normal relations with human beings all over again. The hypomanic elation which often follows the epileptic fit is the joy of rebirth; the previous fixations of libido lying in a more personal layer of experience are removed by recovery from a cataclysmic catastrophe in the depth of the organism. "But," Schilder emphasizes, although "the results of the treatment are psychologically understood, it does not mean that metrazol treatment acts as a psychologic agent in the common sense. Its effects are deeper than the effects of what is called psychic influence. This is an organic treatment reflected in psychologic attitudes. Just as in insulin treatment, the organic processes of regeneration are put in action, metrazol convulsions seem to bring with themselves a reconstruction which also serves the more labile organic structures which serve emotions and which are damaged by the process of schizophrenia. The forces liberated by metrazol and insulin treatment come from layers which are generally not accessible to the processes which are usually called psychic." Flescher feels that the therapeutic process of ECT implies a specific and dynamic pathogenous element which cannot be referred to a higher psychic level such as fear or need of help. He himself tries to understand ECT through the function of epileptic attacks, in which, according to him, considerable amounts of destructive energies are discharged.

Psychoanalytic theories of shock treatment have been formulated by Jelliffe, Glueck, Bychowski, and others. Glueck believes that the shock treatment facilitates emotional catharsis and is a highly condensed recapitulation of the process by means of which the fate of the egodystonic impulses is determined—the process which takes place normally in cases of ontogentic development and artificially in the course of psychoanalytic therapy. Bychowski believes that in the psychoses the pathologic ego dominates the healthy one which experiences a rebirth and fortification through insulin; between these two a battle rages until the shock reduces the pathologic ego. The cathartic abreaction then permits psychoanalytic approach and influence. Frosch and Impastato maintain that the various clinical changes seen during and following shock therapy reflect the degree to which the ego defenses succeed in controlling the emergence of previously repressed libidinous and aggressive impulses consequent to the drastic physical assault of the convulsion and the attendant disorders of memory defect and altered body image.

There have been some who assert that the amnesia produced in convulsive shock treatment is a therapeutic factor. For instance, the theory of Brain and Strauss postulates the presence of faulty electrical patterns in the brain, which are altered by the treatment, the resulting amnesia allowing time for the brain to become accustomed to simplified patterns. It should be pointed out, however, that amnesia does not occur regularly in shock treated patients. It is not often present in the insulin-treated patients, and it is usually temporary. The loss of familiarity which plays a certain role in the psychological literature on ECT (Zubin, Janis) has the same weak point as the amnesia theory, namely, that often the organic symptoms are either not present or clear up in a short time after the treatment, and yet, in many cases the recovery persists. The temporary blotting out of symptoms of all kinds does not affect the ultimate outcome of therapy.

A neurophysiologic-adaptive theory was presented by Fink et al. who stated that in ECT an induced change in brain function precedes the milieu in which behavioral changes can occur depending on the characterologic disposition of the subject. As indices of cerebral function they measured the degree of induced delta activity in the EEG, and changes in orientation and awareness of illness after intravenous injection of amobarbital sodium. In the amobarbital test the patient is asked a standard set of questions, and changes in orientation, denial of illness, confabulation and reduplication are considered as indicative of altered brain function. It was found that patients with high denial scores are those who improve best under ECT. These findings were considered to support the hypothesis advanced by Weinstein and Kahn that the mechanism of therapeutic action of electrically induced convulsions lies in the creation of altered brain function in which the patient might express his problems in a new symbolic fashion, particularly in the form of denial. Other theories also tend to combine physiological and psychological mechanisms. In analogy to similar insulin theories, Benda using Selye's general adaptation syndrome, considers the convulsion as a severe stress to which the body adapts and thereby mobilizes general defences. Ploog applies ideas about psychic counter regulation to ECT. L. Alexander tried to come to a better understanding of the mode of action by means of a study of the distinctive operations of the ego.

In connection with psychogenic theories of shock treatment, it is necessary to discuss again the question of psychotherapy in conjunction with these treatments. The theoretical implication of this question is whether the somatic treatments are treatments in their own right, or whether they are only part of the over-all psychological treatment of the patient, or, as is still claimed by many, an adjunct to psychotherapy. Sakel, in his first publications, designated insulin shock treatment as an organic treatment. He mentioned the fact that probings or psychotherapeutic attempts with respect to hallucinations and delusions, especially in paranoid patients, were unwarranted for they upset the patient and might provoke a relapse. Most workers agree that intensive analytical psychotherapy should not be carried out simultaneously with insulin treatment as the patient is in no condition to digest such material; this is especially true as regards sexual and particularly homosexual conflicts. If psychotherapy is given during insulin treatment, it is best to give reassurance in order to assist the patient in solving some of his superficial conflicts and to discuss with him some of his most disturbing psychotic experiences. The best time to do this is after he wakens, when he is in a state of relaxation and maximum approachability. In patients whose improvement is more stabilized, psychotherapeutic sessions can be held in the afternoons of insulin treatment days. The special aspects of this question in electric shock patients have been discussed in the section on this treatment.

Practically no study is available that proves the necessity of psychotherapy by comparing the results in patients who received psychotherapy with those who did not. Furthermore, psychotherapy covers a wide range of activity from simple reassurance to psychoanalysis, and in many instances it is not stated what type of psychotherapy was applied. In some of those institutions where the best results with shock treatments were obtained and where the largest number of cases was treated, only very superficial psychotherapy was and is applied. Their results were apparently not worse and indeed sometimes even better than those indicated by statistics from hospitals where it was possible to apply intensive psychotherapy in conjunction with or after shock therapy. This question is of great importance and more research should be concentrated on it.

An attempt was made by Knight to designate the organic forms of treatment and especially shock therapy as "strong arm method" in contrast to the "gentle" form of treatment, meaning psychotherapy or psychoanalysis. Hoch took exception to this differentiation of therapy. Shock treatments, lobotomy, and other procedures were not devised to intimidate patients, to purge patients, or to force them to desist from expressing symptoms. The treatments were introduced as the basis of certain theoretical conceptions and, more important, of empirical observations. Some of the theoretical concepts which were offered as a basis of these treatments turned out to be invalid. The same, however, can be said for many psychoanalytic concepts.

Empirically, the organic treatments produced results. The evaluation of these results is naturally open to discussion, and no final determination of their value has as yet been made. Even so, we know approximately what they are able to accomplish. The organic treatments rapidly accumulated considerable statistical material which could be analyzed and criticized. By comparison, the psychotherapeutic approaches have practically no statistics or the number of patients evaluated and reported is very small. Therefore, it is more difficult to appraise the efficacy of these treatments; this is especially true for psychoanalytical treatment in the psychoses. The indiscriminate use of the somatic treatments, particularly of electric shock therapy, must be deplored. However, indiscriminate use of psychotherapy also occurs. For instance, we do not think that treatment with analysis or other psychotherapy is justified in a markedly depressed patient who is not able to establish a good transference with the therapist, and becomes agitated due to a procedure that he is unable to follow and which brings up traumatic material which, in his state of agitation and agony he is unable to digest. These patients often become worse under such treatment but usually very quickly recover with electroshock treatments.

In all theoretical considerations of shock therapy there is a great tendency to single out certain observational factors, such as memory impairment or confusion, unconsciousness, and so on, and to try to explain all the actions of the treatments by one or the other of these changes seen. We are in full agreement with Von Baeyer that the shock treatments are not etiological treatments because the basic personality organization, the matrix on which the psychosis grows, is not touched. The recurrence of manic-depressive psychosis or the frequent relapses in shock-treated schizophrenics indicates that even though symptoms of the disorder can sometimes be fully removed, some of the underlying basic factors are not eliminated. With such special drugs as mescaline, pervitin, etc., it is possible to reactivate the psychosis, which also would indicate that a complete elimination of the etiological mechanisms is not achieved. However, lack of etiological basis should not be assumed as an argument against any form of treatment. Many valuable methods in other fields of medicine are proof that it would be entirely unjustified to reject methods because they are purely symptomatic in nature. It may be said here that this objection has been raised against the psychosurgical procedures, whose theoretical implications will now be discussed.

PSYCHOSURGERY

Theories which try to explain *frontal lobotomy and other psychosurgical procedures* are fewer in number than those brought forward for the shock treatments, and have a better foundation in clinical observation, although it must be repeated that none is entirely satisfactory. The hypothesis of Egaz Moniz, who introduced frontal lobotomy, has been mentioned already. It is in certain ways too general to be useful, and some of his specific statements concerning mental illness as being caused by faulty fiber connections are not generally accepted.

Freeman and Watts demonstrated

that the therapeutic results were obtained by section of the thalamofrontal radiation followed by a degeneration of the dorsal medial nucleus of the thalamus which, in turn, produces a bleaching of the affect. They assume that the dorsal medial nucleus of the thalamus is the physical substrata of emotion. Their explanation that the so-called functional psychoses are produced by worry, which is reduced by the operation because the self-involvement of the patient is reduced, is too simple an explanation on the origin of the functional psychoses, even though a nucleus of truth may be in it. Their belief that without the frontal lobes, which have a tendency to overelaborate on anxiety and worry, no functional psychoses could develop, is open to question: elimination of the frontal lobe functions in many patients does not improve the psychosis, and relapses after frontal lobotomy may occur which would not be the case if existence of frontal lobe function were the sole prerequisite for a functional psychosis. It is probable that the origin of the functional psychoses goes beyond the function of the frontal lobe and involves other than the cortical areas of the brain as well.

Partridge, in his monograph on prefrontal leucotomy, clearly states that the modus operandi of leucotomy is not solved. He believes that the most important change after lobotomy is in the thalamus. He considers the thalamus an organ which integrates perceptions, emotions, and patterns of behavior, and believes it is also linked with the hypothalamus, through which autonomic influences are exerted. Partridge feels the schizophrenic disturbances are due to an impairment of this integrating function, which is seemingly favorably altered after operation. This actually does not solve the complicated question of improvements and personality damage seen after psychosurgery but does focus attention on a part of the brain which is probably implicated in mental sickness. Halstead, Hebb, and lately Landis have offered hypotheses based on their psychological investigations. Their description of the alterations which take place after frontal lobe surgery illuminates some aspects of the impairment of function in the frontal lobes without, however, offering a comprehensive understanding of all the alterations of function which are seen. They do not illuminate the etiology of the disorders involved, and do not actually explain the modus operandi of the surgical procedures.

Studies made on different brain-operated patients indicate that a very intimate relationship exists between the cerebral cortex and thalamus, and that a two-way circuit exists between the cortical gray matter and the subcortical gray matter, which mutually influence each other. Therefore, personality alterations can be achieved by ablating cortex, operating on the thalamus, or by cutting connections between thalamus and cortex. Today the connections between frontal lobe and thalamus are especially emphasized. However, it is necessary to recall that the long association fibers connecting the cortical areas of different lobes are also of great importance. We believe that these twofold connections within the cortical areas, and between cortex and thalamus explain why after frontal lobotomy the alterations of psychic functioning are not more severe. The basic intellectual and emotional functioning of the individual remains intact after frontal lobotomy even though the more subtle cognitive and connative performances are altered. If the basic functions of the person were concentrated in the frontal lobes alone, we could expect personality function after frontal lobotomy to show very serious alterations which actually are not even seen after frontal lobectomy. The changes are much less marked than prior theories of the function of the frontal lobe have indicated. Most likely, when parts of the frontal lobe are separated from other parts of the brain, the other cortical areas are able to take over. We believe that the basic intellectual and emotional life of the individual which is necessary for his personality functioning is not localized in the frontal lobe alone, but is distributed over the whole cortex, with the thalamus also having some function in it. This, of course, does not contradict the observation that the highest symbolic functions, such as creativeness, planning and the fusion of emotional and intellectual performances, depend on normal functioning by the frontal lobes. We do not believe that psychosurgery alters the basic structure of the neurosis or psychosis. Most patients who have undergone psychosurgery show in general unchanged dynamics. The retention of the basic psychodynamic structure is clearly seen in schizophrenic patients, and it is possible with drugs like mescaline to reactivate the original psychosis even some time after the operation. The symptoms which reappear are usually not as intense but are the same in quality. Therefore, we believe that psychosurgery points to an important problem in psychiatric therapy. Most of our treatments, especially the psychotherapeutic ones, mainly consider the qualitative approach to the different disorders. By analyzing the psychodynamic factors in a case we try to find out what conflicts in what constellations produce the emotional disorder. Thus we may overlook the fact that many of these conflicts can be present in a person without emotional disease becoming apparent until the symptoms become so marked that he is obsessed by his fears or dominated by his hallucinations and delusions. Only these dominating symptoms are eliminated or reduced by psychosurgery. An analogy exists in patients who suffer from intract-

able pain, where the pain is not eliminated but the patient's response to the perception of the pain experience is altered by the operation. We think that in psychosurgery we are dealing with a quantitative treatment which leaves many of the underlying disease processes unimpaired; the patient, however, does not perceive his difficulties any more, is no longer disorganized by them, and is thereby enabled to function. The same quantitative approach is applicable to the therapeutic effect of the neuroleptic drugs which may not always remove certain symptoms completely but reduce them sufficiently to allow the patient to live with them.

FINAL REMARKS

The discussion of the theoretical aspects of the various somatic treatments has shown that most of them are poorly understood, or even entirely obscure in their mode of action. The expectation that the newer somatic treatments would throw some light on the etiology of the mental disorders for which they are applied, has not yet been fulfilled. A great deal of research will still be necessary to explain the mode of action of the treatments hitherto available, and thus help us at some future day to arrive at better understood means of treating psychotic disorders. At present, we can say only that we are treating empirically disorders whose etiology is unknown, with methods whose action is also shrouded in mystery.

Psychopharmacologic Drugs

HAROLD E. HIMWICH

The last few years have seen the increasing use of a new group of drugs effective for overactive psychotic patients and presenting interesting and important differences from procedures and drugs previously employed in the management of individuals with such behavioral disorders. In fact, in order to give an appropriate name to these drugs, it was necessary to invent a nomenclature. Many terms, all emphasizing one or another aspect of the actions of these drugs, have been devised. The one most frequently used is *tranquilizer*, indicating a sedative or calming effect without enforcement of sleep. Others are *ataraxic (1)*, denoting peace of mind, and *neuroleptic* and *neuroplegic*, indicating diminutions in the intensity of nerve function. This group of drugs, however, may be regarded as an advance guard of a long-awaited pharmacologic attack not limited only to hyperactive disturbed patients, but also to be directed against other types of behavioral disorders. To this division of drugs the term *psychotropic (2)*, or action on the mind, has been applied. *Neuropharmacologic* refers to the branch of pharmacology to which these drugs belong. The title *psychopharmacologic drugs (3, 4)*, possesses certain advantages, for it indicates a medicine which influences the mind by affecting its morphologic substrate, the brain.

The chief usefulness of the new drugs, which at present lies in the field of psychiatry, is being extended into the many medical and surgical specialties. It is true that a drug not only changes favorably the malfunction of the organ for which it is intended but also acts, perhaps to a lesser extent, on the entire body. Either indirectly, by their influence on the brain, or by their influence on the peripheral nerves, the new drugs exert potent effects on the viscera of the body, including the gastrointestinal tract and the cardiorespiratory system and the endocrine glands.

But the impact of these new drugs has extended far beyond their immediate practical use in the management of disease. They are also employed by the clinical investigator who is seeking to unravel the tangled skein of abnormal behavior as well as by the psychologist who delves into intricacies of accepted normal patterns. Neurochemists and neurophysiologists have taken advantage of the tranquilizers to use them as tools in their investigations and meanwhile are uncovering their physiological actions in the brain and elsewhere in the body. These studies, made on man and lower animals, permit an analysis of the structure and function of the central nervous system, impossible before. Not that the methods are new, but the tranquilization resulting from the application of these drugs has not been previously observed. Perhaps most important, the new drugs may aid in the production of a desirable change in our culture and remove mental disease from the field of mysticism and superstition. They may convince the public that mental disease is not a thing to be ashamed of and that it should be placed in the same category as any other disease which can be treated by medical means.

CLINICAL ASPECTS

At this time it is hardly necessary to emphasize the magnitude of the problem of mental disease. The title of Gorman's recent book, *Every Other Bed (5)*, is suggested by the fact that half of the sickbeds in our country are occupied by mental patients. The finan-

From *Science* 127:59-72, Jan. 10, 1958, by permission of the American Association for the Advancement of Science and the author.

cial requirements for the maintenance of these hospitals are correspondingly great. The money comes chiefly out of the taxpayers' pockets. Only comparatively wealthy families can bear the cost of maintaining one of their members in a private institution.

The growing population of our mental hospitals indicates that advances made prior to the advent of new drugs were not adequate to cope with the problem of mental disease. Much was left to be desired, therefore, from the therapeutic viewpoint. Psychoanalysis is a better weapon in the management of the neuroses than of the psychoses. Electroshock is a comparatively severe procedure, for electrodes are applied to the temples of the patient and a brief, measured current is passed through his brain. The patient becomes momentarily unconscious and undergoes a convulsion. Electroshock greatly benefits patients with depression and is of value in the management of excessively hyperactive patients to maintain the uneasy status quo which characterizes hospitals not using tranquilizing drugs. Insulin hypoglycemia appears to be more effective than electroshock for certain types of schizophrenia but requires highly trained physicians and is costly. In insulin hypoglycemia, the patients receive doses of insulin large enough to reduce the level of sugar in the blood. The brain is thus deprived of its chief foodstuff, and the patient sinks into coma. Another method for treating the distraught patient is to stupefy or anesthetize him with an adequate dose of one of the barbiturate drugs.

Though the immediate situation can thus be met, it is not necessarily followed by improvement in behavior. With the tranquilizing drugs, however, the patient is improved without significant interruption of consciousness—a highly desirable goal in the successful therapeutic process. Even if his manic excitement is extreme and if he must be given a correspondingly large dose, which renders him sleepy, he can be easily awakened and in general can go on with his prescribed hospital activities. With the new drugs, more patients have been returned to society from the state hospitals than with any previous therapeutic regime. We therefore seem to be entering a new era in the treatment of mental disease, and it remains to be seen how far this advance will take us.

SCHIZOPHRENIA

What are the mental disorders to which these new drugs are applied? The field of mental disease is complex. It is not a case of a single mental disease. On the contrary, there are many categories, and each one includes several varieties. Schizophrenia is the chief disorder met with in our psychotic population. We do not know the cause of schizophrenia, and this makes it necessary to limit our attack on it to empirical methods. But this is not unusual in the history of medicine, for the majority of therapeutic successes were produced on an empirical basis; witness the use of quinine long before the plasmodium of malaria was discovered.

Because the origin of schizophrenia is not known, that disease must be characterized chiefly by its symptoms. These are many and varied and, in general, may be divided into four types, which may change and merge into each other. The clinical picture is therefore not constant, and at different times the signs of one or another of these four types predominate. One of the characteristics of schizophrenia is emotional blunting, and this is a prominent change in the *simple* type. The psychiatrist is quick to observe the diagnostic paucity of facial expression and regards it as an outward lack of emotional expression or affect. Some individuals with inadequate personalities, who lose one job after another, belong to this group of patients. Sometimes the patient wears a silly and inappropriate grin. If such a patient, like Mr. M. on one of our wards, exhibit restless hyperactivity, at least that aspect of his disorder can be corrected by a tranquilizing drug.

An abnormality of the thought

process is another characteristic of schizophrenia and is developed most highly in the *hebephrenic* type. Sentences spoken may have meaning for the patient but to others are neither coherent nor logical. In the most serious distortion of the thought process, the spoken word ceases to assume sentence form and is called "word salad." Mrs. H. replies to all questions with the unintelligible statement "16-21 telephone pole." That phrase includes her usual conversational limits. After receiving a new experimental tranquilizer, she informed us, in well constructed sentences, that she was born in a small village, consisting of six homes, and that her home was situated near a telephone pole numbered 16-21.

Delusions or false ideas and hallucinations, or false sensory impressions, are characteristic of the *paranoid* type. Unlike the utterances of the hebephrenic, which cannot be comprehended by the physician, those of the paranoid patient are readily understood but reveal lack of relation to reality. Mrs. G., one of the patients in our hospital, has suffered intensely for a long time from well-developed delusions of a gigantic "crime ring" which is out to get her, even penetrating into the confines of the Galesburg State Research Hospital. Recently, when she was receiving a test drug, a new serenity was observed in her demeanor. When asked about the "crime ring," she smiled, made a deprecating gesture with her hand, and said it did not bother her any more. In fact, she doubted whether it existed. This is an evident amelioration and was maintained as long as the patient remained on this medication.

In general, hallucinations, which also occur in mental disease other than schizophrenia, yield more readily to these drugs than do delusions. Mrs. S. has placed cotton plugs in her ears for many years to shut out the voices that were so hostile and were giving her such a bad time. During a period in which she was receiving one of the test drugs, she came in for an interview without the cotton plugs in her ears. The voices no longer tormented her, or at least not to the same extent as previously.

In the *catatonic* type of schizophrenia there are marked distortions of motor activity. Stupor is one aspect, and whether with or without stupor, posturing and the assumption and maintenance of bizarre positions and mannerisms are observed. After one has raised the arm of such a patient, the patient may keep his arm up for a long time. When he walks he may change his direction by turning at right angles only. A catatonic may also go into a furor, a period of wild overactivity, and become highly destructive.

Here we come to a very important use of tranquilizing drugs—namely, a calming action which is being applied to various kinds of destructive patients and not only to combative schizophrenics. Taking chlorpromazine and reserpine as examples, we find two different kinds of pharmacologic actions characteristic of this group of drugs. The first, which counteracts such symptoms of schizophrenia as dissociated thought, hallucinations, and delusions, has just been described. The second drug effect is of a different type and causes a general toning down of emotional reactions and physical activity. If the ability to correct the thought processes of the hebephrenic and the paranoid patients is regarded as a specific antipsychotic power of chlorpromazine and reserpine, then the use of these drugs to combat excessive activity may be considered a nonspecific result. As has been pointed out by Barsa, these two results do not necessarily occur together; either may be observed without the other (*6*). The calming action of the drug cuts across the diagnostic categories of mental disease, for it is employed in all types of overactive patients, irrespective of the diagnosis. It can even be given to an individual who has no behavioral abnormalities, and in such a normal person a reduction of activity and a diminution in the response to environmental stimuli will be noted.

USE WITH HYPERACTIVE PATIENTS

It must be remembered that patients with psychoses are sent to psychiatric hospitals most often because they display behavior which is not socially compatible. Psychotics who can carry on outside the hospital gates are not necessarily sent to such institutions. When a patient presents behavioral disorders that menace the life and limb of other individuals as well as his own, it is essential that he enter a hospital where he can be properly treated.

Types of hyperactive patients who secure benefits from this sedative influence include the manic, whose disorder is chiefly that of mood or affect, which is greatly elevated; the schizoaffective, in whom abnormal elation is associated with deterioration of mental abilities; and the patient with a toxic psychosis, as in delirium tremens. These patients have their hyperactivity and abnormally increased initiative reduced to more reasonable levels so that they cease to wear themselves out and are no longer a trial to the ward attendants and their fellow-patients. This is a tremendous advantage for hospitals with highly disturbed patients. Isolation rooms, where a dangerous patient was formerly incarcerated, are no longer required. Mechanical restraints, sedative wet packs, electroshock, and deep barbiturate medication are prescribed only infrequently. As a result, many of these patients can now be liberated from physical restraints as well as from the psychological constraints of a locked ward. The ward doors have been opened, and privileges have been given to many patients, permitting them to traverse hospital halls and attend various therapeutic activities—recreational, occupational, and industrial. Thus, treatments have not only been made more humane, with greater benefit to the patient, but have also effected improvement in the staff morale of the mental institutions. A hospital atmosphere is being established in state institutions to an extent that was not previously possible. One now feels that a mental hospital is not a place for the expedient management of an intolerable situation but rather a treatment center for the amelioration of disease, like hospitals devoted to other kinds of disorders.

One patient will receive most benefit from a certain tranquilizing agent, and a second from another. This is not the place to compare the therapeutic efficacy of the various tranquilizers, especially in such an early state of their development, but it is obvious that some produce a deeper sedative action than others. Each of the accepted tranquilizing drugs, when given in adequate dosage, is of aid to disturbed patients, but our experience (7) with hyperactive patients has been widest with chlorpromazine (8) and reserpine (9), drugs which have profound sedative or calming actions. But there is no way to foretell which drug will be most effective for a given patient, and therefore the psychiatrist should be prepared to employ any one in an emergency. Some, like azacyclonol (7, 10), can bring about better social adjustment, so that the atmosphere on the ward becomes friendlier, especially among patients who are only moderately disturbed. The choice of a tranquilizing drug must be decided empirically; the best one for a given patient can be found only by the process of elimination.

The most dramatic improvements are observed in the first acute attack or in the chronic patient who has developed an acute exacerbation of his disorder. At our hospital, however, tranquilizing drugs have also been found to exert marked benefit in patients with schizophrenia of long duration—that is, chronic schizophrenia, as documented in the case histories presented above. But the improvements were mainly seen in patients with obvious active schizophrenic processes—those who had hallucinations and delusions or who were hyperactive, agitated, and tense. Blocked, retarded, and apathetic schizophrenics are more difficult to help. This greater intractability of the so-called "burned-out" patients, who have survived a more active phase of their disorder and who seem free of schizophrenic symptoms and excessive physical activity, is also observed with previous methods of treating deteriorated, passive schizophrenics.

Similarly, senile patients who are irritable, quarrelsome, and apprehensive show greater improvements than patients who exhibit negativism, apathy, and withdrawal. It would appear that tranquilizing drugs are less valuable for the senile patient who does not display signs of agitation. For the same reason, depressions not accompanied by anxiety and tension are less apt to be ameliorated by a psychopharmacologic agent. The treatment of the passive patient is therefore more difficult. In individuals with hypertension, apparently free from behavioral abnormalities, the use of these drugs may lead to a worsening of the mental condition if the profound sadness of a depression is induced.

PSYCHONEUROSES

Mental diseases milder than the psychoses are the psychoneuroses or neuroses, and in some forms of these disorders tranquilizing drugs are of value. In contradistinction to the psychotic patient, the neurotic acts, by and large, as if reality has the same meaning for him as for most people. He is not subjected to persecution by a "crime ring" and does not have other bizarre experiences. He suffers, however, from great anxiety, which may not be readily identified with any particular object. Yet this anxiety is expressed in bodily symptoms: palpitation, breathlessness, weakness of limbs tremors and pains that plague him. For that reason, in some patients, the anxiety is associated with a particular organ: the heart, the lungs, or the stomach. Neurotics who must be active in order to escape their disturbing fears are usually not helped by tranquilizers. In contrast, those with in-ternal tensions, who cannot sleep despite use of such sedative drugs as the barbiturates, often gain relief from a psychopharmacologic agent.

FOR THE "NORMAL" POPULATION

These drugs also exhibit decided usefulness for the members of our so-called normal population who are subjected to intolerable stress. A businessman with a demanding and unreasonable supervisor or a woman with insufficient funds to run her home according to her ideal standard can gradually build up an emotional impasse so that perspective is lost, as the darker side of the situation is increasingly magnified, until a state of panic may develop. Restoration to a more objective evaluation of the situation may be secured by psychotherapeutic discussions with a physician, and an important action of tranquilizing drugs is to render the patient more receptive to other kinds of therapy. In fact, at times a psychopharmacologic drug may be essential for a successful psychiatric interview. Ephemeral disturbances—for example, the anxiety and tension aroused by an impending surgical operation—can be pleasantly dissipated by a small dose of a tranquilizing agent.

SIDE REACTIONS

I have not mentioned the matter of occasional undesirable side reactions of the new drugs (11). In the first place, the drugs cause much less inconvenience than the mental disorder of the psychotic patient. Some patients can be managed by a temporary reduction of dosage—for example, a patient who exhibits an excessive fall of blood pressure. Others can be treated by a drug which counteracts the undesirable changes; a tremor of the hands resembling that of Parkinsonism can be relieved by an anti-Parkinson drug. Patients with brain injury are more likely to exhibit a convulsion than those with an intact organ (12). The production of lactation and menstrual changes by chlorpromazine and reserpine and the power of the latter to impair libido in the male are subjects for research. Fortunately, serious complications occur only rarely. A small number of patients develop jaundice, a sign of liver involvement. In some instances there may be a reduction of white blood cells. A failure in the formation of these cells is dangerous because it diminishes the resistance of the body to disease. But, on the whole, the treatment of thousands of psychotic patients with the new drugs has been relatively safe, because most are resistant to these side effects. This resistance, however, does not apply to neurotic patients, who seem more sensitive to side reactions and even on comparatively low dosage complain of fatigue, prostration, dizziness, and nausea.

It is apparent, then, that state hospitals have been placed on a much better basis by the use of the tranquilizing drugs, especially in the management of highly disturbed patients. The same, however, can not be said of psychiatrists whose private practice is concerned chiefly with neurotic patients. But it is also true that many patients who were formerly sent to a mental institution can now be treated outside the hospital gates. Some psychotic individuals can continue to lead productive lives and need not go to a psychiatric hospital at all. During the acute phase, they may be controlled by tranquilizing drugs in a general hospital and later may be maintained outside the hospital on appropriate doses of these medicines. On the other hand, apathetic psychotics who are not in conflict socially but who are rather withdrawn, inactive, and without signs of agitation, usually cannot be raised to a higher adaptive level. They are still the despair of the psychiatrist. In evaluating the present clinical position of the psychopharmacologic drugs, it must be understood that the production of tranquilization, though a desirable end in itself, also aids other forms of therapy. A potent factor in

the successful treatment of a patient with disorganized or disturbed behavior is a satisfactory relationship with a psychiatrist, and an important result of tranquilization is the facilitation of such a beneficial relationship.

NEUROHORMONAL CHANGES CAUSED BY RESERPINE AND CHLORPROMAZINE

A lead for the pharmacologic attack on schizophrenia comes from a study of indole-containing substances. Not only serotonin but also the tranquilizer reserpine and the psychotomimetic lysergic acid diethylamide (LSD) contain the indole nucleus (see Fig. 1). The data that indoles are associated with schizophrenia is not new (13). In a similar vein, suggestions have been made that serotonin plays a part in brain function (14). A clinical analysis of this problem became available in 1954 with the paper of Hoffer, Osmond, and Smythies (15). These experimenters knew that an adrenaline solution which had become pink after standing in the light for a long period of time had exerted psychotomimetic effects. They also drank a solution containing impure adrenochrome and succumbed to its influence to the extent of revealing schizophreniclike changes in their behavior. They therefore thought that the pink solution might contain a breakdown product of adrenaline, similar to adrenochrome in being indolic in character, and pointed out that some indole-containing substances affect behavior adversely. Thus, again we have the suggestion of the pathogenic importance of indole-containing substances. However, it should be pointed out that not all such compounds evoke aberrant behavior. Moreover, drugs with entirely different chemical structures—for example, hashish—are psychotomimetic in action. Nevertheless, it is instructive to examine the effects of serotonin.

The experiments of Welsh (16) showed that in the clam *Venus merceneria* the accelerator nerve of the heart, for which serotonin is the chem-

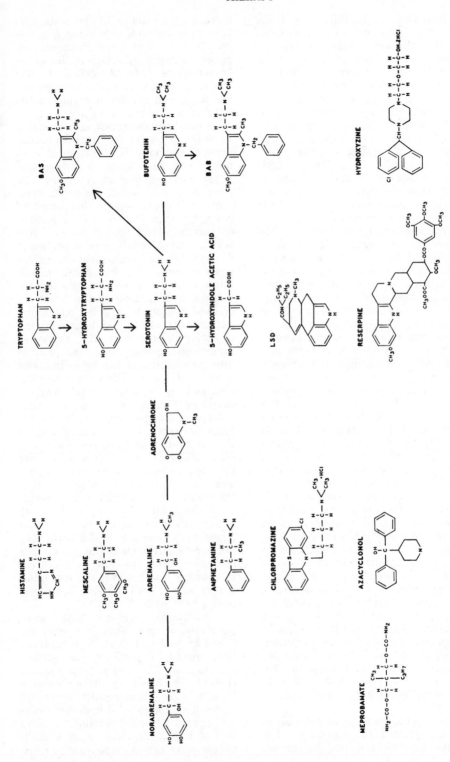

Figure 1. *Structural formulas of some neurohormones, psychotomimetic agents, and tranquilizing drugs.*

ical mediator, is inhibited by LSD. Gaddum and Hameed (17) have demonstrated the antagonism of LSD to the peripheral action of serotonin in mammals and wondered whether or not this antagonism might not also apply in the brain. Wooley and Shaw (18) made the bold hypothesis that LSD produced behavioral abnormalities by interfering with the physiological actions of serotonin in the brain. According to these investigators, LSD is enough like serotonin to be taken up by the serotonin receptors in the brain, yet is different to the extent that LSD fails to evoke serotonin effects.

The Rockefeller workers used the lock-and-key analogy: LSD could be introduced into the same lock as serotonin but, in contrast, could not be used to turn the lock. This suggested, of course, that mental aberrations are produced by an inadequate amount of serotonin at its site of action, the receptors with which serotonin combines. But it is also possible that there may be an excessive concentration of serotonin in some forms of mental disease, and in a later paper these workers showed that LSD could also act like serotonin and, for example, increase the effects of that brain hormone to raise the blood pressure of anesthetized dogs (19). Costa (20), in our laboratory, found that LSD can either diminish or increase the effects of serotonin, depending upon its concentration. The serotonin-evoked contraction of a rat uterus is antagonized by LSD in a solution containing 1.0 microgram per liter but is facilitated by that psychotomimetic agent when its concentration is reduced to 0.2 microgram per liter or less. The latter result suggests that an excess of serotonin, rather than a deficiency, is a disturbing factor in mental disease. In the present status of these investigations it is not possible to decide between these two alternatives. In fact, both may be correct, but each may apply to different kinds of abnormalities.

Reserpine, which is so valuable in the management of combative destructive patients, reduces the concen-

tration of serotonin in the body (21, 22). Furthermore, only those *Rauwolfia* alkaloids which are tranquilizers have this depleting action in the stores of serotonin (23). According to one explanation, the competition between the drug and serotonin displaces the latter from its receptors and, as a result, the neurohormone is eliminated from the depots in the brain and other parts of the body. Restoration of serotonin to normal levels is protracted. After a single dose of reserpine was injected into a rabbit, the brain serotonin was depressed to 10 percent of normal within 4 hours and remained at this low level for 36 hours, after which it rose slowly over a period of 6 days before premedication values were attained (22). Following the administration of reserpine, the concentration of that drug in the brain increased rapidly to a brief maximum, but in contrast to the long-enduring depletion of serotonin (24), reserpine diminished speedily and was practically undetectable in the brain in about 4 hours. These results with reserpine, obtained by a fluorometric method, are in agreement with the concept that reserpine produces pharmacologic effects indirectly by its influence upon the serotonin content of the brain. But other observations (25) with a more sensitive technique, employing isotopically labeled reserpine, disclosed that the radioactive material is extractable from the brain *as reserpine* up to 48 hours after its injection. The long presence of reserpine in the brain does not necessarily exclude the theory that reserpine acts through an indirect mechanism that involves serotonin, but it is in accord with the idea that reserpine acts as such.

Additional evidence that reserpine releases serotonin has been adduced by Valcourt (26), who observed two groups of patients, one schizophrenic and the other mentally defective, at the Galesburg State Research Hospital. A significantly increased urinary excretion of 5-hydroxyindoleacetic acid occurred during the first day of the administration of 4 milligrams of reserpine. Apparently, when

1. ☰☰☰ = .01→.05 γ/gm.

2. ⊙⊙⊙ = .05→.1 γ/gm.

3. ●●● = .1→.3 γ/gm.

4. ▵▵▵ = .3→.6 γ/gm.

5. ▲▲▲ = MORE THAN .6 γ/gm.

16 ᴬEC-17

Figure 2. *Serotonin content of the human brain. The areas with the highest concentration of serotonin, an indole amine, include the hypothalamus. A lower level is observed in the mammillary bodies, fornix, thalamus, and medulla oblongata. Serotonin is found in the cingulate gyrus, hippocampus, and amygdaloid nucleus in greater concentrations than in the neocortex or cerebellum, which contain the least amounts. [Costa and Aprison (32)]*

serotonin does not attain its binding site, it is rendered vulnerable to the amine oxidase enzyme and is metabolized to form 5-hydroxyindoleacetic acid (Fig. 1).

Even if it is proved that serotonin is important to the function of the mind, its action is not a simple one, for that hormone may serve in other ways. Because serotonin can cause smooth muscle—the type of muscle in the walls of arteries and of viscera—to contract, it is thought to be a factor in the production of high blood pressure and in the motility of the gastrointestinal tract. Only 1 percent of the serotonin content of the body is found in the brain (27). Most of it occurs in the spleen and especially in the gastrointestinal tract containing the specialized cells of the enterochromaffin sys-tem, which secrete serotonin (28). A tumor of these cells, called malignant carcinoid, is associated with abnormally high levels of blood serotonin and with an increased excretion of its metabolic product, 5-hydroxyindoleacetic acid, in the urine (29). Behavioral changes are absent, perhaps because of the relative impermeability of the brain to serotonin (30).

The similarities between serotonin, an indole amine, and the catechol amines, noradrenaline and adrenaline, are important. These similarities are not limited to their areas of distribution in the brain (Figs. 2, 3), which in general reveal high concentrations in various subcortical areas and low ones in the cerebral cortex and cerebellum (31, 32), nor are their resemblances confined to their chemical structures (Fig. 1), which disclose that adrenaline can be oxidized to form an indole amine, adrenochrome, and that the latter, plus the appropriate side chain, yields serotonin.

Most striking is the discovery that reserpine exerts an action on noradrenaline and adrenaline similar to that previously disclosed for serotonin— that is, it empties their stores wherever they occur in the body. Even more significant is the observation (33) that the curve for the time relationships for the release of these substances from the brain and the reestablishment to premedication values follow each other closely. Though the results are not the same when different methods for the determination of noradrenaline are used, yet in general there is agreement in the rapid release (34) from the brain and the slow return to normal values. It is obvious, then, that the releases of these amines are closely associated phenomena. Either the amines combine with the same receptor, though not necessarily with the same prosthetic group, or the discharge of one amine initiates the liberation of the other.

One action of reserpine, therefore, involves closely allied substances which may be included in the term *biogenic amines*. Can such a conception be applied to chlorpromazine? An examination of the structure of chlorpromazine (Fig. 1) reveals two chief portions, the phenothiazine nucleus and a side chain

$$N—CH_2—CH_2—CH_2—N$$

Suggestions arise from an examination of both portions of the chlorpromazine molecule. If the phenothiazine nucleus portion is depicted in three dimensions instead of two, it closely resembles the indole nucleus, as observed in serotonin as well as in reserpine. It does not seem, however, that chlorpromazine acts in the same manner as reserpine, for chlorpromazine does not empty the depots of serotonin and the catechol amines. Another lead comes from the examination of the side chain, which is contained in many successful phenothiazine derivatives (35). As has been pointed out by Gyermek and others (35, 36), the same side chain occurs repeatedly in substances which depress the effects of amines. It must not be forgotten that the phenothia-

Figure 3. *Medial sagittal section of a dog's brain, showing the distribution of noradrenaline in micrograms per gram of fresh tissue:* ▲, *1.0* μg/g; +, > *0.4 and* < *1.0* μg/g; O, > *0.3 and* < *0.4* μg/g; −, > *0.2 and* < *0.3* μg/g. *In the dog brain, the catechol amines, noradrenaline and adrenaline, are at their highest concentration in the hypothalamus; then, in decreasing amounts, in the mammillary bodies and the reticular formation. Still lower concentrations are observed in the neocortex and cerebellum.* [Vogt, J. Physiol. (London) (31)]

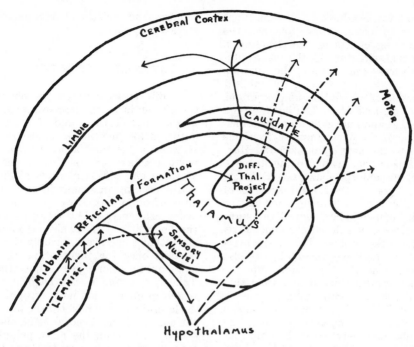

Figure 4. *Mesodiencephalic activating system. Stimulation of the organism evokes impulses which travel by way of the lemnisci to the thalamic sensory nuclei and then to cortical sensory areas. The lemnisci send collateral nerve fibers to the midbrain reticular formation, and by these fibers impulses advance in the reticular formation to the diffuse thalamic projections and arouse the cerebral cortex. Collaterals bearing stimuli from the midbrain reticular formation pass to the hypothalamus, which in turn sends impulses to the cerebral cortex.* [*Himwich*, J. Nervous Mental Disease (3)]

zines belong to the group of antihistaminic drugs and can usually inhibit actions evoked by histamine (Fig. 1). In fact, such a side chain will interfere with the effects of other biogenic amines, including noradrenaline, adrenaline, and serotonin. Chlorpromazine shares with these biogenic amines a side chain of similar construction, and perhaps chlorpromazine attaches itself to the same binding site as do these amines.

If such a generalized action may be attributed to chlorpromazine, the study of the chemical substrates of behavior becomes even broader than the indole viewpoint suggested by the pharmacologic action of reserpine and renders every biogenic amine a fit subject for investigation in the field of behavior. But even these broad possibilities do not account for the chemical aspects of tranquilizers not included in

the reserpine and chlorpromazine groups. As an example, we may cite the experiments of Costa, who showed that the peripheral effects of serotonin were blocked not only by reserpine and chlorpromazine but also by azacyclonol (20). Moreover, meprobamate, hydroxyzine, benactyzine, and many other drugs, each with different chemical constitutions, are effective in various degrees against one mental condition or another. Until the chemical advances catch up with the clinical advances, some of the manifestations can be followed in the form of changes in nerve function.

NEUROHORMONAL EQUILIBRIUM

Marrazzi and Hart (37) propose a theory, depending upon an equilibrium between various hormones, that may account for results with diverse types of tranquilizers. They contrast the stimulating effects of acetylcholine, a chemical mediator of the nerve impulse across the synapse, the junction between two nerves, with the inhibiting action of adrenaline, amphetamine, mescaline, and LSD. The latter group depresses and may even stop the transmission of the nerve impulse from one nerve to the next. Marrazzi and Hart also report that tranquilizing drugs— reserpine, chlorpromazine, and azacyclonol—prevent the inhibitory effect of mescaline on the transmission of the nerve impulse. They regard the signs of psychosis as release phenomena, results of the removal of normal restraints. Their experimental work also discloses that the depressant influence of serotonin is more potent than that of adrenaline, amphetamine, mescaline, or LSD. They therefore suggest that mental derangement is caused by an imbalance between such inhibitory substances as serotonin and the chemical transmitter of the nervous impulse, acetylcholine.

It is known that acetylcholine is active in the function of several cerebral areas, including the mesodiencephalic activating system, which is discussed in the succeeding section of this article (38). In a way, this conception is somewhat like that of Pfeiffer and Jenney, that an increase of acetylcholine may exert an antischizophrenic effect, for raised concentrations of that neurohormone should antagonize the action of serotonin to block the transmission of the nerve impulse (39). But it is not impossible that a dearth of acetylcholine is associated with one type of abnormal behavior, perhaps psychosis, and that an excess of acetylcholine is an accompaniment of another type, neurosis. Jacobsen (40) has suggested that the action of Benactyzine to block acetylcholine may serve a beneficial effect in disturbances associated with supernormal concentrations of acetylcholine (41). Benactyzine exerts little influence on schizophrenic patients but has been termed an antiphobic drug because it is effective against abnormal fears and reduces the emotional reactivity to stress.

ANATOMIC SITES OF ACTION

Differences between the pharmacologic actions of depressant drugs like the barbiturates and of the tranquilizers are mentioned above in the section on "clinical aspects." An important cause for the diverse effects of these two different kinds of drugs is disclosed by an examination of their sites of action. It is well known that every drug may affect many parts of the body, but it must also be emphasized that some areas, usually the important ones for the therapeutic results, are more susceptible than others. Take, for example, the barbiturates, which in general act most strongly on the later-developed parts of the brain— the cortex of the cerebral hemispheres —and least so on the more primitive medulla oblongata, containing vital centers for the control of heart rate, respiration, and blood pressure. Because of their pronounced effects on the cerebral cortex, barbiturates depress functions of the cortical regions concerned with the analyzing mechanisms of vision, audition, and other perceptive functions—the fine coordination of motor movements as well as thought and memory. Though the tranquilizers also affect functions ascribed chiefly to the cerebral cortex, their most potent actions are exerted on the subcortical structures regarded as parts of the anatomic substrate of emotion: the midbrain reticular formation, the hypothalamus, and the components of the rhinencephalon (Figs. 4, 5).

The viewpoint expressed in this article is that the tranquilizing drugs pick out, for their main sites of action, these three cerebral areas, all connected with each other and with the cortex. It would seem that the visceral functions, related to the emotions, were correlated chiefly by the reticular formation in the lower vertebrates. It is also probable that, later in the evolutionary process, other centers in the

Figure 5. *Semidiagrammatic section of human brain. 1, amygdala; 2, anterior nucleus of thalamus; 3, cingulate gyrus; 4, corpus callosum; 5, diagonal band of Broca; 6, fornix; 7, habenula, a nucleus of the thalamus; 8, habenulopeduncular tract; 9, hippocampus; 10, interpeduncular nucleus; 11, lateral olfactory stria; 12, longitudinal stria; 13, mammillary body; 14, mammillothalamic tract; 15, medial olfactory stria; 16, olfactory bulb; 17, olfactory tract; 18, olfactory tubercle; 19, perforating fibers; 20, septum pellucidum; 21, stria medullaris; 22, stria terminalis; 23, subcallosal gyrus; 24, hypothalamus; 25, posterior pituitary gland; 26, anterior pituitary gland; 27, caudate nuclei in depth of brain; 28, septal region. [Adapted from "Physiology and Pharmacology of Emotion," Scope 4, 1 (1955)]*

hypothalamus and especially in the rhinencephalon took over much of the emotional aspect of behavior.

A more detailed description of the midbrain reticular formation reveals that it is an ancient cerebral area, well developed even in the Amphibia, as has been shown by the work of Herrick on the tiger salamander (*42*). In that animal, the midbrain reticular formation probably serves as an important integrating mechanism, coordinating muscular and visceral activities in accordance with the sensory information evoked by changes in the environment. We owe the elucidation of the basic physiology of the reticular formation in mammals and primates to Moruzzi, Magoun, and their students (*43*). These workers showed that the midbrain reticular formation acts in conjunction with diffuse thalamic projections (Fig. 4), as ascribed by Jasper (*44*). Thus, the phyletically older midbrain reticular formation is united functionally with the later-developed diffuse thalamic cortical projections, and the two together form the mesodiencephalic activating system (*38*). This does not mean that the mesodiencephalic activating system is independent of the rest of the brain. On the contrary, its midbrain reticular component probably receives a varying number of stimuli by way of collateral nerve fibers from the lemnisci (Fig. 4). There are therefore two parallel systems. One carries information by way of the lemnisci and the paths of the sensory thalamic nuclei to the cortex, where the messages are analyzed for specific information on the kind of stimulus, its point of application, and similar relationships to the organism. In the other system, the mesodiencephalic activating system, nerve impulses ascend in the reticular formation to the thalamic nuclei, which then send other impulses to the cortex by way of the diffuse thalamic paths. The mesodiencephalic activating system thus affords the emotional cloak which accompanies some kinds of stimulation of the body.

The parts played by the hypothalamus and the rhinencephalon will be considered below, but with this background we can proceed with the psychopharmacologic analysis of the functions of the mesodiencephalic activating system, which has been shown to be sensitive to members of the reserpine group of drugs, to chlorpromazine and other phenothiazine derivatives, and to azacyclonol. A clue to the effect of these drugs on this system is afforded by the electroencephalograph, for stimulation and inhibition are each accompanied by characteristic brainwave patterns. Those associated with inhibition of the reticular formation are also observed, with rest or light dozing in the human being or animal, and are shown on the left side of Fig. 6A. They are characterized by high-amplitude slow waves and spindles of rapid waves. The latter are most prominent in the motor cortex, as is seen in records obtained from a rabbit. This type of activity continues until the animal is exposed to auditory, tactile, or painful stimuli, when rapid low-amplitude waves, particularly in the cortex, appear, while a slower regular rhythm develops in the hippocampus. One the right side of Fig. 6A is seen such an altering or arousal pattern (3, 45). On the other hand, when chlorpromazine is given, the reticular formation is blocked and no longer shows the alerting response (Fig. 6B). This inhibition of the reticular formation does not prevent impulses evoked by a painful stimulus from traversing the lemnisci (Fig. 4), and awareness is thus achieved by way of the cortical mechanisms, but the severity of the associated distressing emotional accompaniment of the stimulus is greatly mitigated.

A clinical example is seen in the use of chlorpromazine for the treatment of the intractable pain associated with inoperable cancer. Surely the patient is aware of the pain, but it has been largely robbed of its harrowing emotional accompaniment. It is not impossible that a patient disturbed by painful hallucinations and upsetting delusions can be similarly rendered relatively free of emotional upheavals. The ability of chlorpromazine to reduce the emotional reactions to painful stimuli is probably due to the depression of the reticular formation. Though azacyclonol is not capable of blocking the pain response, it can prevent and correct the alerting of the electroencephalogram caused by the psychotomimetic drugs, LSD and mescaline (46). In contrast to chlorpromazine, reserpine, in adequate doses, activates the mesodiencephalic activating system and produces the alert pattern (47). It is significant, therefore, that reserpine, despite its tranquilizing action, is not of use in the management of pain. Perhaps the greater sedative effect of chlorpromazine is due to its ability to depress the midbrain reticular formation.

But the fact that reserpine does not inhibit the mesodiencephalic activating system indicates that there are other centers important for tranquilization. We therefore turn next to the consideration of the hypothalamus, which is known to be a part of the brain containing patterns for coordinating visceral functions, increases of blood pressure, heart rate, and respiration in order to support muscular activity. This integration of visceral and muscular activities is especially essential in emergency situations, originally referred to by Cannon as the "fight or flight" reactions (48). This part of the brain, therefore, organizes the visceral manifestations which are overactive in disturbed patients. It would seem probable that the depression of this mechanism acts to mitigate this type of overactivity. The earliest research done on reserpine and chlorpromazine indicated that these drugs inhibited hypothalamic structures, particularly those of the posterior hypothalamic nuclei which regulate the sympathetic nerves to the viscera and blood vessels (49).

The action of reserpine can be explained in part by a depression of the sympathetic representation in the hypothalamus (50), which leaves parasympathetic activity unopposed and thus accounts for the fall in heart rate, drop in blood pressure, constriction of pupils, and the increased intestinal motility frequently observed in patients receiving that drug. These physiological changes are signs of acetylcholine activity. Acetylcholine is not only associated with the chemical transmission of the nerve impulse in parasympathetic nerves to the various organs but also with transmission within the central nervous system. With reserpine, however, the increased effects of acetylcholine may be due to the failure of the opposing effects of adrenaline and noradrenaline. As we have seen in a previous section, this failure may be the result of the emptying of the catechol amine depots by reserpine, in the brain and elsewhere in the body. As a consequence of this depletion, stimuli impinging on the hypothalamus fail to evoke responses from the cerebral representation of the sympathetic nervous system (51). It is also probable that, because of the exhaustion of the adrenaline and noradrenaline deposits in the peripheral sympathetic nerves, these nerves, too, cannot react, and thus the central effects of that drug are accentuated.

In a way, the pharmacologic actions of chlorpromazine may be compared with those of reserpine, for both exert central and peripheral effects. It is true that both drugs inhibit the hypothalamus, but chlorpromazine also depresses peripheral sympathetic nerve centers which help to regulate blood pressure, and this is a second reason for the observed decreases of arterial pressure. But chlorpromazine also exerts a similar impairment on peripheral parasympathetic nerves which usually slow heart rate, and therefore in patients receiving chlorpromazine the heart rate is characteristically rapid. Both peripheral results may be ascribed to interference with the action of acetylcholine in the transmission of the nerve impulse and therefore may be compared with the central operation of chlorpromazine to block the reticular formation (52).

PATHFINDING EXPERIMENTS

The discussion on the parts of the brain affected by chlorpromazine and reserpine will now be extended to include those which were highlighted by the pathfinding experiments of Klüver and Bucy (53). These workers removed the temporal lobes of monkeys, thereby changing these difficult creatures into remarkably tame animals. These primates also exhibited increased oral and sexual proclivities. Objects of all kinds were repeatedly introduced into the mouths of the animals being tested, and males, especially, attempted sexual intercourse frequently, whether or not the animal chosen for these relations was of the appropriate sex or even of the same species.

The temporal lobe includes some structures belonging to the rhinencephalon, which was first regarded as a unified system by Papez (54), in accordance with the schema presented semidiagrammatically in Fig. 5. When the hippocampus is stimulated it gives rise to impulses which initiate the Papez circle. These impulses are transmitted from the hippocampus (No. 9, Fig. 5), through the fornix (No. 6), to the mammillary bodies of the hypothalamus (No. 13). From that area they continue to the anterior thalamic nuclei (No. 2) and attain the cortex of the brain in the cingulate gyrus (No. 3). The functional circle is completed in fibers leaving the cingulate gyrus and returning to the hippocampus.

Again the phyletic point of view is enlightening. When the first air-breathing vertebrates—the amphibians and especially the reptiles—left the oceans for the land, they developed

A

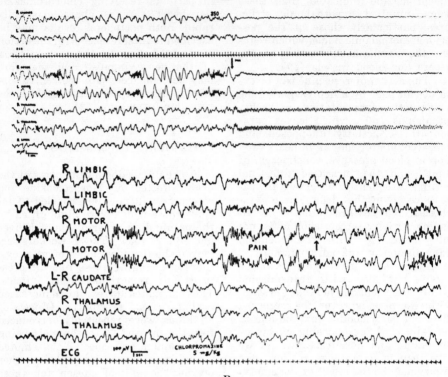

B

Figure 6. *Alert pattern evoked by pain and prevented by chlorpromazine. (A) Bilateral leads are taken from various cerebral structures; on right side, electroencephalographic control pattern of resting rabbit; on left side, the effects of pinching rabbit's leg. (B) Change produced by chlorpromazine (5 mg/kg) in electroencephalographic pattern in response to pain. Note the absence of the alerting reaction to pain. [Himwich, J. Nervous Mental Disease (3)]*

areas of the brain important for smell, the olfactory bulb (No. 16) and the olfactory tract (No. 17). The olfactory tubercle (No. 18), which receives impulses from the midbrain reticular formation, supplies an indirect connection between the latter and Papez' circle. The term *rhinencephalon* originates in the primarily olfactory functions of the bulb and of some of the amygdaloid nuclei (No. 1). These structures are connected, in turn, to others which have been adapted in higher animals to emotional activities. These include the remainder of the amygdaloid and septal nuclei (No. 28). Finally, the latter areas contact Papez' circle in the hippocampus, and awareness of emotional reactions is attained by way of the cingulate gyrus (55). Even today, in man, emotion and olfaction are closely associated, and this is

so despite our mores, which in general require restriction of body odors.

The part of the brain concerned especially with emotional experience and the one least understood is the rhinencephalon, which is also called the limbic system or the visceral brain (56). It must be noted that not only tranquilization but also the reverse reaction of rage was observed when the more forward portions of the rhinencephalon—the septal area and olfactory tubercle—were removed, and similar effects were also reported after the extirpation of the amygdaloid nuclei, the hippocampus, and the fornix (57). Lesions of the septal region alone were also found to produce rage (58). Bilateral extirpation of the amygdaloid complex and the adjacent pyriform lobe rendered animals easily disturbed (59). Many workers, however, have observed placidity and emotional unresponsiveness following the bilateral removal of the amygdala and hippocampus (*60, 61*).

Though these results are apparently contradictory, at present the consensus is veering towards Klüver and Bucy's original conclusions because the pacifying effects of these extirpations are the more frequent findings. With either result, these experiments disclose relationships between the rhinencephalon and the emotional state. From this viewpoint both observations are useful, and in that case the nature of the response may depend on other factors—for example, the immediate social environment, whether or not it is hostile, and whether the animal is being provoked or treated in a friendly fashion. The general reaction characteristic of the animal is also important, for the effects of the operation may be superimposed on an excitable animal, easily aroused, or on a calm and phlegmatic one. Analyses have been made to explain these discordant results (*61, 62*), but for our purposes these reactions serve to point out the type of physiological activity of these parts of the brain and they afford a basis for the appraisal of the effects of drugs upon them.

Killam and Killam report (*63*) spontaneous, seizurelike waves in the rhinencephalon of a cat following the administration of reserpine. These seizures appeared first in the amygdala (*AMG*, Fig. 7) and then spread to the hippocampus (*HIPP*) and to other rhinencephalic structures, including the entorhinal cortex (*ENTO*) and septum (*SEPT*). However, the neocortex, (*MSS* and *SC*) remained free

of such abnormalities. Furthermore, Sigg and Schneider noted that electrically evoked, seizurelike waves in the amygdala were facilitated and prolonged by reserpine without necessarily involving neocortical areas (*64*).

Preston's observations (*65*) with chlorpromazine are similar in some respects to those of the Killiams with reserpine, for he reports that the amygdaloid complex is readily stimulated by chlorpromazine at a time when the activity of the neocortex, including the motor cortex which regulates voluntary muscular movements, is unchanged. The electroencephalographic alterations evoked by single daily injections of chlorpromazine to a cat (10 mg/kg of body weight) for a period of 5 days showed that 20 hours after the last injection there was no obvious effect in the neocortex (*LG* and *MC*, Fig. 8), while the amygdaloid nuclei (*AMG*) revealed spiking.

Thus, the amygdala is the part of the brain most susceptible to both drugs. Rather surprisingly, this amygdaloid hyperactivity was associated with tranquilization. With this dose of chlorpromazine, well within the human therapeutic range, a cat will not pounce upon a mouse placed in its cage but, instead, acts with apparent indifference. Though the convulsive brain waves disclosed in the amygdala were accompanied by a transformation in the behavior of the cat, overt signs of motor activity were not apparent in such animals. In general, it is known that the rhinencephalon is more easily excitable than is the neocortical mantle of the cerebral hemispheres (*66*). With larger doses of chlorpromazine (*65*), which however do not exceed those ad-

Figure 7. *Effect of reserpine (0.1 mg/kg) on brain waves; records of spontaneous rhinencephalic seizures initiated in the amygdala.* [*Killam and Killam*, Brain Mechanisms and Drug Action (63)]

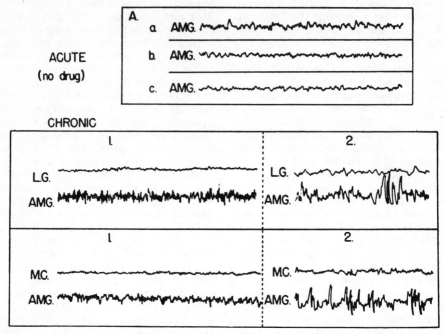

Figure 8. *Comparative effects of chlorpromazine on the amygdala and cerebral cortex.* (A) *Spontaneous activity recorded from the amygdala in three different cats: (1) Records from two cats after a single daily injection of chlorpromazine, 10 mg/kg, for 5 days; (2) spontaneous activity recorded at a later time in the same experiment after 10 mg/kg of chlorpromazine had been injected. Hyperactivity is present in amygdala but not in the neocortex.* [*Preston*, J. Pharmacol. Exptl. Therap. (65)]

ministered to badly disturbed patients (*67*), the electrical hyperactivity spreads from the amygdala (*AMG,* Fig. 9) to other rhinencephalic structures, the septum (*SEPT*) and the hippocampus (*HIPP*). But only when the disturbance extends to neocortical motor areas are the characteristic violent muscular contractions of a major epileptic seizure observed. Perhaps a similar process, the initiation of seizure activity in the amygdala and its spread through the rhinencephalic structures and then to the motor cortex, can explain the convulsive seizure sometimes seen in patients taking reserpine and chlorpromazine (*12*). Penfield has suggested that the phenomena of psychomotor epilepsy may originate in a seizure discharge in the amygdala spreading in the centrencephalic system (*68*). The pharmacologic effects of these two drugs may be compared with the observations of Andy and Akert (*69*), who stimulated the hippocampal formation of a cat electrically and noted that, when the hippocampal discharge was propagated to include the amygdala, the cat was not affected by the presence of the mouse, an apathy which was prolonged for a short period of time after the discharge was completed and which was then replaced by an attack upon the little victim. But there is more than one method by which similar kinds of behavioral results may be obtained. Tranquilization of disturbed psychotic patients can be achieved with meprobamate (*70*), which is neither a phenothiazine derivative nor a reserpine-like drug (Fig. 1). Unlike these tranquilizers, meprobamate does not alter brain wave activity of the amygdala when it is administered in small doses which, however, depress the undulations exhibited by the thalamus (*71*). Though the amygdala does

MC
HIPP
AMG
SEPT
CONTROL

2.
10. mgm./kgm.

3.
20 mgm./kgm.

4.
35.mgm/kgm.

5.
40 mgm./kgm.

CHLORPROMAZINE - IV.

200μV   I sec.

M.C.
AMG.
6. HIPP
SEPT
45mgm./kgm.

Figure 9. *Effects of gradual increases of chlorpromazine upon brain. Seizure spiking is initiated in amygdala and gradually spreads to other areas.* [*Preston*, J. Pharmacol. Exptl. Therap. (65)]

not seem to be a site of activity for meprobamate, yet some portion of the rhinencephalon may be involved, as suggested by experiment with animals. Rats rendered savage by the extirpation of their septal regions are restored to their preoperative behavior by that drug. Apparently meprobamate influenced a portion of the brain which is functionally associated with the septum. It is of more than passing interest that rats that have not been operated on show little or no change in their conduct when the same doses of meprobamate that calm the experimental animals *(72)* are administered.

THEORY FOR THERAPEUTIC EFFECTS

To bridge the gap between our information of the pharmacologic actions of reserpine and chlorpromazine and their therapeutic results is a goal greatly to be desired. Unfortunately, we do not have sufficient data or even

the basic neurophysiologic facts to do this. It is realized that such speculations on the mode of action of tranquilizers in man are largely based on observations of animals—a doubtful procedure. Moreover, there is a genuine logical difficulty, for it has not been proved that the behavioral improvements noted with use of these drugs are due to the pharmacologic effects. The two diverse groups of phenomena may be related to each other only by a common causative factor— namely, the drug. But it is useful to make the assumption that the medicines are causes of the clinical changes as a device to clarify our thinking in seeking indications for the direction of future research in the field of psychopharmacology.

In our analyses of the therapeutic results of reserpine and chlorpromazine, we found that they are of two different kinds: one is a calming of the individual and other is directed against schizophrenic manifestations.

Can each of these two different clinical improvements be related to specific actions of the drugs? The decreased reactivity of tranquilized patients may be ascribed in part to the depletion of the catechol amines, the depletion depriving the organism of part of the mechanism of reactivity. Obviously, tension and anxiety, whether evoked by real or imaginary emergencies, will nevertheless mobilize the autonomic nervous system. Not only adrenaline and noradrenaline but also other hormones, including serotonin and acetylcholine, are probably released during threatening emergencies. Thus, in general, a pharmacologic action of these drugs is to remove part of the mobilization mechanism, and the beneficial results include tranquilization and decreases of anxiety and tension. Turning to the electrophysiological portion of this analysis, we find ourselves examining the parts of the brain which help to regulate the activity of the neurohormones. A neuronal depression of the reticular formation and of the hypothalamus diminishes the actions of these portions of the brain. This depression can only render more profound the decrease in reactivity due to the emptying of the neurohormonal storehouses.

Animal experiments indicate a close relationship between rhinencephalic structure and the emotions, while drug studies have disclosed the sensitivity of the amygdala to chlorpromazine and reserpine. But here we see that a similar final effect of tranquilization is associated with an action which is quite the reverse of that seen in the hypothalamus. Inhibition of nerve function is not observed. On the contrary, the affected areas reveal abnormal hyperactivity. Does the drug-induced aberrant operation of the amygdala interfere with the functions of the rhinencephalon, and, if so, does such an interference afford a basis for the second action of these drugs against schizophrenic symptoms? It would seem that the normal contribution of the amygdala to the economy of the brain cannot continue when that structure is being subjected to seizures

(73). Perhaps the rhinencephalic chain ceases to act physiologically because of the functional failure of the amygdaloid link—a failure which makes for a loss in a connection between the most primitive brain area (concerned with emotion), the midbrain reticular formation, and the later developed rhinencephalon.

The diminution in reactivity of the organism probably influences the quantity or intensity of the emotional impact on the cortex. But it is difficult see how such an amelioration can change the quality of thought so that the dissociated "word salad" of the hebephrenic patient can become less incoherent, more logical and comprehensible. One can appreciate that a decrease in emotional intensity might mitigate the violence in the expression of hallucinatory and delusional material, but again it is more difficult to understand how such a mitigation can cause the correction of schizophrenic mentation. For that change, thinking must be altered in quality.

Though the various parts of the brain work together as a unit in a coordinated manner, we have seen that certain structures, both cortical and subcortical, are more involved than others in our emotional life. Similarly, as is pointed out by Bailey (74), some subcortical regions add a crude awareness, but for the discriminative contribution to that complex function, the cortex must be included in a prominent position. The cingulate gyrus, which is a part not only of the rhinencephalon but also of the cortex, may be the area where the abnormal elements concerned with awareness and thinking enter into discriminative conscious activity. It is not said that rhinencephalic structures do not affect emotional reactions, but it is suggested, as a working hypothesis, that the cessation of rhinencephalic function is a possible factor in the prevention of the morbid thinking of schizophrenia. This would indicate that the disease process of schizophrenia is tied up with the malfunction of certain brain areas and that the rhinencephalic circle carries impulses which are sources of the pathologic psychophysiology of schizophrenia. It is realized that a change of behavior produced by a loss of the contribution from a specific brain area, whether due to a physical extirpation or to functional incapacitation, does not prove that pathology in that area is the source of the disease. The removal of a part of the brain may interfere with the function of another region more directly concerned with the disease process. For example, an origin of the pathologic course may lie within the septal region, as is indicated by the work of Heath and his colleagues (75), or the warped emotional reactions may find their earlier expression in the midbrain reticular formation. But at least it can be said that the anatomic site sensitive to drug action bears a relationship to schizophrenia, because the functional diversion of that area may correct the symptomatology of the disorder.

PATHS OF RESEARCH

A review of the present pharmacologic data can serve to throw light on paths for future exploration. One series of observations has emphasized quantitative changes causing shifts in the neurohormonal balance, involving excesses or deficits of acetylcholine, adrenaline, noradrenaline, serotonin, or serotoninlike substances. Concentrations of serotonin in the brain can be increased by the administration of its precursor, 5-hydroxytryptophan, which provokes disturbances in the electroencephalogram and in the behavior of the rabbit (76) (Fig. 1). Apparently, 5-hydroxytryptophan enters the brain rapidly and, presumably, is transformed into serotonin. But that does not demonstrate that serotonin is excessive in hyperactive psychotic patients (77) or that their improvement is necessarily due to the decrease of serotonin in the brain. On the other hand, there is a recent suggestion that Marsilid, which increases the serotonin content of the brain, benefits depressed patients (78).

Again, that does not prove that patients are depressed because of abnormally low levels of serotonin in the brain. But it must be admitted that this circumstantial evidence is of such interest that it calls for further investigation of these possibilities.

An experiment to throw light on this subject would be to determine the cerebral serotonin contents in the brains of psychotic patients and compare them with those of nonpsychotics. A start has been made. Costa and Aprison have demonstrated that serotonin is a normal constituent of the human brain just as it is of the brain of lower animals (32). However, it can be said conservatively that the suggestion of Woolley and Shaw (18) on the role of serotonin is an attractive one and that it has been useful in turning up new material (79). For example, Shaw and Woolley (80) have synthesized compounds which block serotonin, including BAB, the benzyl analog of bufotenin, and BAS, the benzyl analog of serotonin (Fig. 1). We have employed BAS in the treatment of schizophrenics on the possibility that it may exert a reserpinelike action (79). The salutary results on these psychotic patients were very encouraging, but the side reactions contraindicate the clinical use of BAS.

It is not justifiable, however, to separate the role of serotonin from that of the catechol amines, for both are affected simultaneously by reserpine and probably by other tranquilizing drugs. A strong point in favor of the catechol amines is that one of them, deoxyephedrine, is able to substitute for depleted catechol amines in the brain (81). Mice and monkeys, under the influence of reserpine and showing the depression, reduced mobility, and the hunched posture typically produced by that drug, are dramatically restored to apparently normal activity by deoxyephedrine. Another line of investigation is concerned more with qualitative changes in the neurohormones than with quantitative ones, and it implicates a metabolic factor in schizophrenia. This work cannot be reviewed here, but it involves the more rapid oxidation of adrenaline (82) or the production of abnormal oxidation products of that neurohormone (83). As a result of an abnormal enzyme system, the metabolism of adrenaline is perverted, and an aberrant metabolic product, which may be a pathogenic factor in schizophrenia, is formed (84).

At this time, when theories of schizophrenia are actively multiplying, it would seem that the two different aspects of quantitative and qualitative changes in the hormones are not mutually exclusive. One example is afforded by Hoffer, who suggests that there are two basic conditions for the production of schizophrenia—an increase in the concentration and activity of acetylcholine within the brain and an abnormal metabolic diversion of adrenaline to some aberrant indole compound (85).

The inclusion of electrical changes of brain areas in our field of research diversifies the problem still more. At the present state of development of psychopharmacology it is difficult to apply William of Occam's razor, for each successful drug seems to differ from the others. Perhaps when we know more, the attack will be simplified by a unitary hypothesis on the pharmacologic actions of these drugs. We are therefore left with a number of tempting speculations, and the judgment of the investigator will largely determine which one will be emphasized in his researches.

The fact that we have effective drugs will not stop the production of better ones. In that process, a guiding principle is concerned with a characteristic of the brain—the fact that it, more than any other organ, is sensitive to changes in the chemical structure of a drug (86). Illustrations may be drawn from the phenothiazine derivatives. Profound differences in the intensity of the therapeutic effects and the distribution of the side reactions (35) may be produced either by the replacement of the chlorine (Cl) atom of the nucleus with another chemical or by an alteration in the number of carbon atoms between the two nitrogen atoms (N) of the side chain. We are looking forward to the discovery of compounds of new chemical structures, to be used for types of patients who require not tranquilization but other kinds of therapeutic aid—for example, for the blocked and retarded individual who must be stimulated without an increase of hostility or an activation of hallucinations and delusions.

We have seen, however, that thus far in the field of psychopharmacology, practice has outstripped theory. Through we recognize that tranquilizers correct certain schizophrenic symptoms, there is less agreement on the mechanism by which the improvements are achieved. Whether or not drugs effect cures is a problem for the future. But the practical value of the advance should not be underestimated. It may be compared with the advent of insulin, which counteracts symptoms of diabetes without removing their cause.

References

1. Fabing, H. D. "The dimensions of neurology," presidential address, Am. Acad. of Neurology (1955).
2. Gerard, R. W. Science 125, 201 (1957).
3. Himwich, H. E. J. Nervous Mental Disease 122, 413 (1955).
4. ———, "Discussion of Papers on Basic Observations of New Psychopharmacological Agents." Psychiat. Research Rept. No. 4 (1956), pp. 24-31. Examples include (i) Rauwolfia alkaloids: reserpine (Serpasil, Ciba Pharmaceutical Co.); deserpidine (Harmonyl, Abbott Laboratories); rescinnamine (Moderil, Chas. Pfizer & Co.). (ii) Phenothiazine derivatives: chlorpromazine (Thorazine, Smith, Kline & French Laboratories); promazine (Sparine, Wyeth Laboratories); mepazine (Pacatal, Warner-Chilcott Laboratories); perphenazine (Trilafon, Schering Corp.); proclorperazine (Compazine, Smith, Kline & French Laboratories); thiopropazate (Dartal, G. D. Searle & Co.); triflupromazine (Vesprin, E. R. Squibb & Son; Adazine, Upjohn Co.). (iii) Diphenylmethane derivatives: azacyclonol (Frenquel, William S. Merrell Co.); hydroxyzine (Atarax, R. J. Roerig & Co.); benactyzine (Suavitil, Merck, Sharp & Dohme); phenyltoloxamine (PRN, Bristol Laboratories). (iv) Subtituted propanediols: meprobamate (Miltown, Wallace Laboratories; Equanil, Wyeth Laboratories).

5. Gorman, M. *Every Other Bed* (World, New York, 1956).
6. Barsa, J. A. *Am. J. Psychiat. 114*, 74 (1957.)
7. Rinaldi, F., Rudy, L. H., Himwich, H. E., *ibid. 112*, 678 (1956).
8. Kinross-Wright, V., *ibid. 111*, 907 (1955); Goldman, D. *J. Am. Med. Assoc. 157*, 1274 (1955); Lehman, H. A. *Arch. Neurol. Psychiat. 71*, 227 (1954).
9. Kline, N., Barsa, J., Gosline, E. *Am. J. Psychiat. 17*, 352 (1956).
10. Brown, N. L. *J. Nervous Mental Disease 123*, 130 (1956); Rinaldi, F., Rudy, L. H., Himwich, H. E. *Am. J. Psychiat. 112*, 343 (1955); Rinaldi, F. *et. al.*, in *Tranquilizing Drugs*, Himwich, H. E., Ed. (Am. Assoc. Advance. Sci., Washington, D.C., 1957); Proctor, R. C., in *Alcoholism, Basic Aspects and Treatment*, Himwich, H. E., Ed. (Am. Assoc. Advance. Sci., Washington, D.C., 1957), pp. 133-139.
11. Kline, N. S., Barsa, J., Gosline, E. in *Tranquilizing Drugs*, Himwich, H. E., Ed. (Am. Assoc. Advance. Sci., Washington, D.C., 1957), pp. 149-161; Ferguson, J. T. "The relative values of drugs in the various psychiatric syndromes," *Psychiat. Research Rept. No. 4* (1956), pp. 35-43; Tuteur, W. and Lepson, D. in *Tranquilizing Drugs*, Himwich, H. E., Ed. (Am. Assoc. Advance. Sci., Washington, D.C., 1957), pp. 163-172.
12. Rudy, L. H., Himwich, H. E., Rinaldi, F. "A clinical evaluation of psychopharmacological agents in the management of disturbed mentally defective patients," in *Trans. Soc. Biol. Psychiat. 11*, (1957).
13. Laidlaw, P. P. *Biochem J. (London) 6*, 141 (1912); Alvarez, W. C. *Physiol. Revs. 4*, 352 (1924); Buscaino, V. M. "Extraneurological pathology of schizophrenia," *Proc. 1st Internatl. Congr. Neuropathol.* (1952).
14. Taylor, R. D., Page, I. H., Corcoran, A. C. *Arch. Internal. Med. 88*, 1 (1951); Gaddum, J. H. "Drugs antagonistic to 5-hydroxytryptamine," in *Ciba Symposia: Humoral and Neurogenic Factors*, Wolstenholme, G. E. W., and Cameron, M. P. Eds. (Little, Brown, Boston, Mass., 1954), pp. 75-85.
15. Hoffner, A., Osmond, H. Smythies, J. *J. Mental Sci. 100*, 29 (1954).
16. Welsh, J. H. *Federation Proc. 13*, 162 (1954).
17. Gaddum, J. H., and Hameed, K. A. *Brit. J. Pharmacol. 9*, 240 (1954).
18. Woolley, D. W., and Shaw, E. *Proc. Natl. Acad. Sci. U.S. 40*, 228 (1964).
19. Shaw, E., and Woolley, D. W. *Science 124*, 121 (1956).
20. Costa, E. "The effects of hallucinogenic and tranquilizing drugs on the serotonin evoked uterine contractions," *Psychiat. Research Rept. No. 4* (1956), pp. 11-23.
21. Paasonen, M. K., and Vogt, M. *J. Physiol. 131*, 617 (1956).
22. Pletscher, A., Shore, P. A., Brodie, B. *J. Pharmacol. Exptl. Therap. 116*, 84 (1956).
23. Shore, P. A., Carlsson, A., Brodie, B. B. *Federation Proc. 15*, 483 (1956).
24. Hess, S. M., Shore, P. A., Brodie, B. B. *J. Pharmacol. Exptl. Therap. 118*, 84 (1956).
25. Plummer, A. J., Sheppard, H., Schulert, A. R. "The metabolism of reserprine," presented at the Intern. Symposium of Psychotropic Drugs, Milan, Italy (May 1957).
26. Valcourt, A. J. *Federation Proc. 16*, 130 (1957).
27. Correale, P. *J. Neurochem. 1*, 22 (1956).
28. Erspamer, V. *Pharmacol. Revs. 6*, 425 (1954).
29. Sjoerdsma, A., Weissbach, H., Udenfriend, S. *Am. J. Med. 20*, 520 (1956).
30. Costa, E., and Aprison, M. H. *Federation Proc. 16*, 25 (1957).
31. Vogt, M. *J. Physiol. 123*, 451 (1954).
32. Costa, E., and Aprison, M. H. "Studies on the 5-hydroxytryptamine (serotonin) content in human brain," presented before the Society of Biological Psychiatry, Atlantic City, N.J. (June 1957).
33. Brodie, B. B. *et al.*, *Science 125*, 1293 (1957).
34. Carlsson, A. *et al.*, "Effects of reserprine on the metabolism of catechol amines" presented at the Intern. Symposium of Psychotropic Drugs, Milan, Italy (May 1957).
35. Himwich, H. E., Rinaldi, F., Willis, D. *J. Nervous Mental Disease 124*, 53 (1956).
36. Gyermek, L. *Lancet II*, 724 (1955); Begany, A. J., *et al.*, *Federation Proc. 15*, 399 (1956).
37. Marrazzi, A. S., and Hart, E. R. in *Tranquilizing Drugs*, Himwich, H. E., Ed. (Am. Assoc. Advance. Sci., Washington, D.C., 1957).
38. Rinaldi, F., and Himwich, H. E. *Arch. Neurol Psychiat. 73*, 396 (1955); *ibid. 73*, 387 (1955).
39. Pfeiffer, C. C., and Jenney, E. H. *Ann. N.Y. Acad. Sci. 66*, 753 (1957).
40. Jacobsen, E. *Danish Med. Bull. 2*, 159 (1955).
41. Himwich, H. E., and Rinaldi, F. *Yale J. Biol. Med. 28*, 308 (1955/56).
42. Herrick, C. J. *The Brain of the Tiger Salamander* (Univ. of Chicago Press, Chicago, Ill., 1948).
43. Moruzzi, G., and Magoun, H. W. *Electroencephalog. and Clin. Neurophysiol. 1*, 455 (1949).
44. Jasper, H. H., *ibid. 1*, 405 (1949).
45. Bradley, P. B. "The central action of certain drugs in relation to the reticular formation of the brain," Intern. Symposium—Reticular Formation of the Brain, Detroit, Mich. (1957); Hiebel, G., Bonvallet, M., Dell, P., *Semaine des Hôpitaux de Paris 30*, 2346 (1954).
46. Himwich, H. E. in *Lysergic Acid Diethylamide and Mescaline in Experimental Psychiatry*, Cholden, L., E. (Grune & Stratton, New York, 1956), pp. 19-26; Rinaldi, F. "The Experimental Electroencephalographic Approach to Psychopharmacology," *Psychiatric Research Repts. No. 4* (1956), pp. 1-10.

47. Rinaldi, F., and Himwich, H. E. *Ann. N.Y. Acad. Sci. 61*, 27 (1955).
48. Cannon, W. B. *The Wisdom of the Body* (Norton, New York, 1932).
49. Bein, H. J. *et. al., Schweiz. med. Wochschr. 83*, 1007 (1953); Courvoiser S., *et. al., Arch. intern. pharmacodynamie 92*, 305 (1953).
50. Tripod, J., Bein, H. G., Meier, R. *ibid. 96*, 406 (1954).
51. Weiskrantz, L. "Changes in behaviour under the influence of central acting substances," presented at the Intern. Symposium on Psychotropic Drugs, Milan, Italy (1957).
52. Rinaldi, F., and Himwich, H. E. *Diseases of Nervous System 16*, 3 (1955).
53. Klüver, H., and Bucy, P. C. *Arch. Neurol. Psychiat. 42*, 979 (1939).
54. Papez, J. W., *ibid. 38*, 725 (1937).
55. Pribram, K. H., and Kruger, L. *Ann. N.Y. Acad. Sci. 58*, 109 (1954).
56. MacLean, P. D. *Psychosomat. Med. 11*, 338 (1949); *Electroencephalog. and Clin. Neurophysiol. 4*, 407 (1952).
57. Spiegel, E. A., Miller H. R., Oppenheimer, M. J. *J. Neurophysiol. 3*, 538 (1940).
58. Brady, J. V. "The Paleocortex and Behavioral Motivation" Research Rept. No. WRAIR-30-56 (Walter Reed Army Medical Center, Washington, D.C., 1956).
59. Bard, P., and Mountcastle, V. B. *Research Publs. Assoc. Research Nervous Mental Disease 27*, 362 (1948).
60. Smith, W. K. *Federation Proc. 9*, 118 (1950); Thompson, A. E., and Walker, A. E. *Arch. Neurol. Psychiat. 65*, 251 (1951); Fuller, J. L., Rosvold, H., Pribram, K. H. *J. Comp. and Physiol. Psychol.*, in press.
61. Schreiner, L., and Kling, A. *J. Neurophysiol. 16*, 643 (1953).
62. Rothfield, L., and Harman, P. *J. Comp. Neurol. 101*, 173 (1955).
63. Killam, E. K., and Killam, K. F. in *Brain Mechanisms and Drug Action*, Fields, W. S., Ed. (Thomas, Springfield, Ill., 1957), pp. 71-98.
64. Sigg, E. B., and Schneider, J. A. *Electroencephalog. and Clin. Neurophysiol. 9*, 419 (1957).
65. Preston, J. B. *J. Pharmacol. Exptl. Therap. 118*, 100 (1956).
66. Liberson, W. T., and Akert, K. *Electroencephalog. and Clin. Neurophysiol. 7*, 211 (1955); Green, J. D., and Shimamoto, T. *Arch. Neurol. Psychiat 70*, 687 (1953); Liberson, W. T., and Cadilhac, J. G. *Confinia Neurol. 13*, 278 (1953).
67. Kinross-Wright, V. *Formal Discussion of Chlorpromazine and Mental Health* (Lea & Febiger, Philadelphia, Pa., 1955), pp. 154-157.
68. Penfield, W. *Research Publs. Assoc. Research Nervous Mental Disease 30*, 513 (1950); Gloor, P. *Arch. Neurol. Psychiat. 77*, 247 (1957).
69. Andy, O. R., and Akert, K. *J. Neuropathol. Exptl. Neurol. 14*, 198 (1955).
70. Pennington, V. M. in *Tranquilizing Drugs*, Himwich, H. E., Ed. (Am. Assoc. Advance. Sci., Washington, D.C., 1957), pp. 125-131.
71. Hendley, C. D., Lynes, T. E., Berger, F. M. in *ibid.*, pp. 35-46.
72. Hunt, H. *Ann. N.Y. Acad. Sci. 67*, 712 (1957).
73. Buscaino, M. *Scientia Med. Ital. 5*, 44 (1956).
74 Bailey, P. "Neurosurgical data on states of consciousness," Congr. Neurol. Sci. Brussels, Belgium (1957).
75. Heath, R. B. *et al.*, "Pharmacological and biological psychotherapy," presented at the annual meeting of the American Psychiatric Assoc., Chicago, Ill. (May 1957).
76. Udenfriend, S., Weissbach, H., Bogdanski, D. F. *J. Biol. Chem. 224*, 803 (1956); Shore, P. A., and Brodie, B. B. *Proc. Soc. Explt. Biol. Med. 94*, 433 (1957).
77. Costa, E., Rinaldi, F., Himwich, H. E. "Some relationships between tranquilization indolalkylamines and brain structure," presented at the Intern. Symposium on Psychotropic Drugs, Milan, Italy (May 1957).
78. Saunders, J. C., Radinger, N., Kline, N. S. "A theoretical and clinical approach to treating depressed and regressed patients with iproniazid," paper read at 12th annual meeting, Society of Biological Psychiatry (1957).
79. Rudy, L. H. *et al.* "Clinical evaluation of benzyl analog of serotonin (BAS): a tranquilizing drug," presented before the Society of Biological Psychiatry, Atlantic City, N.J. (June 1957).
80. Shaw, E. N., and Woolley, D. W. *J. Pharmacol, Exptl. Therap. 116*, 164 (1955).
81. Everett, G. M., Toman, J. E. P., Smith, A. H., Jr. *Federation Proc. 16*, 295 (1957).
82. Akerfeldt, S. "Serological reaction of psychiatric patients to n, n-dimethy-p-phenylene diamine," presented at annual meeting of American Psychiatric Assoc. (May 1957).
83. Leach, B. E. *et al., Arch. Neurol. Psychiat. 76*, 635 (1956); Hoffer, A., and Kenyon, M. *ibid. 77*, 437 (1957); Rinkel, M., Hyde, R. W., Solomon H. C. *Diseases of Nervous System 15*, 3 (1954).
84. Heath, R. G. *et al.*, in preparation.
85. Hoffer, A. *J. Clin. Explt. Psychopathol. 18*, 27 (1957).
86 Abood, L. G., and Romanchek, L. *Ann. N.Y. Acad. Sci. 66*, 812 (1957); Grenell, R. G. *ibid. 66*, 826 (1957); Ayd, F. J., Jr. *J. Am. Geriatric Soc. 5*, 1 (1957); Fazekas, J. F. *et al.*, in Alcoholism, Himwich, H. E., Ed. (Am. Assoc. Advance. Sci., Washington, D.C., 1957), pp. 125-132; Gallagher, W. J. *et al.* in *Tranquilizing Drugs*, H. E. Himwich, Ed. (Am. Assoc. Advance. Sci., Washington, D.C., 1957), pp. 133-147; Rudy, L. H., Himwich, H. E., Tasher, D. C. *Am. J. Psychiat. 113*, 979 (1957).

Biophysical Theories:

CRITICAL EVALUATION

The belief that tangible biophysical defects or deficiencies are the cause of mental disorders has not gone unchallenged. Evidence in support of this notion has not been demonstrated convincingly and has spurred adherents of other viewpoints to question the wisdom of pursuing the search for these defects. Thomas Szasz's article, for example, contends that the concept of mental disease itself is merely a myth, a false verbal analogy founded on the erroneous application of a medical model to psychopathology. In contrast, Seymour Kety does not question the legitimacy of the biophysical approach, but merely examines a number of biochemical hypotheses in detail, and finds them either ill-conceived or lacking in empirical support.

The Myth of Mental Illness

THOMAS S. SZASZ

My aim in this essay is to raise the question "Is there such a thing as mental illness?" and to argue that there is not. Since the notion of mental illness is extremely widely used nowadays, inquiry into the ways in which this term is employed would seem to be especially indicated. Mental illness, of course, is not literally a "thing"—or physical object—and hence it can "exist" only in the same sort of way in which other theoretical concepts exist. Yet, familiar theories are in the habit of posing, sooner or later—at least to those who come to believe in them—as "objective truths" (or "facts"). During certain historical periods, explanatory conceptions such as deities, witches, and microorganisms appeared not only as theories but as self-evident *causes* of a vast number of events. I submit that today mental illness is widely regarded in a somewhat similar fashion, that is, as the cause of innumerable diverse happenings. As an antidote to the complacent use of the notion of mental illness—whether as a self-evident phenomenon, theory, or cause—let us ask this question: What is meant when it is asserted that someone is mentally ill?

In what follows I shall describe briefly the main uses to which the concept of mental illness has been put. I shall argue that this notion has outlived whatever usefulness it might have had and that it now functions merely as a convenient myth.

From *Amer. Psychol.* 15:113-118, 1960, by permission of the American Psychological Association and the author.

MENTAL ILLNESS AS A SIGN
OF BRAIN DAMAGE

The notion of mental illness derives its main support from such phenomena as syphilis of the brain or delirious conditions — intoxications, for instance—in which persons are known to manifest various peculiarities or disorders of thinking and behavior. Correctly speaking, however, these are diseases of the brain, not of the mind. According to one school of thought, *all* so-called mental illness is of this type. The assumption is made that some neurological defect, perhaps a very subtle one, will ultimately be found for all the disorders of thinking and behavior. Many contemporary psychiatrists, physicians, and other scientists hold this view. This position implies that people *cannot* have troubles—expressed in what are *now called* "mental illnesses"—because of differences in personal needs, opinions, social aspirations, values, and so on. *All problems in living* are attributed to physicochemical processes which in due time will be discovered by medical research.

"Mental illnesses" are thus regarded as basically no different than all other diseases (that is, of the body). The only difference, in this view, between mental and bodily diseases is that the former, affecting the brain, manifest themselves by means of mental symptoms; whereas the latter, affecting other organ systems (for example, the skin, liver, etc.), manifest themselves by means of symptoms referable to those parts of the body. This view rests on and expresses what are, in my opinion, two fundamental errors.

In the first place, what central nervous system symptoms would correspond to a skin eruption or a fracture? It would *not* be some emotion or complex bit of behavior. Rather, it would be blindness or a paralysis of some part of the body. The crux of the matter is that a disease of the brain, analogous to a disease of the skin or bone, is a neurological defect, and not a problem in living. For example, a *defect* in a person's visual field may be satisfactorily explained by correlating it with certain definite lesions in the nervous system. On the other hand, a person's *belief*—whether this be a belief in Christianity, in Communism, or in the idea that his internal organs are "rotting" and that his body is, in fact, already "dead"— cannot be explained by a defect or disease of the nervous system. Explanations of this sort of occurrence— assuming that one is interested in the belief itself and does not regard it simply as a "symptom" or expression of something else that is *more interesting*—must be sought along different lines.

The second error in regarding complex psychosocial behavior, consisting of communications about ourselves and the world about us, as mere symptoms of neurological functioning is *epistemological*. In other words, it is an error pertaining not to any mistakes in observation or reasoning, as such, but rather to the way in which we organize and express our knowledge. In the present case, the error lies in making a symmetrical dualism between mental and physical (or bodily) symptoms, a dualism which is merely a habit of speech and to which no known observations can be found to correspond. Let us see if this is so. In medical practice, when we speak of physical disturbances, we mean either signs (for example, a fever) or symptoms (for example, pain). We speak of mental symptoms, on the other hand, when we refer to a patient's *communications about himself, others, and the world about him.* He might state that he is Napoleon or that he is being persecuted by the Communists. These would be considered mental symptoms *only* if the observer believed that the patient was *not* Napoleon or that he was *not* being persecuted by the Communists. This makes it apparent that the statement that "*X* is a mental symptom" involves rendering a judgment. The judgment entails, moreover, a covert comparison or matching of the patient's ideas, concepts, or beliefs with those of the observer and the society in which they live. The notion of mental symptom is therefore inextricably tied to the *social* (including *ethical*) *context* in which it is made in much the same way as the notion of bodily symptom is tied to an *anatomical* and *genetic context* (Szasz, 1957a, 1957b).

To sum up what has been said thus far: I have tried to show that for those who regard mental symptoms as signs of brain disease, the concept of mental illness is unnecessary and misleading. For what they mean is that people so labeled suffer from diseases of the brain; and, if that is what they mean, it would seem better for the sake of clarity to say that and not something else.

MENTAL ILLNESS AS A NAME FOR PROBLEMS IN LIVING

The term "mental illness" is widely used to describe something which is very different than a disease of the brain. Many people today take it for granted that living is an arduous process. Its hardship for modern man, moreover, derives not so much from a struggle for biological survival as from the stresses and strains inherent in the social intercourse of complex human personalities. In this context, the notion of mental illness is used to identify or describe some feature of an individual's so-called personality. Mental illness—as a deformity of the personality, so to speak —is then regarded as the *cause* of the human disharmony. It is implicit in this view that social intercourse between people is regarded as something *inherently harmonious*, its disturbance being due solely to the presence of "mental illness" in many people. This is obviously fallacious reasoning, for it makes the abstraction "mental illness" into a *cause*, even though this abstraction was created in the first place to serve only as a shorthand expression for certain types of human behavior. It now becomes necessary to ask: "What kinds of behavior are regarded as indicative of mental illness, and by whom?"

The concept of illness, whether bodily or mental, implies *deviation from some clearly defined norm*. In the case of physical illness, the norm is the structural and functional integrity of the human body. Thus, although the desirability of physical health, as such, is an ethical value, what health *is* can be stated in anatomical and physiological terms. What is the norm deviation from which is regarded as mental illness? This question cannot be easily answered. But whatever this norm might be, we can be certain of only one thing: namely, that it is a norm that must be stated in terms of *psychosocial, ethical,* and *legal* concepts. For example, notions such as "excessive repression" or "acting out an unconscious impulse" illustrate the use of psychological concepts for judging (so-called) mental health and illness. The idea that chronic hostility, vengefulness, or divorce are indicative of mental illness would be illustrations of the use of ethical norms (that is, the desirability of love, kindness, and a stable marriage relationship). Finally, the widespread psychiatric opinion that only a mentally ill person would commit homicide illustrates the use of a legal concept as a norm of mental health. The norm from which deviation is measured whenever one speaks of a mental illness is a *psychosocial and ethical one*. Yet, the remedy is sought in terms of *medical* measures which—it is hoped and assumed—are free from wide differences of ethical value. The definition of the disorder and the terms in which its remedy are sought are therefore at serious odds with one another. The practical significance of this covert conflict between the alleged nature of the defect and the remedy can hardly be exaggerated.

Having identified the norms used to measure deviations in cases of mental illness, we will now turn to the question: "Who defines the norms and hence the deviation?" Two basic answers may be offered: *(a)* It may be the person himself (that is, the patient) who decides that he deviates from a norm. For example, an artist may believe that he suffers from a work inhibition; and he may implement this conclusion by seeking help *for* himself from a psychotherapist. *(b)* It may be someone other than the patient who decides that the latter is deviant (for example, relatives, physicians, legal authorities, society generally, etc.). In such a case a psychiatrist may be hired by others to do something *to* the patient in order to correct the deviation.

These considerations underscore the importance of asking the question "Whose agent is the psychiatrist?" and of giving a candid answer to it (Szasz, 1956, 1958). The psychiatrist (psychologist or nonmedical psychotherapist), it now develops, may be the agent of the patient, of the relatives, of the school, of the military services, of a business organization, of a court of law, and so forth. In speaking of the psychiatrist as the agent of these persons or organizations, it is not implied that his values concerning norms, or his ideas and aims concerning the proper nature of remedial action, need to coincide exactly with those of his employer. For example, a patient in individual psychotherapy may believe that his salvation lies in a new marriage; his psychotherapist need not share this hypothesis. As the patient's agent, however, he must abstain from bringing social or legal force to bear on the patient which would prevent him from putting his beliefs into action. If his *contract* is with the patient, the psychiatrist (psychotherapist) may disagree with him or stop his treatment; but he cannot engage others to obstruct the patient's aspirations. Similarly, if a psychiatrist is engaged by a court to determine the sanity of a criminal, he need not fully share the legal authorities' values and intentions in regard to the criminal and the means available for dealing with him. But the psychiatrist is expressly barred from stating, for example, that it is not the criminal who is "insane" but the men who wrote the law on the basis of which the very actions that are being judged are regarded as "criminal." Such an opinion could be voiced, of course, but not in a courtroom, and not by a psychiatrist who makes it his practice to assist the court in performing its daily work.

To recapitulate: In actual contemporary social usage, the finding of a mental illness is made by establishing a deviance in behavior from certain psychosocial, ethical, or legal norms. The judgment may be made, as in medicine, by the patient, the physician (psychiatrist), or others. Remedial action, finally, tends to be sought in a therapeutic—or covertly medical—framework, thus creating a situation in which *psychosocial, ethical,* and/or *legal deviations* are claimed to be correctible by (so-called) *medical action.* Since medical action is designed to correct only medical deviations, it seems logically absurd to expect that it will help solve problems whose very existence had been defined and established on nonmedical grounds. I think that these considerations may be fruitfully applied to the present use of tranquilizers and, more generally, to what might be expected of drugs of whatever type in regard to the amelioration or solution of problems in human living.

THE ROLE OF ETHICS IN PSYCHIATRY

Anything that people *do*—in contrast to things that *happen* to them (Peters, 1958)—takes place in a context of value. In this broad sense, no human activity is devoid of ethical implications. When the values underlying certain activities are widely shared, those who participate in their pursuit may lose sight of them altogether. The discipline of medicine, both as a pure science (for example, research) and as a technology (for example, therapy), contains many ethical considerations and judgments. Unfortunately, these are often denied, minimized, or merely kept out of focus; for the ideal of the medical profession as well as of the people whom it serves seems to be having a system of medicine (allegedly) free of ethical value. This sentimental notion is expressed by such things as the doctor's willingness to treat and help patients irrespective of their religious or political beliefs, whether they are rich or poor, etc. While there may be some grounds for this belief—albeit it is a view that is not impressively true even in these regards—the fact remains that ethical considerations encompass a vast range of human affairs. By making the practice of medicine neutral in regard to some specific issues of value need not, and cannot, mean that it can be kept free from all such values. The practice of medicine is intimately tied to ethics; and the first thing that we must do, it seems to me, is to try to make this clear and explicit. I shall let this matter rest here, for it does not concern us specifically in this essay. Lest there be any vagueness, however, about how or where ethics and medicine meet, let me remind the reader of such issues as birth control, abortion, suicide, and euthanasia as only a few of the major areas of current ethicomedical controversy.

Psychiatry, I submit, is very much more intimately tied to problems of ethics than is medicine. I use the word "psychiatry" here to refer to that contemporary discipline which is concerned with *problems in living* (and not with diseases of the brain, which are problems for neurology). Problems in human relations can be analyzed, interpreted, and given meaning only within given social and ethical contexts. Accordingly, it *does* make a difference—arguments to the contrary notwithstanding—what the psychiatrist's socioethical orientations happen to be; for these will influence his ideas on what is wrong with the patient, what deserves comment or interpretation, in what possible directions change might be desirable, and so forth. Even in medicine proper, these factors play a role, as for instance, in the divergent orientations which physicians, de-

pending on their religious affiliations, have toward such things as birth control and therapeutic abortion. Can anyone really believe that a psychotherapist's ideas concerning religious belief, slavery, or other similar issues play no role in his practical work? If they do make a difference, what are we to infer from it? Does it not seem reasonable that we ought to have different psychiatric therapies—each expressly recognized for the ethical positions which they embody—for, say, Catholics and Jews, religious persons and agnostics, democrats and communists, white supremacists and Negroes, and so on? Indeed, if we look at how psychiatry is actually practiced today (especially in the United States), we find that people do seek psychiatric help in accordance with their social status and ethical beliefs (Hollingshead & Redlich, 1958). This should really not surprise us more than being told that practicing Catholics rarely frequent birth control clinics.

The foregoing position which holds that contemporary psychotherapists deal with problems in living, rather than with mental illnesses and their cures, stands in opposition to a currently prevalent claim, according to which mental illness is just as "real" and "objective" as bodily illness. This is a confusing claim since it is never known exactly what is meant by such words as "real" and "objective." I suspect, however, that what is intended by the proponents of this view is to create the idea in the popular mind that mental illness is some sort of disease entity, like an infection or a malignancy. If this were true, one could *catch* or *get* a "mental illness," one might *have* or *harbor* it, one might *transmit* it to others, and finally one could get *rid* of it. In my opinion, there is not a shred of evidence to support this idea. To the contrary, all the evidence is the other way and supports the view that what people now call mental illnesses are for the most part *communications* expressing unacceptable ideas, often framed, moreover, in an unusual idiom. The scope of this essay allows me to do no more than mention this alternative theoretical approach to this problem (Szasz, 1957c).

This is not the place to consider in detail the similarities and differences between bodily and mental illnesses. It shall suffice for us here to emphasize only one important difference between them: namely, that whereas bodily disease refers to public, physicochemical occurrences, the notion of mental illness is used to codify relatively more private, sociopsychological happenings of which the observer (diagnostician) forms a part. In other words, the psychiatrist does not stand *apart* from what he observes, but is, in Harry Stack Sullivan's apt words, a "participant observer." This means that he is *committed* to some picture of what he considers reality—and to what he thinks society considers reality—and he observes and judges the patient's behavior in the light of these considerations. This touches on our earlier observation that the notion of mental symptom itself implies a comparison between observer and observed, psychiatrist and patient. This is so obvious that I may be charged with belaboring trivialities. Let me therefore say once more that my aim in presenting this argument was expressly to criticize and counter a prevailing contemporary tendency to deny the moral aspects of psychiatry (and psychotherapy) and to substitute for them allegedly value-free medical considerations. Psychotherapy, for example, is being widely practiced as though it entailed nothing other than restoring the patient from a state of mental sickness to one of mental health. While it is generally accepted that mental illness has something to do with man's social (or inter-personal) relations, it is paradoxically maintained that problems of values (that is, of ethics) do not arise in this process.* Yet, in one

sense, much of psychotherapy may revolve around nothing other than the elucidation and weighing of goals and values—many of which may be mutually contradictory—and the means whereby they might best be harmonized, realized, or relinquished.

The diversity of human values and the methods by means of which they may be realized is so vast, and many of them remain so unacknowledged, that they cannot fail but lead to conflicts in human relations. Indeed, to say that human relations at all levels—from mother to child, through husband and wife, to nation and nation—are fraught with stress, strain, and disharmony is, once again, making the obvious explicit. Yet, what may be obvious may be also poorly understood. This I think is the case here. For it seems to me that—at least in our scientific theories of behavior—we have failed to *accept* the simple fact that human relations are inherently fraught with difficulties and that to make them even relatively harmonious requires much patience and hard work. I submit that the idea of mental illness is now being put to work to obscure certain difficulties which at present may be inherent—not that they need be unmodifiable—in the social intercourse of persons. If this is true, the concept functions as a disguise; for instead of calling attention to conflicting human needs, aspirations, and values, the notion of mental illness provides an amoral and impersonal "thing" (an "illness") as an explanation for *problems in living* (Szasz, 1959). We may recall in this connection that not so long ago it was devils and witches who were held responsible for men's problems in social living. The belief in mental illness, as something other than man's trouble in getting along with his fellow man, is the proper heir to the belief in demonology and witchcraft. Mental illness exists or is "real" in exactly the same sense in which witches existed or were "real."

---

* Freud went so far as to say that: "I consider ethics to be taken for granted. Actually I have never done a mean thing" (Jones, 1957, p. 247). This surely is a strange thing to say for someone who has studied man as a social being as closely as did Freud. I mention it here to show how the notion of "illness" (in the case of psycho-

analysis, "psychopathology," or "mental illness") was used by Freud—and by most of his followers—as a means for classifying certain forms of human behavior as falling within the scope of medicine, and hence (by *fiat*) outside that of ethics!

CHOICE, RESPONSIBILITY, AND PSYCHIATRY

While I have argued that mental illnesses do not exist, I obviously did not imply that the social and psychological occurrences to which this label is currently being attached also do not exist. Like the personal and social troubles which people had in the Middle Ages, they are real enough. It is the labels we give them that concerns us and, having labelled them, what we do about them. While I cannot go into the ramified implications of this problem here, it is worth noting that a demonologic conception of problems in living gave rise to therapy along theological lines. Today, a belief in mental illness implies—nay, requires—therapy along medical or psychotherapeutic lines.

What is implied in the line of thought set forth here is something quite different. I do not intend to offer a new conception of "psychiatric illness" nor a new form of "therapy." My aim is more modest and yet also more ambitious. It is to suggest that the phenomena now called mental illnesses be looked at afresh and more simply, that they be removed from the category of illnesses, and that they be regarded as the expressions of man's struggle with the problem of *how* he should live. The last mentioned problem is obviously a vast one, its enormity reflecting not only man's inability to cope with his environment, but even more his increasing self-reflectiveness.

By problems in living, then, I refer to that truly explosive chain reaction which began with man's fall from divine grace by partaking of the fruit of the tree of knowledge. Man's awareness of himself and of the world about him seems to be a steadily expanding one, bringing in its wake an ever larger *burden of understanding* (an expression borrowed from Susanne Langer, 1953). *This burden,* then, *is to be expected and must not be misinterpreted.* Our only *rational* means for lightening it is *more understanding,* and appropriate *action* based on such understanding. The main alter-native lies in acting as though the burden were not what in fact we perceive it to be and taking refuge in an outmoded theological view of man. In the latter view, man does not fashion his life and much of his world about him, but merely lives out his fate in a world created by superior beings. This may logically lead to pleading nonresponsibility in the face of seemingly unfathomable problems and difficulties. Yet, if man fails to take increasing responsibility for his actions, individually as well as collectively, it seems unlikely that some higher power or being would assume this task and carry this burden for him. Moreover, this seems hardly the proper time in human history for obscuring the issue of man's responsibility for his actions by hiding it behind the skirt of an all-explaining conception of mental illness.

CONCLUSIONS

I have tried to show that the notion of mental illness has outlived whatever usefulness it might have had and that it now functions merely as a convenient myth. As such, it is a true heir to religious myths in general, and to the belief in witchcraft in particular; the role of all these belief-systems was to act as *social tranquilizers,* thus encouraging the hope that mastery of certain specific problems may be achieved by means of substitutive (symbolic-magical) operations. The notion of mental illness thus serves mainly to obscure the everyday fact that life for most people is a continuous struggle, not for biological survival, but for a "place in the sun," "peace of mind," or some other human value. For man aware of himself and of the world about him, once the needs for preserving the body (and perhaps the race) are more or less satisfied, the problem arises as to what he should do with himself. Sustained adherence to the myth of mental illness allows people to avoid facing this problem, believing that mental health, conceived as the absence of mental illness, automatically insures the making of right and safe choices in one's conduct of life. But the facts are all the other way. It is the making of good choices in life that others regard, retrospectively, as good mental health!

The myth of mental illness encourages us, moreover, to believe in its logical corollary: that social intercourse would be harmonious, satisfying, and the secure basis of a "good life" were it not for the disrupting influences of mental illness or "psychopathology." The potentiality for universal human happiness, in this form at least, seems to me but another example of the I-wish-it-were-true type of fantasy. I do believe that human happiness or well-being on a hitherto unimaginably large scale, and not just for a select few, is possible. This goal could be achieved, however, only at the cost of many men, and not just a few being willing and able to tackle their personal, social, and ethical conflicts. This means having the courage and integrity to forego waging battles on false fronts, finding solutions for substitute problems—for instance, fighting the battle of stomach acid and chronic fatigue instead of facing up to a marital conflict.

Our adversaries are not demons, witches, fate, or mental illness. We have no enemy whom we can fight, exorcise, or dispel by "cure." What we do have are *problems in living*— whether these be biologic, economic, political, or sociopsychological. In this essay I was concerned only with problems belonging in the last mentioned category, and within this group mainly with those pertaining to moral values. The field to which modern psychiatry addresses itself is vast, and I made no effort to encompass it all. My argument was limited to the proposition that mental illness is a myth, whose function it is to disguise and thus render more palatable the bitter pill of moral conflicts in human relations.

References

Hollingshead, A. B., and Redlich, F. C. *Social class and mental illness.* New York: Wiley, 1958.

Jones, E. *The life and work of Sigmund Freud.* Vol. III. New York: Basic Books, 1957.

Langer, S. K. *Philosophy in a new key.* New York: Mentor Books, 1953.

Peters, R. S. *The concept of motivation.* London: Routledge & Kegan Paul, 1958.

Szasz, T. S. Malingering: "Diagnosis" or social condemnation? *AMA Arch Neurol. Psychiat.,* 1956, *76,* 432-443.

Szasz, T. S. *Pain and pleasure; A study of bodily feelings.* New York: Basic Books, 1957. (a)

Szasz, T. S. The problem of psychiatric nosology: A contribution to a situational analysis of psychiatric operations. *Amer. J. Psychiat.,* 1957, *114,* 405-413. (b)

Szasz, T. S. On the theory of psychoanalytic treatment. *Int. J. Psycho-Anal.,* 1957, *38,* 166-182. (c)

Szasz, T. S. Psychiatry, ethics and the criminal law. *Columbia Law Rev.,* 1958, *58,* 183-198.

Szasz, T. S. Moral conflict and psychiatry, *Yale Rev.,* 1959, in press.

Biochemical Theories of Schizophrenia: Part A

SEYMOUR S. KETY

The concept of a chemical etiology in schizophrenia is not new. The Hippocratic school attributed certain mental aberrations to changes in the

From *Science 129:*1528-1532, June 5, 1959, and 1590-1596, June 12, 1959, by permission of the American Association for the Advancement of Science and the author.

composition of the blood and disturbances in the humors of the brain, but it was Thudichum (1), the founder of modern neurochemistry, who in 1884 expressed the concept most cogently: 'Many forms of insanity are unquestionably the external manifestations of the effects upon the brain substance of poisons fermented within the body, just as mental aberrations accompanying chronic alcoholic intoxication are the accumulated effects of a relatively simple poison fermented out of the body. These poisons we shall, I have no doubt, be able to isolate after we know the normal chemistry to its uttermost detail. And then will come in their turn the crowning discoveries to which our efforts must ultimately be directed, namely, the discoveries of the antidotes to the poisons and to the fermenting causes and processes which produce them.' In these few words were anticipated and encompassed most of the current chemical formulations regarding schizophrenia.

It may be of value to pause in the midst of the present era of psychochemical activity to ask how far we have advanced along the course plotted by Thudichum. Have we merely substituted 'enzymes' for 'ferments' and the names of specific agents for 'poisons' without altering the completely theoretical nature of the concept? Or, on the other hand, are there some well-substantiated findings to support the prevalent belief that this old and stubborn disorder which has resisted all previous attempts to expose its etiology is about to yield its secrets to the biochemist?

An examination of the experience of another and older discipline may be of help in the design, interpretation, and evaluation of biochemical studies. The concepts of the pathology of schizophrenia have been well reviewed recently (2). As a result of findings of definite histological changes in the cerebral cortex of patients with schizophrenia which were described by Alzheimer at the beginning of the present century and confirmed by a number of others, an uncritical enthusiasm for the theory of a pathological lesion in this disease developed, and this enthusiasm penetrated the thinking of Kraepelin and Bleuler and persisted for 25 years. This was followed by a period of questioning which led to the design and execution of more critically controlled studies and, eventually, to the present consensus that a pathological

lesion characteristic of schizophrenia or any of its subgroups remains to be demonstrated.

Earlier biochemical theories and findings related to schizophrenia have been reviewed by a number of authors, of whom McFarland and Goldstein (3), Keup (4), and Richter (5) may be mentioned (6). Horwitt and others (7-9) have pointed out some of the difficulties of crucial research in this area. It is the purpose of this review to describe the biochemical trends in schizophrenia research of the past few years, to discuss current theories, and to examine the evidence which has been used to support them.

SOURCES OF ERROR

Because of the chronicity of the disease, the prolonged periods of institutionalization associated with its management, and the comparatively few objective criteria available for its diagnosis and the evaluation of its progress, schizophrenia presents to the investigator a large number of variables and sources of error which he must recognize and attempt to control before he may attribute to any of his findings a primary or characteristic significance.

Despite the phenomenological similarities which permitted the concept of schizophrenia as a fairly well defined symptom complex to emerge, there is little evidence that all of its forms have a common etiology or pathogenesis. The likelihood that one is dealing with a number of different disorders with a common symptomatology must be recognized and included in one's experimental design (8, 10, 11). Errors involved in sampling from heterogeneous populations may help to explain the high frequency with which findings of one group fail to be confirmed by those of another. Recognition that any sample of schizophrenics is probably a heterogeneous one would seem to indicate the importance of analyzing data not only for mean values but also for significant deviations of individual values from group values. The biochemical characteristics of phenylketonuria would hardly have been detected in an average value for phenylalanine levels in blood in a large group of mentally retarded patients.

Most biochemical research in schizophrenia has been carried out in patients with a long history of hospitalization in institutions where overcrowding is difficult to avoid and where hygienic standards cannot always be maintained. It is easy to imagine how chronic infections, especially of the digestive tract, might spread among such patients. The presence of amebiasis in a majority of the patients at one large institution has been reported (12), and one wonders how often this condition or a former infectious hepatitis has caused the various disturbances in hepatic function found in schizophrenia. Even in the absence of previous or current infection, the development of a characteristic pattern of intestinal flora in a population of schizophrenic patients living together for long periods and fed from the same kitchen is a possibility which cannot be dismissed in interpreting what appear to be deviant metabolic pathways.

In variety and quality the diet of the institutionalized schizophrenic is rarely comparable to that of the non-hospitalized normal control. Whatever homeostatic function the process of free dietary selection may serve is often lost between the rigors of the kitchen or the budget and the overriding emotional or obsessive features of the disease. In the case of the 'acute' schizophrenic, the weeks and months of emotional turmoil which precede recognition and diagnosis of the disease are hardly conducive to a normal dietary intake. Kelsey, Gullock, and Kelsey (13) confirmed findings of certain abnormalities in thyroid function previously reported in schizophrenia and showed that in their patients these abnormalities resulted from a dietary deficiency of iodine, correctable by the introduction of iodized salt into the hospital diet. It is not surprising that a dietary vitamin deficiency has been found to explain at least two of the biochemical abnormalities recently attributed to schizophrenia (9, 14-16). It is more surprising that the vitamins and other dietary constituents, whose role in metabolism has become so clearly established, should so often be relegated to a position of unimportance in consideration of the intermediary metabolism of schizophrenics. Horwitt (17) has found signs of liver dysfunction during ingestion of a diet containing borderline levels of protein, while nonspecific vitamin therapy accompanied by a high protein and carbohydrate diet has been reported to reverse the impairment of hepatic function in schizophrenic patients (18).

Another incidental factor which sets the schizophrenic apart from the normal control is the long list of therapies to which he may have been exposed. Hypnotic and ataractic drugs and their metabolic products or effects produce changes which have sometimes been attributed to the disease. Less obvious is the possibility of residual electrophysiological or biochemical changes resulting from repeated electroshock or insulin coma.

Emotional stress is known to cause profound changes in man—in adrenocortical and thyroid function (19), in the excretion of epinephrine and norepinephrine (20), and in the excretion of water, electrolytes, or creatinine (21), to mention only a few recently reported findings. Schizophrenic illness is often characterized by marked emotional disturbance even in what is called the basal state and by frequently exaggerated anxiety in response to routine and research procedures. The disturbances in behavior and activity which mark the schizophrenic process would also be expected to cause deviations from the normal in many biochemical and metabolic measures—in volume and concentration of urine, in energy and nitrogen metabolism, in the size and function of numerous organic systems. The physiological and biochemical changes which are secondary to the psychological and behavioral state of the patient are of interest in themselves, and understanding of them contributes to total understanding of the schizophrenic process; it is important, however, not to attribute to them a primary or etiological role.

An additional source of error which must be recognized is one which is common to all of science and which it is the very purpose of scientific method, tradition, and training to minimize—the subjective bias. There are reasons why this bias should operate to a greater extent in this field than in many others. Not only is the motivation heightened by the tragedy of this problem and the social implications of findings which may contribute to its solution, but the measurements themselves, especially of the changes in mental state or behavior, are so highly subjective, and the symptoms are so variable and so responsive to nonspecific factors in the milieu, that only the most scrupulous attention to controlled design will permit the conclusion that a drug, or a diet, or a protein fraction of the blood, or an extract of the brain is capable of causing or ameliorating some of the manifestations of the disease. This is not to suggest that the results of purely chemical determinations are immune to subjective bias; the same vigilance is required there to prevent the hypothesis from contaminating the data. In a field with as many variables as this one, it is difficult to avoid the subconscious tendency to reject for good reason data which weaken a hypothesis while uncritically accepting those data which strengthen it. Carefully controlled and 'double blind' experimental designs which are becoming more widely utilized in this area can help to minimize this bias.

Obvious as many of these sources of error are, it is expensive and difficult, if not impossible, to prevent some of them from affecting results obtained in this field, especially in the preliminary testing of interesting hypotheses. It is in the interpretation of these results, however, and in the formulating of conclusions, that the investigator has the opportunity, and indeed the responsibility, to recognize and evaluate his uncontrolled variables rather than to ignore them, for no one knows better than the investigator himself the possible sources of error in his particular experiment. There are enough unknowns in our guessing game with nature to make it unnecessary for us to indulge in such a sport with one another.

SCHIZOPHRENIA PROGRAM OF THE LABORATORY OF CLINICAL SCIENCE

Since 1956, the Laboratory of Clinical Science of the National Institute of Mental Health has been developing and pursuing a program of biological research in schizophrenia designed to minimize many of the sources of error discussed above while increasing the opportunity to detect, and to correlate with psychiatric and behavioral information, true biological characteristics if they exist. One of the wards houses a group of approximately 14 clearly diagnosed schizophrenic patients, representative of as many clinical subgroups as possible, chosen from a patient population of 14,000. In selecting these patients an attempt was made to minimize the variables of age, sex, race, and physical illness and, on the basis of careful family surveys, to maximize the likelihood of including within the group individuals representative of whatever genetic subgroups of the disease may exist (10). These patients are maintained for an indefinite period of time on a good diet, receiving excellent hygienic, nursing, medical, and psychiatric care. Each patient receives a careful and sophisticated psychiatric and genealogical characterization, and detailed daily records are kept on his psychiatric and behavioral status; these, it is hoped, will be of value in a more complete interpretation of biological findings. No specific therapy is employed or even found to be necessary, and drugs or dietary changes are introduced only for research purposes and for short periods of time. The other ward houses a comparable number of normal controls, who volunteer to remain for protracted periods of time on the same diet and in a reasonably similar milieu. We recognize, of course, that only a few of the variables are thus controlled and that any positive difference which emerges in this preliminary experiment between some or all of the schizophrenics and the normal population will have to be subjected to much more rigorous examination before its significance can be evaluated. Such re-examination has rarely been necessary, since our schizophrenic patients, individually or as a group, have shown little abnormality in the biological studies which have thus far been completed (9, 14, 22-24).

OXYGEN, CARBOHYDRATE, AND ENERGETICS

A decrease in basal metabolism was found in schizophrenia by earlier workers, although more recent work has not confirmed this (5), and theories attributing the disease to disturbances in the fundamental mechanisms of energy supply or conversion in the brain have enjoyed some popularity, but on the basis of extremely inadequate evidence, such as spectroscopic oximetry of the ear lobe or nail bed (25). Our finding of a normal rate of cerebral circulation and oxygen consumption in schizophrenic patients (26) was confirmed by Wilson, Schieve, and Scheinberg (27) and, more recently, in our laboratory by Sokoloff and his associates (28), who also found a normal rate of cerebral glucose consumption in this condition. These studies make it appear unlikely that the moderate decrease in these functions reported by Gordan and his associates (29), but only in patients with longstanding disease, is fundamental to the disease process. These studies do not, of course, rule out a highly localized change in energy metabolism somewhere in the brain, but cogent evidence for such a hypothesis has yet to be presented.

Richter (5) has pointed out the uncontrolled factors in earlier work which indicated that a defect in carbo-hydrate metabolism was characteristic of the schizophrenic disease process. The finding in schizophrenia of an abnormal glucose tolerance in conjunction with considerable other evidence of hepatic dysfunction (30), or evidence of an abnormally slow metabolism of lactate in the schizophrenic (31), do not completely exclude incidental hepatic disease or nutritional deficiencies as possible sources of error. Horwitt and his associates (32) were able to demonstrate and correct similar abnormalities by altering the dietary intake of the B group of vitamins.

Evidence for greater than normal anti-insulin or hyperglycemic activity in the blood or urine of a significant segment of schizophrenic patients was reported in 1942 by Meduna, Gerty, and Urse (33) and as recently as 1958 by Moya and his associates (34). Some progress has been made in concentrating or characterizing such factors in normal (35) urine as well as in urine from schizophrenics (36). Harris (37) has thrown some doubt on the importance of such anti-insulin mechanisms in the pathogenesis of schizophrenia, and it is hoped that further investigation may clarify the nature of the substance or substances involved and their relevance to schizophrenia.

Defects in oxidative phosphorylation have been thought to occur in this disease. Reports of alterations in the phosphorus metabolism of the erythrocyte (38) await further definition and independent confirmation.

Two recent reports of a more normal pattern of carbohydrate metabolism and of clinical improvement following the infusion of glutathione (39) in psychotic patients, some of whom were schizophrenic, are perhaps of interest. There is little verifiable evidence for a reduction in the blood glutathione index in schizophrenia (9); one group which has repeatedly postulated this reduction has done so on the basis of decreasingly convincing data (16, 40), while our laboratory has failed to find it at all (14), and a very recent report publishes identical figures for the schizophrenic and normal groups (41). Clinical and biochemical improvement in a variety of psychoses following glutathione infusion, even if it is accepted without the necessary controls, suggests at best that glutathione is of secondary and nonspecific import.

It is difficult for some to believe that a generalized defect in energy metabolism—a process so fundamental to every cell in the body—could be responsible for the highly specialized features of schizophrenia. On the other hand, a moderate lack of oxygen, an essential requirement of practically every tissue, produces highly selective manifestations involving especially the higher mental functions and as suggestive of schizophrenia as manifestations produced by many of the more popular hallucinogens. It may not, therefore, be completely appropriate that, in a search for biochemical factors etiologically related to schizophrenic psychoses, the center of interest today appears to have shifted to other, more specialized aspects of metabolism.

AMINO ACIDS AND AMINES

The well-controlled studies of the Gjessings (42) on nitrogen metabolism in periodic catatonia arouse considerable interest in that they suggest the possibility of a relationship between intermediary protein metabolism and schizophrenia, although earlier workers had postulated defects in amino acid metabolism in this disease (43). The hallucinogenic properties of some compounds related directly or indirectly to biological amines reawakened this interest, and the techniques of paper chromatography offered new and almost unlimited opportunity for studying the subject.

The first group to report chromatographic studies of the urine of schizophrenic and control groups found certain differences in the amino acid pattern and, in addition, the presence of certain unidentified imidazoles in the urine of schizophrenics (44). Although a normal group of comparable age was used for comparison, there is no indication of the extent to which dietary and other variables were controlled, and the authors were properly cautious in their conclusions. In a more extensive series of studies, another group has reported a significantly higher than normal concentration of aromatic compounds in the urine of schizophrenic patients (45) and has suggested that there are certain qualitative differences in the excretion of such compounds (46). Others have reported the abnormal presence of unidentified amines (47) or indoles (48), and one group has reported the absence of a normally occurring indole (49) in the urine of schizophrenic patients. In some of these studies there appears to have been no control relative to possible drug therapy or to volume or concentration of urine, and in few of them was there control of diet. There are numerous mechanisms whereby vitamin deficiencies may cause substantial changes in the complex patterns of the intermediary metabolism of amino acids. In addition, the fact that a large number of aromatic compounds in the urine have recently been shown to be of dietary origin (50) suggests the need for considerably more caution than has usually been employed in drawing conclusions with regard to this variable. Another point which has not been emphasized sufficiently is that chromatographic procedures which make possible the simultaneous determination of scores of substances, many of them unknown, require statistical analyses somewhat different from those which were developed for the testing of single, well-defined hypotheses. It is merely a restatement of statistical theory to point out that in a determination of 100 different compounds carried out simultaneously in two samples of the *same* population, five would be expected to show a difference significant at the 0.05 level! It is interesting to note that a more recent study was able to demonstrate considerably fewer differences between the urines of normal and schizophrenic populations and drew very limited and guarded conclusions

(51). In our own laboratory, Mann and Labrosse (24) undertook a search for urinary phenolic acids, in terms of quantity excreted in a standard time interval rather than in terms of concentration, which disclosed significantly higher levels of four compounds in the urine of schizophrenics than in that of the normal test subjects. These compounds were found to be known metabolites of substances in coffee, and their presence in the urine was, in fact, better correlated with the ingestion of this beverage than with schizophrenia.

The hypothesis that a disordered amino acid metabolism is a fundamental component of some forms of schizophrenia remains an attractive though fairly general one, chromatography as a means of searching for supporting evidence is convenient and valuable, and preliminary indications of differences are certainly provocative. Proof that any of these differences are characteristic of even a segment of the disease rather than artifactual or incidental has not yet been obtained.

THE EPINEPHRINE HYPOTHESIS

The theory which relates the pathogenesis of schizophrenia to faulty metabolism of epinephrine (52-54) is imaginative, ingenious, and plausible. It postulates that the symptoms of this disease are caused by the action of abnormal, hallucinogenic derivatives of epinephrine, presumably adrenochrome or adrenolutin. By including the concept of an enzymatic, possibly genetic, defect with another factor, epinephrine release, which may be activated by stressful life situations (22), it encompasses the evidence for sociological as well as constitutional factors in the etiology of the schizophrenias.

The possibility that some of the oxidation products of epinephrine are psychotomimetic received support from anecdotal reports of psychological disturbances associated with the therapeutic use of the compound, especially when it was discolored (52), and from some early experiments in which the administration of adrenochrome or adrenolutin in appreciable dosage was followed by certain unusual mental manifestations (54). A number of investigators failed to demonstrate any hallucinogenic properties in adrenochrome (55), and the original authors were not always able to confirm their earlier results.

Meanwhile, reports were emerging from the group at Tulane University, suggesting a gross disturbance in epinephrine metabolism in schizophrenic patients. Five years previously, Holmberg and Laurell (56) had demonstrated a more rapid oxidation of epinephrine in vitro in the presence of pregnancy serum than with serum from the umbilical cord and had suggested that this was due to higher concentrations of ceruloplasmin in the former. There had also been a few reports of an increase in levels of this protein in the blood of schizophrenics. Leach and Heath (57) reported a striking acceleration in the in vitro oxidation of epinephrine in the presence of plasma from schizophrenic patients as compared with that from normal subjects and shortly thereafter implicated ceruloplasmin or some variant of ceruloplasmin as the oxidizing substance (58). Hoffer and Kenyon (59) promptly reported evidence that the substance formed from epinephrine by blood serum in vitro was adrenolutin and pointed out how this strengthened the epinephrine hypothesis.

All of the evidence does not, however, support the epinephrine theory. In the past few years the major metabolites of epinephrine have been identified: 3-methoxy-4-hydroxymandelic acid, by Armstrong and his associates (60), and its precursor, metanephrine, by Axelrod and his coworkers of this laboratory (61), where, in addition, the principal pathways of epinephrine metabolism in animals (62) and man (63) have been demonstrated. The metabolites of C^{14}-labeled epinephrine in the urine of schizophrenic patients (64) and in normal man (65) have been studied independently by others. No evidence has been found for the oxidation of epinephrine via adrenochrome and adrenolutin in any of these populations. Although it has been reported that there are appreciable amounts of adrenochrome in the blood of normal subjects and that these amounts increase considerably following administration of lysergic acid diethylamide (66), Szara, Axelrod, and Perlin, using techniques of high sensitivity, have been unable to detect adrenochrome in the blood of normal test subjects or in that of acute or chronic schizophrenic patients (22). In a recent ingenious study of the rate of destruction of epinephrine in vivo, no difference between normal subjects and schizophrenic patients was found in this regard (67). Finally, it has been shown, by McDonald (9) in our laboratory and by members of the Tulane group themselves (16), that the low level of ascorbic acid in the blood is an important and uncontrolled variable in the rapid in vitro oxidation of epinephrine by plasma from schizophrenic patients. The fact that McDonald has been able to produce wide fluctuations in the epinephrine oxidation phenomenon, from normal to highly abnormal rates, in both normal subjects and schizophrenics merely by altering the level of ascorbic acid in the blood by dietary means, and that this has had no effect on the mental processes of either group, is quite convincing evidence of the dietary and secondary nature of the phenomenon.

It should be pointed out that none of this negative evidence invalidates the theory that some abnormal product of epinephrine metabolism, existing somewhere in the body, produces the major symptoms of schizophrenia; it does, however, considerably weaken the evidence which has been used to support the theory. In addition, there is the bothersome observation of numerous workers (68) that the administration of epinephrine to schizophrenics, which, according to the theory, should aggravate the psychotic symptoms, is not accompanied by appreciably greater mental disturbance than occurs in normal subjects.

Quite recently a new report on inconstant psychotomimetic effects of epinephrine oxidation products in a small number of subjects has appeared (69), with evidence suggesting that the psychotoxic substance is neither adrenochrome nor adrenolutin, that it is active in microgram quantities, and that it is highly labile. This report, like the previous ones which described the psychotomimetic effects of epinephrine products, is highly subjective and incompletely controlled. Even if these conclusions are accepted, the relevance of such hallucinogens to, or their presence in, schizophrenia remains to be demonstrated.

References

1. Thudichum, J. W. L. A Treatise on the Chemical Constitution of the Brain (Balliere, Tindall, and Cox, London, 1884).
2. Peters, G. 'Dementia praecox,' in Handbuch der Speziellen Pathologischen Anatomie und Histologie, Lubarsch, Henke, and Rossle, Eds. (Springer, Berlin, 1956), vol. 13, pt. 4, pp. 1-52; David, G. B. 'The pathological anatomy of the schizophrenias,' in Schizophrenia: Somatic Aspects (Pergamon, London, 1957), pp. 93-130; Dastur, D. K. A.M.A. Arch. Neurol, Psychiat., 81, 601 (1959).
3. McFarland, R. A., and Goldstein, H. Am. J. Psychiat., 95, 509 (1938).
4. Keup, W. Monatsschr. Psychiat. Neurol., 128, 56 (1954).
5. Richter, D. 'Biochemical aspects of schizophrenia,' in Schizophrenia: Somatic Aspects (Pergamon, London, 1957), pp. 53-75.
6. For the most recent review see Benjamin, J. D. Psychosom. Med., 20, 427 (1958).
7. Horwitt, M. K. Science, 124, 429 (1956).
8. Evarts, E. V. Psychiat. Research Repts., 9, 52 (1958).
9. McDonald, R. K. J. Chronic Diseases, 8, 366 (1958).
10. Perlin, S., and Lee, A. R. Am. J. Psychiat., in press.
11. Freedman, D. A. Diseases of Nervous System, 19, 108 (1958).
12. Vestergaard, P., Abbott, M. T., Kline, N. S., Stanley, A. M. J. Clin. Exptl. Psychopathol., 19, 44 (1958).
13. Kelsey, F. O., Gullock, A. H., Kelsey, F. E. A.M.A. Arch. Neurol. Psychiat., 77, 543 (1957).
14. McDonald, R. K. 'Plasma ceruloplasmin and ascorbic acid levels in schizophrenia,' paper presented at the annual meeting of the American Psychiatric Association, Chicago, Ill., 1957.

15. Aprison, M. H., and Grosz, H. J. *A.M.A. Arch. Neurol. Psychiat.*, *79*, 575 (1958).

16. Angel, C., Leach, B. E., Martens, S., Cohen, M., Heath, R. G. *ibid.*, *78*, 500 (1957).

17. Horwitt, M. K. 'Report of Elgin Project No. 3 with Emphasis on Liver Dysfunction,' *Nutrition Symposium Ser. No. 7* (National Vitamin Foundation, New York, 1953), pp. 67-83.

18. Fischer, R., Georgi, F., Weber, R., Piaget, R. M. *Schweiz. med. Wochschr.*, *80*, 129 (1950).

19. Board, F., Persky, H., Hamburg, D. A. *Psychosom. Med.*, *18*, 324 (1956).

20. Elmadjian, R., Hope, J. M., Lamson, E. T. *J. Clin. Endocrinol. and Metabolism*, *17*, 608 (1957).

21. Schottstaedt, W. W., Grace, W. J., Wolff, H. G. *J. Psychosom. Research*, *1*, 147 (1956); *ibid.* *1*, 292 (1956).

22. Szara, S., Axelrod, J., Perlin, S. *Am. J. Psychiat.*, *115*, 162 (1958).

23. Kopin, I. J. *Science*, *129*, 835 (1959); Kornetsky, C. personal communication.

24. Mann, J. D., and Labrosse, E. H. *A.M.A. Arch. Genl. Psychiat.*, in press.

25. Doust, J. W. Lovett. *J. Mental Sci.*, *98*, 143 (1952).

26. Kety, S. S., Woodford, R. B., Harmel, M. H., Freyhan, F. A., Appel, K. E., Schmidt, C. F. *Am. J. Psychiat.*, *104*, 765 (1948).

27. Wilson, W. P., Schieve, J. F., Scheinberg, P. *A.M.A. Arch. Neurol. Psychiat.*, *68*, 651 (1952).

28. Sokoloff, L., Perlin, S., Kornetsky, C., Kety, S. S. *Ann. N.Y. Acad. Sci.*, *66*, 468 (1957).

29. Gordan, G. S., Estess, F. M., Adams, J. E., Bowman, K. M., Simon, A. *A.M.A. Arch. Neurol. Psychiat.*, *73*, 544 (1955).

30. Longo, V., Buscaino, G. A., D'Andrea, F., Uras, A., Ferrari, E., Rinaldi, F., Pasolini, F. *Acta Neurol. (Naples)*, Quad. III, 21 (1953).

31. Altschule, M. D., Henneman, D. H., Holliday, P., Goncz, R. M. *A.M.A. Arch. Internal Med.*, *98*, 35 (1956).

32. Horwitt, M. K., Liebert, E., Kreisler, O., Wittman, P. *Bull. Natl. Research Council (U.S.) No. 116* (1948).

33. Meduna, L. J., Gerty, F. J., Urse, V. G. *A.M.A. Arch. Neurol. Psychiat.*, *47*, 38 (1942).

34. Moya, F., Dewar, J., MacIntosh, M., Hirsch, S., Townsend, R. *Can. J. Biochem. and Psysiol.*, *36*, 505 (1958).

35. Moya, F., Szerb, J. C., MacIntosh, M., *ibid.* *34*, 563 (1956).

36. Morgan, M. S., and Pilgrim, F. J. *Proc. Soc. Exptl. Biol. Med.*, *79*, 106 (1952).

37. Harris, M. M. *A.M.A. Arch. Neurol. Psychiat.*, *48*, 761 (1942).

38. Boszormenyi-Nagy, I., Gerty, F. J., Kueber, J. J. *Nervous Mental Disease*, *124*, 413 (1956); Boszormenyi-Nagy, I., and Gerty, F. J., *ibid.*, *121*, 53 (1955).

39. Altschule, M. D., Henneman, D. H., Holliday, P. D., Goncz, R. M. *A.M.A. Arch. Internal Med.*, *99*, 22 (1957); Surikov, M. P., Ushakov, G. K., Il'ina, B. N., Verbliunskaia, A. A., Khokhlov, L. K. *Zhur. Nevropatol.*, *57*, 237 (1957).

40. Martens, S., Leach, B. E., Heath, R. G., Cohen, M. *A.M.A. Arch. Neurol. Psychiat.* *76*, 630 (1956).

41. Barak, A. J., Humoller, F. L., Stevens, J. D., *ibid.*, *80*, 237 (1958).

42. Gjessing, R. *J. Mental Sci.*, *84*, 608 (1938); ——, *Arch. Psychiat. Nervenkrankh.*, *108*, 525 (1939); Gjessing, L., Bernhardsen, A., Frøshaug, H. *J. Mental Sci.*, *104*, 188 (1958).

43. Buscaino, V. M. *Acta Neurol. (Naples)*, *13*, 1 (1958).

44. Young, H. K., Berry, H. K., Beerstecher, E. *Univ. Texas Publ. No. 5109* (1951), pp. 189-197.

45. McGeer, P. L., McNair, F. E., McGeer, E. G., Gibson, W. C. *J. Nervous Mental Disease*, *125*, 166 (1957).

46. McGeer, E. G., Brown, W. T., McGeer, P. L., *ibid.*, *125*, 176 (1957).

47. Georgi, F., Honegger, C. G., Jordan, D., Rieder, H. P., Rottenberg, M. *Klin. Wochschr.*, *34*, 799 (1956).

48. Riegelhaupt, L. M. *J. Nervous Mental Disease*, *123*, 383 (1956).

49. Cafruny, E. J., and Domino, E. F. *A.M.A. Arch. Neurol. Psychiat.*, *79*, 336 (1958).

50. Armstrong, M. D., and Shaw, K. N. F. *J. Biol. Chem.*, *225*, 260 (1956); ——, Gortatowski, M. J., Singer, H., *ibid.*, *232*, 17 (1958); Armstrong, M. D., Wall, P. E., Parker, V. J., *ibid.*, *218*, 921 (1956); Booth, A. N., Emerson, O. H., Jones, F. T., Deeds, F., *ibid.*, *229*, 51 (1957); Waalkes, T. P., Sjoerdsma, A., Creveling, C. R., Weissbach, H., Undenfriend, S. *Science*, *127*, 648 (1958).

51. Acheson, R. M., Paul, R. M., Tomlinson, R. V. *Can. J. Biochem. Physiol.*, *36*, 295 (1958).

52. Osmond, H. *Diseases of Nervous System*, *16*, 101 (1955).

53. ——and Smythies, J. *J. Mental Sci.*, *98*, 309 (1952); Hoffer, A. *J. Clin. Exptl. Psychopathol.*, *18*, 27 (1957).

54. Hoffer, A., Osmond, H., Smythies, J. *J. Mental Sci.*, *100*, 29 (1954).

55. Rinkel, M., and Solomon, H. C. *J. Clin. Exptl. Psychopathol.*, *18*, 323 (1957).

56. Holmberg, C. G., and Laurell, C. B. *Scand. J. Clin. & Lab. Invest.*, *3*, 103 (1951).

57. Leach, B. E., and Heath, R. G. *A.M.A. Arch. Neurol. Psychiat.*, *76*, 444 (1956).

58. Leach, B. E., Cohen, M., Heath, R. G., Martens, S., *ibid.*, *76*, 635 (1956).

59. Hoffer, A., and Kenyon, M., *ibid.*, *77*, 437 (1957).

60. Armstrong, M. D., McMillan, A., Shaw, K. N. F. *Biochem. et. Biophys. Acta*, *25*, 422 (1957).

61. Axelrod, J., and Tomchick, R. *J. Biol. Chem.*, *233*, 702 (1958).

62. Axelrod, J., Senoh, S., Witkop, B., *ibid.*, *233*, 697 (1958).
63. Labrosse, E. H., Axelrod, J., Kety, S. S. *Science, 128*, 593 (1958).
64. Resnick, O., Wolfe, J. M., Freeman, H., Elmadjian, F., *ibid., 127*, 1116 (1958).
65. Kirshner, N., Goodall, McC., Rosen L. *Proc. Soc. Exptl. Biol. Med., 98*, 627 (1958).
66. Hoffer, A., *Am. J. Psychiat., 114*, 752 (1958).
67. Holland, B., Cohen, G., Goldenberg, M.,

Sha, J., Leifer, L. *Federation Proc., 17*, 378 (1958).
68. Lindemann, E. *Am. J. Psychiat., 91*, 983 (1935); Heath, R. G., Leach, B. E., Byers, L. W., Martens, S., Feigley, C. A., *ibid., 114*, 683 (1958); Dynes, J. B., and Tod, H. *J. Neurol. Psychiat., 3*, 1 (1940); and workers in this laboratory.
69. Taubmann, G., and Jantz, H. *Nervenarzt, 28*, 485 (1957).

Part B

In Part A of this article, an attempt was made to discuss the possible sources of error peculiar to biological research in schizophrenia, including the possible heterogeneity of that symptom complex and the presence of certain biological features—such as adventitious disease, nutritional deficiencies, disturbances associated with abnormal motor or emotional states, and changes brought about by treatment, all of which may be said to result from the disease or from its current management rather than to be factors in its genesis. The difficulty of avoiding subjective bias was emphasized. Some of the hypotheses relating to oxygen, carbohydrate, and energy metabolism, to amino acid metabolism, and to epinephrine were presented, and the existing evidence relevant to them was discussed. Among the recent or current concepts there remain to be discussed those concerned with ceruloplasmin, with serotonin, and with the general genetic aspects of schizophrenic disorders.

CERULOPLASMIN AND TARAXEIN

The rise and fall of interest in ceruloplasmin as a biochemical factor significantly related to schizophrenia is one of the briefest, if not one of the most enlightening, chapters in the history of biological psychiatry. The upsurge of interest can be ascribed to a report that a young Swedish biochemist had discovered a new test for schizophrenia. The test depended upon the oxidation of N,N-dimethyl-p-phenylenediamine by ceruloplasmin (1, 2). It is difficult to understand the exaggerated interest which this report aroused, since Holmberg and Laurell (3) had demonstrated previously that ceruloplasmin was capable of oxidizing a number of substances, including phenylenediamine and epinephrine, and Leach and Heath (4) had already published a procedure based on epinephrine oxidation which was equally valid as a means of distinguishing schizophrenics from normal subjects and had identified the oxidizing substance as ceruloplasmin (5). All of these observations were compatible with earlier reports in the German literature (6) of an increase in serum copper in schizophrenia and with the demonstration that practically all of the serum copper was in the form of ceruloplasmin and that the levels of this compound in blood were elevated during pregnancy and in a large number of diseases (7, 8). There had even been preliminary observations of an increase in blood ceruloplasmin in schizophrenia (8). Following the announcement of the Akerfeldt test, however, interest in copper and ceruloplasmin rose, and very soon a number of investigators reported this reaction, or some modification of it, to be positive in a high percentage of schizophrenics (2, 9), although as a diagnostic test the Akerfeldt procedure was discredited because of the large number of diseases, besides schizophrenia, in which the results were positive. Both Akerfeldt and Heath recognized that ascorbic acid could inhibit the oxidation of phenylenediamine and of epinephrine, respectively, but neither felt that this was crucial to his findings, since each had satisfied himself that the feeding of large doses of ascorbic acid to the patients had not influenced the respective reactions (2). In addition, Abood (9), who used a modification of the Akerfeldt procedure which was not affected by ascorbic acid, was able to obtain a positive reaction indicating abnormally high ceruloplasmin levels in two-thirds of the more than 250 schizophrenics he had examined.

In the past 18 months there has been a remarkable decline in the interest in, and the reported levels of, ceruloplasmin in schizophrenia. In May of 1957, McDonald (10) reported his findings on three groups of schizophrenics, one group from the wards of the National Institute of Mental Health, where the patients had been maintained on a more than adequate diet, and two groups from state hospitals. He performed the Akerfeldt test and the Abood modification of it, as well as independent tests to measure ascorbic acid and copper, on these groups and on three groups of controls. In none of the schizophrenic groups was there an increase in serum copper or other evidence of increase in ceruloplasmin. In the state-hospital patients and one group of controls, however, ascorbic acid levels were low and the results of Akerfeldt tests were positive, whereas in schizophrenic patients from the National Institute of Mental Health, levels of ascorbic acid were normal and the results of Akerfeldt tests were negative. It was clear that a high ceruloplasmin level was not characteristic of schizophrenia and that a positive response to the Akerfeldt test, where it occurred, could be completely explained by a dietary insufficiency of ascorbic acid.

In findings of the Tulane group, the mean values for serum copper in schizophrenia have decreased from a high of 216 micrograms per 100 milliliters in 1956 (5) to 145 micrograms per 100 milliliters at the end of 1957 (4), mean normal values having remained at 122 and 124 micrograms per 100 milliliters during the same period. Other groups have found slight differences or no differences at all with respect to blood levels of ceruloplasmin or copper between schizophrenic and normal subjects (11) and no support for the theory that the Akerfeldt test is a means of distinguishing between schizophrenic and nonschizophrenic patients (12). It is not clear why some schizophrenics apparently show an elevated level of ceruloplasmin in the blood; among suggested explanations are dietary factors, hepatic damage, chronic infection, or the possibility that excitement tends to raise the level of ceruloplasmin in the blood, as preliminary experiments appear to indicate (13).

Quite early in their studies, members of the Tulane group recognized that the potent oxidant effects of the serum of schizophrenics on epinephrine in vitro could not be satisfactorily explained by the ceruloplasmin levels alone (5). Before they recognized the importance to this reaction of ascorbic acid deficiency (14), they had postulated the presence in the blood of schizophrenics of a qualitatively different form of ceruloplasmin (5), which they proceeded to isolate and to test in monkey and man, and to which they have given the name taraxein (from the Greek root tarassein, meaning 'to disturb'). They have reported that when certain batches of this material were tested in monkeys, marked behavioral and electroencephalographic changes occurred. When samples of these active batches were injected intravenously at a rapid rate into carefully selected prisoner volunteers, all of the subjects developed symptoms which have been described as characteristic of schizophrenia—disorganization and fragmentation of thought, autism, feelings of depersonalization, paranoid ideas, auditory hallucinations, and catatonic behavior (15-17).

Demonstration of toxic materials in the blood and in the body fluids of schizophrenic patients is not new. The voluminous and inconclusive work of earlier investigators was well reviewed by Keup in 1954 (6). Since that time, many new reports have appeared, although there has been no extensive substantiation of any of them. The results of one, on the toxicity of serum and urine of schizophrenic patients for the larvae of *Xenopus laevis* (18), were disputed by the laboratory in which the work was done (19). Edisen (20) was unable to demonstrate toxicity of such serum for the species of tadpole previously used, or for other species and other genera. A report that serum from schizophrenic patients is toxic to cells in tissue culture (21) lost some of its significance when 1 year later the same laboratory reported that the sera of surgical patients (22) was of comparable toxicity. Reports that injection of certain extracts of the urine of schizophrenic patients induces electroencephalographic and behavioral changes in rats (23) or disturbances in web construction in spiders (24) have not yet received confirmation in the scientific literature. Such urine, however, has been reported to have no effect on the Siamese fighting fish, which is remarkably sensitive to certain hallucinogens (25). Contrary to earlier findings, a recent attempt to demonstrate behavioral changes in rats following the injection of cerebrospinal fluid from catatonic patients was unsuccessful (26). A highly significant decrease in rope-climbing speed in rats injected with sera from psychotic patients as opposed to sera from nonpsychotic controls has been reported by Winter and Flataker (27). Their later finding (28) that the phenomenon occurs with sera of patients with a wide variety of mental disorders, including mental retardation and alcoholism, and that

there is a considerable variation in this index between similar groups at different hospitals, coupled with the inability of at least one other investigator (29) to demonstrate this phenomenon in the small group of schizophrenic patients under investigation in this laboratory, suggests that the quite real and statistically significant phenomenon originally observed may be related to variables other than those specific for, or fundamental to, schizophrenia. More recently, Ghent and Freedman (29) have reported their inability to confirm the observations of Winter and Flataker.

It has been reported that rabbits pretreated with serum from schizophrenics do not exhibit a pressor response following the local application of an epinephrine solution to the cerebral cortex (30). No difference between the action of sera from normal subjects and that from schizophrenics was demonstrated by means of this procedure in tests of sera from a small number of individuals on our wards.

The significance of all of these studies in animals, whether the studies are successful or unsuccessful in demonstrating a toxic factor in schizophrenia, is quite irrelevant to, and considerably dwarfed by, the implications of the taraxein studies. It is because of the tremendous implications which these results could have in the etiology and rational therapy of this important disorder that a reviewer must evaluate them with even more than the usual care.

In the first place, the important biochemical phenomena originally reported in schizophrenia—lowered blood levels of glutathione and rapid oxidation of epinephrine in vitro—which prompted the search for taraxein and directed work on its isolation toward the ceruloplasmin fraction of serum (15, 16, 17) have since been controverted by data reported by the same group, as well as by others and have been regarded by most workers as spurious or at least unrelated in any direct way to the schizophrenic process (14, 31). This, in itself, does not preclude the possible validity of the taraxein phenomenon, since bona fide discoveries have occasionally been made on the basis of erroneous leads; it does, however, reduce the probability of its occurrence from that involved in a logical interrelationship of sequential proven steps to the extremely small chance of selecting this particular and heretofore unknown substance from the thousands of substances which occur in blood and which might have been chosen.

One attempt by Robins, Smith, and Lowe (32) to confirm the Tulane findings, in tests in which they used comparable numbers and types of subjects and at least equally rigorous controls, was quite unsuccessful. In 20 subjects who at different times received saline or extracts of blood from normal or schizophrenic donors, prepared according to the method for preparing taraxein, there were only five instances of mental or behavioral disturbance resembling those cited in the original report on taraxein, and these occurred with equal frequency following the administration of saline, extracts of normal plasma, or taraxein. It is easy to dismiss the negative findings with taraxein on the basis of the difficulty of reproducing exactly the 29 steps described in its preparation; it is considerably more difficult to dismiss the observation that a few subjects who received only saline or normal blood extract developed psychotic manifestations similar to those reported with taraxein.

During the preliminary investigations it was stated, on the basis of unpublished studies (5), that taraxein was qualitatively different from ceruloplasmin. A physicochemical or other objective characterization of taraxein would do much to dispel some of the confusion regarding its nature. It is possible, for example, that taraxein, is in fact, ceruloplasmin but ceruloplasmin that derives its special properties from the psychosocial characteristics of the situation in which it has been tested? This question was raised more than a year ago (33), and since then additional evidence has become available which tends to support it. This is a detailed report from a psychoanalyst at Tulane of the experience of one of his patients who received taraxein (34). Even though a 'double blind' procedure was said to have been used, there are enough possibilities for the operation of unconscious bias in this one case, if it is at all typical of the means used to demonstrate the psychotomimetic properties of taraxein, to raise some doubts concerning the validity of these properties. The subject, a psychiatric resident, knew before the injection that he was to get either saline or a potent sample of taraxein which had made a monkey catatonic for several hours. Immediately following the injection he noted venous distension, tachycardia, a swollen feeling of the head, and flushing of the head and face, which, a footnote explains, was probably a reaction to the ammonium sulfate in the taraxein solution. Following these symptoms, which the subject could hardly have attributed to saline, there ensued a period of introspective cogitation, with occasional mild mental disturbances quite compatible with the anxiety-producing nature of the situation, with the preparation and cues which the subject had received, and with his anticipation of marked psychotic reactions and not necessarily symptomatic of a chemical toxin at all. The changes were not qualitatively dissimilar to those which Robins and his associates had on a few occasions obtained with their control solutions (32). The report of the observer who injected the material was longer and mentioned more numerous and more bizarre subjective feelings than the subject himself reported. The observer's summary of the subject's reactions as blocking of thought processes, autism, bodily estrangement, and suspiciousness seems incompletely supported by the subject's retrospective report.

The possibility, remote as it may be, that the reported effects of taraxein are the result of a combination of suggestion, nonspecific toxic reactions from ammonium sulfate or other contaminants, and reinforcement of these cues by the unconscious biases of subject and observer through the device of an unstructured interview, is one which has not been ruled out. Hypotheses related to the mechanism of action of this material have moved from concern with abnormalities in the blood to concern with abnormalities in the blood-brain barrier; but the question of whether taraxein acts as a biological cause or as a mediator of some of the symptoms of schizophrenia is by no means resolved. I have already mentioned the only attempt of which I am aware on the part of an independent group to confirm the original results in a controlled series of significant size, and that attempt was unsuccessful.

SEROTONIN

Serotonin, an important derivative of tryptophan, was first shown to exist in the brain in high concentration by Amin, Crawford, and Gaddum (35). Interest in its possible function in the central nervous system and speculation that it might even be related to schizophrenia were inspired by the finding that certain hallucinogens, notably lysergic acid diethylamide, could, in extremely low concentration, block the effects of serotonin on smooth muscle. Thus, Woolley and Shaw in 1954 (36) wrote: 'The demonstrated ability of such agents to antagonize the action of serotonin in smooth muscle and the finding of serotonin in the brain suggest that the mental changes caused by the drugs are the result of a serotonin-deficiency which they induce in the brain. If this be true, then the naturally occurring mental disorders—for example, schizophrenia—which are mimicked by these drugs, may be pictured as being the result of a cerebral serotonin deficiency arising from a metabolic failure. . . .' Simultaneously, in England, Gaddum (37) was speculating, 'it is possible that the HT in our brains plays an essential part in keeping us sane and that the effect of LSD is due

to its inhibitory action on the HT in the brain.' Since that time additional evidence has appeared to strengthen these hypotheses.

Levels of serotonin have been found to be considerably higher in the limbic system and other areas of the brain which appear to be associated with emotional states (38) than elsewhere. Bufotenin, or dimethyl serotonin, extracted from a hallucinogenic snuff of West Indian tribes, was found to have some properties similar to those of lysergic acid diethylamide (39). A major discovery was the finding that the ataractic agent, reserpine, causes a profound and persistent fall in the level of serotonin in the brain (40), a process which more closely parallels the mental effects of reserpine than does its own concentration in the brain. By administration of the precursor, 5-hydroxytryptophan, the levels of serotonin can be markedly elevated in the brain, with behavioral effects described as resembling those of lysergic acid diethylamide (41)—a finding quite at odds with the original hypotheses. On the other hand, administration of this precursor to mental patients, along with a benzyl analog of serotonin to block the peripheral effects of the amine, has been reported, in preliminary trials, to suppress the disease (42), while confusion is compounded by the report that the benzyl analog alone is an effective tranquilizing drug in chronically psychotic patients (43).

Still another bit of evidence supporting the hypotheses of a central function for serotonin was the accidental discovery of toxic psychoses in a certain fraction of tuberculous patients treated with iproniazid (44, 45), which has led to the therapeutic use of this drug in psychic depression. It is known that iproniazid inhibits the action of monoamine oxidase, an enzyme which destroys serotonin, and it has been shown that iproniazid increases the levels of this amine in the brain (41).

There are certain inconsistencies in the data cited above to support the serotonin hypotheses, and no single theory has been found to explain all of the findings, even though full use is made of the concept of 'free' and 'bound' forms and of the common pharmacological principle of stimulant and depressant effects from the same drug under different circumstances. Moreover, certain weaknesses have appeared in each of the main supporting hypotheses, and these should be noted.

Although the ability of the hallucinogen lysergic acid diethylamide to block effects of serotonin on smooth muscle prompted the development of the hypotheses relating serotonin to mental function or disease, a number of lysergic acid derivatives have since been studied, and the correlation between mental effects and antiserotonin activity in the series as a whole is quite poor (46). One of these compounds is 2-bromolysergic acid diethylamide; this has 1.5 times the antiserotonin activity of lysergic acid diethylamide, and through this property, its presence in the brain, after systemic administration, can be demonstrated, but in doses more than 15 times as great it produces none of the mental effects of lysergic acid diethylamide (46). A recent report that, at least in one preparation, lysergic acid diethylamide in low concentration behaves like serotonin and does not antagonize it (47) seems to reconcile some of the empirical inconsistencies in the field, although it is quite at odds with the original hypotheses based on the antagonistic action of lysergic acid diethylamide.

Levels of norepinephrine as well as serotonin are markedly lowered in the brain following administration of reserpine (48). In fact, the brain concentrations of these two amines follow each other so closely in their response to reserpine as to suggest some mechanism common to both and perhaps obtaining as well for other active amines in the brain. In one study, 3,4-dihydroxyphenylalanine, a precursor of norephinephrine, was capable of counteracting the behavioral effects of reserpine, whereas the precursor of serotonin was ineffective (49). More-

over, the effects of iproniazid are not limited to brain serotonin; a comparable effect on norepinephrine has been reported (50), and it is possible that other amines or substances still to be discovered in the brain may be affected by what may be a nonspecific inhibitor of a relatively nonspecific enzyme. Of great interest in this connection are recent studies of Olds and Olds (51) indicating a positive behavioral response for iproniazid injected into the hypothalamus but not for serotonin or norepinephrine.

Chlorpromazine, which has the same therapeutic efficacy as reserpine in disturbed behavior, is apparently able to achieve this action without any known effect on serotonin. In addition, the provocative observation that iproniazid, which elevates serotonin levels in the brain, can cause a toxic psychosis loses some of its impact when one realizes that isoniazid, which does not inhibit monoamine oxidase and can hardly raise the brain serotonin concentration, produces a similar psychosis (45, 52).

It seems reasonable to conclude that the serotonin as well as the norepinephrine in the brain have some important functions there, and the evidence in general supports this thesis, even though it also suggests that their roles still remain to be defined.

If the picture of the role which serotonin plays in central nervous function is blurred, the direct evidence to support the early speculations that it is involved in mental illness is meager and contradictory. From all of the evidence cited above, one could find a basis for predicting that in schizophrenia the serotonin levels in the brain, if they are altered at all, should be quite low or quite high. Results confirming both predictions have been reported.

The urinary excretion of 5-hydroxyindoleacetic acid has been used as an indicator of the portion of ingested tryptophan which is metabolized through serotonin to form that end product. Although excretion of 5-hydroxyindoleacetic acid is normal in schizophrenic patients under ordinary circumstances (53), it may be altered by challenging the metabolic systems with large doses of tryptophan. Zeller and his associates have reported a failure on the part of schizophrenics, under these circumstances, to increase their output of 5-hydroxyindoleacetic acid, while nonpsychotic controls double theirs (54). Banerjee and Agarwal, on the other hand, have reported exactly the opposite results; in their study it was the schizophrenics who doubled their output of the serotonin end product while the output of the controls remained unchanged (55).

Kopin, of our laboratory, has had the opportunity to perform a similar study on schizophrenics and normal controls maintained on a good and reasonably controlled diet and given no drugs. In each group there was a slightly greater than twofold increase in output of 5-hydroxyindoleacetic acid following a tryptophan load, and there was no significant deviation from this pattern in any single case (56).

That the heuristic speculations of Woolley and Shaw, and of Gaddum, have not yet been established does not mean that they are invalid. The widespread experimental activity which they stimulated has broadened and deepened our knowledge of the metabolism and pharmacology of serotonin and of its effects on behavior and may lead the way to definitive evaluation of its possible role in normal and pathological states.

GENETICS AND SCHIZOPHRENIC DISORDERS

Many of the current hypotheses concerning the schizophrenia complex are original and attractive even though, up to this time, evidence directly implicating any one of them in the disease itself is hardly compelling. There is, nevertheless, cogent evidence that is responsible to a large extent for the present reawakening of the long dormant biochemical thinking in this area and sufficiently convincing to promote its continued development.

Genetic studies have recently assumed such a role, and it appears worth while briefly to review them in the present context.

In earlier studies on large populations, a remarkable correlation was reported between the incidence of schizophrenia and the degree of consanguinity in relatives of known schizophrenics (57). These findings were not conclusive, however, since the influence of socioenvironmental factors was not controlled. Better evidence is obtained from the examination of the co-twins and siblings of schizophrenics; a number of such studies have been completed and are summarized in Table 1 (57-59). The concordance rate for schizophrenia is extremely high for monozygotic twins in all the studies, while that for dizygotic twins is low and not significantly different from that in siblings, to which, of course, dizygotic twins are quite comparable genetically. Even these studies, however, are not completely free from possible sources of error, and this makes it difficult to arrive at a definitive conclusion regarding the role of genetic factors in this disease. One cannot assume that environmental similarities and mutual interactions in identical twins, who are always of the same sex and whose striking physical congruence is often accentuated by parental attitudes, play an insignificant role in the high concordance rate of schizophrenia in this group. This factor could be controlled by a study of twins separated at birth (of such twins no statistically valid series has yet been compiled) or by a comparison of the concordance rates in monozygotic twins and in dizygotic twins whose zygosity had been mistakenly evaluated by the twins themselves and by their parents and associates. Another possible means of better controlling the environmental variables would be to make a careful study of schizophrenia in adopted children, with comparison of the incidence in blood relatives and in foster relatives. Perhaps only a survey on a national scale would provide the requisite numbers of cases for any of these studies.

A less satisfactory resolution of this problem can be obtained by an appraisal of environmental similarities in normal fraternal and identical twins. Such a study, on over 100 specific aspects of the environment, has been made (60), and I have assembled the results into a rough index of environmental similarity (Table 2). Although a difference is apparent, in the crude measurement of environmental congruence, between identical and fraternal twins of like sex, it is not statistically significant and can account for only a small fraction of the large difference in concordance with respect to schizophrenia between these types of twins. On the other hand, there is a highly significant difference in environmental similarity between fraternal twins of like and unlike sex which is sufficient to account for the difference in concordance with respect to schizophrenic psychosis between them, for which, of course, there is no tenable genetic explanation.

Two recent reports have been used, but by no means conclusively, in support of the position that too much significance has been attached to environmental factors as determining causes in this disease group. Chapman (61), reporting a case of concordant early infantile autism in identical twins, points out that this disorder has never been reported as concordant in fraternal twins, whereas it has been described in three sets of identical twins. Since fraternal twins occur nearly three times as frequently as identical twins, the evidence cited is suggestive, in spite of the small numbers involved; furthermore, the disease may develop before the personal identifications and interactions peculiar to monozygotic twins have had much chance to operate. Another interesting finding in over 150 families with a single schizophrenic member is that no ordinal position in the family appears to carry specific vulnerability to schizophrenia (62)—a finding completely compatible with genetic theory but more difficult to reconcile with theories of environmental etiology if the assumption is correct that different positions within the family are subject to varying degrees of stress. Of course one may argue quite properly that schizophrenogenic stress exists and can be evaluated only in terms of the reaction between each individual and his own environment, so that any position on a social, economic, occupational, or birth-order scale may be associated with greatly different degrees of stress for different individuals.

Another possible source of error in the twin studies which have been reported is the personal bias of the investigators who made the judgment of zygosity and the diagnosis of schizophrenia in the co-twins. Until a more definitive study is carried out in which these judgments are made independently, a rough evaluation is possible, at least for the diagnosis of schizophrenia, if not for zygosity, on the basis of diagnoses arrived at in the various hospitals to which the co-twins may have been admitted before or irrespective of their involvement in the study—diagnoses which are not likely to have been contaminated by knowledge about their zygosity. Kallmann has been kind enough to review the material collected in his 1946-49 survey from that point of view. Of 174 monozygotic co-twins of schizophrenic index cases, 103, or 59 percent, had been diagnosed schizophrenic by Kallmann, while 87, or 50 percent, had received a psychiatric hospital diagnosis of schizophrenia prior to any examination made by him. On the other hand, he had made the diagnosis of schizophrenia in 47, or 9.1 percent, of 517 dizygotic co-twins as compared to a hospital diagnosis in 31, or 6 percent. Although the concordance rates based only on hospital diagnoses are lower in both types of twins, for obvious reasons, the striking difference between the two concordance rates remains. Slater (59) has published individual protocols of his cases from which I have made judgments of zygosity and schizophrenia. Of 21 pairs of twins who could be considered definitely uniovular, 15, or 75 percent, were concordant with respect to the simple criterion of admission to a mental hospital, whereas in only 12, or 10.3 percent, of 116 binovular or questionably binovular pairs was there a history of the co-twin's having been admitted to a mental hospital for any psychosis. On the basis of this analysis of the two most recent series, it seems that only a small component of the great difference in concordance rates reported for schizophrenia between uniovular and binovular twins can be attributed to the operation of personal bias in the diagnosis of the disease in the co-twin.

Even the most uncritical acceptance of all the genetic data, however, cannot lead to the conclusion that the schizophrenic illnesses are the result of genetic factors alone. In 14 to 30 percent of the cases in which schizophrenia occurs in one of a pair of monozygotic twins, the genetically identical partner is found to be free

of the disorder (Table 1). Attention has already been called (Table 2) to the higher concordance with respect to schizophrenia and the greater environmental similarities in like-sexed fraternal twins or siblings than in those of unlike sex, and from the same source (57) a difference in concordance is reported between monozygotic twins separated some years before the study (77.6 percent) as opposed to those not separated (91.5 percent). Neither of these observations is compatible with a purely genetic etiology of the disease, and both suggest the operation of environmental factors. Rosenthal (63) and Jackson (64) have pointed out the striking preponderance of female over male pairs concordant for schizophrenia in all of the reported series, whether they be monozygotic or dizygotic twins, siblings, or parent-child pairs. If sampling errors resulting from the greater mobility of males

Table 1. *Concordance rates for schizophrenia found in studies of twins.*

Investigator	Number of pairs		Concordance rate* (%)	
	Dizygotic	Monozygotic	Dizygotic	Monozygotic
Luxenburger (1928)	48	17	2	59 (67)
Rosanoff *et al.* (1934)	101	41	10	61
Kallmann (1946)	517	174	10 (15)	69 (86)
Slater (1953)	115	41	11 (14)	68 (76)

* Figures in parentheses indicate rate after correction for the chance that a co-twin, normal at the time of observation, may develop the disease later.

Table 2. *Environmental factors in studies of schizophrenia in twins.*

Sex	Environmental similarity in normal twins* (%)	Number of pairs	Concordance with respect to schizophrenia† (%)	Number of pairs
		Identical twins		
Same	61	70	86	174
		Fraternal twins		
Same	53	69	18	296
Different	26	55	10	221
		Siblings		
Same			16	
Different			12	

* Estimated from data of P. T. Wilson (1934).
† From data of F. J. Kallmann (1946).

are excluded and the observations are taken as a reflection of the true incidence of this phenomenon, several explanations for it on the basis of social interaction can be given, but none based on purely genetic grounds, unless sex linkage is invoked, for which there is no other evidence.

Clausen has critically reviewed the extensive literature supporting the importance of environmental factors in the etiology of schizophrenic disorders (65). The evidence there seems quite as suggestive as the genetic evidence but by no means more conclusive, since few studies in either field have been completely objective or adequately controlled.

It is both interesting and important to note that even if the conclusions of both the genetic and the environmental approaches to the etiology of schizophrenic psychoses are accepted uncritically, they are not mutually exclusive. Both are compatible with the hypothesis that this group of diseases results from the operation of socioenvironmental factors on some hereditary predisposition, or from an interaction of the two, each being necessary but neither alone sufficient. An excellent example of such a relationship is seen in tuberculosis, where the importance of the environmental microbial factor is undisputed and where, as Lurie (66) has shown, genetic susceptibility is likewise important; a population sufficiently heterogeneous with respect to susceptibility and exposure to tuberculosis yields results in contingency and twin studies (67) which, before the discovery of the tubercle bacillus, could easily have been used to prove a primary genetic cause—almost as convincingly as the results of similar studies have been used to prove such a cause in schizophrenia. Interestingly enough, studies of tuberculosis made from the socioenvironmental point of view would obviously provide data offering equally convincing proof that exogenous, social, and economic factors play a part. One hypothesis with respect to the schizophrenic psychoses which remains compatible with all the evidence from the genetic as well as the psychosocial disciplines is that these disorders, like tuberculosis, require the operation of environmental factors upon a genetically determined predisposition.

RÉSUMÉ

Although the evidence for genetic and therefore biological factors as important and necessary components in the etiology of many or all of the schizophrenias is quite compelling, the signposts pointing the way to their discovery are at present quite blurred and, to me at least, illegible.

Genetic factors may operate through some ubiquitous enzyme system to effect general changes in one or another metabolic pathway— changes detectable through studies of blood or urine—and it is to be hoped that the currently active search in these areas will continue.

It is at least equally possible, however, that these genetic factors may operate only through enzymes or metabolic processes peculiar to or confined within the brain, or even within extremely localized areas of the brain. We are in need of new hypotheses such as those of Elkes (68) and many already discussed. In this connection, gamma-amino-butyric acid appears to be just as interesting a substance about which to construct working hypotheses as are the catechols or the indoles. It has been isolated only from nervous tissue, and its metabolism in such tissue has been investigated in some detail (69), while its neurophysiological properties appear to be better defined than are those of the other two groups (70); in addition, its inhibitory properties may have special relevance to diseases where a failure in central inhibition seems to be involved.

Amphetamine possesses remarkable psychotomimetic properties which should not be overlooked. Its ability to produce a clinical syndrome often indistinguishable from schizophrenia (71) and the possible relation of amphetamine to the naturally occurring catechol amines make it at least as interesting as lysergic acid diethylamide.

In addition to techniques at present available in neurochemistry, neurophysiology, and behavioral pharmacology, the development of new methods designed to yield information on processes occurring within the psychotic brain will be needed before our explorations in this field have been exhausted.

But the biochemist must not lose sight of the possibility, which is certainly as great as any of the others, that the genetic factors in schizophrenia operate to determine inappropriate interconnections or interaction between chemically normal components of the brain; if that should prove to be the case, the physiological psychologist, the neurophysiologist, or the anatomist is likely to find meaningful information long before the biochemist does. It would take many biochemists a long time to find a noisy circuit in a radio receiver if they restricted themselves to chemical techniques.

These possibilities are mentioned only to indicate how large is the haystack in which we are searching for the needle; one cannot avoid a feeling of humility when one realizes how slight the chance is that any one of us has already found it, or will find it in a relatively short time.

That is no cause for discouragement, however. It is not necessary that one be convinced of the truth of a particular hypothesis to justify devoting one's energies to testing it. It is enough that one regard it as worth testing, and that the tools be adequate. Modern biochemistry, with its wealth of new knowledge of intermediary metabolism and its array of new techniques for the separation and identification of compounds and the tracing of their metabolic pathways, has provided the biologist interested in mental illness with an armamentarium which his predecessor of only a generation ago could hardly have envisioned. If he chooses from among the approaches which may lead to a definition of the biological factors in schizophrenia those which will in any case lead to a

better understanding of the nervous system and of thought processes and behavior, the present surge of enthusiasm will not have been misdirected.

References

1. Akerfeldt, S. *Science, 125,* 117 (1957).
2. Gibbs, F. A. Ed., *Blood Tests in Mental Illness* (Brain Research Foundation, Chicago, 1957).
3. Holmberg, C. G., and Laurell, C. B. *Scand. J. Clin. & Lab. Invest., 3,* 103 (1951).
4. Leach, B. E., and Heath, R. G. *A.M.A. Arch. Neurol. Psychiat., 76,* 444 (1956).
5. Leach, B. E., Cohen, M., Heath, R. C., Martens, S. *ibid., 76,* 635 (1956).
6. Keup, W. *Monatsschr. Psychiat. Neurol., 128,* 56 (1954).
7. Holmberg, C. G., and Laurell, C. B. *Acta Chem. Scand., 2,* 550 (1948).
8. Markowitz, H., Gubler, C. J., Mahoney, J. P., Cartwright, G. E., Wintrobe, M. M. *J. Clin. Invest., 34,* 1498 (1955).
9. Abood, L. G., Gibbs, F. A., Gibbs, E. *A.M.A. Arch. Neurol. Psychiat., 17,* 643 (1957).
10. McDonald, R. K. 'Plasma ceruloplasmin and ascorbic acid levels in schizophrenia,' paper presented at the annual meeting of the American Psychiatric Association, Chicago, Ill., 1957.
11. Scheinberg, I. H., Morell, A. G., Harris, R. S., Berger, A. *Science, 126,* 925 (1957); Horwitt, M. K., Meyer, B. J., Meyer, A. C., Harvey, C. C., Haffron, D. *A.M.A. Arch. Neurol. Psychiat., 78,* 275 (1957); Frohman, C. E., Goodman, M., Luby, E. D., Beckett, P. G. S., Senf, R. *ibid., 79,* 730 (1958) ; Aprison, M. H., and Grosz, H. J. *ibid., 79,* 575 (1958).
12. Aprison, M. H., and Drew, A. L. *Science, 127,* 758 (1958).
13. Ostfeld, A. M., Abood, L. G., Marcus, D. A. *A.M.A. Arch. Neurol. Psychiat., 79,* 317 (1958).
14. Angel, C., Leach, B. E., Martens, S., Cohen, M., Heath, R. G. *ibid., 79,* 500 (1957).
15. Heath, R. G., Martens, S., Leach, B. E., Cohen, M., Feigley, C. A. *Am. J. Psychiat., 114,* 917 (1958).
16. Heath, R. G., Leach, B. E., Byers, L. W., Martens, S., Feigley, C. A. *ibid., 114,* 683 (1958).
17. Heath, R. G., Martens, S., Leach, B. E., Cohen, M., Angel, C. *ibid., 114,* 14 (1957).
18. Fischer, R. *Proc. Intern. Physiol. Congr., 19th Congr.* (1953), pp. 350-351.
19. Georgi, F., Rieder, H. P., Weber, R. *Science, 120,* 504 (1954).
20. Edisen, C. B. *Diseases of Nervous System, 17,* 77 (1956).
21. Fedoroff, S. *Anat. Record, 121,* 394 (1955).
22. —— and Hoffer, A. *J. Nervous Mental Disease, 124,* 396 (1956).
23. Wada, J. *Proc. Soc. Biol. Psychiatrists, 12th Ann. Conv.* (1957).

24. Rieder, H. P. *Psychiat. et Neurol., 134,* 378 (1957).
25. Smith, K., and Moody, A. C. *Diseases of Nervous System, 17,* 327 (1956).
26. Shapiro, A. K. *J. Nervous Mental Disease, 123,* 65 (1956).
27. Winter, C. A., and Flataker, L. *Proc. Soc. Biol. Psychiatrists, 12th Ann. Conv.* (1957).
28. ———, *A.M.A. Arch. Neurol. Psychiat., 80,* 441 (1958).
29. Kornetsky, C. personal communication: Ghent, L., and Freedman, A. M. *Am. J. Psychiat., 115,* 465 (1958).
30. Minz, B., and Walaszek, E. J. *Compt. rend., 244,* 1974 (1957).
31. McDonald, R. K. *J. Chronic Diseases, 8,* 366 (1958); Barak, A. J., Humoller, F. L., Stevens, J. D. *AMA Arch. Neurol. Psychiat., 80,* 237 (1958).
32. Robins, E., Smith, K., Lowe, I. P., in 'Neuropharmacology,' *Trans. Josiah Macy, Jr. Foundation, 4th Conf.* (1957).
33. Kety, S. S. in *ibid.* (1957).
34. Lief, H. I. *A.M.A. Arch. Neurol. Psychiat., 78,* 624 (1957).
35. Amin, A. H., Crawford, T. B. B., Gaddum, J. H. *J. Physiol. (London), 126,* 596 (1954).
36. Woolley, D. W., and Shaw, E. *Science, 119,* 587 (1954).
37. Gaddum, J. H., in *Ciba Foundation Symposium on Hypertension* (Little, Brown, Boston, 1954).
38. Bogdanski, D. F., Weissbach, H., Udenfriend, S., *J. Neurochem., 1,* 272 (1957); Paasonen, M. K., MacLean, P. D., Giarman, N. J. *ibid., 1,* 326 (1957).
39. Evarts, E. V. *A.M.A. Arch. Neurol. Psychiat., 75,* 49 (1956); Fabing, H. D., and Hawkins, J. R. *Science, 123,* 886 (1956).
40. Shore, P. A., Pletscher, A., Tomich, E. G., Carlsson, A., Kuntzman, R., Brodie, B. B. *Ann. N.Y. Acad. Sci., 66,* 609 (1957).
41. Udenfriend, S., Weissbach, H., Bogdanski, D. F. *ibid., 66,* 602 (1957).
42. Woolley, D. W. *Science, 125,* 752 (1957).
43. Rudy, L. H., Costa, E., Rinaldi, F., Himwich, H. E. *J. Nervous Mental Disease, 126,* 284 (1958).
44. Crane, G. E. *ibid., 124,* 322 (1956).
45. Pleasure, H. *A.M.A. Arch. Neurol. Psychiat., 72,* 313 (1954).
46. Rothlin, E. *Ann. N.Y. Acad. Sci., 66,* 668 (1957).
47. Welsh, J. H., and McCoy, A. C. *Science, 125,* 348 (1957).
48. Holzbauer, M., and Vogt, M. *J. Neurochem., 1,* 8 (1956); Vogt, M., in *Metabolism of the Nervous System,* Richter, D. Ed. (Pergamon, London, 1957), pp. 553-565.

49. Carlsson, A., Lindqvist, M., Magnusson, T. *Nature, 180,* 1200 (1957).
50. Spector, S., Prockop, D., Shore, P. A., Brodie, B. B. *Science, 127,* 704 (1958).
51. Olds, J., and Olds, M. E. *ibid., 127,* 1175 (1958).
52. Jackson, S. L. O. *Brit. Med. J., 2,* 743 (1957).
53. Buscaino, G. A., and Stefanchi, L. *A.M.A. Arch. Neurol. Psychiat., 80,* 78 (1958); Feldstein, A., Hoagland, H., Freeman, H. *Science, 128,* 358 (1958).
54. Zeller, E. A., Bernsohn, J., Inskip, W. M., Lauer, J. W. *Naturwissenschaften, 44,* 427 (1957); Lauer, J. W., Inskip, W. M., Bernsohn, J., Zeller, E. A. *A.M.A. Arch. Neurol. Psychiat., 80,* 122 (1958).
55. Banerjee, S., and Agarwal, P. S. *Proc. Soc. Exptl. Biol. Med., 97,* 657 (1958).
56. Kopin, I. J. *Science, 129,* 835 (1959).
57. Kallmann, F. J. *Am. J. Psychiat., 103,* 309 (1946).
58. Luxenburger, H. *Z. ges. Neurol. Psychiat., 116,* 297 (1928); Rosanoff, A. J., Handy, L. M., Plesset, I. R., Brush, S. *Am. J. Psychiat., 91,* 247 (1934).
59. Slater, E. 'Psychotic and Neurotic Illnesses in Twins,' *Medical Research Council Special Report No. 278* (H. M. Stationery Office, London, 1953).
60. Wilson, P. T. *Human Biology, 6,* 324 (1934).
61. Chapman, A. H. *A.M.A. Arch. Neurol. Psychiat., 78,* 621 (1957).
62. Grosz, H. J., and Miller, I. *Science, 128,* 30 (1958).
63. Rosenthal, D. *J. Nervous Mental Disease,* in press.
64. Jackson, D. D., in *The Study of Schizophrenia,* Jackson, D. D., Ed. (Basic Books, New York, 1960).
65. Clausen, J. A. *Sociology Today,* Merton, Broom, and Cottrell, Eds. (Basic Books, New York, 1959).
66. Lurie, M. B., Abramson, S., Heppelston, A. *J. Exptl. Med., 95,* 119 (1952).
67. Planansky, K., and Allen, G. *Am. J. Human Genet., 5,* 322 (1953).
68. Elkes, J., in 'Neuropharmacology,' *Trans. Josiah Macy, Jr. Foundation, 3rd Conf.* (1956).
69. Roberts, E., and Frankel, S. *J. Biol. Chem., 187,* 55 (1950); Roberts, E., Rothstein, M., Baxter, C. F. *Proc. Soc. Exptl. Biol. Med., 97,* 796 (1958).
70. Purpura, D. P., Girardo, M., Grundfest, H. *Science, 125,* 1200 (1957); Iwama, K., and Jasper, H. H. *J. Physiol. (London), 138,* 365 (1957).
71. Connell, P. H. *Biochem. J., 65,* 7P (1957).

Part II

Intrapsychic Theories

Michael Mazur—*Her Place*. (The Museum of Modern Art, Gift of Mrs. Bertram Smith.)

INTRODUCTION

The emphasis given to early childhood experience by intrapsychic theorists represents their contention that disorders of adulthood are a direct product of the continued and insidious operation of past events. To them, knowledge of the past provides information indispensable to understanding adult difficulties. To the question "What is the basis of adult disorders?" they would answer: the anxieties of childhood and the progressive sequence of defensive maneuvers which were devised to protect against a recurrence of these feelings.

Intrapsychic theorists contend that these two determinants of adult behavior, childhood anxieties and defensive maneuvers, are unconscious, that is, cannot be brought to awareness except under unusual conditions. It is the search for these unconscious processes which is the distinguishing feature of the intrapsychic approach. The obscure and elusive phenomena of the unconscious are the data which they uncover and use for their concepts. These data consist, first, of repressed childhood anxieties that persist within the individual and attach themselves insidiously to ongoing experiences, and, second, of unconscious adaptive processes which protect the individual against the resurgence of these anxieties. The *intrapsychic* label we have attached to these theorists reflects, therefore, their common focus on these two elements of the unconscious.

Intrapsychic Theories:

ORIENTATION

Our presentation of the intrapsychic approach begins with a contribution by Sigmund Freud for two reasons. First, in recognition of the fact that his monumental works are the foundation upon which all other intrapsychic theories are based and, second, to demonstrate the bridge he attempted to build between the biophysical and the intrapsychic orientations. Freud anchored many of his concepts to the biological make-up of man, a view that was rejected or overlooked by several of his followers. In the selection reprinted, drawn from one of his major publications, Freud attempted to summarize the central features of his theoretical work. Here he chose to stress two central ideas: the role and development of the biological instincts and the workings of unconscious processes.

Among the major theorists who have continued and enriched the intrapsychic tradition none has played a more significant or creative role than Heinz Hartmann. Hartmann retained Freud's notion of biological instincts, but proposed that constructive "ego" instincts exist within man which enable him to develop in a healthy and constructive fashion. In contrast to Freud, who believed that disorders arose as a function of destructive instinctual drives, Hartmann contended that pathological development occurs when constructive ego instincts fail to develop. In the article presented here, Hartmann examines the philosophical underpinnings of intrapsychic theory. He outlines the major assumptions of this approach and offers a series of counterarguments to those who have criticized "psychoanalysis" as lacking scientific and theoretical rigor.

The Metapsychology of Instincts, Repression and the Unconscious

SIGMUND FREUD

I: INSTINCTS

The view is often defended that sciences should be built up on clear and sharply defined basal concepts. In actual fact no science, not even the most exact, begins with such definitions. The true beginning of scientific activity consists rather in describing phenomena and then in proceeding to group, classify and correlate them. Even at the stage of description it is not possible to avoid applying certain abstract ideas to the material in hand, ideas derived from various sources

From *Collected Papers of Sigmund Freud* edited by Ernest Jones, Basic Books, Inc., 1959, by permission of the publisher.

and certainly not the fruit of the new experience only. Still more indispensable are such ideas—which will later become the basal concepts of the science—as the material is further elaborated. They must at first necessarily possess some measure of uncertainty; there can be no question of any clear delimitation of their content. So long as they remain in this condition, we come to an understanding about their meaning by repeated references to the material of observation, from which we seem to have deduced our abstract ideas, but which is in point of fact subject to them. Thus, strictly speaking, they are in the nature of conventions; although everything depends on their being chosen in no arbitrary manner, but determined by the important relations they have to the empirical material—relations that we seem to divine before we can clearly recognize and demonstrate them. It is only after more searching investigation of the field in question that we are able to formulate with increased clarity the scientific concepts underlying it, and progressively so to modify these concepts that they become widely applicable and at the same time consistent logically. Then, indeed, it may be time to immure them in definitions. The progress of science, however, demands a certain elasticity even in these definitions. The science of physics furnishes an excellent illustration of the way in which even those 'basal concepts' that are firmly established in the form of definitions are constantly being altered in their content.

A conventional but still rather obscure basal concept of this kind, which is nevertheless indispensable to us in psychology, is that of an *instinct*. Let us try to ascertain what is comprised in this conception by approaching it from different angles.

First, from the side of physiology. This has given us the concept of *stimuli* and the scheme of the reflex arc, according to which a stimulus applied *from the outer world* to living tissue (nervous substance) is discharged by action *towards the outer world*. The action answers the purpose of withdrawing the substance affected from the operation of the stimulus, removing it out of range of the stimulus.

Now what is the relation between 'instinct' and 'stimulus'? There is nothing to prevent our including the concept of 'instinct' under that of 'stimulus' and saying that an instinct is a stimulus to the mind. But we are immediately set on our guard against treating instinct and mental stimulus as one and the same thing. Obviously, besides those of instinctual origin, there are other stimuli to the mind which behave far more like physiological stimuli. For example, a strong light striking upon the eye is not a stimulus of instinctual origin; it is one, however, when the mucous membrane of the œsophagus becomes parched or when a gnawing makes itself felt in the stomach.[1]

We have now obtained material necessary for discriminating between stimuli of instinctual origin and the other (physiological) stimuli which operate on our minds. First, a stimulus of instinctual origin does not arise in the outside world but from within the organism itself. For this reason it has a different mental effect and different actions are necessary in order to remove it. Further, all that is essential in an external stimulus is contained in the assumption that it acts as a single impact, so that it can be discharged by a single appropriate action—a typical instance being that of motor flight from the source of stimulation. Of course these impacts may be repeated and their force may be cumulative, but that makes no difference to our notion of the process and to the conditions necessary in order that the stimulus may be dispelled. An instinct, on the other hand, never acts as a momentary impact but always as a constant force. As it makes its attack not from without but from within the organism, it follows that no flight can avail against it. A better term for a stimulus of instinctual origin is a 'need'; that

---

[1] Assuming, of course, that these internal processes constitute the organic basis of the needs described as thirst and hunger.

which does away with this need is 'satisfaction'. This can be attained only by a suitable (adequate) alteration of the inner source of stimulation.

We thus find our first conception of the essential nature of an instinct by considering its main characteristics, its origin in sources of stimulation within the organism and its appearance as a constant force, and thence we deduce one of its further distinguishing features, namely, that no actions of flight avail against it. Now, in making these remarks, we cannot fail to be struck by a fact which compels us to a further admission. We do not merely accept as basal concepts certain conventions which we apply to the material we have acquired empirically, but we also make use of various complicated postulates to guide us in dealing with psychological phenomena. We have already cited the most important of these postulates; it remains for us expressly to lay stress upon it. It is of a biological nature, and makes use of the concept of 'purpose' (one might say, of adaptation of the means to the end) and runs as follows: the nervous system is an apparatus having the function of abolishing stimuli which reach it, or of reducing excitation to the lowest possible level: an apparatus which would even, if this were feasible, maintain itself in an altogether unstimulated condition. Let us for the present not take exception to the indefiniteness of this idea and let us grant that the task of the nervous system is — broadly speaking — *to master stimuli*. We see then how greatly the simple physiological reflex scheme is complicated by the introduction of instincts. External stimuli impose upon the organism the single task of withdrawing itself from their action: this is accomplished by muscular movements, one of which reaches the goal aimed at and, being the most appropriate to the end in view, is thenceforward transmitted as an hereditary disposition. Those instinctual stimuli which emanate from within the organism cannot be dealt with by this mechanism. Consequently, they make far higher demands upon the nervous

system and compel it to complicated and interdependent activities, which effect such changes in the outer world as enable it to offer satisfaction to the internal source of stimulation; above all, instinctual stimuli oblige the nervous system to renounce its ideal intention of warding off stimuli, for they maintain an incessant and unavoidable afflux of stimulation. So we may probably conclude that instincts and not external stimuli are the true motive forces in the progress that has raised the nervous system, with all its incomparable efficiency, to its present high level of development. Of course there is nothing to prevent our assuming that the instincts themselves are, at least in part, the precipitates of different forms of external stimulation, which in the course of phylogenesis have effected modifications in the organism.

If now we apply ourselves to considering mental life from a biological point of view, an 'instinct' appears to us as a borderland concept between the mental and the physical, being both the mental representative of the stimuli emanating from within the organism and penetrating to the mind, and at the same time a measure of the demand made upon the energy of the latter in consequence of its connection with the body.

We are now in a position to discuss certain terms used in reference to the concept of an instinct, for example, its impetus, its aim, its object and its source.

By the *impetus* of an instinct we understand its motor element, the amount of force or the measure of the demand upon energy which it represents. The characteristic of impulsion is common to all instincts, is in fact the very essence of them. Every instinct is a form of activity; if we speak loosely of passive instincts, we can only mean those whose aim is passive.

The *aim* of an instinct is in every instance satisfaction, which can only be obtained by abolishing the condition of stimulation in the source of the instinct. But although this remains invariably the final goal of every instinct, there may yet be different ways leading to the same goal, so that an instinct may be found to have various nearer or intermediate aims, capable of combination or interchange. Experience permits us also to speak of instincts which are *inhibited in respect of their aim,* in cases where a certain advance has been permitted in the direction of satisfaction and then an inhibition or deflection has occurred. We may suppose that even in such cases a partial satisfaction is achieved.

The *object* of an instinct is that in or through which it can achieve its aim. It is the most variable thing about an instinct and is not originally connected with it, but becomes attached to it only in consequence of being peculiarly fitted to provide satisfaction. The object is not necessarily an extraneous one: it may be part of the subject's own body. It may be changed any number of times in the course of the vicissitudes the instinct undergoes during life; a highly important part is played by this capacity for displacement in the instinct. It may happen that the same object may serve for the satisfaction of several instincts simultaneously, a phenomenon which Adler calls a 'confluence' of instincts. A particularly close attachment of the instinct to its object is distinguished by the term *fixation:* this frequently occurs in very early stages of the instinct's development and so puts an end to its mobility, through the vigorous resistance it sets up against detachment.

By the *source* of an instinct is meant that somatic process in an organ or part of the body from which there results a stimulus represented in mental life by an instinct. We do not know whether this process is regularly of a chemical nature or whether it may also correspond with the release of other, *e.g.* mechanical, forces. The study of the sources of instinct is outside the scope of psychology; although its source in the body is what gives the instinct its distinct and essential character, yet in mental life

we know it merely by its aims. A more exact knowledge of the sources of instincts is not strictly necessary for purposes of psychological investigation; often the source may be with certainty inferred from the aims.

Now what instincts and how many should be postulated? There is obviously a great opportunity here for arbitrary choice. No objection can be made to anyone's employing the concept of an instinct of play or of destruction, or that of a social instinct, when the subject demands it and the limitations of psychological analysis allow of it. Nevertheless, we should not neglect to ask whether such instinctual motives, which are in one direction so highly specialized, do not admit of further analysis in respect of their sources, so that only those primal instincts which are not to be resolved further could really lay claim to the name.

I have proposed that two groups of such primal instincts should be distinguished: the *self-preservative* or *ego*-instincts and the *sexual* instincts. But this proposition has not the weight of a necessary postulate, such as, for instance, our assumption about the biological 'purpose' in the mental apparatus (*v. supra*); it is merely an auxiliary construction, to be retained only so long as it proves useful, and it will make little difference to the results of our work of description and classification if we replace it by another. The occasion for it arose in the course of the evolution of psychoanalysis, which was first employed upon the psychoneuroses, actually upon the group designated transference neuroses (hysteria and obsessional neurosis); through them it became plain that at the root of all such affections there lies a conflict between the claims of sexuality and those of the ego. It is always possible that an exhaustive study of the other neurotic affections (especially of the narcissistic psychoneuroses, the schizophrenias) may oblige us to alter this formula and therewith to make a different classification of the primal instincts. But for the present we do not know what this new formula may be, nor have we met with any argument which seems likely to be prejudicial to the contrast between sexual and ego-instincts.

An attempt to formulate the general characteristics of the sexual instincts would run as follows: they are numerous, emanate from manifold organic sources, act in the first instance independently of one another and only at a late stage achieve a more or less complete synthesis. The aim which each strives to attain is 'organpleasure'; only when the synthesis is complete do they enter the service of the function of reproduction, becoming thereby generally recognizable as sexual instincts. At their first appearance they support themselves upon the instincts of self-preservation, from which they only gradually detach themselves; in their choice of object also they follow paths indicated by the ego-instincts. Some of them remain throughout life associated with these latter and furnish them with libidinal components, which with normal functioning easily escape notice and are clearly recognizable only when disease is present. They have this distinctive characteristic—that they have in a high degree the capacity to act vicariously for one another and that they can readily change their objects. In consequence of the last-mentioned properties they are capable of activities widely removed from their original modes of attaining their aims (sublimation).

Our inquiry into the various vicissitudes which instincts undergo in the process of development and in the course of life must be confined to the sexual instincts, for these are the more familiar to us. Observation shows us that an instinct may undergo the following vicissitudes:

Reversal into its opposite,
Turning round upon the subject,
Repression,
Sublimation.

Since I do not intend to treat of sublimation here and since repression requires a special chapter to itself, it only remains for us to describe and discuss the two first points. Bearing in mind that there are tendencies which are opposed to the instincts pursuing a straightforward course, we may regard these vicissitudes as modes of defence against the instincts.

The *reversal* of an instinct *into its opposite* may on closer scrutiny be resolved into two different processes: a change from active to passive, and a reversal of the content. The two processes, being essentially distinct, must be treated separately.

Examples of the first process are met with in the two pairs of opposites: sadism-masochism and scoptophilia-exhibitionism. The reversal here concerns only the aims of the instincts. The passive aim (to be tortured, or looked at) has been substituted for the active aim (to torture, to look at). Reversal of content is found in the single instance of the change of love into hate.

The *turning round* of an instinct *upon the subject* is suggested to us by the reflection that masochism is actually sadism turned round upon the subject's own ego, and that exhibitionism includes the love of gazing at the subject's own body. Further, analytic observation leaves us in no doubt that the masochist also enjoys the *act* of torturing when this is being applied to himself, and the exhibitionist the exposing of someone in being exposed himself. So the essence of the process is the change of the object, while the aim remains unchanged.

The fact that, at that later period of development, the instinct in its primary form may be observed side by side with its (passive) opposite deserves to be distinguished by the highly appropriate name introduced by Bleuler: *ambivalence*.

These considerations regarding the developmental history of an instinct and the permanent character of the intermediate stages in it should make instinct-development more comprehensible to us. Experience shows that the degree of demonstrable ambivalence varies greatly in individuals, groups and races. Marked ambivalence of an instinct in a human being at the present day may be regarded as an archaic inheritance, for we have reason to suppose that the part played in the life of the instincts by the active impulses in their original form was greater in primitive times than it is on an average to-day.

The transformation of the 'content' of an instinct into its opposite is observed in a single instance only—the changing of *love into hate*. It is particularly common to find both these directed simultaneously towards the same object, and this phenomenon of their co-existence furnishes the most important example of ambivalence of feeling.

The case of love and hate acquires a special interest from the circumstance that it resists classification in our scheme of the instincts. It is impossible to doubt the existence of a most intimate relation between these two contrary feelings and sexual life, but one is naturally unwilling to conceive of love as being a kind of special component-instinct of sexuality in the same way as are the others just discussed. One would prefer to regard loving rather as the expression of the whole sexual current of feeling, but this idea does not clear up our difficulties and we are at a loss how to conceive of an essential opposite to this striving.

Loving admits of not merely one, but of three antitheses. First there is the antithesis of loving—hating; secondly, there is loving—being loved; and, in addition to these, loving and hating together are the opposite of the condition of neutrality or indifference. The second of these two antitheses, loving—being loved, corresponds exactly to the transformation from active to passive and may be traced to a primal situation in the same way as the scoptophilic instinct. This situation is that of *loving oneself,* which for us is the characteristic of narcissism. Then, according to whether the self as object or subject is exchanged for an extraneous one, there results the active aim of loving or the passive one of being loved, the latter remaining nearly related to narcissism.

Perhaps we shall come to a better understanding of the manifold opposites of loving if we reflect that our mental life as a whole is governed by *three polarities,* namely, the following antitheses:

Subject (ego)—Object (external world),

Pleasure—Pain,

Active—Passive.

The antithesis of ego—non-ego (outer), *i.e.* subject—object, is, as we have already said, thrust upon the individual being at an early stage, by the experience that it can abolish external stimuli by means of muscular action but is defenceless against those stimuli that originate in instinct. This antithesis remains sovereign above all in our intellectual activity and provides research with a fundamental situation which no amount of effort can alter. The polarity of pleasure—pain depends upon a feeling-series, the significance of which in determining our actions (will) is paramount and has already been emphasized. The antithesis of active and passive must not be confounded with that of ego-subject—external object. The relation of the ego to the outer world is passive in so far as it receives stimuli from it, active when it reacts to these. Its instincts compel it to a quite special degree of activity towards the outside world, so that, if we wished to emphasize the essence of the matter, we might say that the ego-subject is passive in respect of external stimuli, active in virtue of its own instincts. The antithesis of active—passive coalesces later with that of masculine—feminine, which, until this has taken place, has no psychological significance. The fusion of activity with masculinity and passivity with femininity confronts us, indeed, as a biological fact, but it is by no means so invariably complete and exclusive as we are inclined to assume.

II: REPRESSION

One of the vicissitudes an instinctual impulse may undergo is to meet with resistances the aim of which is to make the impulse inoperative. Under certain conditions, which we shall presently investigate more closely, the impulse then passes into the state of *repression*. If it were a question of the operation of an external stimulus, obviously flight would be the appropriate remedy; with an instinct, flight is of no avail, for the ego cannot escape from itself. Later on, rejection based on judgement (*condemnation*) will be found to be a good weapon against the impulse. Repression is a preliminary phase of condemnation, something between flight and condemnation; it is a concept which could not have been formulated before the time of psycho-analytic research.

It is not easy in theory to deduce the possibility of such a thing as repression. Why should an instinctual impulse suffer such a fate? For this to happen, obviously a necessary condition must be that attainment of its aim by the instinct should produce 'pain' instead of pleasure. But we cannot well imagine such a contingency. There are no such instincts; satisfaction of an instinct is always pleasurable. We should have to assume certain peculiar circumstances, some sort of process which changes the pleasure of satisfaction into 'pain'.

In order the better to define repression we may discuss some other situations in which instincts are concerned. It may happen that an external stimulus becomes internal, for example, by eating into and destroying a bodily organ, so that a new source of constant excitation and increase of tension is formed. The stimulus thereby acquires a far-reaching similarity to an instinct. We know that a case of this sort is experienced by us as *physical pain*. The aim of this pseudo-instinct, however, is simply the cessation of the change in the organ and of the pain accompanying it. There is no other direct pleasure to be attained by cessation of the pain. Further, pain is imperative; the only things which can subdue it are the effect of some toxic agent in removing it and the influence of some mental distraction.

The case of physical pain is too obscure to help us much in our pur-

pose. Let us suppose that an instinctual stimulus such as hunger remains unsatisfied. It then becomes imperative and can be allayed by nothing but the appropriate action for satisfying it; it keeps up a constant tension of need. Anything like a repression seems in this case to be utterly out of the question.

So repression is certainly not an essential result of the tension produced by lack of satisfaction of an impulse being raised to an unbearable degree. The weapons of defence of which the organism avails itself to guard against that situation must be discussed in another connection.

Let us instead confine ourselves to the clinical experience we meet with in the practice of psychoanalysis. We then see that the satisfaction of an instinct under repression is quite possible; further, that in every instance such a satisfaction is pleasurable in itself, but is irreconcilable with other claims and purposes; it therefore causes pleasure in one part of the mind and 'pain' in another. We see then that it is a condition of repression that the element of avoiding 'pain' shall have acquired more strength than the pleasure of gratification. Psycho-analytic experience of the transference neuroses, moreover, forces us to the conclusion that repression is not a defence-mechanism present from the very beginning, and that it cannot occur until a sharp distinction has been established between what is conscious and what is unconscious: that *the essence of repression lies simply in the function of rejecting and keeping something out of consciousness*. This conception of repression would be supplemented by assuming that, before the mental organization reaches this phase, the other vicissitudes which may befall instincts, *e.g.* reversal into the opposite or turning round upon the subject, deal with the task of mastering the instinctual impulses.

It seems to us now that in view of the very great extent to which repression and the unconscious are correlated, we must defer probing more deeply into the nature of repression until we have learnt more about the structure of the various institutions in the mind—and about what differentiates consciousness from the unconscious. Till we have done this, all we can do is to put together in purely descriptive fashion some characteristics of repression noted in clinical practice, even though we run the risk of having to repeat unchanged much that has been said elsewhere.

Psycho-analysis is able to show us something else which is important for understanding the effects of repression in the psychoneuroses. It shows us, for instance, that the instinct-presentation develops in a more unchecked and luxuriant fashion if it is withdrawn by repression from conscious influence. It ramifies like a fungus, so to speak, in the dark and takes on extreme forms of expression, which when translated and revealed to the neurotic are bound not merely to seem alien to him, but to terrify him by the way in which they reflect an extraordinary and dangerous strength of instinct. This illusory strength of instinct is the result of an uninhibited development of it in phantasy and of the damming-up consequent on lack of real satisfaction. The fact that this last result is bound up with repression points the direction in which we have to look for the true significance of the latter.

In reverting to the contrary aspect, however, let us state definitely that it is not even correct to suppose that repression withholds from consciousness all the derivatives of what was primally repressed. If these derivatives are sufficiently far removed from the repressed instinct-presentation, whether owing to the process of distortion or by reason of the number of intermediate associations, they have free access to consciousness. It is as though the resistance of consciousness against them was in inverse proportion to their remoteness from what was originally repressed. During the practice of the psycho-analytic method, we continually require the patient to produce such derivatives of what has been repressed as, in consequence either of their remoteness or of distortion, can pass the censorship of consciousness. Indeed, the associations which we require him to give, while refraining from any consciously directed train of thought or any criticism, and from which we reconstruct a conscious interpretation of the repressed instinct-presentation, are precisely derivatives of this kind. We then observe that the patient can go on spinning a whole chain of such associations, till he is brought up in the midst of them against some thought-formation, the relation of which to what is repressed acts so intensely that he is compelled to repeat this attempt at repression. Neurotic symptoms, too, must have fulfilled the condition referred to, for they are derivatives of the repressed, which has finally by means of these formations wrested from consciousness the right of way previously denied it.

We can lay down no general rule concerning the degree of distortion and remoteness necessary before the resistance of consciousness is abrogated. In this matter a delicate balancing takes place, the play of which is hidden from us; its mode of operation, however, leads us to infer that it is a question of a definite degree of intensity in the cathexis of the unconscious—beyond which it would break through for satisfaction. Repression acts, therefore, in a *highly specific* manner in each instance; every single derivative of the repressed may have its peculiar fate—a little more or a little less distortion alters the whole issue. In this connection it becomes comprehensible that those objects to which men give their preference, that is, their ideals, originate in the same perceptions and experiences as those objects of which they have most abhorrence, and that the two originally differed from one another only by slight modifications. Indeed, as we found in the origin of the fetish, it is possible for the original instinct-presentation to be split into two, one part undergoing repression, while the remainder, just on account of its intimate association with the other, undergoes idealization.

The same result as ensues from an increase or a decrease in the degree of distortion may also be achieved at the other end of the apparatus, so to speak, by a modification in the conditions producing pleasure and 'pain.' Special devices have been evolved, with the object of bringing about such changes in the play of mental forces that what usually gives rise to 'pain' may on this occasion result in pleasure, and whenever such a device comes into operation the repression of an instinct-presentation that is ordinarily repudiated is abrogated. The only one of these devices which has till now been studied in any detail is that of joking. Generally the lifting of the repression is only transitory; the repression is immediately re-established.

Observations of this sort, however, suffice to draw our attention to some further characteristics of repression. Not only is it, as we have just explained, *variable* and *specific,* but it is also exceedingly *mobile.* The process of repression is not to be regarded as something which takes place once for all, the results of which are permanent, as when some living thing has been killed and from that time onward is dead; on the contrary, repression demands a constant expenditure of energy, and if this were discontinued the success of the repression would be jeopardized, so that a fresh act of repression would be necessary. We may imagine that what is repressed exercises a continuous straining in the direction of consciousness, so that the balance has to be kept by means of a steady counter-pressure. A constant expenditure of energy, therefore, is entailed in maintaining a repression, and economically its abrogation denotes a saving. The mobility of the repression, incidentally, finds expression also in the mental characteristics of the condition of sleep which alone renders dream-formation possible. With a return to waking life the repressive cathexes which have been called in are once more put forth.

Finally, we must not forget that after all we have said very little about an instinctual impulse when we state it to be repressed. Without prejudice to the repression such an impulse may find itself in widely different conditions; it may be inactive, *i.e.* cathected with only a low degree of mental energy, or its degree of cathexis (and consequently its capacity for activity) may vary. True, its activity will not result in a direct abrogation of the repression, but it will certainly set in motion all the processes which terminate in a breaking through into consciousness by circuitous routes. With unrepressed derivatives of the unconscious the fate of a particular idea is often decided by the degree of its activity or cathexis. It is an everyday occurrence that such a derivative can remain unrepressed so long as it represents only a small amount of energy, although its content is of such a nature as to give rise to a conflict with conscious control. But the quantitative factor is manifestly decisive for this conflict; as soon as an idea which is fundamentally offensive exceeds a certain degree of strength, the conflict takes on actuality, and it is precisely activation of the idea that leads to its repression. So that, where repression is concerned, an increase in energic cathexis operates in the same way as an approach to the unconscious, while a decrease in that energy operates like distance from the unconscious or like distortion. We understand that the repressing tendencies can find a substitute for repression in a weakening or lessening of whatever is distasteful to them.

We now wish to gain some insight into the mechanism of the process of repression, and especially we want to know whether it has a single mechanism only, or more than one, and whether perhaps each of the psychoneuroses may be distinguished by a characteristic repression-mechanism peculiar to itself. At the outset of this inquiry, however, we encounter complications. The mechanism of a repression becomes accessible to us only when we deduce it from its final results. If we confine our observations to the results of its effect on the ideational part of the instinct-presentation, we discover that as a rule repression creates a *substitute-formation.* What then is the mechanism of such a substitute-formation, or must we distinguish several mechanisms here also? Further, we know that repression leaves *symptoms* in its train. May we then regard substitute-formation and symptom-formation as coincident processes, and, if this is on the whole possible, does the mechanism of substitute-formation coincide with that of repression? So far as we know at present, it seems probable that the two are widely divergent, that it is not the repression itself which produces substitute-formations and symptoms, but that these latter constitute indications of a *return of the repressed* and owe their existence to quite other processes. It would also seem advisable to examine the mechanisms of substitute- and symptom-formation before those of repression.

Obviously there is no ground here for speculation to explore: on the contrary, the solution of the problem must be found by careful analysis of the results of repression observable in the individual neuroses. I must, however, suggest that we should postpone this task, too, until we have formed reliable conceptions of the relation of consciousness to the unconscious.

III: THE UNCONSCIOUS

Psycho-analysis has taught us that the essence of the process of repression lies, not in abrogating or annihilating the ideational presentation of an instinct, but in withholding it from becoming conscious. We then say of the idea that it is in a state of 'unconsciousness,' of being not apprehended by the conscious mind, and we can produce convincing proofs to show that unconsciously it can also produce effects, even of a kind that finally penetrate to consciousness. Everything that is repressed must remain unconscious, but at the very outset let us state that the repressed does not comprise the whole unconscious. The unconscious has the greater compass: the repressed is a part of the unconscious.

How are we to arrive at a knowledge of the unconscious? It is of course only as something conscious that we know anything of it, after it has undergone transformation or translation into something conscious. The possibility of such translation is a matter of everyday experience in psycho-analytic work. In order to achieve this, it is necessary that the person analysed should overcome certain resistances, the very same as those which at some earlier time placed the material in question under repression by rejecting it from consciousness.

In many quarters our justification is disputed for assuming the existence of an unconscious system in the mind and for employing such an assumption for purposes of scientific work. To this we can reply that our assumption of the existence of the unconscious is *necessary* and *legitimate,* and that we possess manifold *proofs* of the existence of the unconscious. It is necessary because the data of consciousness are exceedingly defective; both in healthy and in sick persons mental acts are often in process which can be explained only by presupposing other acts, of which consciousness yields no evidence. These include not only the parapraxes[1] and dreams of healthy persons, and everything designated a mental symptom or an obsession in the sick; our most intimate daily experience introduces us to sudden ideas of the source of which we are ignorant, and to results of mentation arrived at we know not how. All these conscious acts remain disconnected and unintelligible if we are determined to hold fast to the claim that every single mental act performed within us must be consciously experienced; on the other hand, they fall into a demonstrable connection if we interpolate the unconscious acts that we infer. A gain in meaning and connection, however, is a perfectly justifiable motive, one which may well carry us beyond the limitations of direct experience. When, after this, it appears that the assumption of the unconscious helps us to construct a highly successful practical method, by which we are enabled to

---

[1] [*E.g.* slips of the tongue, mislaying of objects, etc.—TRANS.]

exert a useful influence upon the course of conscious processes, this success will have won us an incontrovertible proof of the existence of that which we assumed. We become obliged then to take up the position that it is both untenable and presumptuous to claim that whatever goes on in the mind must be known to consciousness.

We can go further and in support of an unconscious mental state allege that only a small content is embraced by consciousness at any given moment, so that the greater part of what we call conscious knowledge must in any case exist for very considerable periods of time in a condition of latency, that is to say, of unconsciousness, of not being apprehended by the mind. When all our latent memories are taken into consideration it becomes totally incomprehensible how the existence of the unconscious can be gainsaid. We then encounter the objection that these latent recollections can no longer be described as mental processes, but that they correspond to residues of somatic processes from which something mental can once more proceed. The obvious answer to this should be that a latent memory is, on the contrary, indubitably a residuum of a mental process. But it is more important to make clear to our minds that this objection is based on the identification—not, it is true, explicitly stated but regarded as axiomatic—of conscious and mental. This identification is either a *petitio principii* and begs the question whether all that is mental is also necessarily conscious, or else it is a matter of convention, of nomenclature. In this latter case it is of course no more open to refutation than any other convention. The only question that remains is whether it proves so useful that we must needs adopt it. To this we may reply that the conventional identification of the mental with the conscious is thoroughly unpractical. It breaks up all mental continuity, plunges us into the insoluble difficulties of psychophysical parallelism, is open to the reproach that without any manifest grounds it overestimates the part played by consciousness, and finally it forces us

prematurely to retire from the territory of psychological research without being able to offer us any compensation elsewhere.

At any rate it is clear that the question—whether the latent states of mental life, whose existence is undeniable, are to be conceived of as unconscious mental states or as physical ones—threatens to resolve itself into a war of words. We shall therefore be better advised to give prominence to what we know with certainty of the nature of these debatable states. Now, as far as their physical characteristics are concerned, they are totally inaccessible to us: no physiological conception nor chemical process can give us any notion of their nature. On the other hand, we know for certain that they have abundant points of contact with conscious mental processes; on being submitted to a certain method of operation they may be transformed into or replaced by conscious processes, and all the categories which we employ to describe conscious mental acts, such as ideas, purposes, resolutions and so forth, can be applied to them. Indeed, of many of these latent states we have to assert that the only point in which they differ from states which are conscious is just in the lack of consciousness of them. So we shall not hesitate to treat them as objects of psychological research, and that in the most intimate connection with conscious mental acts.

The stubborn denial of a mental quality to latent mental processes may be accounted for by the circumstance that most of the phenomena in question have not been objects of study outside psycho-analysis. Anyone who is ignorant of the facts of pathology, who regards the blunders of normal persons as accidental, and who is content with the old saw that dreams are froth[2] need only ignore a few more problems of the psychology of consciousness in order to dispense with the assumption of an unconscious mental activity. As it happens, hypnotic experiments, and especially post-hyp-

---

[2] [*'Träume sind Schäume.'*]

notic suggestion, had demonstrated tangibly even before the time of psycho-analysis the existence and mode of operation of the unconscious in the mind.

The assumption of an unconscious is, moreover, in a further respect a perfectly *legitimate* one, inasmuch as in postulating it we do not depart a single step from our customary and accepted mode of thinking. By the medium of consciousness each one of us becomes aware only of his own states of mind; that another man possesses consciousness is a conclusion drawn by analogy from the utterances and actions we perceive him to make, and it is drawn in order that this behaviour of his may become intelligible to us. (It would probably be psychologically more correct to put it thus: that without any special reflection we impute to everyone else our own constitution and therefore also our consciousness, and that this identification is a necessary condition of understanding in us.) This conclusion—or identification—was formerly extended by the ego to other human beings, to animals, plants, inanimate matter and to the world at large, and proved useful as long as the correspondence with the individual ego was overwhelmingly great; but it became more untrustworthy in proportion as the gulf between the ego and the non-ego widened. To-day, our judgment is already in doubt on the question of consciousness in animals; we refuse to admit it in plants and we relegate to mysticism the assumption of its existence in inanimate matter. But even where the original tendency to identification has withstood criticism—that is, when the non-ego is our fellow-man—the assumption of a consciousness in him rests upon an inference and cannot share the direct certainty we have of our own consciousness.

Now psycho-analysis demands nothing more than that we should apply this method of inference to ourselves also—a proceeding to which, it is true, we are not constitutionally disposed. If we do this, we must say that all the acts and manifestations which I notice in myself and do not know how to link up with the rest of my mental life must be judged as if they belonged to someone else and are to be explained by the mental life ascribed to that person. Further, experience shows that we understand very well how to interpret in others (*i.e.* how to fit into their mental context) those same acts which we refuse to acknowledge as mentally conditioned in ourselves. Some special hindrance evidently deflects our investigations from ourselves and interferes with our obtaining true knowledge of ourselves.

Now this method of inference, applied to oneself in spite of inner opposition, does not lead to the discovery of an unconscious, but leads logically to the assumption of another, second consciousness which is united in myself with the consciousness I know. But at this point criticism may fairly make certain comments. In the first place, a consciousness of which its own possessor knows nothing is something very different from that of another person and it is questionable whether such a consciousness, lacking, as it does, its most important characteristic, is worthy of any further discussion at all. Those who have contested the assumption of an unconscious system in the mind will not be content to accept in its place an unconscious consciousness. Secondly, analysis shows that the individual latent mental processes inferred by us enjoy a high degree of independence, as though each had no connection with another, and knew nothing about any other. We must be prepared, it would appear, to assume the existence not only of a second consciousness in us, but of a third and fourth also, perhaps of an infinite series of states of consciousness, each and all unknown to us and to one another. In the third place—and this is the most weighty argument of all—we have to take into account that analytic investigation reveals some of these latent processes as having characteristics and peculiarities which seem alien to us, or even incredible, and running directly counter to the well-known attributes of consciousness. This justifies us in modifying our inference about ourselves and saying that what is proved is not a second consciousness in us, but the existence of certain mental operations lacking in the quality of consciousness. We shall also, moreover, be right in rejecting the term 'subconsciousness' as incorrect and misleading. The known cases of *'double conscience'* (splitting of consciousness) prove nothing against our view. They may most accurately be described as cases of a splitting of the mental activities into two groups, whereby a single consciousness takes up its position alternately with either the one or the other of these groups.

In psycho-analysis there is no choice for us but to declare mental processes to be in themselves unconscious, and to compare the perception of them by consciousness with the perception of the outside world through the sense-organs; we even hope to extract some fresh knowledge from the comparison.

Psychoanalysis As a Scientific Theory

HEINZ HARTMANN

When some forty-five years ago Freud (12) wrote for the first time about the philosophical interests in analysis, his main point was that philosophy could not avoid taking fully into account what he then called "the hypothesis of unconscious mental activities." He also mentioned that philosophers may be interested in the interpretation of philosophical thought in terms of psychoanalysis—adding, though, here as elsewhere, that the fact that a theory or doctrine is determined by psychological processes of many kinds does not necessarily invalidate its scientific truth. Since then, the knowledge of human behavior and motivation we owe to analysis has greatly increased, has become much more comprehensive but also more specific; and this development has certainly influenced not only social science, anthropology, and medicine, but also philosophy in a broad sense. This does not, though, necessarily mean that analysis can "answer" what one usually calls philosophical problems; it usually means that it leads to looking at them from a new angle. Some of its potentialities in this respect have been made use of only rather scantily so far. I am thinking, for example, of its possible contribution toward a better understanding of ethical problems. The interest psychoanalysis may have for philosophers has clearly two aspects: it resides partly in the new psychological findings and theories of analysis, but also in certain questions of methodology raised by Freud's and other psychoanalysts' approach to the study of man.

In speaking of psychoanalysis one often refers to a therapeutic technique. One may also refer to a method of psychological investigation whose main aspects are free association and interpretation; or, finally, to a body of facts and theories (Freud, 13). In this last sense, we would certainly consider as psychoanalytical any knowledge gained directly by Freud's method of investigation; but many of us would today consider analysis to include related procedures such as the application of psychoanalytic insights to data of

Abridged from *Psychoanalysis, Scientific Method and Philosophy* edited by S. Hcok, pages 3-35, New York University Press, 1959, by permission of the publisher and the author.

direct child observation, a field which has grown in importance in the last two decades. Of the three aspects just mentioned, it is the method of exploration that has undergone the least change; it is commonly used in a situation defined by a certain set of rules and referred to as the psychoanalytic situation or the psychoanalytic interview. The therapeutic technique has been repeatedly modified, and psychoanalytic theory has gone through a series of more or less radical modifications, by Freud and by others. I want to emphasize that the interrelations among these three aspects are, in analysis, a central topic—though in the context of this presentation I can refer to them only occasionally.

The theories of psychoanalysis follow principles of systematization, as do theories in other fields. Freud, however, did not speak of analysis as a "system," but rather accentuated its unfinished character, its flexibility, and the tentative nature of a considerable part of it. Actually, adjustments and reformulations of various aspects of theory have repeatedly become necessary. There are chapters such as the psychology of the dream, of libidinal development, of anxiety, and of symptom formation, that have been more systematically worked out than others. Psychoanalysis is obviously far from being a closed system of doctrines, though it has sometimes been represented as such. Also, though some fundamental tenets of psychoanalysis are accepted by all (Freudian) analysts, agreement on all of them is obviously lacking.

There is in analysis a hierarchy of hypotheses as to their closeness to observation, their generality, and the degree to which they have been confirmed. It appears that a neater classification as to these points and a higher degree of systematization (considering the different levels of theorizing) than exist today would not only facilitate my task in discussing psychoanalysis as a scientific theory but also clarify the standing of analysis as a scientific discipline. Promising efforts in this direction have been made and

are being made by analysts and also by nonanalysts, but as yet no complete and systematical outline drawn from this angle is available; a recent work by David Rapaport (30), soon to be published, may come close to performing this task. This is probably the reason, or one of the reasons, that in more or less general presentations of psychoanalysis references to its history abound, and the reader will forgive me if they do in this paper too, at least in its first part. I shall mostly refer to the work of Freud, because most of the more general theories of analysis have their origin in it, and because he is in many ways more representative of psychoanalytic thinking than anybody else.

Often historical explanations are substituted for system; an attempt is made to clarify the function of propositions in their relation to others by tracing their place in the development of analysis. Also, without such historical reference it happens over and over again that analytical hypotheses are dealt with on one level, so to say, which belong to different phases of theory formation, and some of which have actually been discarded and replaced by others. Again, because of the comparatively low level of systematization, I think it is true that even today a thorough knowledge of at least some chapters of analytic theory cannot be acquired without knowledge of its history (Hartmann, 16).

From the beginning, explanations of human behavior in terms of propositions about unconscious mental processes have been an essential part and one characteristic feature of psychoanalysis. I may, then, start by introducing Freud's concepts of unconscious processes. He makes a distinction between two forms of unconscious mental activity. The one, called preconscious, functions more or less as conscious activities do. It is not conscious, in a descriptive sense, but can become conscious without having to overcome powerful counterforces. Where such overcoming of resistances is necessary, as is the case with repressed material, we speak of unconscious processes in the stricter, the dynamic, sense of the word. The dynamic impact of these latter unconscious processes on human behavior —and not only in the case of mental disease—is one main tenet of Freud's theory of unconscious mental activities.

There is rather wide agreement that conscious data are insufficient for the explanation of a considerable part of behavior, and particularly of those aspects that were first studied in analysis. However, its critics have repeatedly claimed that the introduction of unconscious processes is superfluous. The explanation needed could be stated, or should be sought for, in terms of the more reliable data of brain physiology. The question here is not just whether, and why, explanations based on such data would be per se more reliable, nor why psychological hypotheses about mental processes ought not to be introduced in explaining human behavior. We have also to consider the fact that, given the actual state of brain physiology, many and even comparatively simple aspects of behavior of the kind we are dealing with in analysis cannot be explained. To rely on brain physiology alone would mean to renounce explanation of the greatest part of the field that psychoanalysis has set out to explain. Or, if one should insist on attempting an explanation on physiological grounds, the resultant hypotheses would of necessity be considerably more tenuous and more speculative even than psychoanalytic hypotheses are suspected to be by its critics today.

Freud, well trained in the anatomy and physiology of the brain, actually started out by attempting to devise a physiological psychology that could provide him with concepts and hypotheses to account for his clinical insights. But beyond a certain point this approach proved of no use. He was thus led to replace it by a set of psychological hypotheses and constructs; and this step represents probably the most important turning point in the history of psychoanalysis. It was the

beginning in analysis of psychological theory, the heuristic value of which he found to be greatly superior—a point that, I think, has been corroborated by its subsequent development.

But it is true that even after this radical turn in his approach Freud held on to the expectation, shared by many analysts, that one day the development of brain physiology would make it possible to base psychoanalysis on its findings and theories. He did not think this would happen during his lifetime, in which he proved to be right. In the meantime certain, though limited, parallels between analytic propositions and discoveries in the physiology of the brain have become apparent. Also, the usefulness of some psychoanalytic hypotheses for their field has been recognized by at least some representatives of brain research (Adrian, 1). As to the psychology of unconscious processes, I think it can be said that Freud in developing that part of analysis was much less interested in the ultimate "nature" or "essence" of such processes—whatever this may mean—than in finding a suitable conceptual framework for the phenomena he had discovered.

While Freud, after the first years of his scientific work, relinquished the attempt to account for his findings in terms of physiology, it is nevertheless characteristic of some of his psychoanalytic theorizing that he used physiological models. He was guided by the trend in German physiology which has been designated as the physicalist school (Bernfeld, 5), whose representatives were, among others, Helmholtz and Bruecke, the latter being one of Freud's teachers. Certain aspects of the psychology of neurosis, for example, led him to introduce into psychoanalysis the concept of regression (to earlier stages of development), which had been used in the physiology of his day; this concept, though, acquired new meaning in the context in which he used it. Also, in making "function" the criterion for defining what he called the mental systems (ego, id, superego), Freud used physiology as a model. But this no longer implies any correlation to any specific physiological organization (Hartmann, Kris, Loewenstein, 21). The value of such borrowings or analogies has, of course, to be determined in every single instance by confronting their application with tested knowledge (data and hypotheses). Physiological models (also occasionally physical models, as is obvious, for instance, in Freud's concept of a "mental apparatus") have been used also by other psychoanalysts (see Kubie in a recent lecture) in order to illustrate certain characteristics of mental phenomena or to suggest a new hypothesis. The use even of metaphors need not of necessity lead into muddled thinking once their place in theory has been clearly delineated. The danger that earlier implications of those model concepts might impair their fruitful use in the new context of psychoanalysis has on the whole been successfully avoided (Hartmann-Kris-Loewenstein).

The broadening of the scope of psychology that came about as the consequence of the inclusion of propositions about unconscious mental processes meant, first of all, that many aspects of a person's life history that had never been explained before—and that, as a matter of fact, one had not even tried to explain—could be accounted for in terms of the individual's experience and dispositions. Causation in the field of personality is traceable only at its fringes without this broadening of theory. Freud was a strict determinist and often stated that to fill that gap in earlier psychological approaches, partly because of which the study of personality had been unsatisfactory, was one of his primary aims in developing analytic theory. More recently it has been said, by the mathematician von Mises (29), that the observations correspond rather to statistical than to causal relations. I may mention at this point that this interest in the causation of mental phenomena included, quite naturally, also the interest in what we call the genetic viewpoint, since Freud's attention had been drawn to many facts of

early childhood which had been unknown, and regularities in the relationships between early childhood situations and the behavior of the adult had become apparent. With Freud, the investigation of highly complex series of experience and behavior, extending over long periods of time, soon moved into the center of interest. Developmental research was to become equally important for psychoanalytic theory and practice. It is significant that the reconstructive approach in analysis led not only to the discovery of a great wealth of childhood material in every individual case, but also to the ascertainment of typical sequences of developmental phases. The genetic approach has become so pervasive, not only in psychopathology but also in psychoanalytic psychology in general, that in analysis phenomena are often grouped together, not according to their descriptive similarities but as belonging together if they have a common genetic root (oral character, anal character). It was only much later that this predominance of a genetic conceptualization was counterbalanced by a sharper distinction between genesis and function, to which I shall shortly return in speaking of the structural point of view.

Here I want to add that while I just spoke of the study of the individual's "life history," it would be misleading (though it actually has been done) to classify this aspect of analysis as an historical discipline. This misinterpretation may be traceable to its comparison with archaeology, which Freud occasionally uses. It is true that most analytical knowledge has been gained in the psychoanalytic interview and that the concern with developmental problems refers primarily to the history of individuals. But this should not obfuscate the fact that the aim of these studies is (besides its therapeutic purpose) to develop lawlike propositions which then, of course, transcend individual observations.

At this point I should like briefly to summarize the role of psychoanalysis as a psychology of motivation, bearing in mind that nowadays psychoanalysis takes into consideration the interaction of the individual with his environment, as well as his so-called "inner-psychic" processes. The study of these psychic processes constitutes what, in analysis, we call "metapsychology," a term that signifies not (as it might seem) that which is beyond psychology altogether, but simply those psychological investigations that are not limited to conscious phenomena, and that formulate the most general assumptions of analysis on the most abstract level of theory. Metapsychology is concerned with the substructures of personality, with the ego, the id, and the superego which are defined as units of functions. The id refers to the instinctual aspect, the ego to the reality principle and to the "centralization of functional control" (to borrow a term from brain physiology). The superego has its biological roots in the long dependency on the parents and in the helplessness of the human child; it develops out of identification with the parents; and it accounts for the fact that moral conflict and guilt feelings become a natural and fundamental aspect of human behavior. The theoretical and clinical advantage of the structural formulations, referring to the distinction of ego, id, superego, has several reasons. The most important is probably that the demarcation lines of the three systems, ego, id, superego are geared to the typical conflicts of man: conflicts with the instinctual drives, with moral conscience, and with the outside world. The paramount importance on neurotic *and* normal development of these conflicts, and of the ways to solve them, was one of the earliest discoveries of Freud and has remained central in psychoanalytic practice and theory ever since.

Critics of analysis often tend to underrate the wealth of individual data on which it is built. But on the other hand, it also happens that the theoretical nature of concepts like libido is not fully realized; for example, libido is often identified with sexual experience, or as a mere generalization of some observable connections.

In the beginnings of psychoanalysis (even after the importance of unconscious processes had been realized), Freud still adhered more or less strictly to associationism. But when he found conflict to be a primary motivating force of behavior, and specifically an important etiological agent in neurosis, he gradually developed the concept of mental tendencies and purposive ideas. Psychoanalysis became a psychology of motivation, the motives being partly, but not generally, considered in analogy with those consciously experienced. There originated the idea of wishes, in certain circumstances, warded off by defensive techniques. He discovered the role of repression and later of other defense mechanisms, like projection, isolation, undoing, and so on. The consideration of mental processes from this angle of synergistic or antagonistic motivating forces is what has been known since as the dynamic aspect of psychoanalysis. The systematic and objective study of conflict has remained one of its essential aspects and has proved a necessary and fruitful avenue to the explanation of human behavior. This was a second bold step in the development of psychoanalysis. The importance of "conflict" had, of course, been known in religious and philosophical doctrines and in literature, but scientific psychology before Freud had had no means to approach the subject.

The dynamic factors involved in both sides of a conflict were, for some time, rather poorly defined. It was, then, again primarily data of analytical observation that led to the realization of the dominance of the instinctual drives among the motivating forces. I am referring here to Freud's discovery of infantile sexuality. This discovery was, at the time, considered by many as the product of revolting imagination; today, it can easily be confirmed in every nursery.

Even at the period when instinctual motivation seemed to be pretty much ubiquitous, the basic fact of conflict was not overlooked. Self-preservative instinctual drives were, at the time, thought of as the opponents of sexuality. Besides this, the concept of overdetermination, referring to the multiple motivation of all human behavior, continued also through the phase in which motivation was, on the level of general theory, nearly always considered instinctual.

Again, to fit it to his field of observation Freud has to modify the concept of "instinct" commonly used in other fields. His term, in German, *Trieb*, in English, "instinctual drive," or "drive," is certainly not identical with what one refers to in speaking of the instincts of lower animals. His concept of drives had to prove its usefulness with respect to human psychology. Here, the sources of the drives are of much less importance than their aims and their objects. The lesser rigidity of the human drives, the comparatively easy shift of the aims, the freeing of many activities from a rigid connection with one definite instinctual tendency, the comparative independence from and variety of possible response to outer and inner stimuli have to be taken into account in considering the role of the drives in human psychology. Still, the psychoanalytic theory of instinctual drives is broad enough to show also many impressive parallels with the findings of a modern school of zoologists (ethnologists).

The concept of a continuity of this driving force allows the consideration of a great variety of mental acts from the angle of their investment with drive energy. Also in this way it is possible to understand the close relationship of many mental processes which, looked at from the surface, would appear to be entirely heterogeneous. The capacity for displacement or transformation into various kinds of human activities; also the motivational role traceable through and specific on all levels of man's growth from birth to maturity; their central role in typical conflicts; and the fact that they involve relations to human objects—these are some of the psycho-

logically essential aspects of the psychoanalytic concept of human drives. According to Freud, sexuality and aggression are, among all the drives one could describe, those that come closest to fulfilling the demands psychoanalysis makes on a concept of drives.

The concept of mental energy was then elaborated in the sense that it is the drives that are the main sources of energy in what Freud calls the "mental apparatus." However, a strictly speaking quantifying approach to these energic problems has so far not been developed. Or rather: while it is possible to speak of a greater or lesser degree of, let's say, a resistance (against the uncovering of some hidden material), we have no way of measuring it. To account for the difference in the unconscious and the conscious (and preconscious) processes Freud postulated two forms of energy distribution, conceptualized as, respectively, primary and secondary processes. The primary processes represent a tendency to immediate discharge, while the secondary processes are guided by the consideration of reality. This distinction is again both theoretically significant and clinically quite helpful. The thesis that behavior is to be explained also in terms of its energic cathexis is what we call, in analysis, the economic viewpoint.

The regulation of energies in the mental apparatus is assumed to follow the pleasure principle, the reality principle (derived from the pleasure principle under the influence of ego-development), and a tendency to keep the level of excitation constant or at a minimum. There are parallels to this in hypotheses formulated by others, and again the use of physical and physiological models played a role in the Freudian concepts.

The three aspects of psychoanalytic theory I have mentioned so far— the topographical (conscious-preconscious-unconscious), the dynamic, and the economic (energic)—represent Freud's first approach to what he called "metapsychology." It is postulated that a satisfactory explanation of human behavior includes its consideration in relation to all aspects of metapsychology. The "meta" in this term points to a theory going "beyond" the investigation of conscious phenomena. The word, generally accepted in psychoanalysis, has proved misleading for many outside analysis. Actually, "metapsychology" is nothing but a term for the highest level of abstraction used in analytic psychology.

A fourth aspect of metapsychology, called structural, was explicitly stated considerably later, though it was implicit in earlier theoretical thinking on mental conflicts. The forces opposing the drives in typical conflict formations, warding them off and forcing them to compromise formations (of which the neurotic symptom may serve as an example), are today conceptualized as an essential aspect of what we call the ego. At the core of this concept formation is the recognition of the relevant differences between instinctual tendencies which strive for discharge, and other tendencies that enforce postponement of discharge and are modifiable by the influence of the environment. This means, of course, that the dynamic and economic viewpoints can no longer be limited to the vicissitudes of instinctual drives. The original concept of a defensive ego had to be broadened to include in the ego those nondefensive functions of the mental apparatus that are noninstinctual in character. Many of these are not, or not necessarily, part of the conflictual set-up; we call them today "the nonconflictual sphere of the ego" (Hartmann, 15). Here belong (though they too may be involved in conflict, without, however, originating in it) perception, thinking, memory, action, and so on. It is likely that in man not only instinctual factors are in part determined by heredity, but also the apparatus of the ego underlying the functions just mentioned. We speak of the primary autonomous functions of the ego. It is true that analysis is, due to its method, directly dealing with environmental factors and with reactions to them,

but this has never implied a denial on principle, of heredity. It is in this sense that we speak of a drive constitution, and today also of constitutional elements in the ego, and of the role of maturational factors in the typical sequence of developmental phases.

To those noninstinctual functions that we attribute to the ego belongs also what one can call the centralized functional control which integrates the different parts of personality with each other and with outer reality. This function (synthetic function or organizing function) is in a way similar to what, since Cannon, we call homeostasis, and may represent one level of it.

The ego is, then, a substructure of personality and is defined by its functions. The instinctual aspect of personality is today conceptualized as the id. Through the development of the ego it becomes possible that the pleasure principle, dominant with the instinctual drives, can be modified to that consideration of reality, in thinking and action, that makes adaptation possible and is termed, as I said before, the reality principle. Through recent work, the relation between adaptation to outer reality and the state of integration of inner reality has become more accessible. This development in psychoanalytic theory has thus led to an improved understanding of man's relations to his environment, and to the most significant part of it, his fellowmen—which is, however, not to say that the socio-cultural aspects of mental functions and development had been overlooked in earlier analysis. Psychoanalysis, in contradistinction to some other schools of psychology, has never considered "innerpsychic" processes only, but also, and not only accidentally, includes the consideration of the individual's interactions with the environment. At any rate, the study of object relations in human development has more recently become one of the most fruitful centers of analytic interest ("new environmentalism," Kris, 25). Ego psychology represents a more balanced consideration of the biological and the social and cultural aspects of human behavior. We may say that in analysis cultural phenomena are often studied in their biological context and significance and biological phenomena in relation to the socio-cultural environment (Hartmann, 19). But this aspect will be discussed more fully later.

Some of the functions of the ego have, in the course of development, to be wrested from the influence of the drives. Gradually, they then reach, through a change of function, a certain degree of independence from instinctual origins and of resistance against reinvolvement with the drives (secondary autonomy—see Hartmann, 15, 17). A similar concept, though less specific in relation to psychoanalytic propositions, has been introduced by G. Allport (2). This relative independence of the ego is also energically conceptualized, with respect to the sources of energy at the disposal of ego functions. The necessity to distinguish function from genesis more clearly is one of the main implications of the structural viewpoint.

The third unit of functions, considered a substructure of personality, is called the superego. To it we attribute the functions of self-criticism, conscience and the formation of ideals. The acceptance of moral standards is considered a natural step in ontogenesis. Moral conflict, and the guilt feelings that are an expression of it, are, from the time when the superego has been instituted, one fundamental aspect of human behavior. The superego has a biological root in the comparatively long dependency and helplessness of the child of the human species, which also means increased importance of the parents for its development. The superego develops out of identification with them, to which, in subsequent layers of development, identifications with others are added. Also obvious in its genesis is a socio-cultural factor, which accounts for an important segment of tradition formation. The acceptance of certain moral demands, the rejection of others, the

degree of severity of the superego and its capacity to enforce its demands can very frequently be traced in clinical investigation.

Structural hypotheses are in many ways more comprehensive, but also, if I may say so, more elegant than earlier formulations of partly the same problems. They have also a considerable value in clinical thinking, because they are particularly fit to account for what has remained dominant in clinical work, that is, the various forms of typical conflict situations. Actually, the demarcation lines of those units of functions, or systems, or substructures of personality are so drawn that they correspond to the main conflicts of man, which we now describe as conflicts between ego and id, superego and ego, and ego and reality. It was in this respect that Freud found the older topographical model, the layer model (conscious-preconscious-unconscious), rather disappointing, though in other respects it still retains a certain degree of significance. Defenses as well as drives can be unconscious; thus differences between conscious and unconscious processes cannot be used to account for these conflicts.

I thought it advisable to begin by giving a picture of certain fundamentals of psychoanalytic theory, and of the degree of its comprehensiveness, by indicating at least some of its dimensions, and also the relations between different parts of these theories. Its comprehensiveness means also its actual or potential importance in many neighboring fields. My survey shows also at least some of the points at which questions can be raised from the viewpoint of a philosophy of science. There would have been an alternative to the way of presentation I chose. I could have shown how, in the analysis of a symptom or a dream, our observations lead to anticipations, and how the various levels of our conceptual tools are brought to bear on them; also, how in this process theoretical thinking is constantly brought back to the observables. But this alternative would inevitably demand the introduction of a great number of variables and a discussion of the analytic method and the analytic situation much broader than I am able to give here. Of course, a sector of psychoanalytic propositions can be tested outside analysis, and some have been tested in this way; but it is still true that it is, in the field of analysis, extremely difficult to assay the suitability of the hypotheses for the purposes for which they have been primarily devised without the use, in the analytic situation, of the analytic method.

Generally, Freud's views on introspection have not always been clearly appreciated. They are, though, evident already in the kind of psychoanalytic thinking that is comparatively close to observational data, as in Freud's ideas on the psychopathology of everyday life. In a slip of the tongue, for instance, when, in place of a word we consciously intended to use, another one, not consciously intended, appears, we use the behavioral aspect in evaluating the psychological situation—we use it, that is, in taking the word actually spoken as an indication of an unconscious motivation that takes precedence over the conscious one.

The data gathered in the psychoanalytic situation with the help of the psychoanalytic method are primarily behavioral data; and the aim is clearly the exploration of human behavior. The data are mostly the patient's verbal behavior, but include other kinds of action. They include his silences, his postures (F. Deutsch, 7), and his movements in general, more specifically his expressive movements. While analysis aims at an explanation of human behavior, those data, however, are interpreted in analysis in terms of mental processes, of motivation, of "meaning"; there is, then, a clear-cut difference between this approach and the one usually called "behavioristic," and this difference is even more marked if we consider the beginnings of behaviorism, rather than its more recent formulations.

As to the data, it is hard to give, outside the analytic process itself, an impression of the wealth of observational data collected in even one single "case." One frequently refers to the comparatively small number of cases studied in analysis and tends to forget the very great number of actual observations on which we base, in every individual case, the interpretations of an aspect of a person's character, symptoms and so on.*

By keeping certain variables in the analytic situation, if not constant, as close to constancy as the situation allows, it becomes easier to evaluate the significance of other variables that enter the picture. The best-studied example of this is what is called the "passivity" of the analyst, in contradistinction to the considerably more pronounced activity of the psychotherapist. This is not to claim that psychoanalysis is an experimental discipline. However, there are situations where it comes close to it. At any rate, there is sufficient evidence for the statement that our observations in the psychoanalytic situation, set in the context of psychoanalytic experience and hypotheses, make predictions possible—predictions of various degrees of precision or reliability, but as a rule superior to any others that have been attempted in the psychology of personality. Due to the emphasis on the genetic viewpoint, many predictions are what has been called "predictions of the past," (Hartmann, Kris, 20) that is, reconstructions of the past which can often be confirmed in astonishing detail (Bonaparte, 6). One obvious limitation of our predictive potential is, of course, the great number of factors determining, according to psychoanalytic theory, every single element of behavior—what Freud has termed "overdetermination." Still, our technique is constantly directed by tentative predictions of the patient's reaction. Also, studies in developmental psychology by means of direct child observation, such as have been conducted by E. Kris and other psychoanalysts (M. Kris, 26), are guided by the formulation of expectations and their checking in individual

---

* Thus every single clinical "case" represents, for research, hundreds of data of observed regularities, and in hundreds of respects.

cases. Here I just want to point to one way in which psychoanalytic hypotheses can be used vis-à-vis individual cases and how they may be confirmed in clinical experience. I may mention here that problems of validation of psychoanalytic hypotheses ought not to be equated, as has too often been done, with the problem of therapeutic success.

A further difficulty results from the fact that psychoanalytic theory has also to deal with the relation between observer and observed in the analytic situation. There are personality layers, if you will excuse this term, that in the average case the observed cannot reach without the help of the observer and his method of observation. But the insight of the observer ought not to be confused with the insight of the observed. Some of these problems belong in a theory of psychoanalytic technique. But there is also the problem of the "personal equation" (Hartmann, 18; Kris, 25). The field of observation includes not only the patient, but also the observer who interacts with the former ("participant observation"). The interaction of analyst and analysand are accounted for in the theories of transference and countertransference. As to the potential handicaps of observations traceable to the mental processes of the observer, they are subject to the constant scrutiny of the analyst. Some such handicaps of psychological observation can certainly be eliminated by the personal analysis of the observer, and this is one of the reasons that a didactic analysis is an essential element in the training of our students of analysis. Thus, what I want to say here is not that in the psychology of personality objectivity is impossible. It is rather than psychoanalysis has discovered potential sources of error and found a way to combat them.

Another aspect of the clinical origins of psychoanalytic theory is the fact that more was found, in the beginning, about pathological than about normal behavior. The etiology of neurosis was studied before the etiology of health, though psychoanalysis has,

on principle, always aimed at a comprehensive general psychology. Also, as I mentioned, more became known, in the first attempts to deal with the field, about the instinctual drives, especially about sexuality and its development, than about the forces opposing the drives in the typical ego-id conflicts. This, however, has changed in the last two or three decades, and analysis thus has today come closer to what it always was intended to be, though not every aspect and not every implication of its very comprehensive conceptual frame has so far been actually developed.

In clinical work, one is used to being guided by signs and symptoms in forming an opinion on the presence or absence of a pathological process. But the question of the significance and the use of signs for purposes of explanation is, of course, logically of much wider relevance. Different meanings can be attributed to the terms sign, signal, expressive sign, symbol, and so on, and these differences are important also in psychoanalysis. However, I don't propose to deal with this problem here. Suffice it to say that a considerable part of psychoanalytic work can be described as the use of signs—a series of associations, a dream, an affect vis-à-vis the analyst —as indications of mental processes. In this sense one speaks of the psychoanalytic method as a method of interpretation (Hartmann, 14; Bernfeld, 4; Loewenstein, 28). This has both a cognitive and a therapeutic aspect. They partly coincide, that is, in so far as a therapeutic agent of foremost significance in analysis is making the patient aware of, and capable of integrating, previously unconscious and, through defense, split-off processes. Some of those signs, for example, some of the symbols we find in dreams, have a rather ubiquitous meaning, while the interpretation of others requires a closer scrutiny of the individual under observation. At any rate, there are many situations in which the relation between a sign and what it signifies becomes easily recognizable, for instance in the associations immediately following the observation of some detail of behavior. In others, various levels of theory have to be introduced to explain the connection. Such sign systems are used today not only in the psychoanalytic situation, but also in the study by analysts, by means of direct observation, of child development. Many childhood situations of incisive significance for the formation of the adult personality have a low probability of direct manifestation. One tries to learn about the sign function of data of child behavior for a recognition of the central, and often unconscious, development that we know from the psychoanalytic interview (Hartmann, 18). At this point it is possible, or even likely, that a misunderstanding may occur of what I have said about a low probability of manifestation outside analysis of certain processes investigated in analysis. I want, then, to add explicitly that this was not meant to be a general statement. Many phenomena first studied in the analytic situation could later be studied also in the direct observation of psychotics, in so-called applied psychoanalysis, or in the direct observation of children. What I want to emphasize in this context is that the comparative study of reconstructive data and data of direct observation of children leads, on the one hand, to the confirmation of analytical propositions; on the other hand it leads to the formulation of more specific hypotheses.

The essential importance of constructs for the coherence of the psychoanalytic system (or whatever we choose to call it) can be gathered already from the brief outline I have given in the first part of this discussion. Theories, or hypotheses of a different order, connect them with observational data. That these constructs, which are introduced because of their explanatory value, cannot be directly defined in terms of observational data, but that inferences from the constructs can be tested by observation, has long been known in psychoanalysis (Hartmann, 14). Still, some of these constructs seem particularly

suspect to many critics of analysis. An occasional lack of caution in the formulation of its propositions, or Freud's liking for occasional striking metaphors, has led to the accusation against analysis of an anthropomorphization of its concepts. But in all those cases a more careful formulation can be substituted which will dispel this impression.

There is, then, the question whether and in what sense such constructs are considered "real"; and, more specifically, the question has often been asked whether and in what sense Freud considered constructs like libido, the "system unconscious," and the substructures of personality in the sense of structural psychology, as real. He said that the basic concepts of science form rather the roof than the foundation of science and ought to be changed when they no longer seem able to account for experience; also that they have the character of conventions. But he certainly thought that what he meant to cover by these basic concepts had effects which could be observed. He was in no danger of confusing concepts with realities; he was a "realist" in a different sense. He does not seem to have thought that "real" means just "the simplest theoretical presentation of our experiences," but rather that those basic concepts pointed to something real in the ordinary sense of the word.

As to the genetic propositions of analysis, the direct observation of children has not only become a rich source of information, but also given us the possibility to make our hypotheses more specific and to check their validity. A great number of Freud's hypotheses on childhood could be confirmed by direct observation of children. But to validate more completely our genetic propositions, "systematic observations of life histories from birth on" are necessary. "If the longitudinal observation in our own civilization were to be systematized and the study of life histories were to be combined with that of the crucial situations in Freud's sense, many hunches might be formulated as propositions, and others might be discarded" (Hartmann and Kris, 20).

The literature on experimental research, both in animals and in man, devised for the purpose of testing propositions derived from psychoanalysis has become very extensive. It has been repeatedly reviewed (Sears, 31; Kris, 24; Benjamin, 3; Frenkel-Brunswik, 10; and others), and I do not think I should go into it in any detail here. The following remarks are, then, random remarks and do not attempt to be in any way systematic. The classical animal experiments of Hunt, Levy, Miller, Masserman are probably known to many of you. Many of the animal experiments were conducted with considerable insight and great skill. Where the experimental set-up is adequate, the frequency of "confirmation" is impressive. Or, as Hilgard (22) states, "It has been possible to parallel many psychoanalytic phenomena in the laboratory. When this is done, the correspondence between predictions according to psychoanalytic theory and what is found is on the whole very satisfactory."

References

1. Adrian, E. D., "The Mental and the Physical Origins of Behaviour," *International Journal of Psychoanalysis*, XXVII, 1946.
2. Allport, G., *Personality*. New York: Henry Holt, 1937.
3. Benjamin, J., "Methodological Considerations in the Validation and Elaboration of Psychoanalytical Personality Theory." *American Journal of Orthopsychiatry, 20*, 1950.
4. Bernfeld, S., "Der Begriff der Deutung in der Psychoanalyse," *Zeitschrift fur Angewandte Psychologie*, XLII, 1932.
5. ——, "Freud's Earliest Theories and the School of Helmholtz," *Psychoanalytic Quarterly*, XIII, 1944.
6. Bonaparte, M., "Notes on the Analytical Discovery of a Primal Scene," *Psychoanalytic Study of the Child*, I, 1945
7. Deutsch, F., "Analytic Posturology." *Psychoanalytic Quarterly*, XXI, 1952.
8. Dollard, J. and Miller, N. E., *Personality and Psychotherapy*. New York: McGraw-Hill, 1950.
9. Ellis, A., *An Introduction to the Principles of Scientific Psychoanalysis*, Genetic Psychology Monograph, *41*, 1950.
10. Frenkel-Brunswik, E., *Psychoanalysis and the Unity of Science*, Proceedings of the American Academy of Arts and Sciences, *80*, 1954.
11. Freud, A., "The Contributions of Psychoanalysis to Genetic Psychology," *American Journal of Orthopsychiatry*, XXI, 1951.
12. Freud, S., *The Claim of Psychoanalysis to Scientific Interest*. London: Hogarth Press, Standard Edition, Vol. XIII.
13. ——, *Psycho-Analysis*. London: Hogarth Press, Standard Edition, Vol. XVIII.
14. Hartmann, H., *Die Grundlagen der Psychoanalyse*. Leipzig, 1927.
15. ——, "Ichpsychologie und Anpassungsproblem," *Internationale Zeitschrift fur Psychoanalyse*, XXIV, 1939. Partly translated in: D. Rapaport, *Organization and Pathology of Thought*. New York: Columbia University Press, 1951.
16. ——, "Comments on the Psychoanalytic Theory of Instinctual Drives," *Psychoanalytic Quarterly*, XVII, 1948.
17. ——, "Comments on the Psychoanalytic Theory of the Ego," *Psychoanalytic Study of the Child*, V, 1950.
18. ——, "Psychoanalysis and Developmental Psychology." *Psychoanalytic Study of the Child*, V, 1950.
19. ——, "The Development of the Ego Concept in Freud's Work," *International Journal of Psychoanalysis*, XXXVII, 1956.
20. —— and Kris, E., "The Genetic Approach in Psychoanalysis," *Psychoanalytic Study of the Child*, I, 1945.
21. ——, Kris, E. and Loewenstein, R., "Comments on the Formation of Psychic Structure," *Psychoanalytic Study of the Child*, II, 1946.
22. Hilgard, E., "Experimental Approaches to Psychoanalysis," in: *Psychoanalysis as Science*, ed. E. Pumpian-Mindlin. Stanford University Press, 1952.
23. Klein, G., "Cognizant Style and Motivation," in: *Assessment of Human Motives*, ed. G. Lindzey. New York: Rinehart, 1958.
24. Kris, E., "The Nature of Psychoanalytic Propositions and their Validation," in: *Freedom and Experience*, ed. S. Hook and M. R. Konvitz, Cornell University Press, 1947.
25. ——, "Notes on the Development and on some Current Problems of Psychoanalytic Child Psychology," *Psychoanalytic Study of the Child*, V, 1950.
26. Kris, M., "The Use of Prediction in a Longitudinal Study," *Psychoanalytic Study of the Child*, XII, 1957.
27. Kubie, L., "Problems and Techniques of Psychoanalytic Validation and Progress," in: *Psychoanalysis as Science*, ed. E. Pumpian-Mindlin. Stanford University Press, 1952.
28. Loewenstein, R., "Some Thoughts on In-

terpretation in the Theory and Practice of Psychoanalysis," *Psychoanalytic Study of the Child,* XII, 1957.

29. Mises, R. v., *Kleines Lehrbuch des Positivismus.* The Hague, 1939.

30. Rapaport, D., "The Structure of Psychoanalytic Theory (A Systematizing Attempt)," in: *Psychology: A Study of a*

Science, ed. S. Koch. New York: McGraw-Hill, 1958, Vol. III.

31. Sears, R., "Survey of Objective Studies of Psychoanalytic Concepts," Social Sciences Research Council *Bulletin,* 1943, 51.

32. Wisdom, J., *Philosophy and Psycho-Analysis.* New York: Philosophical Library, 1953.

Intrapsychic Theories:

ETIOLOGY AND DEVELOPMENT

The key to the development of pathological behavior, according to the intrapsychic theorist, can be found in faulty experiences in early life. Each child is born with a variety of drives or instincts which require nourishment and stimulation. Deprivation or conflicts associated with these needs result in feelings of anxiety and insecurity. In an effort to handle these feelings, the child adopts a variety of defensive maneuvers which ultimately lead to maladaptive behavior.

Carl Jung, an early disciple of Freud who broke from the main stream of psychoanalysis, retained Freud's focus on the role of unconscious processes. He posited the existence of a collective unconscious to represent a hypothetical pattern of inborn dispositions bequeathed by the ancestral past of mankind. Failure to find adequate expression for these dispositions was viewed by Jung to be the crux of psychopathology. In the paper presented here, Jung discusses in detail the pros and cons for a psychological interpretation of schizophrenia. His article can be viewed as a companion piece to the paper presented earlier by Eugen Bleuler. It represents, in part, a rebuttal to Bleuler's conviction that the basic etiology of schizophrenia is organic.

Erik Erikson, one of the major contemporary figures in "ego psychology," has formulated a model for ego development which parallels Freud's conception of the stages of psychosexual development. In the selection reprinted here, he outlines, with a clarity rare among intrapsychic writers, the major phases of early interpersonal experience. Disruptions in the sequence of this developmental pattern often lead to pathological development, according to Erikson.

On the Psychogenesis of Schizophrenia

CARL G. JUNG

It is just twenty years ago that I read a paper on the "Problem of Psychogenesis in Mental Disease" before

From *J. of Mental Science 85*: 993-1011, 1939, by permission of the Royal Medico-Psychological Association.

this Society. William McDougall, whose recent death we all deplore, was in the chair. What I then said about psychogenesis could be safely repeated to-day, for it has left no visible traces, or other noticeable consequences, either in text-books or in clinics. Although I hate to repeat myself, it is almost impossible to say something wholly new and different about a subject which has not changed its face in the many years that have gone by. My experience, however, has increased and some of my views have matured, but I could not say that my standpoint has had to undergo any radical change. I am therefore in the somewhat uncomfortable situation of one who, on the one hand, believes that he has a well-founded conviction, but, on the other hand, is afraid to indulge in the habit of repeating old stories. Although psychogenesis has been discussed long ago, it is still a modern, even an ultra-modern, problem.

There is little doubt nowadays about the psychogenesis of hysteria and other neuroses, although thirty years ago some brain enthusiasts still cherished vague suspicions that at bottom "there was something organically wrong even with neuroses." But the *consensus doctorum* in their vast majority has admitted the psychical causation of hysteria and similar neuroses. Concerning mental diseases, however, and especially concerning schizophrenia, they agreed unanimously upon an essentially organic aetiology, although for a long time specific destruction of the brain-matter could not be proved. Even in our days the question of how far schizophrenia itself can destroy brain-cells is not satisfactorily answered; much less the more specific question of how far primary organic disintegrations account for the symptomatology of schizophrenia. I quite agree with Bleuler that the great majority of symptoms are of a secondary nature and are chiefly due to psychical causes. For the primary symptoms, however, Bleuler assumes the existence of an organic cause. As the *primary symptom* he points to a peculiar disturbance of the association process which is difficult to describe. According to his description it is a matter of a sort of disintegration, inasmuch as the associations seem to be peculiarly mutilated and disjointed. He refuses to adopt Wernicke's concept of *sejunc-*

tio on account of its anatomical implications. He prefers to term it "schizophrenia", obviously understanding by this concept a more *functional* disturbance. Such disturbances, or at least very similar ones, can be observed in delirious conditions of various kinds. Bleuler himself points out the remarkable likeness between schizophrenic associations and the association phenomena in dreams and half-waking conditions. From his description it becomes sufficiently clear, that the primary symptom coincides with the condition which Pierre Janet has formulated as *abaissement du niveau mental*. It is due to a peculiar *faiblesse de la volonté*. If we are permitted to call the main guiding and controlling force of our mental life *will-power*, then one can agree that Janet's concept of the *abaissement* explains a psychical condition in which a train of thought is not carried through to its logical end, or where it is interrupted by strange contents insufficiently inhibited. Though Bleuler does not refer to Janet, I hold that Janet's notion of the *abaissement* aptly formulates Bleuler's views on the primary symptoms.

It is true, however, that Janet uses his hypothesis chiefly in order to explain the symptomatology of hysteria and other neuroses, which are indubitably psychogenic and different from schizophrenia. Yet there are certain noteworthy analogies between the neurotic and the schizophrenic mental condition. If you study the association tests of neurotics, for instance, you find that the normal associations are disturbed by the spontaneous interference of complex contents typical of an *abaissement*. The dissociation can even go so far as the creation of one, or of several, secondary personalities with an apparently complete segregation of consciousness. But the fundamental difference from schizophrenia consists in the maintenance of the potential unity of the personality. Despite the fact that consciousness can be split up into several personal consciousnesses, the unity of all the dissociated fragments is not only visible to the professional eye, but it can also be re-established by means of hypnosis. This is not the case with schizophrenia. The general picture of an association test of a schizophrenic may be very similar to the test of a neurotic, but a close exploration reveals the fact that in a schizophrenic patient the connection between the ego and certain complexes is more or less completely lost. The split is not relative, it is rather absolute. A hysterical patient might suffer from a sort of persecution mania very similar to a real paranoia, but the difference is that in the case of hysteria one can bring the delusion back under the control of consciousness, whereas it is impossible to do this in paranoia. A neurosis, it is true, is characterized by a relative autonomy of its complexes, but in schizophrenia the complexes have become disjointed and autonomous fragments, which either do not reintegrate to the psychical totality, or, in the case of a remission, are unexpectedly joined together, as if nothing had happened before.

The dissociation in schizophrenia is not only far more serious, but very often it is also irreversible. The dissociation is no longer *liquid and changeable*, as it is in a neurosis, but is more like a mirror broken up into splinters. The unity of personality which lends a humanly understandable character to its own secondary personalities in a case of hysteria is definitely severed into fragments. In a hysterical multiple personality there is an almost smooth, even a tactful, co-operation between the different persons, who neatly keep their role and, if possible, do not bother each other. One feels the presence of an invisible *spiritus rector*, or a central manager, who arranges the stage for the different figures in an almost rational way, often in the form of a more or less sentimental drama. Each figure has a suggestive name and an admissible character, and they are just as nicely hysterical and as sentimentally biased as the patient's consciousness.

The picture of a personality dissociation in schizophrenia is quite a different matter. The split-off figures assume banal, grotesque or highly exaggerated names and characters and are often objectionable in many ways. They do not, moreover, co-operate with the patient's consciousness. They are not tactful and they have no respect for sentimental values. On the contrary, they break in and make a disturbance at any time, they torture the ego in a hundred ways; all and sundry are objectionable and shocking either in their noisy and impertinent behaviour, or in their grotesque cruelty and obscenity. There is an apparent chaos of inconsistent visions, voices and characters of an overwhelmingly strange and incomprehensible nature. If there is a drama at all, it is certainly far beyond the patient's understanding. In most cases it transcends even the physician's mind, so much so that he is inclined to suspect anybody's mental sanity who sees anything more than mere madness in the ravings of a lunatic.

The autonomous figures have liberated themselves from the control of the ego so thoroughly that their original participation in the patient's mental make-up has vanished beyond recognition. The *abaissement* has reached a degree unheard of in the sphere of neuroses. A hysterical dissociation is bridged-over by a unity of the personality which still functions, whereas in schizophrenia the very foundations of the personality are injured.

The *abaissement* causes:

1. A loss of whole regions of normally controlled contents.
2. It thus produces split-off fragments of the personality.
3. It hinders the normal train of thought from being consistently carried through and completed.
4. It decreases the responsibility and the adequate reaction of the ego.
5. It causes incomplete realizations and thus produces insufficient and inadequate emotional reactions.
6. It lowers the threshold of consciousness and thus allows nor-

mally inhibited contents of the unconscious mind to enter consciousness in the form of autonomous intrusions.

We meet all these effects of the *abaissement* in neuroses as well as in schizophrenia. But in neuroses the unity of personality is at least potentially preserved, whereas in schizophrenia it is more or less damaged. On account of this fundamental injury the cleavage between dissociated psychical elements amounts to a real destruction of their former connections.

Psychogenesis of schizophrenia, therefore, in the first place means the question: Can the primary symptom, viz. the extreme *abaissement* be considered as an effect of psychological conflicts and other disorders of an emotional nature or not? I do not think that it is necessary to discuss at length the question of whether *secondary symptoms,* as Bleuler describes them, owe their existence and their specific form to psychological determination or not. Bleuler himself is fully convinced that they derive their form and contents, i. e. their individual phenomenology, entirely from emotional complexes. I agree with Bleuler, whose experience of the psychogenesis of secondary symptoms coincides with my own, for we were collaborating in the years which preceded his famous book on dementia praecox. As a matter of fact I began as early as 1903 to analyse cases of schizophrenia for theoretical purposes. There can, indeed, be no doubt about the psychological determination of secondary symptoms. Their structure and derivation is in no way different from those of neurotic symptoms, with, of course, the significant exception that they exhibit all the characteristics of mental contents no longer subordinated to the supreme control of a complete personality. There is, as a matter of fact, hardly one secondary symptom which does not show signs of the typical *abaissement* in some ways. This character, however, does not depend upon psychogenesis, but it derives entirely from the primary symptom. Psychological

causes, in other words, produce secondary symptoms exclusively on the basis of the primary condition.

In dealing with the question of psychogenesis in schizophrenia we can dismiss the secondary symptoms altogether. There is only one problem, viz., the psychogenesis of the primary condition, i. e., the extreme *abaissement,* which is, from the psychological point of view, the root of the schizophrenic disorder. We ask therefore: Is there any reason to believe that such an *abaissement* can be due to causes which are strictly psychological? An *abaissement* can be produced—as we well know—by many causes: by fatigue, normal sleep, intoxication, fever, anaemia, intense affects, shocks, organic diseases of the central nervous system, induction through mob psychology or primitive mentality or religious and political fanaticism, etc. It can also be due to constitutional and hereditary factors.

The general and more frequent form of *abaissement* does not touch the unity of the personality, at least not seriously. Thus all dissociations and other psychical phenomena derived from this general form of *abaissement* carry the seal of the integral personality.

Neuroses are specific consequences of an *abaissement;* as a rule they derive from a habitual or chronic form of it. Where they appear to be the effect of an acute form, a more or less latent psychological disposition always existed previous to the *abaissement,* so that the latter does not mean more than a conditional cause.

Now there is no doubt that an *abaissement* which leads to a neurosis is produced either by exclusively psychological factors or by those in conjunction with other, perhaps more physical, conditions. Any *abaissement,* particularly one that leads to a neurosis, means in itself that there is a weakening of the supreme control. A neurosis is a relative dissociation, a conflict between the ego and a resistant force based upon unconscious contents. Those contents are relatively severed from the connection with the psychical totality. They form parts, and the loss of them means a depotentiation of the conscious personality. The intense conflict on the other side, however, expresses an equally acute desire to re-establish the severed connection. There is no cooperation, but there is at least a violent conflict, which functions instead of a positive connection. Every neurotic fights for the maintenance and supremacy of his ego-consciousness and for the subjugation of the resistant unconscious forces. But a patient who allows himself to be swayed by the intrusions of strange contents from the unconscious, a case that does not fight, that even identifies with the morbid elements, immediately exposes himself to the suspicion of schizophrenia. His *abaissement* has reached the fatal extreme degree, where the ego loses all power of resistance against the inimical onslaught of an apparently more powerful unconscious.

Neurosis lies this side of the critical point, schizophrenia is beyond it. We do not doubt that psychological motives can bring about an *abaissement* which eventually results in a neurosis. A neurosis approaches the danger line, yet it somehow manages to remain on the hither side. If it should transgress the lines it would cease to be a neurosis. Yet are we quite certain that neurosis never steps beyond the danger line? You know that there are such cases, neuroses to all appearances for many years, and then it suddenly happens that the patient steps beyond the line and clearly transforms himself into a real psychotic.

Now, what do we say in such a case? We say that it has always been a psychosis, a "latent" one, or one concealed or camouflaged by an apparent neurosis. But what has really happened? For many years the patient fought for the maintenance of his ego, for the supremacy of his control and for the unity of his personality. But at last he gave out—he succumbed to the invader, whom he could suppress no longer. He is not merely overcome by a violent emotion, he is really drowned in a flood of insurmountably strong forces and thought forms, which are far beyond any ordinary emotion, no matter how violent. These unconscious forces and contents existed long ago and he had wrestled with them successfully for years. As a matter of fact such strange contents are not confined to the patient alone, they exist in other peoples' unconscious just as well, who, however, are fortunate enough to be profoundly ignorant of them. These forces did not originate in our patient out of the nowhere. They are most emphatically not the result of poisoned brain-cells, but are normal constituents of our unconscious minds. They appeared in numberless dreams, in the same or a similar form, at a time of life when seemingly nothing was wrong. And they appear even in the dreams of normal people, who never get anywhere near to a psychosis. But if such a normal individual should suddenly undergo a dangerous *abaissement,* his dreams would instantly seize upon him and make him think, feel and act exactly like a lunatic. And he would be one, like the man in one of Andreyev's stories, who thought he could safely bark at the moon, because he knew that he was perfectly normal. But when he barked he lost consciousness of the little difference between normal and crazy, and thus the other side overwhelmed him and he became mad.

What happened to our case was an attack of weakness—in reality it is often just a sudden panic—it made him hopeless or desperate, and then all the suppressed material welled up and drowned him.

In my experience of almost forty years I have seen quite a number of cases who developed either a psychotic interval or a lasting psychosis out of a neurotic condition. Let us assume for the time being that they really suffered from a *latent psychosis* concealed in the cloak of a neurosis. What, then, is a latent psychosis exactly? It is obviously nothing but the possibility that an individual may become mentally deranged at some period of his life. The existence of strange unconscious material proves nothing of all.

You find the same with neurotics, modern artists and poets, and also with fairly normal people, who have submitted to a careful investigation of their dreams. Moreover, you find most suggestive parallels in the mythology and symbolism of all races and times. The possibility of a future psychosis has nothing to do with the peculiar contents of the unconscious mind. But it has everything to do with the question of whether the individual can stand a certain panic, or the chronic strain of a psyche at war with itself. Very often it is merely the question of a little bit too much, i. e. of the drop that falls into a vessel already full, or of the spark that incidentally lands upon a heap of gunpowder.

Under the effect of an extreme *abaissement* the psychical totality falls asunder and splits up into complexes, and the ego-complex ceases to play the important role among these. It is just one among several or many complexes which are equally important, or perhaps even more important, than the ego is. All these complexes assume a certain personal character, although they remain fragments. It is understandable that people get panicky or that they eventually become demoralized under a chronic strain or that they despair of their hopes and expectations. It is also comprehensible when their willpower weakens and their self-control becomes slack and begins to lose its grip upon circumstances, moods and thoughts. It is quite consistent with such a state of mind when some particularly unruly parts of the patient's psyche assume a certain amount of autonomy.

Thus far schizophrenia does not behave in any way differently from a merely psychological disorder. We should search in vain for anything characteristic of our ailment in this part of the symptomatology. The real trouble begins with the disintegration of the personality and the divestment of the ego-complex from its habitual supremacy. As I have already pointed out, not even multiple personality, or certain religious or "mystical" phenomena, can be compared to what happens in schizophrenia. The primary symptom seems to have no analogy with any kind of functional disturbance. It is just as if the very basis of the psyche were giving way, as if an explosion or an earthquake were tearing asunder the structure of a normally built house. I use this allegory on purpose, because it is suggested through the symptomatology of the initial stages. Sollier has given us a vivid description of these *"troubles cénesthésiques,"* which are compared to explosions, pistol-shots and other violent noises in the head. Their projected appearance are earthquakes, cosmic catastrophes, such as the fall of the stars, the splitting of the sun, the falling asunder of the moon, the transformation of people into corpses, the freezing of the universe, and so on.

I have just said that the primary symptom appears to have no analogy with any kind of functional disturbance, yet I have omitted to mention the phenomena of the *dream*. Dreams can produce similar pictures of great catastrophes. They can show all stages of personal disintegration, so it is no exaggeration when we say that the dreamer is normally insane, or that insanity is a dream which has replaced normal consciousness. To say that insanity is a dream which has become real is no metaphor. The phenomenology of the dream and of schizophrenia is almost identical, with certain difference of course; for the one state occurs normally under the condition of sleep, while the other upsets the waking or conscious state. Sleep is also an *abaissement du niveau mental* which leads into a more or less complete oblivion of the ego. The psychical mechanism, therefore, which is destined to bring about the normal extinction and disintegration on consciousness, is a normal function which almost obeys our will. It seems as if this function were set in motion in order to bring about that sleep-like condition in which consciousness becomes reduced to the level of dreams, or where dreams are intensified to a degree paramount to that of consciousness.

Yet even if we knew that the primary symptom is produced by the aid of an always present normal function, we should still have to explain why a pathological condition ensues instead of the normal effect, viz. sleep. It must, however, be emphasized that it is precisely not sleep which is produced, but something which disturbs sleep, namely, the dream. Dreams are due to an incomplete extinction of consciousness, or to a somewhat excited state of the unconscious which interferes with sleep. Sleep is bad if too many remnants of consciousness go stirring; or if there are unconscious contents with too much energic charge, for they then rise above the threshold and create a relatively conscious state. Thus it is better to explain many dreams from the remnants of conscious impressions, while others derive directly from unconscious sources which have never existed in consciousness. The former dreams have a personal character and agree with the rules of a personalistic psychology; the latter have a collective character, inasmuch as they exhibit a peculiarly mythological, legendary or generally archaic imagery. One must turn to historical or primitive symbology in order to explain such dreams.

Both types of dream mirror themselves in the symptomatology of schizophrenia. There is a mixture of personal and collective material just as there is in dreams. But in contradistinction to normal dreams the collective material seems to prevail. This is particularly obvious in the so-called "dream states" or delirious intervals, and in paranoid conditions. It seems also to prevail in katatonic phases, in so far as we can succeed in getting a certain insight into the inner experiences of such patients. Whenever collective material prevails under normal conditions it is matter of important dreams. Primitives call them "big dreams" and consider them of tribal importance. You find the same in the Greek and Roman civilizations, where such dreams were reported to the Areopagos or to the Senate. One meets these dreams frequently in the decisive moments or periods of life: in childhood from the 3rd to the 6th year, at the time of puberty, from 14 to 16, of maturity from 20 to 25, in the middle of life from 35 to 40, and before death. They occur also when it is a matter of particularly important psychological situations. It seems that such dreams come chiefly at the moments or periods where antique or primitive mentality deemed it necessary to celebrate certain religious or magic rites, in order to produce favourable issues, or to propitiate the gods for the same end.

We may safely assume that important personal matters and worries account sufficiently for personal dreams. We are not so sure of our ground, however, when we come to collective dreams with their often weird and archaic imagery, which it is impossible to trace back to personal sources. Yet historical symbology yields the most surprising and most enlightening parallels, without which we could never follow up the often remarkable meaning of such dreams.

This fact lets one feel how inadequate the psychological training of the alienist is. It is, of course, impossible to appreciate the importance of comparative psychology for the theory of delusions without a detailed knowledge of historical and ethnical symbology. No sooner did we begin with the qualitative analysis of schizophrenic conditions at the Psychiatric Clinic in Zürich than we realized the need of such additional information. We naturally started with an entirely personalistic medical psychology, mainly as presented by Freud. But we soon came up against the fact that, in its basic structure, the human psyche is as little personalistic as the body. It is rather an inherited and universal affair. The logic of our mind, the *"raison du coeur,"* the emotions, the instincts, the basic images and forms of imagination, have in a way more resemblance to Kant's table of *a priori* categories or to Plato's *eida,* than to the scurrilities, circumstantialities, whims and tricks of our personal mind. It is especially schizophrenia that yields an immense harvest of collective symbology, neuroses yield far less, for, with a few exceptions, they show a predominantly personal psychology. The fact that schizophrenia upsets the foundations accounts for the abundance of collective symbolism, because it is the latter material that constitutes the basic structure of personality.

From this point of view we might conclude that the schizophrenic state of mind, in so far as it yields archaic material, has all the characteristics of a "big dream"—in other words, that it is an important event, exhibiting the same "numinous" quality which primitive civilizations attribute to the corresponding magic ritual. As a matter of fact, the insane person has always enjoyed the prerogative of being the one possessed by spirits or haunted by a demon, which is, by the way, a correct rendering of his psychical condition, for he is invaded by autonomous figures and thought-forms. The primitive evaluation of insanity, moreover, points out a certain characteristic which we should not overlook: it ascribes personality, initiative and wilful intention to the unconscious— again a true interpretation of the obvious facts. From the primitive standpoint it is perfectly clear that the unconscious, out of its own volition, has taken possession of the ego. According to this view the ego is not primarily enfeebled, on the contrary, it is the unconscious that is strengthened through the presence of a demon. The primitive theory, therefore, does not seek the reason for insanity in a primary weakness of consciousness, but rather in an inordinate strength of the unconscious.

I must admit it is exceedingly difficult to decide the intricate question of whether it is a matter of primary weakness and a corresponding dissociability of consciousness or of a primary strength of the unconscious. The latter possibility cannot easily be dismissed, since it is not unthinkable that the abundant archaic material might be the expression of a still existing infantile, as well as primitive, mentality. It might be a question of *atavism*. I seriously consider the possibility of a so-called *"développement arrêté,"* where a more than normal amount of primitive psychology remains intact and does not become adapted to modern conditions. It is natural that under such conditions a considerable part of the psyche should not catch up with the normal progress of consciousness. In the course of years the distance between the unconscious and the conscious mind increases and produces a latent conflict at first. But when a particular effort at adaptation is needed, and when consciousness should draw upon its unconscious instinctive resources, the conflict becomes manifest; and the hitherto latent primitive mind suddenly bursts forth with contents that are too incomprehensible and too strange for assimilation to be possible. As a matter of fact, such a moment marks the beginning of the psychosis in a great number of cases.

But one should not disregard the fact that many patients seem to be quite capable of producing a modern and sufficiently developed consciousness, sometimes of a particularly concentrated, rational and obstinate kind. However one must add quickly that such a consciousness shows early signs of a self-defensive nature. This is a symptom of weakness, not of strength.

It may be that a normal consciousness is confronted with an unusually strong unconscious; it may also be that the consciousness is just weak and therefore unable to succeed in keeping back the inflow of unconscious material. Practically I must allow for the existence of two groups of schizophrenia: the one with a weak consciousness and the other with a strong unconscious. We have here a certain analogy with neuroses, where we also find plenty of cases with a markedly weak consciousness and little willpower, and other patients, who enjoy a remarkable energy, but who are confronted with an almost overwhelmingly strong unconscious determination. This is particularly the case where creative (artistic or otherwise) impulses are coupled with unconscious incompatibilities.

If we return now to our original question, viz. the psychogenesis of schizophrenia, we reach the conclusion that the problem itself is rather complicated. At all events we ought to make it clear, that the term "psychogenesis" consists of two different things: (1) It means an exclusive psychological origin. (2) It means a number of psychological and psychical conditions. We have dealt with the second point, but we have not yet touched upon the first. This point envisages psychogenesis from the standpoint of the *causa efficiens*. The question is: Is the sole and absolute reason for a schizophrenia a psychological one or not?

In the whole field of medicine such a question is, as you know, more than awkward. Only in a very few cases can it be answered positively. The usual aetiology consists of a competition of various conditions. It has been urged, therefore, that the word causality or cause should be struck off the medical vocabulary and replaced by the term "conditionalism." I am absolutely in favour of such a measure, since it is well-nigh impossible to prove, even approximately, that schizophrenia is an organic disease to begin with. It is equally impossible to make an exclusively psychological origin evident. We may have strong suspicions as to the organic aspect of the primary symptom, but we cannot omit the well-established fact that there are many cases which developed out of an emotional shock, a disappointment, a difficult situation, a reverse of fortune, etc., and also that many relapses as well as improvements are due to psychological conditions. What shall we say about a case like this: A young student experiences a great disappointment in a love affair. He has a katatonic attack, from which he recovers after months. He then finishes his studies and becomes a successful academical man. After a number of years he returns to Zürich, where he

had experienced his love affair. Instantly he is seized by a new and very similar attack. He says that he believes he saw the girl somewhere. He recovers and avoids Zürich for several years. Then he returns and in a few days he is back in the clinic with a katatonic attack, again because he is under the impression that he has seen the girl, who by that time is married and has children.

My teacher, Eugen Bleuler, used to say that a psychological cause can only release the symptoms of the disease, but not the disease itself. This statement may be profound or the reverse. At all events it shows the alienist's perplexity. One could say, for instance, that our patient returned to Zürich when he felt the disease coming on, and one thinks that one has said something clever. He denies it—naturally, you will say. But it is a fact that this man is still deeply in love with his girl. He never went near another woman and his thoughts kept on returning to Zürich. What could be more natural than that once in a while he should give way to his unconquered longing to see the streets, the houses, the walks again, where he had met her, insanity or not? We do not know, moreover, what ecstasies and adventures he experienced during insanity and what unknown expectation tempted him to seek the experience once more. I once treated a schizophrenic girl who told me that she hated me because I had made it impossible for her to return into her beautiful psychosis. . . .

I admit that I cannot imagine, how "merely" psychical events can cause an *abaissement* which destroys the unity of personality, only too often beyond repair. But I know from long experience not only that the overwhelming majority of symptoms are due to psychological determination, but also that the beginning of an unlimited number of cases is influenced by, or at least coupled with, psychical facts which one would not hesitate to declare as causal in a case of neurosis. Statistics in this respect prove nothing to me, for I know that even in a neurotic case one runs the risk of only discovering the true anamnesis after months of careful analysis. Psychiatric anamnesis often suffers from a lack of psychological knowledge which is sometimes appalling. I do not say that physicians in general should have a knowledge of psychology, but if the alienist aims at psychotherapy at all he certainly ought to have a proper psychological education. What we call "medical psychology" is unfortunately a very one-sided affair. It may give you some knowledge of every-day complexes, but it knows far too little beyond the medical department. Psychology does not consist of medical rules of thumb,

it has far more to do with the history of civilisation, of philosophy, or religion and quite particularly with primitive mentality. The pathological mind is a vast, almost unexplored, area and little has been done in this field, whereas the biology, anatomy and physiology of schizophrenia have had all the attention they want. And with all this work, what exact knowledge have we about heredity or the nature of the primary symptom? I should say: Let us discuss the question of psychogenesis once more when the psychical side of schizophrenia has had a fair deal.

Growth and Crises

ERIK H. ERIKSON

BASIC TRUST VERSUS BASIC MISTRUST

For the first component of a healthy personality I nominate a sense of *basic trust,* which I think is an attitude toward oneself and the world derived from the experiences of the first year of life. By "trust" I mean what is commonly implied in reasonably trustfulness as far as others are concerned and a simple sense of trustworthiness as far as oneself is concerned. When I say "basic," I mean that neither this component nor any of those that follow are, either in childhood or in adulthood, especially conscious. In fact, all of these criteria, when developed in childhood and when integrated in adulthood, blend into the total personality. Their crises in childhood, however, and their impairment in adulthood are clearly circumscribed.

In describing this growth and its crises as a development of a series of alternative basic attitudes, we take recourse to the term *"a sense of."* Like a "sense of health" or a "sense of not being well," such "senses" pervade surface and depth, consciousness and the unconscious. They are ways of conscious *experience,* accessible to introspection (where it develops); ways of *behaving,* observable by others; and unconscious *inner states* determinable by test and analysis. It is important to keep these three dimensions in mind, as we proceed.

In *adults* the impairment of basic trust is expressed in a *basic mistrust.* It characterizes individuals who withdraw into themselves in particular ways when at odds with themselves and with others. These ways, which often are not obvious, are more strikingly represented by individuals who regress into psychotic states in which they sometimes close up, refusing food and comfort and becoming oblivious to companionship. In so far as we hope to assist them with psychotherapy, we must try to reach them again in specific ways in order to convince them

From *Psychological Issues* edited by G.S. Klein, pages 54-94, International Universities Press, 1959, by permission of the publisher. The original verion of this paper appeared in *Symposium on the Healthy Personality,* Supplement II; Problems of Infancy and Childhood, Transactions of Fourth Conference, March, 1950, M.J.E. Senn, ed., New York: Josiah Macy, Jr. Foundation.

that they can trust the world and that they can trust themselves (Fromm-Reichmann, 1950).

It is from the knowledge of such radical regressions and of the deepest and most infantile layers in our not-so-sick patients that we have learned to regard basic trust as the cornerstone of a healthy personality. Let us see what justifies our placing the crisis and the ascendancy of this component at the beginning of life.

As the newborn infant is separated from his symbiosis with the mother's body, his inborn and more or less coordinated ability to take in by mouth meets the mother's more or less coordinated ability and intention to feed him and to welcome him. At this point he lives through, and loves with, his mouth; and the mother lives through, and loves with, her breasts.

For the mother this is a late and complicated accomplishment, highly dependent on her development as a woman; on her unconscious attitude toward the child; on the way she has lived through pregnancy and delivery; on her and her community's attitude toward the act of nursing—and on the response of the newborn. To him the mouth is the focus of a general first approach to life—the *incorporative* approach. In psychoanalysis this stage is usually referred to as the "oral" stage. Yet it is clear that, in addition to the overwhelming need for food, a baby is, or soon becomes receptive in many other respects. As he is willing and able to suck on appropriate objects and to swallow whatever appropriate fluids they emit, he is soon also willing and able to "take in" with his eyes whatever enters his visual field. His tactual senses, too, seem to "take in" what feels good. In this sense, then, one could speak of an *"incorporative stage,"* one in which he is, relatively speaking, receptive to what he is being offered. Yet many babies are sensitive and vulnerable, too. In order to ensure that their first experience in this world may not only keep them alive but also help them to coordinate their sensitive breathing and their metabolic and circulatory rhythms, we must see to it

that we deliver to their senses stimuli as well as food in the proper intensity and at the right time; otherwise their willingness to accept may change abruptly into diffuse defense—or into lethargy.

Now, while it is quite clear what *must* happen to keep a baby alive (the minimum supply necessary) and what *must not* happen, lest he be physically damaged or chronically upset (the maximum early frustration tolerable), there is a certain leeway in regard to what *may* happen; and different cultures make extensive use of their prerogatives to decide what they consider workable and insist upon calling necessary. Some people think that a baby, lest he scratch his own eyes out, must necessarily be swaddled completely for the better part of the day and throughout the greater part of the first year; also, that he should be rocked or fed whenever he whimpers. Others think that he should feel the freedom of his kicking limbs as early as possible, but also that he, as a matter of course, be forced to cry "please" for his meals until he literally gets blue in the face. All of this (more or less consciously) seems related to the culture's general aim and system. I have known some old American Indians who bitterly decried the way in which we often let our small babies cry because we believe that "it will make their lungs strong." No wonder (these Indians said) that the white man, after such an initial reception, seems to be in a hurry to get to the "next world." But the same Indians spoke proudly of the way their infants (breast fed into the second year) became blue in the face with fury when thumped on the head for "biting" the mother's nipples; here the Indians, in turn, believed that "it's going to make good hunters of them."

There is some intrinsic wisdom, some unconscious planning and much superstition in the seemingly arbitrary varieties of child training: what is "good for the child," what *may* happen to him, depends on what he is supposed to become and where.

At any rate, it is already in his

earliest encounters that the human infant meets up with the basic modalities of his culture. The simplest and the earliest modality is *"to get,"* not in the sense of *"go and get"* but in that of receiving and accepting what is given; and this sounds easier than it is. For the groping and unstable newborn's organism learns this modality only as he learns to regulate his readiness to get with the methods of a mother who, in turn, will permit him to coordinate his means of getting as she develops and coordinates her means of giving. The mutuality of relaxation thus developed is of prime importance for the first experience of friendly otherness: from psychoanalysis one receives the impression that in thus *getting what is given,* and in learning to *get somebody to do* for him what he wishes to have done, the baby also develops the necessary groundwork to *get to be* the giver, to "identify" with her.

Where this *mutual regulation* fails, the situation falls apart into a variety of attempts to control by duress rather than by reciprocity. The baby will try to get by random activity what he cannot get by central suction; he will activate himself into exhaustion or he will find his thumb and damn the world. The mother's reaction may be to try to control matters by nervously changing hours, formulas, and procedures. One cannot be sure what this does to a baby; but it certainly is our clinical impression that in some sensitive individuals (or in individuals whose early frustration was never compensated for) such a situation can be a model for a radical disturbance in their relationship to the "world," to "people," and especially to loved or otherwise significant people.

There are ways of maintaining reciprocity by giving to the baby what he can get through other forms of feeding and by making up for what is missed orally through the satiation of other than oral receptors: his pleasure in being held, warmed, smiled at, talked to, rocked, and so forth. Besides such *"horizontal" compensation* (compensation during the same stage of development) there are many *"longitudinal"* *compensations* in life: compensations emerging from later stages of the life cycle.[1]

During the "second oral" stage the ability and the pleasure in a more active and more directed incorporative approach ripen. The teeth develop and with them the pleasure in biting *on* hard things, in biting *through* things, and in biting *off* things. This *active-incorporative* mode characterizes a variety of other activities (as did the first incorporative mode). The eyes, first part of a passive system of accepting impressions as they come along, have now learned to focus, to isolate, to "grasp" objects from the vaguer background and to follow them. The organs of hearing similarily have learned to discern significant sounds, to localize them, and to guide an appropriate change in position (lifting and turning the head, lifting and turning the upper body). The arms have learned to reach out determinedly and the hands to grasp firmly. We are more interested here in the over-all *configuration and final integration* of developing approaches to the world than in the *first appearance of specific abilities* which are so well described in the child-development literature.[2]

With all of this a number of interpersonal patterns are established which center in the social modality of *taking* and *holding on to* things—things which are more or less freely

---

[1] My participation in the longitudinal research of the Institute of Child Welfare at the University of California (see Macfarlane, 1938; Erikson, 1951b) has taught me the greatest respect for the resiliency and resourcefulness of individual children who, with the support of an expanding economy and of a generous social group, learned to compensate for grievous early misfortunes of a kind which in our clinical histories would suffice to explain malfunctioning rather convincingly. The study gave me an opportunity to chart a decade of the life histories of about fifty (healthy) children, and to remain somewhat informed about the further fortunes of some of them. However, only the development of the identity concept (see this volume, pp. 101-164) has helped me to approach an understanding of the mechanisms involved. I hope to publish my impressions.

[2] The reader trained in child development may want to pay special attention to the fact that one can think of a stage as the time when a capacity *first appears* (or appears in testable form) or as that period when it is so well *established* and integrated (has become an available apparatus for the ego, as we would say) that the next step in development can safely be initiated.

offered and given, and things which have more or less a tendency to slip away. As the baby learns to change positions, to roll over, and very gradually to establish himself on the throne of his sedentary kingdom, he must perfect the mechanisms of grasping and appropriating, holding and chewing all that is within his reach.

The *crisis* of the oral stage (during the second part of the first year) is difficult to assess and more difficult to verify. It seems to consist of the coincidence in time of three developments: (1) a physiological one: the general tension associated with a more violent drive to incorporate, appropriate, and observe more actively (a tension to which is added the discomfort of "teething" and other changes in the oral machinery); (2) a psychological one: the infant's increasing awareness of himself as a distinct person; and (3) an environmental one: the mother's apparent turning away from the baby toward pursuits which she had given up during late pregnancy and postnatal care. These pursuits include her full return to conjugal intimacy and may soon lead to a new pregnancy.

Where breast feeding lasts into the biting stage (and, generally speaking, this has been the rule) it is now necessary to learn how to continue sucking without biting, so that the mother may not withdraw the nipple in pain or anger. Our clinical work indicates that this point in the individual's early history provides him with some sense of basic loss, leaving the general impression than once upon a time one's unity with a material matrix was destroyed. Weaning, therefore, should not mean sudden loss of the breast and loss of the mother's reassuring presence too, unless, of course, other women can be depended upon to sound and feel much like the mother. A drastic loss of accustomed mother love without proper substitution at this time can lead (under otherwise aggravating conditions) to acute infantile depression (Spitz, 1945) or to a mild but chronic state of mourning which may give a depressive undertone

to the whole remainder of life. But even under more favorable circumstances, this stage seems to introduce into the psychic life a sense of division and a dim but universal nostalgia for a lost paradise.

It is against the combination of these impressions of having been deprived, of having been divided, and of having been abandoned, all of which leave a residue of basic mistrust, that basic trust must be established and maintained.[3]

What we here call "trust" coincides with what Therese Benedek has called "confidence." If I prefer the word "trust," it is because there is more naïveté and more mutuality in it: an infant can be said to be trusting, but it would be assuming too much to say that he "has confidence." The general state of trust, furthermore, implies not only that one has learned to rely on the sameness and continuity of the outer providers but also that one may trust oneself and the capacity of one's own organs to cope with urges; that one is able to consider oneself trustworthy enough so that the providers will not need to be on guard or to leave.

In the psychiatric literature we find frequent references to an "oral character," which is a characterological

---

[3] One of the chief misuses of the schema presented here is the connotation that the sense of trust (and all the other *positive* senses to be postulated) is an *achievement*, secured once and for all at a given stage. In fact, some writers are so intent on making an *achievement scale* out of these stages that they blithely omit all the *negative* senses (basic mistrust, etc.) which are and remain the dynamic counterpart of the positive senses throughout life. (See, for example, the "maturation chart" distributed at the National Congress of Parents and Teachers in Omaha, Nebraska [1958], which omits any reference to crises, and otherwise "adapts" the stages presented here.)

What the child acquires at a given stage is a certain *ratio* between the positive and the negative which, if the balance is toward the positive, will help him to meet later crises with a better chance for unimpaired total development. The idea that at any stage a *goodness* is achieved which is impervious to new conflicts within and changes without is a projection on child development of that success ideology which so dangerously pervades our private and public daydreams and can make us inept in the face of a heightened struggle for a meaningful existence in our time.

Only in the light of man's inner division and social antagonism is a belief in his essential resourcefulness and creativity justifiable and productive.

deviation based on the unsolved conflicts of this stage. Wherever oral pessimism becomes dominant and exclusive, infantile fears, such as that of "being left empty," or simply of "being left," and also of being "starved of stimulation," can be discerned in the depressive forms of "being empty" and of "being no good." Such fears, in turn, can give orality that particular avaricious quality which in psychoanalysis is called "oral sadism," that is, a cruel need to get and to take in ways harmful to others. But there is an optimistic oral character, too, one which has learned to make giving and receiving the most important thing in life; and there is "orality" as a normal substratum in all individuals, a lasting residuum of this first period of dependency on powerful providers. It normally expresses itself in our dependencies and nostalgias, and in our all too hopeful and all too hopeless states. The integration of the oral stage with all the following ones results, in adulthood, in a combination of faith and realism.

The pathology and irrationality of oral trends depend entirely on the degree to which they are integrated with the rest of the personality and the degree to which they fit into the general cultural pattern and use approved interpersonal techniques for their expression.

Here, as elsewhere, we must therefore consider as a topic for discussion the expression of *infantile urges* in *cultural patterns* which one may (or may not) consider a pathological deviation in the total economic or moral system of a culture or a nation. One could speak, for example, of the invigorating belief in "chance," that traditional prerogative of American trust in one's own resourcefulness and in Fate's store of good intentions. This belief, at times, can be seen to degenerate—in large-scale gambling, or in "taking chances" in the form of an arbitrary and often suicidal provocation of Fate, or in the insistence that one has not only the right to an equal chance but also the privilege of being preferred over all other investors in

the same general enterprise. In a similar way all the pleasant reassurances which can be derived (especially in good company) from old and new taste sensations, from inhaling and imbibing, from munching and swallowing and digesting, can turn into mass addictions neither expressive of, nor conducive to, the kind of basic trust which we have in mind.

Here we are obviously touching on phenomena the analysis of which would call for a comprehensive approach both to personality and to culture. This would be true also for an epidemiological approach to the problem of the more or less malignant elaboration of the oral character in "schizoid" characters and the mental diseases seemingly expressive of an underlying weakness in oral reassurance and basic trust. A related problem is the belief (reflected in much of contemporary obstetric and pediatric concern with the methods of child care) that the establishment of a basic sense of trust in earliest childhood makes adult individuals less dependent on mild or malignant forms of addiction, on self-delusion, and on avaricious appropriation. Of this, little is known; and the question remains whether healthy orality makes for a healthy culture or a healthy culture makes for healthy orality—or both.

At any rate, the psychiatrists, obstetricians, pediatricians, and anthropologists, to whom I feel closest, today would agree that the *firm establishment of enduring patterns for the balance of basic trust over basic mistrust* is the first task of the budding personality and therefore first of all a task for maternal care. But it must be said that the *amount of trust* derived from earliest infantile experience does not seem to depend on absolute *quantities of food or demonstrations of love* but rather on the *quality* of the maternal relationship. Mothers create a sense of trust in their children by that kind of administration which in its quality combines sensitive care of the baby's individual needs and a firm sense of personal trustworthiness within the trusted framework of their community's life style. (This forms the basis in the child for a sense of identity which will later combine a sense of being "all right," of being oneself, and of becoming what other people trust one will become.) Parents must not only have certain ways of guiding by prohibition and permission; they must also be able to represent to the child a deep, an almost somatic conviction that there is a meaning to what they are doing. In this sense a traditional system of child care can be said to be a factor making for trust, even where certain items of that tradition, taken singly, may seem irrational or unnecessarily cruel. Here much depends on whether such items are inflicted on the child by the parent in the firm traditional belief that this is the only way to do things or whether the parent misuses his administration of the baby and the child in order to work off anger, alleviate fear, or win an argument, with the child or with somebody else (mother-in-law, doctor, or priest).

In times of change—and what other times are there, in our memory? —one generation differs so much from another that items of tradition often become disturbances. Conflicts between mother's ways and one's own self-made ways, conflicts between the expert's advice and mother's ways, and conflicts between the expert's authority and one's own self-willed ways may disturb a mother's trust in herself. Furthermore, all the mass transformations in American life (immigration, migration, and Americanization; industrialization, urbanization, mechanization, and others) are apt to disturb young mothers in those tasks which are so simple yet so far-reaching. No wonder, then, that the first section of the first chapter of Benjamin Spock's (1945) book is entitled "Trust Yourself." But while it is true that the expert obstetrician and pediatrician can do much to replace the binding power of tradition by giving reassurance and guidance, he does not have the time to become the father-confessor for all the doubts and fears, angers and arguments, which can fill the minds of lonely young parents. Maybe

a book like Spock's needs to be read in study groups where the true psychological spirit of the town meeting can be created; that is, where matters are considered to be agreed upon not because somebody said so, but because the free airing of opinions and emotions, of prejudices and of errors has led to a general area of relative consent and of tolerant good will.

This chapter has become unduly long. In regard to the matters discussed here, it is too bad that one must begin with the beginning. We know so little of the beginnings, of the deeper strata of the human mind. But since we have already embarked on general observations, a word must be said about one cultural and traditional institution which is deeply related to the matter of trust, namely, religion.

It is not the psychologist's job to decide whether religion should or should not be confessed and practiced in particular words and rituals. Rather the psychological observer must ask whether or not in any area under observation religion and tradition are living psychological forces creating the kind of faith and conviction which permeates a parent's personality and thus reinforces the child's basic trust in the world's trustworthiness. The psychopathologist cannot avoid observing that there are millions of people who cannot really afford to be without religion, and whose pride in not having it is that much whistling in the dark. On the other hand, there are millions who seem to derive faith from other than religious dogmas, that is, from fellowship, productive work, social action, scientific pursuit, and artistic creation. And again, there are millions who profess faith, yet in practice mistrust both life and man. With all of these in mind, it seems worth while to speculate on the fact that religion through the centuries has served to restore a sense of trust at regular intervals in the form of faith while giving tangible form to a sense of evil which it promises to ban. All religions have in common the periodical childlike surrender to a Provider or providers who dispense earthly fortune as well as spiritual health; the demonstration of one's smallness and dependence through the medium of reduced posture and humble gesture; the admission in prayer and song of misdeeds, of misthoughts, and of evil intentions; the admission of inner division and the consequent appeal for inner unification by divine guidance; the need for clearer self-delineation and self-restriction; and finally, the insight that individual trust must become a common faith, individual mistrust a commonly formulated evil, while the individual's need for restoration must become part of the ritual practice of many, and must become a sign of trustworthiness in the community.

Whosoever says he has religion must derive a faith from it which is transmitted to infants in the form of basic trust; whosoever claims that he does not need religion must derive such basic faith from elsewhere.

AUTONOMY VERSUS SHAME AND DOUBT

A survey of some of the items discussed in Spock's book under the headings "The One-Year-Old" and "Managing Young Children" will enable those of us who, at this time, do not have such inquisitive creatures in our homes to remember our skirmishes, our victories, and our defeats:

Feeling his oats.

The passion to explore.

He gets more dependent and more independent at the same time.

Arranging the house for a wandering baby.

Avoiding accidents.

Now's the time to put poisons out of reach.

How do you make him leave certain things alone?

Dropping and throwing things.

Children learn to control their own aggressive feelings.

Biting humans.

Keeping bedtime happy.

The small child who won't stay in bed at night.

My selection is intended to convey the inventory and range of problems described though I cannot review here either the doctor's excellent advice or his good balance in depicting the remarkable ease and matter-of-factness with which the nursery may be governed at this as at any other stage. Nevertheless, there is an indication of the sinister forces which are leashed and unleashed, especially in the guerilla warfare of unequal wills; for the child is often unequal to his own violent drives, and parent and child unequal to each other.

The over-all significance of this stage lies in the maturation of the muscle system, the consequent ability (and doubly felt inability) to coordinate a number of highly conflicting action patterns such as "holding on" and "letting go," and the enormous value with which the still highly dependent child begins to endow his autonomous will.

Psychoanalysis has enriched our vocabulary with the word "anality" to designate the particular pleasurableness and willfulness which often attach to the eliminative organs at this stage. The whole procedure of evacuating the bowels and the bladder as completely as possible is, of course, enhanced from the beginning by a premium of "feeling good" which says in effect, "well done." This premium, at the beginning of life, must make up for quite frequent discomfort and tension suffered as the bowels learn to do their daily work. Two developments gradually give these anal experiences the necessary volume: the arrival of better formed stool and the general coordination of the muscle system which permits the development of voluntary release, of dropping and throwing away. This new dimension of approach to things, however, is not restricted to the sphincters. A general ability, indeed, a violent need, develops to drop and to throw away and to alternate withholding and expelling at will.

As far as anality proper is concerned, at this point everything depends on whether the cultural environment wants to make something of it. There are cultures where the parents ignore anal behavior and leave it to older children to lead the toddler out to the bushes so that his compliance in this matter may coincide with his wish to imitate the bigger ones. Our Western civilization, and especially certain classes within it, have chosen to take the matter more seriously. It is here that the machine age has added the ideal of a mechanically trained, faultlessly functioning, and always clean, punctual, and deodorized body. In addition it has been more or less consciously assumed that early and rigorous training is absolutely necessary for the kind of personality which will function efficiently in a mechanized world which says "time is money" and which calls for orderliness, punctuality, and thrift. Indications are that in this, we have gone too far; that we have assumed that a child is an animal which must be broken or a machine which must be set and tuned —while, in fact, human virtues can grow only by steps. At any rate our clinical work suggests that the neurotics of our time include the "overcompulsive" type, who is stingy, retentive, and meticulous in matters of affection, time, and money, as well as in matters concerning his bowels. Also, bowel and bladder training has bcome the most obviously disturbing item of child training in wide circles of our society.

What, then, makes the anal problem potentially important and difficult?

The anal zone lends itself more than any other to the expression of stubborn insistence on conflicting impulses because, for one thing, it is the model zone for two contradictory modes which must become alternating; namely, *retention* and *elimination*. Furthermore, the sphincters are only part of the muscle system with its general ambiguity of rigidity and relaxation, of flexion and extension. This whole stage, then, becomes a battle for *autonomy*. For as he gets ready to stand on his feet more firmly,

the infant delineates his world as "I" and "you," "me" and "mine." Every mother knows how astonishingly pliable a child may be at this stage, if and when he has made the decision that he *wants* to do what he is supposed to do. It is impossible, however, to find a reliable formula for making him want to do just that. Every mother knows how lovingly a child at this stage will snuggle and how ruthlessly he will suddenly try to push the adult away. At the same time the child is apt both to hoard things and to discard them, to cling to possessions and to throw them out of the windows of houses and vehicles. All of these seemingly contradictory tendencies, then, we include under the formula of the retentive-eliminative modes.

The matter of mutual regulation between adult and child now faces its severest test. If outer control by too rigid or too early training insists on robbing the child of his attempt *gradually* to control his bowels and other functions willingly and by his free choice, he will again be faced with a double rebellion and a double defeat. Powerless in his own body (sometimes afraid of his bowels) and powerless outside, he will again be forced to seek satisfaction and control either by regression or by fake progression. In other words, he will return to an earlier, oral control, that is, by sucking his thumb and becoming whiny and demanding; or he will become hostile and willful, often using his feces (and, later, dirty words) as ammunition; or he will pretend an autonomy and an ability to do without anybody to lean on which he has by no means really gained.

This stage, therefore, becomes decisive for the ratio between love and hate, for that between cooperation and willfulness, and for that between the freedom of self-expression and its suppression. From a sense of *self-control without loss of self-esteem* comes a lasting sense of autonomy and pride; from a sense of muscular and anal impotence, of loss of self-control, and of parental overcontrol comes a lasting sense of doubt and shame.

To develop autonomy, a firmly developed and a convincingly continued stage of early trust is necessary. The infant must come to feel that basic faith in himself and in the world (which is the lasting treasure saved from the conflicts of the oral stage) will not be jeopardized by this sudden violent wish to have a choice, to appropriate demandingly, and to eliminate stubbornly. *Firmness* must protect him against the potential anarchy of his as yet untrained sense of discrimination, his inability to hold on and to let go with circumspection. Yet his environment must back him up in his wish to "stand on his own feet" lest he be overcome by that sense of having exposed himself prematurely and foolishly which we call shame, or that secondary mistrust, that "doubletake," which we call doubt.

Shame is an infantile emotion insufficiently studied. Shame supposes that one is completely exposed and conscious of being looked at—in a word, self-conscious. One is visible and not ready to be visible; that is why we dream of shame as a situation in which we are stared at in a condition of incomplete dress, in night attire, "with one's pants down." Shame is early expressed in an impulse to bury one's face, or to sink, right then and there, into the ground. This potentiality is abundantly utilized in the educational method of "shaming" used so exclusively by some primitive peoples, where it supplants the often more destructive sense of guilt to be discussed later. The destructiveness of shaming is balanced in some civilizations by devices for *"saving face."* Shaming exploits an increasing sense of being small, which paradoxically develops as the child stands up and as his awareness permits him to note the relative measures of size and power.

Too much shaming does not result in a sense of propriety but in a secret determination to try to get away with things when unseen, if, indeed, it does not result in deliberate *shamelessness*. There is an impressive American ballad in which a murderer to be hanged on the gallows before the eyes of the community, instead of feeling appropriately afraid or ashamed, begins to berate the onlookers, ending every salvo of defiance with the words, "God damn your eyes." Many a small child, when shamed beyond endurance, may be in a mood (although not in possession of either the courage or the words) to express defiance in similar terms. What I mean by this sinister reference is that there is a limit to a child's and an adult's individual endurance in the face of demands which force him to consider himself, his body, his needs, and his wishes as evil and dirty, and to believe in the infallibility of those who pass such judgment. Occasionally he may be apt to turn things around, to become secretly oblivious to the opinion of others, and to consider as evil only the fact that they exist: his chance will come when they are gone, or when he can leave them.

Many a defiant child, many a young criminal, is of such makeup, and deserves at least an investigation into the conditions which caused him to become that way.

To repeat: muscular maturation sets the stage for experimentation with two simultaneous sets of social modalities—*holding on* and *letting go*. As is the case with all of these modalities, their basic conflicts can lead in the end either to hostile or to benign expectations and attitudes. Thus, "to hold" can become a destructive and cruel retaining or restraining, and it can become a pattern of care: "to have and to hold." To "let go," too, can turn into an inimical letting loose of destructive forces, or it can become a relaxed "to let pass" and "to let be." Culturally speaking, these modalities are neither good nor bad; their value depends on whether their hostile implications are turned against enemy or fellow man —or against the self.

The last-named danger is the one best known to psychiatry. Denied the gradual and well-guided experience of the autonomy of free choice, or weakened by an initial loss of trust, the sensitive child may turn against himself all his urge to discriminate and to manipulate. He will *overmanipulate himself,* he will develop a *precocious conscience.* Instead of taking possession of things in order to test them by repetitive play, he will become obsessed by his own repetitiveness; he will want to have everything "just so," and only in a given sequence and tempo. By such infantile obsessiveness, by dawdling, for example, or by becoming a stickler for certain rituals, the child then learns to gain power over his parents and nurses in areas where he could not find large scale mutual regulation with them. Such hollow victory, then, is the infantile model for a compulsion neurosis. As for the consequences of this for adult character, they can be observed in the classical compulsive character which we have mentioned. We must add to this the character dominated by the wish to "get away with" things—yet unable to get away even with the wish. For while he learns evasion from others, his precocious conscience does not let him really get away with anything, and he goes through life habitually ashamed, apologetic, and afraid to be seen; or else, in a manner which we call "overcompensatory," he evinces a defiant kind of autonomy. Real inner autonomy, however, is not carried on the sleeve.

But it is time to return from these considerations of the abnormal to a study of the headings which transmit the practical and benevolent advice of the children's doctor. They all add up to this: be firm and tolerant with the child at this stage, and he will be firm and tolerant with himself. He will feel pride in being an autonomous person; he will grant autonomy to others; and now and again he will even let himself get away with something.

Why, then, if we know how, do we not tell parents in detail what to do to develop this intrinsic, this genuine autonomy? The answer is: because when it comes to human values, nobody knows how to fabricate or manage the fabrication of the genuine article. My own field, psychoanalysis, having studied particularly the excessive increase of guilt feelings beyond any

normal rhyme or reason, and the consequent excessive estrangement of the child from his own body, attempted at least to formulate what should *not* be done to children. These formulations, however, often aroused superstitious inhibitions in those who were inclined to make anxious rules out of vague warnings. Actually, we are learning only gradually what exactly *not* to do with *what kind* of children at *what age.*

People all over the world seem convinced that to make the right (meaning *their*) kind of human being, one must consistently introduce the senses of shame, doubt, guilt and fear into a child's life. Only the patterns vary. Some cultures begin to restrict early in life, some late, some abruptly, others more gradually. Until enough comparative observations are available, we are apt to add further superstitions, merely because of our wish to *avoid* certain pathological conditions, without even knowing definitely all the factors which are responsible for these conditions. So we say: Don't wean too early; don't train too early. But what is too early and what is too late seem to depend not only on the pathologies we wish to avoid but also on the values we wish to create, or, to put it more honestly, on the values we wish to live by. For no matter what we do in detail, the child will feel primarily what we live by, what makes us loving, cooperative, and firm beings, and what makes us hateful, anxious, and divided in ourselves.

There are of course a few matters of necessary avoidance which become clear from our basic epigenetic point of view. It will be remembered that every new development carries with it its own specific vulnerability. For example, at around eight months the child seems to be somehow more aware, as it were, of his *separateness;* this prepares him for the impending sense of autonomy. At the same time he becomes more cognizant of his mother's features and presence and of the strangeness of others. Sudden or prolonged separation from his mother at that time apparently can cause a sensitive child to experience an aggravation of the experience of division and abandonment, arousing violent anxiety and withdrawal. Again, in the first quarter of the second year, if everything has gone well, the infant just begins to become aware of the autonomy discussed in this chapter. The introduction of bowel training at this time may cause him to resist with all his strength and determination, because he seems to feel that his budding will is being "broken." To avoid this feeling is certainly more important than to insist on his being trained just then because there is a time for the stubborn ascendancy of autonomy and there is a time for the partial sacrifice of secure autonomy, but obviously the time for a meaningful sacrifice is *after* one has acquired and reinforced a core of autonomy and has also acquired more insight.

The more exact localization in time of the most critical growth periods of the personality is becoming established only now. Often, the unavoidable cause of trouble is not one event but the coincidence in time of a number of changes which upset the child's orientation. He may have been involved in a special growth period when the family moved to a new place. Perhaps he was forced to conceive of his first words all over again when the grandmother who had taught him these words suddenly died. A trip on the part of the mother may have exhausted her because she happened to be pregnant at the time, and thus unable, on returning, to make proper amends. Given the right spirit toward life and its vicissitudes, a parent can usually handle such matters, if necessary with the help of the pediatrician or guidance expert. The expert's job, however, should be (to quote Frank Fremont-Smith) *"to set the frame of reference within which choice is permissible and desirable."* For in the last analysis (as comparative studies in child training have convinced many of us) the kind and degree of a sense of autonomy which parents are able to grant their small children depends on the dignity and the sense of personal independence which they derive from their own lives. Again, just as the sense of trust is a reflection of the parents' sturdy and realistic faith, so is the sense of autonomy a reflection of the parents' dignity as individuals.

As was the case with "oral" personality, the compulsive personality (often referred to as "anal" in the psychiatric literature) has its normal aspects and its abnormal exaggerations. If well integrated with other compensatory traits, some compulsiveness is useful in the administration of matters in which order, punctuality, and cleanliness are essential. The question is always whether we remain the masters of the rules by which we want to make things more manageable (not more complicated) or whether the rules master the ruler. But it often happens, in the individual as well as in group life, that the letter of the rules kills the spirit which created them.

We have related basic trust to the institution of religion. The basic need of the individual for a delineation of his *autonomy* in the adult order of things seems, in turn, to be taken care of by the *principle of "law and order,"* which in daily life as well as in the high courts of law apportions to each his privileges and his limitations, his obligations and his rights. The sense of autonomy which arises, or should arise, in the second stage of childhood, is fostered by a handling of the small individual which expresses a sense of rightful dignity and lawful independence on the part of the parents and which gives him the confident expectation that the kind of autonomy fostered in childhood will not be frustrated later. This, in turn, necessitates a relationship of parent to parent, of parent to employer, and of parent to government which reaffirms the parent's essential dignity within the hierarchy of social positions. It is important to dwell on this point because much of the shame and doubt, much of the indignity and uncertainty which is aroused in children is a consequence of the parents' frustrations in marriage, in work, and in citizenship. Thus, the sense of autonomy in the child (a sense richly fostered in American childhood in general) must be backed up by the preservation in economic and political life of a high sense of autonomy and of self-reliance.

Social organization assigns with the power of government certain privileges of leadership and certain obligations of conduct; while it imposes on the ruled certain obligations of compliance and certain privileges of remaining autonomous and self-determining. Where this whole matter becomes blurred, however, the matter of individual autonomy becomes an issue of mental health, as well as one of economic reorientation. Where large numbers of people have been prepared in childhood to expect from life a high degree of personal autonomy, pride, and opportunity, and then in later life find themselves ruled by superhuman organizations and machinery too intricate to understand, the result may be deep chronic disappointment not conducive to healthy personalities willing to grant each other a measure of autonomy. All great nations (and all the small ones) are increasingly challenged by the complication and mechanization of modern life, and are being enveloped in the problems of the organization of larger units, larger spheres, and larger interdependencies which by necessity redefine the role of the individual. It is important for the spirit of this country, as it is for that of the world, than an increased consciousness of equality and individuality may grow out of the necessity for divided function within the increasing complexity of organization; for otherwise a number of fears are aroused which find expression in anxiety on a large scale, often individually slight and hardly conscious, but nevertheless strangely upsetting to people who seemingly, on the surface, have what they want or what they seem to have a right to expect. Besides irrational fears of losing one's autonomy—"don't fence me in"—there are fears of being sabotaged in one's free will by inner enemies; of being restricted and constricted in one's autonomous initiative;

and, paradoxically enough, at the same time of not being completely controlled enough, of not being told what to do. While many such fears are, of course, based on the realistic appraisal of dangers inherent in complex social organizations and in the struggle for power, safety, and security, they seem to contribute to psychoneurotic and psychosomatic disturbances on the one hand, and, on the other, to the easy acceptance of slogans which seem to promise alleviation of conditions by excessive and irrational conformity.

INITIATIVE VERSUS GUILT

Having found a firm solution of his problem of autonomy, the child of four and five is faced with the next step—and with the next crisis. Being firmly convinced that he *is* a person, the child must now find out *what kind* of a person he is going to be. And here he hitches his wagon to nothing less than a star: he wants to be like his parents, who to him appear very powerful and very beautiful, although quite unreasonably dangerous. He "identifies with them," he plays with the idea of how it would be to be them. Three strong developments help at this stage, yet also serve to bring the child closer to his crisis: (1) he learns to *move around* more freely and more violently and therefore establishes a wider and, so it seems to him, an unlimited radius of goals; (2) his sense of *language* becomes perfected to the point where he understands and can ask about many things just enough to misunderstand them thoroughly; and (3) both language and locomotion permit him to expand his *imagination* over so many things that he cannot avoid frightening himself with what he himself has dreamed and thought up. Nevertheless, out of all this he must emerge with a sense of *unbroken initiative* as a basis for a high and yet realistic sense of ambition and independence.

One may ask here—one may, indeed—what are the criteria for such an unbroken sense of initiative? The criteria for all the senses discussed here are the same: a crisis, beset with fears, or at least a general anxiousness or tension, seems to be resolved, in that the child suddenly seems to "grow together" both psychologically and physically. He seems to be "more himself," more loving and relaxed and brighter in his judgment (such as it is at this stage). Most of all, he seems to be, as it were, self-activated; he is in the free possession of a certain surplus of energy which permits him to forget failures quickly and to approach what seems desirable (even if it also seems dangerous) with undiminished and better aimed effort. In this way the child and his parents face the next crisis much better prepared.

We are now approaching the end of the third year, when walking is getting to be a thing of ease, or vigor. The books tell us that a child "can walk" much before this; but from the point of view of personality development he cannot really walk as long as he is only able to accomplish the feat more or less well, with more or fewer props, for short spans of time. He has made walking and running an item in his sphere of mastery when gravity is felt to be *within,* when he can forget that he is doing the walking and instead can find out what he can do *with it.* Only then do his legs become an unconscious part of him instead of being an external and still unreliable ambulatory appendix. Only then will he find out with advantage what he now *may* do, along with what he *can* do.

To look back: the first way-station was prone relaxation. The trust based on the experience that the basic mechanisms of breathing, digesting, sleeping, and so forth have a consistent and familiar relation to the foods and comforts offered gives zest to the developing ability to raise oneself to a sitting and then to a standing position. The second way-station (accomplished only securely but, as it were, untiringly, a feat which permits the muscle system gradually to be used for finer discrimi-

nation and for more autonomous ways of selecting and discarding, of piling things up—and of throwing them away with a bang.

The third way-station finds the child able to move independently and vigorously. He is ready to visualize himself as being as big as the perambulating grownups. He begins to make comparisons and is apt to develop untiring curiosity about differences in sizes in general, and sexual differences in particular. He tries to comprehend possible future roles, or at any rate to understand what roles are worth imitating. More immediately, he can now associate with those of his own age. Under the guidance of older children or special women guardians, he gradually enters into the infantile politics of nursery school, street corner, and barnyard. His learning now is eminently intrusive and vigorous: it leads away from his own limitations and into future possibilities.

The *intrusive mode,* dominating much of the behavior of this stage, characterizes a variety of configurationally "similar" activities and fantasies. These include the intrusion into other bodies by physical attack; the intrusion into other people's ears and minds by aggressive talking; the intrusion into space by vigorous locomotion; the intrusion into the unknown by consuming curiosity.

This is also the stage of infantile sexual curiosity, genital excitability, and occasional preoccupation and overconcern with sexual matters. This "genitality" is, of course, rudimentary, a mere promise of things to come; often it is not particularly noticeable as such. If not specifically provoked into precocious manifestation by especially strict and pointed prohibitions ("if you touch it, the doctor will cut it off") or special customs (such as sex play in groups), it is apt to lead to no more than a series of fascinating experiences which soon become frightening and pointless enough to be repressed. This leads to the ascendancy of that human specialty which Freud called the "latency" period, that is, the long delay separating infantile sexuality (which in animals is followed by maturity) and physical sexual maturation.

The sexual orientation of the boy is focused on the phallus and its sensations, purposes, and meanings. While erections undoubtedly occur earlier (either reflexively or in response to things and people who make the child feel intensively), a focused interest may now develop in the genitalia of both sexes, as well as an urge to perform playful sex acts, or at least acts of sexual investigation. The increased locomotor mastery and the pride in being big now and *almost* as good as father and mother receives its severest setback in the clear fact that in the genital sphere one is vastly inferior; furthermore, it receives an additional setback in the fact that not even in the distant future is one ever going to be father in sexual relationship to mother, or mother in sexual relationship to father. The very deep emotional consequences of this insight and the magic fears associated with it make up what Freud has called the oedipus complex.

Psychoanalysis verifies the simple conclusion that boys attach their first genital affection to the maternal adults who have otherwise given comfort to their bodies and that they develop their first sexual rivalry against the persons who are the sexual owners of those maternal persons. The little girl, in turn, becomes attached to her father and other important men and jealous of her mother, a development which may cause her much anxiety, for it seems to block her retreat to that selfsame mother, while it makes the mother's disapproval ever so much more magically dangerous because unconsciously "deserved."

Girls often have a difficult time at this stage, because they observe sooner or later that, although their locomotor, mental, and social intrusiveness is increased equally with, and is as adequate as, that of the boys, thus permitting them to become perfect tomboys, they lack one item: the penis; and with it, important prerogatives in some cultures and classes. While the boy has this visible, erectable, and comprehensible organ to which he can attach dreams of adult bigness, the girl's clitoris only poorly sustains dreams of sexual equality. She does not even have breasts as analogously tangible tokens of her future, her maternal drives are relegated to play fantasy or baby tending. On the other hand, where mothers dominate households, the boy, in turn, can develop a sense of inadequacy because he learns at this stage that while a boy can do well in play and work, he will never boss the house, the mother, and the older sisters. His mother and sisters, in fact, might get even with him for vast doubts in themselves by making him feel that a boy (with his snails and puppy-dog tails) is really an inferior if not a repulsive creature. Both the girl and the boy are now extraordinarily appreciative of any convincing promise of the fact that someday they will be as good as father or mother—perhaps better; and they are grateful for sexual enlightenment, a little at a time, and patiently repeated at intervals. Where the necessities of economic life and the simplicity of its social plan make the male and female roles and their specific powers and rewards comprehensible, the early misgivings about sexual differences are, of course, more easily integrated in the culture's design for the differentiation of sexual roles.

This stage adds to the inventory of basic social modalities in both sexes that of "making" in the older and today slangier sense of "being on the make." There is no simpler, stronger word to match the social modalities previously enumerated. The word suggests enjoyment of competition, insistence on goal, pleasure of conquest. In the boy the emphasis remains on "making" by head-on attack; in the girl it may change to "making" by making herself attractive and endearing. The child thus develops the prerequisites for *masculine* and *feminine initiative,* that is, for the selection of social goals and perseverance in approaching them. Thus the stage is all set for entrance into life, except that life must first be school life. The child here must repress or forget many of his fondest hopes and most energetic wishes, while his exuberant imagination is tamed and he learns the necessary self-restraint and the necessary interest in impersonal things—even the three R's. This often demands a change of personality that is sometimes too drastic for the good of the child. This change is not only a result of education but also of an inner reorientation, and it is based on a biological fact (the delay of sexual maturation) and a psychological one (the repression of childhood wishes). For those sinister oedipal wishes (so simply and so trustingly expressed in the boy's assurance that he will marry mother and make her proud of him and in the girl's that she will marry father and take much better care of him), in consequence of vastly increased imagination and, as it were, the intoxication of increased locomotor powers, seem to lead to secret fantasies of terrifying proportions. The consequence is a deep sense of *guilt*—a strange sense, for it forever seems to imply that the individual has committed crimes and deeds which, after all, were not only not committed but also would have been biologically quite impossible.

While the struggle for autonomy at its worst concentrated on keeping rivals out, and was therefore more an expression of *jealous rage* most often directed against encroachments by *younger* siblings, initiative brings with it *anticipatory rivalry* with those who were there first and who may therefore occupy with their superior equipment the field toward which one's initiative is directed. Jealousy and rivalry, those often embittered and yet essentially futile attempts at demarcating a sphere of unquestioned privilege, now come to a climax in a final contest for a favored position with one of the parents; the inevitable and necessary failure leads to guilt and anxiety. The child indulges in fantasies of being a giant and a tiger, but in his dreams he runs in terror for dear life. This, then, is the stage of fear for life and limb, including the fear of losing (or on the

part of the girl the conviction that she may have lost) the male genital as punishment for the fantasies attached to infantile genital excitement.

All of this may seem strange to readers who have only seen the sunnier side of childhood and have not recognized the potential powerhouse of destructive drives which can be aroused and temporarily buried at this stage, only to contribute later to the inner arsenal of a destructiveness so ready to be used when opportunity provokes it. By using the words "potential," "provoke" and "opportunity," I mean to emphasize that there is little in these inner developments which cannot be harnessed to constructive and peaceful initiative if only we learn to understand the conflicts and anxieties of childhood and the importance of childhood for mankind. But if we should choose to overlook or belittle the phenomena of childhood, or to regard them as "cute" (even as the individual forgets the best and the worst dreams of his childhood), we shall forever overlook one of the eternal sources of human anxiety and strife.

It is at this stage of initiative that the great governor of initiative, namely, *conscience,* becomes firmly established. Only as a dependent does man develop conscience, that dependence on himself which makes him, in turn, dependable; and only when thoroughly dependable with regard to a number of fundamental values can he become independent and teach and develop tradition.

The child now feels not only ashamed when found out but also afraid of being found out. He now hears, as it were, God's voice without seeing God. Moreover, he begins automatically to feel guilty even for mere thoughts and for deeds which nobody has watched. This is the cornerstone of morality in the individual sense. But from the point of view of mental health, we must point out that if this great achievement is overburdened by all too eager adults, it can be bad for the spirit and for morality itself. For the conscience of the child *can* be primitive, cruel, and uncompromising, as may be observed in instances where children learn to constrict themselves to the point of over-all inhibition; where they develop an obedience more literal than the one the parent wishes to exact; or where they develop deep regressions and lasting resentments because the parents themselves do not seem to live up to the new conscience which they have fostered in the child. One of the deepest conflicts in life is the hate for a parent who served as the model and the executor of the conscience but who (in some form) was found trying to "get away with" the very transgressions which the child can no longer tolerate in himself. These transgressions often are the natural outcome of the existing inequality between parent and child. Often, however, they represent a thoughtless exploitation of such inequality; with the result that the child comes to feel that the whole matter is not one of universal goodness but of arbitrary power. The suspiciousness and evasiveness which is thus mixed in with the all-or-nothing quality of the superego, that organ of tradition, makes moralistic man a great potential danger to himself and to his fellow men. It is as if morality, to him, became synonymous with vindictiveness and with the suppression of others.

It is necessary to point to the source of such moralism (not to be mistaken for morality) in the child of this age because infantile moralism is a stage to be lived through and worked through. The consequences of the guilt aroused at this stage (guilt expressed in a deep-seated conviction that the child as such, or drive as such, is essentially bad) often do not show until much later, when conflicts over initiative may find expression in a self-restriction which keeps an individual from living up to his inner capacities or to the powers of his imagination and feeling (if not in relative sexual impotence or frigidity). All of this, of course, may in turn be "overcompensated" in a great show of tireless initiative, in a quality of "go-at-itive-ness" at all cost. Many adults feel that

their worth as people consists entirely in *what they are doing,* or rather in *what they are going to do next,* and not in what they are, as individuals. The strain consequently developed in their bodies, which are always "on the go," with the engine racing, even at moments of rest, is a powerful contribution to the much-discussed psychosomatic diseases of our time.

Pathology, however, is only the sign that valuable human resources are being neglected, that they have been neglected first of all in childhood. The problem is again one of mutual regulation. Where the child, now so ready to overrestrict himself, can gradually develop a sense of responsibility, where he can gain some simple feeling for the institutions, functions, and roles which will permit him to anticipate his responsible participation as an adult, he will soon find pleasurable accomplishment in wielding miniature tools and weapons, in manipulating meaningful toys, and in taking care of himself—and of younger children.

For such is the wisdom of the ground plan that at no time is the individual more ready to learn quickly and avidly, to become big in the sense of sharing obligation, discipline, and performance rather than power, in the sense of *making things, instead of "making" people,* than during this period of his development. He is also eager and able to *make things together,* to combine with other children for the purpose of constructing and planning, instead of trying to boss and coerce them; and he is able and willing to profit fully by the association with teachers and ideal prototypes.

Parents often do not realize why some children suddenly seem to think less of them and seem to attach themselves to teachers, to the parents of other children, or to people representing occupations which the child can grasp: firemen and policemen, gardeners and plumbers. The point is that children do not wish to be reminded of the principal inequality with the parent of the same sex. They remain identified with this same parent; but for the present they look for opportunities where superficial identification seems to promise a field of initiative without too much conflict or guilt.

Often, however (and this seems more typical of the American home than of any other in the world), the child can be guided by the parent himself into a second, a more realistic identification based on the spirit of equality experienced in doing things together. In connection with comprehensible technical tasks, a companionship may develop between father and son, an experience of essential *equality in worth*, in spite of the *inequality in time schedules.* Such companionship is a lasting treasure not only for parent and child but for mankind, which so sorely needs an alleviation of all those hidden hatreds which stem from the exploitation of weakness because of mere size or schedule.

Only a combination of early prevention and alleviation of hatred and guilt in the growing being, and the consequent handling of hatred in the free collaboration of people who feel *equal in worth although different in kind or function or age,* permits a peaceful cultivation of initiative, a truly free sense of enterprise. And the word "enterprise" was deliberately chosen. For a comparative view of child training suggests that it is the prevalent economic ideal, or some of its modifications, which is transmitted to the child at the time when, in identification with his parent, he applies the dreams of early childhood to the as yet dim goals of an active adult life.

INDUSTRY VERSUS INFERIORITY

One might say that personality at the first stage crystallizes around the conviction "I am what I am given," and that of the second, "I am what I will." The third can be characterized by "I am what I can imagine I will be." We must now approach the fourth: "I am what I learn." The child now wants to be shown how to get busy with something and how to be busy with others.

This trend, too, starts much earlier, especially in some children. They want to watch how things are done and to try doing them. If they are lucky they live near barnyards or on streets around busy people and around many other children of all ages, so that they can watch and try, observe and participate as their capacities and their initiative grow in tentative spurts. But now it is time to *go to school.* In all cultures, at this stage, children receive some systematic instruction, although it is by no means always in the kind of school which literate people must organize around teachers who have learned how to teach literacy. In preliterate people much is learned from adults who become teachers by acclamation rather than by appointment; and very much is learned from older children. What is learned in more primitive surroundings is related to the basic skills of *technology* which are developed as the child gets ready to handle the utensils, the tools, and the weapons used by the big people: he enters the technology of his tribe very gradually but also very directly. More literate people, with more specialized careers, must prepare the child by teaching him things which first of all make him literate. He is then given the widest possible basic education for the greatest number of possible careers. The greater the specialization, the more indistinct the goal of initiative becomes; and the more complicated the social reality, the vaguer the father's and mother's role in it. Between childhood and adulthood, then, our children go to school; and school seems to be a world all by itself, with its own goals and limitations, its achievements and disappointments.

Grammar-school education has swung back and forth between the extreme of making early school life an extension of grim adulthood by emphasizing self-restraint and a strict sense of duty in doing what one is *told* to do, and the other extreme of making it an extension of the natural tendency in childhood to find out by playing, to learn what one must do by doing steps which one *likes* to do. Both methods work for some children at times but not for all children at all times. The first trend, if carried to the extreme, exploits a tendency on the part of the preschool and grammar-school child to become entirely dependent on pre-scribed duties. He thus learns much that is absolutely necessary and he develops an unshakable sense of duty; but he may never unlearn again an unnecessary and costly self-restraint with which he may later make his own life and other people's lives miserable, and in fact spoil his own children's natural desire to learn and to work. The second trend, when carried to an extreme, leads not only to the well-known popular objection that children do not learn anything any more but also to such feelings in children as are expressed in the by now famous re-mark of a metropolitan child who apprehensively asked one morning: "Teacher, *must* we do today what we *want* to do?" Nothing could better express the fact that children at this age *do* like to be mildly but firmly coerced into the adventure of finding out that one can learn to accomplish things which one would never have thought of by oneself, things which owe their attractiveness to the very fact that they are *not* the product of play and fantasy but the product of reality, practicality, and logic; things which thus provide a token sense of participation in the real world of adults. In discussions of this kind it is common to say that one must steer a middle course between play and work, between childhood and adult-hood, between old-fashioned and pro-gressive education. It is always easy (and it seems entirely satisfactory to one's critics) to say that one plans to steer a middle course, but in practice it often leads to a course charted by avoidances rather than by zestful goals. Instead of pursuing, then, a course which merely avoids the extremes of easy play or hard work, it may be worth while to consider what play is and what work is, and then learn to dose and alternate each in such a way that *play is play and work is work.* Let

us review briefly what play may mean at various stages of childhood and adulthood.

The adult plays for purposes of recreation. He steps out of his reality into imaginary realities for which he has made up arbitrary but nonetheless binding rules. But an adult rarely gets away with being a playboy. Only he who works shall play—if, indeed, he can relax his competitiveness.

The playing child, then, poses a problem: whoever does not work shall not play. Therefore, to be tolerant of the child's play the adult must invent theories which show either that child-hood play is really the child's work or that it does not count. The most popu-lar theory, and the easiest on the observer, is that the child is nobody yet and that the nonsense of his play reflects it. According to Spencer, play uses up surplus energy in the young of a number of mammalians who do not need to feed or protect themselves be-cause their parents do it for them. Others say that play is either prepara-tion for the future or a method of working off past emotion, a means of finding imaginary relief for past frustrations.

It is true that the content of individual play often proves to be the infantile way of thinking over difficult experiences and of *restoring a sense of mastery*, comparable to the way in which we repeat, in ruminations and in endless talk, in daydreams and in dreams during sleep, experiences that have been too much for us. This is the rationale for play observation, play diagnosis, and play therapy. In watch-ing a child play, the trained observer can get an impression of what it is the child is "thinking over," and what faulty logic, what emotional dead end he may be caught in. As a diagnostic tool such observation has become in-dispensable.

The small world of manageable toys is a harbor which the child estab-lishes, returning to it when he needs to overhaul his ego. But the thing-world has its own laws: it may resist rearrangement or it may simply break to pieces; it may prove to belong to somebody else and be subject to confiscation by superiors. Thus, play may seduce the child into an unguarded expression of dangerous themes and attitudes which arouse anxiety and lead to sudden *disruption of play*. This is the counterpart, in waking life, of the anxiety dream; it can keep children from trying to play just as the fear of night terror can keep them from going to sleep. If thus frightened or disappointed, the child may regress into daydreaming, thumb sucking, masturbating. On the other hand, if the first use of the thing-world is successful and guided properly, the *pleasure of mastering toy things* becomes associated with the *mastery of the conflicts* which were projected on them and with the *prestige* gained through such mastery.

Finally, at nursery-school age playfulness reaches into the world *shared with others*. At first these others are treated as things; they are inspected, run into, or forced to "be horsie." Learning is necessary in order to discover what potential play content can be admitted only to fantasy or only to play by and with oneself; what content can be successfully represented only in the world of toys and small things; and what content can be shared with others and even forced upon them.

What is infantile play, then? We saw that it is not the equivalent of adult play, that it is not recreation. The playing adult steps sideward into another, an artificial reality; the playing child advances forward to new stages of *real mastery*. This new mastery is not restricted to the technical mastery of toys and *things*; it also includes an infantile way of mastering *experience* by meditating, experimenting, planning, and sharing.

While all children at times need to be left alone in solitary play (or later in the company of books and radio, motion pictures and video, all of which, like the fairy tales of old, at least *sometimes* seem to convey what fits the needs of the infantile mind), and while all children need their hours and days of make-believe in games, they all, sooner or later, become dis-satisfied and disgruntled without a sense of being useful, without a sense of being able to make things and make them well and even perfectly: this is what I call the *sense of industry*. Without this, the best entertained child soon acts exploited. It is as if he knows and his society knows that now that he is psychologically already a rudimentary parent, he must begin to be somewhat of a worker and potential provider before becoming a biological parent. With the oncoming latency period, then, the normally advanced child forgets, or rather "sublimates" (that is, applies to more useful pursuits and approved goals) the necessity of "making" people by direct attack or the desire to become father or mother in a hurry: he now learns to win recognition by *producing things*. He develops industry, that is, he adjusts himself to the inorganic laws of the tool world. He can become an eager and absorbed unit of a productive situation. To bring a productive situation to completion is an aim which gradually supersedes the whims and wishes of his idiosyncratic drives and personal disappointments. As he once untiringly strove to walk well, and to throw things away well, he now wants to make things well. He develops the pleasure of *work completion* by steady attention and persevering diligence.

The danger at this stage is the development of a sense of *inadequacy and inferiority*. This may be caused by an insufficient solution of the preceding conflict: he may still want his mummy more than knowledge; he may still rather be the baby at home than the big child in school; he still compares himself with his father, and the comparison arouses a sense of guilt as well as a sense of anatomical inferiority. Family life (small family) may not have prepared him for school life, or school life may fail to sustain the promises of earlier stages in that nothing that he has learned to do well already seems to count one bit with the teacher. And then, again, he may be potentially able to excel in ways which are dormant and which, if not evoked now, may develop late or never.

Good teachers, healthy teachers, relaxed teachers, teachers who feel trusted and respected by the community, understand all this and can guide it. They know how to alternate play and work, games and study. They know how to recognize special efforts, how to encourage special gifts. They also know how to give a child time, and how to handle those children to whom school, for a while, is not important and rather a matter to endure than to enjoy; or the child to whom, for a while, other children are much more important than the teacher.

Good parents, healthy parents, relaxed parents feel a need to make their children trust their teachers, and therefore to have teachers who can be trusted. It is not my job here to discuss teacher selection, teacher training, and the status and payment of teachers in their communities—all of which is of direct importance for the development and the maintenance in children of a *sense of industry* and of a positive identification with those who *know* things and know how to *do* things. Again and again I have observed in the lives of especially gifted and inspired people that one teacher, somewhere, was able to kindle the flame of hidden talent.

The fact that the majority of teachers in the elementary school are women must be considered here in passing, because it often leads to a conflict with the "ordinary" boy's masculine identification, as if knowledge were feminine, action masculine. Both boys and girls are apt to agree with Bernard Shaw's statement that those who can, do, while those who cannot, teach. The selection and training of teachers, then, is vital for the avoidance of the dangers which can befall the individual at this stage. There is, first, the above-mentioned sense of inferiority, the feeling that one will never be any good—a problem which calls for the type of teacher who knows how to emphasize what a child *can* do, and who knows a psychiatric problem when she sees one. Second, there is the danger of the child's identifying too strenuously with a too

virtuous teacher or becoming the teacher's pet. What we shall presently refer to as his sense of identity can remain prematurely fixed on being nothing but a good little worker or a good little helper, which may not be all he *could* be. Third, there is the danger (probably the most common one) that throughout the long years of going to school he will never acquire the enjoyment of work and the pride of doing at least one kind of thing well. This is particularly of concern in relation to that part of the nation who do not complete what schooling is at their disposal. It is always easy to say that they are born that way; that there must be less educated people as background for the superior ones; that the market needs and even fosters such people for its many simple and unskilled tasks. But from the point of the healthy personality (which, as we proceed, must now include the aspect of playing a constructive role in a healthy society), we must consider those who have had just enough schooling to appreciate what more fortunate people are learning to do but who, for one reason or another, have lacked inner or outer support of their stick-to-itiveness.

It will have been noted that, regarding the period of a developing sense of industry, I have referred to *outer hindrances* but not to any crisis (except a deferred inferiority crisis) coming from the inventory of basic human drives. This stage differs from the others in that it does not consist of a swing from a violent inner upheaval to a new mastery. The reason why Freud called it the latency stage is that violent drives are normally dormant at that time. But it is only a lull before the storm of puberty.

On the other hand, this is socially a most decisive stage: since industry involves doing things beside and with others, a first sense of *division of labor* and of *equality of opportunity* develops at this time. When a child begins to feel that it is the color of his skin, the background of his parents, or the cost of his clothes rather than his wish and his will to learn which will decide his social worth, lasting harm may ensue for the *sense of identity*, to which we must now turn.

IDENTITY VERSUS IDENTITY DIFFUSION

With the establishment of a good relationship to the world of skills and to those who teach and share the new skills, childhood proper comes to an end. Youth begins. But in puberty and adolescence all sameness and continuities relied on earlier are questioned again because of a rapidity of body growth which equals that of early childhood and because of the entirely new addition of physical genital maturity. The growing and developing young people, faced with this physiological revolution within them, are now primarily concerned with attempts at consolidating their social roles. They are sometimes morbidly, often curiously, preoccupied with what they appear to be in the eyes of others as compared with what they feel they are and with the question of how to connect the earlier cultivated roles and skills with the ideal prototypes of the day. In their search for a new sense of continuity and sameness, some adolescents have to refight many of the crises of earlier years, and they are never ready to install lasting idols and ideals as guardians of a final identity.

The integration now taking place in the form of the ego identity is more than the sum of the childhood identifications. It is the inner capital accrued from all those experiences of each successive stage, when successful identification led to a successful alignment of the individual's *basic drives* with his *endowment* and his *opportunities*. In psychoanalysis we ascribe such successful alignments to "ego synthesis"; I have tried to demonstrate that the ego values accrued in childhood culminate in what I have called *a sense of ego identity*. The sense of ego identity, then, is the accrued confidence that one's ability to maintain inner sameness and continuity (one's ego in the psychological sense) is matched by the sameness and continuity of one's meaning for others. Thus, self-esteem, confirmed at the end of each major crisis, grows to be a conviction that one is learning effective steps toward a tangible future, that one is developing a defined personality within a social reality which one understands. The growing child must, at every step, derive a vitalizing sense of reality from the awareness that his individual way of mastering experience is a successful variant of the way other people around him master experience and recognize such mastery.

In this, children cannot be fooled by empty praise and condescending encouragement. They may have to accept artificial bolstering of their self-esteem in lieu of something better, but what I call their accruing ego identity gains real strength only from wholehearted and consistent recognition of real accomplishment, that is, achievement that has meaning in their culture. On the other hand, should a child feel that the environment tries to deprive him too radically of all the forms of expression which permit him to develop and to integrate the next step in his ego identity, he will resist with the astonishing strength encountered in animals who are suddenly forced to defend their lives. Indeed, in the social jungle of human existence, there is no feeling of being alive without a sense of ego identity. To understand this would be to understand the trouble of adolescents better, especially the trouble of all those who cannot just be "nice" boys and girls, but are desperately seeking for a satisfactory sense of belonging, be it in cliques and gangs here in our country or in inspiring mass movements in others.

Ego identity, then, develops out of a gradual integration of all identifications, but here, if anywhere, the whole has a different quality than the sum of its parts. Under favorable circumstances children have the nucleus of a separate identity in early life; often they must defend it against any pressure which would make them overidentify with one of their parents. This is difficult to learn from patients, because the neurotic ego has, by definition, fallen prey to overidentification and to faulty identifications with disturbed parents, a circumstance which isolated the small individual both from his budding identity and from his milieu. But we can study it profitably in the children of minority-group Americans who, having successfully graduated from a marked and well-guided stage of autonomy, enter the most decisive stage of American childhood: that of initiative and industry.

Minority groups of a lesser degree of Americanization (Negroes, Indians, Mexicans, and certain European groups) often are privileged in the enjoyment of a more sensual early childhood. Their crises come when their parents and teachers, losing trust in themselves and using sudden correctives in order to approach the vague but pervasive Anglo-Saxon ideal, create violent discontinuities; or where, indeed, the children themselves learn to disavow their sensual and overprotective mothers as temptations and a hindrance to the formation of a more American personality.

On the whole, it can be said that American schools successfully meet the challenge of training children of play-school age and of the elementary grades in a spirit of self-reliance and enterprise. Children of these ages seem remarkably free of prejudice and apprehension, preoccupied as they still are with growing and learning and with the new pleasures of association outside their families. This, to forestall the sense of individual inferiority, must lead to a hope for "industrial association," for equality with all those who apply themselves wholeheartedly to the same skills and adventures in learning. Many individual successes, on the other hand, only expose the now overly encouraged children of mixed backgrounds and somewhat deviant endowments to the shock of American adolescence: the standardization of individuality and the intolerance of "differences."

The emerging ego identity, then, bridges the early childhood stages, when the body and the parent images were given their specific meanings, and the later stages, when a variety of social roles becomes available and increasingly coercive. A lasting ego identity cannot begin to exist without the trust of the first oral stage; it cannot be completed without a promise of fulfillment which from the dominant image of adulthood reaches down into the baby's beginnings and which creates at every step an accruing sense of ego strength.

The danger of this stage is *identity diffusion*; as Biff puts it in Arthur Miller's *Death of a Salesman,* "I just can't take hold, Mom, I can't take hold of some kind of a life." Where such a dilemma is based on a strong previous doubt of one's ethnic and sexual identity, delinquent and outright psychotic incidents are not uncommon. Youth after youth, bewildered by some assumed role, a role forced on him by the inexorable standardization of American adolescence, runs away in one form or another; leaving schools and jobs, staying out all night, or withdrawing into bizarre and inaccessible moods. Once "delinquent," his greatest need and often his only salvation, is the refusal on the part of older friends, advisers, and judiciary personnel to type him further by pat diagnoses and social judgments which ignore the special dynamic conditions of adolescence. For if diagnosed and treated correctly, seemingly psychotic and criminal incidents do not in adolescence have the same fatal significance which they have at other ages. Yet many a youth, finding that the authorities expect him to be "a bum" or "a queer," or "off the beam," perversely obliges by becoming just that.

In general it is primarily the inability to settle on an occupational identity which disturbs young people. To keep themselves together they temporarily overidentify, to the point of apparent complete loss of identity, with the heroes of cliques and crowds. On the other hand, they become remarkably clannish, intolerant, and cruel in their exclusion of others who are "different," in skin color or cultural background, in tastes and gifts, and often in entirely petty aspects of dress and gesture arbitrarily selected as *the* signs of an in-grouper or out-grouper. It is important to understand (which does not mean condone or participate in) such intolerance as the necessary *defense against a sense of identity diffusion,* which is unavoidable at a time of life when the body changes its proportions radically, when genital maturity floods body and imagination with all manners of drives, when intimacy with the other sex approaches and is, on occasion, forced on the youngster, and when life lies before one with a variety of conflicting possibilities and choices. Adolescents help one another temporarily through such discomfort by forming cliques and by stereotyping themselves, their ideals, and their enemies.

It is important to understand this because it makes clear the appeal which simple and cruel totalitarian doctrines have on the minds of the youth of such countries and classes as have lost or are losing their group identities (feudal, agrarian, national, and so forth) in these times of worldwide industrialization, emancipation, and wider intercommunication. The dynamic quality of the tempestuous adolescences lived through in patriarchal and agrarian countries (countries which face the most radical changes in political structure and in economy) explains the fact that their young people find convincing and satisfactory identities in the simple totalitarian doctrines of race, class, or nation. Even though we may be forced to win wars against their leaders, we still are faced with the job of winning the peace with these grim youths by convincingly demonstrating to them (by living it) a democratic identity which can be strong and yet tolerant, judicious and still determined.

But it is increasingly important to understand this also in order to treat the intolerances of our adolescents at home with understanding and guidance rather than with verbal stereotypes or prohibitions. It is difficult to be tolerant if deep down you are not quite sure that you are a man (or

a woman), that you will ever grow together again and be attractive, that you will be able to master your drives, that you really know who you are,[4] that you know what you want to be, that you know what you look like to others, and that you will know how to make the right decisions without, once for all, committing yourself to the wrong friend, sexual partner, leader, or career.

Democracy in a country like America poses special problems in that it insists on *self-made identities* ready to grasp many chances and ready to adjust to changing necessities of booms and busts, of peace and war, of migration and determined sedentary life. Our democracy, furthermore, must present the adolescent with ideals which can be shared by youths of many backgrounds and which emphasize autonomy in the form of independence and initiative in the form of enterprise. These promises, in turn, are not easy to fulfill in increasingly complex and centralized systems of economic and political organization, systems which, if geared to war, must automatically neglect the "self-made" identities of millions of individuals and put them where they are most needed. This is hard on many young Americans because their whole upbringing, and therefore the development of a healthy personality, depends on a certain degree of *choice,* a certain hope for an individual *chance,* and a certain conviction in freedom of *self-determination.*

We are speaking here not only of high privileges and lofty ideas but also of psychological necessities. Psychologically speaking, a gradually accruing ego identity is the only safeguard against the *anarchy of drives* as well as the *autocracy of conscience,* that is, the cruel overconscientiousness which is the inner residue in the adult of his past inequality in regard to his parent. Any loss of a sense of identity exposes the individual to his own childhood

---

[4] On the wall of a cowboys' bar in the wide-open West hangs a saying: "I ain't what I ought to be, I ain't what I'm going to be, but I ain't what I was."

conflicts—as could be observed, for example, in the neuroses of World War II among men and women who could not stand the general dislocation of their careers or a variety of other special pressures of war. Our adversaries, it seems, understand this. Their psychological warfare consists in the determined continuation of general conditions which permit them to indoctrinate mankind within their orbit with the simple and yet for them undoubtedly effective identities of class warfare and nationalism, while they know that the psychology, as well as the economy, of free enterprise and of self-determination is stretched to the breaking point under the conditions of long-drawn-out cold and lukewarm war. It is clear, therefore, that we must bend every effort to present our young men and women with the tangible and trustworthy promise of opportunities for a rededication to the life for which the country's history, as well as their own childhood, has prepared them. Among the tasks of national defense, this one must not be forgotten.

I have referred to the relationship of the problem of trust to matters of adult faith; to that of the problem of autonomy to matters of adult independence in work and citizenship. I have pointed to the connection between a sense of initiative and the kind of enterprise sanctioned in the economic system, and between the sense of industry and a culture's technology. In searching for the social values which guide identity, one confronts the problem of aristocracy, in its widest possible sense which connotes the conviction that the best people rule and that that rule develops the best in people. In order not to become cynically or apathetically lost, young people in search of an identity must somewhere be able to convince themselves that those who succeed thereby shoulder the obligation of being the best, that is, of personifying the nation's ideals. In this country, as in any other, we have those successful types who become the cynical representatives of the "inside track," the "bosses" of impersonal machinery. In a culture once pervaded with the value of the self-made man, a special danger ensues from the idea of a synthetic personality: as if you are what you can appear to be, or as if you are what you can buy. This can be counteracted only by a system of education that transmits values and goals which determinedly aspire beyond mere "functioning" and "making the grade."

Intrapsychic Theories:

PATHOLOGICAL PATTERNS

Intrapsychic theorists recognize that pathological behavior represents, in large measure, an adaptive strategy developed by patients in response to feelings of anxiety and threat. The bizarre and maladaptive behavior they display is not viewed as functionless or random, but as an intricate, albeit self-defeating, maneuver to relieve oneself of anguish, humiliation, and insecurity. In childhood, a youngster will cope with anxiety by a variety of spontaneous strategies; he may be submissive, hostile, ambitious, avoidant, exploitive, or independent, shifting from one to the other at different times. Eventually, a dominant pattern of adaptive behavior emerges. The excerpts from the works of Karen Horney and Erich Fromm, two of the better known neo-Freudians, illustrate the typical characteristics of several of these ingrained adaptive personality patterns.

Culture and Neurosis

KAREN HORNEY

In the psychoanalytic concept of neuroses a shift of emphasis has taken place: whereas originally interest was focussed on the dramatic symptomatic picture, it is now being realized more and more that the real source of these psychic disorders lies in character disturbances, that the symptoms are a manifest result of conflicting character traits, and that without uncovering and straightening out the neurotic character structure we cannot cure a neurosis. When analyzing these character traits, in a great many cases one is struck by the observation that, in marked contrast to the divergency of the symptomatic pictures, character difficulties invariably center around the same basic conflicts.

These similarities in the content of conflicts present a problem. They suggest, to minds open to the importance of cultural implications, the question of whether and to what extent neuroses are moulded by cultural processes in essentially the same way as "normal" character formation is determined by these influences; and, if so, how far such a concept would necessitate certain modifications in Freud's views of the relation between culture and neurosis.

In the following remarks I shall try to outline roughly some characteristics typically recurring in all our neuroses. The limitations of time will allow us to present neither data—good case histories—nor method, but only results. I shall try to select from the extremely complex and diversified observational material the essential points.

From *Amer. Sociol. Review* 1:221-230, 1936, by permission of the American Sociological Association.

There is another difficulty in the presentation. I wish to show how these neurotic persons are trapped in a vicious circle. Unable to present in detail the factors leading up to the vicious circle, I must start rather arbitrarily with one of the outstanding features, although this in itself is already a complex product of several interrelated, developed mental factors. I start, therefore, with the problem of competition.

The problem of competition, or rivalry, appears to be a never-failing center of neurotic conflicts. How to deal with competition presents a problem for everyone in our culture; for the neurotic, however, it assumes dimensions which generally surpass actual vicissitudes. It does so in three respects:

(1) There is a constant measuring-up with others, even in situations which do not call for it. While striving to surpass others is essential for all competitive situations, the neurotic measures up even with persons who are in no way potential competitors and have no goal in common with him. The question as to who is the more intelligent, more attractive, more popular, is indiscriminately applied towards everyone.

(2) The content of neurotic ambitions is not only to accomplish something worth while, or to be successful, but to be absolutely best of all. These ambitions, however, exist in fantasy mainly—fantasies which may or may not be conscious. The degree of awareness differs widely in different persons. The ambitions may appear in occasional flashes of fantasy only. There is never a clear realization of the powerful dramatic role these ambitions play in the neurotic's life, or of the great part they have in accounting for his behavior and mental reactions. The challenge of these ambitions is not met by adequate efforts which might lead to realization of the aims. They are in queer contrast to existing inhibitions towards work, towards assuming leadership, towards all means which would effectually secure success. There are many ways in which these fantastic ambitions influence the emotional lives of the persons concerned: by hypersensitivity to criticism, by depressions or inhibitions following failures, etc. These failures need not necessarily be real. Everything which falls short of the realization of the grandiose ambitions is felt as failure. The success of another person is felt as one's own failure.

This competitive attitude not only exists in reference to the external world, but is also internalized, and appears as a constant measuring-up to an ego-ideal. The fantastic ambitions appear on this score as excessive and rigid demands towards the self, and failure in living up to these demands produces depressions and irritations similar to those produced in competition with others.

(3) The third characteristic is the amount of hostility involved in neurotic ambition. While intense competition implicitly contains elements of hostility—the defeat of a competitor meaning victory for oneself—the reactions of neurotic persons are determined by an insatiable and irrational expectation that no one in the universe other than themselves should be intelligent, influential, attractive, or popular. They become infuriated, or feel their own endeavors condemned to futility, if someone else writes a good play or a scientific paper or plays a prominent role in society. If this attitude is strongly accentuated, one may observe in the analytical situation, for example, that these patients regard any progress made as a victory on the part of the analyst, completely disregarding the fact that progress is of vital concern to their own interests. In such situations they will disparage the analyst, betraying, by the intense hostility displayed, that they feel endangered in a position of paramount importance to themselves. They are as a rule completely unaware of the existence and intensity of this "no one but me" attitude, but one may safely assume and eventually always uncover this attitude from reactions observable in the analytical situation, as indicated above.

This attitude easily leads to a fear of retaliation. It results in a fear of success and also in a fear of failure: "If I want to crush everyone who is successful, then I will automatically assume identical reactions in others, so that the way to success implies exposing me to the hostility of others. Furthermore: if I make any move towards this goal and fail, then I shall be crushed." Success thus becomes a peril and any possible failure becomes a danger which must at all costs be avoided. From the point of view of all these dangers it appears much safer to stay in the corner, be modest and inconspicuous. In other and more positive terms, this fear leads to a definite recoiling from any aim which implies competition. This safety device is assured by a constant, accurately working process of automatic self-checking.

This self-checking process results in inhibitions, particularly inhibitions towards work, but also towards all steps necessary to the pursuit of one's aims, such as seizing opportunities, or revealing to others that one has certain goals or capacities. This eventually results in an incapacity to stand up for one's own wishes. The peculiar nature of these inhibitions is best demonstrated by the fact that these persons may be quite capable of fighting for the needs of others or for an impersonal cause. They will, for instance, act like this:

When playing an instrument with a poor partner, they will instinctively play worse than he, although otherwise they may be very competent. When discussing a subject with someone less intelligent than themselves, they will compulsively descend below his level. They will prefer to be in the rank and file, not to be identified with the superiors, not even to get an increase in salary, rationalizing this attitude in some way. Even their dreams will be dictated by this need for reassurance. Instead of utilizing the liberty of a dream to imagine themselves in glorious situations, they will actually see themselves, in their dreams, in humble or even humiliating situations.

This self-checking process does not restrict itself to activities in the pursuit of some aim, but going beyond that, tends to undermine the self-confidence, which is a prerequisite for any accomplishment, by means of self-belittling. The function of self-belittling in this context is to eliminate oneself from any competition. In most cases these persons are not aware of actually disparaging themselves, but are aware of the results only as they feel themselves inferior to others and take for granted their own inadequacy.

The presence of these feelings of inferiority is one of the most common psychic disorders of our time and culture. Let me say a few more words about them. The genesis of inferiority feelings is not always in neurotic competition. They present complex phenomena and may be determined by various conditions. But that they do result from, and stand in the service of, a recoiling from competition, is a basic and ever-present implication. They result from a recoiling inasmuch as they are the expression of a discrepancy between high-pitched ideals and real accomplishment. The fact, however, that these painful feelings at the same time fulfill the important function of making secure the recoiling attitude itself, becomes evident through the vigor with which this position is defended when attacked. Not only will no evidence of competence or attractiveness ever convince these persons, but they may actually become scared or angered by any attempt to convince them of their positive qualities.

The surface pictures resulting from this situation may be widely divergent. Some persons appear thoroughly convinced of their unique importance and may be anxious to demonstrate their superiority on every occasion, but betray their insecurity in an excessive sensitivity to every criticism, to every dissenting opinion, or every lack of responsive admiration. Others are just as thoroughly convinced of their incompetence or unworthiness, or of being unwanted or unappreciated; yet they betray their actually great demands in that they react with open or concealed hostility to every frustration of their unacknowledged demands. Still others will waver constantly in their self-estimation between feeling themselves all-important and feeling, for instance, honestly amazed that anyone pays any attention to them.

If you have followed me thus far, I can now proceed to outline the particular vicious circle in which these persons are moving. It is important here, as in every complex neurotic picture, to recognize the vicious circle, because, if we overlook it and simplify the complexity of the processes going on by assuming a simple cause-effect relation, we either fail to get an understanding of the emotions involved, or attribute an undue importance to some one cause. As an example of this error, I might mention regarding a highly emotion-charged rivalry attitude as derived directly from rivalry with the father. Roughly, the vicious circle looks like this:

The failures, in conjunction with a feeling of weakness and defeat, lead to a feeling of envy towards all persons who are more successful, or merely more secure or better contented with life. This envy may be manifest or it may be repressed under the pressure of the same anxiety which led to a repression of, and a recoiling from, rivalry. It may be entirely wiped out of consciousness and represented by the substitution of a blind admiration; it may be kept from awareness by a disparaging attitude towards the person concerned. Its effect, however, is apparent in the incapacity to grant to others what one has been forced to deny oneself. At any rate, no matter to what degree the envy is repressed or expressed, it implies an increase in the existing hostility against people and consequently an increase in the anxiety, which now takes the particular form of an irrational fear of the envy of others.

The irrational nature of this fear is shown in two ways: (1) it exists regardless of the presence or absence of envy in the given situation; and (2) its intensity is out of proportion to the dangers menacing from the side of the envious competitors. This irrational side of the fear of envy always remains unconscious, at least in non-psychotic persons, therefore it is never corrected by a reality-testing process, and is all the more effective in the direction of reinforcing the existing tendencies to recoil.

Consequently the feeling of own insignificance grows, the hostility against people grows, and the anxiety grows. We thus return to the beginning, because now the fantasies come up, with about this content: "I wish I were more powerful, more attractive, more intelligent than all the others, then I should be safe, and besides, I could defeat them and step on them." Thus we see an ever-increasing deviation of the ambitions towards the stringent, fantastic, and hostile.

This pyramiding process may come to a standstill under various conditions, usually at an inordinate expense in loss of expansiveness and vitality. There is often some sort of resignation as to personal ambitions, in turn permitting the diminution of anxieties as to competition, with the inferiority feelings and inhibitions continuing.

It is now time, however, to make a reservation. It is in no way self-evident that ambition of the "no-one-but-me" type must necessarily evoke anxieties. There are persons quite capable of brushing aside or crushing everyone in the way of their ruthless pursuit of personal power. The question then is: Under what special condition is anxiety invoked in neurotically competitive people?

The answer is that they at the same time want to be loved. While most persons who pursue an asocial ambition in life care little for the affection or the opinion of others, the neurotics, although possessed by the same kind of competitiveness, simultaneously have a boundless craving for affection and appreciation. Therefore, as soon as they make any move towards self-assertion, competition, or success, they begin to dread losing the affection of others, and must automatically check their aggressive impulses. This conflict between ambition and affection is one of the gravest and most typical dilemmas of the neurotics of our time.

Why are these two incompatible strivings so frequently present in the same individual? They are related to each other in more than one way. The briefest formulation of this relationship would perhaps be that they both grow out of the same sources, namely, anxieties, and they both serve as a means of reassurance against the anxieties. Power and affection may both be safeguards. They generate each other, check each other, and reinforce each other. These interrelations can be observed most accurately within the analytic situation, but sometimes are obvious from only a casual knowledge of the life history.

In the life history may be found, for instance, an atmosphere in childhood lacking in warmth and reliability, but rife with frightening elements—battles between the parents, injustice, cruelty, over-solicitousness — generation of an increased need for affection —disappointments—development of an outspoken competitiveness—inhibition —attempts to get affection on the basis of weakness, helplessness, or suffering. We sometimes hear that a youngster has suddenly turned to ambition after an acute disappointment in his need for affection, and then given up the ambition on falling in love.

Particularly when the expansive and aggressive desires have been severely curbed in early life by a forbidding atmosphere, the excessive need for reassuring affection will play a major role. As a guiding principle for behavior this implies a yielding to the wishes or opinions of others rather than asserting one's own wishes or opinions; an overvaluation of the significance for one's own life of expressions of fondness from others, and a dependence on such expressions. And similarly, it implies an overvaluation of signs of rejection and a reacting to such signs with apprehension and defensive hostility. Here again a vicious circle begins easily and reinforces the

single elements: In diagram it looks somewhat like this:

> Anxiety plus repressed hostility
> Need for reassuring affection
> Anticipation of, sensitivity to, rejection
> Hostile reactions to feeling rejected

These reactions explain why emotional contact with others that is attained on the basis of anxiety can be at best only a very shaky and easily shattered bridge between individuals, and why it always fails to bring them out of their emotional isolation. It may, however, serve to cope with anxieties and even get one through life rather smoothly, but only at the expense of growth and personality development, and only if circumstances are quite favorable.

Let us ask now, which special features in our culture may be responsible for the frequent occurrence of the neurotic structures just described?

We live in a competitive, individualistic culture. Whether the enormous economic and technical achievements of our culture were and are possible only on the basis of the competitive principle is a question for the economist or sociologist to decide. The psychologist, however, can evaluate the personal price we have paid for it.

It must be kept in mind that competition not only is a driving force in economics activities, but that it also pervades our personal life in every respect. The character of all our human relationships is moulded by a more or less outspoken competition. It is effective in the family between siblings, at school, in social relations (keeping up with the Joneses), and in love life.

In love, it may show itself in two ways: the genuine erotic wish is often overshadowed or replaced by the merely competitive goal of being the most popular, having the most dates, love letters, lovers, being seen with the most desirable man or woman. Again, it may pervade the love relationship itself. Marriage partners, for example, may be living in an endless struggle for supremacy, with or without being aware of the nature or even of the existence of this combat.

The influence on human relations of this competitiveness lies in the fact that it creates easily aroused envy towards the stronger ones, contempt for the weaker, distrust towards everyone. In consequence of all these potentially hostile tensions, the satisfaction and reassurance which one can get out of human relations are limited and the individual becomes more or less emotionally isolated. It seems that here, too, mutually reinforcing interactions take place, so far as insecurity and dissatisfaction in human relations in turn compel people to seek gratification and security in ambitious strivings, and vice versa.

Another cultural factor relevant to the structure of our neurosis lies in our attitude towards failure and success. We are inclined to attribute success to good personal qualities and capacities, such as competence, courage, enterprise. In religious terms this attitude was expressed by saying that success was due to God's grace. While these qualities may be effective—and in certain periods, such as the pioneer days, may have represented the only conditions necessary—this ideology omits two essential facts: (1) that the possibility for success is strictly limited; even external conditions and personal qualities being equal, only a comparative few can possibly attain success; and (2) that other factors than those mentioned may play the decisive role, such as, for example, unscrupulousness or fortuitous circumstances. Inasmuch as these factors are overlooked in the general evaluation of success, failures, besides putting the person concerned in a factually disadvantageous position, are bound to reflect on his self-esteem.

The confusion involved in this situation is enhanced by a sort of double moral. Although, in fact, success meets with adoration almost without regard to the means employed in securing it, we are at the same time taught to regard modesty and an undemanding, unselfish attitude as social or religious virtues, and are rewarded for them by praise and affection. The particular difficulties which confront the individual in our culture may be summarized as follows: for the competitive struggle he needs a certain amount of available aggressiveness; at the same time, he is required to be modest, unselfish, even self-sacrificing. While the competitive life situation with the hostile tensions involved in it creates an enhanced need of security, the chances of attaining a feeling of safety in human relations— love, friendship, social contacts—are at the same time diminished. The estimation of one's personal value is all too dependent on the degree of success attained, while at the same time the possibilities for success are limited and the success itself is dependent, to a great extent, on fortuitous circumstances or on personal qualities of an asocial character.

Perhaps these sketchy comments have suggested to you the direction in which to explore the actual relationship of our culture to our personality and its neurotic deviations. Let us now consider the relation of this conception to the views of Freud on culture and neurosis.

The essence of Freud's views on this subject can be summarized, briefly, as follows: Culture is the result of a sublimation of biologically given sexual and aggressive drives—"sexual" in the extended connotation Freud has given the term. Sublimation presupposes unwitting suppression of these instinctual drives. The more complete the suppression of these drives, the higher the cultural development. As the capacity for sublimating is limited, and as the intensive suppression of primitive drives without sublimation may lead to neurosis, the growth of civilization must inevitably imply a growth of neurosis. Neuroses are the price humanity has to pay for cultural development.

The implicit theoretical presupposition underlying this train of thought is the belief in the existence of biologically determined human nature, or, more precisely, the belief that oral, anal, genital, and aggressive drives exist in all human beings in approximately equal quantities.[1] Variations in character formation from individual to individual, as from culture, are due, then, to the varying intensity of the suppression required, with the addition that this suppression can affect the different kinds of drives in varying degrees.

This viewpoint of Freud's seems actually to encounter difficulties with two groups of data. (1) Historical and anthropological findings[2] do not support the assumption that the growth

_____

[1] I pass over Freud's recognition of individual constitutional difference.

[2] Ruth Benedict, *Patterns of Culture;* Margaret Mead, *Sex and Temperament in Three Savage Societies.*

of civilization is in a direct ratio to the growth of instinct suppression. (2) Clinical experience of the kind indicated in this paper suggests that neurosis is due not simply to the quantity of suppression of one or the other instinctual drives, but rather to difficulties caused by the conflicting character of the demands which a culture imposes on its individuals. The differences in neuroses typical of different cultures may be understood to be conditioned by the amount and quality of conflicting demands within the particular culture.

In a given culture, those persons are likely to become neurotic who have met these culturally determined difficulties in accentuated form, mostly through the medium of childhood experiences; and who have not been able to solve their difficulties, or have solved them only at great expense to personality.

Non-Productive Character Orientations

ERICH FROMM

Freud tried to account for this dynamic nature of character traits by combining his characterology with his libido theory. In accordance with the type of materialistic thinking prevalent in the natural sciences of the late nineteenth century, which assumed the energy in natural and psychical phenomena to be a substantial not a relational entity, Freud believed that the sexual drive was the source of energy of the character. By a number of complicated and brilliant assumptions he explained different character traits as "sublimations" of, or "reaction formations" against, the various forms of the sexual drive. He interpreted the *dynamic nature* of character traits as an expression of their *libidinous source.*

_____

From *Man For Himself* by Erich Fromm. Copyright 1947 by Erich Fromm. Reprinted by permission of Holt, Rinehart and Winston, Inc.

The progress of psychoanalytic theory led, in line with the progress of the natural and social sciences, to a new concept which was based, not on the idea of a primarily isolated individual, but on the *relationship* of man to others, to nature, and to himself. It was assumed that this very relationship governs and regulates the energy manifest in the passionate strivings of man. H. S. Sullivan, one of the pioneers of this new view, has accordingly defined psychoanalysis as a "study of interpersonal relations."

The theory presented in the following pages follows Freud's characterology in essential points: in the assumption that character traits underlie behavior and must be inferred from it; that they constitute forces which, though powerful, the person may be entirely unconscious of. It follows

Freud also in the assumption that the fundamental entity in character is not the single character trait but the total character organization from which a number of single character traits follow. These character traits are to be understood as a syndrome which results from a particular organization or, as I shall call it, orientation of character. I shall deal only with a very limited number of character traits which follow immediately from the underlying orientation. A number of other character traits could be dealt with similarly, and it could be shown that they are also direct outcomes of basic orientations or mixtures of such primary traits of character with those of temperament. However, a great number of others conventionally listed as character traits would be found to be not character traits in our sense but pure temperament or mere behavior traits.

The main difference in the theory of character proposed here from that of Freud is that the fundamental basis of character is not seen in various types of libido organization but in specific kinds of a person's relatedness to the world. In the process of living, man relates himself to the world (1) by acquiring and assimilating things, and (2) by relating himself to people (and himself). The former I shall call the process of assimilation; the latter, that of socialization. Both forms of relatedness are "open" and not, as with the animal, instinctively determined. Man can acquire things by receiving or taking them from an outside source or by producing them through his own effort. But he must acquire and assimilate them in some fashion in order to satisfy his needs. Also, man cannot live alone and unrelated to others. He has to associate with others for defense, for work, for sexual satisfaction, for play, for the upbringing of the young, for the transmission of knowledge and material possessions. But beyond that, it is necessary for him to be related to others, one with them, part of a group. Complete isolation is unbearable and incompatible with sanity. Again man can relate himself to

others in various ways: he can love or hate, he can compete or cooperate; he can build a social system based on equality or authority, liberty or oppression; but he must be related in some fashion and the particular form of relatedness is expressive of his character.

These orientations, by which the individual relates himself to the world, constitute the core of his character; character can be defined as the (*relatively permanent*) *form in which human energy is canalized in the process of assimilation and socialization.* This canalization of psychic energy has a very significant biological function. Since man's actions are not determined by innate instinctual patterns, life would be precarious, indeed, if he had to make a deliberate decision each time he acted, each time he took a step. On the contrary, many actions must be performed far more quickly than conscious deliberation allows. Furthermore, if all behavior followed from deliberate decision, many more inconsistencies in action would occur than are compatible with proper functioning. According to behavioristic thinking, man learns to react in a semiautomatic fashion by developing habits of action and thought which can be understood in terms of conditioned reflexes. While this view is correct to a certain extent, it ignores the fact that the most deeply rooted habits and opinions which are characteristic of a person and resistant to change grow from his character structure: they are expressive of the particular form in which energy has been canalized in the character structure. The character system can be considered the human substitute for the instinctive apparatus of the animal. Once energy is canalized in a certain way, action takes place "true to character." A particular character may be undesirable ethically, but at least it permits a person to act fairly consistently and to be relieved of the burden of having to make a new and deliberate decision every time. He can arrange his life in a way which is geared to his character and thus create a certain degree of compatibility between the inner and the outer situation. Moreover, character has also a selective function with regard to a person's ideas and values. Since to most people ideas seem to be independent of their emotions and wishes and the result of logical deduction, they feel that their attitude toward the world is confirmed by their ideas and judgments when actually these are as much a result of their character as their actions are. This confirmation in turn tends to stabilize their character structure since it makes the latter appear right and sensible.

Not only has character the function of permitting the individual to act consistently and "reasonably"; it is also the basis for his adjustment to society. The character of the child is molded by the character of its parents in response to whom it develops. The parents and their methods of child training in turn are determined by the social structure of their culture. The average family is the "psychic agency" of society, and by adjusting himself to his family the child acquires the character which later makes him adjusted to the tasks he has to perform in social life. He acquires that character which makes him want to do what he has to do and the core of which he shares with most members of the same social class or culture. The fact that most members of a social class or culture share significant elements of character and that one can speak of a "social character" representing the core of a character structure common to most people of a given culture shows the degree to which character is formed by social and cultural patterns. But from the social character we must differentiate the individual character in which one person differs from another within the same culture. These differences are partly due to the differences of the personalities of the parents and to the differences, psychic and material, of the specific social environment in which the child grows up. But they are also due to the constitutional differences of each individual, particularly those of temperament. Genetically, the formation of individ-

ual character is determined by the impact of its life experiences, the individual ones and those which follow from the culture, on temperament and physical constitution. Environment is never the same for two people, for the difference in constitution makes them experience the same environment in a more or less different way. Mere habits of action and thought which develop as the result of an individual's conforming with the cultural pattern and which are not rooted in the character of a person are easily changed under the influence of new social patterns. If, on the other hand, a person's behavior is rooted in his character, it is charged with energy and changeable only if a fundamental change in a person's character takes place.

In the following analysis *non-productive orientations* are differentiated from the *productive orientation*. It must be noted that these concepts are "ideal-types," not descriptions of the character of a given individual. Furthermore, while, for didactic purposes, they are treated here separately, the character of any given person is usually a blend of all or some of these orientations in which one, however, is dominant. Finally, I want to state here that in the description of the nonproductive orientations only their negative aspects are presented.

THE RECEPTIVE ORIENTATION

In the receptive orientation a person feels "the source of all good" to be outside, and he believes that the only way to get what he wants—be it something material, be it affection, love, knowledge, pleasure—is to receive it from that outside source. In this orientation the problem of love is almost exclusively that of "being loved" and not that of loving. Such people tend to be indiscriminate in the choice of their love objects, because being loved by anybody is such an overwhelming experience for them that they "fall for" anybody who gives them love or what looks like love. They are exceedingly sensitive to any withdrawal or rebuff they experience on the part of the loved person. Their orientation is the same in the sphere of thinking: if intelligent, they make the best listeners, since their orientation is one of receiving, not of producing, ideas; left to themselves, they feel paralyzed. It is characteristic of these people that their first thought is to find somebody else to give them needed information rather than to make even the smallest effort of their own. If religious, these persons have a concept of God in which they expect everything from God and nothing from their own activity. If not religious, their relationship to persons or institutions is very much the same; they are always in search of a "magic helper." They show a particular kind of loyalty, at the bottom of which is the gratitude for the hand that feeds them and the fear of ever losing it. Since they need many hands to feel secure, they have to be loyal to numerous people. It is difficult for them to say "no," and they are easily caught between conflicting loyalties and promises. Since they cannot say "no," they love to say "yes" to everything and everybody, and the resulting paralysis of their critical abilities makes them increasingly dependent on others.

They are dependent not only on authorities for knowledge and help but on people in general for any kind of support. They feel lost when alone because they feel that they cannot do anything without help. This helplessness is especially important with regard to those acts which by their very nature can only be done alone— making decisions and taking responsibility. In personal relationships, for instance, they ask advice from the very person with regard to whom they have to make a decision.

This receptive type has great fondness for food and drink. These persons tend to overcome anxiety and depression by eating or drinking. The mouth is an especially prominent feature, often the most expressive one; the lips tend to be open, as if in a state of continuous expectation of being fed. In their dreams, being fed is a fre-

quent symbol of being loved; being starved, an expression of frustration or disappointment.

By and large, the outlook of people of this receptive orientation is optimistic and friendly; they have a certain confidence in life and its gifts, but they become anxious and distraught when their "source of supply" is threatened. They often have a genuine warmth and a wish to help others, but doing things for others also assumes the function of securing their favor.

THE EXPLOITATIVE ORIENTATION

The exploitative orientation, like the receptive, has as its basic premise the feeling that the source of all good is outside, that whatever one wants to get must be sought there, and that one cannot produce anything oneself. The difference between the two, however, is that the exploitative type does not expect to receive things from others as gifts, but to take them away from others by force or cunning. This orientation extends to all spheres of activity.

In the realm of love and affection these people tend to grab and steal. They feel attracted only to people whom they can take away from somebody else. Attractiveness to them is conditioned by a person's attachment to somebody else; they tend not to fall in love with an unattached person.

We find the same attitude with regard to thinking and intellectual pursuits. Such people will tend not to produce ideas but to steal them. This may be done directly in the form of plagiarism or more subtly by repeating in different phraseology the ideas voiced by others and insisting they are new and their own. It is a striking fact that frequently people with great intelligence proceed in this way, although if they relied on their own gifts they might well be able to have ideas of their own. The lack of original ideas or independent production in otherwise gifted people often has its explanation in this character orientation, rather than in any innate lack of originality. The same statement holds true with regard to their orientation to material things. Things which they can take away from others always seem better to them than anything they can produce themselves. They use and exploit anybody and anything from whom or from which they can squeeze something. Their motto is: "Stolen fruits are sweetest." Because they want to use and exploit people, they "love" those who, explicitly or implicitly, are promising objects of exploitation, and get "fed up" with persons whom they have squeezed out. An extreme example is the kleptomaniac who enjoys things only if he can steal them, although he has the money to buy them.

This orientation seems to be symbolized by the biting mouth which is often a prominent feature in such people. It is not a play upon words to point out that they often make "biting" remarks about others. Their attitude is colored by a mixture of hostility and manipulation. Everyone is an object of exploitation and is judged according to his usefulness. Instead of the confidence and optimism which characterizes the receptive type, one finds here suspicion and cynicism, envy and jealousy. Since they are satisfied only with things they can take away from others, they tend to overrate what others have and underrate what is theirs.

THE HOARDING ORIENTATION

While the receptive and exploitative types are similar inasmuch as both expect to get things from the outside world, the hoarding orientation is essentially different. This orientation makes people have little faith in anything new they might get from the outside world; their security is based upon hoarding and saving, while spending is felt to be a threat. They have surrounded themselves, as it were, by a protective wall, and their main aim is to bring as much as possible into this fortified position and to let as little as possible out of it. Their miserliness refers to money and material things as well as to feelings and thoughts. Love

is essentially a possession; they do not give love but try to get it by possessing the "beloved." The hoarding person often shows a particular kind of faithfulness toward people and even toward memories. Their sentimentality makes the past appear as golden; they hold on to it and indulge in the memories of bygone feelings and experiences. They know everything but are sterile and incapable of productive thinking.

One can recognize these people too by facial expressions and gestures. Theirs is the tight-lipped mouth; their gestures are characteristic of their withdrawn attitude. While those of the receptive type are inviting and round, as it were, and the gestures of the exploitative type are aggressive and pointed, those of the hoarding type are angular, as if they wanted to emphasize the frontiers between themselves and the outside world. Another characteristic element in this attitude is pedantic orderliness. The hoarder will be orderly with things, thoughts, or feelings, but again, as with memory, his orderliness is sterile and rigid. He cannot endure things out of place and will automatically rearrange them. To him the outside world threatens to break into his fortified position; orderliness signifies mastering the world outside by putting it, and keeping it, in its proper place in order to avoid the danger intrusion. His compulsive cleanliness is another expression of his need to undo contact with the outside world. Things beyond his own frontiers are felt to be dangerous and "unclean"; he annuls the menacing contact by compulsive washing, similar to a religious washing ritual prescribed after contact with unclean things or people. Things have to be put not only in their proper place but also into their proper time; obsessive punctuality is characteristic of the hoarding type; it is another form of mastering the outside world. If the outside world is experienced as a threat to one's fortified position, obstinacy is a logical reaction. A constant "no" is the almost automatic defense against intrusion; sitting tight, the answer to the danger of being pushed. These people tend to feel that they possess only a fixed quantity of strength, energy, or mental capacity, and that this stock is diminished or exhausted by use and can never be replenished. They cannot understand the self-replenishing function of all living substance and that activity and the use of one's powers increase strength while stagnation paralyzes; to them, death and destruction have more reality than life and growth. The act of creation is a miracle of which they hear but in which they do not believe. Their highest values are order and security; their motto: "There is nothing new under the sun." In their relationship to others intimacy is a threat; either remoteness or possession of a person means security. The hoarder tends to be suspicious and to have a particular sense of justice which in effect says: "Mine is mine and yours is yours."

THE MARKETING ORIENTATION

The marketing orientation developed as a dominant one only in the modern era. In order to understand its nature one must consider the economic function of the market in modern society as being not only analogous to this character orientation but as the basis and the main condition for its development in modern man.

Barter is one of the oldest economic mechanisms. The traditional local market, however, is essentially different from the market as it has developed in modern capitalism. Bartering on a local market offered an opportunity to meet for the purpose of exchanging commodities. Producers and customers became acquainted; they were relatively small groups; the demand was more or less known, so that the producer could produce for this specific demand.

The modern market is no longer a meeting place but a mechanism characterized by abstract and impersonal demand. One produces for this market, not for a known circle of customers; its verdict is based on laws of supply and demand; and it determines whether the commodity can be sold and at what price. No matter what the *use value* of a pair of shoes may be, for instance, if the supply is greater than the demand, some shoes will be sentenced to economic death; they might as well not have been produced at all. The market day is the "day of judgment" as far as the exchange *value* of commodities is concerned.

The reader may object that this description of the market is oversimplified. The producer does try to judge the demand in advance, and under monopoly conditions even obtains a certain degree of control over it. Nevertheless, the regulatory function of the market has been, and still is, predominant enough to have a profound influence on the character formation of the urban middle class and, through the latter's social and cultural influence, on the whole population. The market concept of value, the emphasis on exchange value rather than on use value, has led to a similar concept of value with regard to people and particularly to oneself. The character orientation which is rooted in the experience of oneself as a commodity and of one's value as exchange value I call the marketing orientation.

In our time the marketing orientation has been growing rapidly, together with the development of a new market that is a phenomenon of the last decades—the "personality market." Clerks and salesmen, business executives and doctors, lawyers and artists all appear on this market. It is true that their legal status and economic positions are different: some are independent, charging for their services; others are employed, receiving salaries. But all are dependent for their material success on a personal acceptance by those who need their services or who employ them.

The principle of evaluation is the same on both the personality and the commodity market: on the one, personalities are offered for sale; on the other, commodities. Value in both cases is their exchange value, for which use value is a necessary but not a sufficient condition. It is true, our economic system could not function if people were not skilled in the particular work they have to perform and were gifted only with a pleasant personality. Even the best bedside manner and the most beautifully equipped office on Park Avenue would not make a New York doctor successful if he did not have a minimum of medical knowledge and skill. Even the most winning personality would not prevent a secretary from losing her job unless she could type reasonably fast. However, if we ask what the respective weight of skill and personality as a condition for success is, we find that only in exceptional cases is success predominantly the result of skill and of certain other human qualities like honesty, decency, and integrity. Although the proportion between skill and human qualities on the one hand and "personality" on the other hand as prerequisites for success varies, the "personality factor" always plays a decisive role. Success depends largely on how well a person sells himself on the market, how well he gets his personality across, how nice a "package" he is; whether he is "cheerful," "sound," "aggressive," "reliable," "ambitious"; furthermore what his family background is, what clubs he belongs to, and whether he knows the right people. The type of personality required depends to some degree on the special field in which a person works. A stockbroker, a salesman, a secretary, a railroad executive, a college professor, or a hotel manager must each offer different kinds of personality that, regardless of their differences, must fulfill one condition: to be in demand.

The fact that in order to have success it is not sufficient to have the skill and equipment for performing a given task but that one must be able to "put across" one's personality in competition with many others shapes the attitude toward oneself. If it were enough for the purpose of making a living to rely on what one knows and what one can do, one's self-esteem would be in proportion to one's capacities, that is, to one's use value; but since success depends largely on how

one sells one's personality, one experiences oneself as a commodity or rather simultaneously as the seller *and* the commodity to be sold. A person is not concerned with his life and happiness, but with becoming salable. This feeling might be compared to that of a commodity, of handbags on a counter, for instance, could they feel and think. Each handbag would try to make itself as "attractive" as possible in order to attract customers and to look as expensive as possible in order to obtain a higher price than its rivals. The handbag sold for the highest price would feel elated, since that would mean it was the most "valuable" one; the one which was not sold would feel sad and convinced of its own worthlessness. This fate might befall a bag which, though excellent in appearance and usefulness, had the bad luck to be out of date because of a change in fashion.

Like the handbag, one has to be in fashion on the personality market, and in order to be in fashion one has to know what kind of personality is most in demand. This knowledge is transmitted in a general way throughout the whole process of education, from kindergarten to college, and implemented by the family. The knowledge acquired at this early stage is not sufficient, however; it emphasizes only certain general qualities like adaptability, ambition, and sensitivity to the changing expectations of other people. The more specific picture of the models for success one gets elsewhere. The pictorial magazines, newspapers, and newsreels show the pictures and life stories of the successful in many variations. Pictorial advertising has a similar function. The successful executive who is pictured in a tailor's advertisement is the image of how one should look and be, if one is to draw down the "big money" on the contemporary personality market.

The most important means of transmitting the desired personality pattern to the average man is the motion picture. The young girl tries to emulate the facial expression, coiffure, gestures of a high-priced star as the most promising way to success. The young man tries to look and be like the model he sees on the screen. While the average citizen has little contact with the life of the most successful people, his relationship with the motion-picture stars is different. It is true that he has no real contact with them either, but he can see them on the screen again and again, can write them and receive their autographed pictures. In contrast to the time when the actor was socially despised but was never-theless the transmitter of the works of great poets to his audience, our motion-picture stars have no great works or ideas to transmit, but their function is to serve as the link an average person has with the world of the "great." Even if he can not hope to become as successful as they are, he can try to emulate them; they are his saints and because of their success they embody the norms for living.

Since modern man experiences himself both as the seller and as the commodity to be sold on the market, his self-esteem depends on conditions beyond his control. If he is "success-ful," he is valuable; if he is not, he is worthless. The degree of insecurity which results from this orientation can hardly be overestimated. If one feels that one's own value is not constituted primarily by the human qualities one possesses, but by one's success on a competitive market with ever-changing conditions, one's self-esteem is bound to be shaky and in constant need of confirmation by others. Hence one is driven to strive relentlessly for success, and any setback is a severe threat to one's self-esteem; helplessness, insecu-rity, and inferiority feelings are the result. If the vicissitudes of the market are the judges of one's value, the sense of dignity and pride is destroyed.

But the problem is not only that of self-evaluation and self-esteem but of one's experience of oneself as an inde-pendent entity, of one's *identity with oneself*. The mature and productive individual derives his feeling of iden-tity from the experience of himself as the agent who is one with his powers; this feeling of self can be briefly ex-pressed as meaning *"I am what I do."* In the marketing orientation man encounters his own powers as com-modities alienated from him. He is not one with them but they are masked from him because what matters is not his self-realization in the process of using them but his success in the process of selling them. Both his powers and what they create become estranged, something different from himself, something for others to judge and to use; thus his feeling of identity becomes as shaky as his self-esteem; it is constituted by the sum total of roles one can play: *"I am as you desire me."*

Intrapsychic Theories:

THERAPY

Pathological behavior, according to the intrapsychic theorists, reflects the operation of unconscious anxieties and defensive maneuvers which have persisted from early childhood. The task of therapy, then, is to bring these residues of the past into consciousness where they can be reevaluated and reworked in a constructive fashion. The excerpt chosen from Lewis Wolberg's excellent book, The Technique of Psychotherapy, summarizes the logic and the technical procedures utilized to accomplish this goal. Harry Stack Sullivan, one of the outstanding theorists of the intrapsychic persuasion, presents in the excerpt reproduced here a detailed statement of the roles and activities assumed by patient and therapist in the treatment of schizophrenia. This paper is especially important in light of the fact that many critics suggest that the psychoanalytic approach is of little value in the therapy of psychotic patients.

Technique of Reconstructive Therapy

LEWIS R. WOLBERG

Freud contended that the essence of a neurosis was a repression of infantile fears and experiences which continually forced the individual to act in the present as if he were living in the past. The neurotic seemed to be dominated by past anxieties that, split off, operated autonomously and served no further function in reality.

Internal dangers were constantly threatened by the efforts of the id to discharge accumulated tension. Such discharge was opposed by the mental force of the super-ego in the form of repression to prevent the release of tension. Repression was a dynamic force which attempted to seal off internal dangers. However, the maintenance of repression required an

From Lewis R. Wolberg *Technique of Psychotherapy*, pages 58-63, Grune & Stratton, Inc., 1954, by permission of the publisher and author.

enormous expenditure of energy. The ego derived this energy from the id in a subversive manner. Thus, an idea or tendency invested with libido (cathexis) would be stripped of libido and this energy used to oppose the idea or tendency (anti-cathexis).

Subtle mechanisms such as symbolization, condensation, distortion and displacement were employed to evade repressive forces and to provide a substitutive discharge of repressed energy, and a consequent relief of tension. Fantasies, dreams and symptoms were expressions of such mechanisms. Where the substitutive expression was in harmony with social values and super-ego ideals, it provided a suitable means of relief (sublimation). Where it was not in harmony, conflict resulted and repressive mechanisms were again invoked.

If repression proved ineffective in mediating tension, a regression to earlier modes of adaptation was possible. This happened particularly where the individual was confronted by experiences similar to, or representative of, those which initiated anxiety in childhood. The ego reacted automatically to these experiences, as if the reality conditionings of later years had had no corrective effect on the original danger situation. It responded with essentially the same defenses of childhood, even though these were now inappropriate.

A retention of a relationship to reality at the expense of an intrapsychic balance produced a psychoneurotic disturbance. The existing conflict here was between the ego and the id. If an intrapsychic balance developed at the expense of reality relationships, the consequence was psychosis. The latter resulted when the ego was overwhelmed by id forces, the conflict being between the ego and the environment.

In addition to the libido theory described above, Freud elaborated the theory of the death instinct to account for phenomena not explicable in terms of libido. He postulated that an instinct existed in the id which prompted aggressive and destructive drives. This instinct manifested itself in a "repetition compulsion" to undo the forward evolutionary development of the organism, and to its primordial inorganic state. The death instinct, though sometimes libidinized(sadism) was totally different from the sexual instinct.

Freudian psychoanalytic therapy is based on the libido theory described above. It rests on the hypothesis that neurotic illness is nurtured by the repression of vital aspects of the self and its experiences; particularly oral, anal and sexual (including Oedipal) experiences in relation to important parental agencies. This repression is sponsored by fear of the loss of love or of punishment from the parents, which has been internalized in the super-ego. Repressed feelings, attitudes and fears, and the early experi-ences associated with them, continue to strive for conscious recognition, but are kept from awareness by dread of repetition of parental loss of love or punishment now invested in the super-ego. The removal from the mainstream of consciousness makes it impossible for the individual to come to grips with basic conflicts. These remain in their pristine state, uncorrected by reality and by later experiences. The energy required to maintain repression, as well as to sustain other defenses against anxiety, robs the individual of energy that could be utilized to nurture psychosexual development.

Therapy, of necessity, consists of restoring to consciousness that which was removed by repression, and which has been draining off energies needed to foster personality growth. In therapy, the relationship with the therapist helps strengthen the ego to a point where it can eventually cope with anxiety, mobilized by the return of the repressed to awareness. It is essential that the patient recognize the derivatives of the repressed, since these represent in an attenuated form, the warded-off material. To minimize the distortion of these derivatives, the obtrusion of current situations and other reality influences must be kept at a minimum. This is fostered by certain technical procedures, such as "free association," the assumption of the couch position, passivity of the therapist, encouragement of transference, the use of dreams, and the focusing of the interview away from reality considerations.

The basis of Freudian psychoanalysis lies in what is perhaps Freud's most vital discovery, that of transference. As has previously been indicated, Freud found that the patient, if not interfered with, inevitably projected into the therapeutic situation, feelings and attitudes that were parcels of his past. Sometimes transference manifestations became so intense that the patient actually reproduced and reenacted with the therapist important conflictual situations and traumatic experiences (transference neurosis) which had been subject to infantile amnesia. By recovering and recognizing these repressed experiences and conflictual situations that had never been resolved, and by living them through with a new, less neurotic and non-punitive parental agency, the superego was believed to undergo modification. The individual became tolerant of his id, and more capable of altering ego defenses that had crippled his adaptation. There occurred, finally, a mastery of his early conflicts and a liberation of fixated libido which could then enter into the development of a mature personality.

Since the Oedipus complex is considered by Freud to be the nucleus of every neurosis, its analysis and resolution in transference constitutes a primary focus. Where the Oedipus complex is not revealed, where its pathologic manifestations are not thoroughly analyzed and worked through, and where forgotten memories of early childhood experiences are not restored, treatment is considered incomplete.

Because Freudian psychoanalysis *is* transference analysis, all means of facilitating transference are employed. These include the assumption by the therapist of an extremely passive role, the verbalization by the patient of a special kind of communication—"free association"—the analysis of dream material, the maintenance of an intense contact with the patient on the basis of no less than five visits weekly, and the employment of the recumbent couch position.

Passivity on the part of the therapist is judiciously maintained even through long periods of silence. The therapist also refrains from reacting emotionally, or responding positively or negatively to any verbalized or non-verbalized attitude or feeling expressed by the patient. Strict anonymity is observed, no personal information being supplied to the patient irrespective of how importunate he may become. A non-judgmental, non-punitive, non-condoning attitude by the therapist is adhered to, dogmatic utterances of any kind being forbidden.

The only "rule" the patient is asked to obey is the "basic rule" or "fundamental rule" of verbalizing whatever comes to his mind, however fleeting, repulsive or seemingly inconsequential it may seem (free association). This undirected kind of thinking is a most important means of tapping the unconscious, and of reviving unconscious conflicts and the memories that are related to their origin. Most importantly, free association, like passivity, enhances the evolution of transference. So long as the patient continues to associate freely, the therapist keeps silent, even though entire sessions may pass without a comment. The therapist fights off all temptations toward "small talk" or impulses to expound on theory. Only when resistances to free association develop, does he interfere, and only until the patient proceeds with his verbalizations.

Dream analysis is utilized constantly as another means of penetrating the unconscious. By activating repressed material and working on defenses as they are revealed in dream structure, the therapist aids the development of transference.

The frequency of visits in Freudian psychoanalysis is important. To encourage transference, no fewer than five visits weekly are required. In some cases four visits may suffice. Fewer visits than this encourage "acting-out" and other resistances to transference.

The use of the recumbent couch position enables the patient to concentrate on the task of free association with as few encumbrances of reality as possible. It helps the therapist, also, to focus on the unconscious content underlying the patient's verbalizations without having to adjust himself to the demands such as would exist in a face-to-face position. Concentrating on his inner life rather than on external reality, helps to bring on the phenomenon of transference.

During the early stages of analysis, the main task is to observe—from his free associations and dreams— unconscious conflicts, and the types of defenses employed by the patient, which form a kind of blueprint of the unconscious problems of the patient. This blueprint is utilized later at the stage of transference. Since repression is threatened by the operation of exploring the unconscious, anxiety is apt to appear, stimulating defensive mechanisms. These function as resistances to productivity, and even to verbalization. Free association may consequently cease, and the patient may exhibit other manifestations that oppose cooperation with the treatment endeavor. Such resistances are dealt with by interpretation. Through interpretation the patient is brought to an awareness of how and why he is resisting, and the conflicts that make resistance necessary.

Sooner or later the patient will "transfer" past attitudes and feelings into the present relationship with the analyst. Observance of the "basic rule," the attack on his resistances through interpretation, and the consideration of unconscious material in dreams and free associations, remove habitual protective devices and façades that permit the patient to maintain a conventional relationship. Toward the therapist he is most apt to express strivings rooted in past experiences, perhaps even reproducing his past in the present. Thus, a revival of pathogenic past conflicts develops. Unlike supportive and re-educative therapy, in which transference may be utilized as a therapeutic vehicle, the transference is interpreted to the patient in order to expose its nature. This is the chief means of resolving resistance, of bringing the individual to an awareness of the warded off content, and of realizing the historical origin of his conflicts.

The development of transference may occur insidiously and manifest itself indirectly, or it may suddenly break out in stark form. It often shows itself in changes in the content of free associations, from inner feel-ings and past relationships with parents, to more innocuous topics, like current events and situations. This shift is evidence of resistance to deeper material activated by the erupting transference feelings. Sometimes free association may cease entirely, with long stubborn silences prevailing which are engendered by an inability to talk about feelings in relation to the therapist. The purpose of superficial talk or silence is to keep from awareness repressed emotions and forgotten memories associated with early childhood, particularly the Oedipus complex. Until these can be brought out into the open, the emotions relating to them discharged, and the associated memories revived, the conflictual base of neurosis will remain. The transference neurosis offers an opportunity for this revival, since, in the relationship with the therapist, the patient will "act-out" his loves, fears and hates, which were characteristic of his own experiences during the Oedipal period.

Transference, however, acts as a source of powerful resistances that impede therapeutic progress. Once the patient is in the grip of such resistances, he is usually determined to cling to them at the expense of any other motivation, including that of getting well. On the positive side, transference is important diagnostically, since it reveals a most accurate picture of the patient's inner conflicts. Additionally, it induces a coming to grips with and a working-through in a much more favorable setting of those unresolved conflicts that have blocked maturation. The resolution of transference is felt by Freudian psychoanalysts to be the most powerful vehicle known today for producing structural alterations in the personality.

Active interpretations of the transference are essential to its resolution. These include the interpretation of its manifestations, its origin, and its original and present purposes. The working-through of transference is accompanied by a recollection of forgotten infantile and childhood experiences—a recounting of distortions in relationships with parents or parental surrogates. Interpretations will usually be denied at first as part of the resistance manifestation. Acknowledgment of the unreal nature of transference is usually opposed by the patient, because this either constitutes too great a threat for him, or because he does not want to relinquish transference gratifications which are deemed essential to life itself. So long as he continues to accept transference as factual, the analysis will remain interminable, unless forcefully terminated by either participant. With persistence on the part of the therapist, interpretations usually take hold, and the patient is rewarded with greater insight, an increased sense of mastery, liberation from neurotic symptoms, and a genuine growth in maturity.

The therapist must also constantly guard against manifestations of counter-transference, which may be both disguised and varied, and which are mobilized by unresolved problems and pressing needs within the therapist himself. Common forms of counter-transference are subtle sadistic attacks on the patient, impulses to be pompous and omnipotent, or desires to reject the patient or to detach oneself from the relationship. Because of counter-transference, a personal analysis is considered essential for the analyst in order that he can deal with his own unconscious tendencies and resistances precipitated by his contact with his patients.

As the ego of the patient is strengthened by an alliance with the therapist, it becomes more and more capable of tolerating less and less distorted derivatives of unconscious conflict. The continued interpretation by the therapist of the patient's unconscious feelings and attitudes, as well as the defensive devices that he employs against them, enables the patient to work-through his problems by seeing how they condition every aspect of his life. In the medium of the therapeutic relationship, the individual is helped to come to grips with early fears and misconceptions, resolving these by living them through in the transference. The patient is finally able to resolve libidinal fixations, and to liberate energy that should originally have gone into the formation of a mature sexual organization.

Disagreement with certain psychoanalytic concepts is legion. Even those analysts who consider themselves to be "orthodox" Freudians are not in complete accord with Freud in theory and method. For instance, there are many analysts who challenge the death instinct hypothesis. Insofar as technique is concerned, practically every analyst implements psychoanalytic methods in his own specific way. An extensive questionnaire distributed by Glover to a representative group of practicing psychoanalysts demonstrated that deviations from orthodox techniques were extensive. There were differences in the form, timing, amount and depth of interpretation. The degree of adherence to free association varied, as did the assumption of passivity and anonymity, the use of reassurance, and the management of transference. Variation in methods of doing psychoanalysis was indicated by the fact that out of eighty-two questions, there was general agreement on only six, and even here there was not complete conformity.

Criticism of Freudian psychoanalysis is voiced both by those who have had no intimate contact with the psychoanalytic technique, as well as by well-trained psychoanalysts who have been thoroughly schooled in Freudian principles. Lines of disagreement will be discussed in the next section on non-Freudian psychoanalysis. One commonly voiced criticism of the Freudian method is that some analysts insist upon wedging their patients into a preconceived theoretic structure. When the patient does not produce appropriate material that substantiates accepted notions of dynamics, or when he refuses to accept interpretations, he is credited as being in an obstinate state of resistance. Another criticism expressed by non-Freudians is that, in their eagerness to smuggle "deep" insights into patients, certain "orthodox" analysts make dogmatic interpretations which the patient feels obliged to accept. These may mobilize intense anxiety, which disorganizes patients with weak ego structures. A third criticism is that many Freudian analysts are intolerant toward those who practice any therapies other than Freudian psychoanalysis, considering these to be superficial and of little real value. Accordingly, they are inclined to depreciate the results of treatment by non-analysts, as well as by analysts of non-Freudian orientation.

Freudian psychoanalysis is taught extensively in this country, being sponsored by the American Psychoanalytic Association and by most of the current schools of psychoanalytic training.

The Modified Psychoanalytic Treatment of Schizophrenia

HARRY STACK SULLIVAN

In this presentation, an attempt will be made to contribute some factual material bearing on the nature of the schizophrenic mental disorders, and on their treatment by a procedure rather intimately related to the psychoanalytic method of Sigmund Freud. No argument will be offered as to the propriety of the use of "psychoanalytic" in referring to a definite variation from Dr. Freud's technique, nor will a review of the orthodox Freudian contributions to the schizophrenia problem be undertaken. The former cannot but remain a matter of personal opinion. For the latter we may await a presently forthcoming study by Dr. William V. Silverberg. Since a session of our current meeting has been devoted to the subject of schizophrenia, and since some of the views expressed therein are doubtless not consonant with those of the present writer, some attention must also be devoted to the meaning of schizophrenia as hereinafter used. No importance is attached, however, to the magnificent expression of my personal prejudices in these matters.[1]

Firstly, it is held that if there is any difference between the "schizoid" and the "schizophrenic" mental disturbances, the difference is wholly one of degree, and not one of kind. The writer is no more entertained by "thobbing" about an essential organic disorder in schizophrenia, than is he by tedious speculation as to the relations of organic anomaly or defect to particular psychoses with mental deficiency. In contradistinction, for example, to Schilder's contribution at the earlier session,[*] this paper is intended to deal with consensually valid information about actual patients and actual procedures of therapy, rather than with ingenuity of thinking about hypotheses concerning possibilities of an unknown order of probability. It must follow the tedious scientific rather than the spectacular philosophic road, and its verbiage must be so carefully organized and so adequately elucidated as

[1] The reader is respectfully referred to the perhaps redundant but no less relevant "Thobbing" of Henshaw Ward (New York: Bobbs-Merrill, 1926). To *thob* is to *th*ink out something, which opinion is glorified as an extravasation of one's personality, and most vigorously *b*elieved and "defended," thereafter.

[*Paul Schilder, "Scope of Psychotherapy in Schizophrenia," *Amer. J. Psychiatry* (1931–32) 88:1181–1187.]

From *Amer. J. Psychiat. 88*:519-540, 1931-1932, by permission of the American Psychiatric Association.

to provide the psychiatric reader with a formulation useful to himself and his patients. It does not set up any new frame of reference by use of which one can achieve a high percentage of "hits" at the game of prognostic prophecy: to the writer, the future of any particular person is a highly contingent matter, unless the subject-person be psychobiologically an adult—and in the latter case, unless also he be approaching the *senium*, the degree of contingency of his future is *distinct* if not still *high*. Had we persisted for many generations in an agrarian culture, and had this, improbably, been accompanied by extensive, well-integrated psychobiological research, so that we came to know a great deal about the living of our people, then, perchance, we would have come to a fair acquaintance with the actualities of *human probability*. Translated, however, in a few generations from such a culture to the unprecedented industrial situation, we are now in a state of almost complete ignorance of these facts of living, and therefore without any basis for prophecy as to the outcome of this or that poorly envisaged complex of more or less important but partly unrecognized factors. The future of each physico-chemical organism may subsist in some reality underlying our hypothetical time-dimension, but the future of each *person* must be recognized as a function of the eternally changing configuration of the cultural-social present. Conceivably, the identical germ plasm evolving in monozygotic twins may be representative in the present of a path in the future such that the twins shall arrive synchronously at a physico-chemical fiasco in the shape of appendicial inflammation. Conceivably, it was in some ultimately comprehensible fashion ordained at the moment of the writer's conception that he shall cease to live owing to rupture of the middle meningeal artery at the age of 57 years, three months and five days, plus or minus less than 100 hours. But that the present fact of his condemning what

Dr. Gregory Stragnell has so aptly dubbed the scholasticism of certain psychoanalytically inclined psychiatrists—in this particular case Paul Schilder about real and pseudo-schizophrenia—that this activity was determined more remotely than the occasion of the last meeting of the Association for Research in Nervous and Mental Diseases, is not true.[2]

No one could conceivably demonstrate any preordination of the effect on the protagonist's future of this situation, prior to the date first named. That which at least two people cannot demonstrate cannot be utilized in scientific procedure. It seems therefore fairly proven that the effects of the current interpersonal situation on the future of Dr. Paul Schilder, arise *de novo* from the configuration of the present; this in turn, in so far as it is focused in the writer, arising from configurations *actually existing* at particular moments on certain dates in the recent past; these, in further turn, arising from streams of events so complex in themselves, and so complex in their interrelations, that any prophecy of the current situation, on a date more distant than six months ago, would have been fantastic in the extreme.[3]

[2] The most significant determining factors in this particular situation, *so far as the writer is chiefly concerned*, may be "dated" as follows: March 12, 1931, psychiatric meeting at which the protagonist "presented" a case illustrating the alleged relations of the organic and the functional; March 18, 1931, dinner discussion; April 10, 1931, psychiatric meeting, as previous; April 24, 1931, psychiatric meeting, as previous; April 28, 1931, protagonist's discussion of "The Pathogenesis of Schizophrenia" by Dr. Gregory Zilboorg, New York Psychoanalytic Society; May 13, 1931, reading of summary of protagonist's paper in the program of the current meeting; May 17, 1931, realization that someone must be made a "goat" for illustrating pseudopsychiatric contributions; May 21, 1931, conclusion that the ends justified the risk of this sort of illustration before so kindly and democratic an audience as the present one.

The *situation* under discussion is *interpersonal;* involving, as major nexus, (a) the writer variously expanded, (b) his "impersonal" hearers and readers, (c) the person, Paul Schilder as protagonist, auditor, reader, and reactor, and secondarily those who "side" with him in the alleged "controversy" which many conceive all psychiatric criticism to be, (d) the body of valid and other information that is the psychiatry of schizophrenia; and so forth.

[3] The best that could have been ventured is something as follows: The present writer, being

To return now to the crux of this point: *either no one* of the acutely schizophrenic young men received by the research service of the Sheppard and Enoch Pratt Hospital in the past two years was in fact schizophrenic but instead all were "schizoid"—in which case we might perhaps assume that schizophrenia *the* disease is not shown by native-born males before the age of 25—*or* there is no great importance to be attached to the organic substratum of personality in young acute schizophrenics, but rather great stress to be laid on the socio-psychiatric treatment to which they are exposed, in our studying of the factors relevant to outcome. It is my opinion that a consensus of qualified observers can be secured in support of the latter conclusion. The question of an "organic disorder" is therefore irrelevant to this consideration of schizophrenia.[4]

Secondly, in further delimitation of the term, schizophrenia, it is held

that these disorders have not been defined psychoanalytically. It is necessary, before adumbrating the original communication herein attempted, to discountenance any conclusion that the writer's study of schizophrenia has "proven" or "disproven" psychoanalytic theory, or any part or parcel thereof, other than the doctrine of narcissistic neurosis. The psychoanalytic terms hereinafter utilized are terms as to the meaning of which, in the writer's opinion, a consensus of competent observers could be obtained. That these consensually defined meanings would be identical with or quite different from the most orthodox Freudian definitions, is unknown. Psychoanalytic formulations are extremely individualistic, in the sense that they are largely Prof. Freud's opinions about his experience with his patients, in the formation of which opinions—as in the great part of all psychiatric opinions—the social and cultural aspects of the thinker's opinion-formation have mostly been ignored. There could not be a meaningful use of the term schizophrenia in regard of a man who had grown from birth into adolescence in utter detachment from any person or personally organized culture. Again, it is possible so to organize a society that the living of its persons, normal to each other, would be regarded as schizophrenic by psychiatrists who studied any one of its members in sufficiently alien surroundings. In brief, schizophrenia is meaningful only in an *interpersonal context;* its characteristics can only be established by a study of the interrelation of the schizophrenic with schizophrenic, less schizophrenic, and nonschizophrenic others. A "socially recovered" schizophrenic is often still psychotic, but is certainly *less* schizophrenic than is a patient requiring active institutional supervision. To isolate the *non*-schizophrenic individual, however, is no small problem. It implies criteria of presence or absence of these processes, of which criteria there seems to be a marked dearth. One might use the following as a fun-

---

deeply interested in schizophrenia, and having amassed consensually valid information which he interprets as evidence convincing to any intelligent observer to the effect that *no such illness of acute onset is apt to manifest a dependable sign of bad outcome regardless of treatment*, being moreover activated by a drive to insure the active attention of all concerned to the importance of early care in determining the outcome of schizophrenic disorders, being also interested in the growth of psychiatric knowledge and its refinement from fantasy, *will to a considerable probability*, sooner or later, subject the views of the protagonist to more or less effective criticism. If suitable occasion arise, this will doubtless occur in the course of a psychiatric meeting. Since the writer will be activated to reach the largest audience, it will probably occur at a meeting of The American Psychiatric Association. After reading the program of the current meeting—a prophecy the more probable in that it is but a few weeks "ahead of" the events—an astute prognostician might have said, "It is *quite probable* that this situation will arise on June 3 or 5, 1931." Even if, on May 27, he had read this paper, he would have had clearly in mind the fact that the occurrence of the present situation *continued to be contingent* on many actually unpredictable factors.

[4] The acuteness or insidiousness of *onset of the observed psychosis*, however, may finally give the question of underlying organic state new relevance. It is quite *possible*, in the writer's opinion, that an ultimately measurable something of great prognostic significance may be found to underlie these insidious disintegrations of personality attended by more or less of schizophrenic phenomena, that are now lumped with disorders of acute *observed onset*. Statistics of the Sheppard experience indicate so great a difference in course of the two groups, that one cannot but wish that effort might be directed to the comparative study of individuals of acute *versus* insidious observed onset.

damental basis for classification: the non-schizophrenic individual, in his interaction with other persons, behaves and thinks in complete consonance with their mutual cultural make-up. Then, to the extent that one's behavior and thought in dealing with another diverges from the mutual culture—traditions, conventions, fashions—to that extent he would be schizophrenic. This seems to be a good working hypothesis, but it has not yet ensued in much consensually valid information. There is, as yet, no measuring of mutual culture; we know that being exposed to culture does not necessarily imply its incorporation in a personality; we know that there are certain personality differentials that greatly affect the incorporation of cultural entities; but we have not paid much attention to evolving techniques for distinguishing the cultural aspects of individual personalities.[5]

There is, however, an indirect approach to this problem—one, moreover, that has seemed to be of practical application. We know that the dream-life of the individual is to a very great degree, purely personal. This consideration applies to a lesser extent to the waking fantasy-life. While there is probably very little indeed of the waking fantasy that is uninfluenced by environing persons or personal entities not wholly of the self, we can assume that certain "primitive" dreams are almost entirely without external reference. We therefore conclude that the more like the dream of deep sleep a given content is, the more purely of the self it is. We can then surmise that a rough approximation to our basis for division into the schizophrenic and the nonschizophrenic can be hypothecated on the consideration of the more purely personal *versus* the consensually valid apperception of a given interpersonal situation. If the "contact" with external reality is wholly unintelligible

per se to the presumably fairly sane observer, then the subject-individual manifests a content indistinguishable from a dream, and is either in a state of serious disorder of the integrating systems, or is schizophrenic. An individual manifesting behavior when not fully awake would thus be clearly schizophrenic. An individual suffering the disorder of interest manifested in severe fatigue would likewise come under this rubric.

A psychiatrist's initial reaction to this formulation can scarcely be one of instant acceptance. He knows of people who "awaken" in nightmares and have trouble in throwing off the content of the dream. He knows that most of these folk are comparatively normal, in their daily life. He is not ready to identify their transitory disturbance of consciousness on occasional nights with the mental disorder shown 18 hours or so per day, day in and day out by the "dementia præcox" patients in the wards of the mental hospital. It is the writer's opinion that neither phenomenologically nor dynamically can distinction be shown between the two situations. Schizophrenics, in the first hours or days of the frank illness, show just as abrupt transitions among distinguishable states as does our troubled dreamer. The dream-state in their case tends to become habitual, or at least frequently recurrent, and whenever this occurs, the individual is definitely schizophrenic.[6]

The questions that would seem to require answer before acceptance of this formulation of schizophrenia are somewhat as follows: How does it happen that most of us are able to sort out our dreams and our waking experience with a very high degree of success, while the schizophrenic fails in this? Why do only some of those who have night-terror or nightmares progress into chronic schizophrenic states? And, from the organicist, why, if this

---

[5] The development of this topic—*viz.*, the cultural entities built into and going to make up the individual personality—is to be found in the writer's forthcoming text, "The Sickness of The Modern Mind: The Psychopathology of Interpersonal Relations" [probably *Personal Psychopathology*].

[6] That this conception of schizophrenia is broad enough to include the clinical entity, *hysteria*, has not escaped the writer. This is not the occasion on which to develop the implications of a classification of levels of consciousness, nor of the dynamics underlying major and minor dissociations.

definition is approximately correct, should not a treatment by alternation of rest and the use of a powerful cerebral stimulant like caffeine bring about at least a suspension of the schizophrenic state? As to the first of these questions, the actual sorting out of *some little* of our dream-life from waking experience is a difficult or impossible task. The little that is "hard to locate" as to whether dream or "reality" is often quite transparently related to important but none too well recognized tendency systems within the personality concerned. We come thus to the answer of questions one and two: To the extent that important tendency systems of the personality *have* to discharge themselves in sleep, to that extent the dream-processes tend to exaggerated personal importance, and to augmented "reality value." That which permits tendency systems no direct manifestation except during sleep and other states of altered consciousness is their condition of *dissociation* by other tendency systems of the personality—systems apparently invariably represented in the self. At this point, a digression must be made anent a fairly popular psychoanalytic "thob" about the "strength" *versus* "weakness" of the ego. We learn that the superego is "weak" in the schizophrenic; also, that it is "strong" in the schizophrenic; that the ego and the ideal of ego are weak or strong; that the feeble ego is ground between the powerful id of instinctual cravings and the superego; and so forth. Leaving aside the fact that there is plenty of clinical material to be observed by anyone seriously interested in *finding out* what this is all about—there being at least 250,000 patients diagnosed as schizophrenic in the hospitals of the United States—the writer would point out that no night-terror, nightmare, or schizophrenic disorder *can occur* unless there is a waking dissociation of some one powerful tendency system by another powerful tendency system. And, by direct implication of the formula, a continued dream-state, schizophrenia, cannot occur unless there is continued an approximation to a dynamic balance between the tendency system manifesting in the conscious self and the one dissociated from such manifestation.[7] As to the chemotherapeutic employment of agents to provide rest alternating with cerebral stimulants of the caffeine group, it may be noted that this very program, applied during the first hours of schizophrenic collapse, does delay the disaster. The cerebrum and the other areas responding to caffeine stimulation, however, are not solely the province of the conscious self, and the raised threshold of function is not solely at the service of the *dissociating* system. This topic, together with that of delirifacient drugs and of ethyl alcohol, has been discussed by the writer, elsewhere.

It appears, then, that no well-integrated personality—in whom there is no dissociation of an important tendency system—can show schizophrenic processes of more than momentary duration; and that any personality in whom there is a chronic dissociation of a powerful tendency system may show persisting schizophrenia after any event that destroys the balance by strengthening the dissociated tendency system, or by enfeebling the dissociating system. Physiological maturation and toxic-exhaustive states are frequent factors in this connection.

The partition of time to the schizophrenic processes — whether they occupy but moments during the time ordinarily devoted to sleep, or instead persist days on end in active psychosis —is determined by the balance between the dissociated and the dissociating systems. The "healing" process that ordinarily occurs in night-terror and nightmare is the source of an important insight into this matter. One "recovers" from the failing dissociation manifesting more or less lucidly in the nightmare, by reintegrating one's consciousness of circumambient reality, including one's "place," status, etc. If the pressure of the dissociated

---

[7] Since it is not the present purpose to discuss the strength or weakness of the ego and so forth, no comment will be made on, for example, the highly relevant data provided by psychopathic personalities.

system is great, one "knows better" than to return to sleep until one has strengthened the dissociating system by a readjustment of interest and attention to one's waking world. In night-terror, the healing process is less conscious, but usually more directly *interpersonal*. In any case, in the writer's opinion, the restoration of balance in favor of the dissociating system is achieved by some *adjustment of interpersonal relations*. On the other hand, a persisting dream-state represents a failure of interpersonal adjustment, such that the tendency system previously dissociated is now as powerful in integrating interpersonal situations as is the previously successful dissociating system. The augmentation of the one may alternate somewhat with that of the other; the *degree* of consciousness may vary, but conflict and a consciously perceived threat of eruption of the dissociated system is sustained. It is evident that these dynamics may lead to the phenomena delineated in the paper of Dr. Mary O'Malley earlier in the program. It is equally clear that the "retreat" from the personal realities of others, the "seclusiveness" and the inaccessibility to easy personal contacts that are so classically schizophrenic are but the avoidance of accentuated conflict between the tendency systems, which integrate or "strive" to integrate the sufferer into mutually incongruous interpersonal relations, with the appearance of most distressing interests and attention.

We may proceed from this theoretic formulation of the facts of schizophrenia to consideration of the treatment of these disorders. It is to be noted that the basic formula of all psychotherapy is that of interpersonal relations, and their effects on the further growth of tendency systems within the patient-personality. Observation of the processes shown in improvements and aggravations of personality disorder is clearly in line with this formulation. One sees that there is no *essential* difference between psychotherapeutic achievement and achievements in other forms of education. There is, in each, an alteration in the cultural-social part of the affected personality, to a state of better adaptation to the physico-chemical, social, and cultural environment. No essential difference exists between the better integration of a personality to be achieved by way of psychoanalytic personality study, and the better integration to be achieved by an enlightened teacher of physics in demonstrating to his student the properties of matter. There are several differences in the technique required, but these are superficial rather than fundamental, and are to be regarded as determined by actual early training of the patient, in the end reducible to the common denominator of *experience incorporated into the self*. The principal factors responsible for the apparent gap between the ordinary good educative techniques and the orthodox psychoanalytic procedures are to be found in the peculiar characteristics of very early experience—*viz.*, that of the first 18 to 30 months of extra-uterine life.[8] Since the characteristics of this material are discussed in various psychoanalytic contributions—including that of Dr. Gregory Zilboorg in this session—and since the purpose of this paper is to present the necessary steps preliminary to dealing with the infantile and early childhood experience, we shall proceed immediately to a consideration of the *interpersonal requirements* for the successful therapy of the schizophrenic.

Psychotherapy, like all experience, functions by promoting personality growth, *with or without* improvement of personality integration. Pure suggestion therapy, if such there be, merely adds experience to one or more of the important tendency systems of the personality, thereby perhaps altering the dynamic summation manifested in behavior and thought. Even such a therapy could perhaps be useful in preschizophrenic personalities and, conceivably, even in acute psychosis.

---

[8] Consideration of these factors is not directly relevant to the contribution herein attempted, and has been outlined elsewhere [*Personal Psychopathology*].

A purely rational therapy would be directed to the better integration of the personality systems, as well as to the provision of additional experience. Since it could apply only at the level of verbal communication, it should scarcely be expected to produce great affect in the field of extra-conscious processes. Hortatory therapy would generally be directed to the augmentation of the superego aspects of personality. This includes persuasion and the all too prevalent "bucking up" treatment. None of these procedures is in line with the information which we have secured as to the growth and function of personality.

Treatment in states of reduced consciousness, notably under hypnosis, could be more nearly adjusted to the total personality. Unfortunately, however, the integration of the treatment situation implied by the occurrence of the hypnotic or even the hypnoid states imposes a great responsibility on the physician. Unless he is expert indeed in dealing with the earlier experience incorporated in each personality, the net result of the treatment is sadly disappointing. Either there is little more achieved than could have been secured by a fairly rational exhortation, or there is disturbance of the superego functions and an increased severity of conflict. The integration of the hypnosis situation in the incipient or acute schizophrenic is difficult in extreme. This manipulation of the personality is therefore for us chiefly of theoretic importance. The attempt at hypnotizing distressed preschizophrenics should perhaps be emphatically discouraged, as the mandatory—even if self-determined—submission to the other personality is almost certain to cause a severe emotional upheaval, with the hypnotist thereafter in an unenviable role as chief personification of the goal of the dissociated system.

The only tools that have shown results that justify any enthusiasm in regard of the treatment of schizophrenia are the *psychoanalytic* procedures and the *socio-psychiatric* program which the writer has evolved from them. Before taking up these procedures, however, it may be well to note that the process of benefit by psychoanalysis seems none too clearly envisaged by many of its practitioners. One might be led to assume from the literature that a "cure" is achieved by a releasing of the libido from its "point of the fixation" existing somewhere in the past of the individual. A steadily increasing complexity of the map of possible fixation points is leading some of the outstanding thinkers in this field to doubt the importance of the doctrine of fixation. The writer has long since indicated his inability to discover anything corresponding to a point of fixation in schizophrenia, and has come to believe that "releasing the libido from its fixations" is but a figure of speech for something that occurs in recovery under analysis. Observation shows that psychoanalytic therapy consists of two major processes, the combination of which leads to growth and improved integration of personality. These are, firstly, a retrospective survey of the experiential basis of tendencies that conflict with the simple adaptation of the person to others with resulting growth to a more adult character; and secondly, the provision of experience that facilitates the reorganization of the undeveloped or warped tendencies such that adaptation becomes more successful. The achievement of this double process requires the establishment between the physician and patient of the situation called by Freud the "transference."

There has been a good deal written about "transference," and many peculiarities of technique have been originated with view to its cultivation and management. There seems to the writer to be nothing other than *the purpose* of the interpersonal situation which distinguishes the psychoanalytic transference relation from other situations of interpersonal intimacy. In other words, it seems to be a special case of interpersonal adaptation, distinguished chiefly by the role of subordination to an enlightened physician skilled in penetrating the self-deceptions to which man is uniquely susceptible, with a mutually accepted purpose of securing the patient an increased skill in living. Like almost all other situations tending towards intimacy the early stages of the psychoanalytic situation include a great body of fantasy processes that are not directly helpful to the achievement of the goal of the physician. Like all other interpersonal relations, this one includes a good deal of intercommunication by channels other than that of spoken propositions. As it is ordinarily applied, the psychoanalytic situation involves a patient the organization of whose self is not satisfactory, and whose self-regard is inadequate. This is very much the case in preschizophrenic and incipiently and acutely (catatonic) schizophrenic patients. By reason of the extreme distress caused by any threatened (or fantasied) reduction of the already distressingly small self-regard of these patients, and also by reason of specific painful experience with all previously significant persons, these patients are extremely uneasy about any situation in which the favorable cooperation of another is required for its resolution. The appearance of strong positive tendency towards the physician is thus attended by an extraordinary augmentation of attention for unfavorable signs, and very slight provocation may lead to a reversal of the tendency— from positive to negative, love to hate.

Before proceeding to develop the implications of these facts for the actual management of these patients, reemphasis must be made of the writer's distinction of schizophrenia from hebephrenic deterioration and from paranoid maladjustments. In brief, the patients to whom therapy may be applied with high probability of success are, firstly, patients in whom there has been a rather rapid change from a state of partial adjustment, to one of apparent psychosis, a matter of weeks, not months or years—this transition being the incipient schizophrenic state; secondly, patients who have not progressed into that regression of interests to early childhood or late infancy levels, to which we refer as the hebephrenic; and thirdly, patients who

have not made a partial recovery by massive projection and transfer of blame, the "paranoid schizophrenic," or paranoid state with more or less of residual schizophrenic phenomena. The case of the chronic catatonic state is of potentially good outcome, this seeming to be but a chronic continuation of the purely schizophrenic state, but the actual duration in illness is a factor that is not to be ignored.

The procedure of treatment begins with removing the patient from the situation in which he is developing difficulty, to a situation in which he is encouraged to renew efforts at adjustment with others. This might well be elsewhere than to an institution dealing with a cross-section of the psychotic population; certainly, it should not be to a large ward of mental patients of all sorts and ages. The sub-professional personnel with whom the patient is in contact must be aware of the principal difficulty—viz., the extreme sensitivity underlying whatever camouflage the patient may use. They must be activated by a well-integrated purpose of helping in the re-development or development de novo of self-esteem as an individual attractive to others. They must possess sufficient insight into their own personality organization to be able to avoid masked or unconscious sadism, jealousies, and morbid expectations of results. They must be free from the more commonplace ethical delusions and superstitions. Admittedly, this is no small order, and the creation of this sort of situation is scarcely to be expected either from chance or from the efforts of a commonplace administrative agent.

Given the therapeutic environment, the first stage of therapy by the physician takes the form of providing an orienting experience. After the initial, fairly searching, interview, the patient is introduced to the new situation in a matter-of-fact fashion, with emphasis on the personal elements. In other words, he is made to feel that he is now one of a group, composed partly of sick persons—the other patients—and partly of well folk

—the physician and all the others concerned. Emphasis is laid on the fact that something is the matter with the patient, and—once this is at least clearly understood to be the physician's view—that regardless of the patient's occasional or habitual surmise to the contrary, everyone who is well enough to be a help will from thenceforth be occupied in giving him a chance to get well. From the start, he is treated as a *person among persons*.

There is never to be either an acceptance of his disordered thought and behavior as *outré* or "crazy," or a "never-mind" technique that ignores the obvious. Everyone is to regard the outpouring of thought or the doing of acts as at least *valid* for the patient, and to be considered seriously as something that at least he should understand. The individualism of the patient's performances is neither to be discouraged nor encouraged, but instead, when they seem clearly morbid, to be noted and perhaps questioned. The questioning must not arise from ethical grounds, nor from considerations of mere convenience, but from a desire to center the patient's attention on the discovery of the factors concerned. If there is violence, it is to be discouraged, *unemotionally,* and in the clearly expressed interest of the general or special good. If, as is often the case, violence arises from panic, the situation must be dealt with by the physician. If, however, the patient seems obviously to increase in comfort without professional attention after the introduction to care, the physician can profitably await developments. A considerable proportion of these patients proceed in this really human environment to the degree of social recovery that permits analysis, without much contact with the supervising physician. Moreover, in the process, they become aware of their need for insight into their previous difficulties, and somewhat cognizant of the nature of the procedures to be used to that end. They become not only ready but prepared for treatment.

If the patient does not respond in so gratifying a fashion to the special environment, the physician must discover the difficulty. In some cases, the previously dissociated tendency system is integrating personal situations that precipitate panic or panicky states. This requires reassurance by a technique of realistic acceptance of the underlying tendencies, a bringing out into the open of the cause for the fear experienced by the self, with the resulting beneficent effects of a new feeling of group solidarity in that the harsh appraisal of the tendency incorporated in the patient's personality is temporarily suspended or enfeebled, by acquaintance with people to whom the situation is a commonplace of life. In all too many cases, the ideal-organization is such that the appearance of this solidarity-reaction is judged by the self to be ominous, and the attempt to diminish the violence of reaction to the previously dissociated tendency system fails. It is necessary, however, that the conflict be abated, otherwise the development of interpersonal security that is absolutely necessary for a social recovery cannot be achieved. In such cases, recourse is had to chemotherapeutic agencies, notably ethyl alcohol, which impair the highly discriminative action of the more lately acquired tendency systems, and permit the at least rudimentary functioning of the more primitive, without much stress. After from three to ten days of continuous mild intoxication, almost all such patients, in the writer's experience, have effected a considerable readjustment. The *modus operandi* may be indicated roughly by remarking that these patients discover by actual experience that the personal environment is not noxious, and, having discovered this, have great difficulty in subsequently elaborating convictions of menace, plots, fell purposes, etc. It is the rule to have several interviews with the patient during the period of intoxication, and in them to carry out the reassuring technique above indicated.

Occasionally, an acute schizophrenic, showing a marked tendency to paranoid maladjustment, proceeds all the more rapidly in this direction

under the type of care thus far outlined. Several devices have been used
in combating the process, but the
results are not yet satisfactory. It has
become clear that this eventuality
requires an extraordinary intervention, if the patient is to be saved; and
some pioneering work has been done
in this connection. The principle involved, however, is one sufficiently
startling to justify hesitancy in reporting but two patients. For the present,
it must suffice that patients who show
progressively deepening paranoid developments or those who are received
in florid paranoid states should not
remain with the group under active
treatment.

As the patient improves, and as
his acceptance of the need for help
grows, the efforts of the physician
become more direct in their application. Energy is expended chiefly in
*reconstructing the actual chronology
of the psychosis.* All tendencies to
"smooth over" the events are discouraged, and free-associational technique is introduced at intervals to fill
in "failures of memory." The role of
significant persons and their doings is
emphasized, the patient being constantly under the influence of the formulation above set forth—*viz.,* that
however mysteriously the phenomena
originated, everything that has be-
fallen him is related to his actual living
among a relatively small number of
significant people, in a relatively simple
course of events. Psychotic phenomena
recalled from the more disturbed periods are subjected to study as to their
relation to these people. Dreams are
studied under this guide. During this
phase of the work, the patient may or
may not grasp the dynamics of his
difficulty as they become apparent to
the physician. Interpretations are
never to be forced on him, and preferably none are offered excepting as
statistical findings. In other words, if
the patient's actual insight seems to
be progressing at a considerable pace,
it can *occasionally* be offered that thus-
and-so has, in some patients, been
found to be the result of this-and-that,

with a request for his associations to
this comment.

One of perhaps three situations
now develops. Firstly, if the patient is
doing very well, the family insist on
taking him home, and generally ignore
advice as to further treatment. Secondly, the chronology of the course of
recent events running into the psychosis is rather well recovered, and
the patient is found to have great
difficulty in coming to insight. He is
then discharged into regular treatment at the hands of a suitable psychoanalyst, experienced in the psychiatry of schizophrenia—and not too
rigid in devotion to technique. Thirdly,
the stage of chronology-perfecting is
accompanied by so much growth of
insight that it is shifted gradually to
a close approximation to regular analytic sessions that follow a liberal variant
of the orthodox technique.

In the writer's experience, covering some 11 years, there have been
regrettable events to be charged off to
precipitate and to rigid techniques of
psychotherapy. From these mistakes
and from the singular opportunities
provided by patients themselves, the
sociopsychiatric technique above indicated has finally evolved. When physical facilities were made available, it
was tried out rather thoroughly. The
condition of no patient was aggravated
by its use, and the social and real
recovery rates obtained were extremely
gratifying. It would seem that, for the
group as defined above, schizophrenia
is an illness of excellent prognosis. The
treatment required, however, is obviously far from widely available, and
the schizophrenia problem therefore
continues to be very urgently one of
prevention.

Certain considerations bearing on
the professional personnel for working
with schizophrenics may not be amiss.
In the first place, it seems quite clearly
demonstrated in the Sheppard experience that the therapeutic situations
must be integrated between individuals of the same sex. Two male patients treated by woman physicians
did remarkably badly, while "cooperat-

ing" much better than the average. A number of women, treated by the writer, also "cooperated" nicely, as they progressed into deterioration or paranoid maladjustments. Male patients treated by the writer are not as comfortable in the treatment situation as were these women. But they are correspondingly more successful in achieving actual rather than fantastic results.

In the second place, the unanalyzed psychiatrist and the psychiatrist filled with the holy light of his recent analysis are in general not to be considered for this work. The former have generally a rigid system of taboos and compromises which are rather obvious to the schizophrenic intuition, so that the patient comes early to be treating the physician, and to be fearing him. The analytic zealot knows so many things that are not so that the patient never makes a beginning.

Thirdly, the philosophical type of person is a poor candidate for success as a therapist of schizophrenics; they too love philosophizing—it is so much safer to "think" than to go through the mill of observation and understanding. Also, most of these people get systematized so early that they are blind to experience less than a personal psychosis.

Fourthly, those elsewhere identified as the "resistant homosexual types" are poor material for schizophrenia therapists; they are too busy finding "homosexual components" in everyone to note the facts flowing past them.

Fifthly, the reformer element, who "know" how life should be lived, and what is good and bad, if they must do psychiatric work, should keep far from the schizophrenic. Perhaps the manic-depressive psychosis is their ideal field.

Sixthly, perhaps of all the people least fitted for this work are those that are psychiatrists because it gives them powers and principalities over their fellows; to them should go the obsessional neurotics.

Lastly, sadly enough, those to whom life has brought but a pleasant flood of trifling problems without any spectacular disturbances, who have grown up in quiet backwashes far from the industrial revolution, within the tinted half-lights of the passing times —these are afield in undertaking the schizophrenia problem. It is one up to the last minute in its ramifications, and can but bring them a useless gloom and pessimism about youth and the times. There are some ecclesiasts who find joy in tinkering with the mild mental disorders, in Church Healing Missions and the like. These folk might learn much from, for example, the Rev. Anton Boisen, Chaplain of the Worcester State Hospital, who has come by the tedious and often deeply disturbing road of observation and experimentation to a sane grasp of the relations of religious thoughts and techniques to the schizophrenia problem.

In conclusion, it may be restated that, at least in the case of the male, fairly young schizophrenic patients whose divorcement from fairly conventional behavior and thought has been rather abrupt, when received under care before they have progressed either into hebephrenic dilapidation or durable paranoid maladjustments, are to be regarded as of good outlook for recovery and improvement of personality, if they can be treated firstly to the end of socialization, and thereafter by more fundamental reorganization of personality.

Intrapsychic Theories:

CRITICAL EVALUATION

*Intrapsychic theorists have created a highly compli-
cated superstructure of concepts and propositions to
amplify their notions. Although the intricacies of man's
behavior are infinite, intrapsychic theorists appear to
incorporate an excessive number of principles and terms
to account for them. Critics are especially prone to note
the rather shoddy empirical foundation upon which these
concepts are based. They contend that the line of reasoning connecting dubious clinical observations to the theory
progresses through a series of highly tenuous and obscure
steps. In short, not only is the source of intrapsychic data
suspect, but the sequence of reasoning which ties it to the
conceptual system seems excessively involved and impre-
cise. The papers by B. F. Skinner, the well-known behaviorist, and N. S. Lehrman, a practicing therapist, articulate
these points persuasively.*

Critique of Psychoanalytic Concepts and Theories

B. F. SKINNER

Freud's great contribution to
Western thought has been described
as the application of the principle of
cause and effect to human behavior.
Freud demonstrated that many features of behavior hitherto unexplained
—and often dismissed as hopelessly
complex or obscure—could be shown
to be the product of circumstances in
the history of the individual. Many of
the causal relationships he so convincingly demonstrated had been
wholly unsuspected—unsuspected, in
particular, by the very individuals
whose behavior they controlled. Freud
greatly reduced the sphere of accident
and caprice in our considerations of
human conduct. His achievement in

this respect appears all the more
impressive when we recall that he was
never able to appeal to the quantitative proofs characteristic of other sciences. He carried the day with sheer
persuasion—with the massing of instances and the delineation of surprising parallels and analogies among
seemingly diverse materials.

This was not, however, Freud's
own view of the matter. At the age
of seventy he summed up his achievement in this way: "My life has been
aimed at one goal only: to infer or
guess how the mental apparatus is
constructed and what forces interplay
and counteract in it." (2) It is difficult
to describe the mental apparatus he
refers to in noncontroversial terms,
partly because Freud's conception
changed from time to time and partly

From the *Scientific Monthly* 79:300-305, Novem-
ber, 1954, by permission of the American Association
for the Advancement of Science and the author.

because its very nature encouraged misinterpretation and misunderstanding. But it is perhaps not too wide of the mark to indicate its principal features as follows: Freud conceived of some realm of the mind, not necessarily having physical extent, but nevertheless capable of topographic description and of subdivision into regions of the conscious, co-conscious, and unconscious. Within this space, various mental events—ideas, wishes, memories, emotions, instinctive tendencies, and so on—interacted and combined in many complex ways. Systems of these mental events came to be conceived of almost as subsidiary personalities and were given proper names: the id, the ego, and the superego. These systems divided among themselves a limited store of psychic energy. There were, of course, many other details.

No matter what logicians may eventually make of this mental apparatus, there is little doubt that Freud accepted it as real rather than as a scientific construct or theory. One does not at the age of seventy define the goal of one's life as the exploration of an explanatory fiction. Freud did not use his "mental apparatus" as a postulate system from which he deduced theorems to be submitted to empirical check. If there was any interaction between the mental apparatus and empirical observations, such interaction took the form of modifying the apparatus to account for newly discovered facts. To many followers of Freud the mental apparatus appears to be equally as real as the newly discovered facts, and the exploration of such an apparatus is similarly accepted as the goal of a science of behavior. There is an alternative view, however, which holds that Freud did not discover the mental apparatus but rather invented it, borrowing part of its structure from a traditional philosophy of human conduct but adding many novel features of his own devising.

There are those who will concede that Freud's mental apparatus was a scientific construct rather than an observable empirical system but who,

nevertheless, attempt to justify it in the light of scientific method. One may take the line that metaphorical devices are inevitable in the early stages of any science and that although we may look with amusement today upon the "essences," "forces," "phlogistons," and "ethers," of the science of yesterday, these nevertheless were essential to the historical process. It would be difficult to prove or disprove this. However, if we have learned anything about the nature of scientific thinking, if mathematical and logical researches have improved our capacity to represent and analyze empirical data, it is possible that we can avoid some of the mistakes of adolescence. Whether Freud could have done so is past demonstrating, but whether we need similar constructs in the future prosecution of a science of behavior is a question worth considering.

Constructs are convenient and perhaps even necessary in dealing with certain complicated subject matters. As Frenkel-Brunswik shows (1), Freud was aware of the problems of scientific methodology and even of the metaphorical nature of some of his own constructs. When this was the case, he justified the constructs as necessary or at least highly convenient. But awareness of the nature of the metaphor is no defense of it, and if modern science is still occasionally metaphorical, we must remember that, theorywise, it is also still in trouble. The point is not that metaphor or construct is objectionable but that particular metaphors and constructs have caused trouble and are continuing to do so. Freud recognized the damage worked by his own metaphorical thinking, but he felt that it could not be avoided and that the damage must be put up with. There is reason to disagree with him on this point.

Freud's explanatory scheme followed a traditional pattern of looking for a cause of human behavior inside the organism. His medical training supplied him with powerful supporting analogies. The parallel between the excision of a tumor, for example, and the release of a repressed wish from the unconscious is quite compelling and must have affected Freud's thinking. Now, the pattern of an inner explanation of behavior is best exemplified by doctrines of animism, which are primarily concerned with explaining the spontaneity and evident capriciousness of behavior. The living organism is an extremely complicated system behaving in an extremely complicated way. Much of its behavior appears at first blush to be absolutely unpredictable. The traditional procedure has been to invent an inner determiner, a "demon," "spirit," "homunculus," or "personality" capable of spontaneous change of course or of origination of action. Such an inner determiner offers only a momentary explanation of the behavior of the outer organism, because it must, of course, be accounted for also, but it is commonly used to put the matter beyond further inquiry and to bring the study of a causal series of events to a dead end.

Freud, himself, however, did not appeal to the inner apparatus to account for spontaneity or caprice because he was a thoroughgoing determinist. He accepted the responsibility of explaining, in turn, the behavior of the inner determiner. He did this by pointing to hitherto unnoticed external causes in the environmental and genetic history of the individual. He did not, therefore, need the traditional explanatory system for traditional purposes; but he was unable to eliminate the pattern from his thinking. It led him to represent each of the causal relationships he had discovered as a series of three events. Some environmental condition, very often in the early life of the individual, leaves an effect upon the inner mental apparatus, and this in turn produces the behavioral manifestation or symptom. Environmental event, mental state or process, behavioral symptom—these are the three links in Freud's causal chain. He made no appeal to the middle link to explain spontaneity or caprice. Instead he used it to bridge the gap in space and time between the events he had proved to

be causally related.

A possible alternative, which would have had no quarrel with established science, would have been to argue that the environmental variables leave *physiological* effects that may be inferred from the behavior of the individual, perhaps at a much later date. In one sense, too little is known at the moment of these physiological processes to make them useful in a legitimate way for this purpose. On the other hand, too much is known of them, at least in a negative way. Enough is known of the nervous system to place certain dimensional limits upon speculation and to clip the wings of explanatory fiction. Freud accepted, therefore, the traditional fiction of a mental life, avoiding an out-and-out dualism by arguing that eventually physiological counterparts would be discovered. Quite apart from the question of the existence of mental events, let us observe the damage that resulted from this maneuver.

We may touch only briefly upon two classical problems that arise once the conception of a mental life has been adopted. The first of these is to explain how such a life is to be observed. The introspective psychologists had already tried to solve this problem by arguing that introspection is only a special case of the observation upon which all science rests and that man's experience necessarily stands between him and the physical world with which science purports to deal. But it was Freud himself who pointed out that not all of one's mental life was accessible to direct observation—that many events in the mental apparatus were necessarily inferred. Great as this discovery was, it would have been still greater if Freud had taken the next step, advocated a little later by the American movement called Behaviorism, and insisted that conscious, as well as unconscious, events were inferences from the facts. By arguing that the individual organism simply reacts to its environment, rather than to some inner experience of that environment, the bifurcation of nature into physical and psychic can be avoided.*

A second classical problem is how the mental life can be manipulated. In the process of therapy, the analyst necessarily acts upon the patient only through physical means. He manipulates variables occupying a position in the first link of Freud's causal chain. Nevertheless, it is commonly assumed that the mental apparatus is being directly manipulated. Sometimes it is argued that processes are initiated within the individual himself, such as those of free association and transference, and that these in turn act directly upon the mental apparatus. But how are these mental processes initiated by physical means? The clarification of such a causal connection places a heavy and often unwelcome burden of proof upon the shoulders of the dualist.

The important disadvantages of Freud's conception of mental life can be described somewhat more specifically. The first of these concerns the environmental variables to which Freud so convincingly pointed. The cogency of these variables was frequently missed because the variables were transformed and obscured in the course of being represented in mental life. The physical world of the organism was converted into conscious and unconscious experience, and these experiences were further transmuted as they combined and changed in mental processes. For example, early punishment of sexual behavior is an observable fact that undoubtedly leaves behind a changed organism. But when this change is represented as a state of conscious or unconscious anxiety or guilt, specific details of the punishment are lost. When, in turn, some unusual characteristic of the sexual behavior of the adult individual is related to the supposed guilt, many specific features of the relationship

may be missed that would have been obvious if the same features of behavior had been related to the punishing episode. Insofar as the mental life of the individual is used as Freud used it to represent and to carry an environmental history, it is inadequate and misleading.

Freud's theory of the mental apparatus had an equally damaging effect upon his study of behavior as a dependent variable. Inevitably, it stole the show. Little attention was left to behavior per se. Behavior was relegated to the position of a mere mode of expression of the activities of the mental apparatus or the symptoms of an underlying disturbance. Among the problems not specifically treated in the manner that was their due, we may note five.

1. The nature of the act as a unit of behavior was never clarified. The simple *occurrence* of behavior was never well represented. "Thoughts" could "occur" to an individual; he could "have" ideas according to the traditional model; but he could "have" behavior only in giving expression to these inner events. We are much more likely to say that "the thought occurred to me to ask him his name" than that "the act of asking him his name occurred to me." It is in the nature of thoughts and ideas that they occur to people, but we have never come to be at home in describing the emission of behavior in a comparable way. This is especially true of verbal behavior. In spite of Freud's valuable analysis of verbal slips and of the techniques of wit and verbal art, he rejected the possibility of an analysis of verbal behavior in its own right rather than as the expression of ideas, feelings, or other inner events, and therefore missed the importance of this field for the analysis of units of behavior and the conditions of their occurrence.

The behavioral nature of perception was also slighted. To see an object as an object is not mere passing sensing; it is an act, and something very much like it occurs when we see an object although no object is present.

* Although it was Freud himself who taught us to doubt the face value of introspection, he appears to have been responsible for the view that another sort of direct experience is required if certain activities in the mental apparatus are to be comprehended. Such a requirement is implied in the modern assertion that only those who have been psychoanalyzed can fully understand the meaning of transference or the release of a repressed fear.

Fantasy and dreams were for Freud not the perceptual *behavior* of the individual but pictures painted by an inner artist in some atelier of the mind which the individual then contemplated and perhaps then reported. This division of labor is not essential when the behavioral component of the act of seeing is emphasized.

2. The dimensions of behavior, particularly its dynamic properties, were never adequately represented. We are all familiar with the fact that some of our acts are more likely to occur upon a given occasion than others. But this likelihood is hard to represent and harder to evaluate. The dynamic changes in behavior that are the first concern of the psychoanalyst are primarily changes in probability of action. But Freud chose to deal with this aspect of behavior in other terms —as a question of "libido," "cathexis," "volume of excitation," "instinctive or emotional tendencies," "available quantities of psychic energy," and so on. The delicate question of how probability of action is to be quantified was never answered, because these constructs suggested dimensions to which the quantitative practices of science in general could not be applied.

3. In his emphasis upon the genesis of behavior, Freud made extensive use of processes of learning. These were never treated operationally in terms of changes in behavior but rather as the acquisition of ideas, feelings, and emotions later to be expressed by, or manifested in, behavior. Consider, for example, Freud's own suggestion that sibling rivalry in his own early history played an important part in his theoretical considerations as well as in his personal relationships as an adult.

An infant brother died when Freud himself was only one and a half years old, and as a young child Freud played with a boy somewhat older than himself and presumably more powerful, yet who was, strangely enough, in the nominally subordinate position of being his nephew. To classify such a set of circumstances as sibling rivalry obscures, as we have seen, the many specific properties of the circumstances themselves regarded as independent variables in a science of behavior. To argue that *what was learned* was the effect of these circumstances upon unconscious or conscious aggressive tendencies or feelings of guilt works a similar misrepresentation of the dependent variable. An emphasis upon behavior would lead us to inquire into the specific acts plausibly assumed to be engendered by these childhood episodes. In very specific terms, how was the behavior of the young Freud *shaped* by the special reinforcing contingencies arising from the presence of a younger child in the family, by the death of that child, and by later association with an older playmate who nevertheless occupied a subordinate family position? What did the young Freud *learn to do* to achieve parental attention under these difficult circumstances? How did he avoid aversive consequences? Did he exaggerate any illness? Did he feign illness? Did he make a conspicuous display of behavior that brought commendation? Was such behavior to be found in the field of physical prowess or intellectual endeavor? Did he learn to engage in behavior that would in turn increase the repertoires available to him to achieve commendation? Did he strike or otherwise injure young children? Did he learn to injure them verbally by teasing? Was he punished for this, and if so, did he discover other forms of behavior that had the same damaging effect but were immune to punishment?

We cannot, of course, adequately answer questions of this sort at so late a date, but they suggest the kind of inquiry that would be prompted by a concern for the *explicit shaping of behavioral repertoires* under childhood circumstances. What has survived through the years is not aggression and guilt, later to be manifested in behavior, but rather patterns of behavior themselves. It is not enough to say that this is "all that is meant" by sibling rivalry or by its effects upon the mental apparatus. Such an expression obscures, rather than illuminates, the nature of the behavioral changes taking place in the childhood learning process. A similar analysis could be made of processes in the fields of motivation and emotion.

4. An explicit treatment of behavior as a datum, of probability of response as the principal quantifiable property of behavior, and of learning and other processes in terms of changes of probability is usually enough to avoid another pitfall into which Freud, in common with his contemporaries, fell. There are many words in the layman's vocabulary that suggest the activity of an organism yet are not descriptive of behavior in the narrower sense. Freud used many of these freely; for example, the individual is said to discriminate, remember, infer, repress, decide, and so on. Such terms do not refer to specific acts. We say that a man discriminates between two objects when he behaves differently with respect to them; but discriminating is not itself behavior. We say that he represses behavior which has been punished when he engages in other behavior *just because* it displaces the punished behavior; but repressing is not action. We say that he decides upon a course of conduct either when he enters upon one course to the exclusion of another, or when he alters some of the variables affecting his own behavior in order to bring this about; but there is no other "act of deciding." The difficulty is that when one uses terms which suggest an activity, one feels it necessary to invent an actor, and the subordinate personalities in the Freudian mental apparatus do, indeed, participate in just these activities rather than in the more specific behavior of the observable organism.

Among these activities are conspicuous instances involving the process of self-control—the so-called "Freudian mechanisms." These need not be regarded as activities of the individual or any subdivision thereof —they are not, for example, what happens when a skillful wish evades a censor—but simply as ways of representing relationships among responses

and controlling variables. I have elsewhere tried to demonstrate this by restating the Freudian mechanisms without reference to Freudian theory (3).

5. Since Freud never developed a clear conception of the behavior of the organism and never approached many of the scientific problems peculiar to that subject matter, it is not surprising that he misinterpreted the nature of the observation of one's own behavior. This is admittedly a delicate subject, which presents problems that no one, perhaps, has adequately solved. But the act of self-observation can be represented within the framework of physical science. This involves questioning the reality of sensations, ideas, feelings, and other states of consciousness which many people regard as among the most immediate experiences of their life. Freud himself prepared us for this change. There is, perhaps, no experience more powerful than that which the mystic reports of his awareness of the presence of God. The psychoanalyst explains this in other ways. He himself, however, may insist upon the reality of certain experiences that others wish to question. There are other ways of describing what is actually seen or felt under such circumstances.

Each of us is in particularly close contact with a small part of the universe enclosed within his own skin. Under certain limited circumstances, we may come to react to that part of the universe in unusual ways. But it does not follow that that particular part has any special physical or nonphysical properties or that our observations of it differ in any fundamental respect from our observations of the rest of the world. I have tried to show elsewhere (3) how self-knowledge of this sort arises and why it is likely to be subject to limitations that are troublesome from the point of view of physical science. Freud's representation of these events was a particular personal contribution influenced by his own cultural history. It is possible that science can now move on to a different description of them. If it is impossible to be wholly nonmetaphorical, at least we may improve upon our metaphors.

The crucial issue here is the Freudian distinction between the conscious and unconscious mind. Freud's contribution has been widely misunderstood. The important point was not that the individual was often unable to describe important aspects of his own behavior or identify important causal relationships, but that his ability to describe them was irrelevant to the occurrence of the behavior or to the effectiveness of the causes. We begin by attributing the behavior of the individual to events in his genetic and environmental history. We then note that because of certain cultural practices, the individual may come to describe some of that behavior and some of those causal relationships. We may say that he is conscious of the parts he can describe and unconscious of the rest. But the act of self-description, as of self-observation, plays no part in the determination of action. It is superimposed upon behavior. Freud's argument that we need not be aware of important causes of conduct leads naturally to the broader conclusion that awareness of cause has nothing to do with causal effectiveness.

In addition to these specific consequences of Freud's mental apparatus in obscuring important details among the variables of which human behavior is a function and in leading to the neglect of important problems in the analysis of behavior as a primary datum, we have to note the most unfortunate effect of all. Freud's methodological strategy has prevented the incorporation of psychoanalysis into the body of science proper. It was inherent in the nature of such an explanatory system that its key entities would be unquantifiable in the sense in which entities in science are generally quantifiable, but the spatial and temporal dimensions of these entities have caused other kinds of trouble.

One can sense a certain embarrassment among psychoanalytic writers with respect to the primary entities of the mental apparatus. There is a predilection for terms that avoid the embarrassing question of the spatial dimensions, physical or otherwise, of terms at the primary level. Although it is occasionally necessary to refer to mental events and their qualities and to states of consciousness, the analyst usually moves on in some haste to less committal terms such as *forces, processes, organizations, tensions, systems,* and *mechanisms.* But all these imply terms at a lower level. The notion of a conscious or unconscious "force" may be a useful metaphor, but if this is analogous to force in physics, what is the analogous mass that is analogously accelerated? Human behavior is in a state of flux and undergoing changes that we call "processes," but what is changing in what direction when we speak of, for example, an affective process? Psychological "organization," "mental systems," "motivational interaction"—these all imply arrangements or relationships among *things,* but what are the things so related or arranged? Until this question has been answered the problem of the dimensions of the mental apparatus can scarcely be approached. It is not likely that the problem can be solved by working out independent units appropriate to the mental apparatus, although it has been proposed that such a step be undertaken in an attempt to place psychoanalysis on a scientific footing.

Before one attempts to work out units of transference, or scales of anxiety, or systems of mensuration appropriate to the regions of consciousness, it is worth asking whether there is not an alternative program for a *rapprochement* with physical science that would make such a task unnecessary. Freud could hope for an eventual union with physics or physiology only through the discovery of neurological mechanisms that would be the analogues of, or possibly only other aspects of, the features of his mental apparatus. Since this depended upon the prosecution of a science of neurology far beyond its current state of knowledge, it was not an attractive future. Freud appears never to have considered the possibility of bringing the concepts and theories of a psychological science into contact with the rest of physical and biological science by the simple expedient of an operational definition of terms. This would have placed the mental apparatus in jeopardy as a life goal, but it would have brought him back to the observable, manipulable, and pre-eminently physical variables with which, in the last analysis, he was dealing.

References

1. Frenkel-Brunswik, Else. "Meaning of Psychoanalytic Concepts and Confirmation of Psychoanalytic Theories," *Scientific Monthly*, 79:293-300 (1954).
2. Jones, E. *Life and Work of Sigmund Freud*, Vol. 1. New York: Basic Bks., 1953.
3. Skinner, B. F. *Science and Human Behavior*. New York: Macmillan, 1953.

Precision in Psychoanalysis

N. S. LEHRMAN

The purpose of this paper is: (a) to show that precise definition of terms is necessary if psychoanalysis is to become more scientific and useful, and (b) to demonstrate two contrascientific trends within classical psychoanalysis resulting from its lack of precision: a refusal to face facts, and a tendency to retreat to a therapeutically-nihilistic "elite" status(1). These retreating trends tend to evoke hopeless abandonment of the interpersonal search for the cause and cure of mental illness, thereby leaving the field to chemists, geneticists and physiologists whose tools, though refined, appear unsuited for the analysis of human feelings and mental illness.

We shall first attempt to define the word "scientific," and to indicate the role of precision in scientific work. Second, we shall examine a recent classical psychoanalytic conceptualization to demonstrate its lack of precision and its unverifiability. Third, we shall try to show that a scientific reformulation of this conceptualization may make experimental and clinical verification possible. Fourth, we shall examine Freud's metaphorical method to show that it lacked precision and

frequently confused reiterated hypotheses for proved facts. Finally, we shall examine Freud's unscientific justification of his opposition to precise definitions, and shall seek the consequences in American classical psychoanalysis today.

WHAT DOES "SCIENTIFIC" MEAN?

The Merriam-Webster Unabridged Dictionary defines "scientific" as "conducted . . . strictly according to the principles and practice . . . of exact science, especially as designed to establish incontestably sound conclusions and generalizations by absolute accuracy of investigation."

The phrase "incontestably sound" includes the basic concept of verifiability. Descartes' scientific concept of how the brain worked, as the neurophysiologist H. S. Magoun notes(2), "was so clearly put as to possess the danger of permitting easy determination of its truth."

If "scientific" means "conducted according to the principles and practice . . . of exact science," we can examine the practice and principles of an exact science for guidance. Nobel Laureate Robert A. Millikan(3), writes:

From *Amer. J. Psychiat.* *116*:1097-1103, 1960, by permission of the American Psychiatric Association and the author.

The first principle of the physicist, when he uncovers a new phenomenon, is to determine *what* he is to measure; the next is to devise *means* to measure it(3a) . . . All scientific investigations which have led to real progress have begun . . . by the treatment of simple and specific problems with quantitative exactness, not by making deductions from general philosophical schemes or *a priori* principles(3b).

One of the cardinal principles of scientific work, therefore, is precision, both in definitions and in measurements.

A RECENT VAGUE PSYCHOANALYTIC CONCEPTUALIZATION

Percival Bailey's recent Academic Lecture(4) criticizing classical psychoanalysis drew an almost definitive reply from Ostow(1), one of the ablest of the classical psychoanalysts. Let us apply the principles of scientific methodology which Millikan has just described to one of Ostow's key statements.

As a hypothesis, Ostow offers the psychoanalytic proposition that *"every man has a tendency to enjoy a physical, sexual relationship with his mother."* Verification of this statement requires, as Millikan indicates, determining *what* is to be measured, and then determining *how* it is to be measured.

As is unfortunately so frequent in psychoanalytic statements, many words in Ostow's hypothesis have rather vague meanings. His use of the word "every" would mean the proposition disproved if one man on earth lacked this tendency. Does the word "man" mean an adult male, or does it mean *all* human males, or does it mean all young human males, *i.e.*, boys? I believe Ostow is really referring to boys rather than to men.

But the key word in Ostow's hypothesis is "tendency"; what does it mean? The total proposition cannot be scientifically examined until we know *what* this "tendency" is which we are measuring and against what yardstick.

The word "tendency" itself is an example of the fuzziness of definition so frequently seen in psychoanalytic writings. A "tendency" has a self-initiated efferent quality quite similar to that present in the psychoanalytic concepts of wishes, drives, impulses and instincts. But all these efferent concepts have two separate aspects: that which is either innately or experientially responsive to stimuli, and that which is mystically self-propelled, as were Freud's life and death instincts. Failure to distinguish between the responsive and self-initiated aspects makes Ostow's meaning rather unclear.

For the sake of discussion, let us assume we know what Ostow's "tendency" means. How do we verify its existence?

We are usually told that the hypothesis is validly confirmed by patients' productions in psychoanalytic treatment. But Grinker(5) denies that such confirmation is valid. He says:

Using the tools of psychoanalysis, (psychoanalysts) find what they search for and little else. . . . The patient is the psychoanalyst's biased collaborator. Each interpretation may be a hypothesis . . . but there are no alternatives and little possibility that the patient-collaborator will refute it, although theoretically much is made of the patient's behavior as an index of correctness or refutation of interpretations. We have demonstrated in our experiments . . . (that) the patient-subject interprets almost everything that the psychiatrist states as having therapeutic meaning. The patient is not an unbiased scientific colleague.

Verification of a psychoanalyst's hypothesis by his patients' responses is, therefore, not a scientifically valid, independent confirmation of the hypothesis, particularly when the analyst determines whether the student-patient progresses in his course of psychoanalytic training. Instead, it may well be part of a closed philosophical system.

What other means are there of direct verification of hypotheses such as Ostow's? Is selecting(4a) "from a mass of data of observation those items which support (one's) thesis" worth while? Such a selection is valid in the formulation of hypotheses, but not valid in proving them.

Isaac Newton(6) pointed to the lack of validity of "proofs" arrived at by such selection of data. He wrote:

The best and safest method of philosophizing certainly seems to be, first, to inquire diligently into the properties of things, and to establish these properties by experiments.

Psychoanalysis has had relatively few such experiments. Newton continues:

Then, [one should] proceed more slowly to hypotheses for the explanation of them. For *hypotheses* ought to be used only in explaining the properties of things, and ought not to be assumed for determining them, *except where they are able to furnish experiments*. For if from the possibility of *hypotheses* alone, anyone makes a conjecture concerning the true nature of things, I do not see by what means it is possible to determine certainty in any science, since it is always possible to devise any number of hypotheses, which will seem to overcome new difficulties.

Hence, selection of data to fit a hypothesis by no means proves it; confirming a hypothesis is more important than, and should precede, elaborations upon it.

Is the "general opinion" of the correctness of psychoanalytic concepts proof of its validity? If this were so, the earth suddenly became spheroidal in 1492, after having previously been flat, and no one needed psychoanalytic aid before Freud appeared. "General opinion" therefore lacks validity as scientific proof. Consequently we must conclude that there are no direct proofs for the validity of Ostow's imprecisely formulated psychoanalytic hypothesis.

The only indirect proof for the classical psychoanalytic hypotheses lies in the value of the procedure in helping patients. Yet Teuber(7), discussing the Cambridge-Somerville experiment, points out that "the burden of proof is on anyone who claims specific results for a given form of therapy." But when the American Psychoanalytic Association examined its members' treatment results, it could not prove the value of the classical psychoanalytic treatment. Weinstock, chairman of the survey committee, stated(8), "It is not that the figures can be used to prove analytic therapy effective or

ineffective." Hence indirect therapeutic proof of the classical psychoanalytic hypotheses is also lacking.

Consequently, there is no proof, direct or indirect, for Ostow's imprecisely formulated psychoanalytic Oedipal hypothesis.

A VERIFIABLE REFORMULATION OF THE OEDIPAL HYPOTHESIS

Is there sexual attraction (a more precise formulation than "a tendency to enjoy a sexual relationship") between a boy and his mother? I believe there is, because there are apparently inborn sexual responses in all of us to members of the opposite sex which may well be mediated outside of conscious awareness, and at least partly through the sense of smell(9). Since the mother is the female with whom the boy has most contact, his inborn sexual responses will probably be directed mostly toward her, but there may well be a corresponding unconscious sexual response on her part toward him as well. These concepts, unlike classical formulations such as Ostow's, can perhaps be experimentally tested and quantitatively measured. But until such testing confirms them, they must be regarded as hypotheses only, no matter how many times our patients may confirm them, unless, perhaps, it can be clearly shown that using them is statistically helpful in accomplishing cure.

AN EXAMPLE OF FREUD'S METAPHORICAL VAGUENESS

Let us now examine an example of Freud's metaphorical method, to see the lack of precision characterizing much of his work. That this led to later mysticism, with life and death instincts in eternal unverifiable conflict, is well known. We shall, however, take an example from the more scientific early part of his career.

In his "Interpretation of Dreams," he discusses the behavior of a hungry infant, and states(10), "nothing prevents us from assuming that there was a primitive state of the psychical apparatus . . . in which wishing ended in hallucinating." In this connection, let us recall Newton's statement(6) that "it is always possible to devise any number of hypotheses which will *seem* to overcome new difficulties."

Freud maintains, essentially, that since the baby has been fed before, when he is again hungry, the memory image of the previous feeding might be experienced as a hallucination. But there is quantitatively a far cry between the memory trace of a previous feeding in a two-day-old baby, and the relatively adult quality of a hallucination. An hallucination of milk involves the anticipatory differentiation of milk from non-milk, something utterly beyond the capacity of a two-day-old infant. Moreover, while perhaps(10) "nothing prevents us from assuming" this hallucination, scientific method demands, as Newton(6) points out, that such hypotheses "ought *not* to be assumed for determining (the properties of things), *except where they are able to furnish experiments.*" In the 59 years since Freud's assumption of infantile hallucinations, what experiments have been made to prove or disprove them? Yet this and many other unprovable assumptions continue to be accepted in psychoanalytic thinking because one great man postulated them.

But here, and elsewhere as well, Freud's lack of precision led him down an unverifiable and therefore unscientific path. Was this imprecision accidental? Perhaps it was at first, but it was later explicitly justified.

We have seen how Millikan insisted that hypotheses cannot be verified until *after* they have been rigorously defined, and that hypotheses cannot themselves be defined until their fundamental terms and basic concepts have previously been rigorously defined. But psychoanalysis consciously and explicitly declines to define its terms rigorously; it is as if Freud's statements are, *ipso facto*, sometimes exempted from the scientific requirement for objective verification. In reality, however, it is a long way from "nothing prevents us from assuming" to proven fact.

FREUD'S JUSTIFICATION FOR "ELASTIC" DEFINITIONS

The question of "clear and sharply defined basal concepts" is discussed in Freud's 1915 paper, "Instincts and Their Vicissitudes"(11). His concept of scientific method differs quite sharply from that of the exact scientists already quoted. It also differs sharply from Osler(12), who wrote that "the leaven of science gives to men habits of mental accuracy . . . which enlarge the mental vision."

In his 1915 paper, Freud correctly points out that concepts are changed as a science progresses. Continued investigation reveals conceptual imperfections, and the concepts and definitions are therefore changed accordingly. Because, at the beginning of a scientific investigation, we do not know its final concepts with *absolute* accuracy, Freud incorrectly denied the necessity of precise definition of the *relatively* accurate conceptual tools with which the investigation begins.

When we deal with precisely defined concepts such as Newton's or Descartes', we can fairly easily determine the accuracies and inaccuracies within them. Such determinations result in more precise formulations, which are then subjected to the same evaluative process, leading to still greater precision.

When, however, we have no firm definitions with which to work, we find ourselves without a valid starting point. We are consequently attempting to dissect warm air with empty hands. The fact that concepts and definitions become altered as the result of investigation is very different from the idea that *working* definitions, like scissors, should be elastic.

Hence Freud's statement(11) that "the progress of science demands a certain elasticity even in . . . definitions" is unscientific. Working definitions are points of reference, but not rubber bands; they can be and are changed, but they are not elastic. They become *different* definitions after their alteration, rather than merely being somewhat stretched. A sexually altered dog is sexually quite different from what it used to be; there is no question of elasticity whatsoever. Just as an oak is quite different from the acorn from which it has grown, so is an hallucination quite different from an infantile memory trace.

But, it might be said, psychoanalysis differs from physics and mathematics inasmuch as it deals with the unconscious, with feelings and with instincts. Ernst Mach(13) categorically rejected abdication of scientific method to the "instinctive." He wrote:

Instinctive knowledge is very frequently the starting-point of investigations. . . . This by no means compels us, however, to create a new mysticism out of the instinctive in science and to regard this factor as infallible. That it is not infallible, we very easily discover. . . . The instinctive is just as fallible as the distinctly conscious.

Freud failed to separate meticulously the mystical, self-initiatory aspects in his concept of instinct from its scientific responsive aspects. This failure, continued by some of his followers, has helped lead to the pessimistic religious trend which has pervaded much of classical psychoanalysis for so long. Indeed, the psychologist Joseph Lyons(14) recently noted that

If there is one all-pervading faith that binds twentieth century western man, it may be found in his uncritical acceptance of the value of psychotherapy. If there is a universal answer offered in these times for the anxiety that is supposed to be the mark of the age, it lies in the role of the patient in psychotherapy. It is our new religion, arising out of and efficiently tailored to the moral crisis of the day.

THE RESULTS OF IMPRECISION IN CLASSICAL PSYCHOANALYSIS TODAY

Freud's refusal, continued by his followers, to define terms meticulously has led, in part, to the rather poor estimation other scientists hold of psychoanalysis. James R. Newman(15), author of *The World of Mathematics*, recently reviewed a new psychological and psychoanalytic dictionary. Referring to these fields, he wrote:

A discipline cannot live without words, but words can corrupt and destroy it. This explains the importance of good science dictionaries, which are as much works of criticism as they are guides to usage. No subjects are in greater need for such services than psychology and psychoanalysis. The vocabularies of both these wildly flourishing branches of study are plagued by amateurishness, pretentiousness and a general professional weakness for fancy terms. As Goethe wrote in Faust, "When ideas fail, words come in very handy."

This is one example of an exact scientist's view of psychoanalysis today.

Percival Bailey(4a), the distinguished neurosurgeon happily turned psychiatrist, wrote:

I know that there are attempts to prove that psychoanalysis is a science. They do not convince me and have convinced very few objective observers(4b). Even Freud(4c) admitted that it is only a sort of post-dictive science, lacking in power of synthesis and prediction. Science cannot be built on the insights of visionaries or on the mutual titillation of interdisciplinary minds at Palo Alto, or elsewhere, Science can be built only by the cautious, laborious verification, step by step, of one's hypotheses, establishing each one solidly before passing on to the next. As Jones says(4d), Freud had no patience with such a method.

There is another example of an exact scientist's view of psychoanalysis today.

TWO UNFORTUNATE PSYCHOANALYTIC RESPONSES

Two important contra-scientific trends can be seen within classical psychoanalysis in response to its general scientific vagueness and to its specific failure to prove its therapeutic effectiveness. The first trend declines to reveal the data about its lack of therapeutic effectiveness, and seeks to rationalize away this anti-scientific suppression of data. The second trend maintains that only a psychoanalytic "elite" are capable of meaningfully evaluating both themselves and their results.

The first trend is exemplified in Weinstock's explanation of the American Psychoanalytic's decision not to publish its survey results. "The material on which either opinion is based (whether or not psychoanalysis is therapeutically effective) is inadequately established, and controversial publicity on such material cannot be of benefit in any way." This fear of "controversial publicity" includes refusal to allow investigators who are not members of the American Psychoanalytic even to see the report unless they pledge in advance to keep the material "confidential." This is material which has already been circularized to the membership of the American Psychoanalytic, and which has already been described in detail in the *New York Herald Tribune*.

How scientific is this point of view?

Avoidance of "controversy" (*i.e.,* disagreement) and suppression of data because they might support the "wrong" side still occur in politics, but have not been in style in astronomy, for example, for about 350 years. At that time, Tycho Brahe spent 25 years making astronomical observations to destroy the Copernican heliocentric theory. His observations were, however, available to Kepler, who used them to prove the Copernican doctrine, and to place it on a firm foundation.

It would appear to me that the general public and the healing professions in particular would greatly benefit from the publication of the results of treatment at the hands of members of the American Psychoanalytic Association. The Bible says, "The truth shall make you free." It seems to me that the only people to whom "publicity on such material cannot be of benefit in any way" (8) would be individuals who, for some reason, may be afraid of what the truth will show. But science itself is more important than the reputation of any individual

scientific worker, or of any particular group of workers.

The second unfortunate trend in classical psychoanalysis maintains that only the psychoanalytic "elite" (1) are capable of meaningfully evaluating both themselves and their results.

The analyzed are an elite . . . in the sense that they have had certain filters removed from their visual apparatus so that they can now see clearly what they previously could not see at all, or could see only with serious distortion (1).

While training analyses are often helpful, ascription of such crystal-clear thinking only to the products of "authentic" psychoanalysis (which Ostow contrasts with the "shoddy perversions and dilutions that usurp its name"), suggests a defensive device more than a statement of scientific fact.

For Ostow's statement to be completely accurate and for all the filters to be removed, a perfect training analyst would be required. But no human being is perfect.

Indeed, there are data suggesting that the training analysis may even *add* visual filters not previously present. Edward Glover, as "authentic" an analyst as there is, writes (16),

Training analysts' methods of analyzing candidates are influenced by their own character formations and peculiarities, and by the training they (themselves) have undergone. These peculiarities they, in their turn, are quite likely to transvey to their pupils.

I have known several analysts both before their training analyses began and since they have finished them. It seems to me, as an observant friend, that most of them are stiffer, less courageous and less human after their supposedly successful analyses than they were before. Some are members of the "authentic" American Psychoanalytic, and some are not. From my own small sample (hardly enough for a hypothesis, and certainly not for an assertion), those who have been "authentically" analyzed by training analysts of the "approved" New York institutes seem, in general, to be less warm, less spontaneous, less human and far more arrogant than those friends whose analyses were conducted under the aegis of one or another of "the shoddy perversions and dilutions that usurp the name" of psychoanalysis.

If classical psychoanalysts wish to make a secular religious cult of themselves, nobody can stop them, even if the consequences affect our entire society. It is also their privilege disdainfully to flee the epidemic of mental illness which Dr. Gunnar Gundersen, President of the American Medical Association, describes as sweeping our country.

But, as "authentic" Allen Wheelis writes(17), "Knowledgeable moderns put their backs to the couch, and in so doing may fail occasionally to put their shoulders to the wheel." Might not those who "authentically" worship Freud's great courage be more useful if they emulated it as well?

The more widespread the classical psychoanalytic retreat from American psychiatric realities, the more the classical analysts leave the field of investigation of mental illness to chemists, geneticists and physiologists, whose tools are not designed for the best available understanding of human feelings. There is some danger that this classical psychoanalysts' retreat from reality will tend toward the abandonment of perhaps the greatest contribution by Freud to psychiatry: his recognition that mental illness arises from distorted interpersonal relationships, beginning with the family of origin.

This retreat of some classical psychoanalysts also abandons the most potent tool there is in the field, a tool scientifically defined by Freud's genius, and used, although in part incorrectly, by him and his followers: the emotional interaction between patient and doctor. This retreat also abandons one of the most effective curative techniques yet devised in psychiatry: free association into the past to discover the "reminiscences" still plaguing patients.

All of these potent contributions to human welfare would be jettisoned should all of classical psychoanalysis withdraw to sulk in elite secrecy. It could then perhaps join other self-proclaimed aristocracies, such as Virginia Woolf's "aristocracy of sensibility." But is not retreat into such "elitism" an abdication of the physician's responsibility to the patients needing his aid?

I believe the science of interpersonal relationships which Freud founded can, when properly modified, lay open the causes and nature of functional mental illness. I believe that only psychoanalysis has forged the scientific tools able to overcome the effects of man's inhumanity to man, perhaps the prime cause of human fear and mental illness.

Fortunately, despite the negative trends mentioned above, psychoanalysis is far from dead. The incisive work of Ackerman(18) and others on intra-family interactions, the distinguished studies which Spitz(19) has made on insufficiently fondled children, Ferenczi's(20) demonstration that the analyst's warmth is a necessary condition for cure, and Fromm-Reichmann's(21) brilliant sensitivity with schizophrenics all encourage the hope that precise knowledge of the effects of interpersonal warmth at the breast, in the home and role-appropriate warmth in the office can help us fulfill our task of preventing and curing mental illness. But for us to do so, we must also return to scientific precision, even in the presence of human warmth.

SUMMARY

Scientific precision has far too often been consciously excluded from classical psychoanalysis, because Freud rejected it. In consequence, classical psychoanalysis has assumed many of the trappings of a religion, and lost many of the essential characteristics of a science. Two anti-scientific trends in the field, defensive secrecy and arrogant "elitism," seem to have occurred in part as a result of perpetuation of this lack of precision.

References

1. Ostow, M.: Am. J. Psychiat., *113*: 844, 1957.
2. Margoun, H. W.: The Waking Brain. Springfield, Ill.: C. C Thomas, 1958, p. 11.
3. Millikan, R. A., Roller, W., and Watson, E. C.: Mechanics, Molecular Physics, Heat and Sound: Boston: Ginn and Co., 1937. a. p. 3. b. plate 4, following p. 35.
4. Bailey, P.: Am. J. Psychiat., *113*: 387, 1956. a. p. 394. b. Sears, R. R.: Survey of Objective Studies of Psychoanalytic Concepts. New York: Social Science Research Council, 1943 (Bailey reference #146). c. Freud, S.: The Psychogenesis of a Case of Homosexuality in a Woman. Collected Papers, II. London, 1933 (Bailey reference #56). d. Jones, E.: The Life and Work of Sigmund Freud. New York: Basic Books, 1945-46. Vol. I, pp. 34, 40 (Bailey reference #100).
5. Grinker, R. R.: A Philosophical Appraisal of Psychoanalysis. *In* Masserman, J. H.: Science and Psychoanalysis. New York: Grune and Stratton, 1958, p. 137.
6. Newton, Isaac: Philosophical Transactions, 7: 5014, 1672. Quoted in Millikan *et al.* (3), p. 52.
7. Teuber, H. L., and Powers, E.: Res. Publ. Assoc. Nerv. Ment. Dis., *31*: 138, 1953.
8. Ubell, Earl: Psychiatric Treatment Results Are Measured. New York Herald Tribune, July 7, 1958, p. 1.
9. Bieber, Irving: Olfaction in Sexual Development and Sexual Organization. Paper read before Academy of Psychoanalysis, New York, December 7, 1958. To be published.
10. Freud, S.: The Interpretation of Dreams. Translated by James Strachey. N.Y.: Basic Books, 1955, p. 566.
11. Freud, S.: Instincts and Their Vicissitudes. *In* Collected Papers of Sigmund Freud. London: Hogarth Press, 1949. Vol. 4, p. 61.
12. Osler, W.: Aequanimitas. Philadelphia: Blakiston, 1932, p. 93.
13. Mach, E.: The Science of Mechanics. The Open Court Publishing Co., 1893, pp. 26-27. Quoted in Millikan *et al.* (3), p. 64.
14. Lyons, Joseph: Midstream, 5: 46, Spring 1959.
15. Newman, J. R.: Unsigned Book Review of "A Comprehensive Dictionary of Psychological and Psychoanalytic Terms," by H. B. and A. C. English. Scient. Am., *199*: 146, Oct. 1958.
16. Glover, E.: Technique of Psychoanalysis. New York: International Universities Press, 1955, p. 6.
17. Wheelis, Allen: J. Am. Psychoanal. Assn., 4: 289, 1956.
18. Ackerman, N. W.: Psychodynamics of Family Life. New York: Basic Books, 1958.
19. Spitz, R.: Child Development, *20*: 146, Sept. 1949.
20. Ferenczi, S.: Further Contributions to the Theory and Technique of Psychoanalysis. London: Hogarth Press, 1926.
21. Fromm-Reichmann, F.: Principles of Intensive Psychotherapy. Chicago: University of Chicago Press, 1950.

Part III

Phenomenological Theories

Marco Prassinos—*Cellist*. (The Museum of Modern Art, Gift of Victor S. Riesenfeld.)

INTRODUCTION

Phenomenologists stress that the individual reacts to the world only in terms of his unique perception of it. No matter how transformed or unconsciously distorted this perception may be, it is the person's way of perceiving events which determines his behavior. Concepts and propositions must be formulated, therefore, not in terms of objective realities or unconscious processes, but in accordance with how events actually are consciously perceived by the individual; concepts must not disassemble these experiences into depersonalized or abstract categories.

The phenomenon of consciousness is one of the most controversial topics in both psychological and philosophical literature. No one doubts that self-awareness exists, but how can phenomenological reality as experienced by another person be categorized, measured, or even sensed? At best, observers must adopt an empathic attitude, a sensing in one's self of what another may be experiencing. But this method is justly suspect,

fraught with the distortions and insensitivities of the observer. To obviate this difficulty, phenomenologists assume that the verbal statements of the individual accurately reflect his phenomenal reality. Any datum which represents the individual's portrayal of his experience is grist, therefore, for the phenomenologist's mill. They contend that an individual's verbal reports reveal the most important influences upon his behavior. Is it not simple efficiency to ask a person directly what is disturbing him and how this disturbance came to pass? Is his report more prone to error than an observer's speculations gathered from the odds and ends of a case history study? Is it less reliable than deductions which are drawn from dreams and free-associations? The fact that some verbal recollections and feelings are misleading is not reason to dismiss them as useless; they summarize events in terms closest to the individual's experience of them and often embody knowledge that is not otherwise available.

Phenomenological Theories:

ORIENTATION

*Phenomenologists believe that the distinctive charac-
teristics of each individual's conscious experience should be
the primary focus of clinical science. The selection by Rollo
May, the primary exponent of the "existential" school in
America, represents a direct and convincing application of
phenomenological philosophy to the study of mental disorders. In it, he draws upon his own experiences to illustrate the central phenomenological concepts of anxiety and
self. F. J. J. Buytendijk, the eminent European phenomenologist, outlines the philosophical and psychological basis
for this view and illustrates its particular value in the
study of feeling and emotion. His essay argues in a clear
and straightforward way why the personal experience of
the patient cannot be overlooked in the science of psychopathology.*

Existential Psychology

ROLLO MAY

Existentialism means centering
upon the *existing* person; it is the
emphasis on the human being as he is
emerging, becoming. The word "existence" comes from the root *ex-sistere*,
meaning literally "to stand out,
emerge." Traditionally in Western culture, *existence* has been set over
against *essence*, the latter being the
emphasis upon immutable principles,
truth, logical laws, etc., that are supposed to stand above any given existence. In endeavoring to separate
reality into its discrete parts and to
formulate abstract laws for these
parts, Western science has by and
large been *essentialist* in character;
mathematics is the ultimate, pure
form of this essentialist approach. In

psychology, the endeavors to see human beings in terms of forces, drives,
conditioned reflexes, and so on, illustrate the approach via essences.

The emphasis on essences was
dominant in Western thought and
science—with such notable exceptions, to name only a few, as Socrates,
Augustine, and Pascal—until roughly
a hundred years ago. The "peak" was
reached, the most systematic and comprehensive expression of "essentialism," in Hegel's panrationalism, an
endeavor to encompass all reality in a
system of concepts that identified
reality with abstract thought. It was
against Hegel that Kierkegaard, and
later Nietzsche, revolted so strenuously.

But in the decades since World
War I, the existential approach has
emerged from the status of stepchild
of Western culture to a dominant position in the center of Western art,

literature, theology, and philosophy. It has gone hand in hand with the new developments in science, particularly the physics of Bohr and Heisenberg.

The extreme of the existentialist position is found in Jean Paul Sartre's statement that "existence precedes essence," the assertion that only as we affirm our existence do we have any essence at all. This is a consistent part of Sartre's great emphasis on decision: "We *are* our choices."

My own position, and that of most psychologists who appreciate the great value of this existential revolution, is not so extreme as Sartre's. "Essences" must not be ruled out—they are presupposed in logic, mathematical forms, and other aspects of truth which are not dependent upon any individual's decision or whim. But that is not to say that you can adequately describe or understand a living human being, or any living organism, on an "essentialist" basis. *There is no such thing as truth or reality for a living human being except as he participates in it, is conscious of it, has some relationship to it.* We can demonstrate at every moment of the day in our psychotherapeutic work that only the truth that comes alive, becomes more than an abstract idea, and is "felt on the pulse," only the truth that is genuinely experienced on all levels of being, including what is called subconscious and unconscious and never excluding the element of conscious decision and responsibility—only this truth has the power to change a human being.

The existentialist emphasis in psychology does not, therefore, deny the validity of the approaches based on conditioning, the formulation of drives, the study of discrete mechanisms, and so on. It only holds that you can never explain or understand any *living* human being on that basis. And the harm arises when the image of man, the presuppositions about man himself are exclusively based on such methods. There seems to be the following "law" at work: the more accurately and comprehensively you can

describe a given mechanism, the more you lose the existing person. *The more absolutely and completely you formulate the forces or drives, the more you are talking about abstractions and not the existing, living human being.* For the living person (who is not hypnotized or drugged or in some other way placed in an artificial position, such as in a laboratory, in which his element of decision and his responsibility for his own existence are temporarily suspended for the purposes of the experiment) always transcends the given mechanism and always experiences the "drive" or "force" in his unique way. The distinction is whether the "person has meaning in terms of the mechanism" or the "mechanism has meaning in terms of the person." The existential emphasis is firmly on the latter. And it holds that the former can be integrated within the latter.

True, the term "existentialist" is dubious and confused these days, associated as it is with the beatnik movement at one extreme and with esoteric, untranslatable, Germanic, philosophical concepts at the other. True also, the movement collects the "lunatic fringe" groups—to which existential psychology and psychiatry are by no means immune. I often ask myself whether in some quarters the term has become so dubious as to be no longer useful. But "existence" does have the important historical meanings outlined above and probably, therefore, can and ought to be saved from its deteriorated forms.

In psychology and psychiatry, the term demarcates an *attitude*, an approach to human beings, rather than a special school or group. It is doubtful whether it makes sense to speak of "*an* existential psychologist or psychotherapist" in contradistinction to other schools; it is not a system of therapy but an attitude toward therapy, not a set of new techniques but a concern with the understanding of the structure of the human being and his experience that must underlie all techniques. This is why it makes sense, if I may say so without being misunderstood, to say that every psychotherapist is existential to the extent that he is a good therapist, i.e., that he is able to grasp the patient in his reality and is characterized by the kinds of understanding and presence that will be discussed below.

I wish, after these sallies at definition, to *be* existentialist in this essay and to speak directly from my own experience as a person and as a practicing psychoanalytic psychotherapist. Some fifteen years ago, when I was working on my book, *The Meaning of Anxiety*, I spent a year and a half in bed in a tuberculosis sanatorium. I had a great deal of time to ponder the meaning of anxiety— and plenty of first hand data in myself and my fellow patients. In the course of this time, I studied the only two books written on anxiety till our day, *The Problem of Anxiety* by Freud and *The Concept of Dread* by Kierkegaard. I valued Freud's formulations: namely, his first theory, that anxiety is the re-emergence of repressed libido, and his second, that anxiety is the ego's reaction to the threat of the loss of the loved object. Kierkegaard, on the other hand, described anxiety as the struggle of the living being against non-being— which I could immediately experience there in my struggle with death or the prospect of being a life-long invalid. He went on to point out that the real terror in anxiety is not this death as such, but the fact that each of us within himself is on both sides of the fight, that "anxiety is a desire for what one dreads," as he put it; thus, like an "alien power it lays hold of an individual, and yet one cannot tear one's self away."

What struck me powerfully then, was that Kierkegaard was writing about *exactly what my fellow patients and I were going through*. Freud was not; he was writing on a different level, giving formulations of the psychic mechanisms by which anxiety comes about. Kierkegaard was portraying what is immediately experienced by human beings in crisis. It was, specifically, the crisis of life

against death, which was completely real to us patients, but he was writing about a crisis that I believe is not in its essential form different from the various crises of people who come for therapy, or the crises that all of us experience in much more minute form a dozen times a day, even though we push the ultimate prospect of death far from our minds. Freud was writing on the technical level, where his genius was supreme; perhaps more than any man up to his time, he *knew about anxiety*. Kierkegaard, a genius of a different order, was writing on the existential, ontological level; he *knew anxiety*.

This is not a value dichotomy; obviously both are necessary. Our real problem, rather, is given us by our cultural-historical situation. We in the Western world are the heirs of four centuries of technical achievement in power over nature and now over ourselves; this is our greatness and, at the same time it is also our greatest peril. We are not in danger of repressing the technical emphasis (of which Freud's tremendous popularity in this country is proof if any were necessary). But rather we repress the opposite. If I may use terms which I shall be discussing and defining more fully later, we repress the *sense of being,* the *ontological sense.* One consequence of this repression of the sense of being is that modern man's image of himself, his experience and concept of himself as a responsible individual have likewise disintegrated.

I make no apologies in admitting that I take very seriously, as will have been evident already, the dehumanizing dangers in our tendency in modern science to make man over into the image of the machine, into the image of the techniques by which we study him. This tendency is not the fault of any "dangerous" men or "vicious" schools; it is rather a crisis brought upon us by our particular historical predicament. Karl Jaspers, both psychiatrist and existentialist philosopher, holds that we are actually in process of losing self-consciousness and that we may well be in the last age of historical man. William Whyte, in his *Organization Man*, cautions that modern man's enemies may turn out to be a "mild-looking group of therapists, who . . . would be doing what they did to help you." He refers here to the tendency to use the social sciences in support of the social ethic of our historical period; and thus the process of helping people may actually make them conform and tend toward the destruction of individuality. We cannot brush aside the cautions of such men as unintelligent or antiscientific; to try to do so would make *us* the obscurantists. There is a real possibility that we may be helping the individual adjust and be happy at the price of loss of his being.

One may agree with my sentiments here but hold that the existentialist approach, with these terms "being" and "non-being," may not be of much help. Some readers will already have concluded that their suspicion was only too right, that this so-called existential approach to psychology is hopelessly vague and horribly muddled. Carl Rogers remarks in a later chapter that many American psychologists must find these terms abhorrent because they sound so general, so philosophical, so untestable. Rogers goes on to point out, however, that he had no difficulty in putting the existential principles in therapy into empirically testable hypotheses.

But I would go further and hold that *without* some concepts of "being" and "non-being" we cannot even understand our most commonly used psychological mechanisms. Take for example, *repression, resistance*, and *transference*. The usual discussions of these terms hang in midair, it seems to me, unconvincing and psychologically unreal, precisely because we have lacked an underlying structure on which to base them. The term "repression," for example, obviously refers to a phenomenon we observe all the time, a dynamism which Freud clearly, and in many forms, described. The mechanism is generally explained

by saying that the child represses into unconsciousness certain impulses, such as sex and hostility, because the culture, in the form of parental figures, disapproves, and the child must protect his own security with those figures. But this culture which assumedly disapproves is made up of the very same people who do the repressing. Is it not an illusion, therefore, and much too simple to speak of the culture over against the individual in such fashion and to make it our whipping boy? Furthermore, where did we get the idea that children or adults are so concerned with security and libidinal satisfactions? Are these not carryovers from our work with the *neurotic, anxious* child and the *neurotic* adult?

Certainly the neurotic, anxious child *is* compulsively concerned with security, for example; and certainly the neurotic adult, and we who study him, read our later formulations back into the unsuspecting mind of the child. But is not the normal child just as truly interested in moving out into the world, exploring, following his curiosity and sense of adventure—going out "to learn to shivver and to shake," as the nursery rhyme puts it? And if you block these needs of the child, do you not get a traumatic reaction from him just as you do when you take away his security? I, for one, believe we vastly overemphasize the human being's concern with security and survival satisfactions because they so neatly fit our cause-and-effect way of thinking. I believe Nietzsche and Kierkegaard were more accurate when they described man as *the organism who makes certain values—prestige, power, tenderness, love —more important than pleasure and even more important than survival itself.**

---

* This is the point Binswanger is making in the case of *Ellen West*, translated in the volume *Existence*. By means of the discussion of the psychological illness and suicide of Ellen West, he asks whether there are times when an existence, in order to fulfill itself, must destroy its existence. In this case, Binswanger, like so many of his European psychiatric and psychological colleagues, discusses a case for the purpose of delving into the understanding of some problem about human

The implication of our argument here is that we can understand such a mechanism as repression, for example, only on the deeper level of the meaning of the human beings' potentialities. In this respect, "being" is to be defined as the *individual's unique pattern of potentialities*. These potentialities will be partly shared with other individuals but will in every case form a unique pattern for this particular person.

We must ask these questions, therefore, if we are to understand repression in a given person: What is this person's relation to his own potentialities? What goes on that he chooses, or is forced to choose, to block off from his awareness something that he knows, and on another level *knows that he knows?* In my own work in psychotherapy, there appears more and more evidence that anxiety in our day arises not so much out of fear of lack of libidinal satisfactions or security, but rather out of the patient's fear of his own powers and the conflicts that arise from that fear. This may well be the particular "neurotic personality of our time"—the neurotic pattern of contemporary "outer-directed," organizational man.

The "unconscious," then, is not to be thought of as a reservoir of impulses, thoughts, and wishes that are culturally unacceptable. I define it rather as *those potentialities for*

beings rather than for the purpose of illustrating how the case should or should not be managed therapeutically. In presenting the case, we assumed, as editors of *Existence*, that it, like the other cases, would be understood on the basis of the purposes and assumptions of its author in writing it; this was an unrealistic assumption. The case is almost universally discussed—and from that point of view justly criticized—in this country from the point of view of what therapy should have been given Ellen West. If it had been Binswanger's purpose to discuss techniques of therapy, he would not have taken a case from the archives of four and a half decades ago in his sanatorium. He seeks, rather, to ask this most profound of all questions: Does the human being have needs and values that transcend its own survival, and are there not situations when the existence, in order to fulfill itself, needs to destroy itself? The implication of this question is in the most radical way to question simple adaptation, length of life, and survival as ultimate goals. It is similar to Nietzsche's point referred to above, and also similar to Maslow's emphasis when he brings out that the "self-actualizing personalities" that he studied resist acculturation.

knowing and experiencing that the individual cannot or will not actualize. On this level, we shall find that the simple mechanism of repression, which we blithely started with, is infinitely less simple than it looks; that it involves a complex struggle of the individual's *being* against the possibility of *non-being;* that it cannot be adequately comprehended in "ego" and "not-ego" terms, or even "self" and "not-self"; and that it inescapably raises the question of the human being's freedom with respect to his own potentialities. This margin of freedom must be assumed if one is to deal with an existing person. In this margin resides the individual's responsibility for himself, which even the therapist cannot take away.

Thus, every mechanism or dynamism, every force or drive, presupposes an underlying structure that is infinitely greater than the mechanism, drive, or force itself. And note that I do not say it is the "sum total" of the mechanisms, et cetera. It is not the "sum total," though it includes all the mechanisms, drives, or forces: it is the underlying structure from which they derive their meaning. This structure is, to use one definition proposed above, the *pattern of potentiality* of the living individual man *of whom* the mechanism is one expression; the given mechanism is one of a multitude of ways in which he actualizes his potentiality. Surely, you can abstract a given mechanism like "repression" or "regression" for study and arrive at formulations of forces and drives which seem to be operative; but your study will have meaning only if you say at every point, "I am abstracting such and such a form of behavior," and if you also make clear at every point *what* you are abstracting *from,* namely the living man who *has* these experiences, the man *to whom* these things happen.

In a similar vein, I have, for a number of years, been struck, as a practicing therapist and teacher of therapists, by how often our concern with trying to understand the patient in terms of the mechanisms by which his behavior takes place blocks our understanding of what he really is experiencing. Here is a patient, Mrs. Hutchens, who comes into my office for the first time, a suburban woman in her middle thirties, who tries to keep her expression poised and sophisticated. But no one could fail to see in her eyes something of the terror of a frightened animal or a lost child. I know, from what her neurological specialists have already told me, that her presenting problem is hysterical tenseness of the larynx, as a result of which she can talk only with a perpetual hoarseness. I have been given the hypothesis from her Rorschach that she has felt all her life, "If I say what I really feel, I'll be rejected; under these conditions it is better not to talk at all." During this first hour with her, I also get some hints of the genetic *why* of her problem as she tells me of her authoritarian relation with her mother and grandmother and of *how* she learned to guard firmly against telling any secrets at all.

But if, as I sit here, I am chiefly thinking of these *whys* and *hows* of the way the problem came about, I will have grasped everything *except the most important thing of all, the existing person*. Indeed, I will have grasped everything except the only real source of data I have, namely, this experiencing human being, this person now emerging, becoming, "building world," as the existential psychologists put it, immediately in this room with me.

This is where *phenomenology*, the first stage in the existential psychotherapeutic movement, has been a helpful breakthrough for many of us. Phenomenology is the endeavor to take the phenomena as given. It is the disciplined effort to clear one's mind of the presuppositions that so often cause us to see in the patient only our own theories or the dogmas of our own systems, the effort to experience instead the phenomena in their full reality as they present themselves. It is the attitude of openness and readiness to hear—aspects of the art of listening in psychotherapy that are generally taken for granted and sound so easy but are exceedingly difficult.

Note that we say *experience* the phenomena and not *observe;* for we need to be able, as far as possible, to catch what the patient is communicating on many different levels; these include not only the words he utters but his facial expressions, his gestures, the distance from us at which he sits, various feelings which he will have and communicate subtly to the therapist and will serve as messages even though he cannot verbalize them directly, ad infinitum. And there is always a great deal of subliminal communication on levels below what either the patient or therapist may be conscious of at the moment. This points toward a controversial area in therapy which is most difficult in the training and practice of therapists, but which is unavoidable because it is so important, namely, subliminal, empathetic, "telepathic" communication. We shall not go into it here; I wish only to say this experiencing of the communications of the patient on many different levels at once is one aspect of what the existential psychiatrists like Binswanger call *presence*.

Phenomenology requires an "attitude of disciplined naïveté," in Robert MacLeod's phrase. And commenting on this phrase, Albert Wellek adds his own, "an ability to *experience critically*." It is not possible, in my judgment, to listen to any words or even to give one's attention to anything without some assumed concepts, some constructs in one's own mind by which he hears, by which he orients himself in his world at that moment. But the important terms "disciplined" in MacLeod's phrase and "critically" in Wellek's refer, I take it, to the difficult attainment of objectivity—that while one must have constructs as he listens, one's aim in therapy is to make one's own constructs sufficiently flexible so that he can listen in terms of the patient's constructs and hear in the patient's language.

Phenomenology has many complex ramifications, particularly as developed by Edmund Husserl, who decisively influenced not only the philosophers Heidegger and Sartre but also the psychiatrists Minkowski, Straus, and Binswanger, the psychologists Buytendijk, Merleau-Ponty, and many others. We shall not go into these ramifications here.

Sometimes the phenomenological emphasis in psychotherapy is used as a disparagement of the learning of technique or as a reason for not studying the problems of diagnosis and clinical dynamics. I think this is an error. What is important, rather, is to apprehend the fact that the technical and diagnostic concerns are on a different level from the understanding that takes place in the immediate encounter in therapy. The mistake is in confusing them or letting one absorb the other. The student and practicing psychologist must steer his course between the Scylla of letting knowledge of techniques be a substitute for direct understanding and communication with the patient and the Charybdis of assuming that he acts in a rarified atmosphere of clinical purity without any constructs at all.

Certainly it is true that students learning therapy often become preoccupied with techniques; this is the strongest anxiety-allaying mechanism available to them in the turmoil-fraught encounters in psychotherapy. Indeed, one of the strongest motivations for dogmatism and rigid formulations among psychotherapeutic and analytic schools of all sorts lies right here—the technical dogma protects the psychologist and psychiatrist from their own anxiety. But to that extent, the techniques also protect the psychologist or psychiatrist from understanding the patient; they block him off from the full presence in the encounter which is essential to understanding what is going on. One student in a case seminar on existential psychotherapy put it succinctly when he remarked that the chief thing he had learned was that "understanding

does not follow knowledge of dynamics."

There is, however, a danger of "wild eclecticism" in these phenomenological and existential approaches to therapy when they are used without the rigorous clinical study and thought which precedes any expertness. Knowledge of techniques and the rigorous study of dynamics in the training of the psychotherapist should be presupposed. Our situation is analogous to the artist: long and expert training is necessary, but if, at the moment of painting, the artist is preoccupied with technique or technical questions—a preoccupation every artist knows arises exactly at those points at which some anxiety overtakes him—he can be sure nothing creative will go on. Diagnosis is a legitimate and necessary function, particularly at the beginning of therapy; but it is a function different from the therapy itself and requires a different attitude and orientation to the patient. There is something to be said for the attitude that once one gets into therapy with a patient and has decided on the general direction, one forgets for the time being the diagnostic question. By the same token, questions of technique will arise in the therapist's mind from time to time as the therapy proceeds, and one of the characteristics of existential psychotherapy is that the technique changes. These changes will not be hit and miss, however, but will depend on the needs of the patient at given times.

If this discussion sounds unconcluded and gives the appearance of straddling the issue of "technique" on one side and "understanding" on the other, the appearance is indeed correct. The whole topic of the "technical-objective" versus the "understanding-subjective" attitude has been on a false dichotomized basis in our psychological and psychiatric discussions. It needs to be restated on the basis of the concept of the existence of the patient as *being-in-the-world*, and the therapist as existing in and participating in this world. I shall not essay such a restatement here, but I wish only to state my conviction that such a reformulation is possible and gives promise of taking us out of our present dichotomy on this topic. And in the meantime, I wish as a practical expedient to take my stand against the nascent anti-rational tendencies in the existential approach. Though I believe that therapists are born and not made, it inheres in one's integrity to be cognizant of the fact that there also is a great deal we can learn!

Another question that has perennially perplexed many of us in psychology has already been implied above, and we now turn to it explicitly. What are the presuppositions which underlie our science and our practice? I do not say "scientific method" here; already a good deal of attention has been paid, and rightly, to the problem of methodology. But every method is based on certain presuppositions—assumptions about the nature of man, the nature of his experience, and so forth. These presuppositions are partially conditioned by our culture and by the particular point in history at which we stand. As far as I can see, this crucial area is almost always covered over in psychology: we tend to assume uncritically and implicitly that our particular method is true for all time. The statement that science has built-in self-corrective measures—which is partially true—cannot be taken as a reason for overlooking the fact that our particular science is culturally and historically conditioned and is thereby limited even in its self-corrective measures.

At this point, the existential insistence is that, because every psychology, every way of understanding man, is based upon certain presuppositions, the psychologist must continually analyze and clarify his own presuppositions. One's presuppositions always limit and constrict what one sees in a problem, experiment, or therapeutic situation; from this aspect

of our human "finiteness" there is no escape. The naturalist perceives in man what fits his naturalistic spectacles; the positivist sees the aspects of experience that fit the logical forms of his propositions; and it is well known that different therapists of different schools will see in the same dream of a single patient the dynamics that fit the theory of their particular school. The old parable of the blind men and the elephant is writ large on the activities of men in the enlightened twentieth century as well as those of earlier, more "benighted" ages. Bertrand Russell puts the problem well with respect to physical science: "Physics is mathematical not because we know so much about the physical world but because we know so little; it is only its mathematical properties that we can discover."

No one, physicist, psychologist, or anyone else, can leap out of his historically conditioned skin. But the one way we can keep the presuppositions underlying our particular method from undue biasing effect is to know consciously what they are and so not to absolutize or dogmatize them. Thus we have at least a chance of refraining from forcing our subjects or patients upon our "procrustean couches" and lopping off, or refusing to see, what does not fit.

In Ludwig Binswanger's little book relating his conversations and correspondence with Freud, *Sigmund Freud: Reminiscences of a Friendship,* there are some interesting interchanges illustrating this point. The friendship between Freud, the psychoanalyst, and Binswanger, a leading existential psychiatrist of Switzerland, was lifelong and tender, and it marks the only instance of Freud's continuing friendship with someone who differed radically with him.

Shortly before Freud's eightieth birthday, Binswanger wrote an essay describing how Freud's theory had radically deepened clinical psychiatry, but he added that Freud's own existence as a person pointed beyond the deterministic presuppositions of his theory. "Now [with Freud's psychoanalytic contribution] man is no longer merely an animated organism, but a 'living being' who has origins in the finite life process of this earth, and who dies its life and lives its death; illness is no longer an externally or internally caused disturbance of the 'normal' course of a life on the way to its death." But Binswanger went on to point out that as a result of his interest in existential analysis, he believed that in Freud's theory man is not yet man in the full sense of the word:

. . . for to be a man does not mean merely to be a creature begotten by living-dying life, cast into it and beaten about, and put in high spirits or low spirits by it; it means to be a being that looks its own and mankind's fate in the face, a being that is "steadfast," i.e., one taking its own stance, or one standing on its own feet. . . . The fact that our lives are determined by the forces of life, is only one side of the truth; the other is that we determine these forces as our fate. Only the two sides together can take in the full problem of sanity and insanity. Those who, like Freud, have forged their fates with the hammer—the work of art he has created in the medium of language is sufficient evidence of this—can dispute this fact least of all.

Then, on the occasion of Freud's eightieth birthday, the Viennese Medical Society invited Binswanger, along with Thomas Mann, to deliver papers at the anniversary celebration. Freud himself did not attend, not being in good health and also, as he wrote Binswanger, not being fond of anniversary celebrations. ("They seem to be on the American model.") Binswanger spent two days with Freud in Vienna at the time of this birthday and remarked that in these conversations he was again impressed by how far Freud's own largeness and depth of humanity as a man surpassed his scientific theories.

In his paper at the celebration, Binswanger gave credit to Freud for having enlarged and deepened our insight into human nature more, perhaps, than anyone since Aristotle. But he went on to point out that these insights wore "a theoretic-scientific garb that as a whole appeared to me too 'one-sided' and narrow." He held that Freud's great contribution was in the area of *homo natura*, man in relation to nature (*Umwelt*)—drives instincts, and similar aspects of experience. And as a consequence, Binswanger believed that in Freud's theory there was only a shadowy, epiphenomenal understanding of man in relation to his fellowmen (*Mitwelt*) and that the area of man in relation to himself (*Eigenwelt*) was omitted entirely.

Binswanger sent a copy of the paper to Freud and a week later received a letter from him containing the following sentences:

As I read it I was delighted with your beautiful language, your erudition, the vastness of your horizon, your tactfulness in contradicting me. As is well known, one can put up with vast quantities of praise. . . . *Naturally, for all that you have failed to convince me.** I have always confined myself to the ground floor and basement of the edifice. You maintain that by changing one's point of view, one can also see the upper story, in which dwell such distinguished guests as religion, art, etc. . . . I have already found a place for religion, by putting it under the category of "the neurosis of mankind." But probably we are speaking at cross purposes, and our differences will be ironed out only after centuries. In cordial friendship, and with greetings to your charming wife, your Freud.

Binswanger then adds in his book—and this is the central reason we quote the interchange—"As can be seen from the last sentence, Freud looked upon our differences as something to be surrounded by empirical investigation, not as something bearing upon the transcendental** conceptions that underly all empirical research."

In my judgment, Binswanger's point is irrefutable. One can gather empirical data, let us say on religion and art, from now till doomsday, and one will never get any closer to understanding these activities if, to start with, his presuppositions shut out what the religious person is dedicated

---

* Binswanger's italics.

** By "transcendental," Binswanger of course does not refer to anything ethereal or magical: he means the underlying presuppositions which "point beyond" the given fact, the presuppositions which determine the goals of one's activity.

to and what the artist is trying to do. Deterministic presuppositions make it possible to understand everything about art except the creative act and the art itself; mechanistic naturalistic presuppositions may undercover many facts about religion, but, as in Freud's terms, religion will always turn out to be more or less a neurosis, and what the genuinely religious person is concerned with will never get into the picture at all.

The point we wish to make in this discussion is the necessity of analyzing the presuppositions one assumes and of making allowance for the sectors of reality—which may be large indeed—that one's particular approach necessarily leaves out. In my judgment, we in psychology have often truncated our understanding and distorted our perception by failure consciously to clarify these presuppositions.

I vividly recall how, back in my graduate days in psychology some twenty years ago, Freud's theories tended to be dismissed as "unscientific" because they did not fit the methods then in vogue in graduate schools of psychology. I maintained at the time that this missed the point: Freud had uncovered realms of human experience of tremendous importance, and if they did not fit our methods, so much the worse for our methods; the problem was to devise new ones. In actual fact, the methods did catch up—perhaps, one should add, with a vengeance, until, as Rogers has stated, Freudianism is now the dogma of American clinical psychology. Remembering my own graduate-school days, I am therefore inclined to smile when someone says that the concepts of existential psychology are "unscientific" because they do not fit the particular methods *now* in vogue.

It is certainly clear that the Freudian mechanisms invite the separation into discrete cause-and-effect formulations which fit the deterministic methodology dominant in American psychology. But what also needs to be seen is that this making of Freudianism into the dogma of psychology has been accomplished at the price of omitting essential and vitally important aspects of Freud's thought. There is at present a three-cornered liaison, in tendency and to some extent in actuality, between Freudianism, behaviorism in psychology, and positivism in philosophy. An example of the first side of the liaison is the great similarity between Hull's drive-reduction theory of learning and Freud's concept of pleasure, the goal of behavior, as consisting of the reduction of stimuli. An example of the second is the statement of the philosopher Herman Feigl in his address at a recent annual convention of the American Psychological Association, that Freud's specific mechanisms could be formulated and used scientifically, but such concepts as the "death instinct" could not be.

But the trouble there is that such concepts as the "death instinct" in Freud were precisely what saved him from the full mechanistic implications of his system; these concepts always point beyond the deterministic limitations of his theory. They are, in the best sense of the word, a mythology. Freud was never content to let go of this mythological dimension to his thinking despite his great effort at the same time to formulate psychology in terms of his nineteenth-century biological presuppositions. In my judgment, his mythology is fundamental to the greatness of his contribution and essential to his central discoveries, such as "the unconscious." It was likewise essential to his radical contribution to the new image of man, namely, man as pushed by demonic, tragic, and destructive forces. I have tried elsewhere to show that Freud's tragic concept of the Oedipus is much closer to the truth than our tendency to interpret the Oedipus complex in terms of discrete sexual and hostile relationships in the family. The formulation of the "death instinct" as a biological instinct makes no sense, of course, and in this sense is rightly rejected by American behaviorism and positivism. But as a psychological and spiritual statement of the tragic nature of man, the idea has very great importance indeed and transcends any purely biological or mechanistic interpretation.

Methodology always suffers from a cultural lag. Our problem is to open our vision to more of human experience, to develop and free our methods so that they will as far as possible do justice to the richness and breadth of man's experience.

The Phenomenological Approach to the Problem of Feelings and Emotions

F. J. J. BUYTENDIJK

During the many years of my investigations of animal behavior I have become more and more convinced that we ought to understand the observable vital phenomena such as actions and expressions. Behavior can never be reduced to physiological processes and explained as a result of the integration of reflexes. The reflex is a reduced action, stabilized by the constant signification, for example the dangerousness, of the situation in which it occurs. The characteristics and the entire signification of behavior become intelligible in the light of their relation to the essence of the animal being in general and the definite mode of existence of the species.[1] The proper content or signification of the concept of behavior presupposes that being an animal is absolutely different from being a crystal, à drop of water, or a plant.[2] These ideas and views resulting from concrete experiments and observations have made me appreciate the value of the phenomenological approach and apply the phenomenological method to the problems of psychology.[3] Animals and men are observable subjects,[4] because we understand behavior as a system of intentional acts.

Husserl's phenomenological method[5] is founded on the irreducible fact that consciousness must necessarily be consciousness of something toward which it is intentionally directed and which therefore has a meaning. Consequently consciousness is not considered to be an "interiority," an imaginary space with certain contents and processes, interacting with the physical being and with a sensorially appearing outer world. This conception, implied in various images, has entered psychology as a means of interpreting consciousness (or the self or the ego) as "something" existing (res cogitans) that enters into relationship with an existing world (res extensa).

Psychology as a positive science has become dogmatic and lacks the radicalism of doubt. The unprejudiced return to the "things themselves," i.e., inspection of knowledge "itself"

[1] F. J. J. Buytendijk. Wege zum Verständnis der Tiere. Zurich: 1938.

[2] Explained in an excellent way by Merleau-Ponty, La structure du comportement (Pr. Un. Fr.).

[3] F. J. J. Buytendijk. (1) Das Spiel von Mensch und Tier. Berlin: Kurt Wolff, 1933. (2) Over de Pijn ("On pain"). Utrecht: 1943. (3) Algemene Theorie der menselijke Houding en Beweging ("General theory of human attitude and movement"). Utrecht: 1948.

[4] V. von Weizsäcker. Angeschaute Subjecktivität. Leipzig: Der Gestaltkreis, 1943.

[5] A very good survey of Husserl's ideas is to be found in Marvin Farber, The foundations of phenomenology (Cambridge, Mass.: Harvard Univ. Press, 1943), and Marvin Farber (Ed.), Philosophical essays in memory of Edmund Husserl (Cambridge, Mass.: Harvard Univ. Press, 1940). A short but very clear explanation of the concept of intentionality has been published by J. P. Sartre in Situations I (N.R.F.), Une idée fondamentale de la phénoménologie de Husserl: l'intentionnalité.

Abridged from Feelings and Emotions edited by M. L. Reymert, pages 127-141, copyright 1950, used by permission of McGraw-Hill Book Company.

as given to us *directly*, with nothing mediating or interfering, reveals the intentionality or act-character of all behavior. Feeling, *e.g.*, being pleased, is an act, in which there is reference —not a causal relation—to an object that is intentionally *present*. It may occur without the object existing, for this object is merely *meant* in the act of feeling.

Perhaps, someone might remark, psychology as a pure science has nothing to do with a theoretical conception concerning consciousness, neither the Cartesian nor the phenomenological idea. Science should be limited to establishing *facts*. I can agree with this conception of science, but then, I think, we are obliged to ask what a fact is. Is feeling a fact? Or is it an abstraction? And is it a fact that there exist men who have feeling in certain situations? If we take this question seriously, we should have to know what we *mean* by "exist," "situation," "feeling." This is exactly what it is the aim of phenomenology to reveal.

When we should like, for example, to institute a statistical inquiry into "happy and unhappy marriages," we have to know *what* a marriage is. We can arrange to take it for granted that a marriage can be defined by certain characteristics or properties, just as we identify a substance as oxygen or gold. I will not insist on the dubious value of such an objective determination of a human relationship such as marriage. But what are happiness and unhappiness? Should we calculate in our statistics the subjective opinions of everyone who is asked whether he is happy or unhappy or should we try to know what may be the essential characteristics of the sense of happiness as a pure phenomenon, given to us directly as something that shows itself in itself, with all its immanent characteristics and also its reference to the situation of being married? This analysis of the intentional experience is the phenomenological approach to feelings and emotions.

In phenomenology we should like to know what the significations of the acts of hating, loving, desiring, rage, joy, etc., are; and we are convinced that these significations or meanings are the real essence of the feelings. Every feeling is feeling of something, and the human attitude in which a feeling is experienced in a positional, not reflective, consciousness results in fuller understanding.

Our feelings are no senseless states of consciousness or psychic facts, but modes to detect the signification of situations, to *know* what is savory, disgusting, alarming, distressing, lovely, etc. Human reality is equivalent to being conscious and this can be defined only as open to the world, as cast upon the world. Being conscious is *s'éclater dans le monde,* to use Sartre's image of this kind of being. A pure description of purified knowledge of the affected and feeling self, of the situation and the concrete mode of existence in this situation, ignores all actual facts, for example, psychogenetic laws and physiological conditions.

In phenomenological psychology man is considered as existing. All mental experiences—perception, remembrance, thinking, dreaming, and also feeling—are relations of an existing human being and his world. They presuppose both the human being and his world, and we ought to know what is meant by these concepts. To discover the definite significance, *i.e.*, the essence of a feeling, we have to start from a conception of human existence. Consciousness exists to the exact extent that it is consciousness to exist. It would be a misunderstanding to think that the a priori concept of existence can be interpreted as a dogmatic a priori, that is, a statement about human existence of irrefutable validity.

Surely all phenomenological analysis of feelings and emotions, such as Scheler's investigations of the modes of sympathy,[6] the research on

---

[6] Max Scheler. *Wesen und Forme der Sympathie*. Bonn.

normal and abnormal feelings by such psychiatrists as Rümke,[7] Binswanger,[8] Minkowski,[9] Kunz,[10] and others, and the analysis of laughing and crying by Plessner,[11] presuppose a certain implicit idea about human reality and man's existence in the world, but this conception becomes explicit in the progress of the phenomenological analysis itself. If the psychologists in their modesty are animated by the laudable hope of realizing later, on the solid ground of their research work, an anthropological synthesis, they are in full contradiction with themselves (Sartre[12]). The traditional theories of feeling and emotion, even all descriptions of these phenomena, are based on the a priori conception of man as a "mundane ego," that is, a constituted object among other objects in the world. We do not agree with this conception.

The phenomenological approach to feelings and emotions starts from the undeniable fact that consciousness is always a being conscious of something else and that we are conscious of our existing, that means our being physically subjected to a given situation. This "being subjected" is not a causal relation, but it means that the situation must be responded to. The reply is the attitude, the feeling, the intentional act and not a reaction in a physiological sense. The fact that we find ourselves as subjects (in our "this-ness") only by standing apart and viewing ourselves in the situations in which we are involved is the profoundest basis of the phenomenon of feeling. Feeling and emotion are the affirmations of our attitudes toward situations, and the pure phenomenon of feeling reveals the human being as always projecting it and always projecting the world. The pure description of a feeling is the description of an existing human being in his well-defined attitude toward a situation. The projection is the signification of the act of feeling, a spontaneous movement (*s'éclater vers* —ejecting himself toward), which implies a totality of relations and their development. Feeling is a mode of replying to a situation and transforming it as a projected new world, in which unknown qualities are categorically experienced. There are as many feelings as there are situations, and the situation is created by the mode in which I have accepted it, *i.e.*, by my chosen projection. Of course this projection is not the result of reasoning and my choice is not arbitrary. I choose my emotional attitude in the same unreflective, nonconsidering (thematic, not thetic) mode of consciousness as I choose my words in speaking or writing.

The attitude toward the situation, confirmed by the feeling, is a true reply that is elicited. It is always my own unreflected act. There are, for example, many kinds of being irritated, angry, or furious, in which we choose and project ourselves in the mode of an efficacious revolt, just as I choose the more tasty of two apples. I have no motive in mind for my choice, but still there is in the situation and the backward reference to my existential history an antecedent that works *only* by its signification and hence is no cause.

When the normal impassive contemplative attitude becomes too difficult, so that we cannot meet the exigencies of the situation, we may choose to become angry and to change the situation and our attitude to it by this feeling.[13] Every feeling has a signification that makes us find the thing that is signified. Both the dynamic quality of the immediately experienced feeling and the essential characteristics of the expression refer to the signification and the thing signified. Even joy is not an automatic

[7] H. C. Rümke. Zur Phaenomenologie und Klinik des Glücksgefühls. *Monogr. Gesamtgebeit Neurol. Psychiat.*, 1924, 39.

[8] L. Binswanger, *e.g.* Uber die manische Lebensform. *Schweiz. Med. Wschr.*, 1945, 75.

[9] E. Minkowski. *Vers une cosmologie.* Paris: Aubier.

[10] H. Kunz, *Aggressivität und Zärtlichkeit.* Bern: 1946.

[11] H. Plessner, *Lachen und Weinen.* Arnhem: 1946.

[12] J. P. Sartre, *Esquisse d'une théorie des émotions.* Paris: Hermann, 1939. P. 5.

[13] *Ibid.*, p. 22.

reaction to an impression. Joy may be cheerfulness, high spirits, radiant expansion, dilatation, illumination, elevation.

All these dynamic elements may be the invariant content of a certain kind of joy. They denote the act, by which I affirm my choice of the positive value concealed in the situation and now revealed by my feeling joyous. The phenomenology of feeling has taken only the first step on the way of analyzing the various kinds of joyous feelings. We know—and it is important for psychopathology—that there exists a silent, quiet joy, large, placid, voluminous, embracing as a climate and signifying the mode of possessing and concealing a value which structures our entire existence.

There is also a leaping joy, a being animated, when we shout, jubilate, dance. This joy is allied to and impregnated with impatience (Sartre). It signifies the anticipation, a reaching, longing for some value that is approaching, that is expected.

I will try to give a provisional short sketch of a possible phenomenological genetic analysis of feeling and emotion, starting from the conception of Ruckmick[14] that the affective life begins with consciousness itself. In every concrete existence this "being conscious" is consciousness of existing physically, *i.e.*, being limited. The pure phenomenon of existing is the immediate act of experience of its own limit and this experience includes necessarily the experience of a possible transcendence of this limit. Conscious existing contains (in its own limitation) the possibility of feeling in its original signification of close relationship to the act of touching.

The sense of touch is the "father" of all senses (Lavelle,[15] Nogué[16]). Touching is the discovery

of our real existence in its own limitation. It reveals at the same time the physical self as touched, moved, and something that is touched by our self-movement. Touching is the most original mode of the experience of participation and feeling. In this encounter, for example, feeling the smoothness, slipperiness, stickiness, angularity, roundness, the shape and form of an object, we are intentionally involved in an anticipated developing situation. The act, the answer to the encounter, may be in the direction of the discovery of the qualities felt or of the feeling of something or in the direction of being emotionally stirred up and disturbed. It depends on the situation and our approach to it, whether feeling or emotion will prevail. Every new encounter is at the same time the abolishing of a former mode of being-in-the-world and this former existence is stirred, moved, and emotionalized. Awareness of emotion and also of excitation, I believe, is a nonintentional element of every feeling, just as it may be an element in the act of touching. It depends on the situation and the projection of our mode of relation to it, if feeling, emotion, or excitement prevails. The original signification of the act of feeling and the disturbing function of emotion and irritation, which are included in touching, the most original act of being-for-self in the individual's limited physical existence, inhibit themselves in the manifold situations in which a human being chooses to be engaged. These situations are the affective ones which elicit rage, fright, terror, astonishment, sorrow, joy, shame, jealousy, hate, sympathy, compassion, etc., and unlimited variations of sentiments, passion, and moods. In all these cases the phenomenological analysis will have to detect the full content of the significant formation and the essential history of significance. Many such investigations have appeared in the literature. Typical examples are given by Sartre, who showed the magical transformation of the world by feeling and emotion. He also speaks

[14] C. A. Ruckmick, *Psychology of feeling and emotion.* New York and London: McGraw-Hill, 1936. P. 214.
[15] L. Lavelle, *Dialectique du monde sensible.* Strassbourg: 1921.
[16] J. Nogué, *Esquisse d'un système de qualités sensibles.* Pr. Un. Fr: 1943. *La signification du sensible.* Aubier: 1936.

of the projection of the affective significations on the environment and mentions that consciousness "lives in the new world which it has just constituted. Consciousness is the victim of the trap it has set itself. Consciousness is moved by its own emotion."

Emotion is not an intentional act, but allied to sensation, irritation, and excitation. We may come to understand this fact in the following way: we have only consciousness of ourselves (regaining ourselves in the vision of things). When I admire something or hate someone, I, in *one* intentional act of feeling, project both myself as admiring or hating and the qualitative structure of the object or person. The created situation is not a static pattern, but an animated, vivid, lively unity that appeals to me by the claims of its qualities, provoked by my feeling. As has been demonstrated by V. von Weizsäcker for the act of touching, there is a functional circle of movement and being moved, in which the *Gestalt* is developed. Exactly as in touching, there is in the act of feeling a *closed* reciprocal relation between the subject and its intentional object. Consciousness is shut up with something and isolated from the rest of the world. The *rebound* of my projection of feeling against the created intentional experience has the character of being moved, *i.e.,* of emotion (possibly in the modality of excitation, excitement, or irritation). The result is penetration of feeling with emotion, of emotion with feeling, a stabilization, a continuity of the affected relation, with a certain analogy to the standing vibrations in a closed resonator or the standing waves on a limited surface of water. Thus we conclude that there is no emotion without the act of feeling, but the emotion itself is not an intentional act. It is the specific quality of our own existence, revealed in the regaining of ourselves in the act of feeling.

This may be the reason that I prefer to say: *I am* admiring this picture, *I am* hating that person, and I am moved *by* the beauty of the picture, *by* the untrustworthiness of that person. We must be aware that in every language the verbal expressions are ambiguous. The reason is that the dialectic and reciprocal relation of the involvement of affect makes it possible to describe the experience in a different way. It may happen that the repercussion of the (created) object to my act of feeling is so intense that I am conscious of my existence as a purely-passive-entity-being-moved and that this emotion totally hides the original intentional act that was the creator and also is the maintainer of the emotion. Therefore Sartre could write, "Pain is quite free from intentionality."[17] This is true, but there is no pain without a preceding, original attitude toward our existence as a physical-being-in-the-world. In our well-balanced life this attitude of ours is so "normal" that we forget its intentional character, but the simple fact of being painless in fighting or in hysteria reminds us that the condition of undergoing the sensation of pain is to be *with* ourselves, means to be conscious of our existence. Pain is not a feeling (act) but an emotional sensation only possible in the intentional experience of existence.

Continuing our sketch of a genetic analysis of feeling and emotion, we ought to realize that the encounter of our existence with something that limits it takes place in different intentional experiences. There are, so far as I can see, two extreme possibilities. The intentional object to which we are directed in the act of recognition of our own limitation is presented either as a resistance or as no resistance. The experience of resistance signifies our obstructed existence. The experience of no resistance in the encounter signifies our expanding existence. It seems to me that in grasping the sense of these phenomena we can distinguish four modes of feeling pleasant and four modes of feeling unpleasant, corresponding to the experience of different modes of existence. The four modes of

---

[17] *Op. cit.,* p. 398.

existence that are presented in the feeling of being pleased are (1) being-with-something, that is, being one with something or someone (*e.g.*, in love), (2) flowing-on, flowing-out existence, (3) expansion of the accentuated self, and (4) taking to one's self, assimilating, including as one's own. These four dynamic contents are in outline four kinds of feeling pleasant which are involved in the most different concrete feelings actually experienced in life.

The encounter with a resistance has also a fourfold typical dynamic structure, corresponding to four modes of unpleasantness. They are (1) being thrown back, (2) being subdued, (3) being injured, and (4) losing a part of one's self, abandoning part or all of one's self. Of course the phenomenological analysis of the different types of pleasantness and unpleasantness should be continued. My few remarks will try only to indicate the direction of approach.

Generally we think of feeling and emotion as spontaneous acts. It may be important, especially for applied psychology and psychotherapeutics, to make clear that *what* a feeling, an attitude, an expressive movement or a gesture means can be changed by the situation-creating power of our words. Here I do not think of the intellectualization of feelings, exposed by Dugas.[18] It was Brice Parain[19] who explained that we create a situation by our speaking. When I say (or write), "It is now night," I choose to project an image of a world and at the same time a definite nuance of feeling. It is another feeling and another world from when I say, "It is becoming night." We are able to change, to strengthen, or to weaken our feelings by our language. We may further the genuineness, the truth, and the reality of our feelings or their falseness. Saying "I am hungry" serves to communicate to myself and to others that my trouble is being

hungry. By this determination I call forth a situation with many consequences. My words—for example, saying to anyone, "I love you"— throw me into an adventure of affections and a series of situations and also serve to present me in a certain mode of existence. A word is not only a communication concerning a concrete attitude and situation; it also creates new situations, attitudes, and feelings.

To understand the value of the phenomenological approach to the problem of feelings and emotions, we have to establish the value of description in general and distinguish between the introspective and the phenomenological methods. Introspection is always an inspection of subjective experience. I describe this kind of experience exactly in the same way as any observer gives a report on his sensory simultaneous and successive perceptions. In both cases we observe facts, their positions in time, and in a real or imaginary space. When I should like to describe the mutual relations of these facts, I must have a categorical system of references, for example, the physical concept of causality or the metaphoric and often mythological notions used in physiology and psychology. The phenomenological description, however, is directed immediately toward experienced phenomena, as well as toward the different acts—the acts of perception, remembering, thinking, feeling, etc. All these phenomena are taken exactly as they belong to the phenomenal world. This world is given to us directly and shows itself in itself, in its meaning. The question whether the phenomenon is real or not is disregarded. The only interest of the phenomenologist is directed toward the *essential* structure, the intrinsic connections, and the self-revelation of the significance in the full context of the phenomenal field. So the question, "*What* is happiness or shame?" is the same question as the one put in common life: "What is a chair or a box?" or "What is red?" In both cases we are not satisfied with the indications

---

[18] Dugas, La logique des sentiments. *Nouveau Traité de Psychologie*, VI fasc. 1. Alcan, 1937.

[19] Brice Parain, *Recherche sur la nature et les fonctions du langage*. N.R.F., 1942.

of the conditions necessary to produce these phenomena, neither with the description of the material of which they are made nor with the result of an investigation into the causal relations to other things. I want to know exactly what kind of thing a chair or a box is, what it signifies in the world, where chairs and boxes are experienced, and what is the inner *essential* structure by which these significations are clarified. Just as in common life, phenomenology wants an evident insight in the sense of experience, for example, in feelings and emotions.

The continued research on feelings and emotions as stimulated by the phenomenological approach will require exact and repeated observation of the phenomenon in the above-mentioned sense of this notion. This observation or contemplation must be performed with the aim of penetrating to the essential sense as it is presented in the intentional act itself. Of course our experience is never complete. Everyone who has read the *Farbenlehre* of Goethe will have learned how "rich" the content of a simple perception of color is. The word "red" or "violet" is neither only a sign to indicate something nor only an abstract notion, but we use these words also to express our direct experience of these colors. In daily life as well as in science a word generally functions like a chain to get hold of a dog, to have the dog near us, and to do with it what we like. The phenomenologist, however, is not interested in the chain but in the dog itself. This is what Valéry meant when he wrote: "Every word is a bottomless pit."

In this way we understand that development of the phenomenologically orientated psychology depends on the dialectic relations between exemplary contemplation and the verbal expressions in living language developed out of unreflected intuitive views, signifying the essential sense. Perhaps one would assume from this that the phenomenology of feelings and emotions may be better furthered

by artists than by psychologists. First of all I should like to reply that art has proved its high value for psychology; second, that psychology requires the most thorough description of experience; and third, that applied psychology has proved the importance of the phenomenological method along with the analytic, functional, statistical viewpoints. It is impossible to know what an abnormal feeling is without an insight into the essential significance of normal feeling in the context of human existence. It is impossible to understand or even to describe sex relations when we do not know the essence and meaning of sexuality, bodily existence, femininity or masculinity. Pedagogics requires understanding the full content of sense of the phenomenon of play as well as of the mode of existence of the adolescent.

We are at the beginning of the phenomenological approach to all these matters and to the feelings and emotions in particular, but it is desirable for us to be aware of the richness of phenomenological analysis gathered in ancient and recent psychological literature, for example, in the publications of *Gestalt* psychologists.

An important starting point for further research is, among other things, the statement of William James: "We ought to say a feeling of *and*, a feeling of *if*, a feeling of *but*, and a feeling of *by*, quite as readily as we say a feeling of blue or a feeling of cold." And he adds: "Yet we do not: so inveterate has our habit become of recognizing the existence of the substantive parts alone, that language almost refuses to lend itself to any other use."[20]

The progress of phenomenological analysis of feeling and emotion depends on the discovery of the invariance which occurs during the continual experience concerning a feeling in various situations in relation to the modes of existence of normal and

---

[20] W. James. *Principles of Psychology*. Vol. I, pp. 245-246.

also of neurotic individuals, of men, women, children, primitive people, and animals.

The implicit conception of human reality and of the characteristics of human existence must become explicit during such a research through the evidence of insight into the signification of every intentional act of a concrete mode of feeling.

Repeatedly the question has been raised as to what is the guarantee that the phenomenological statement is true and not a pure subjective opinion. The answer to this is simple. The evidence of a statement about the essence and sense of a phenomenon can be proved only by the affirmation of everyone who, without prejudice, directs himself to the phenomenon in question. It is possible that some observer will find new, more detailed, more specific essential characteristics. Scheler, who has enriched us with so many phenomenological analyses—for example, about repentance, resentment, and sympathy—once said that the phenomenological approach offers the advantage of a continuous progress of insight after every return to the "thing-itself in its thisness." Such progress is the aim of science.

Phenomenological Theories:

ETIOLOGY AND DEVELOPMENT

Phenomenologists stress that every individual is the center of his changing world of experiences; experiences must be viewed, therefore, only in terms of their relevance to the individual. As the individual matures, a portion of his experience becomes differentiated into a conscious perception of the self-as-object. Once this self-concept is established, it influences the perceptions, memories, and thoughts of the individual. If experiences are inconsistent with the self-image, they are ignored or disowned.

Carl Rogers, the major American exponent of "self theory," details this process of growth and indicates the points at which "breakdown and disorder" arise. Rogers contends that psychopathology occurs when the individual abandons his inherent potentials and feelings and adopts values that are imposed upon him by others. Abraham Maslow's paper argues strongly for the healthy potential that exists within each individual, believing that if the child is encouraged to "actualize" his inherent potentials, he will develop into a mature and well-integrated adult.

A Theory of Personality

CARL R. ROGERS

In endeavoring to order our perceptions of the individual as he appears in therapy, a theory of the development of personality, and of the dynamics of behavior, has been constructed. It may be well to repeat the warning previously given, and to note that the initial propositions of this theory are those which are furthest from the matrix of our experience and hence are most suspect. As one reads on, the propositions become steadily closer to the experience of

From "A Theory of Therapy, Personality, and Interpersonal Relationships, as Developed in the Client-centered Framework," pages 221-231. In *Psychology: A Study of a Science* edited by S. Koch, Vol. 3, copyright 1959, used by permission of McGraw-Hill Book Company.

therapy. As before, the defined terms and constructs are italicized, and are to be understood as previously defined.

A. POSTULATED CHARACTERISTICS OF THE HUMAN INFANT

It is postulated that the individual, during the period of infancy, has at least these attributes.

1. He perceives his *experience* as reality. His *experience* is his reality.

    a. As a consequence he has greater potential *awareness* of what reality is for him than does anyone else, since no one else can completely assume his *internal frame of reference.*

2. He has an inherent tendency toward *actualizing* his organism.

3. He interacts with his reality in terms of his basic *actualizing* tendency. Thus his behavior is the goal-directed attempt of the organism to satisfy the experienced needs for *actualization* in the reality as *perceived*.

4. In this interaction he behaves as an organized whole, as a gestalt.

5. He engages in an *organismic valuing process*, valuing *experience* with reference to the *actualizing tendency* as a criterion. *Experiences* which are *perceived* as maintaining or enhancing the organism are valued positively. Those which are *perceived* as negating such maintenance or enhancement are valued negatively.

6. He behaves with adience toward positively valued *experiences* and with avoidance toward those negatively valued.

Comment. In this view as formally stated, the human infant is seen as having an inherent motivational system (which he shares in common with all living things) and a regulatory system (the valuing process) which by its "feedback" keeps the organism "on the beam" of satisfying his motivational needs. He lives in an environment which for theoretical purposes may be said to exist only in him, or to be of his own creation.

This last point seems difficult for some people to comprehend. It is the perception of the environment which constitutes the environment, regardless as to how this relates to some "real" reality which we may philosophically postulate. The infant may be picked up by a friendly, affectionate person. If his perception of the situation is that this is a strange and frightening experience, it is this perception, not the "reality" or the "stimulus" which will regulate his behavior. To be sure, the relationship with the environment is a transactional one, and if his continuing experience contradicts his initial perception, then in time his perception will change. But the effective reality which influences behavior is at all times the perceived

reality. We can operate theoretically from this base without having to resolve the difficult question of what "really" constitutes reality.

Another comment which may be in order is that no attempt has been made to supply a complete catalogue of the equipment with which the infant faces the world. Whether he possesses instincts, or an innate sucking reflex, or an innate need for affection, are interesting questions to pursue, but the answers seem peripheral rather than essential to a theory of personality.

B. THE DEVELOPMENT OF THE SELF

1. In line with the tendency toward differentiation which is a part of the *actualizing tendency*, a portion of the individual's *experience* becomes differentiated and *symbolized* in an *awareness* of being, *awareness* of functioning. Such awareness may be described as *self-experience*.

2. This representation in *awareness* of being and functioning, becomes elaborated, through interaction with the environment, particularly the environment composed of significant others, into a *concept of self*, a perceptual object in his *experiential field*.

Comment. These are the logical first steps in the development of the self. It is by no means the way the construct developed in our own thinking, as has been indicated in the section of definitions.

C. THE NEED FOR POSITIVE REGARD

1. As the awareness of self emerges, the individual develops a *need for positive regard*. This need is universal in human beings, and in the individual, is pervasive and persistent. Whether it is an inherent or learned need is irrelevant to the theory. Standal, who formulated the concept, regards it as the latter.

a. The satisfaction of this need

is necessarily based upon inferences regarding the experiential field of another.

(1) Consequently it is often ambiguous.

b. It is associated with a very wide range of the individual's *experiences*.

c. It is reciprocal, in that when an individual discriminates himself as satisfying another's need for *positive regard,* he necessarily experiences satisfaction of his own need for *positive regard.*

(1) Hence it is rewarding both to satisfy this need in another, and to experience the satisfaction of one's own need by another.

d. It is potent, in that the *positive regard* of any social other is communicated to the total *regard complex* which the individual associates with that social other.

(1) Consequently the expression of positive regard by a significant social other can become more compelling than the *organismic valuing process,* and the individual becomes more adient to the *positive regard* of such others than toward *experiences* which are of positive value in *actualizing* the organism.

D. THE DEVELOPMENT OF THE NEED FOR SELF-REGARD

1. The positive regard satisfactions or frustrations associated with any particular *self-experience* or group of *self-experiences* come to be *experienced* by the individual independently of *positive regard* transactions with social others. *Positive regard experienced* in this fashion is termed *self-regard.*

2. A *need for self-regard* develops as a learned need developing out of the association of *self-experiences* with the satisfaction or frustration of the *need for positive regard.*

3. The individual thus comes to *experience positive regard* or loss of *positive regard* independently of transactions with any social other. He becomes in a sense his own significant social other.

4. Like *positive regard, self-regard* which is *experienced* in relation to any particular *self-experience* or group of *self-experiences,* is communicated to the total *self-regard complex.*

E. THE DEVELOPMENT OF CONDITIONS OF WORTH

1. When *self-experiences* of the individual are discriminated by significant others as being more or less worthy of *positive regard,* then *self-regard* becomes similarly selective.

2. When a *self-experience* is avoided (or sought) solely because it is less (or more) worthy of *self-regard,* the individual is said to have acquired a *condition of worth.*

3. If an individual should *experience* only *unconditional positive regard,* then no *conditions of worth* would develop, *self-regard* would be unconditional, the needs for *positive regard* and *self-regard* would never be at variance with *organismic evaluation,* and the individual would continue to be *psychologically adjusted,* and would be fully functioning. This chain of events is hypothetically possible, and hence important theoretically, though it does not appear to occur in actuality.

Comment. This is an important sequence in personality development, stated more fully by Standal. It may help to restate the sequence in informal, illustrative, and much less exact terms.

The infant learns to need love. Love is very satisfying, but to know whether he is receiving it or not he must observe his mother's face, gestures, and other ambiguous signs. He develops a total gestalt as to the way he is regarded by his mother and each new experience of love or rejection tends to alter the whole gestalt. Consequently each behavior on his mother's part such as a specific disapproval of a specific behavior tends to be experienced as disapproval in general. So important is this to the infant that he comes to be guided in his behavior not by the degree to which an experience maintains or enhances the organism, but by the likelihood of receiving maternal love.

Soon he learns to view himself in much the same way, liking or disliking himself as a total configuration. He tends, quite independently of his mother or others, to view himself and his behavior in the same way they have. This means that some behaviors are regarded positively which are not actually experienced organismically as satisfying. Other behaviors are regarded negatively which are not actually experienced as unsatisfying. It is when he behaves in accordance with these introjected values that he may be said to have acquired conditions of worth. He cannot regard himself positively, as having worth, unless he lives in terms of these conditions. He now reacts with adience or avoidance toward certain behaviors solely because of these introjected conditions of self-regard, quite without reference to the organismic consequences of these behaviors. This is what is meant by living in terms of introjected values (the phrase formerly used) or conditions of worth.

It is not theoretically necessary that such a sequence develop. If the infant always felt prized, if his own feelings were always accepted even though some behaviors were inhibited, then no conditions of worth would develop. This could at least theoretically be achieved if the parental attitude was genuinely of this sort: "I can understand how satisfying it feels to you to hit your baby brother (or to defecate when and where you please, or to destroy things) and I love you and am quite willing for you to have those feelings.

But I am quite willing for me to have my feelings, too, and I feel very distressed when your brother is hurt, (or annoyed or sad at other behaviors) and so I do not let you hit him. Both your feelings and my feelings are important, and each of us can freely have his own." If the child were thus able to retain his own organismic evaluation of each experience, then his life would become a balancing of these satisfactions. Schematically he might feel, "I enjoy hitting baby brother. It feels good. I do not enjoy mother's distress. That feels dissatisfying to me. I enjoy pleasing her." Thus his behavior would sometimes involve the satisfaction of hitting his brother, sometimes the satisfaction of pleasing mother. But he would never have to disown the feelings of satisfaction or dissatisfaction which he experienced in this differential way.

F. THE DEVELOPMENT OF INCONGRUENCE BETWEEN SELF AND EXPERIENCE

1. Because of the need for *self*-regard, the individual *perceives* his *experience* selectively, in terms of the *conditions of worth* which have come to exist in him.

   a. Experiences which are in accord with his *conditions of worth* are *perceived* and symbolized accurately in *awareness*.

   b. Experiences which run contrary to the *conditions of worth* are *perceived* selectively and distortedly as if in accord with the *conditions of worth*, or are in part or whole, *denied to awareness*.

2. Consequently some experiences now occur in the organism which are not recognized as *self-experiences*, are not accurately *symbolized*, and are not organized into the *self-structure* in *accurately symbolized* form.

3. Thus from the time of the first selective *perception* in terms of

conditions of worth, the states of *incongruence between self and experience,* of *psychological maladjustment* and of *vulnerability,* exist to some degree.

Comment. It is thus because of the distorted perceptions arising from the conditions of worth that the individual departs from the integration which characterizes his infant state. From this point on his concept of self includes distorted perceptions which do not accurately represent his experience, and his experience includes elements which are not included in the picture he has of himself. Thus he can no longer live as a unified whole person, but various part functions now become characteristic. Certain experiences tend to threaten the self. To maintain the self-structure defensive reactions are necessary. Behavior is regulated at times by the self and at times by those aspects of the organism's experience which are not included in the self. The personality is henceforth divided, with the tensions and inadequate functioning which accompany such lack of unity.

This, as we see it, is the basic estrangement in man. He has not been true to himself, to his own natural organismic valuing of experience, but for the sake of preserving the positive regard of others has now come to falsify some of the values he experiences and to perceive them only in terms based upon their value to others. Yet this has not been a conscious choice, but a natural—and tragic—development in infancy. The path of development toward psychological maturity, the path of therapy, is the undoing of this estrangement in man's functioning, the dissolving of conditions of worth, the achievement of a self which is congruent with experience, and the restoration of a unified organismic valuing process as the regulator of behavior.

G. THE DEVELOPMENT OF DISCREPANCIES IN BEHAVIOR

1. As a consequence of the incongruence between self and experience described in *F,* a similar incongruence arises in the behavior of the individual.

    a. Some behaviors are consistent with the *self-concept* and maintain and actualize and enhance it.

        (1) Such behaviors are *accurately symbolized* in *awareness.*

    b. Some behaviors maintain, enhance, and actualize those aspects of the experience of the organism which are not assimilated into the *self-structure.*

        (1) These behaviors are either unrecognized as *self-experiences* or *perceived* in distorted or selective fashion in such a way as to be *congruent* with the *self.*

H. THE EXPERIENCE OF THREAT AND THE PROCESS OF DEFENSE

1. As the organism continues to *experience,* an *experience* which is incongruent with the self-structure (and its incorporated *conditions of worth,* is *subceived* as *threatening.*

2. The essential nature of the *threat* is that if the *experience* were *accurately symbolized* in *awareness,* the *self-concept* would no longer be a consistent gestalt, the *conditions of worth* would be violated, and the *need for self-regard* would be frustrated. A state of *anxiety* would exist.

3. The process of *defense* is the reaction which prevents these events from occurring.

    a. This process consists of the selective *perception* or *distortion* of the *experience* and/or the *denial to awareness* of the *experience* or some portion thereof, thus keeping the total *perception* of the *experience* consistent with the individual's *self-structure,* and consistent with his *conditions of worth.*

4. The general consequences of the process of *defense*, aside from its preservation of the above consistencies, are a rigidity of *perception*, due to the necessity of distorting *perceptions*, an inaccurate *perception* of reality, due to distortion and omission of data, and *intensionality*.

Comment. Section *G* describes the psychological basis for what are usually thought of as neurotic behaviors, and Section *H* describes the mechanisms of these behaviors. From our point of view it appears more fundamental to think of defensive behaviors (described in these two sections) and disorganized behaviors (described below). Thus the defensive behaviors include not only the behaviors customarily regarded as neurotic—rationalization, compensation, fantasy, projection, compulsions, phobias, and the like—but also some of the behaviors customarily regarded as psychotic, notably paranoid behaviors and perhaps catatonic states. The disorganized category includes many of the "irrational" and "acute" psychotic behaviors, as will be explained below. This seems to be a more fundamental classification than those usually employed, and perhaps more fruitful in considering treatment. It also avoids any concept of neurosis and psychosis as entities in themselves, which we believe has been an unfortunate and misleading conception.

Let us consider for a moment the general range of the defensive behaviors from the simplest variety, common to all of us, to the more extreme and crippling varieties. Take first of all, rationalization. ("I didn't really make that mistake. It was this way....") Such excuses involve a perception of behavior distorted in such a way as to make it congruent with our concept of self (as a person who doesn't make mistakes). Fantasy is another example. ("I am a beautiful princess, and all the men adore me.") Because the actual experience is threatening to the concept of self (as an adequate person, in this example), this experience is denied,

and a new symbolic world is created which enhances the self, but completely avoids any recognition of the actual experience. Where the incongruent experience is a strong need, the organism actualizes itself by finding a way of expressing this need, but it is perceived in a way which is consistent with the self. Thus an individual whose self-concept involves no "bad" sexual thoughts may feel or express the thought "I am pure, but you are trying to make me think filthy thoughts." This would be thought of as projection or as a paranoid idea. It involves the expression of the organism's need for sexual satisfactions, but it is expressed in such a fashion that this need may be denied to awareness and the behavior perceived as consistent with the self. Such examples could be continued, but perhaps the point is clear that the incongruence between self and experience is handled by the distorted perception of experience or behavior, or by the denial of experience in awareness (behavior is rarely denied, though this is possible), or by some combination of distortion and denial.

I. THE PROCESS OF BREAKDOWN AND DISORGANIZATION

Up to this point the theory of personality which has been formulated applies to every individual in a lesser or greater degree. In this and the following section certain processes are described which occur only when certain specified conditions are present.

1. If the individual has a large or significant degree of *incongruence between self and experience* and if a significant experience demonstrating this *incongruence* occurs suddenly, or with a high degree of obviousness, then the organism's process of *defense* is unable to operate successfully.

2. As a result *anxiety* is *experienced* as the *incongruence* is subceived. The degree of *anxiety* is dependent upon the extent of the *self-structure* which is *threatened*.

3. The process of *defense* being

unsuccessful, the *experience* is *accurately symbolized* in *awareness*, and the gestalt of the *self-structure* is broken by this *experience* of the *incongruence* in *awareness*. A state of disorganization results.

4. In such a state of disorganization the organism behaves at times in ways which are openly consistent with experiences which have hitherto been distorted or denied to awareness. At other times the self may temporarily regain regnancy, and the organism may behave in ways consistent with it. Thus in such a state of disorganization, the tension between the concept of self (with its included distorted perceptions) and the experiences which are not accurately symbolized or included in the concept of self, is expressed in a confused regnancy, first one and then the other supplying the "feedback" by which the organism regulates behavior.

Comment. This section, as will be evident from its less exact formulation, is new, tentative, and needs much more consideration. Its meaning can be illuminated by various examples.

Statements 1 and 2 above may be illustrated by anxiety-producing experiences in therapy, or by acute psychotic breakdowns. In the freedom of therapy, as the individual expresses more and more of himself, he finds himself on the verge of voicing a feeling which is obviously and undeniably true, but which is flatly contradictory to the conception of himself which he has held. Anxiety results, and if the situation is appropriate (as described under *J*) this anxiety is moderate, and the result is constructive. But if, through overzealous and effective interpretation by the therapist, or through some other means, the individual is brought face to face with more of his denied experiences then he can handle, disorganization ensues and a psychotic break occurs, as described in statement 3. We have known this to happen when an individual has sought "therapy" from several different sources simultaneously. It has also

been illustrated by some of the early experience with sodium pentathol therapy. Under the drug the individual revealed many of the experiences which hitherto he had denied to himself, and which accounted for the incomprehensible elements in his behavior. Unwisely faced with the material in his normal state he could not deny its authenticity, his defensive processes could not deny or distort the experience, and hence the self-structure was broken, and a psychotic break occurred.

Acute psychotic behaviors appear often to be describable as behaviors which are consistent with the denied aspects of experience rather than consistent with the self. Thus the person who has kept sexual impulses rigidly under control, denying them as an aspect of self, may now make open sexual overtures to those with whom he is in contact. Many of the so-called irrational behaviors of psychosis are of this order.

Once the acute psychotic behaviors have been exhibited, a process of defense again sets in to protect the organism against the exceedingly painful awareness of incongruence. Here I would voice my opinion very tentatively as to this process of defense. In some instances perhaps the denied experiences are now regnant, and the organism defends itself against the awareness of the self. In other instances the self is again regnant, and behavior is consistent with it, but the self has been greatly altered. It is now a self concept which includes the important theme, "I am a crazy, inadequate, unreliable person who contains impulses and forces beyond my control." Thus it is a self in which little or no confidence is felt.

It is hoped that this portion of the theory may be further elaborated and refined and made more testable in the future.

J. THE PROCESS OF REINTEGRATION

In the situations described under sections *G* and *H,* (and probably in situations of breakdown as described under *I,* though there is less evidence on this) a process of reintegration is possible, a process which moves in the direction of increasing the *congruence* between *self* and *experience.* This may be described as follows:

1. In order for the process of *defense* to be reversed—for a customarily *threatening experience* to be *accurately symbolized* in *awareness* and assimilated into the *self-structure,* certain conditions must exist.

   a. There must be a decrease in the *conditions of worth.*

   b. There must be an increase in *unconditional self-regard.*

2. The communicated *unconditional positive regard* of a significant other is one way of achieving these conditions.

   a. In order for the *unconditional positive regard* to be communicated, it must exist in a context of *empathic* understanding.

   b. When the individual *perceives* such *unconditional positive regard,* existing *conditions of worth* are weakened or dissolved.

   c. Another consequence is the increase in his own *unconditional positive self-regard.*

   d. Conditions *2a* and *2b* above thus being met, *threat* is reduced, the process of *defense is reversed,* and *experiences* customarily *threatening* are *accurately symbolized* and integrated into the *self concept.*

3. The consequences of 1 and 2 above are that the individual is less likely to encounter *threatening experiences;* the process of *defense* is less frequent and its consequences reduced; *self* and *experience* are more *congruent; self-regard* is increased; *positive regard* for others is increased; *psychological adjustment* is increased; the *organismic valuing process* becomes increasingly the basis of regulating behavior; the individual becomes nearly fully functioning.

Comment. This section is simply the theory of therapy which we presented earlier, now stated in a slightly more general form. It is intended to emphasize the fact that the reintegration or restoration of personality occurs always and only (at least so we are hypothesizing) in the presence of certain definable conditions. These are essentially the same whether we are speaking of formal psychotherapy continued over a considerable period, in which rather drastic personality changes may occur or whether we are speaking of the minor constructive changes which may be brought about by contact with an understanding friend or family member.

One other brief comment may be made about item *2a,* above. Empathic understanding is always necessary if unconditional positive regard is to be fully communicated. If I know little or nothing of you, and experience an unconditional positive regard for you, this means little because further knowledge of you may reveal aspects which I cannot so regard. But if I know you thoroughly, knowing and empathically understanding a wide variety of your feelings and behaviors, and still experience an unconditional positive regard, this is very meaningful. It comes close to being fully known and fully accepted.

Defense and Growth

ABRAHAM H. MASLOW

This chapter is an effort to be a little more systematic in the area of growth theory. For once we accept the notation of growth, many questions of detail arise. Just how does growth take place? Why do children grow or not grow? How do they know in which direction to grow? How do they get off in the direction of pathology?

After all, the concepts of self-actualization, growth and self are all high-level abstractions. We need to get closer to actual processes, to raw data, to concrete, living happenings.

These are far goals. Healthily growing infants and children don't live for the sake of far goals or for the distant future; they are too busy enjoying themselves and spontaneously living for the moment. They are *living*, not *preparing* to live. How can they manage, just being, spontaneously, not *trying* to grow, seeking only to enjoy the present activity, nevertheless to move forward step by step? i.e., to grow in a healthy way? to discover their real selves? How can we reconcile the facts of Being with the facts of Becoming? Growth is not in the pure case a goal out ahead, nor is self-actualization, nor is the discovery of Self. In the child, it is not specifically purposed; rather it just happens. He doesn't so much search as find. The laws of deficiency-motivation and of purposeful coping do not hold for growth, for spontaneity, for creativeness.

The danger with a pure Being-psychology is that it may tend to be static, not accounting for the facts of movement, direction and growth. We tend to describe states of Being, of self-actualization as if they were Nirvana states of perfection. Once you're there, you're there, and it seems as if

From *Merrill-Palmer Quarterly* 3:36-47, 1956, by permission of the publisher and the author.

all you could do is to rest content in perfection.

The answer I find satisfactory is a simple one, namely, that growth takes place when the next step forward is subjectively more delightful, more joyous, more intrinsically satisfying than the last; that the only way we can ever know what is right for us is that it feels better subjectively than any alternative. The new experience validates *itself* rather than by an outside criterion. It is self-justifying, self-validating.

We don't do it because it is good for us, or because psychologists approve, or because somebody told us to, or because it will make us live longer, or because it is good for the species, or because it will bring external rewards, or because it is logical. We do it for the same reason that we choose one dessert over another. I have already described this as a basic mechanism for falling in love, or for choosing a friend, i.e., kissing one person gives more delight than kissing the other, being friends with *a* is more satisfying subjectively than being friends with *b*.

In this way, we learn what we are good at, what we really like or dislike, what our tastes and judgments and capacities are. In a word, this is the way in which we discover the Self and answer the ultimate questions Who am I? What am I?

The steps and the choices are taken out of pure spontaneity, from within outward. The healthy infant or child, just Being, as *part* of his Being, is randomly, and spontaneously curious, exploratory, wondering, interested. Even when he is non-purposeful, non-coping, expressive, spontaneous, not motivated by any deficiency of the ordinary sort, he tends to try out his powers, to reach out, to be absorbed, fascinated, interested, to play, to wonder, to manipulate the world. *Exploring, manipulating, experiencing*, being interested, choosing, delighting, *enjoying* can all be seen as attributes of pure Being, and yet lead to Becoming, though in a serendipitous way, fortuitously, unplanned, unanticipated. Spontaneous, creative experience can and does happen without expectations, plans, foresight, purpose, or goal.[1] It is only when the child sates himself, becomes bored, that he is ready to turn to other, perhaps "higher," delights.

Then arise the inevitable questions. What holds him back? What prevents growth? Wherein lies the conflict? What is the alternative to growth forward? Why is it so hard and painful for some to grow forward? Here we must become more fully aware of the fixative and regressive power of ungratified deficiency-needs, of the attractions of safety and security, of the functions of defense and protection against pain, fear, loss, and threat, of the need for courage in order to grow ahead.

Every human being has *both* sets of forces within him. One set clings to safety and defensiveness out of fear, tending to regress backward, hanging on to the past, *afraid* to grow away from the primitive communion with the mother's uterus and breast, *afraid* to take chances, afraid to jeopardize what he already has, *afraid* of independence, freedom and separateness. The other set of forces impels him forward toward wholeness of Self and uniqueness of Self, toward full functioning of all his capacities, toward confidence in the face of the external world at the same time that he can accept his deepest, real, unconscious Self.

I can put all this together in a schema, which though very simple, is

also very powerful, both heuristically and theoretically. This basic dilemma or conflict between the defensive forces and the growth trends I conceive to be existential, imbedded in the deepest nature of the human being, now and forever into the future. If it is diagrammed like this:

Safety $\longleftarrow<$ PERSON $>\longrightarrow$ Growth

then we can very easily classify the various mechanisms of growth in an uncomplicated way as

> a. Enhancing the growthward vectors, e.g., making it more attractive and delight producing,
> b. Minimizing the fears of growth,
> c. Minimizing the safetyward vectors, i.e., making it less attractive,
> d. Maximizing the fears of safety, defensiveness, pathology and regression.

We can then add to our basic schema these four sets of valences:

Enhance the dangers Enhance the attractions
Safety $\leftarrow<$PERSON$>\rightarrow$Growth
Minimize the attractions Minimize the dangers

Therefore we can consider the process of healthy growth to be a never ending series of free choice situations, confronting each individual at every point throughout his life, in which he must choose between the delights of safety and growth, dependence and independence, regression and progression, immaturity and maturity. Safety has both anxieties and delights; growth has both anxieties and delights. We grow forward when the delights of growth and anxieties of safety are greater than the anxieties of growth and the delights of safety.

So far it sounds like a truism. But it isn't to psychologists who are mostly trying to be objective, public, behavioristic. And it has taken many experiments with animals and much theorizing to convince the students of animal motivation that they must invoke what P. T. Young called a hedonic factor, over and above need-reduction, in order to explain the results so far obtained in free-choice experimentation. For example, saccharin is not need-reducing in any way and yet white rats will choose it over plain water. Its (useless) taste *must* have something to do with it.

---

[1] "But paradoxically, the art experience cannot be effectively *used* for this purpose or any other. It must be a purposeless activity, as far as we understand "purpose'. It can only be an experience in *being*—being a human organism doing what it must and what it is privileged to do—experiencing life keenly and wholly, expending energy and creating beauty in its own style—and the increased sensitivity, integrity, efficiency, and feeling of well-being are by-products."

Furthermore, observe that subjective delight in the experience is something that we can attribute to *any* organism, e.g., it applies to the infant as well as the adult, to the animal as well as to the human.

The possibility that then opens for us is very enticing for the theorist. Perhaps all these high-level concepts of Self, Growth, Self-realization, and Psychological Health can fall into the same system of explanation with appetite experiments in animals, free choice observations in infant feeding and in occupational choice, and the rich studies of homeostasis.

Of course this formulation of growth-through-delight also commits us to the necessary postulation that what tastes good is also, in the growth sense, "better" for us. We rest here on the faith that if free choice is *really* free and if the chooser is not too sick or frightened to choose, he will choose wisely, in a healthy and growthward direction, more often than not.

For this postulation there is already much experimental support, but it is mostly at the animal level, and much more detailed research is necessary with free choice in humans. We must know much more than we do about the reasons for bad and unwise choices, at the constitutional level and at the level of psychodynamics.

There is another reason why my systematizing side likes this notion of growth-through-delight. It is that then I find it possible to tie it in nicely with dynamic theory, with *all* the dynamic theories of Freud, Adler, Jung, Schachtel, Horney, Fromm and Rank, as well as The Self theories of Rogers, Buhler, Combs, Angyal, Allport, Goldstein and of the Growth-and-Being school, Dewey, Rasey, Kelley, Moustakas, Wilson, Perls, Lee, Mearns, etc.

I criticize the classical Freudians for tending (in the extreme instance) to pathologize everything and for not seeing clearly enough the healthward possibilities in the human being, for seeing everything through brown-colored glasses. But the growth school (in the extreme instance) is equally vulnerable, for they tend to see through rose-colored glasses and generally slide over the problems of pathology, of weakness, of *failure* to grow. One is like a theology of evil and sin exclusively; the other is like a theology without any evil at all, and is therefore equally incorrect and unrealistic.

One additional relationship between safety and growth must be specially mentioned. Apparently growth forward customarily takes place in little steps, and each step forward is made possible by the feeling of being safe, of operating out into the unknown from a safe home port, of daring because retreat is possible. We may use as a paradigm the toddler venturing away from his mother's knee into strange surroundings. Characteristically, he first clings to his mother as he explores the room with his eyes. Then he dares a little excursion, continually reassuring himself that the mother-security is intact. These excursions get more and more extensive. In this way, the child can explore a dangerous and unknown world. If suddenly the mother were to disappear, he would be thrown into anxiety, would cease to be interested in exploring the world, would wish only the return of safety, and might even lose his abilities, e.g., instead of daring to walk, he might creep.

I think we may safely generalize this example. Assured safety permits higher needs and impulses to emerge and to grow towards mastery. To endanger safety, means regression backward to the more basic foundation. What this means is that in the choice between giving up safety or giving up growth, safety will ordinarily win out. Safety needs are prepotent over growth needs. This means an expansion of our basic formula. In general, only a child who feels safe dares to grow forward healthily. His safety needs must be gratified. He can't be *pushed* ahead, because the ungratified safety needs will remain forever underground, always calling for satisfaction. The more safety needs are gratified, the less valence they have for the child, the less they will beckon, and lower his courage.

Now, how can we know when the child feels safe enough to dare to choose the new step ahead? Ultimately, the only way in which we can know is by *his* choices, which is to say only *he* can ever really know the right moment when the beckoning forces ahead overbalance the beckoning forces behind, and courage outweighs fear.

Ultimately the person, even the child, must choose for himself. Nobody can choose for him too often, for this itself enfeebles him, cutting his self-trust, and confusing his *ability* to perceive his own internal delight in the experience, his *own* impulses, judgments, and feelings, and to differentiate them from the interiorized standards of others.[2]

---

[2] "From the moment the package is in his hands, he feels free to do what he wants with it. He opens it, speculates on what it is, recognizes what it is, expresses happiness or disappointment, notices the arrangement of the contents, finds a book of directions, feels the touch of the steel, the different weights of the parts, and their number, and so on. He does all this before he has attempted to do a thing with the set. Then comes the thrill of doing something with it. It may be only matching one single part with another. Thereby alone he gets a feeling of having done something, that he can do something, and that he is not helpless with that particular article. Whatever pattern is subsequently followed, whether his interest extends to the full utilization of the set and therefore toward further gaining a feeling of greater and greater accomplishment, or whether he completely discards it, his initial contact with the erector set has been meaningful.

"The results of active experiencing can be summarized approximately in the following way. There is physical, emotional, and intellectual self-involvement; there is a recognition and further exploration of one's abilities; there is initiation of activity or creativeness; there is finding out one's own pace and rhythm and the assumption of enough of a task for one's abilities at that particular time, which would include the avoidance of taking on too much; there is gain in skill which one can apply to other enterprises, and there is an opportunity each time that one has an active part in something, no matter how small, to find out more and more what one is interested in.

"The above situation may be contrasted with another in which the person who brings home the erector set says to the child, 'Here is an erector set, let me open it for you.' He does so, and then points out all the things in the box, the book of directions, the various parts, etc., and, to top it off, he sets about building one of the complicated models, let us say, a crane. The child may be much interested in what he has seen being done, but let us focus on one aspect of what has really

If this is all so, if the child himself must finally make the choice by which he grows forward, since only he can know his subjective delight experience, then how can we reconcile this ultimate necessity for trust in the inner individual with the necessity for help from the environment? For he does need help. Without help he will be too frightened to dare. How can we help him to grow? Equally important, how can we endanger his growth?

The opposite of the subjective experience of delight (trusting himself), so far as the child is concerned, is the opinion of other people (love, respect, approval, admiration, reward from others, trusting others rather than himself). Since others are so important and vital for the helpless baby and child, fear of losing them (as providers of safety, food, love, respect, etc.) is a primal, terrifying danger. Therefore, the child, faced with a difficult choice between his own delight experiences and the experience of approval from others, must generally choose approval from others, and then handle his delight by repression or letting it die, or not noticing it or controlling it by will-power. In general, along with this will develop a disapproval of the delight experience, or shame and embarrassment and secre-

---

been happening. The child has had no opportunity to get himself involved with the erector set, with his body, his intelligence, or his feelings, he has had no opportunity to match himself up with something that is new for him, to find out what he is capable of or to gain further direction for his interests. The building of the crane for him may have brought in another factor. It may have left the child with an implied demand that he do likewise without his having had an opportunity to prepare himself for any such complicated task. The end becomes the object instead of the experience involved in the process of attaining the objective. Also, whatever he may subsequently do by himself will look small and mean compared to what had been made for him by someone else. He has not added to his total experience for coming up against something new for the next time. In other words, he has not grown from within but has had something superimposed from the outside. . . . Each bit of active experiencing is an opportunity toward finding out what he likes or dislikes, and more and more what he wants to make out of himself. It is an essential part of his progress toward the stage of maturity and self-direction."

tiveness about it, with finally, the inability even to experience it.[3]

The primal choice, the fork in the road, then, is between others' and one's own self. If the only way to maintain the self is to lose others, then the ordinary child will give up the self. This is true for the reason already mentioned, that safety is a most basic and prepotent need for children, more primarily necessary by far than independence and self-actualization. If adults force this choice upon him, of choosing between the loss of one (lower) vital necessity or another (higher) vital necessity, the child must choose safety even at the cost of giving up self and growth.

---

[3] "How is it possible to lose a self? The treachery, unknown and unthinkable, begins with our secret psychic death in childhood—if and when we are not loved and are cut off from our spontaneous wishes. (Think: what is left?) But wait —victim might even "outgrow" it—but it is a perfect double crime in which he him-it is not just this simple murder of a psyche. That might be written off, the tiny self also gradually and unwittingly takes part. He has not been accepted for himself, *as he is*. "Oh, they 'love' him, but they want him or force him or expect him to be different! Therefore he *must be unacceptable*. He himself learns to believe it and at last even takes it for granted. He has truly given himself up. No matter now whether he obeys them, whether he clings, rebels or withdraws—his behavior, his performance is all that matters. His center of gravity is in 'them,' not in himself—yet if he so much as noticed it he'd think it natural enough. And the whole thing is entirely plausible; all invisible, automatic, and anonymous!

"This is the perfect paradox. Everything looks normal; no crime was intended; there is no corpse, no guilt. All we can see is the sun rising and setting as usual. But what has happened? He has been rejected, not only by them, but by himself. (He is actually without a self.) What has he lost? Just the one true and vital part of himself: his own yes-feeling, which is his very capacity for growth, his root system. But alas, he is not dead. 'Life' goes on, and so must he. From the moment he gives himself up, and to the extent that he does so, all unknowingly he sets about to create and maintain a pseudo-self. But this is an expediency —a 'self' without wishes. This one shall be loved (or feared) where he is despised, strong where he is weak; it shall go through the motions (oh, but they are caricatures!) not for fun or joy but for survival; not simply because it wants to move but because it has to obey. This necessity is not life— not his life—it is a defense mechanism against death. It is also the machine of death. From now on he will be torn apart by compulsive (unconscious) *needs* or ground by (unconscious) conflicts into paralysis, every motion and every instant canceling out his being, his integrity; and all the while he is disguised as a normal person and expected to behave like one!

"In a word, I saw that we *become* neurotic seeking or defending a pseudo-self, a self-system; and we *are* neurotic to the extent that we are self-less."

(In principle there is no need for forcing the child to make such a choice. People just *do* it often, out of their own sicknesses and out of ignorance. We know that it is not necessary because we have examples enough of children who are offered all these goods simultaneously, at no vital cost, who can have safety and love *and* respect too.)

Here we can learn important lessons from the therapy situation, the creative educative situation, creative art education and I believe also creative dance education. Here where the situation is set up variously as permissive, admiring, praising, accepting, safe, gratifying, reassuring, supporting, unthreatening, non-valuing, non-comparing, that is, where the person can feel completely safe and unthreatened, then it becomes possible for him to work out and express all sorts of lesser delights, e.g., hostility, neurotic dependency. Once these are sufficiently catharted, he then tends spontaneously to go to other delights which outsiders perceive to be "higher" or growthward, e.g., love, creativeness, and which he himself will prefer to the previous delights, once he has experienced them both. (It often makes little difference what kind of explicit theory is held by the therapist, teacher, helper, etc. The really good therapist who may espouse a pessimistic Freudian theory, *acts* as if growth were possible. The really good teacher who espouses verbally a completely rosy and optimistic picture of human nature, will *imply* in actual teaching, a complete understanding and respect for regressive and defensive forces. It is also possible to have a wonderfully realistic and comprehensive philosophy and belie it in practice, in therapy, or teaching or parenthood. Only the one who respects fear and defense can teach; only the one who respects health can do therapy.)

Part of the paradox in this situation is that in a very real way, even the "bad" choice is "good for" the neurotic chooser, or at least understandable and even necessary in terms of his own dynamics. We know that tearing away a functional neurotic symptom by force, or by too direct a confrontation or interpretation, or by a stress situation which cracks the person's defenses against too painful an insight, can shatter the person altogether. This involves us in the question of *pace* of growth. And again the good parent, or therapist or educator *practices* as if he understood that gentleness, sweetness, respect for fear, understanding of the naturalness of defensive and regressive forces, are necessary if growth is not to look like an overwhelming danger instead of a delightful prospect. He implies that he understands that growth can emerge only from safety. He *feels* that if a person's defenses are very rigid this is for a good reason and he is willing to be patient and understanding even though knowing the path in which the child "should" go.

Seen from the dynamic point of view, ultimately *all* choices are in fact wise, if only we grant two kinds of wisdom, defensive-wisdom and growth-wisdom. Defensiveness can be as wise as daring; it depends on the particular person, his particular status and the particular situation in which he has to choose. The choice of safety is wise when it avoids pain that may be more than the person can bear at the moment. If we wish to help him grow (because we know that consistent safety-choices will bring him to catastrophe in the long run, and will cut him off from possibilities that he himself would enjoy if only he could savor them), then all we can do is help him if he asks for help out of suffering, or else simultaneously allow him to feel safe and beckon him onward to *try* the new experience like the mother whose open arms invite the baby to try to walk. We can't *force* him to grow, we can only *coax* him to, make it more possible for him, in the trust that simply experiencing the new experience will make him prefer it. *Only* he can prefer it; no one can prefer it for him. If it is to become part of him, *he* must like

it. If he doesn't, we must gracefully concede that it is not for him at this moment.

This means that the sick child must be respected as much as the healthy one, so far as the growth process is concerned. Only when his fears are accepted respectfully, can he dare to be bold. We must understand that the dark forces are as "normal" as the growth forces.

This is a ticklish task, for it implies simultaneously that we know what is best for him (since we *do* beckon him on in a direction we choose), and also that only he knows what is best for himself in the long run. This means that we must *offer* only, and rarely force. We must be quite ready, not only to beckon forward, but to respect retreat to lick wounds, to recover strength, to look over the situation from a safe vantage point, or even to regress to a previous mastery or a "lower" delight, so that courage for growth can be regained.

And this again is where the helper comes in. He is needed, not only for making possible growth forward in the healthy child (by being "available" as the child desires) and getting out of his way at other times, but much more urgently, by the person who is "stuck" in fixation, in rigid defenses, in safety measures which cut off the possibilities of growth. Neurosis is self-perpetuating; so is character structure. We can either wait for life to prove to such a person that his system doesn't work, i.e., by letting him eventually collapse into neurotic suffering, or else by understanding him and helping him to grow by respecting and understanding both his deficiency needs and his growth needs.

This amounts to a revision of Taoistic "let-be," which often hasn't worked because the growing child needs help. It can be formulated as "helpful let-be." It is a *loving* and *respecting* Taoism. It recognizes not only growth and the specific mechanism which makes it move in the right direction, but it also recognizes and respects the fear of growth, the slow pace of growth, the blocks, the pathology, the reasons for not growing. It recognizes the place, the necessity and the helpfulness of the outer environment without yet giving it control. It implements inner growth by knowing its mechanisms and by being willing to help *it* instead of merely being hopeful or passively optimistic about it.

All the foregoing may now be related to the general motivation theory, set forth in my *Motivation and Personality*, particularly the theory of need gratification, which seems to me to be the most important single principle underlying all healthy human development. The single holistic principle that binds together the multiplicity of human motives is the tendency for a new and higher need to emerge as the lower need fulfills itself by being sufficiently gratified. The child who is fortunate enough to grow normally and well gets satiated and *bored* with the delights that he has savored sufficiently, and *eagerly* (without pushing) goes on to higher more complex, delights as they become available to him without danger or threat.

This principle can be seen exemplified not only in the deeper motivational dynamics of the child but also in microcosm in the development of any of his more modest activities, e.g., in learning to read, or skate, or paint, or dance. The child who masters simple words enjoys them intensely but doesn't stay there. In the proper atmosphere he spontaneously shows eagerness to go on to more and more new words, longer words, more complex sentences, etc. If he is forced to stay at the simple level he gets bored and restless with what formerly delighted him. He *wants* to go on, to move, to grow. Only if frustration, failure, disapproval, ridicule come at the next step does he fixate or regress and we are then faced with the intricacies of pathological dynamics and of neurotic compromises, in which the impulses remain alive but unfulfilled,

or even of loss of impulse and of capacity.[4]

What we wind up with then is a subjective device to add to the principle of the hierarchical arrangement of our various needs, a device which guides and directs the individual in the direction of "healthy" growth. The principle holds true at any age. Recovering the ability to perceive one's own delights is the best way of rediscovering the sacrificed self even in adulthood. The process of therapy helps the adult to discover that the childish (repressed) necessity for the approval of others no longer need exist in the childish form and degree, and that the terror of losing these others with the accompanying fear of being weak, helpless and abandoned is no longer realistic and justified as it was for the child. For the adult, others can be and should be less important than for the child.

---

[4] I think it is possible to apply this general principle to Freudian theory of the progression of libidinal stages. The infant in the oral stage, gets most of his delights through the mouth. And one in particular which has been neglected is that of mastery. We should remember that the *only* thing an infant can do well and efficiently is to suckle. In all else he is inefficient, incapable and if, as I think, this is the earliest precursor of self esteem (feeling of mastery), then this is the *only* way in which the infant can experience the delight of mastery (efficiency, control, self expression, volition.)

But soon he develops other capacities for mastery and control. I mean here not only anal control which though correct, has, in my opinion, been overplayed. Motility and sensory capacities also develop enough during the so-called "anal" stage to give feelings of delight and mastery. But what is important for us here is that the oral infant tends to play out his oral mastery and to become bored with it, just as he becomes bored with milk alone. In a free choice situation, he tends to give up the breast milk in favor of the more complex activities and tastes, or anyway, to add to the breast these other "higher" developments. Given sufficient gratification, free choice and lack of threat, he "grows" out of the oral stage and renounces it himself. He doesn't have to be "kicked upstairs," or forced on to maturity as is so often implied. He *chooses* to grow on to higher delights, to become bored with older ones. Only under the impact of danger, threat, failure, frustration, or stress does he tend to regress or fixate; only then does he prefer safety to growth. Certainly renunciation, delay in gratification and the ability to withstand frustration are also necessary for strength, and we know that unbridled gratification is dangerous. And yet it remains true that these qualifications are *subsidiary* to the principle that sufficient gratification of basic needs is *sine qua non*.

Our final formula then has the following elements:

1. The healthily spontaneous child, in his spontaneity, from within out, in response to his own inner Being, reaches out to the environment in wonder and interest, and expresses whatever skills he has,

2. To the extent that he is not crippled by fear, to the extent that he feels safe enough to dare.

3. In this process, that which gives him delight-experience is fortuitously encountered, or is offered to him by helpers.

4. He must be safe and self-accepting enough to be able to choose and prefer these delights, instead of being frightened by them.

5. If he *can* choose these experiences which are validated by the experience of delight, then he can return to the experience, repeat it, savor it to the point of repletion, satiation or boredom.

6. At this point, he shows the tendency to go on to more complex, richer experiences and accomplishments in the same sector (again, if he feels safe enough to dare.)

7. Such experiences not only mean moving on, but have a feedback effect on the Self, in the feeling of certainty ("This I like; that I don't, for *sure*"); of capability, mastery, self-trust, self-esteem.

8. In this never ending series of choices of which life consists, the choice may generally be schematized as between safety (or, more broadly, defensiveness) and growth, and since only that child doesn't need safety who already has it, we may expect the growth choice to be made by the safety-need gratified child. Only he can afford to be bold.

9. In order to be able to choose in accord with his own nature and to develop it, the child must be permitted to retain the subjective experiences of delight and boredom, as *the* criteria of the correct choice for him. The alternative criterion is making the choice in terms of the wish of another person. The Self is lost when this happens. Also this constitutes restricting the choice to safety alone, since the child will give up trust in his own delight-criterion out of fear (of losing protection, love, etc.).

10. If the choice is really a free one, and if the child is not crippled, then we may expect him ordinarily to choose progression forward.[5]

11. The evidence indicates that what delights the healthy child, what tastes good for him, is also, more frequently than not, "best" for him in terms of far goals as perceivable by the spectator.

12. In this process the environment (parents, therapists, teachers) is important in various ways, even though the ultimate choice must be made by the child:

   a. it can gratify his basic needs for safety, belongingness, love and respect, so that he can feel unthreatened, autonomous, interested and spontaneous and thus dare to choose the unknown;

   b. it can help by making the growth choice positively attractive and less dangerous, and by making the regressive choice less attractive and more costly.

13. In this way the psychology of Being and the psychology of Becoming can be reconciled, and the child, simply being himself, can yet move forward and grow.

---

[5] A kind of pseudo-growth takes place very commonly when the person tries (by repression, denial, reaction-formation, etc.) to convince himself that an ungratified basic need has really been gratified, or doesn't exist. He then permits himself to grow on to higher-need-levels, which of course, forever after, rest on a very shaky foundation. I call this "pseudo-growth by bypassing the ungratified need." Such a need perseverates forever as an unconscious force (repetition compulsion).

Phenomenological Theories:

PATHOLOGICAL PATTERNS

Phenomenological theorists express particular concern that contemporary man is trapped in a mechanistic mass society. Exposure to such an impersonal atmosphere results in feelings of social isolation and a sense of alienation from one's "true" self. Without a sure grasp of self, the individual lacks an identity, and cannot experience what is termed "being in the world." Unable to sense his own inner world, he cannot sense the inner world of others, and without meaningful social relationships, cannot break the vicious circle to expand experience and develop a sense of identity. Eventually, he may succumb to "nothingness" and disorder.

Arthur Combs has been a leading exponent of the phenomenological approach to the study of personality. In the article reprinted here, he applies the phenomenological rationale to the problems of adjustment and mental disorder. To him, it is more fruitful to approach disorders in terms of the patient's personal experiences than in terms of abstract theoretical concepts and psychiatric categories. The paper by R. D. Laing, a British existential psychiatrist, illuminates the nature of these personal experiences of isolation and anxiety. Beneath the sense of social loneliness lies a deep and profound alienation from one's self.

A Phenomenological Approach to Adjustment Theory

ARTHUR W. COMBS

To state that personality theory and the practice of psychotherapy should be closely interwoven seems obvious. Yet, amazingly enough, until recent years we have behaved almost as though this conspicuous relationship did not exist. In the past there has been some justification for this separation. For, on the one hand, traditional normative personality theory contributed little that was very helpful to the psychotherapist in dealing

From *J. Abnormal & Social Psychol.* 44:29-35, 1949, by permission of the American Psychological Association and the author.

with his unique client. On the other hand, the psychotherapists were so busy developing and comparing methods that they were blind to the importance of sound personality theory. But all this is changing. We seem now to be developing a new group of theorists who are therapists, and therapists who are theorists, which promises much for both theory and practice. We are discovering now that the microcosm of therapy can both stimulate and test the concepts of theory (10). At the same time we are beginning to understand that effective methods of therapy must find their justification in accurate and consistent personality theory.

In this paper I should like to add what impetus I can to the movement by developing more fully several concepts of personality organization discussed in separate papers by Rogers (10) and by Combs (3) at the 1947 meetings of the American Psychological Association. In particular, I should like to explore the concepts of adjustment and maladjustment as these appear from a phenomenological point of view. The position I have taken grows out of a dual interest in personality theory and the practice of therapy and seems to me to have implications for both fields of psychology. It is based upon a number of concepts and principles already widely held in many areas of psychological thought and represents an attempt to integrate these in a consistent organization.

TWO FRAMES OF REFERENCE FOR OBSERVING BEHAVIOR

There seem to be two possible frames of reference from which we can examine the problem of adjustment. The first we might call the external or objective approach and the second, the *personal* or *phenomenological* point of view.

1. The *external* or *objective* frame of reference is the traditional method of psychology. In this approach we attempt to observe the behavior of adjusted or maladjusted individuals from the viewpoint of an outside observer. When we make our observations in this way we usually arrive at either of two positions: (*a*) We describe the individual's behavior in normative or statistical terms in which people who conform to social expectancies are described as normal while those who do not are considered to be maladjusted. Or (*b*), examining behavior more closely, we describe adjustment as a frustration when confronted with a barrier to need satis-

faction. Both descriptions have been useful but have also had serious limitations when applied to the practical problems of therapy. The normative position has little to offer the psychotherapist, who must deal with clients just as apt to be the exception as the rule. The frustration concept also does not help us very much, for it describes *all* behavior in these terms and does not help us to understand the unique character of maladjustment in terms of which an adequate therapy must be developed.

2. The second frame of reference from which we may observe the dynamics of adjustment is from the point of view of the individual himself. This approach has been called by Rogers (10), in connection with therapy, *"the client-centered approach,"* and by Snygg and Combs (11), in a more general sense, *"the phenomenological frame of reference."* In this frame of reference we are concerned with the client's perceptions of himself and his environment rather than the way in which things appear to an outside observer. When we examine adjustment and maladjustment in this way, we arrive at a very different concept of adjustment and one that seems to offer a more adequate guide to the practical problems of therapy. In this paper let us examine the dynamics of adjustment as they seem to appear from the subject's own viewpoint.

MALADJUSTMENT AS A FUNCTION OF PERCEIVED THREAT

The most universally described characteristic of maladjustment from an external point of view is the tension under which "maladjusted" people appear to be operating. In fact the term "tension states" is often used almost synonymously with maladjustment. Tension states, however, are mere descriptions of the client's condition and are not adequate for the construction of therapy. Tension, itself, is caused and it is necessary for us to understand how such conditions come about.

When we examine these tensions through the client's own eyes, they appear to be produced by the individual's perception of threat to his self. The presence of threatening perceptions seems to force upon the individual an emergency situation which must be dealt with. His body responds to this emergency by going on what Cannon (2) has called a "war footing" and produces the tension states characteristic of maladjustment. This effect of threatening perceptions is well known to all of us. We can observe it in our own reactions to things which worry or concern us and we can observe it in the reactions of others when they feel afraid or angry. As psychologists, we even make practical use of this principle in our experiments with "lie detection." It would thus appear from a phenomenological point of view that a maladjusted personality is equivalent to a threatened one. Conversely, a well-adjusted personality seems to be one unthreatened by its perceptions.

Describing maladjustment as a function of the perception of threat, however, is not enough. We need to know specifically what it is that is threatened. We have described threat to this point as a threat to self. Yet, when we observe the behavior of individuals from their own point of view, it does not seem to be their physical selves, alone, which they are attempting to preserve. For the most part, threats to our physical selves are seldom of long duration in our society and most of us have learned to deal with them smoothly and effectively. The more serious and long-lasting threats which we experience seem to arise out of social and personal situations that threaten, not our physical selves, but our perceptions of ourselves. Most of our perceptions of threat appear to occur when we are faced with humiliation, the loss of love or prestige, or from a thousand other threats to the way we see ourselves.

THE CONCEPT OF SELF IN ADJUSTMENT

This perceived self Raimy (9) has defined as a complex organization of perceptions about self made up of many perceptions of greater or lesser degree of importance to the individual and defining his relationships to the world as he sees it. Many psychologists have come to feel that the concept of self gives consistency to behavior and lies at the very core of personality (6, 7, 10). A great deal, if not all, of our behavior appears to be governed by our self-concepts in the myriad life-situations in which we find ourselves. In my own case, for example, when I see myself as a professor, I behave in ways appropriate to my concept of what a professor should be like. At other times I behave in terms of my concept of myself as a parent, as a husband, as a host, as a cigarette smoker, or as a man who enjoys reading "lil Abner," to name but a few of the many concepts I have of myself. Not all of these concepts will be of equal importance in the total organization of my self-concept but all are aspects in terms of which I behave at one time or another.

This principle of the determining effect of the self-concept upon behavior has been demonstrated experimentally in many studies. Piaget (8), for example, has shown how the child's concept of himself selects his perceptions in conformity with the self-concept held. The same phenomenon has been demonstrated by Frenkel-Brunswik (4) with young adults and in a fascinating experiment by Bruner and Goodman (1) showing differences in children's perception of coin sizes.

THE CENTRAL CHARACTER OF THE SELF-CONCEPT IN THE INDIVIDUAL ECONOMY

In the personal economy of any individual, the concept of self seems to represent the individual's guide to every behavior. Its development is the result of long and arduous experience and stands, at any moment, as the individual's personal frame of reference. Indeed, it is himself from his own point of view. To the individual the concept of self seems a very precious thing to be maintained or enhanced at all costs. As Gardner Murphy (7) has expressed it: "This cherished possession must forever be made more adequate, more worthy; and it must forever be defended against stain and injury whether from the acts of others or of the . . . organism (itself)." Snygg and Combs (11) have suggested that the need to maintain and enhance the concept of self is, in fact, the basic human need.

In terms of this analysis, it seems to be the self-concept which the individual perceives to be threatened rather than his self as he appears to others. Almost any psychotherapist has among his clients many individuals who from an external point of view seem to be living satisfactory lives. There may even be some who feel a need of therapy themselves, although, they are described by other people as "remarkably well adjusted" and may, even, be pointed out to our youth as notable examples, worthy of emulation. Yet these same persons often reveal themselves in the therapy sessions to be deeply threatened and unhappy. It matters very little what things look like to others. The crucial factor is the individual's own perception of threat to his concept of self. Knowing that other people think he is unthreatened does not produce less threat for the individual. It merely proves how little other people really understand him!

SOME IMPLICATIONS OF THE PERCEPTIVE VIEW OF BEHAVIOR FOR THERAPY

If the client comes to the therapist believing he is being picked on by his boss, this perception of self in relation to his world must be the subject of therapy. Whether the client is *really* being picked on, as others may see it, is unimportant insofar as that individual is concerned.[1] Indeed, it is even possible that, if the therapist makes an investigation and discovers that the objective facts in the case are that the boss is *not* picking on his client, he may end by convincing his client that the therapist has joined the boss in the "picking on" process.

If it is true that human behavior is a function of the individual's perceptions, then it seems necessary to change our concept of therapy. Therapy in the light of this theoretical position becomes a technique for changing perception, rather than a way of changing the client's behavior. Since perceptions lie within the client and are not open to direct manipulation, the therapist cannot change behavior directly. He can only create a situation in which the client can change himself. The task of therapy thus becomes, not so much one of *changing the client's behavior*, as one of *creating a situation in which change in perception is facilitated and encouraged*. This will be true whether we are speaking of individual or environmental treatment, whether we attempt to induce some specific and predetermined change in perception, or whether we are content to let the client choose his own direction of change.

To construct such a therapy it will be necessary for us to understand thoroughly the dynamics of change in perception, and that is a job for personality theory. If we can develop a satisfactory understanding of these dynamics the development of therapeutic techniques for its best implementation should quickly become clear to us. Without such an understanding, it seems likely we shall remain mired in the confusion of methodologies in which we now find ourselves. The fundamental question in the construction of any therapeutic method is, not "what method shall I

---

[1] It is not unimportant, of course, from a social point of view.

use?" but; "what are the dynamics of behavior?" If we can answer the latter question, methods should easily follow.

THE CONCEPT OF THE
ADEQUATE SELF

Up to this point I have described maladjustment as a function of perceived threat to the self. We have not yet, however, examined why, and under what conditions, the self is perceived as threatened. From our observations of behavior, both in and out of therapy, the experience of threat seems to be at a minimum when the concept of self is perceived as being adequate to deal with the perception of events. For example, the person who sees himself as a successful public speaker feels unthreatened by the necessity for making a speech. Indeed, he may even feel enhanced by an invitation to appear before an audience. Feeling adequate to his task, he can accept his perceptions into his organization and feels unthreatened by them. He operates smoothly and effectively and with a minimum of tension. Rogers (10) has described the results of this feeling of adequacy as follows:

It would appear that when all of the ways in which the individual perceives himself—all perceptions of the qualities, abilities, impulses and attitudes of the person and all perceptions of himself in relation to others —are accepted into the organized conscious concept of self, then this achievement is accompanied by feelings of comfort and freedom from tension which are experienced as psychological adjustment.

The person with an inadequate self-definition, however, finds himself in a very different position. Feeling inadequate to deal effectively with his perceptions, he is more or less seriously threatened by them. The person who feels himself inadequate or unable to speak in public finds his perception of the necessity for making a speech a threatening and disturbing experience. He feels more and more threatened as the time for action approaches. This is an experi-ence common to many of us who at one time or another have suffered from stage fright. The experience of threat appears to be the result of a self-concept inadequate to cope with the perception. What is more, the threat continues so long as the self is defined as inadequate to cope with the perception or the perception remains in the field.

Since the individual is always under the necessity for maintaining and enhancing the self-concept, perceptions which threaten the self cannot be accepted into the personal organization. Unfortunately, this failure to accept a perception does not eliminate the threat. It continues the threat, for the individual will feel threatened so long as the perception remains in figure and the self is defined in a manner inadequate to cope with it. The mother who feels inadequate to handle her child, for example, remains threatened by the perception of her child whether the youngster is present in the flesh or not. Until either the child is removed or the mother defines herself as adequate to cope with her responsibility she will continue to feel threatened and disturbed.

It follows from this discussion that therapy may attempt to produce change in the perception of self, or the perception of external events, or both. It will often be possible to change the perception of external events by changing the client's environment and may even be possible to induce changes in the concept of self by environmental treatment. But the possibilities of environmental treatment will often be drastically restricted, for there are limits to the degree to which we can change our society for a single individual. More often than not, it will be necessary for us to find ways of aiding threatened individuals to develop more adequate concepts of self. If we could do this well, it is even possible that environmental treatment, in many cases, would be unnecessary.

The development of an adequate concept of self, however, is greatly complicated by the selective effect upon perceptions that any concept of self exerts. We have already observed in the studies of Bruner (1) and others that the concepts of self we hold tend to select perceptions in terms of existing self-definitions. This effect is true of inadequate perceptions of self as well. Seeing himself inadequately, the individual selects his perceptions in terms of his self-definitions and so perpetuates his errors of perception. The child who feels he is rejected is likely to see his parents' slightest reprimand as proof of what he already thinks—that his parents don't love him. In the same way, the housewife who feels inadequate in giving a tea is likely to be far more engrossed with her own social errors than with the fact that the affair was generally successful. An inadequate perception of self tends to select its perceptions in such a way as to conform with its definition and makes new perceptions of self more difficult to achieve.

THE EFFECTS OF THREAT UPON PERCEPTION

To assist clients to the development of a more adequate concept of self it will be necessary for us to discover ways of freeing the client to make new perceptions of self more adequate than those he has previously held. Unfortunately, the very existence of threat in the perceptive field seems to have effects which complicate and obstruct change in perception. For successful therapy, it will be necessary to develop methods by which these effects can be eliminated or reduced.

If the maintenance and enhancement of the self-concept is as important in the dynamics of behavior as Snygg and Combs (11) have suggested, it follows that any threat to this concept must be resisted by the client. A self under threat has no choice but to defend itself. It is a common saying that "nobody ever wins an argument." In fact, the more strongly we are threatened, the more

we seem driven to defend ourselves and the positions we have taken. This leaves us with a fine dilemma in therapy. We have theorized that an inadequate self is threatened, and the perception of threat forces the self to maintain its position. Clearly, so long as the individual is under the necessity for defending himself, the self-concept is not likely to change. Yet, therapy, to be successful, must result in change in the concept of self, not in the maintenance of the status quo.

It appears that, in order to break into this vicious circle, it will be necessary somehow to shield the client from threat. This seems to be the major principle upon which nondirective therapy depends in its attempt to create a warm, permissive, accepting atmosphere for the client. The transference phenomenon of psychoanalysis also appears to have this effect at least in part. It also seems to be true of other forms of therapy which shelter the client from threat, such as play therapy, some forms of group therapy, and, in a more limited way, some types of environmental treatment like foster-home placement. By shielding the client from threat in the therapeutic relationship these therapies seem to make it possible for the client to arrive at new self-perceptions. It would appear that absolute respect for the integrity of the client is not only a fine democratic principle but just good business in therapy. If this theoretical position is sound, it also raises grave doubts about the effects of certain types of highly traumatic therapies. If our argument that threat forces the self to defend itself is accurate, it is conceivable that traumatic therapies may even result in driving some clients deeper into their maladjustments.

A second result of threat to the self is its restrictive effect upon the field of perceptions. This is a common phenomenon often observed in work on emotion and has been given the name "tunnel vision." It is also familiar to most of us in our daily lives. When we feel threatened, the field of our perceptions is greatly narrowed to the vicinity of the perceptions which appear threatening to us. For example, in a situation where we are frightened or angry, our perceptions are narrowed to the immediate field of the threatening object and we may be totally unaware of other factors in the situation to which we would normally have attended. It is a common observation in therapy too, that clients who have seriously threatening problems are deeply engrossed in these matters. And no wonder. A threat to self is no laughing matter. It cannot be shrugged off. It must be attended to. In this sense it is understandable that maladjusted persons should be egocentric. This restrictive effect of threat upon perceptions appears to be responsible for much of the perseverative character of maladjusted behavior.

In a restricted perceptive field the number of possibilities for new perceptions is sharply delimited. Yet this restrictive effect of threat upon perception is exactly the opposite of what we desire for therapy. In therapy we want to help our clients to explore freely a wide variety of perceptions from which they may discover better and more satisfying ways of behaving. Anything which prevents such exploration is contrary to the goal of therapy. For effective therapy we must find ways of freeing the individual from threat so that free exploration of the field is possible. To make this possible it will be necessary to understand the dynamics of threat and to discover ways of controlling the effects of threat in the therapeutic process.

In this paper I have attempted to outline some of the dynamics of adjustment and maladjustment as these appear from a phenomenological frame of reference. While this approach represents a considerable departure from traditional concepts of adjustment, it is often true that new frames of reference provide new perspective upon old problems. Parts of this theoretical position have already been corroborated by research. Others remain to be demonstrated. In the final analysis, such hypotheses as I have presented here must stand the test of experimental demonstration, theoretical consistency, and demonstration in the practical test of therapy.

References

1. Bruner, J. S., and Goodman, C. C. Value and need as organizing factors in perception. This *Journal*, 1947, 42, 33-44.
2. Cannon, W. B. *The wisdom of the body.* New York: Norton, 1932.
3. Combs, A. W. Phenomenological concepts in non-directive therapy. *J. consult. Psychol.* August, 1948.
4. Frenkel-Brunswik, E. Mechanisms of self deception. *J. soc. Psychol.*, 1939, 10, 409-420.
5. Kelley, E. *Education for what is real.* New York: Harper, 1948.
6. Lecky, L. *Self consistency.* New York: Island Press, 1945.
7. Murphy, G. *Personality: A biosocial approach to origins and structure.* New York: Harper, 1947.
8. Piaget, J. *The child's conception of the world.* New York: Harcourt, Brace, 1929.
9. Raimy, V. C. The self concept as a factor in counseling and personality organization. Unpublished doctoral thesis, Ohio State University, 1943.
10. Rogers, C. R. The organization of personality. *Amer. Psychologist*, 1947, 2, 358-368.
11. Snygg, D., and Combs, A. W. *Individual behavior: A new frame of reference for psychology.* New York: Harper (in press).

Ontological Insecurity

R. D. LAING

A man may have a sense of his presence in the world as a real, alive, whole, and, in a temporal sense, continuous person. As such, he can live out into the world and meet others: a world and others experienced as equally real, alive, whole, and continuous.

Such a basically *ontologically*[1] secure person will encounter all the hazards of life, social, ethical, spiritual, biological, from a centrally firm sense of his own and other people's reality and identity. It is often difficult for a person with such a sense of his integral selfhood and personal identity, of the permanency of things, of the reliability of natural processes, of the substantiality of natural processes, of the substantiality of others, to transpose himself into the world of an individual whose experiences may be utterly lacking in any unquestionable self-validating certainties.

This study is concerned with the issues involved where there is the partial or almost complete absence of the assurances derived from an existential position of what I shall call *primary ontological security*: with anxieties and dangers that I shall suggest arise *only* in terms of *primary ontological insecurity*; and with the consequent attempts to deal with such anxieties and dangers.

The literary critic, Lionel Trilling (1955), points up the contrast that I wish to make between a *basic existential position of ontological security* and one of *ontological insecurity* very clearly in comparing the worlds of Shakespeare and Keats on the one hand, and of Kafka on the other:

> . . . for Keats the awareness of evil exists side by side with a very strong sense of personal identity and is for that reason the less immediately apparent. To some contemporary readers, it will seem for the same reason the less intense. In the same way it may seem to a contemporary reader that, if we compare Shakespeare and Kafka, leaving aside the degree of genius each has, and considering both only as expositors of man's suffering and cosmic alienation, it is Kafka who makes the more intense and complete exposition. And, indeed, the judgment may be correct, exactly because for Kafka the sense of evil is not contradicted by the sense of personal identity. Shakespeare's world, quite as much as Kafka's, is that prison cell which Pascal says the world is, from which daily the inmates are led forth to die; Shakespeare no less than Kafka forces upon us the cruel irrationality of the conditions of human life, the tale told by an idiot, the puerile gods who torture us not for punishment but for sport; and no less than Kafka, Shakespeare is revolted by the fetor of the prison of this world, nothing is more characteristic of him than his imagery of disgust. But in Shakespeare's cell the company is so much better than in Kafka's, the captains and kings and lovers and clowns of Shakespeare are alive and complete before they die. In Kafka, long before the sentence is executed, even long before the malign legal process is even instituted, something terrible has been done to the accused. We all know what that is—he has been stripped of all that is becoming to a man except his abstract humanity, which, like his skeleton, never is quite becoming to a man. He is without parents, home, wife, child, commitment, or appetite; he has no connection with power, beauty, love, wit, courage, loyalty, or fame, and the pride that may be taken in these. So that we may say that Kafka's knowledge of evil exists without the contradictory knowledge of the self in its health and validity, that Shakespeare's knowledge of evil exists with that contradiction in its fullest possible force (pp. 38-9).

We find, as Trilling points out, that Shakespeare does depict characters who evidently experience themselves as real and alive and complete however riddled by doubts or torn by conflicts they may be. With Kafka

---

From *The Divided Self*, chapter 3, copyright 1960, by permission of the author, Penguin Books and Tavistock Publications, Limited.

[1] Despite the philosophical use of "ontology" (by Heidegger, Sartre, Tillich, especially), I have used the term in its present empirical sense because it appears to be the best adverbial or adjectival derivative of "being."

this is not so. Indeed, the effort to communicate what being alive is like in the absence of such assurances seems to characterize the work of a number of writers and artists of our time. Life, without feeling alive.

With Samuel Beckett, for instance, one enters a world in which there is no contradictory sense of the self in its "health and validity" to mitigate the despair, terror, and boredom of existence. In such a way, the two tramps who wait for Godot are condemned to live:

> ESTRAGON: We always find something, eh, Didi, to give us the impression that we exist?
> VLADIMIR (impatiently): Yes, yes, we're magicians. But let us persevere in what we have resolved, before we forget.

In painting, Francis Bacon, among others, seems to be dealing with similar issues. Generally, it is evident that what we shall discuss here clinically is but a small sample of something in which human nature is deeply implicated and to which we can contribute only a very partial understanding.

To begin at the beginning:

Biological birth is a definitive act whereby the infant organism is precipitated into the world. There it is, a new baby, a new biological entity, already with its own ways, real and alive, from *our* point of view. But what of the baby's point of view? Under usual circumstances, the physical birth of a new living organism into the world inaugurates rapidly ongoing processes whereby within an amazingly short time the infant *feels* real and alive and has a *sense* of being an entity, with continuity in time and a location in space. In short, physical birth and biological aliveness are followed by the baby becoming existentially born as real and alive. Usually this development is taken for granted and affords the certainty upon which all other certainties depend. This is to say, not only do adults see children to be real biologically visible entities but they experience themselves as whole persons who are real and alive, and conjunctively experience other human beings as real and alive. These are self-validating data of experience.

The individual, then, may experience his own being as real, alive, whole; as differentiated from the rest of the world in ordinary circumstances so clearly that his identity and autonomy are never in question; as a continuum in time; as having an inner consistency, substantiality, genuineness, and worth; as spatially co-extensive with the body; and, usually, as having begun in or around birth and liable to extinction with death. He thus has a firm core of ontological security.

This, however, may not be the case. The individual in the ordinary circumstances of living may feel more unreal than real; in a literal sense, more dead than alive; precariously differentiated from the rest of the world, so that his identity and autonomy are always in question. He may lack the experience of his own temporal continuity. He may not possess an over-riding sense of personal consistency or cohesiveness. He may feel more insubstantial than substantial, and unable to assume that the stuff he is made of is genuine, good, valuable. And he may feel his self as partially divorced from his body.

It is, of course, inevitable that an individual whose experience of himself is of this order can no more live in a "secure" world than he can be secure "in himself." The whole "physiognomy" of his world will be correspondingly different from that of the individual whose sense of self is securely established in its health and validity. Relatedness to other persons will be seen to have a radically different significance and function. To anticipate, we can say that in the individual whose own being is secure in this primary experiential sense, relatedness with others is potentially gratifying; whereas the ontologically insecure person is preoccupied with himself: the ordinary circumstances of living threaten his *low threshold* of security.[2]

If a position of primary ontological security has been reached, the ordinary circumstances of life do not afford a perpetual threat to one's own existence. If such a basis for living has not been reached, the ordinary circumstances of everyday life constitute a continual and deadly threat.

Only if this is realized is it possible to understand how certain psychoses can develop.

If the individual cannot take the realness, aliveness, autonomy, and identity of himself and others for granted, then he has to become absorbed in contriving ways of trying to be real, of keeping himself or others alive, of preserving his identity, in efforts, as he will often put it, to prevent himself losing his self. What are to most people everyday happenings, which are hardly noticed because they have no special significance, may become deeply significant in so far as they either contribute to the sustenance of the individual's being or threaten him with non-being. Such an individual, for whom the elements of the world are coming to have, or have come to have, a different hierarchy of significance from that of the ordinary person, is beginning, as we say, to "live in a world of his own," or has already come to do so. It is not true to say, however, without careful qualification that he is losing "contact with" reality, and withdrawing into himself. External events no longer affect him in the same way as they do others: it is not that they affect him less; on the contrary, frequently they affect him more. It is frequently not the case that he is becoming "indifferent" and "withdrawn." It may, however, be that the world of his experience comes to be one he can no longer share with other people.

But before these developments are explored, it will be valuable to characterize under three headings three forms of anxiety encountered by the ontologically insecure person: engulfment, implosion, petrification.

ENGULFMENT

An argument occurred between two patients in the course of a session in an analytic group. Suddenly, one of the protagonists broke off the argument to say, "I can't go on. You are arguing in order to have the pleasure of triumphing over me. At best you win an argument. At worst you lose an argument. *I am arguing in order to preserve my existence.*"

This patient was a young man who I would say was sane, but, as he stated, his activity in the argument, as in the rest of his life, was not designed to gain gratification but to "preserve his existence." Now, one might say that if he did, in fact, really imagine the loss of an argument would jeopardize his existence, then he was "grossly out of touch with reality" and was virtually psychotic. But this is simply to beg the question without making any contribution towards understanding the patient. It is, however, important to know that if you were to subject this patient to a type of psychiatric interrogation recommended in many psychiatric textbooks, within ten minutes his behaviour and speech would be revealing "signs" of psychosis. It is quite easy to evoke such "signs" from such a person whose threshold of basic security is so low that practically any relationship with another person, however tenuous or however apparently "harmless," threatens to overwhelm him.

A firm sense of one's own autonomous identity is required in order that one may be related as one human being to another. Otherwise, any and every relationship threatens the individual with loss of identity. One form this takes can be called engulfment. In this the individual dreads relatedness as such, with anyone or anything or, indeed, even with himself, because

---

[2] This formulation is very similar to those of H. S. Sullivan, Hill, F. Fromm-Reichmann, and Arieti in particular. Federn, although expressing himself very differently, seems to have advanced a closely allied view.

his uncertainty about the stability of his autonomy lays him open to the dread lest in any relationship he will lose his autonomy and identity. Engulfment is not simply envisaged as something that is liable to happen willy-nilly despite the individual's most active efforts to avoid it. The individual experiences himself as a man who is only saving himself from drowning by the most constant, strenuous, desperate activity. Engulfment is felt as a risk in being understood (thus grasped, comprehended), in being loved, or even simply in being seen. To be hated may be feared for other reasons, but to be hated as such is often less disturbing than to be destroyed, as it is felt, through being engulfed by love.

The main manœuvre used to preserve identity under pressure from the dread of engulfment is isolation. Thus, instead of the polarities of separateness and relatedness based on individual autonomy, there is the antithesis between complete loss of being by absorption into the other person (engulfment), and complete aloneness (isolation). There is no safe third possibility of a dialectical relationship between two persons, both sure of their own ground and, on this very basis, able to "lose themselves" in each other. Such merging of being can occur in an "authentic" way only when the individuals are sure of themselves. If a man hates himself, he may wish to lose himself in the other: then being engulfed by the other is an escape from himself. In the present case it is an ever-present possibility to be dreaded. It will be shown later, however, that what at one "moment" is most dreaded and strenuously avoided can change to what is most sought.

This anxiety accounts for one form of a so-called "negative therapeutic reaction" to apparently correct interpretation in psychotherapy. To be understood correctly is to be engulfed, to be enclosed, swallowed up, drowned, eaten up, smothered, stifled in or by another person's supposed all-embracing comprehension. It is lonely and painful to be always misunderstood, but there is at least from this point of view a measure of safety in isolation.

The other's love is, therefore, feared more than his hatred, or rather all love is sensed as a version of hatred. By being loved one is placed under an unsolicited obligation. In therapy with such a person, the last thing there is any point in is to pretend to more "love" or "concern" than one has. The more the therapist's own necessarily very complex motives for trying to "help" a person of this kind genuinely converge on a concern for him which is prepared to "let him be" and is not *in fact* engulfing or merely indifference, the more hope there will be in the horizon.

There are many images used to describe related ways in which identity is threatened which may be mentioned here, as closely related to the dread of engulfment, e.g., being buried, being drowned, being caught and dragged down into quicksand. The image of fire recurs repeatedly. Fire may be the uncertain flickering of the individual's own inner aliveness. It may be a destructive alien power which will devastate him. Some psychotics say in the acute phase that they are on fire, that their bodies are being burned up. A patient describes himself as cold and dry. Yet he dreads any warmth or wet. He will be engulfed by the fire or the water, and either way be destroyed.

IMPLOSION

This is the strongest word I can find for the extreme form of what Winnicott terms the *impingement* of reality. Impingement does not convey, however, the full terror of the experience of the world as liable at any moment to crash in and obliterate all identity, as a gas will rush in and obliterate a vacuum. The individual feels that, like the vacuum, he is empty. But this emptiness is him. Although in other ways he longs for the emptiness to be filled, he dreads the possibility of this happening because he has come to feel that all he can be is the awful nothingness of just this very vacuum. Any "contact" with reality is then in itself experienced as a dreadful threat because reality, as experienced from this position, is necessarily *implosive* and thus, as was relatedness in engulfment, *in itself* a threat to what identity the individual is able to suppose himself to have.

Reality, as such, threatening engulfment or implosion, is the persecutor.

In fact, we are all only two or three degrees Fahrenheit from experiences of this order. Even a slight fever, and the whole world can begin to take on a persecutory, impinging aspect.

PETRIFICATION AND DEPERSONALIZATION

In using the term "petrification," one can exploit a number of the meanings embedded in this word:

1. A particular form of terror, whereby one is petrified, i.e., turned to stone.
2. The dread of this happening: the dread, that is, of the possibility of turning, or being turned, from a live person into a dead thing, into a stone, into a robot, an automaton, without personal autonomy of action, an *it* without subjectivity.
3. The "magical" act whereby one may attempt to turn someone else into stone, by "petrifying" him; and, by extension, the act whereby one negates the other person's autonomy, ignores his feelings, regards him as a thing, kills the life in him. In this sense one may perhaps better say that one depersonalizes him, or reifies him. One treats him not as a person, as a free agent, but as an *it*.

Depersonalization is a technique that is universally used as a means of dealing with the other when he becomes too tiresome or disturbing. One no longer allows oneself to be responsive to his feelings and may be prepared to regard him and treat him as though he had no feelings. The people in focus here both tend to feel themselves as more or less depersonalized and tend to depersonalize others; they are constantly afraid of being depersonalized by others. The act of turning him into a thing is, *for him,* actually petrifying. In the face of being treated as an *it,* his own subjectivity drains away from him like blood from the face. Basically he requires constant confirmation from others of his own existence as a person.

A partial depersonalization of others is extensively practised in everyday life and is regarded as normal if not highly desirable. Most relationships are based on some partial depersonalizing tendency in so far as one treats the other not in terms of any awareness of who or what he might be in himself but as virtually an android robot playing a role or part in a large machine in which one too may be acting yet another part.

It is usual to cherish if not the reality, at least the illusion that there is a limited sphere of living free from this dehumanization. Yet it may be in just this sphere that the greater risk is felt, and the ontologically insecure person experiences this risk in highly potentiated form.

The risk consists in this: if one experiences the other as a free agent, one is open to the possibility of experiencing oneself as an *object* of his experience and thereby of feeling one's own subjectivity drained away. One is threatened with the possibility of becoming no more than a thing in the world of the other, without any life for oneself, without any being for oneself. In terms of such anxiety, the very act of experiencing the other as a person is felt as virtually suicidal. Sartre discusses this experience brilliantly in Part 3 of *Being and Nothingness.*

The issue is in principle straightforward. One may find oneself enlivened and the sense of one's own being enhanced by the other, or one may experience the other as deadening and impoverishing. A person may have come to anticipate that any possible relationship with another will have the latter consequences. Any other is then a threat to his "self" (his capacity to act autonomously) not by reason of anything he or she may do or not do specifically, but by reason of his or her very existence.

Some of the above points are illustrated in the life of James, a chemist, aged twenty-eight.

The complaint he made all along was that he could not become a "person." He had "no self." "I am only a response to other people, I have no identity of my own." He felt he was becoming more and more "a mythical person." He felt he had no weight, no substance of his own. "I am only a cork floating on the ocean."

This man was very concerned about not having become a person: he reproached his mother for this failure. "I was merely her emblem. She never recognized my identity." In contrast to his own belittlement of and uncertainty about himself, he was always on the brink of being overawed and crushed by the formidable reality that other people contained. In contrast to his own light weight, uncertainty, and insubstantiality, *they* were solid, decisive, emphatic, and substantial. He felt that in every way that mattered others were more "large scale" than he was.

At the same time, in practice he was not easily overawed. He used two chief manœuvres to preserve security. One was an outward compliance with the other. The second was an inner intellectual Medusa's head he turned on the other. Both manœuvres taken together safeguarded his own subjectivity which he had never to betray openly and which thus could never find direct and immediate expression for itself. Being secret, it was safe. Both techniques together were designed to avoid the dangers of being engulfed or depersonalized.

With his outer behaviour he forestalled the danger to which he was perpetually subject, namely that of becoming someone else's *thing*, by pretending to be no more than a cork. (After all, what safer thing to be in an ocean?) At the same time, however, he turned the other person into a thing in his own eyes, thus magically nullifying any danger to himself by secretly totally disarming the enemy. By destroying, in his own eyes, the other person as a person, he robbed the other of his power to crush him. By depleting him of his personal aliveness, that is, by seeing him as a piece of machinery rather than as a human being, he undercut the risk to himself of this aliveness either swamping him, imploding into his own emptiness, or turning him into a mere appendage.

This man was married to a very lively and vivacious woman, highly spirited, with a forceful personality and a mind of her own. He maintained a paradoxical relationship with her in which, in one sense, he was entirely alone and isolated and, in another sense, he was almost a parasite. He dreamt, for instance, that he was a clam stuck to his wife's body.

Just because he could dream thus, he had the more need to keep her at bay by contriving to see her as no more than a machine. He described her laughter, her anger, her sadness, with "clinical" precision, even going so far as to refer to her as "it," a practice that was rather chilling in its effect. "It then started to laugh." She was an "it" because everything she did was a predictable, determined response. He would, for instance, tell her (it) an ordinary funny joke and when she (it) laughed this indicated her (its) entirely "conditioned," robot-like nature, which he saw indeed in much the same terms as certain psychiatric theories would use to account for all human actions.

I was at first agreeably surprised by his apparent ability to reject and disagree with what I said as well as to agree with me. This seemed to indicate that he had more of a mind of his own then he perhaps realized and that he was not too frightened to display some measure of autonomy. However, it became evident that his apparent capacity to act as an autonomous person with me was due to his secret manœuvre of regarding me not as a live human being, a person in my own right with my own selfhood, but as a sort of robot interpreting device to which he fed input and which after a quick commutation came out with a verbal message to him. With this secret outlook on me as a thing he could appear to be a "person." What he could not sustain was a person-to-person relationship, experienced as such.

Dreams in which one or other of the above forms of dread is expressed are common in such persons. These dreams are not variations on the fears of being eaten which occur in ontologically secure persons. To be eaten does not necessarily mean to lose one's identity. Jonah was very much himself even within the belly of the whale. Few nightmares go so far as to call up anxieties about actual loss of identity, usually because most people, even in their dreams, still meet whatever dangers are to be encountered as persons who may perhaps be attacked or mutilated but whose basic existential core is not itself in jeopardy. In the classical nightmare the dreamer wakes up in terror. But this terror is not the dread of losing the "self." Thus a patient dreams of a fat pig which sits on his chest and threatens to suffocate him. He wakes in terror. At worst, in this nightmare, he is threatened with suffocation, but not with the dissolution of his very being.

The defensive method of turning the threatening mother- or breast-figure into a *thing* occurs in patients' dreams. One patient dreamt recurrently of a small black triangle which originated in a corner of his room and grew larger and larger until it seemed about to engulf him—whereupon he always awoke in great terror. This was a psychotic young man who stayed with my family for several months, and whom I was thus able to get to know rather well. There was only one situation as far as I could judge in which he could let himself "go" without anxiety at not recovering himself again, and that was in listening to jazz.

The fact that even in a dream the breast-figure has to be so depersonalized is a measure of its potential danger to the self, presumably on the basis of its frightening original personalizations and the failure of *a normal process of depersonalization.*

Medard Boss (1957a) gives examples of several dreams heralding psychosis. In one, the dreamer is engulfed by fire:

A woman of hardly thirty years dreamt, at a time when she still felt completely healthy, that she was afire in the stables. Around her, the fire, an ever larger crust of lava was forming. Half from the outside and half from the inside her own body she could see how the fire was slowly becoming choked by this crust. Suddenly she was entirely outside this fire and, as if possessed, she beat the fire with a club to break the crust and to let some air in. But the dreamer soon got tired and slowly she (the fire) became extinguished. Four days after this dream she began to suffer from acute schizophrenia. In the details of the dream the dreamer had exactly predicted the special course of her psychosis. She became rigid at first and, in effect, encysted. Six weeks afterwards she defended herself once more with all her might against the choking of her life's fire, until finally she became completely extinguished both spiritually and mentally. Now, for some years, she has been like a burnt-out crater (p. 162).

In another example, petrification of others occurs, anticipating the dreamer's own petrification:

. . . a girl of twenty-five years dreamt that she had cooked dinner for her family of five. She had just served it and she now called her parents and her brothers and sisters to dinner. Nobody replied. Only her voice returned as if it were an echo from a deep cave. She found the sudden emptiness of the house uncanny. She rushed upstairs to look for her family. In the first bedroom, she could see her two sisters sitting on two beds. In spite of her impatient calls they remained in an unnaturally rigid position and did not even answer her. She went up to her sisters and wanted to shake them. Suddenly she noticed that they were stone statues. She escaped in horror and rushed into her mother's room. Her mother too had turned into stone and was sitting inertly in her armchair staring into the air with glazed eyes. The dreamer escaped into the room of her father. He stood in the middle of it. In her despair she rushed up to him and, desiring his protection, she threw her arms round his neck. But he too was made of stone and, to her utter horror, he turned into sand when she embraced him. She awoke in absolute terror, and was so stunned by the dream experience that she could not move for some minutes. This same horrible dream was dreamt by the patient on four successive occasions within a few days. At that time she was apparently the picture of mental and physical health. Her parents used to call her the sunshine of the whole family. Ten days after the fourth repetition of the dream, the patient was taken ill with an acute form of schizophrenia displaying severe catatonic symptoms. She fell into a state which was remarkably similar to the physical petrification of her family that she had dreamt about. She was now overpowered in waking life by behaviour patterns that in her dreams she had merely observed in other persons (pp. 162-3).

It seems to be a general law that at some point those very dangers most dreaded can themselves be encompassed to forestall their actual occurrence. Thus, to forgo one's autonomy becomes the means of secretly safeguarding it; to play possum, to feign death, becomes a means of preserving one's aliveness (see Oberndorf, 1950). To turn oneself into a stone becomes a way of not being turned into a stone by someone else. "Be thou hard," exhorts Nietzsche. In a sense that Nietzsche did not, I believe, himself intend, to be stony hard and thus far dead forestalls the danger of being turned into a dead thing by another person. Thoroughly to understand oneself (engulf oneself) is a defense against the risk involved in being sucked into the whirlpool of another person's way of comprehending oneself. To consume oneself by one's own love prevents the possibility of being consumed by another.

It seems also that the preferred method of attack on the other is based on the same principle as the attack felt to be implicit in the other's relationship to oneself. Thus, the man who is frightened of his own subjectivity being swamped, impinged upon, or congealed by the other is fre-

quently to be found attempting to swamp, to impinge upon, or to kill the other person's subjectivity. The process involves a vicious circle. The more one attempts to preserve one's autonomy and identity by nullifying the specific human individuality of the other, the more it is felt to be necessary to continue to do so, because with each denial of the other person's ontological status, one's own ontological security is decreased, the threat to the self from the other is potentiated and hence has to be even more desperately negated.

In this lesion in the sense of personal autonomy there is both a failure to sustain the sense of oneself as a person with the other, and a failure to sustain it alone. There is a failure to sustain a sense of one's own being without the presence of other people. It is a failure *to be* by oneself, a failure to exist alone. As James put it, "Other people supply me with my existence." This appears to be in direct contradiction to the aforementioned dread that other people will deprive him of his existence. But contradictory or absurd as it may be, these two attitudes existed in him side by side, and are indeed entirely characteristic of this type of person.

The capacity to experience oneself as autonomous means that one has really come to realize that one is a separate person from everyone else. No matter how deeply I am committed in joy or suffering to someone else, he is not me, and I am not him. However lonely or sad one may be, one can exist alone. The fact that the other person in his own actuality is not me, is set against the equally real fact that my attachment to him is a part of me. If he dies or goes away, he has gone, but my attachment to him persists. But in the last resort I cannot die another person's death for him, nor can he die my death. For that matter, as Sartre comments on this thought of Heidegger's, he cannot love for me or make my decisions, and I likewise cannot do this for him. In short, he cannot be me, and I cannot be him.

If the individual does not feel himself to be autonomous this means that he can experience neither his separateness from, nor his relatedness to, the other in the usual way. A lack of sense of autonomy implies that one feels one's being to be bound up in the other, or that the other is bound up in oneself, in a sense that transgresses the actual possibilities within the structure of human relatedness. It means that a feeling that one is in a position of ontological dependency on the other (i.e., dependent on the other for one's very being), is substituted for a sense of relatedness and attachment to him based on genuine mutuality. Utter detachment and isolation are regarded as the only alternatives to a clam- or vampire-like attachment in which the other person's life-blood is necessary for one's own survival, and yet is a threat to one's survival. Therefore, the polarity is between complete isolation or complete merging of identity rather than between separateness and relatedness. The individual oscillates perpetually between the two extremes, each equally unfeasible. He comes to live rather like those mechanical toys which have a positive tropism that impels them towards a stimulus until they reach a specific point, whereupon a built-in negative tropism directs them away until the positive tropism takes over again, this oscillation being repeated *ad infinitum*.

Other people were necessary for his existence, said James. Another patient, in the same basic dilemma, behaved in the following way: he maintained himself in isolated detachment from the world for months, living alone in a single room, existing frugally on a few savings, day-dreaming. But in doing this, he began to feel he was dying inside; he was becoming more and more empty, and observed "a progressive impoverishment of my life mode." A great deal of his pride and self-esteem was implicated in thus existing on his own, but as his state of depersonalization progressed he would emerge into social life for a brief foray in order to get a "dose" of other people, but "not an overdose." He was like an alcoholic who goes on sudden drinking orgies between dry spells, except that in his case his addiction, of which he was as frightened and ashamed as any repentant alcoholic or drug-addict, was to other people. Within a short while, he would come to feel that he was in danger of being caught up or trapped in the circle he had entered and he would withdraw again into his own isolation in a confusion of frightened hopelessness, suspicion, and shame.

Some of the points discussed above are illustrated in the following two cases:

CASE 1. ANXIETY AT FEELING ALONE

Mrs. R.'s presenting difficulty was a dread of being in the street (agoraphobia). On closer inspection, it became clear that her anxiety arose when she began to feel on her own in the street or elsewhere. She could *be* on her own, as long as she did not feel that she was really alone.

Briefly, her story was as follows: she was an only and a lonely child. There was no open neglect or hostility in her family. She felt, however, that her parents were always too engrossed in each other for either of them ever to take notice of her. She grew up wanting to fill this hole in her life but never succeeded in becoming self-sufficient, or absorbed in her own world. Her longing was always to be important and significant *to someone* else. There always had to be someone else. Preferably she wanted to be loved and admired, but, if not, then to be hated was much to be preferred to being unnoticed. She wanted to be *significant* to someone else in whatever capacity, in contrast to her abiding memory of herself as a child that she did not really matter to her parents, that they neither loved nor hated, admired nor were ashamed of her very much.

In consequence, she tried looking

at herself in her mirror but never managed to convince herself that she was *somebody*. She never got over being frightened if there was no one there.

She grew into a very attractive girl and was married at seventeen to the first man who really noticed this. Characteristically, it seemed to her, her parents had not noticed that any turmoil had been going on in their daughter until she announced that she was engaged. She was triumphant and self-confident under the warmth of her husband's attentions. But he was an army officer and shortly posted abroad. She was not able to go with him. At this separation she experienced severe panic.

We should note that her reaction to her husband's absence was not depression or sadness in which she pined or yearned for him. It was panic (as I would suggest) because of the dissolution of something in her, which owed its existence to the presence of her husband and his continued attentions. She was a flower that withered in the absence of one day's rain. However, help came to her through a sudden illness of her mother. She received an urgent plea for help from her father, asking her to come to nurse her mother. For the next year, during her mother's illness, she had never been, as she put it, so much herself. She was the pivot of the household. There was not a trace of panic until after her mother's death when the prospect of leaving the place where she had at last come to mean so much, to join her husband, was very much in her mind. Her experience of the last year had made her feel for the first time that she was now her parents' child. Against this, being her husband's wife was now somehow superfluous.

Again, one notes the absence of grief at her mother's death. At this time she began to reckon up the chances of her being alone in the world. Her mother had died; then there would be her father; possibly her husband: "beyond that — nothing." This did not depress her, it frightened her.

She then joined her husband abroad and led a gay life for a few years. She craved for all the attention he could give her but this became less and less. She was restless and unsatisfied. Their marriage broke up and she returned to live in a flat in London with her father. While continuing to stay with her father she became the mistress and model of a sculptor. In this way she had lived for several years before I saw her when she was twenty-eight.

This is the way she talked of the street: "In the street people come and go about their business. You seldom meet anyone who recognizes you; even if they do, it is just a nod and they pass on or at most you have a few minutes' chat. Nobody knows who you are. Everyone's engrossed in themselves. No one cares about you." She gave examples of people fainting and everyone's casualness about it. "No one gives a damn." It was in this setting and with these considerations in mind that she felt anxiety.

This anxiety was at being in the street alone or rather at feeling on her own. If she went out with or met someone who really knew her, she felt no anxiety.

In her father's flat she was often alone but there it was different. There she never felt *really* on her own. She made his breakfast. Tidying up the beds, washing up, was protracted as long as possible. The middle of the day was a drag. But she didn't mind too much. "Everything was familiar." There was her father's chair and his pipe rack. There was a picture of her mother on the wall looking down at her. It was as though all these familiar objects somehow illumined the house with the presence of the people who possessed and used them or had done so as a part of their lives. Thus, although she was by herself at home, she was always able to have someone with her in a magical way. But this magic was dispelled in the noise and anonymity of the busy street.

An insensitive application of what is often supposed to be the classical psychoanalytic theory of hysteria to this patient might attempt to show this woman as unconsciously libidinally bound to her father; with, consequently, unconscious guilt and unconscious need and/or fear of punishment. Her failure to develop lasting libidinal relationships away from her father would seem to support the first view, along with her decision to live with him, to take her mother's place, as it were, and the fact that she spent most of her day, as a woman of twenty-eight, actually thinking about him. Her devotion to her mother in her last illness would be partly the consequences of unconscious guilt at her unconscious ambivalence to her mother; and her anxiety at her mother's death would be anxiety at her unconscious wish for her mother's death coming true. And so on.[3]

However, the central or pivotal issue in this patient's life is not to be discovered in her "unconscious"; it is lying quite open for her to see, as well as for us (although this is not to say that there are not many things about herself that this patient does not realize).

The pivotal point around which all her life is centered is her *lack of ontological autonomy*. If she is not in the actual presence of another person who knows her, or if she cannot succeed in evoking this person's presence in his absence, her sense of her own identity drains away from her. Her panic is at the fading away of her being. She is like Tinker Bell. In order to exist she needs someone else to believe in her existence. How necessary that her lover should be a sculptor and that she should be his model! How inevitable, given this basic premise of her existence, that when her existence was not recognized she should be suffused with anxiety. For her, *esse* is *percipi*; to be seen, that

is, not as an anonymous passer-by or casual acquaintance. It was just that form of seeing which *petrified* her. If she was seen *as* an anonymity, *as* no one who especially mattered or as a *thing*, then she *was* no one in particular. She was as she was seen to be. If there was no one to see her, at the moment, she had to try to conjure up someone (father, mother, husband, lover, at different times in her life) to whom she felt she mattered, for whom she was a *person*, and to imagine herself in his or her presence. If this person on whom her being depended went away or died, it was not a matter for grief, it was a matter for panic.

One cannot transpose her central problem into "the unconscious." If one discovers that she has an unconscious phantasy of being a prostitute, this does not explain her anxiety about street-walking, or her preoccupation with women who fall in the street and are not helped to get on their feet again. The conscious phantasy is, on the contrary, to be explained by and understood in terms of the central issue implicating her self-being, her being-for-herself. Her fear of being alone is not a "defense" against incestuous phantasies or masturbation. She had incestuous phantasies. *These phantasies were a defense against the dread of being alone*, as was her whole "fixation" on being a daughter. They were a means of overcoming her anxiety at being by herself. The unconscious phantasies of this patient would have an entirely different meaning if her basic existential position were such that she had a starting-point in herself that she could leave behind, as it were, in pursuit of gratification. As it was, *her sexual life and phantasies were efforts, not primarily to gain gratification, but to seek first ontological security*. In love-making an illusion of this security was achieved, and on the basis of this illusion gratification was possible.

It would be a profound mistake to call this woman narcissistic in any

---

[3] For extremely valuable psychoanalytic contributions to apparently "hysterical" symptom-formation, see Segal (1954).

proper application of the term. She was unable to fall in love with her own reflection. It would be a mistake to translate her problem into phases of psychosexual development, oral, anal, genital. She grasped at sexuality as at a straw as soon as she was "of age." She was not frigid. Orgasm could be physically gratifying if she was temporarily secure in the prior ontological sense. In intercourse with someone who loved her (and she was capable of believing in being loved by another), she achieved perhaps her best moments. But they were short-lived. She could not be alone or let her lover be alone with her.

Her need to be taken notice of might facilitate the application of a further cliché to her, that she was an exhibitionist. Once more, such a term is only valid if it is understood existentially. Thus, and this will be discussed in greater detail subsequently, she "showed herself off" while never "giving herself away." That is, she exhibited herself while always holding herself in (inhibited). She was, therefore, always alone and lonely although superficially her difficulty was not in being together with other people; her difficulty was *least in evidence* when she was most together with another person. But it is clear that her realization of the autonomous existence of other people was really quite as tenuous as her belief in her own autonomy. If they were not there, they ceased to exist for her. Orgasm was a means of possessing herself, by holding in her arms the man who possessed her. But she could not be herself, by herself, and so could not really be herself at all.

CASE 2

A most curious phenomenon of the personality, one which has been observed for centuries, but which has not yet received its full explanation, is that in which the individual seems to be the vehicle of a personality that

is not his own. Someone else's personality seems to "possess" him and to be finding expression through his words and actions, whereas the individual's own personality is temporarily "lost" or "gone." This happens with all degrees of malignancy. There seem to be all degrees of the same basic process from the simple, benign observation that so-and-so "takes after his father," or "That's her mother's temper coming out in her," to the extreme distress of the person who finds himself under a compulsion to take on the characteristics of a personality he may hate and/or feel to be entirely alien to his own.

This phenomenon is one of the most important in occasioning disruption in the sense of one's own identity when it occurs unwanted and compulsively. The dread of this occurring is one factor in the fear of engulfment and implosion. The individual may be afraid to like anyone, for he finds that he is under a compulsion to become like anyone he likes.

The way in which the individual's self and personality are profoundly modified even to the point of threatened loss of his or her own identity and sense of reality by engulfment by such an alien sub-identity, is illustrated in the following case:

Mrs. D., a woman of forty, presented the initial complaint of vague but intense fear. She said she was frightened of everything, "even of the sky." She complained of an abiding sense of dissatisfaction, of unaccountable accesses of anger towards her husband, in particular of a "lack of a sense of responsibility." Her fear was "as though somebody was trying to rise up inside and was trying to get out of me." She was very afraid that she was like her mother, whom she hated. What she called "unreliability" was a feeling of bafflement and bewilderment which she related to the fact that nothing she did had ever seemed to please her parents. If she did one thing and was told it was wrong, she would do another thing and would find that they still said that was wrong. She was unable to discover, as she put it, "what they wanted me to be." She reproached her parents for this above all, that they hadn't given her any way of knowing who or what she really was or had to become. She could be neither bad nor good with any "reliability" because her parents were, or she felt they were, completely unpredictable and unreliable in their expressions of love or hatred, approval or disapproval. In retrospect, she concluded that they hated her; but at the time, she said, she was too baffled by them and too anxious to discover what she was expected to be to have been able to hate them, let alone love them. She now said that she was looking for "comfort." She was looking for a line from me that would give her an indication of the path she was to follow. She found my non-directive attitude particularly hard to tolerate since it seemed to her to be so clearly a repetition of her father's attitude: "Ask no questions and you'll be told no lies." For a spell, she became subject to compulsive thinking, in which she was under a necessity to ask such questions as, "What is this for?" or "Why is this?" and to provide herself with the answers. She interpreted this to herself as her effort to get comfort from her own thoughts since she could derive comfort from no one. She began to be intensely depressed and to make numerous complaints about her feelings, saying how childish they were. She spoke a great deal about how sorry she was for herself.

Now it seemed to me "she" was not really sorry for her own true self. She sounded to me much more like a querulous mother complaining about a difficult child. Her mother, indeed, seemed to be "coming out of her" all the time, complaining about "her" childishness. Not only was this so as regards the complaints which "she" was making about herself, but in other respects as well. For instance, like her mother, she kept screaming

at her husband and child; like her mother,[4] she hated everyone; and like her mother she was for ever crying. In fact, life was a misery to her by the fact that she could never be herself but was always being her mother. She knew, however, that when she felt lonely, lost, frightened, and bewildered she was more her true self. She knew also that she gave her complicity to becoming angry, hating, screaming, crying, or querulous, for if she worked herself up into being like that (i.e., being her mother), she did not feel frightened any more (at the expense, it was true, of being no longer herself). However, the backwash of this manœuvre was that she was oppressed, when the storm had passed, by a sense of futility (at not having been herself) and a hatred of the person she had been (her mother) and of herself for her self-duplicity. To some extent this patient, once she had become aware of this false way of overcoming the anxiety she was exposed to when she was herself, had to decide whether avoiding experiencing such anxiety, by avoiding being herself, was a cure worse than her disease. The frustration she experienced with me, which called out intense hatred of me, was not fully to be explained by the frustration of libidinal or aggressive drives in the transference, but rather it was what one could term the existential frustration that arose out of the fact that I, by withholding from her the "comfort" she sought to derive from me, in that *I did not tell her what she was to be*, was imposing upon her the necessity to make her own decision about the person she was to become. Her feeling that she had been denied her birthright because her parents had not discharged their responsibility towards her by giving her a definition of herself that could act as her starting-point in life was intensified by my refusal to offer this "comfort."

---

[4] That is, like her notion of what her mother was. I never met her mother and have no idea whether her phantasies of her mother bore any resemblance to her mother as a real person.

But only by withholding it was it possible to provide a setting in which she could take this responsibility into herself.

In this sense, therefore, the task in psychotherapy was to make, using Jasper's expression, an appeal to the freedom of the patient. A good deal of the skill in psychotherapy lies in the ability to do this effectively.

References

Boss, M., *Analysis of Dreams*, London, Rider & Co., 1957.

Oberndorf, C. P., "The Role of Anxiety in Depersonalization," *International Journal of Psychoanalysis*, 1950, Vol. 31.

Segal, H., "Schizoid Mechanisms Underlying Phobia Formation," *International Journal of Psychoanalysis*, 1954, Vol. 35.

Trilling, Lionel, *The Opposing Self*, London, 1955, Secker & Warburg.

Phenomenological Theories:

THERAPY

The goal of therapy, according to phenomenological theorists, should not be to understand the causes or to remove the symptoms of pathological behavior, but rather to free the patient to develop a constructive and confident image of his self-worth. Patients should be led to appreciate their "true identity" and encouraged to venture forth to test their personal tastes and values free of the narrow constraints of a mechanistic society. When the patient is liberated to fulfill himself, he will judge his behavior not in terms of what others believe, but in terms of what he senses is right for him. As his confidence in his self-worth grows, he will be more able to make decisions and commit himself to actions that correspond to his personal value system.

The Swiss psychiatrists Ludwig Binswanger and Medard Boss have modified Freudian psychoanalytic therapy in line with this philosophy. Binswanger studied with Eugen Bleuler at the turn of the century and corresponded frequently with Freud in the ensuing years. He was profoundly influenced by the major works of the existential philosopher Martin Heidegger in the 1920's and subsequently altered his views of both psychotherapy and psychopathology. In this recent essay, Binswanger summarized his position on Daseinsanalyse *and compares it with traditional intrapsychic therapy. The development of Boss' ideas are remarkably similar to those of Binswanger. In the present paper, he argues for a new basis for psychotherapy, one founded on the therapist's appreciation of the patient's total personality. Only by assuming a phenomenological attitude, according to Boss, can the therapist grasp the full nature of the patient's dilemmas and anxieties.*

Existential Analysis and Psychotherapy

LUDWIG BINSWANGER

Zürich is the birthplace of existential analysis *(Daseinsanalyse)* as a psychiatric-phenomenologic re-

From *Progress in Psychotherapy* edited by F. Fromm-Reichmann and J. L. Moreno, 1956, Grune and Stratton, Inc., Vol. I, by permission of the publisher.

search method. I emphasize the term *research method*, for if the psychoanalytic theory of Freud or the teaching of Jung arose out of a dissatisfaction with preceding psychotherapy, thus owing their origin and development predominantly to psychotherapeutic impulses and aims, the existential research orientation in psychiatry arose from dissatisfaction with the prevailing efforts to gain scientific understanding in psychiatry; so that existential analysis owes its origin and development to an attempt to gain a new scientific understanding of the concerns of psychiatry, psychopathology and psychotherapy, on the basis of the analysis of existence (*Daseinsanalytik*) as it was developed in the remarkable work of Martin Heidegger: "Being and Time" *(Sein und Zeit)*, in the year 1927. Psychology and psychotherapy, as sciences, are admittedly concerned with "man," but not at all primarily with mentally *ill* man, but with *man as such*. The new understanding of man, which we owe to Heidegger's analysis of existence, has its basis in the new conception that man is no longer understood in terms of some theory—be it a mechanistic, a biologic or a psychological one—but in terms of a purely phenomenologic elucidation of the total structure or total articulation of existence as BEING-IN-THE-WORLD *(In-der-Welt-sein)*. What this expression, fundamental for existential analysis, means, I unfortunately cannot develop here; be it only emphasized that it encompasses alike the individual's own world and the simultaneous and coextensive relationships with and to other people and things. Nor can I go into the difference between an ontologic-phenomenologic analysis of existence, an empiric-phenomenologic existential analysis, and an empiric discursive description, classification and explanation.

Once, in his interpretation of dreams, Freud said that psychiatrists had "forsaken the stability of the psychic structure too early." Existential analysis could say the same thing, albeit with an altogether different meaning. Freud, as is well known, had in mind the stability of the articulation of the life-history with the psychic structure, in contrast to the psychiatrists of his day who, at the very first opportunity, considered the psychic structure to be disrupted, and

who resorted instead to physiologic processes in the cerebral cortex. Existential analysis, on the other hand, does not have in mind the solidity of the structure of the inner life-history, but rather the solidity of the transcendental structure preceding or underlying, a priori, all psychic structures as the very condition of this possibility. I regret that I cannot explain in fuller detail these philosophic expressions, already employed by Kant but here used in a much wider sense; those among you conversant with philosophy will readily understand me. I want to emphasize only that philosophy is not here in any way being introduced into psychiatry or psychotherapy, but rather that the philosophic bases of these sciences are being laid bare. Obviously, this in turn has an effect upon one's understanding of what constitutes their scientific object or field. This effect reveals itself in the fact that we have learned to understand and to describe the various psychoses and neuroses as specific *deviations* of the a priori, or the transcendental, structure of man's humanity, of the *condition humaine*, as the French say.

Be it noted in passing that the existential-analytic research method in psychiatry had to investigate the structure of existence as being-in-the-world, as Heidegger had outlined and delineated it still further and along various new paths. Such, for instance, are its studies of various existential "dimensions," i.e., height, depth and width, thingness and resistance *(Materialität)*, lighting and coloring of the world, fullness or emptiness of existence, etc. The investigation of psychotic or neurotic world-projects and existential structures such as, for example, those which we designate as manic, depressive, schizophrenic, or compulsive, have so occupied all of us who are engaged upon this work that only suggestions are at hand with regard to the significance of existential-analytic research for psychotherapy. I should like now very cursorily to indicate a few of the main trends of this relationship.

(1) A psychotherapy on existential-analytic bases investigates the life-history of the patient to be treated, just as any other psychotherapeutic method, albeit in its own fashion. It does not explain this life-history and its pathologic idiosyncrasies according to the teachings of any school of psychotherapy, or by means of its preferred categories. Instead, it *understands* this life-history as modifications of the total structure of the patient's being-in-the-world, as I have shown in my studies "On Flight of Ideas" (*Uber Ideenflucht*), in my studies of schizophrenia, and most recently in the case of "Suzanne Urban."

(2) A psychotherapy on existential-analytic bases thus proceeds *not* merely by showing the patient where, when and to what extent he has failed to realize the fullness of his humanity, but it tries to make him *experience* this as radically as possible—how, like Ibsen's master-builder, Solness, he has lost his way and footing in "airy heights" or "ethereal worlds of fantasy." In this case the psychotherapist could be compared to someone who is informed, e.g., a mountain guide, familiar with the particular terrain, who attempts the trip back to the valley with the unpracticed tourist who no longer dares either to proceed or to return. And inversely, the existential-analytically-oriented therapist seeks to enable the depressed patient to get out of his cavernous subterranean world, and to gain footing "upon the ground" once more, by revealing it to him as being the only mode of existence in which the fullness of human possibilities can be realized. And further, the existential-analytically-oriented therapist will lead the twisted schizophrenic out of the autistic world of distortion and askewness in which he lives and acts, into the shared worlds, the *koinos kosmos* of Heraclitus; or he will strive to help a patient who, in her own words, lives "in two speeds" to "synchronize" these (again using her own expression). Yet, another time the therapist will see (as happened in

one of Roland Kuhn's cases of anorexia mentalis) that the goal may be reached much more rapidly if one explores not the temporal but the spatial structures of a particular patient's world. It came as a surprise to us to find how easily some otherwise not particularly intelligent or educated patients proved accessible to an existential-analytic kind of exploration, and how thoroughly they felt understood by it in their singularity. This is, after all, an altogether indispensable prerequisite for any kind of psychotherapeutic success.

(3) Regardless of whether the existential analyst is predominantly psychoanalytic or predominantly jungian in orientation, he will always stand on the same plane with his patients—the plane of common existence. He will therefore not degrade the patient to an object toward which he is subject, but he will see in him an existential partner. He will therefore not consider the bond between the two partners to be as that of two electric batteries—a "psychic contact" —but as an *encounter* on what Martin Buber calls the "sharp edge of existence," an existence which *essentially* "is in the world," not merely as a self but also as a being-together with one another—relatedness and love. Also what has, since *Freud*, been called transference is, in the existential-analytic sense, a kind of encounter. For encounter is a being-with-others in *genuine presence*, that is to say, in the present which is altogether continuous with the *past* and bears within it the possibilities of a *future*.

(4) Perhaps you will also be interested in hearing what is the position of existential analysis toward the *dream*, and this again particularly with regard to psychotherapy. Here again it is removed from any theoretic "explanation" of the dream, especially from the purely sexual exegesis of dream contents in psychoanalysis; rather, it understands the dream, as I emphasized a long time ago, as a specific way of being-in-the-world, in other words, as a specific world and a specific way of existing. This amounts

to saying that in the dream we see the whole man, the *entirety* of his problems, in a different existential modality than in waking, but against the background and with the structure of the a priori articulation of existence, and therefore the dream is also of paramount therapeutic importance for the existential analyst. For precisely by means of the structure of dreams he is enabled first of all to show the patient the structure of his being-in-the-world in an over-all manner, and secondly, he can, on the basis of this, free him for the *totality* of existential possibilities of being, in other words, for open resoluteness (*Entschlossenheit*); he can, to use Heidegger's expression, "retrieve" *(zurückholen)* existence from a dream existence to a genuine capacity for being itself. For the time being, I will refer you to Roland Kuhn's paper, "On the Existential Structure of a Neurosis" in Gebsattel's *Jahrbuch für Psychologie und Psychotherapie.* I only ask of you not to imagine existential structure as something static, but as something undergoing constant change. Similarly, what we call neurosis represents a changed existential *process*, as compared with the healthy. Thus, existential analysis understands the task of psychotherapy to be the opening up of new structural possibilities to such altered existential processes.

As you see, existential analysis, instead of speaking in theoretic concepts, such as "pleasure principle" and "reality principle," investigates and treats the mentally-ill person with regard to the structures, struc-tural articulations and structural alterations of his existence. Hence, it has not, by any means, consciousness as its sole object, as has been erroneously stated, but rather the whole man, prior to any distinction between conscious and unconscious, or even between body and soul; for the existential structures and their alterations permeate man's entire being. Obviously, the existential analyst, insofar as he is a therapist, will not, at least in the beginning of his treatment, be able to dispense with the distinction between conscious and unconscious, deriving from the psychology of consciousness and bound up with its merits and its drawbacks.

(5) Taking stock of the relationship between existential analysis and psychotherapy, it can be said that existential analysis cannot, over long stretches, dispense with the traditional psychotherapeutic methods; that, however, it can, as such, be therapeutically effective only insofar as it succeeds in opening up to the sick fellow man an understanding of the structure of human existence, and allows him to find his way back from his neurotic or psychotic, lost, erring, perforated or twisted mode of existence and world into the freedom of being able to utilize his own capacities for existence. This presupposes that the existential analyst, insofar as he is a psychotherapist, not only is in possession of existential-analytic and psychotherapeutic competence, but that he must dare to risk committing his own existence in the struggle for the freedom of his partner's.

"Daseinsanalysis" and Psychotherapy

MEDARD BOSS

MODERN PSYCHOTHERAPY IN NEED OF A BASIS

All problems, answers and resulting actions are invariably guided by the prescientific notions about the general nature and goal of man which each investigator carries within himself. No matter whether he is explicitly aware of his "philosophical" assumptions or whether he rejects all "philosophy" and attempts to be a "pure empiricist," the fact remains that such more or less hidden philosophical presuppositions, which are at the root of all science, are of fundamental importance. Up to now modern psychologists believed that their therapeutic approaches had found a sound basis in terms of their various psychodynamic theories about the human psyche. Freud thought of the human being as a telescope-like psychic apparatus; Reich, Alexander and Horney on the other hand attempt to explain all instinctual reactions in terms of a Total I or a Total Personality; for Jung the "Psyche" is a self-regulating libidinal system controlled by the archetypes of the "Collective Unconscious"; Sullivan conceives of man as the product of interactions between him and his fellowmen; Fromm and others speak of man as a Self molded by society. Yet all these modern anthropologic theories can't possibly warrant an adequate understanding of the psychotherapeutic processes. For none of them answers what ought to be the first and foremost questions: what would have to be the nature of such a "Psyche," such a psychic apparatus, such a human I or Self or total personality in order that something like a mere per-

ception of an object and of a human being, or even something like object relations and interpersonal and social relations, be at all possible? How should a telescope-like psychic apparatus or a self-regulating libidinal system be able to perceive or understand the meaning of anything, or to love or to hate somebody? Even less can such anonymous psychic structures or forces develop a transference or a resistance in the course of psychotherapy. Yet all these phenomena are central factors for a true healing.

MARTIN HEIDEGGER'S "DASEINSANALYSIS" REVEALING MAN'S BASIC NATURE

The eminent importance of the "Daseinsanalysis" in the sense of Martin Heidegger's fundamental ontology for psychology and psychotherapy lies in the fact that it helps overcome just these shortcomings of the basic anthropologic concepts of our psychological thinking, shortcomings which until now actually kept us groping in the dark. The "Daseinsanalysis" is able to do so because its concept of man's basic nature is nothing more or less than an explicit articulation of that understanding of man which has always guided our therapeutic actions, independent of all secondary theories, although secretly only and without our awareness. Therefore, the daseinsanalytic understanding of man helps us comprehend directly and fundamentally why therapists *can* demand of their patients what they have in fact been asking all along, and why they even *must* demand it if they want to cure at all. In all their endeavors psychotherapists rely on the peculiar ability of man to exist in a variety of instinctual, feeling, thinking and

From *Progress in Psychotherapy* edited by J. H. Masserman and J. L. Moreno, 1957, Grune and Stratton, Inc., Vol. II, by permission of the publisher and the author.

acting relationships to the things and in social and interpersonal patterns of behavior towards the fellowmen of his world. The therapist tacitly counts on this human ability when he asks of his patient—and tries to help him achieve it by this or that psychotherapeutic method—that he knowingly and responsibly seize and adopt all his potentialities of relationships so that they no longer remain frozen in unconscious neurotic mental or physical symptoms because of early childhood inhibitions and repressions.

In order to gain real insight into these preconditions and this goal of all practical psychotherapeutic approaches, the daseinsanalytic thinking had to guard against approaching man dogmatically with preconceived notions about his reality, no matter how self-evident they might seem. It also had to avoid forcing man blindly, by means of such preconceived ideas, into categories whereby he would be nothing but a "Psyche," a "Person" or "Consciousness." On the contrary, the daseinsanalysis had to learn again to see man unbiased, in the manner in which he directly reveals himself, and, in so doing, it made a very simple but all the more significant discovery about the fundamental nature of man. It found that man exists only *in* his relations and *as* his relations to the objects and fellowmen of his world. In order to exist in such manner, however, man must intrinsically possess a fundamental understanding of the fact that something *is* and can *be* at all. Man's special manner of being-in-the-world can therefore only be compared to the shining of a light, in the brightness of which the presence of all that is can occur, in which all things can appear and reveal themselves in their own, proper nature. Man is fundamentally an essentially spiritual brightness and as such he genuinely exists in the world. As this world-revealing brightness he is claimed by the ultimate be-ness. If a primordial understanding of be-ness were not the very essence of man, where would he suddenly find the ability to acquire any special knowledge

and insight? In fact, each single comprehension of the meaning of all the different encountering objects and all actual dealing with them is possible only because man is intrinsically "brightness" in the sense of being a primordial understanding of be-ness. This holds true in an all-embracing way: it is the prerequisite for the possibility to be concretely touched and affected by something as well as for all emotional experience and all conscious or unconscious instinctual behavior toward something: without it there can be no handling and grasping of mechanical tools, nor can there be conceptual grasping of scientific matters. This also refutes the widely heard objection that the daseinsanalysis is relevant only for the psychology of the conscious mind. The intrinsic ability of the human "dasein" to be open to the world in this way does not just discover things which can be located somewhere in space and time. It also opens up ways for the direct and immediate understanding of beings, who, as human beings, not only are altogether different from the things, but who, according to their manner of being as "dasein," are in the world in the same way as I am. These other human beings are likewise there and together with me. Humanity, as a whole, therefore, is best comparable to the full brightness of the day which also consists of the shining-together of all individual sun rays. Because of this being-together-in-the-world the world is always that which I share with others, the world of "dasein" is world-of-togetherness ("Mitwelt").[1]

Just as the objects cannot reveal themselves without such brightness of man, man cannot exist as that which he is without the presence of all he encounters. For if he did not find his proper place in the encounter with the objects, plants, animals and fellowmen, in his ability to be with them, in his relationship to them, how else could men be in this world as such brightening understanding of be-

[1] M. Heidegger: *Sein und Zeit*. Halle, 1927. p. 118.

ness? Even physical light cannot appear as light unless it encounters an object and can make it shine.

THE DASEINSANALYTICALLY ORIENTED PSYCHOTHERAPIST

This then, is the anthropological essence of Martin Heidegger's Existential Analysis (Daseinsanalysis). Meanwhile, the term "existential analysis" has come to include a variety of philosophical, scientific, psychopathologic and psychotherapeutic schools of thought. Although they differ in their methods and goals, they are all derivatives of Heidegger's Daseinsanalysis. At least they received from it their initial impetus even if, as in the case of J.-P. Sartre's philosophy, they have turned the real substance of the "Daseinsanalysis" into its complete opposite, namely, an extreme, subjectivistic Cartesianism.

The psychotherapist who lets himself be thoroughly pervaded by Heidegger's ontologic insight will not be able to derive new words or phrases from the daseinsanalysis for his psychopathologic descriptions. But he will win by it a tacit, but all the more reliable and all-embracing attitude toward his patient and the therapeutic process. If the therapist really understands that man is intrinsically a world-unfolding and world-opening being in the sense that in him, as the bright sphere of be-ness, comparable to a glade in a forest, all things, plants, animals and fellowmen can show and reveal themselves directly and immediately in all their significance and correlations, then he will have an unceasing reverence for the proper value of each phenomenon he encounters. At the same time he will have become aware that this way of being is the prerequisite that our destiny could claim man as a being who should care for the things and his fellowmen in the manner that all that is and may be can best unfold and develop. To exist in this sense is man's intrinsic task in life. How else

could it be that his conscience tells him so relentlessly whenever he falls short of fulfilling it? This call from the conscience and this guilt feeling will not abate until man has taken over and responsibly accepted all those possibilities which constitute him, and has borne and carried them out in taking care of the things and fellowmen of his world. Thus, he has completed his full dasein and hence can consummate his individual, intrinsic temporality in a good death. The daseinsanalytic understanding of man makes the analyst gain so deep a respect for all phenomena he encounters that it bids him to abide even more fully and more firmly by the chief rule of psychoanalysis than Freud himself could, handicapped as he still was by theoretical prejudices. The therapist will now, according to Freud's technical prescriptions, really to able to accept as equally genuine all the new possibilities for communication which grow "on the playground of transference," without mutilating them through his own intellectual and theoretical prejudices and his personal affective censure. The daseinsanalytically oriented psychoanalyst will have a clear conscience if he remains unpartial to all unproved scientific theories and abstractions and therefore refrains from attributing sole and only reality to one kind of behavior—the instinctual reactions, for instance—and does not consider them more "real" than all other potentialities. Thus, the danger of a so-called unresolved transference can often be avoided. This therapeutic difficulty usually develops only because the analyst has attempted to interpret and thereby reduce a new possibility of communication which unfolded for the first time in the therapeutic situation to a mere repetition of a relationship which existed earlier in life, considering this one primary and causal. Therefore, this new possibility can never properly unfold and mature and thus must inevitably remain in its embryonic state, i.e., the "transference fixation." How different, though, if one respects for instance the divine, which also reveals itself during psychoanalysis, in its divineness, just as one is ready to concede to the earthly its earthliness, and does not degrade the divine to a mere product of sublimation of an infantile-libidinal fixation, nor to a mere subjectivistic "psychic reality" produced by some supposed archetypal structure in the psyche of a human subject.

Of equally decisive influence on the attitude of the analyst is a thorough daseinsanalytic understanding of the fact that man is intrinsically and essentially always together with others. Heidegger's fundamental ontology helps us understand this in terms of a primary participation of all men in being the same open sphere of the be-ness. This insight teaches us that there is a being-together which is of such intrinsic and essential nature that no man can in fact perceive another even in the distance, without being already—through the mere art of perceiving—involved in the other's particular world-relatedness in some specific way. Thus, from the very first encounter between the therapist and patient the therapist is already together with his patient in the patient's way of existing, just as the patient already partakes in the therapist's manner of living, no matter whether, either on the part of the therapist or the patient, their being-together manifests itself for some time only in aloof observation, indifference or even intense resistance.

Already the knowledge of just this one essential trait of man provides an enormous impetus and a firm basis even for psychotherapeutic endeavors which formerly were a venture requiring an almost blind courage. For, only in the primordial being-together as it was brought to light by Heidegger's "Daseinsanalysis" we are able now to recognize the very foundation of all psychotherapeutic possibilities. Owing to this basic structure of man's existence, the most seriously ill schizophrenic patient, for instance, partakes in some way or other as human being in the wholesome mode of living of his psychotherapist; hence, such a patient's fundamental possibility of being cured by the adequate being-together of a psychotherapeutic situation through which he may recollect his true self again.[2]

Apart from the confidence which we derive from the daseinsanalytic insights for our practical dealings with such difficult patients, the daseinsanalytic way of thinking affords us also some important "theoretical" gain. For example, it helps us understand such central phenomena as "psychic projection" and "transference." Until now modern psychology could conceive of them only in terms of a tossing-out and carrying-over of psychic contents from within a "psyche" into something in the external world. Those concepts, however, are entirely unexplainable and can only be maintained on the basis of abstract intellectual constructions. The daseinsanalytic thinking allows us to understand these phenomena simply and with full justice to reality out of the primary, intrinsic being-together of all men in the same world.[3]

[2] M. Boss: *Psychoanalyse und Daiseinsanalytik.* Bern, Hans Huber, 1957.
[3] M. Boss: *The Dream and Its Interpretation.* London, 1957.

References

Binswanger, L.: Freud's Auffassung vom Menschen im Lichte der Anthropologie. Bern, A. Francke, 1947.

Boss, M.: The Dream and Its Interpretation. London, Rider, 1957.

———: Einfuhrung in die psychosomatische Medizin. Bern, Huber, 1957.

———: Psychoanalyse und Daseinsanalytik. Bern, Huber, 1957.

Heidegger, M.: Sein and Zeit. Tubingen, Niemeyer, 1927.

———: Ueber den Humanismus. Frankfurt a.M, Klostermann, 1953.

———: Einfuhrung in die Metaphysik, Tübingen, Niemeyer, 1933.

———: Was heisst Denken? Tübingen, Niemeyer, 1947.

Phenomenological Theories:

Critical Evaluation

The phenomenologist's portrayal of the dilemmas of man is striking, but we must distinguish between skillful literary depiction and effective theorizing. No matter how compelling and vivid a theory may be, the crucial test does not lie in elegant persuasion, but in explicit hypothesis. Although phenomenologists are among the most acute observers of the human condition, their formulation of these observations into a theory is sporadic and casual. Perhaps these formulations should not be thought of as theory, but as a set of loosely connected observations and notions. So discursive a body of work, little concerned with problems of integration, structure, and continuity, lacking in tautness of systematic argument, cannot be viewed as a scientific theory at all. At best, it represents a consistent point of view; at worst, it is an ill-constructed social commentary.

Other critics object not to the loose structure of phenomenological theory but to what these theories propose. Particular exception is taken to their idealistic conception of man's inherent nature. The notion that man would be a constructive, rational, and socially conscious being, were he free of the malevolent distortions of society, seems not only sentimental but invalid. There is something grossly naïve in exhorting man to live life to the fullest and then expecting socially beneficial consequences to follow. What evidence is there that one's inherent self-interest would not clash with the self-interests of others? There is something as banal as the proverbialism of a fortune cookie in the suggestion "be thyself." Conceiving man's emotional disorders as a failure to "be thyself" seems equally naïve and banal.

The critiques of M. Brewster Smith and Robert Holt presented here are not entirely unfriendly to the phenomenological position. Rather they argue against a number of naïve and romantic assumptions common among phenomenologists which would preclude the development of an adequate science of personality and psychopathology.

The Phenomenological Approach in Personality Theory: Some Critical Remarks

M. BREWSTER SMITH

The "phenomenological approach" has recently come to be something of a rallying cry to a number of psychologists who share the "tender-minded" bias that psychology must, after all, come to terms with human experience, and who go so far as to believe that careful attention to this experience will leave the science of psychology not merely more satisfying to like-minded people, but also better science. Sharing this point of view and agreeing heartily with the program recommended by MacLeod (1947) in his article on "The Phenomenological Approach in Social Psychology," the present writer has been dismayed by some recent publications which, it seems to him, misconstrue the appropriate role of a phenomenological approach in a way that invites the critical to reject a humanized psychology lock, stock, and barrel. Since the writer would regard such an outcome as highly unfortunate, he feels that a clarification of the issues is badly needed, and herewith makes an attempt in this direction.

The position with which he would take particular issue is that of Snygg and Combs (1949; Combs, 1949) whose point of view has also been espoused by Rogers (1947). These authors contrast the objective or external frame of reference in psychology with the phenomenological, or internal frame of reference, and, declaring their stand firmly with phenomenology, proceed to muster on their side the names of Lewin, Lecky, Allport, Murphy, and Angyal, among others, even including the seemingly less tractable father-figure of Freud.

From *J. Abnormal & Social Psychol.* 45: 516-522, 1950, by permission of the American Psychological Association and the author.

In essence, their contention is that the locus of psychological causation lies entirely within the phenomenal field of conscious experience, and that it therefore behooves the psychological theorist—and therapist—to formulate his problems and concepts accordingly. Snygg and Combs give much attention to the individual's perceptual-cognitive field, particularly to the *self*, as its most salient feature. Written from this standpoint, psychology comes close to a rapprochement with common sense.

While applauding their emphasis on perception and the self, the present writer proposes that they are confusing phenomenology with what may be termed the subjective frame of reference. Sharply maintained, this distinction further helps to clarify certain persistent ambiguities in the theory of ego and self.

PHENOMENOLOGY AND COMMON SENSE

One of the genuine merits of the phenomenological approach is that it brings psychology somewhat closer to the world of common sense. There is always the danger that psychology, in its concern for rigor and neatness, may divorce itself too completely from this source of problems and partial insights. Focussing scientific attention on the phenomenal world as it is presented to us, the world from which common sense also takes its start, the phenomenological approach can bring into the ken of the psychologist data and problems too often left to common sense by default. Like common sense, and unlike some current varieties of psychological theory, it does deal with experience, and thus presents itself as an attractive alternative to those who find a behavioristic psychology uncongenial.

But phenomenology is not common sense, nor can it rightly be called upon to justify a common-sense psychology. In MacLeod's phrase, the phenomenological approach "involves the adoption of what might be called an attitude of disciplined naïveté" (1947, p. 194). In many respects, its result may run exactly counter to common-sense conclusions. Common sense, with its preconceived categories and stock explanations, neither disciplined nor naïve, is full of pseudo-scientific theory, while phenomenology limits its concern to the unprejudiced *description* of the world of phenomena. To take the phenomenal world presented in conscious experience as completely explanatory of behavior is closer to common sense than to phenomenology or adequate science.

Yet this is essentially what Snygg and Combs have done in their attempt to rewrite psychology in a "phenomenological frame of reference." *"All behavior, without exception,"* they say, *"is completely determined by and pertinent to the phenomenal field of the behaving organism"* (1949, p. 15, italics theirs). And they go on to explain that

by the phenomenal field we mean the entire universe, including himself, as it is experienced by the individual at the instant of action. . . . Unlike the "objective" physical field, the phenomenal field is not an abstraction or an artificial construction. It is simply the universe of naive experience in which each individual lives, the everyday situation of self and surroundings which each person takes to be reality (1949, p. 15).

While they bow unnecessarily to current prejudice in avoiding the word *consciousness*, their meaning is clear, and their index spells it out: "Consciousness, *see* Phenomenal field."

It is one variant of common sense that consciousness completely explains behavior, but at this juncture, it is hard to see how such a view can be regarded as an acceptable scientific postulate. Quite apart from the meta-

physical controversy about the status of consciousness as "real" or respectable, we have behind us Würzburg and we have behind us Freud, to mention but two major sources of evidence that a psychology of experience or consciousness has distinct explanatory limits. Where is the determining tendency represented in the phenomenal field? What of the inacceptable strivings that warp our behavior, what of our defensive techniques of adjustment that so often prove most effective precisely when we are least aware of them? It is no satisfactory solution to speak, as Snygg and Combs do, of a "unified field of figure-ground phenomena of which the individual is more or less conscious . . . [in which] the vague and fuzzy aspects of behavior correspond to and are parts of the vague and incompletely differentiated aspects of the field" (1949, p. 17). The clinical literature abounds with instances of unconsciously determined behavior which, far from being "vague and fuzzy," is on the contrary highly differentiated.

One suspects that such a psychology of consciousness has an element of common-sense appeal not unlike the attraction of allied forms of psychotherapy. It does make sense to the layman: it accords with what he is ready and able to recognize in himself. And it has distinct value within limits that it refuses to recognize. Because it over-states its claims, however, it may tend to promote the state of affairs away from which we have been striving—every man his own psychologist.

But McLeod has already made the relevant point succinctly: "The phenomenological method, in social psychology as in the psychology of perception [and we would add, psychology generally] can never be more than an approach to a scientific inquiry" (1947, p. 207). It provides certain kinds of data, not *all* the data. It furnishes the basis for certain valuable theoretical constructs; it does not give birth to them in full concreteness. It sets some problems and provides some clues; the psychologist, theorist or clinician, must *infer* the answers.

SUBJECTIVE CONSTRUCTS AND THE OBSERVER'S FRAME OF REFERENCE

Here we reach the crux of the matter. If a psychology consciousness is necessarily incomplete yet we do not abandon our hope for a psychology that comes to terms with human experience, what is the solution? A discussion of two lesser questions may indicate the nature of the answer. In the first place, does the decision to frame our psychological concepts and theories in terms appropriate to the "private world" of the behaving person commit us to the exclusive use of phenomenal concepts? Secondly, what is the appropriate role of the phenomenological approach in the service of this kind of theory-building?

Lewin, whose psychological life space Snygg and Combs equate to their phenomenal field (1949, p. 15), was entirely clear in maintaining a sharp distinction between the two concepts. He said:

> It is likewise doubtful whether one can use consciousness as the sole criterion of what belongs to the psychological life space at a given moment in regard to social facts and relationships. The mother, the father, the brothers and sisters are not to be included as real facts in the psychological situation of the child only when they are immediately present. For example, the little child playing in the garden behaves differently when he knows his mother is at home than when he knows she is out. One cannot assume that this fact is continually in the child's consciousness. Also a prohibition or a goal can play an essential role in the psychological situation without being clearly present in consciousness. . . . Here, as in many other cases it is clear that one must distinguish between "appearance" and the "underlying reality" in a dynamic sense. In other words, the phenomenal properties are to be distinguished from the conditional-genetic characteristics of objects and events, that is, from the properties which determine their causal relationships. . . . As far as the conceptual derivation is concerned, one may use effectiveness as the criterion for existence: *"What is real is what has effects"* (1936, p. 19).

Lewin's life space, then, is *not* merely the phenomenal field. And he adds to our previous considerations cogent reasons for thinking that a psychology of the phenomenal field cannot be adequately explanatory. His life space is not immediately given in the concreteness of experience; it is an abstract, hypothetical construct, inferred by the psychologist-observer to account for the individual's behavior.

It is, however, a construct of a type that differs from constructs of behavioristic psychology. It is formulated in terms of what is behaviorally real to the acting individual, not primarily in terms of what is physically observable to the scientist. Hence it is legitimate to speak of theories like Lewin's as anchored in a *subjective* (not phenomenological) *frame of reference.* Lewin's concepts and many of Freud's are in this sense *subjective constructs,* not because they are built of the stuff of conscious experience, but because they attempt to deal with what is effectively real to the individual, even when it is real to the scientific observer only in this secondary, indirect way.

The subjective frame of reference in theory construction is to be contrasted with the *objective frame of reference,* wherein concepts are chosen so as to be rooted as closely as possible in effective realities shared by any qualified observer. This is the distinction that Snygg and Combs seek, which makes them see both Freud and Lewin as precursors. There is no absolute difference between the two frames of reference; it is rather a question of which criteria are weighted most strongly in the selection of constructs.

Both the subjective and objective frames of reference pertain to the choice of constructs and the theoretical context in which they are embedded. They in no sense conflict with what has been called the *observer's frame of reference,* which, indeed, lies at the foundation of all science. The problem of establishing a bridge between the point of view of the observer and *either* subjective or objective inferential constructs is the familiar one of operational definition. It cannot, in the last analysis, be avoided unless one chooses the alternative of claiming *direct* access to the point of view of the observed. This is the position of intuitionism, which asserts that the observer's and subject's points of view can be merged. But is this science? Not in the sense of a systematic search for understanding that can withstand the equally systematic doubt of the man from Missouri.

Subjective constructs framed in terms of the "private world" of the behaving individual remain constructs, and as such must ultimately be rooted in data accessible to the observer's frame of reference. There is no reason at all why their source should be restricted to the data of communicated conscious experience, in answer to our first question. But the phenomenological approach, or, more generally, any means of access to the experience of the subject, is of course crucial to the formulation of subjective constructs and the investigation of their relationships. Perhaps the point has been labored, but it is an essential one: the phenomenological approach, the clinical interview, the projective protocol, the behavioral observation—none of these yield direct knowledge of psychological constructs, subjective or objective, while all of them can provide the basis for inferring explanatory constructs and their relationships. If the canons of inference can be made sufficiently explicit, they provide the operational definitions that secure the constructs in the scientific home base of the observer's frame of reference.

Methods that get the subject to reveal his private world as he sees it need to be supplemented by others which permit the observer to infer effective factors that are distorted or disguised in the subject's awareness. But the broadly phenomenological methods remain a signally important source of data. Certain important subjective constructs such as the *self*, moreover, are anchored fairly directly in the data of phenomenological report.

EGO, SELF, AND PHENOMENOLOGY

Although there is still considerable confusion in usage, a degree of consensus seems to be emerging to employ the term *self* for the phenomenal content of the experience of personal identity. A salient feature of the phenomenal field that has figured largely in personality theory, the self in this sense has the conceptual properties of a phenomenal object. Murphy (1947) and Chein (1944) use it with this meaning. Snygg and Combs agree, writing with somewhat franker circularity:

Of particular importance in the motivation of behavior will be those parts of the phenomenal field perceived by him to be part or characteristic of himself. To refer to this important aspect of the total field we have used the term *phenomenal self* (1949, p. 111).

Within the phenomenal self, they distinguish as a stable core the *self-concept:* "Those parts of the phenomenal field which the individual has differentiated as definite and fairly stable characteristics of himself" (1949, p. 112).

Sharing with Murphy a strong emphasis on responses to the self as fundamental to motivational theory, Snygg and Combs go so far as to state that the basic human need is "the preservation and enhancement of the phenomenal self" (1949, p. 58). Changes in the perception of the self play a major role in the theory of the therapeutic process that they share with Rogers (1947).

Let us look more closely, however, at how these writers actually use the term. Passages like the following can readily be found:

. . . when the self is free from any threat of attack or likelihood of attack, then it is possible for the self to consider these hitherto rejected perceptions, to make new differentiations, and to reintegrate the self in such a way as to include them (Rogers, 1947, p. 365).

A self threatened by its perceptions may deny the perception by simply refusing to enter the situation where such a perception is forced upon him (Snygg and Combs, 1949, p. 148).

Can a phenomenal self consider perceptions and reintegrate itself; can a threatened phenomenal self deny perceptions; or is this rather double-talk resulting from the attempt to make one good concept do the work of two? If, as this writer suspects, the latter is the case, what is the nature of the hidden second concept, which evidently is not merely a percept or phenomenal entity? To give it a name he would suggest the conventional term *ego*, realizing that usage in this respect is even more ambiguous than with the term *self*. The important point is that the concept, implicit in the writings of Rogers and of Snygg and Combs, is a subjective construct but does not refer to a phenomenal entity, whereas the self, on the other hand, is a coordinate subjective construct that does. The relation between the two will bear closer examination.

It is not necessary, at this juncture, to propose a definitive theory of the ego, nor to enter into an involved discussion of alternative views about its nature. What is relevant is that starting from an attempt to write a psychology in phenomenal terms, our authors in spite of themselves give implicit recognition to organizing, selective processes in the personality which are somehow guided by the nature and status of the self (among other things) and somehow, in turn, have an influence in its nature and status. So conceived, the relation of ego and self is highly interdependent[1] but by no means an identity. The distinction is that between a dynamic configuration of on-going processes, inferred from many facts of biography and behavior, and a phenomenal entity resulting from these processes and affecting them in turn, inferred primarily (but not exclusively) from phenomenological report.

Approaching the problem on a slightly different tack, we may find it rewarding to consider three of the eight conceptions of the ego listed by Allport (1943, p. 459) in the light of the distinction just made: the ego "as one segregated behavioral system among others," "as knower," and "as object of knowledge." The fundamental conception advanced here is not unlike the first of these senses, if one reads into it a dynamic quality not expressed in Allport's formulation. As an on-going system of organizing and selective processes mediating the individual's intercourse with reality, it includes a variety of processes without being coterminous with the total personality.[2] Among these processes or functions is that of the ego as "knower," which the writer would take in a less metaphysical sense than Allport's to embrace the cognitive-perceptual functions of personality. These have been described with reason in psychoanalytic theory (Freud, 1933, pp. 105-106) as an integral aspect of the ego system. Among the phenomena that the ego "knows" is the *self*, Allport's "ego as object of knowledge." Like any cognitive-perceptual object, the self only imperfectly mirrors the physical, psychological, and social facts that underlie the perception. And also like similar phenomenal objects it serves as a guide to appropriate behavior. But the relation of self to ego-processes is no more and no less obscure than the relation of cognitive structures to behavior generally.

"EGO-INVOLVEMENTS" AND "EGO DEFENSE"

We have sought to reinstate the ego as a subjective but non-phenomenal construct mainly through an examination of the pitfalls encountered by the attempt to avoid such a con-

---

[1] The writer doubts that it is advisable to construct the ego as narrowly around the self as do Chein (1944) and Murphy (1947).

[2] How to distinguish within the personality between *ego* and *non-ego* is, of course, an important problem, though it will not be attempted here. The distinction, however, is not the same as the phenomenal one between the *self* and *notself* (often described, confusingly, as *ego-alien*).

cept. If the ego-self distinction as outlined above is worth making, however, it should make a difference in the formulation of other knotty problems. Does it? Two such problems— the nature of "ego-involvements" and of the "mechanisms of defense"—will be examined briefly as test cases.

As it emerges in the work of Sherif and Cantril (1947), the concept of ego-involvement lacks clarity and focus. Widely divergent sorts of psychological facts turn out to be embraced by the term, which, like so many in popular psychological currency, rather identifies a disparate group of problems than clarifies them. More often than not, ego-involvement means the involvement of a person's pride and self-esteem in a task; he feels put to the test and ready to be ashamed of a poor performance. In other instances, the term is invoked to cover immersion in a cause, or falling in love—cases in which the person, to be sure, cares as deeply about outcomes as in the first type, but may be engrossed to the point of losing self-awareness.

Now the present self-ego distinction makes excellent sense when applied here. Since the distinctive character of the first sort of examples lies in the fact that the individual's conception of his self and its worth is at stake, these can aptly be described as *self-involvement*. The second type of case can often still be called ego-involvement without inconsistency. The situation in the latter instances touches on the person's central system of on-going psychological processes so closely that he may lose himself in it. Similar engrossment can, to be sure, result from the involvement of equally imperative non-ego processes: who is to say, without intimate acquaintance with the principals, whether being in love should be called ego-involvement or "id-involvement"! However that may be, note that self-involvement and ego-involvement thus conceived may vary independently. A person may care about a task both because of its intrinsic meaning for him and with after-thought for its bearing on

his prestige and self-esteem. Or either or neither may be the case. The behavioral conditions and consequences of ego- and self-involvement should furthermore be quite distinct.

The situation is somewhat different in regard to the theoretical status of the mechanisms of defense. Here the classical formulation by Anna Freud (1946) regards the defense mechanisms as employed by the ego (the term is used essentially in our sense) to protect itself, primarily from disruption by strong unassimilated urges, but also from threats from the external world. As a more or less precariously balanced system mediating between inner strivings and outer reality, the ego, in this view, has recourse to these sometimes drastic techniques in order to preserve its balance, and maintain the course of behavior at a lower level of adjustment if need be rather than run the risk of its catastrophic disruption. Murphy (1947), and later Snygg and Combs (1949), on the other hand, say in effect that it is rather the self that is defended. Under conditions of threat, enhancement and preservation of the self may be achieved by the classical defense mechanisms. Is it necessary to choose between these divergent formulations, or can the conflict be resolved?

The present writer would maintain that the mechanisms of defense can ultimately all be conceived as defenses of the ego, since they serve to bolster up the ego's adjustive compromise. As contributors to this compromise, they can also best be regarded as a part of the activity included in the ego system. But in a more immediate sense, any particular one of an individual's defenses may or may *not* be a *self*-defense mechanism. Since the maintenance of a favorable self-image is important to sound ego functioning, though not its only requisite, the end of ego defense can often be served most efficiently by self-defense mechanisms. Certain mechanisms, like identification, may, indeed, always take effect through the defense of the self. There are, however, instances of ego-defense mechanisms which involve the self only indirectly if at all. In regression, for example, one can hardly suppose that the self is enhanced in any way. What is more likely is that by retreating to an earlier, more deeply established, or simpler level of ego organization, the person seeks, perhaps ineptly, to cope with disturbing experiences that, by reason of circumstance, constitution, or previous learning, he has not the strength to meet maturely. In most cases, the relative significance of the self in the defensive process probably cannot be assessed in any simple way, since changes in the self for better or worse may be the *consequence* of the fortunes of the ego and its defenses, as well as the focus of defensive techniques.

A formulation of this sort, which seems to agree with present clinical experience, again suggests the usefulness of a distinction between phenomenal and non-phenomenal (shall we say *functional?*) subjective constructs, with both employed in proper coordination. A purely phenomenological psychology, on the other hand, cannot adequately describe *all* the defensive processes, since neither all the effective threats to the ego nor all the defenses against them are registered accurately in conscious awareness. Indeed, it is largely the consequence of "silent" defensive processes that phenomenological reports must be viewed with so much circumspection in personality research.

CONCLUSIONS

Starting from a discussion of Snygg and Combs' proposal of a phenomenological frame of reference for psychology (1949) the writer has sought to establish the following major points:

1. While common sense may favor an explanatory psychology framed entirely in terms of conscious experience, such a psychological system does violence to currently available knowledge.

2. Phenomenology, as distinct from common sense, is descriptive, not explanatory. It is an approach or method ancillary to the formulation of problems and derivation of constructs, and does not give birth to these constructs full blown.

3. The subjective and objective frames of reference, which denote relatively different alternative contexts within which constructs may be selected, are both entirely compatible with the observer's frame of reference. Subjective constructs to be scientifically admissible must ultimately be anchored in the data of observation.

4. The phenomenological approach provides one method of deriving subjective constructs. But not all subjective constructs need represent phenomenal entities. They may, thus, denote functional entities that are either absent from the phenomenal field or inaccurately presented in it.

5. The coordinate use of phenomenal and non-phenomenal subjective constructs, maintained in clear distinction from one another, serves to clarify the theory of the ego and the self. It is proposed that an adequate theory of personality must distinguish, among other constructs,

a. the *ego*, a *non-phenomenal* subjective construct representing a configuration of on-going processes, among which is the cognitive-perceptual function. Through exercise of this function, the ego "knows," among other things,

b. the *self*, a *phenomenal* subjective construct.

6. When carried into current problems concerning the nature of "ego-involvement" and of the "mechanisms of defense," the above distinction seems productive.

References

Allport, G. W. The ego in contemporary psychology. *Psychol. Rev.*, 1943, *50*, 451-478.

Chein, I. The awareness of self and the structure of the ego. *Psychol. Rev.*, 1944, *51*, 304-314.

Combs, A. W. A phenomenological approach to adjustment. *J. abnorm. soc. Psychol.*, 1949, *44*, 29-35.

Freud, A. *The ego and the mechanisms of defense.* New York: International Universities Press, 1946.

Freud, S. *New introductory lectures on psy-*

choanalysis. New York: Norton, 1933.

Lewin, K. *Principles of topological psychology.* New York: McGraw-Hill, 1936.

MacLeod, R. B. The phenomenological approach to social psychology. *Psychol. Rev.,* 1947, *54,* 193-210.

Murphy, G. *Personality: A biosocial approach to origins and structure.* New York: Harper, 1947.

Rogers, C. R. Some observations on the organization of personality. *Amer. Psychologist,* 1947, *2,* 358-368.

Sherif, M., and Cantril, H. *The psychology of ego-involvements.* New York: Wiley, 1947.

Snygg, D., and Combs, A. W. *Individual behavior: A new frame of reference for psychology.* New York: Harper, 1949.

The Logic of the Romantic Point of View in Personology

ROBERT R. HOLT

Let us now consider each of the main propositions that make up the romantic point of view, and state the logical objections to them systematically.

1. *The goal of personology must be understanding, not prediction and control.* The goal of those who profess an idiographic point of view is not anything so antiseptic and inhuman as a family of curves; it is *understanding.* In one sense, it is proper to say that we understand poliomyelitis when we have isolated the responsible viruses and have identified the conditions under which they attack and cripple a person, but this is not *Verstehen.* That conception is an empathic, intuitive *feeling* of knowing a phenomenon from the inside, as it were. To take a more congenial example, we do not understand why a particular boy becomes delinquent from knowing that he comes from a neighborhood that an ecological survey has determined to be economically deprived and socially disorganized; whereas after we have read Farrell's *Studs Lonigan* and have seen such conditions and the embeddedness of delinquency in them portrayed with artistic power and vividness, then we understand (in the sense of *Verste-*

hen) the relation between these phenomena.

From this example, it should be clear that the feeling of understanding is a subjective effect aimed at by artists, not scientists. In science, when we say we understand something, we mean that we can predict and control it, but such aims are foreign to the romantic viewpoint. When Allport says (as of course Freud and many others have said also) that novelists and poets have been great intuitive psychologists, in some ways the greatest psychologists, the statement has two (not necessarily coexistent) meanings: that literary men have known many significant variables of and propositions about personality (e.g., the role of unconscious incestuous wishes in determining many kinds of behavior), or, that they have been able to create the most vivid, compelling portraits of people, which give us the sense of knowing and understanding them. The latter effect is achieved by judicious selection and artful distortion, not by exhaustive cataloguing and measurement of traits, motives, or structural relations. Indeed, the idea of a catalogue is the very antithesis of art, just as a painful realism that tries to copy nature slavishly is the death of an artistic endeavor.

Here we see the issues drawn clearly. Is personology to be an art,

Abridged from "Individuality and Generalization in the Psychology of Personality," *J. Personality 30:*377-402, 1962, by permission of the publisher and the author.

devoted to word portraits that seek to evoke in the reader the thrill of recognition, the gratifying (if perhaps illusory) feeling of understanding unique individuals? Or is it to be a science, which enables us to study these same persons in all their uniqueness and to derive from such study general propositions about the structure, development, and other significant aspects of personality? If we elect for a science, we must abandon art whenever it takes us in a different direction than the one demanded by the scientific method, and we must recognize that the ideal of an idiographic science is a will-o'-the-wisp, an artistic and not a scientific goal. Science may be supplemented by art, but not combined with it.

There is a legitimate art of personality, literary biography. An artist like André Maurois is not hindered by not being a scientist of any kind. We should recognize that an artist's quest for "truth" differs from a scientist's in being a striving not for strict verisimilitude but for allusive illumination; its criterion is the effect on some audience—something to which science must remain indifferent.

Since some personologists (notably Freud, Murphy, Allport, and Murray) have had much of the artist in them as well as the scientist and have been masters of prose writing, it is no wonder that at times the artistic side of their identities has come uppermost. If Allport had been less aesthetically sensitive, he might not have failed to distinguish between artistic and scientific goals. Often, too, poor scientists are at the same time poor writers, and an inferior case study may be poor either because its facts are wrong and its interpretations undiscerning, or because it is poorly put together and lacks the literary touch that can put the breath of life into even a routine case report. The more art a scientist possesses—so long as he does not let it run away with him—the more effective a scientist he can be, because he can use his aesthetic sense in constructing theory as well as in communicating his findings and ideas to others.

2. *The proper methods of personology are intuition and empathy, which have no place in natural science.* As has been indicated above, intuition and empathy were used by the romantics as ways of gaining direct and definitive understanding, and were considered to be complete scientific methods. The contemporary personologist has no quarrel with their use in the practical arts of clinical psychology and psychoanalysis, nor as ways of making discoveries and formulating hypotheses. Indeed, the more secure scientists are in their methodological position, the more respect they usually have for intuition (and in psychology for the closely related methods of empathy and recipathy). Thus, the claim that these operations have no place in natural science is false; they are used by all scientists in the most exciting and creative phase of scientific work: when they decide what to study, what variables to control, what empirical strategies to use, and when they make discoveries within the structure of empirical data. As to their sufficiency, I need only remind the reader that the methodology of verification, the hypothesis-testing phase of scientific work, involves well-developed rules and consensually established procedures, and that intuition and empathy have no place in it.

3. *Personology is a subjective discipline as contrasted to objective branches of psychology, being concerned with values and meanings, which cannot be subjected to quantification.* Elsewhere (Holt, 1961), I have dealt with the contention that there is a fundamental methodological difference between disciplines that deal with verbal meanings and values, and those that deal with objective facts. Briefly, the argument is the familiar one that objectivity is only intersubjectivity, and that meanings (including values) may be perceived and dealt with in essentially the same ways as the data of natural science, which must be discriminated and recognized also. Moreover, a logi-

cal analysis of the operations carried out in disciplines such as literature, concerned with the understanding of individual works and little (if at all) with generalization, shows that these workers outside of science use many of the *same* methods of analyzing texts as the quantitative content-analysis of social psychology, with their exclusive concern with generalization. Their work has shown that meanings may be quantified and in other ways treated as objectively as any other facts of nature. Other objections to quantification grow out of antipathy to abstract variables of analysis, and will be considered in the following section.

4. *The concepts of personology must be individualized, not generalized as are the concepts of natural science.* The belief that the concern of personology with unique individuals (see below) contrasts fundamentally with the exclusive concern of nomothetic science with generalities logically implies that the two types of discipline must have different types of concepts. As the chief spokesman for the romantic point of view in psychology, Allport calls for the use of individual traits, which are specific to the person being studied, not common traits, which are assumed to be present to some degree in all persons. But to describe an individual trait, we have to take one of two courses: either we create a unique word (a neologism) for each unique trait, or we use a unique configuration of existing words. The first approach is clearly impossible for communication, let alone science; personology would be a complete Babel. The second solution, however, turns out to be a concealed form of nomothesis, for what is a unique configuration of existing words but a "fallacious attempt to capture something ineffably individual by a complex net of general concepts"? Allport himself has explicitly ruled out this possibility:

. . . each psychologist tends to think of individuals as combinations of whatever abstractions he favors for psychological analysis. This procedure, common as it is, is wholly unsuitable for the psychology of personality. For one thing, such abstract units are not distinctively *personal* (1937a, p. 239).*

An idiographic discipline thus must be a dumb or an incomprehensible one, for intelligible words—even some of Allport's favorite, literary ones, like *Falstaffian*, which he does consider "personal"—abstract and generalize, proclaiming a general pattern of resemblance between at least two unique individuals, Falstaff and the case being described. Any such trait thus becomes common, not individual.

One of the great methodologists of social science, Max Weber (1949) developed an apposite analysis of scientific concepts and their development in reaction against the romantic movement in his country at the turn of the century (cf. Parsons, 1957). He had the insight to see that the exponents of *Geisteswissenschaft* were trying to do the impossible: to capture the full richness of reality. There are three identifiable stages in the scientific study of anything, Weber said. To begin with, one selects from nature the historical individual (or class thereof) one wishes to focus on; for example, the Boston Massacre, the personality of Einstein, the cathedral at Chartres. Even though limited, each of these is infinitely rich in potentially specifiable aspects and configurations. One could study one of these, or even a tiny "flower in a crannied wall," until doomsday and not exhaust everything that could be known about it. Without doing any more abstracting than focusing on a particular topic, one can only contemplate it; and this is where the idiographic approach logically must stop. The method of intuition or *Verstehen* is essentially a wordless act of identification with the object, or some other attempt to "live in it" without analyzing its Gestalt.

---

* Allport wrote these words in the context of rejecting Murray's system of needs (1937a) ; yet elsewhere (Allport, 1937b) he praises as "strikingly personal" such concepts (or dimensions) of W. Stern (1938) as depth-surface, embeddedness-salience, nearness-remoteness, and expectancy-retrospect!

The second stage, that of the ideal type, is a rudimentary attempt to see similarities between historical individuals, while staying as close as possible to their concrete particularity. Ideal types are much used in psychology, especially in diagnosis, for any syndrome such as schizophrenia is a complex of identifiably separate but loosely covarying elements, never encountered in exact textbook form. The lure of ideal types is that they give the brief illusion of getting you close to the individual while still allowing a degree of generality. But this advantage is illusory, the apparent advantage of a compromise that denies satisfaction to either party. Concrete reality (fidelity to the unique individual) *is* forsworn, and the advantages of truly general concepts are not attained. An ideal type does not fit any particular case exactly, and the failure of fit is different in kind as well as degree from one case to another. For an ideal type "is a conceptual construct which is neither historical reality nor even the 'true' reality. It is even less fitted to serve as a schema under which a real situation or action is to be subsumed as one *instance*. It has the significance of a purely ideal *limiting* concept with which the real situation or action is compared and surveyed for the explication of certain of its significant components" (Weber, 1949, p. 93).

The final stage of scientific development, therefore, is the fractionation of ideal types into their constituent dimensions and elements, which Weber called abstract analytical variables. Paradoxically, only a truly abstract concept can give an exact fit to any particular individual! I cannot say exactly how Falstaffian or how schizophrenic or how big any particular subject may be, but I can name a particular value of an abstract analytical variable, height, that fits him as closely as his skin. The example would be less convincing if chosen from psychology because we do not have as well-established, unitary dimensions as the physical ones, and not as

simple and unarguable operations for measuring them as the use of the meter stick; the principle, however, is the same.

The fit is exact, of course, only because an abstract analytical concept does not purport to do more than one thing. If I try to measure the breadth of a person's interests, I make no pretensions to have "captured the essence of his personality." Not having tried, I cannot properly be accused of failing. But I have chosen a variable that can be measured, and thus potentially its relations to other aspects of personality can be discovered and precisely stated. Curiously, Allport attacks general variables on the ground that they "merely *approximate* the unique cleavages which close scrutiny shows are characteristic of each separate personality" (Allport, 1946; his emphasis). His preferred *ad hoc* approach may seem less approximate because many of the general variables used in personology are ideal types, lacking true abstract generality. The solution, however, lies in a direction diametrically opposed to the one toward which Allport beckons. And it does not consist in escaping from approximation. Scientific models of reality can *never* fit perfectly; the attempt to force such identity between concept and referent sacrifices the flexibility and power of abstract concepts in a chimerical quest for the direct grasp of noumena.

Parenthetically, the recent vogue of existentialism and Zen Buddhism in psychology may be partly attributed to the promise they extend of providing a way of grasping the total richness of reality. Part of the lure of *satori* or any other mystical ecstasy of a direct contact with the world, unmediated by concepts, may stem from the necessary distance imposed by the scientific necessity to abstract. But despite their confusing jargons, which make them seem superficially quite different from the late nineteenth-century romantic movement we have been considering, both of these fashionable doctrines suffer from the same fallacies. Mystical experience, like aesthetic experience, offers nothing to the scientist qua scientist except an interesting phenomenon that may be subjected to scientific study.

5. *The only kind of analysis allowable in personology is structural, not abstract, while natural science is not concerned with structure.* It is true that the scientific psychology of Dilthey's heyday had no place for structural analysis in the sense introduced by the romantics. Psychology dealt with a number of functions, which were treated implicitly or explicitly as quite independent of one another. It had no methods parallel to those of exegetic Biblical scholarship or literary criticism, which seek out the internal organization of ideas in a specific text. And the reductionistic enthusiasts for analyzing things were not interested in putting the pieces back together again, nor very clear themselves that analysis need not mean dismemberment. This state of affairs made it easy to think that analysis could be destructive, and that structural relations between the parts of the personality could be studied only in concrete, unique individuals, so that structure* seemed to be an exclusive concern of idiographic disciplines.

There are really two points here: the distrust of analysis, and the emphasis on structure. The first of these has been partly dealt with in the preceding section; it was based on a misunderstanding of the nature of abstract concepts.

On the second point, structural concepts and structural analyses are commonplace in science at large today. Such structural disciplines as stereochemistry and circuit design were (at best) in their infancy at the time of the idiographic manifestoes.

---

* Ironically, in psychology the adherents of structuralism were among those who carried atomistic, reductionistic analysis to its most absurd extreme: the Titchenerian introspectionists. The Gestalt psychologists, though appalled by the equally atomistic behaviorism and structuralism alike, concentrated their efforts on perceptual patterning, leaving untouched most of the structural problems that concern personology, particularly the enduring invariances of molar behavior.

Today, natural science uses abstract, structural, and dispositional concepts simultaneously with a minimum of confusion. Presumably, the same may be true of personology someday, too.

One merit of the romantic tradition in personology is that it has consistently highlighted the problem of structure. At the time Allport was taking his position on these matters (in the late 1920's and early 1930's), the predominant American conceptions of personality were "and-summative" (the sum total of a person's habits, traits, etc.), and the problem of structure was ignored. The early academic personologists who concentrated their efforts on personality inventories, single variables, or factor analyses, all tended to disregard entirely the structuring of these elements or to assume simple, universal answers (e.g., orthogonal factor-structure).

At the same time, however, Freud (1947) was developing the structural point of view in psychoanalysis, and today psychoanalytic psychology is increasingly concerned with the problem and has developed a variety of variables to deal with it (cf. Rapaport and Gill, 1959; Holt, 1960; and see the recent work of G. S. Klein and his associates on cognitive controls as structural variables: Gardner *et al.*, 1959). Drawing on this tradition and that of psychopathology generally, psychodiagnosis concerns itself with structural variables and their constellation into a limited number of ideal types (e.g., the obsessive-compulsive type of ego-structure) which, in the best practice, are used not as pigeonholes but as reference-points in terms of which the clinician creates individualized analyses of personality structure.

6. *There can be no general laws of personality because of the role of chance and free will in human affairs.* There are hardly any contemporary personologists who openly espouse this argument. It played an important part in the development of the romantic point of view, as we have seen, and persists in Catholic psychology. It

is generally admitted, however, that scientific work requires the basic assumption of strict determinism throughout. Closely examined, chance becomes ignorance; when we discover systematic effects where "error" existed before, the chance (at least in part) disappears. Theoretically, the exact path of a bolt of lightning and the exact events of a human life could be predicted rigorously, if we only had all of the necessary data at hand.

7. *General laws are not possible in personology because its subject matter is unique individuals, which have no place in natural science.* It is not difficult to dispose of this last, supposedly critical point of difference between *Naturwissenschaft* and *Geisteswissenschaft*.

The mechanistic, pre-field theoretical science of Windelband's day contained a curious dictum that has been one of the principal sources of confusion on this whole issue: *Scientia non est individuorum*—science does not deal with individual cases. This hoary slogan dates back to the days when Aristotle was the last word on matters scientific, and the whole point of view it expresses is outdated in the physical sciences. According to this philosophy, the individual case was not lawful, since laws were conceived of as empirical regularities. This is the point of view (Plato's idealism or what Popper calls *essentialism*) that considers an average to be the only fact, and all deviation from it mere error.

Freud and Lewin have taught us that psychic determinism is thoroughgoing (see above), and the individual case is completely lawful. It is just difficult to know what the laws *are* from a study of one case, no matter how thorough. We can surmise (or, if you will, intuit) general laws from a single case in the hypothesis-forming phase of scientific endeavor, but we can verify them only by resorting to experimental or statistical inquiry or both.

There is truth in the old adage only in one sense, then: We cannot carry out the complete scientific process by the study of an individual. It is true that in certain of the disciplines concerned with man, from anatomy to sensory psychology, it has usually been assumed that the phenomena being studied are so universal that they can be located for study in any single person, and so autonomous from entanglement in idiosyncratically variable aspects of individuals that the findings of intensive investigation will have general applicability to people at large. Every so often, however, these assumptions turn out not to be tenable. For example, when Boring repeated Head's study (in one case, himself) of the return of sensation after the experimental section of a sensory nerve in his arm, he did not find the protopathic-epicritic sequential recovery, which had been so uncritically accepted as to be firmly embedded in the literature. No matter how intensively prolonged, objective, and well-controlled the study of a single case, one can never be sure to what extent the lawful regularities found can be generalized to other persons, or in what ways the findings will turn out to be contingent on some fortuitously present characteristic of the subject—until the investigation is repeated on an adequate sample of persons. As excellent a way as it is to make discoveries, the study of an individual cannot be used to establish laws; bills of attainder (that is, laws concerned with single individuals) are as unconstitutional in science as in jurisprudence. Note, however, that law of either kind, when promulgated, is still conceived as holding quite rigorously for the single individual.

Science is defined by its methods, not its subject matter; to maintain the opposite, as Skaggs (1945) did in an attack on Allport, is to perpetuate the confusion, not resolve it, and Allport (1946) was an easy victor in the exchange. There can be and is scientific study of all sorts of individuals. Particular hurricanes are individualized to the extent of being given personal names and are studied by all the scientific means at the meteorologist's command. A great part of the science of astronomy is given over to the study of a number of unique individuals: the sun, moon, and planets, and even individual stars and nebulae. There may not be another Saturn, with its strange sets of rings, in all of creation,* yet it is studied by the most exact, quantitative and—if you must —nomothetic methods, and no one has ever considered suggesting that astronomy is for these reasons not a science nor that there should be two entirely different astronomical sciences, one to study individual heavenly bodies and the other to seek general laws. Further examples are easily available from geology, physics, and biology. Once we realize that individuals are easily within the realm of orthodox scientific study, and that science does not strive for artistic illusions of complete understanding, the issue is easily seen as a pseudoproblem. Psychology as a science remains methodologically the same, whether its focus be on individual cases or on general laws.

Granted, then, that individual personalities may and must be studied by the scientific method in personology, with the use of general concepts, what is the role of general laws in such a science? Where does it get us to make scientific studies of personalities, if each is unique, and if that uniqueness is the heart of the matter?

Personalities *are* in many ways unique, but as Kluckhohn and Murray (1953) point out, every man is also like all men in some ways and like a limited number of others in still other ways, making generalization possible. If every personality structure were as much a law unto itself as Allport implies, it would be impossible to gain useful information in this field;

there would be no transfer from one case study to another. As anyone knows who has tried it, there is a great deal.

It is a mistake to focus personology on just those aspects of a person that are unique, as Weber (1949) saw clearly half a century ago. "The attempt to understand 'Bismarck,'" he said for example, "by leaving out of account everything which he has in common with other men and keeping what is 'particular' to him would be an instructive and amusing exercise for beginners. One would in that case ... preserve, for example, as one of those 'finest flowers' [of such an analysis of uniqueness] his 'thumbprint,' that most specific indication of 'individuality.'" And some of the most critical points about him for predicting his behavior would have to be excluded because he shared them with other persons. Indeed, in contemporary psychodiagnosis, it is considered most useful to treat as a quantitative variable the degree to which a person's responses resemble those of the group as a whole.

The only kind of law that Allport could conceive for personology was one (like his principle of functional autonomy) that describes how uniqueness comes about. Personology has not been much restrained from seeking general relationships among its variables by this narrow view, however; the journals are full of investigations in which aspects of personality are studied genetically (that is, are related to the abstract variable of age) or are correlated, one with another. Once one treats uniqueness not with awe but with the casual familiarity due any other truistic fact of life, it ceases to pose any difficulty for personology.

Writing intensive case studies (on the genesis and structure of individual personalities) turns out not to be a particularly fruitful method, except for the generation of hypotheses. This is a very important exception, but the point is that personology does not proceed mainly by adding one ex-

---

* After these words had been written, I was amused to find that Cournot used this same example, and even similar wording, in supporting his position that "it is no longer necessary to accept to the letter the aphorism of the ancients to the effect that the individual and particular have no place in science" (1956, p. 443).

haustive scientific biography to another, looking for generalizations afterwards. The Gestaltist taboo on studying any variable out of its context in
the individual life is an overstate-
ment. There is, of course, such a phenomenon as the interaction of variables, but it is not so far-reachingly
prevalent as to make impossible any
study of two variables at a time. As
Falk (1956) has shown, this condition of interactive nonsummativeness
is found in many other kinds of subject matter besides personality and
creates no major difficulties of method
or procedure.

In summary, in this section we
have looked at the major propositions
of the romantic point of view as
applied to personology, and have
found that the "basic differences"
between this field and natural science
are completely illusory. No basis for a
separate methodology exists, and the
objections to applying the general
methodology of science to personalities turn out to be based on misunderstandings or on a narrow conception
of natural science that is an anachro-
nism today.

References

Allport, G. W. *Personality, a psychological
interpretation.* New York: Holt, 1937a.
Allport, G. W. The personalistic psychology
of William Stern. *Char. & Pers.*, 1937b,
5, 231-246.
Allport, G. W. Personalistic psychology as
science: A reply. *Psychol. Rev.*, 1946, 53,
132-135.
Cournot, A. A. *An essay on the foundations
of our knowledge.* (Trans. by M. H.
Moore.) New York: Liberal Arts Press,
1956.
Falk, J. L. Issues distinguishing nomothetic
from idiographic approaches to personality theory. *Psychol. Rev.*, 1956, 63, 53-62.
Freud, S. *The ego and the id.* London:
Hogarth, 1947.
Gardner, R., Holzman, P. S., Klein, G. S.,
Linton, Harriet B., and Spence, D. P.
Cognitive control: A study of individual
consistencies in cognitive behavior. *Psy-
chol. Issues*, 1959, 1, No. 4.
Holt, R. R. Recent developments in psycho-
analytic ego psychology and their impli-
cations for diagnostic testing. *J. proj.
Tech.*, 1960, 24, 254-266.
Holt, R. R. Clinical judgment as a disciplined
inquiry. *J. nerv. ment. Dis.*, 1961, 133,
369-382.
Kluckhohn, C., and Murray, H. A. Personal-
ity formation: The determinants. In C.
Kluckhohn and H. A. Murray (Eds.),
*Personality in nature, society, and cul-
ture.* New York: Knopf, 1953.
Parsons, T. *The structure of social action.*
Glencoe, Ill.: Free Press, 1957.
Rapaport, D., and Gill, M. M. The points of
view and assumptions of metapsychology.
Int. J. Psychoanal., 1959, 40, 153-162.
Skaggs, E. B. Personalistic psychology as
science. *Psychol. Rev.*, 1945, 52, 234-238.
Stern, W. *General psychology from a per-
sonalistic standpoint.* (Trans. by H. D.
Spoerl.) New York: Macmillan, 1938.
Weber, M. *The methodology of the social
sciences.* (Trans. and ed. by E. A. Shils
and H. A. Finch.) Glencoe, Ill.: Free
Press, 1949. (The material collected here
was originally published from 1904 to
1917.)

Part IV

Behavioral
Theories

Jacob Lawrence — No. 48 in the series, *Migration of the Negro.*

INTRODUCTION

Taken in its strictest form, the behavioral approach requires that all concepts and propositions be anchored precisely to measurable properties in the empirical world. That behavioral concepts are, in fact, not always formulated as operational concepts is a concession to the limits of practicality. Nevertheless, empirically unanchored speculation is anathema to behaviorists; hypothetical constructs, which abound in intrapsychic and phenomenological theories, are rarely found in behavioral theories.

Behaviorism originated with the view that subjective introspection was "unscientific" and that it should be replaced by the use of objectively observable behavior. Further, all environmental influences upon behavior were likewise to be defined objectively. If unobservable processes were thought to exist within the individual, they were to be defined strictly in terms of observables which indicate their existence.

Recent theories of behavioral pathology have included concepts generated originally in experimental learning research. They are not simple translations of psychoanalytic concepts into behavioral terminology, as were earlier theories of behavioral pathology, but are based on the ostensible "empirical" laws of learning. Theorists using these concepts lay claim to the virtues of science since their heritage lies with the objective studies of systematic learning research and not with the dubious methods of clinical speculation.

That learning concepts are helpful in understanding pathology cannot be denied, but behavioral theorists take a stronger position. They state that pathological behavior is learned behavior that develops according to the same laws as those governing the development of normal behavior. Disturbed behavior differs from normal behavior only in magnitude, frequency, and social adaptiveness. Were these behavior patterns more adaptive, or less frequent and extreme, they would possess no other distinguishing features.

Behavioral Theories:

ORIENTATION

The first theory to restrict its conception of pathology entirely to objective behavioral processes, eschewing all reference to internal phenomena such as the unconscious or innate anxiety dispositions, was formulated by the eminent learning theorist B. F. Skinner and his disciples. According to strict behaviorism, as presented in the paper reprinted here, it is unnecessary and misleading to posit the existence of unobservable emotional states to account for pathological behavior. The excerpt from the paper by Leonard Ullmann and Leonard Krasner elaborates what they refer to as the "psychological model" of psychopathology. They discard all reference to hypothetical inner states and offer a formulation based solely in terms of stimulation and reinforcement. Reinforcements shape the behavioral repertoire of the individual, and differences between adaptive and maladaptive behavior results from differences in the reinforcement pattern to which individuals were exposed.

What Is Psychotic Behavior?

B. F. SKINNER

Since my field of specialization lies some distance from psychiatry, it may be well to begin with credentials. The first will be negative. In the sense in which my title is most likely to be understood, I am wholly unqualified to discuss the question before us. The number of hours I have spent in the presence of psychotic people (assuming that I am myself sane) is negligible compared with what many of you might claim, and the time I have spent in relevant reading and discussion would suffer equally from the same comparison. I am currently interested in some research on psychotic subjects, to which I shall refer again

From *Theory and Treatment of the Psychoses,* pages 77-99, 1956, Washington University Studies, by permission of the Washington University Press and the author.

later, but my association with that program in no way qualifies me as a specialist.

Fortunately, I am not here to answer the question in that sense at all. A more accurate title would have been "What is *behavior?*—with an occasional reference to psychiatry." Here I will list such positive credentials as seem appropriate. I have spent a good share of my professional life in the experimental analysis of the behavior of organisms. Almost all my subjects have been below the human level (most of them rats or pigeons) and all, so far as I know, have been sane. My research has not been designed to test any theory of behavior, and the results cannot be evaluated in terms of the statistical significance of such proofs. The object has been to discover the functional relations which prevail between measurable aspects of behavior and various conditions and events in the life of the organism. The success of such a venture is gauged by the extent to which behavior can, as a result of the relationships discovered, actually be predicted and controlled. Here we have, I think, been fortunate. Within a limited experimental arrangement, my colleagues and I have been able to demonstrate a lawfulness in behavior which seems to us quite remarkable. In more recent research it has been possible to maintain—actually, to sharpen—this degree of lawfulness while slowly increasing the complexity of the behavior studied. The extent of the prediction and control which has been achieved is evident not only in "smoothness of curves" and uniformity of results from individual to individual or even species to species, but in the practical uses which are already being made of the techniques —for example, in providing baselines for the study of pharmacological and neurological variables, or in converting a lower organism into a sensitive psychophysical observer.

Although research designed in this way has an immediate practical usefulness, it is not independent of one sort of theory. A primary concern has been to isolate a useful and expedient measure. Of all the myriad aspects of behavior which present themselves to observation, which are worth watching? Which will prove most useful in establishing functional relations? From time to time many different characteristics of behavior have seemed important. Students of the subject have asked how well organized behavior is, how well adapted it is to the environment, how sensitively it maintains a homeostatic equilibrium, how purposeful it is, or how successfully it solves practical problems or adjusts to daily life. Many have been especially interested in how an individual compares with others of the same species or with members of other species in some arbitrary measure of the scope, complexity, speed, consistency, or other property of behavior. All these aspects may be quantified, at least in a rough way, and any one may serve as a dependent variable in a scientific analysis. But they are not all equally productive. In research which emphasizes prediction and control, the topography of behavior must be carefully specified. Precisely what is the organism doing? The most important aspect of behavior so described is its probability of emission. How likely is it that an organism will engage in behavior of a given sort, and what conditions or events change this likelihood? Although probability of action has only recently been explicitly recognized in behavior theory, it is a key concept to which many classical notions, from reaction tendencies to the Freudian wish, may be reduced. Experimentally we deal with it as the *frequency* with which an organism behaves in a given way under specified circumstances, and our methods are designed to satisfy this requirement. Frequency of response has proved to be a remarkably sensitive variable, and with its aid the exploration of causal factors has been gratifyingly profitable.

One does not engage in work of this sort for the sheer love of rats or pigeons. As the medical sciences illustrate, the study of animals below the level of man is dictated mainly by convenience and safety. But the primary object of interest is always man. Such qualifications as I have to offer in approaching the present question spring about equally from the experimental work just mentioned and from a parallel preoccupation with human behavior, in which the principles emerging from the experimental analysis have been tested and put to work in the interpretation of empirical facts. The formal disciplines of government, education, economics, religion, and psychotherapy, among others, together with our everyday experience with men, overwhelm us with a flood of facts. To interpret these facts with the formulation which emerges from an experimental analysis has proved to be strenuous but healthful exercise. In particular, the nature and function of *verbal* behavior have taken on surprisingly fresh and promising aspects when reformulated under the strictures of such a framework.

In the long run, of course, mere interpretation is not enough. If we have achieved a true scientific understanding of man, we should be able to prove this in the actual prediction and control of his behavior. The experimental practices and the concepts emerging from our research on lower organisms have already been extended in this direction, not only in the experiments on psychotic subjects already mentioned, but in other promising areas. The details would take us too far afield, but perhaps I can indicate my faith in the possibilities in a single instance by hazarding the prediction that we are on the threshold of a revotionary change in methods of education, based not only upon a better understanding of learning processes, but upon a workable conception of knowledge itself.

Whether or not this brief personal history seems to you to qualify me to discuss the question before us, there is no doubt that it has created a high probability that I will do so, as shown by the fact that I am here. What I have to say is admittedly methodological. I can understand a certain impatience with such discussion particularly when, as in the field of psychiatry, many pressing problems call for action. The scientist who takes time out to consider human nature when so many practical things need to be done for human welfare is likely to be cast in the role of a Nero, fiddling while Rome burns. (It is quite possible that the fiddling referred to in this archetypal myth was a later invention of the historians, and that in actual fact Nero had called in his philosophers and scientists and was discussing "the fundamental nature of combustion" or "the epidemiology of conflagration.") But I should not be here if I believed that what I have to say is remote

from practical consequences. If we are now entering an era of research in psychiatry which is to be as extensive and as productive as other types of medical research, then a certain detachment from immediate problems, a fresh look at human behavior in general, a survey of applicable formulations, and a consideration of relevant methods may prove to be effective practical steps with surprisingly immediate consequences.

The study of human behavior is, of course, still in its infancy, and it would be rash to suppose that anyone can foresee the structure of a well-developed and successful science. Certainly no current formulation will seem right fifty years hence. But although we cannot foresee the future clearly, it is not impossible to discover in what direction we are likely to change. There are obviously great deficiencies in our present ways of thinking about men; otherwise we should be more successful. What are they, and how are they to be remedied? What I have to say rests upon the assumption that the behavior of the psychotic is simply part and parcel of human behavior, and that certain considerations which have been emphasized by the experimental and theoretical analysis of behavior in general are worth discussing in this special application.

It is important to remember that I am speaking as an experimental scientist. A conception of human behavior based primarily on clinical information and practice will undoubtedly differ from a conception emanating from the laboratory. This does not mean that either is superior to the other, or that eventually a common formulation will not prove useful to both. It is possible that questions which have been suggested by the exigencies of an experimental analysis may not seem of first importance to those of you who are primarily concerned with human behavior under therapy. But as psychiatry moves more rapidly into experimental research and as laboratory results take on a greater clinical significance, cer-

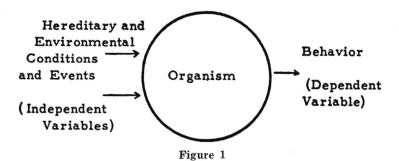

Figure 1

tain problems in the analysis of behavior should become common to researcher and therapist alike, and should eventually be given common and cooperative solutions.

The study of behavior, psychotic or otherwise, remains securely in the company of the natural sciences so long as we take as our subject matter the observable activity of the organism, as it moves about, stands still, seizes objects, pushes and pulls, makes sounds, gestures, and so on. Suitable instruments will permit us to amplify small-scale activities as part of the same subject matter. Watching a person behave in this way is like watching any physical or biological system. We also remain within the framework of the natural sciences in explaining these observations in terms of external forces and events which act upon the organism. Some of these are to be found in the hereditary history of the individual, including his membership in a given species as well as his personal endowment. Others arise from the physical environment, past or present. We may represent the situation as in Figure 1. Our organism emits the behavior we are to account for, as our dependent variable, at the right. To explain this, we appeal to certain external, generally observable, and possibly controllable hereditary and environmental conditions, as indicated at the left. These are the independent variables of which behavior is to be expressed as a function. Both input and

output of such a system may be treated within the accepted dimensional systems of physics and biology. A complete set of such relations would permit us to predict and, insofar as the independent variables are under our control, to modify or generate behavior at will. It would also permit us to *interpret* given instances of behavior by inferring plausible variables of which we lack direct information. Admittedly the data are subtle and complex, and many relevant conditions are hard to get at, but the program as such is an acceptable one from the point of view of scientific method. We have no reason to suppose in advance that a complete account cannot be so given. We have only to try and see.

It is not, however, the subtlety or complexity of this subject matter which is responsible for the relatively undeveloped state of such a science. Behavior has seldom been analyzed in this manner. Instead, attention has been diverted to activities which are said to take place within the organism. All sciences tend to fill in causal relationships, especially when the related events are separated by time and space. If a magnet affects a compass needle some distance away, the scientist attributes this to a "field" set up by the magnet and reaching to the compass needle. If a brick falls from a chimney, releasing energy which was stored there, say, a hundred years ago when the chimney was built, the result is explained by saying that the brick has all this time possessed a certain amount of "potential energy." In order to fill such spa-

Hereditary Variables

    Species   Instincts

    Individual   Traits and Abilities

Environmental Variables

                            Memories

    Personal History   Needs

                            Emotions

    Present Circumstances   Perceptual Experience

Figure 2

tial and temporal gaps between cause and effect, nature has from time to time been endowed with many weird properties, spirits, and essences. Some have proved helpful and have become part of the subject matter of science, especially when identified with events observed in other ways. Others have proved dangerous and damaging to scientific progress. Sophisticated scientists have usually been aware of the practice and alert to its dangers. Such inner forces were, indeed, the hypotheses which Newton refused to make.

Among the conditions which affect behavior, hereditary factors occupy a primary position, at least chronologically. Differences between members of different species are seldom, if ever, disputed, but differences between members of the same species, possibly due to similar hereditary factors, are so closely tied up with social and ethical problems that they have been the subject of seemingly endless debate. In any event, the newly conceived organism begins at once to be influenced by its environment; and when it comes into full contact with the external world, environmental forces assume a major role. They are the only conditions which can be changed so far as the individual is concerned. Among these are the events we call "stimuli," the various interchanges between organism and environment such as occur in breathing or eating, the events which

generate the changes in behavior we call emotional, and the coincidences between stimuli or between stimuli and behavior responsible for the changes we call learning. The effects may be felt immediately or only after the passage of time—perhaps of many years. Such are the "causes"—the independent variables—in terms of which we may hope to explain behavior within the framework of a natural science.

In many discussions of human behavior, however, these variables are seldom explicitly mentioned. Their place is taken by events or conditions within the organism for which they are said to be responsible (see Figure 2). Thus, the species status of the individual is dealt with as a set of instincts, not simply as patterns of behavior characteristic of the species, but as biological drives. As one text puts it, "instincts are innate biological forces, urges, or impulsions driving the organism to a certain end." The individual genetic endowment, if not carried by body-type or other observable physical characteristic, is represented in the form of inherited traits or abilities, such as temperament or intelligence. As to the environmental variables, episodes in the past history of the individual are dealt with as memories and habits, while certain conditions of interchange between organism and environment are represented as needs or wants. Certain inciting episodes are

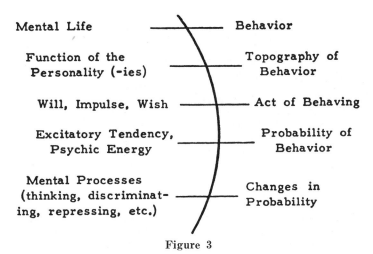

Figure 3

dealt with as emotions, again in the sense not of patterns but of active causes of behavior. Even the present environment as it affects the organism is transmuted into "experience," as we turn from what is the case to what "seems to be" the case to the individual.

The same centripetal movement may be observed on the other side of the diagram (see Figure 3). It is rare to find behavior dealt with as a subject matter in its own right. Instead it is regarded as evidence for a mental life, which is then taken as the primary object of inquiry. What the individual does—the topography of his behavior—is treated as the functioning of one or more personalities. It is clear, especially when personalities are multiple, that they cannot be identified with the biological organism as such, but are conceived of, rather, as inner behavers of doubtful status and dimensions. The act of behaving in a given instance is neglected in favor of an impulse or wish, while the probability of such an act is represented as an excitatory tendency or in terms of psychic energy. Most important of all, the changes in behavior which represent the fundamental behavioral processes are characterized as mental activities —such as thinking, learning, discriminating, reasoning, symbolizing, projecting, identifying, and repressing.

The relatively simple scheme shown in the first figure does not, therefore, represent the conception of human behavior characteristic of most current theory. The great majority of students of human behavior assume that they are concerned with a series of events indicated in the expanded diagram of Figure 4. Here the hereditary and environmental conditions are assumed to generate instincts, needs, emotions, memories, habits, and so on, which in turn lead the personality to engage in various activities characteristic of the mental apparatus, and these in turn generate the observable behavior of the organism. All four stages in the diagram are accepted as proper objects of inquiry. Indeed, far from leaving the inner events to other specialists while confining themselves to the end terms, many psychologists and psychiatrists take the mental apparatus as their primary subject matter.

Perhaps the point of my title is now becoming clearer. Is the scientific study of behavior—whether normal or psychotic—concerned with the behavior of the observable organism under the control of hereditary and environmental factors, or with the functioning of one or more personalities engaged in a variety of mental processes under the promptings of instincts, needs, emotions, memories, and habits? I do not want to raise the

Figure 4

question of the supposed *nature* of these inner entities. A certain kinship between such an explanatory system and primitive animism can scarcely be missed, but whatever the historical sources of these concepts, we may assume that they have been purged of dualistic connotations. If this is not the case, if there are those who feel that psychiatry is concerned with a world beyond that of the psychobiological or biophysical organism, that conscious or unconscious mind lacks physical extent, and that mental processes do not affect the world according to the laws of physics, then the following arguments should be all the more cogent. But the issue is not one of the nature of these events, but of their usefulness and experience in a scientific description.

It can scarcely be denied that the expansion of subject matter represented by Figure 4 has the unfortunate effect of a loss of physical status. This is more than a question of prestige or "face." A subject matter which is unquestionably part of the field of physics and biology has been relinquished for one of doubtful characteristics. This cannot be corrected merely by asserting our faith in the ultimately physical nature of inner processes. To protest that the activities of the conscious and unconscious mind are only in some sense an aspect of the biological functioning of the organism will not answer the practical question. In abandoning the dimensional systems of physics and biology, we abandon the techniques of

measurement which would otherwise be a natural heritage from earlier achievements in other sciences. This is possibly an irreparable loss. If we come out flatly for the existence of instincts, needs, memories, and so on, on the one hand, and the mental processes and functions of the personality on the other, then we must accept the responsibility of devising methods of observing these inner events and of discovering dimensional systems according to which they can be measured. The loss of the opportunity to measure and manipulate in the manner characteristic of the physical sciences would be offset only by some extraordinary advantage gained by turning to inner states or conditions.

It is possible, however, to argue that these inner events are merely ways of representing the outer. Many theorists will contend that a habit is only a sort of notation useful in reporting a bit of the history of the individual, just as so-called "mental processes" are ways of talking about changes in behavior. This is a tempting position, for we may then insist that the only dimensional systems required are those appropriate to the terminal events. But if we are to take that line, a great deal still needs to be done to put our house in scientific order. The concepts which one encounters in current behavior theory represent the observable events in an extremely confusing way. Most of them have arisen from theoretical or practical considerations which have little reference to their validity or usefulness as scientific constructs, and they bear the scars of such a history. For example, Freud pointed to important relationships between the behavior of an adult and certain episodes in early childhood, but he chose to bridge the very considerable gap between cause and effect with activities or states of the mental apparatus. Conscious or unconscious wishes or emotions in the adult represent the earlier episodes and are said to be directly responsible for their effect upon behavior. The adult is said, for example, to be suffering from conscious or unconscious anxiety generated when as a child he was punished for aggressive behavior toward a sibling. But many details of the early episode are glossed over (and may, as a result, be neglected) in attributing the disturbances in his behavior to a current anxiety rather than to the earlier punishment. The number of references to anxiety in treatises on behavior must greatly exceed the number of references to punishing episodes, yet we must turn to the latter for full details. If the details are not available, nothing can take their place.

Other kinds of independent variables provide similar examples. Everyone is familiar with the fact that, in general, organisms eat or do not eat depending upon a recent history of deprivation or ingestion. If we can establish that a child does not eat his dinner because he has recently eaten other food, there may seem to be no harm in expressing this by saying that "he is not hungry," provided we explain this in turn by pointing to the history of ingestion. But the concept of hunger represents quite inadequately the many features of schedules of deprivation and other conditions and events which alter the behavior of eating. In the same way the inner surrogates of hereditary variables function beyond the line of duty. We often have no other explanation of a given bit of behavior than that, like other features of anatomy and physiology, it is characteristic of a species; but when we choose instead

to attribute this behavior to a set of instincts, we obscure the negative nature of our knowledge and suggest more active causes than mere species status warrants. Similarly, we accept the fact that individuals differ in their behavior, and we may, in some instances, show a relation between aspects of the behavior of successive generations, but these differences and relationships are optimistically misrepresented when we speak of hereditary traits and abilities. Again, the term "experience" incorrectly represents our information about a stimulating field. It has often been observed, for example, that some trivial incident generates a reaction altogether out of proportion to its magnitude. A person seems to be reacting, not to the physical world as such, but to what the world "means to him." Eventually, of course, the effect must be explained—for example, by pointing to some earlier connection with more important events. But whatever the explanation, it is almost certainly not adequately expressed by the notion of a momentary experience. There are obvious difficulties involved in representing a physical environment *plus a personal history* as a current psychological environment alone.

So far as our independent variables are concerned, then, the practice we are examining tends to gloss over many important details and complexities. The conceptual structure conceals from us the inadequacy of our present knowledge. Much the same difficulty is encountered with respect to the dependent variable, when observable behavior takes second place to mental functionings of a personality. Just as the physical environment is transmuted into experience, so physical behavior comes to be described in terms of its purpose or meaning. A man may walk down the street in precisely the same way upon two occasions, although in one instance he is out for exercise and in another he is going to mail a letter. And so it is thought necessary to consider, not the behavior itself, but "what it means" to the behaving individual. But the additional information we are trying to convey is not a property of behavior but of an independent variable. The behavior we observe in the two cases *is* the same. In reading meaning or intention into it, we are speculating about some of its causes. To take another example, it is commonly said that we can "see" aggression. But we "see" it in two steps: (1) we observe the behavior of an organism, and (2) we relate it to observed or inferred variables having to do with injurious consequences and with the kinds of circumstances which make such behavior probable. No behavior is itself aggressive by nature, although some forms of behavior are so often a function of variables which make them aggressive that we are inclined to overlook the inferences involved. Similarly, when we observe two or more behavioral systems in the same individual and attribute them to different personalities, we gain a considerable advantage for certain descriptive purposes. For example, we can then describe oppositions between such systems as we would between different persons. But we have almost certainly suggested a unity which is not justified by the observed systems of behavior, and we have probably made it more difficult to represent the actual extent of any conflict as well as to explain its origins. And when we observe that the behavior of a person is characterized by a certain responsiveness or probability of responding and speak instead of a given amount of psychic energy, we neglect many details of the actual facts and dodge the responsibility of finding a dimensional system. Lastly, mental processes are almost always conceived of as simpler and more orderly than the rather chaotic material from which they are inferred and which they are used to explain. The "learning process" in experimental psychology, for example, does not give us an accurate account of measured changes in behavior.

We look inside the organism for a *simpler* system, in which the causes of behavior are less complex than the actual hereditary and environmental events and in which the behavior of a personality is more meaningful and orderly than the day-to-day activity of the organism. All the variety and complexity of the input in our diagram seems to be reduced to a few relatively amorphous states, which in turn generate relatively amorphous functions of the personality, which then suddenly explode into the extraordinary variety and complexity of behavior. But the simplification achieved by such a practice is, of course, illusory, for it follows only from the fact that a one-to-one correspondence between inner and outer events has not been demanded. It is just this lack of correspondence which makes such an inner system unsuitable in the experimental analysis of behavior. If "hunger" is something which is produced by certain schedules of deprivation, certain drugs, certain states of health, and so on, and if in turn it produces changes in the probability of a great variety of responses, then it must have very complex properties. It cannot be any simpler than its causes or its effects. If the behavior we observe simply expresses the functioning of a personality, the personality cannot be any simpler than the behavior. If some common learning process is responsible for the changes observed in a number of different situations, then it cannot be any simpler than these changes. The apparent simplicity of the inner system explains the eagerness with which we turn to it, but from the point of view of scientific method it must be regarded as a spurious simplicity, which foreshadows ultimate failure of such an explanatory scheme.

There is another objection. Although speculation about what goes on within the organism seems to show a concern for completing a causal chain, in practice it tends to have the opposite effect. Chains are left incomplete. The layman commonly feels that he has explained behavior when he has attributed it to something in the organism—as in saying "He went *because* he wanted to go," or "He could not work *because* he was worried about his health." Such statements may have value in suggesting the relevance of one set of causes as against another, but they do not give a full explanation until it is explained *why* the person wanted to go, or *why* he was worried. Frequently this additional step is taken, but perhaps just as often these incomplete explanations bring inquiry to a dead stop.

No matter how we may wish to represent such a sequence of causal events, we cannot satisfy the requirements of interpretation, prediction, or control unless we go back to events acting upon the organism from without—events, moreover, which are observed as any event is observed in the physical and biological sciences. It is only common sense, therefore, as well as good scientific practice, to make sure that the concepts which enter into a theory of behavior are explicitly and carefully related to such events. What is needed is an operational definition of terms. This means more than simple translation. The operational method is commonly misused to patch up and preserve concepts which are cherished for extraneous and irrelevant reasons. Thus it might be possible to set up acceptable definitions of instincts, needs, emotions, memories, psychic energy, and so on, in which each term would be carefully related to certain behavioral and environmental facts. But we have no guarantee that these concepts will be the most useful when the actual functional relationships are better understood. A more reasonable program at this stage is to attempt to account for behavior without appeal to inner explanatory entities. We can do this within the accepted framework of biology, gaining thereby not only a certain personal reassurance from the prestige of a well-developed science, but an extensive set of experimental practices and dimensional

systems. We shall be prevented from oversimplifying and misrepresenting the available facts because we shall not transmute our descriptions into other terms. The practical criteria of prediction and control will force us to take into account the complete causal chain in every instance. Such a program is not concerned with establishing the existence of inferred events, but with assessing the state of our knowledge.

This does not mean, of course, that the organism is conceived of as actually empty, or that continuity between input and output will not eventually be established. The genetic development of the organism and the complex interchanges between organism and environment are the subject matters of appropriate disciplines. Some day we shall know, for example, what happens when a stimulus impinges upon the surface of an organism, and what happens inside the organism after that, in a series of stages the last of which is the point at which the organism acts upon the environment and possibly changes it. At that point we lose interest in this causal chain. Some day, too, we shall know how the ingestion of food sets up a series of events, the last of which to engage our attention is a reduction in the probability of all behavior previously reinforced with similar food. Some day we may even know how to bridge the gap between the behavioral characteristics common to parents and offspring. But all these inner events will be accounted for with techniques of observation and measurement appropriate to the physiology of the various parts of the organism, and the account will be expressed in terms appropriate to that subject matter. It would be a remarkable coincidence if the concepts now used to refer inferentially to inner events were to find a place in that account. The task of physiology is not to find hungers, fears, habits, instincts, personalities, psychic energy, or acts of willing, attending, repressing, and so on. Nor is that task to find entities or processes of which all these could be said to be other "aspects." Its task is to account for the causal relations between input and output which are the special concern of a science of behavior. Physiology should be left free to do this in its own way. Just to the extent that current conceptual systems fail to represent the relationships between terminal events correctly, they misrepresent the task of these other disciplines. A comprehensive set of causal relations stated with the greatest possible precision is the best contribution that we, as students of behavior, can make in the co-operative venture of giving a full account of the organism as a biological system.

But are we not overlooking one important source of knowledge? What about the direct observation of mental activity? The belief that the mental apparatus is available to direct inspection anticipated the scientific analysis of human behavior by many hundreds of years. It was refined by the introspective psychologists at the end of the nineteenth century into a special theory of knowledge which seemed to place the newly created science of consciousness on a par with natural science by arguing that all scientists necessarily begin and end with their own sensations and that the psychologist merely deals with these in a different way for different purposes. The notion has been revived in recent theories of perception, in which it has been suggested that the study of what used to be called "optical illusions," for example, will supply principles which help in understanding the limits of scientific knowledge. It has also been argued that the especially intimate empathic understanding which frequently occurs in psychotherapy supplies a kind of direct knowledge of the mental processes of other people. Franz Alexander and Lawrence Kubie have argued in this manner in defense of psychoanalytic practices. Among clinical psychologists Carl Rogers has actively defended a similar view. Something

of the same notion may underlie the belief that the psychiatrist may better understand the psychotic if, through the use of lysergic acid, for example, he may temporarily experience similar mental conditions.

Whether the approach to human behavior which I have just outlined ignores some basic fact, whether it is unable to take into account the "stubborn fact of consciousness," is part of a venerable dispute which will not be settled here. Two points may be made, however, in evaluating the evidence from direct "introspection" of the mental apparatus. Knowledge is not to be identified with how things look to us, but rather with what we do about them. Knowledge is power because it is action. How the surrounding world soaks into the surface of our body is merely the first chapter of the story and would be meaningless were it not for the parts which follow. These are concerned with behavior. Astronomy is not how the heavens look to an astronomer. Atomic physics is not the physicist's perception of events within the atom, or even of the macroscopic events from which the atomic world is inferred. Scientific knowledge is what people *do* in predicting and controlling nature.

The second point is that knowledge depends upon a personal history. Philosophers have often insisted that we are not aware of a difference until it makes a difference, and experimental evidence is beginning to accumulate in support of the view that we should probably not know anything at all if we were not forced to do so. The discriminative behavior called knowledge arises only in the presence of certain reinforcing contingencies among the things known. Thus, we should probably remain blind if visual stimuli were never of any importance to us, just as we do not hear all the separate instruments in a symphony or see all the colors in a painting until it is worth while for us to do so.

Some interesting consequences follow when these two points are made with respect to our knowledge of events within ourselves. That a small part of the universe is enclosed within the skin of each of us, and that this constitutes a private world to which each of us has a special kind of access can scarcely be denied. But the world with which we are in contact does not for that reason have any special physical or metaphysical status. Now, it is presumably necessary to learn to observe or "know" events within this private world just as we learn to observe or "know" external events, and our knowledge will consist of doing something about them. But the society from which we acquire such behavior is at a special disadvantage. It is easy to teach a child to distinguish between colors by presenting different colors and reinforcing his responses as right or wrong accordingly, but it is much more difficult to teach him to distinguish between different aches or pains, since the information as to whether his responses are right or wrong is much less reliable. It is this limited accessibility of the world within the skin, rather than its nature, which has been responsible for so much metaphysical speculation.

Terms which refer to private events tend to be used inexactly. Most of them are borrowed in the first place from descriptions of external events. (Almost all the vocabulary of emotion, for example, has been shown to be metaphorical in origin.) The consequences are well known. The testimony of the individual regarding his mental processes, feeling, needs, and so on, is, as the psychiatrist above all others has insisted, unreliable. Technical systems of terms referring to private events seldom resemble each other. Different schools of introspective psychology have emphasized different features of experience, and the vocabulary of one may occasionally be unintelligible to another. This is also true of different dynamic theories of mental life. The exponent of a "system" may show extraordinary conviction in his use of terms and in his defense of a given

set of explanatory entities, but it is usually easy to find someone else showing the same conviction and defending a different and possibly incompatible system. Just as experimental psychology once found it expedient to train observers in the use of terms referring to mental events, so the education of experimental psychologists, educators, applied psychologists, psychotherapists, and many others concerned with human behavior is not always free from a certain element of indoctrination. Only in this way has it been possible to make sure that mental processes will be described by two or more people with any consistency.

Psychiatry itself is responsible for the notion that one need not be aware of the feelings, thoughts, and so on, which are said to affect behavior. The individual often behaves *as if* he were thinking or feeling in a given way although he cannot himself say that he is doing so. Mental processes which do not have the support of the testimony supplied by introspection are necessarily defined in terms of, and measured as, the behavioral facts from which they are inferred. Unfortunately, the notion of mental activity was preserved in the face of such evidence with the help of the notion of an unconscious mind. It might have been better to dismiss the concept of mind altogether as an explanatory fiction which had not survived a crucial test. The modes of inference with which we arrive at knowledge of the unconscious need to be examined with respect to the conscious mind as well. Both are conceptual entities, the relations of which to observed data need to be carefully reexamined.

In the long run the point will not be established by argument, but by the effectiveness of a given formulation in the design of productive research. An example of research on psychotic subjects which emphasizes the end terms in our diagram is the project already mentioned. This is not the place for technical details, but the rationale of this research may be relevant.* In these experiments a patient spends one or more hours daily, alone, in a small pleasant room. He is never coerced into going there, and is free to leave at any time. The room is furnished with a chair, and contains a device similar to a vending machine, which can be operated by pushing a button or pulling a plunger. The machine delivers candies, cigarettes, or substantial food, or projects colored pictures on a translucent screen. Most patients eventually operate the machine, are "reinforced" by what it delivers, and then continue to operate it daily for long periods of time—possibly a year or more. During this time the behavior is reinforced on various "schedules"—for example, once every minute or once for every thirty responses—in relation to various stimuli. The behavior is recorded in another room in a continuous curve which is read somewhat in the manner of an electrocardiogram and which permits a ready inspection and measurement of the rate of responding.

The isolation of this small living space is, of course, not complete. The patient does not leave his personal history behind as he enters the room, and to some extent what he does there resembles what he does or has done elsewhere. Nevertheless, as time goes on, the conditions arranged by the experiment begin to compose, so to speak, a special personal history, the important details of which are known. Within this small and admittedly artificial life space, we can watch the patient's behavior change as we change conditions of reinforcement, motivation, and to some extent emo-

* Dr. Harry Solomon of the Boston Psychopathic Hospital has served as co-director of the project, although the preceding arguments do not necessarily represent his views. Ogden R. Lindsley is in immediate charge and responsible for much of the over-all experimental design as well as for the actual day-to-day conduct of the experiments. Support has been provided by the Office of Naval Research and by the National Institute of Mental Health. The work is being carried out at the Metropolitan State Hospital in Waltham, Massachusetts, with the co-operation of Dr. William McLaughlin, Superintendent, and Dr. Meyer Asakoff, Director of Research.

tion. With respect to these variables the behavior becomes more and more predictable and controllable or—as characteristic of the psychotic subject —fails to do so in specific ways.

The behavior of the patient may resemble that of a normal human or infrahuman subject in response to similar experimental conditions, or it may differ in a simple quantitative way—for example, the record may be normal except for a lower over-all rate. On the other hand, a performance may be broken by brief psychotic episodes. The experimental control is interrupted momentarily by the intrusion of extraneous behavior. In some cases it has been possible to reduce or increase the time taken by these interruptions, and to determine where during the session they will occur. As in similar work with other organisms, this quantitative and continuous account of the behavior of the individual under experimental control provides a highly sensitive base line for the observation of the effects of drugs and of various forms of therapy. For our present purposes, however, the important thing is that it permits us to apply to the psychotic a fairly rigorous formulation of behavior based upon much more extensive work under the much more propitious control of conditions obtained with other species. This formulation is expressed in terms of input and output without reference to inner states.

The objection is sometimes raised that research of this sort reduces the human subject to the status of a research animal. Increasing evidence of the lawfulness of human behavior only seems to make the objection all the more cogent. Medical research has met this problem before, and has found an answer which is available here. Thanks to the parallel work on animals, it has been possible, in some cases at least, to generate healthier behavior in men, even though at this stage we are not directly concerned with such a result.

Another common objection is that we obtain our results only through an oversimplification of conditions, and that they are therefore not applicable to daily life. But one always simplifies at the start of an experiment. We have already begun to make our conditions more complex and will proceed to do so as rapidly as the uniformity of results permits. It is possible to complicate the task of the patient without limit, and to construct not only complex intellectual tasks but such interactions between systems of behavior as are seen in the Freudian dynamisms.

One simplification sometimes complained of is the absence of other human beings in this small life space. This was, of course, a deliberate preliminary measure, for it is much more difficult to control social than mechanical stimulation and reinforcement. But we are now moving on to situations in which one patient observes the behavior of another working on a similar device, or observes that the other patient receives a reinforcement whenever he achieves one himself, and so on. In another case the patient is reinforced only when his behavior corresponds in some way to the behavior of another. Techniques for achieving extraordinarily precise competition and co-operation between two or more individuals have already been worked out with lower organisms, and are applicable to the present circumstances.

This project has, of course, barely scratched the surface of the subject of psychotic behavior. But so far as it has gone, it seems to us to have demonstrated the value of holding to the observable data. Whether or not you will all find them

significant, the data we report have a special kind of simple objectivity. At least we can say: this is what a psychotic subject did under these circumstances, and this is what he failed to do under circumstances which would have had a different effect had he not been psychotic.

Although we have been able to describe and interpret the behavior observed in these experiments without reference to inner events, such refences are, of course, not interdicted. Others may prefer to say that what we are actually doing is manipulating habits, needs, and so on, and observing changes in the structure of the personality, in the strength of the ego, in the amount of psychic energy available, and so on. But the advantage of this over a more parsimonious description becomes more difficult to demonstrate, as evidence of the effectiveness of an objective formulation accumulates. In that bright future to which research in psychiatry is now pointing, we must be prepared for the possibility that increasing emphasis will be placed on immediately observable data and that theories of human behavior will have to adjust themselves accordingly. It is not inconceivable that the mental apparatus and all that it implies will be forgotten. It will then be more than a mere working hypothesis to say—to return at long last to my title—that psychotic behavior, like all behavior, is part of the world of observable events to which the powerful methods of natural science apply and to the understanding of which they will prove adequate.

The Psychological Model

LEONARD P. ULLMANN and LEONARD KRASNER

In the following parts of this section, we shall discuss the psychological model, starting with a brief review of elementary learning concepts. This review will be at a level that the student who used an elementary text such as Kendler (1962), Munn (1961), Hilgard (1962), or Morgan (1961) should have no difficulty. Next, we shall take up the major topics we have discussed in terms of the medical model: formulation of maladaptive behavior and the alteration of maladaptive behavior. Specifically, the parts of this section will deal with learning concepts, the formulation of maladaptive behavior, methods of behavior modification, and characteristics of the behavior therapist. The burden of the argument throughout will be that maladaptive behavior is both learned and unlearned in the same manner as all other behavior.

LEARNING THEORY CONCEPTS

At present, only the broadest, most thoroughly established concepts, those common to all learning theories, are used in a clinical setting. This may be supported by two examples of authors writing about the clinical application of learning theory. Dollard and Miller (1950) state: "All that is needed for the present purpose is a reinforcement theory in the broadest sense of those words," and Eysenck (1959): "Those points about which argument rages are usually of academic interest rather than of practical importance . . . there would be general agreement in any particular case about the optimum methods of achieving a quick rate of condi-

tioning, or extinction. . . ."

In this book, more of those authors dealing with hospitalized subjects or children are likely to use terms derived from the work of B. F. Skinner, while authors of articles dealing with adult neurotic or sexual problems are more likely to use the language and concepts of Hull's system. One of the authors in giving the rationale on which he based his treatment, makes use of concepts drawn from Guthrie. The point is that psychologists engaged in behavior modification make use of a variety of learning theories, but their actual operations can be described with ease by any one of a number of learning theories, the fine points that differentiate the theories being relatively minute and not at present reflected in psychologists' behavior in clinical settings.

Basic to concepts of learning is the acquisition of a functional connection between an environmental stimulus and some subject response. Two major, albeit parallel, forms of learning may be noted: classical, or Pavlovian, or respondent conditioning, in which the stimulus elicits the response, and operant conditioning in which the subject must emit the response to the situation prior to the environmental event that becomes associated with and alters its frequency of occurrence in the future either by contiguity or reinforcement.*

* Guthrie's concept of contiguity avoids a theoretical difficulty involved in a strict reinforcement theory: we will say that a reinforcing stimulus is one which alters the frequency of an emitted behavior, and then at times imply that a reinforcing stimulus is defined by its effect on the frequency of behavior. This can easily lead to an embarrassing circular definition situation, which, as Dr. Lloyd Humphreys has pointed out to the authors, makes the contiguity theory preferable. While the authors agree, the preponderance of reinforcement theorists among authors in this volume led to the selection of the easier didactic procedure of a reinforcement rather than contiguity frame of reference.

In the Pavlovian or respondent conditioning situation, a stimulus that initially has no power to elicit a respondent behavior may come to have such power if it is associated with a stimulus that does have the power to elicit the respondent. In this situation, the pairing of the conditioned and the unconditioned stimuli is called *reinforcement* because any tendency for the response to the conditioned stimulus is facilitated by the presence of the unconditioned stimulus and the response to it. Once formed, the conditioned response undergoes systematic changes in strength depending upon the arrangement of the environment. If the unconditioned stimulus is repeatedly omitted, the conditioned response gradually diminishes, and the repetition of the conditioned stimulus without reinforcement is called *extinction*. This is not a passive disappearance, but rather there is learned an inhibition or tendency not to respond. When a conditioned response to one stimulus has been acquired, other similar stimuli will also evoke the response. This observed behavior leads to the concept of *generalization*, a reaction to novel situations in accordance with their degree of similarity to familiar ones. The amount of generalization decreases as the second stimulus becomes less similar to the original conditioned stimulus. A process complementary to *generalization* is *discrimination*. Conditioned discrimination is brought about through selective reinforcement and extinction so that of two stimuli similar to each other, the one reinforced (followed by the unconditioned stimulus) will elicit the respondent while the one extinguished will not elicit the respondent.

In general, respondent behavior is associated with involuntary musculature and operant behavior is associated with voluntary musculature. From birth, the individual makes massive, random responses, both verbal and motoric. He literally "operates" on his environment, hence the Skinnerian term "operant." An operant behavior that is closely followed by a reinforcing stimulus is likely to be changed in frequency of emission. If the reinforcing stimulus is a pleasant one, for example, one that reduces some current deprivation, it is a positive reinforcement, one that increases the likelihood, when the environmental setting is repeated, of the emission of the act with which it was associated. If the reinforcing stimulus is unpleasant or aversive, the emitted behavior is less likely to occur on repetition of the circumstances. Withdrawal of an aversive stimulus is a positive reinforcing event. It is crucial to state explicitly that frequency of emitted behavior is the prime operational definition of reinforcing stimuli (although latency and amplitude may, at times, be used also). Where positive reinforcement increases emission, and negative reinforcement decreases emission, repeated absence of reinforcement leads to extinction and a return of the rate of response emission to the level observed prior to reinforcement.

We may talk of discriminative stimuli: any stimulus that marks a time or place of reinforcement, positive or negative, being presented or removed, is a discriminative stimulus. A discriminative stimulus marks the time or place when an operant will have reinforcing consequences. A discriminative stimulus does not elicit a response. Elicitation is a characteristic that holds only for respondents, that is, the green traffic light, a discriminative stimulus, does not set people going across the street in the same way that a bright light flashed in their eyes constricts their pupils. A discriminated operant is one controlled by a preceding discriminative stimulus. A person who typically responds under the control of discriminative stimuli is said to be discriminating, and the procedure of bringing an operant under such control is called discrimination. Whenever some particular stimulus, through association with reinforcement, takes on discriminative stimulus properties, then other stimuli (although not directly associated with reinforcement) will also take on discriminative stimulus properties to the extent they are similar to the original discriminative stimulus. This phenomenon is called *operant stimulus generalization.*

Discriminative stimuli may become reinforcing. On highways in California pedestrians are able to press a traffic button that will change the light for them. In order to obtain the discriminative stimulus, the green light, they perform operants, that is, push buttons. Discriminative stimuli become reinforcers with adults and comprise the major environmental stimuli that are systematically associated with reinforcement, for example, money. Reinforcers that have achieved their reinforcing powers through their prior service as discriminative stimuli are called *acquired or secondary reinforcers.*

As will be seen in this volume, particularly in Ayllon's work with hospitalized psychiatric patients and in the Harris, *et al.* work with nursery school children, attention is a very strong acquired or secondary reinforcer. For the child, it is usually necessary to obtain an adult's attention before satisfaction of other needs can be obtained. Once established, a secondary reinforcer can strengthen responses other than those used during its original establishment, and can do so with motives other than the motive prevailing during the original training.

The rate at which reinforcements are delivered may follow different patterns, and these patterns are called *schedules of reinforcement.* Reinforcement can be presented upon completion of acts or at the completion of time intervals. A ratio of reinforcement (one reinforcement for one act, one every two acts, and so forth) or an interval of reinforcement (one every ten seconds, one every minute) may be talked about. Further, these programs may be "fixed" every nth act (a fixed ratio) or "variable" (randomly on a one-third or one-tenth ratio). Similarly, there may be fixed interval or variable interval schedules. In general,

learning is more resistant to extinction if the reinforcement is intermittent and/or variable.

An important aspect of work applying operant conditioning techniques is the method of *approximations or shaping.* Isaacs, Thomas, and Goldiamond's article in this volume describes and makes use of shaping. The experimenter reinforces only those responses that move in the direction of the final performance, which is the goal, and he extinguishes or does not reinforce all other responses. In shaping the responses, he may, in many instances, only approximate the final desired behaviors. Such selective reinforcement is a powerful tool in bringing about a "new" behavior.

A final note should be made of another technique, that of *response chaining,* in which an increasingly long set of responses is gradually built up prior to the reinforcement. It should be explicit that a schedule of reinforcement, as well as the behavior reinforced, may gradually be changed during the course of time. These procedures, all of which depend eventually upon response contingent reinforcement, both help explain the development of maladaptive behavior and provide tools for its change.

The range of acquired reinforcers, discriminative stimuli, and complex performances is great indeed. Perhaps the most important, and certainly the one given the greatest attention in traditional therapy, is language. While research reports and experimental (as distinct from theoretical) foundations do not fall within the scope of the present work, it is worthwhile to note that the vocal behavior of chickens (Lane, 1961), cats (Molliver, 1963), and dogs (Salzinger and Waller, 1962) have been brought under control of reinforcing stimuli, and that infants' smiling (Brackbill, 1958) and vocalizations (Rheingold, Gewirtz, and Ross, 1959) have been increased through response contingent social reinforcement.

Simple performances, once established, may become parts of more complex ones. Both the increasing demands of the person's society, and his increased range due to language and communicated experience (lectures, readings) lead to increasingly complex performances which become techniques for solving further problems. Skinner (1963) talks of plans and logical analyses as discriminative stimuli, Miller and Dollard (1941) demonstrate the learning of a relationship, imitation in animals, and Berger (1961), Kanfer and Marston (1963) and particularly Bandura and Walters (1963) have investigated, within social reinforcement terms, vicarious reinforcement and modeling.

The learning concepts we have just reviewed are those of Skinner. The most frequent alternative formulation is that of Hull. While for the present purposes, as we have mentioned, the differences between the two schools are of relatively little importance, we will now turn to Hull's formulations. Where Skinner's concepts are based on the frequency of emission of overt behaviors, Hull distinguishes between performance, the overt behavior, and habit, the modification of the central nervous system, which mediates learning and which is not directly measurable. A performance is the product of habit strength and drives such as hunger or thirst. Important concepts for behavior therapy, particularly of tics, are those of reactive inhibition and conditioned inhibition. All activity produces some fatigue and this fatigue produces a drive (reactive inhibition which decreases with rest) and a negative habit (conditioned inhibition). The Hullian system with its concept of drive and mediation through habit is perhaps a stronger explanatory tool than Skinner's system and certainly lends itself more readily (compare Dollard and Miller, 1950) to the translation of psychoanalytic concepts. The Skinnerian system with its orientation to what Boring called "an empty organism" is more likely to focus on the stimulus environment rather than the internal state of the organism. With a concept of media-

tion and autonomic responses associated with meanings, the Hullian system may rely more heavily on Pavlovian or respondent conditioning than Skinnerian formulations. Hull's system certainly facilitates the comprehension of Wolpe's systematic desensitization procedure in which a conditioned drive, anxiety, may be inhibited by associating the appropriate stimulus with an image or other cue mediating the response to the anxiety provoking stimulus.

In closing this brief section we must add a few related points. The first is that while we have discussed operant and respondent behavior as though they were separate, in reality the two are usually intertwined and operant behaviors have respondent consequences. Especially for the behavior change techniques reported in this book, the concepts of operant and respondent conditioning, role learning and modeling, serve to complement each other. A behavior such as acting pleasantly may have genuine conditioned respondent consequences through prior association with the effects of such behavior, for example, an increase in the positive reinforcing stimuli emitted by other people (Ullmann, Krasner, and Gelfand, 1963). This leads to the concept that an important aspect of the individual's stimulus environment is composed of his own behavior. Performing an appropriate behavior, studying for an exam, may, because of prior experience, lead to an increase in reinforcing stimuli. The operant behavior, studying, may reduce the autonomic consequences of being unprepared. In discussing appropriate behavior of such a molar nature we arrive at a concept of role, a group of behaviors that have been shaped by the environment to meet the expectation of others (that is, to be reinforced) as appropriate for an individual in a given situation. Just as in typing, telegraphy, or piano playing increasing skill leads to larger functional units in which particular enactments may serve as stimuli for subsequent actions, so a complex social response may be developed from fine discriminations of the stimulus situation and generalization from previous situations. The person may learn to identify situations and use his own verbal responses as stimuli, which indicate the similarity or difference of a present situation to ones which were previously punishing or rewarding. This formulation may also include the labeling of patterns of behaviors that have previously been useful such as "Do what the other person is doing" or "It is likely that what happens to him will happen to me" or "This situation—exam—is likely to be painful." The subject responds to the situation with a vocal behavior that in turn is a discriminative stimulus. Finally, just as we noted the complex association of operant and respondent behaviors at the beginning of this paragraph, we should note that the human stimulus situation is considerably more uncontrolled, complex, changeable, and filled with more useful and more irrelevant stimuli than a Skinner box. A small and selected sample of these cues is probably used to match current situations with past ones and provide the self-stimulus of a label. Responses based on self-stimulation are necessary for reasonably prompt social responses, but they may well be inaccurate, superstitious, and self-validating. However, these responses, or the stimuli that control them, may be identified and reconditioned. It is this line of reasoning, the individual's own behavior as a source of stimuli and the patterning of social behavior into roles as units of behavior that we think may offer a fruitful extension of reinforcement theory into increasingly complex areas of social behavior.

MALADAPTIVE BEHAVIOR: A PSYCHOLOGICAL FORMULATION

Maladaptive behaviors are learned behaviors, and the development and maintenance of a maladaptive behavior is no different from the development and maintenance of any other behavior. There is no discontinuity between desirable and undesirable modes of adjustment or between "healthy" and "sick" behavior. The first major implication of this view is the question of how a behavior is to be identified as desirable or undesirable, adaptive or maladaptive. The general answer we propose is that because there are no disease entities involved in the majority of subjects displaying maladaptive behavior, the designation of a behavior as pathological or not is dependent upon the individual's society. Specifically, while there are no single behaviors that would be said to be adaptive in all cultures, there are in all cultures definite expectations or roles for functioning adults in terms of familial and social responsibility. Along with role enactments, there are a full range of expected potential reinforcements. The person whose behavior is maladaptive does not fully live up to the expectations for one in his role, does not respond to all the stimuli actually present, and does not obtain the typical or maximum forms of reinforcement available to one of his status. The difference between the types of reinforcement that maintain adaptive and maladaptive behavior is that the latter is maintained by more direct and immediate forms of reinforcement than the former. Behavior that one culture might consider maladaptive, be it that of the Shaman or the paranoid, is adaptive in another culture if the person so behaving is responding to all the cues present in the situation in a manner likely to lead to his obtaining reinforcement appropriate to his status in that society. Maladaptive behavior is behavior that is considered inappropriate by those key people in a person's life who control reinforcers. Such maladaptive behavior leads to a reduction in the range or the value of positive reinforcement given to the person displaying it.

In a major article, Scott (1958) reviewed definitions of mental health in order to determine if there was available an operational definition of mental health or illness that could be used for purposes of research. His conclusion was that the current definitions were unworkable and at variance with each other. Such findings are not surprising in view of the questionable model on which a concept of "mental health" is based. Definitions of adjustment must be situation specific. In particular, by definition, a person comes to the therapist or to a hospital because someone wants to change him. That someone may be the person himself, his relatives, friends, employer, or authorities empowered to make the judgment that his behavior is a danger to himself or others so that he or his society would benefit from his treatment. This set of circumstances means that the definition of adjustment is not absolute but shifts from time to time and place to place. Further as the number of mental health professionals increases, it is likely that the number of people specified as requiring treatment will also increase. Jerome Frank (1961, pp. 6-7) summarizes this concept as follows:

An interesting, if somewhat unfortunate, consequence of the fact that social attitudes play such a big role in the definition of mental illness is that mental health education may be a two-edged sword. By teaching people to regard certain types of distress or behavioral oddities as illnesses rather than as normal reactions to life's stresses, harmless eccentricities, or moral weaknesses, it may cause alarm and increase the demand for psychotherapy. This may explain the curious fact that the use of psychotherapy tends to keep pace with its availability. The greater the number of treatment facilities and the more widely they are known, the larger the number of persons seeking their help. Psychotherapy is the only form of treatment which, at least to some extent, appear to create the illness it treats.

The next question becomes one of how we can account for the regularities of behavior seen in the "mentally ill" that compose the body of descriptive psychiatry. At a first level, as we have previously implied, these regularities may be far less frequent than is generally supposed. The grouping of people as exemplars of underlying causes or illness is a matter leading to a great deal of argument and con-

stant revision, and expansion under sociological pressures. Textbook cases are hard to find in the psychiatric hospital because most cases manifest only a few of the specific symptoms that compose a syndrome, while many hospitalized people show specific behaviors that belong to more than one syndrome. A factor analytic approach to the question of the covariation of symptomatic behaviors is likely to indicate that classic syndromes are infrequent and may even be labels that do not reflect the behavior actually present. Another instance of this is the increasing use of the concept of premorbid adjustment (Phillips, 1953) or the process-reactive continuum (Ullmann and Giovannoni, 1964) to predict differential responses to stimulus situations either within or across major diagnostic categories. In short, the regularities presupposed by a medical model may not exist.

At a second level there is a matter of role learning. Any behavior that increases positive reinforcement or helps reduce aversive stimuli is likely to be increased. A person who is "sick" is considered unlucky, excused from responsibility, and a proper object of pity and forebearance. In our society, the patient is one who bears or endures suffering without complaint, who is long-suffering, and who is acted upon and receives treatment. At the present time, the person who is a mental patient is frequently considered incompetent legally and yet is in a position to demand attention and forgiveness from his peers. Just as the manifestations of the hypnotic role have changed over time, so have the manifestations of the mentally ill role changed over time and, during the same period, from one social class to another. Illustrations of this are the greater frequency of psychosomatic ills among officers than enlisted men during World War II, the decrease of hysterical symptoms, and the different patterns of maladaptive behavior in different social classes. Kelly (1955, p. 366) notes: "It seemed to the writer, in comparing the complaints of psychologically sophisticated people with those of the psychologically naive, that there was a definite tendency, once a person had chosen a psychological name for his discomfort, to display all of the symptoms in whatever book he had read, even if he had to practice them diligently. It suggested that psychological symptoms may frequently be interpreted as the rationale by which one's chaotic experiences are given a measure of structure and meaning."

The psychiatrist or other mental health professional may do much to foster the regularities supposedly seen in mental illness. During the diagnostic interview, the psychiatrist will focus on, and thereby reinforce with attention, the material that is meaningful to him. Hollingworth (1930, pp. 233-236) makes this point very clearly in his discussion of symptoms rendered vivid by attention. He describes how a medical examination may emphasize complaints: "... it is astonishing to find how many bodily sensations have hitherto escaped attention and now clamor for report. Fixation upon them, prolonged attention to them, minute scrutiny of them, increases their vividness, and they now stand out with distinctness. This is the characteristic effect of attention everywhere." (p. 234). If there is pressure to admit a person to the hospital, the psychiatrist will look for behaviors that are symptomatic and permit the statement that a particular syndrome exists. Once this has been accomplished, he can make a medical decision, a diagnosis, and hospitalize the individual. The patient is shaped into giving the physician what is wanted and expected.

Once within the hospital, there are strong pressures on the individual to assume the proper passive, nontroublesome "good patient" role. In particular, the nursing assistants or attendants have the responsibility to keep large groups of patients safe, clean, quiet, and cooperative. The aide culture (Belknap, 1956; Dunham and Weinberg, 1960; Goffman, 1961; Lehrman, 1961) can impose a strong

set of explicit reinforcements to obtain expected behavior. Among these are the granting of privileges such as freedom of movement, passes, better accommodations, and the threat of punishment such as electroconvulsive therapy and transfer to a ward peopled by more disturbed patients. The apathy and withdrawal that are the most difficult and prognostically unfavorable symptoms of schizophrenia may well arise from the training given the patient not to be assertive or insistent upon his legitimate human rights. In the typical hospital setting, there is also a marked decrease in normal social contact and sensory stimulation. A number of authors have hypothesized that the social and sensory deficits involved in this situation parallel the production of behaviors similar to psychoses observed in sensory deprivation experiments (McReynolds, Acker, and Daily, 1959). The psychological correlates of playing a particular role and the physical conditions of diet, exercise, and living accommodations may lead to biochemical similarities that are the results and not the cause of hospitalization (Kety, 1960).

While perhaps less severe, there is definite role training observed in out-patient treatment. We shall return to this matter, particularly in the work of Goldstein (1962), when we discuss traditional therapy as behavior therapy. At this point we merely wish to indicate that is it possible to build a case for patients learning the regularities expected of them.

Let us turn to a more intensive analysis of the development of specific symptoms within a learning theory context. Again, for purposes of exposition, we will make distinctions between operant and respondent behavior when in fact the two are intertwined.

In terms of respondent or "surplus conditioned reactions" (Eysenck, 1959), we shall describe the concepts and terminology of Wolpe (1954). However, we have reservations about the usefulness of a drive concept; and the concept of "anxiety" currently has so many extraneous and poorly defined uses as to be a hindrance at times rather than an aid in communication (English and English, 1958, p. 35; Sarbin, 1963). To quote Wolpe (1954) : "By 'anxiety' is meant the autonomic response pattern or patterns that are characteristically part of the organism's response to noxious stimulation.... An anxiety response is unadaptive when it is evoked in circumstances in which there is objectively no threat." Such responses occur within the paradigm of classic or Pavlovian conditioning. A noxious stimulus is paired with a previously indifferent stimulus, and at a later time the previously neutral stimulus alone elicits the response appropriate to the prior situation (when the noxious stimulus was present), but which is no longer adaptive or appropriate. Watson and Rayner (1920) present the experimental development of a phobia, complete with generalization, by this technique. Moss (1924) used a similar procedure to establish food aversion in two children and anecdotal material illustrative of this point abounds (Burnham, 1924). On a more general level, we may quote Eysenck (1959) :

Many conditioned responses are unadaptive, and consequently may embarrass the individual and even drive him into a mental hospital if sufficiently intense. Yet other conditioned responses are obviously necessary and desirable; indeed, many of them are indispensable for survival. It has been argued very strongly that the whole process of socialization is built up on the principle of conditioning; the overt display of aggressive and sexual tendencies is severely punished in the child, thus producing conditioned fear and pain responses (anxiety) to situations in which the individual is likely to display such tendencies. He consequently refrains from acting in the forbidden manner . . . because only by not indulging, and physically removing himself can he relieve the very painful conditioned anxiety responses to the whole situation. Anxiety thus acts as a mediating drive. . . .

Another way in which this might be put is that the behaviors that reduce the likelihood of aversive stimuli are positively reinforcing and likely to recur. A result is the avoidance of objects, situations, acts, and so forth, that have been associated with noxious stimuli. However, there is likely to be generalization, and in the very nature of withdrawal, a failure to differentiate between those elements of a situation from which it is adaptive to withdraw and those from which it is maladaptive to withdraw. Similarly, a behavior that has been associated with termination of aversive stimuli is likely to be repeated, even if such a behavior had no association with the reinforcement other than contiguity. Other responses may be continued because they were once appropriate to situations that were similar in some aspect irrelevant to the realities of the current situation. The reader's attention is called to our previous comment that the human stimulus situation is uncontrolled, complex, changeable, and filled with cues that are both relevant and irrelevant. This situation leads to responses to situations based on a limited sample of the available cues. Hollingworth's formulation of maladaptive behavior as redintegrated reactions (Hollingworth, 1930, pp. 249-255) is particularly germane. A major difference between physical and mental reactions is the response to symbols of the situation rather than reinstitution of all the original stimuli. "Mental processes . . . are those in which a partial stimulus serves adequately or approximately to provoke responses formerly occasioned only by more elaborate situations." (Hollingworth, 1930, p. 249). The eliciting of a response by a partial detail of its former antecedent is what Hollingworth means by redintegration. Hollingworth (1930, p. 250) writes:

. . . the response may be overdetermined by the detail, without due regard to other features now occurring with it. The response is thus determined by past contexts rather than by present contexts. It is therefore likely to be bizarre, inutile, maladjusted, and hence neurotic. Prepotency of special cues or fragments of a situation may thus result in ineffective adjustment to that situation. Effective adjustment demands that all present facts be allowed to constellate, to *determine jointly* the nature of the response. Individuals in whom this synergy or adequate cooperation of all the details of a situation does not effectively take place are lacking in a characteristic which we may for convenience call *scope* or *sagacity*.

For purposes of exposition, we may distinguish between an adaptive response that has not been learned and a maladaptive response that now must be changed.

In terms of deficient prior learning, we may conceive of a person who was isolated and socially withdrawn as a child. Such a person is less likely to have practiced, been reinforced for, and learned effective social skills. This deficit in training may make future social situations less rewarding and lead to the development of a vicious cycle. The development of attention and interest is exemplified by Birnbrauer *et al.* in the present volume. Another example of this area is the treatment of enuresis. The association between bladder tension and wakefulness may be taught within a simple conditioning paradigm. In terms of symptom substitution, it is interesting that Mowrer and Mowrer (1938) who made the major breakthrough in this area write: "Personality changes, when any have occurred as a result of the application of the present method of treating enuresis, have uniformly been in a favorable direction. In no case has there been any evidence of 'symptom substitution.'" Morgan and Witmer (1939), Davidson and Douglass (1950), and Geppert (1953) are among authors who also remark on the general personality improvement associated with overcoming enuresis by conditioning techniques. In short, there may have been a simple failure to learn a particular behavior that can be taught easily.

A second group of maladaptive behaviors may be learned through operant conditioning. The behavior is associated with positive reinforcement of some sort. In the present volume, the child in the report by Wolf, *et al.* found that the maladaptive behavior, vomiting, through misguided kindness, led to release from a potentially uncomfortable situation. When the reinforcement maintaining the behavior, release from the situation, ceased, the maladaptive response to the situation decreased and finally ceased. Mees (1964) summarizes the general principle: "If you want an explanation for this behavior—this monster behavior—I believe we can account for all of it with one general principle: *it pays off*. It pays off for the individual who can't seem to find other, nonmonstrous behaviors to get him what he wants."

Patterns of behaviors are increased, shaped, and maintained through reinforcement. If a person emits a behavior and reinforcement follows soon after, the frequency with which that behavior will be emitted in the future is altered. In terms of the development of maladaptive behavior, we have mentioned the work of Watson and Rayner (1920) and Moss (1924). To this, we may add the Haughton and Ayllon work on the production and elimination of symptomatic behavior printed in this book. In this work, a person for whom cigarettes were reinforcing was handed a broom and given a cigarette. Broom holding became a stimulus associated with being given cigarettes, and the person developed the "bizarre, maladaptive" behavior of holding a broom and refusing to let it go. In another article, Ayllon and Haughton (1964) systematically manipulated the symptomatic verbal behavior of three patients. When the staff responded with interest and attention to bizarre talk, these verbalizations increased in frequency. Withholding social reinforcement (extinction) resulted in a decrease in the frequency of symptomatic verbal responses. The articles in the first section of this book illustrate operant techniques to promote adjustive responses, but, by implication, if adjustive responses are under stimulus control, we may hypothesize that so are maladjustive ones. In studies in which either control groups or periods of no reinforcement (extinction) have been used, Salzinger and Pisoni (1958, 1961) and Weiss, Krasner, and Ullmann (1963) have illustrated that affect self-references and use of emotional words by hospitalized patients may be altered by reinforcement. Many people have posited that a crucial symptom in schizophrenia is disorganization of thinking. Sommer, Witney, and Osmond (1962) have increased, through selective reinforcement of desirable responses, the frequency of common associations of hospitalized patients in a word association situation. Ullmann, Krasner, and Edinger (1964) replicated this result, and perhaps as noteworthy, found that even with long-term schizophrenic patients, the nonreinforced control group decreased in their rate of emission of common associations. Work on nursery school behavior, Allen *et al.* with social isolation, Harris *et al.* with regressed crawling, and Hart *et al.* with operant crying, illustrate with the same paradigm used by Ayllon and Haughton (1964) that these behaviors may be increased or decreased contingent upon adult attention. These three studies of nursery school behavior indicate clearly how a behavior "paying off" may lead to its increase. Finally, avoidance of aversive stimuli is reinforcing: stuttering was instigated in three normally fluent subjects when a persistent shock was introduced and its cessation for a brief period was made contingent upon nonfluent verbal behavior (Flanagan, Goldiamond, and Azrin, 1959). In our introductions to specific groups of case histories, we shall offer additional material, but at the present, we may point to the instigation and manipulation (both increase and decrease) of maladaptive behavior through procedures of reinforcement. While there are relatively few studies that set out to develop maladaptive responses to stimuli, every article that utilizes a psychological technique for the direct alteration of adaptive behavior buttresses by implication this formulation of the development of maladaptive behavior.

A question that follows the development of maladaptive responses is why, or more accurately how, these behavior patterns are maintained. The answer is by the same manner, reinforcement, as they were developed. Some of the evidence for this may be found in the articles cited in the previous paragraph. Further evidence comes from the effect of removing reinforcement (such as attention) in articles such as those of Ayllon and Ayllon and Michael. Additional material appears in the Isaacs, Thomas, and Goldiamond article in which a previously mute patient verbalized his wishes with those people who did not respond to his gestures, but continued to be mute with those people with whom the nonverbal behavior was effective. Williams' article on temper tantrums provides an instance of a relapse, a naturalistic experiment similar to the systematic instances reported in the group of nursery school papers previously cited. In Ayllon, "emotional responses" which, if reinforced, might have become highly frequent behaviors, did not become so due to being ignored. The current reinforcement obtained for maladaptive behavior need not be the same as the reinforcement that led to the development of the behavior: *all* that is argued is that the maladaptive behavior is maintained by some reinforcement. An example may make this point clear. A person known to the authors once had a roommate who snored. To drown out the snoring he started using a second pillow to cover his ear. A pillow over the ear was associated with reinforcement, going to sleep, and became a discriminative stimulus for sleeping. Ten years after the original situation he continued to have difficulty going to sleep without a second, covering pillow. Although the original stimulus, the snoring roommate, was no longer present, the behavior continued because it was still associated with a pleasant stimulus, that is, going to sleep. Reinforcing stimuli can, particularly in humans, be different from the stimuli in the original situation. It is neither parsimonious nor necessary to explain behavior by either functional autonomy or underlying causes. It goes without saying that we doubt whether analyzing the dynamics of the comfort pattern of clinging to a soft, white object, such as a pillow, first observed when the subject was separated from his home and mother, would be particularly useful in changing the behavior.

We have noted that because there is no distinction between the development and maintenance of adaptive and maladaptive behavior, what we say of one applies to the other. For this reason, in line with our discussion of the maintenance of maladaptive behavior, we would now like to turn to the generalization of gains made in the professional behavior modification setting to the extra-therapy environment. The explicit techniques for the alteration of maladaptive behavior and fostering of new, more adaptive behavior, will be discussed in the next part of this introduction. But if we assume that the new behavior has developed, we may offer a number of means by which it is maintained.

First and foremost, the new behavior pays off. It is more likely to lead to reinforcement. Lazarus' case (1959) of a boy treated with Wolpe's (1958, pp. 184-185) anxiety-relief technique for sleeping with his mother is an example. The new behavior was welcomed by both parents and the siblings, and the entire family situation was changed. In short, because the subject's behavior leads to responses from other people, a new pattern of behavior by the subject puts him in a new environment. This point is important because evocative therapists typically argue that the person must be "basically" changed (for example, his ego strengthened) before he can withstand the stress of returning to the environment in which he had previously developed a pattern of maladaptive behavior. Using this concept as a solution, alternative, or supplement, expressive therapists are likely to press for the treatment of parents so that they will solve *their* problems.

People who are likely to be important in regard to the maintenance of new adaptive behavior can be taught and literally programed as alternate therapists. In the present volume there are many examples of this. In Ayllon and Michael's and Bachrach, Erwin, and Mohr's articles we will see the nurse being given instructions as to her behavior toward hospitalized patients. In Wolf, Risley, and Mees' article, an aide who worked with the child in the hospital went home with him to teach the parents. Davison discusses the training of college undergraduates for work with severely disturbed children. Parents play a key role in selecting and reinforcing behavior in papers by Rickard and Mundy (stuttering), Patterson (school phobia), Williams (temper tantrums), Bentler (phobia), Peterson and London, and Madsen (toilet training). School teachers play a key role in the majority of the work with children in social situations, and retardates. Finally, in Sulzer's paper we will see the subject's friends making their reinforcing behavior contingent on his not drinking. It is important to note that this approach is readily understandable to parents and other significant people in the child's environment and thus may lead to a rapid and hearty adoption by them. For example, Jersild and Holmes (1935) discuss the techniques that parents devised to overcome children's fears, and the most effective of these closely parallel the reconditioning techniques that are presented in this book. A second point is that these techniques are more likely to be accepted and utilized by those members of the lower social classes who are likely to have difficulty in utilizing more traditional forms of psychotherapy (Hollingshead and Redlich, 1958). There are many parents who do not value self-insight and neither understand nor believe in the efficacy of working on their basic problems to alleviate their child's maladaptive behavior. For those people, who may well expect prescription and direction, withdrawal from therapy follows a rigid approach which assumes that the focus of difficulty lies in them. By accepting whatever the parent has been doing as evidence of good faith, the person interested in behavior modification can reduce the parents' feelings of inadequacy and pave the way for the development of more effective parental responses to the child's behavior. The therapist's goal is to program the parents to respond to and nurture the desired changes toward adaptive behavior. Behavior therapy may extend the number of cases the therapist is likely to undertake. For example, Phillips notes that with his assertion-structured therapy 53 of 59 patients entered therapy and 51 of these 53 obtained benefit in an average of less than eight sessions. In contrast, at the same clinic, and with no noticeable bias of assignment, of 190 cases initially interviewed 103 were judged unsuitable for treatment by psychoanalytically oriented therapists, 42 refused therapy themselves, and the remaining 45 completed a course of therapy averaging 17 sessions. For approximately 75 percent of these 45 cases, benefit was reported. Aside from the difference in the rate of benefit of those actually undergoing treatment, the assertion-structured approach was found serviceable in a far greater proportion of the population that came for help. Thus behavior therapy may have an additional value in terms of the scope of the population served. Finally, behavior may be maintained by subject feedback. An obvious aspect of this is the increase of positive environmental reinforcement. Another aspect is that certain new behaviors are inconsistent with other maladaptive behaviors. An example may be found in the Ayllon and Michael article in which, with self-feeding and a considerable weight gain, an "untreated" delusion of poisoned food ceased. It seems reasonable to hypothesize that hearty self-feeding is a behavior incompatible with the claim of poisoned food. There is also a matter of generalization: as Eysenck (1959) has noted, removal of one symptom, rather than exacerbating or leading to development of new symptoms, fa-

cilitates removal of other maladaptive behaviors. On one level, the person observes that he can be different and can change. On a different level of abstraction, it seems reasonable that if maladaptive responses can generalize, a technique that has been adaptive in one situation will also be tried out as a response to other situations. Finally, as we noted in our discussion of learning concepts, operant and respondent behaviors are intertwined and a considerable portion of the subject's environment is composed of his own behavior. We may hypothesize that this part of the environment is appreciably changed for the better as he emits more adaptive responses. In short, there are many ways in which behavior, whether adaptive or maladaptive, can be maintained without reference to an underlying, historical cause.

References

Ayllon, T., and Haughton, E. Control of the behavior of schizophrenic patients by food. *J. exp. Anal. Behav.*, 1962, 5, 343-352.

Bandura, A., and Walters, R. H. *Social learning and personality development.* New York: Holt, Rinehart and Winston, Inc., 1963.

Belknap, I. *Human problems of a state mental hospital.* New York: McGraw-Hill, 1956.

Berger, S. M. Incidental learning through vicarious reinforcement. *Psychol. Rep.*, 1961, 9, 477-491.

Brackbill, Yvonne. Extinction of the smiling response in infants as a function of reinforcement schedule. *Child Develpm.*, 1958, 29, 115-124.

Burnham, W. H. *The normal mind.* New York: Appleton, 1924.

Davidson, J. R., and Douglass, E. Nocturnal enuresis: a special approach to treatment. *Brit. Med. J.*, 1950, 1, 1345-1347.

Dollard, J., and Miller, N. E. *Personality and psychotherapy.* New York: McGraw-Hill, 1950.

Dunham, H. W., and Weinberg, S. K. *The culture of the state mental hospital.* Detroit: Wayne State University Press, 1960.

English, H. B., and English, Ava C. *A comprehensive dictionary of psychological and psychoanalytical terms: a guide to usage.* New York: Longmans, 1958.

Eysenck, H. J. Learning theory and behaviour therapy. *J. ment. Sci.*, 1959, 105, 61-75. (In Eysenck, 1960a)

Flanagan, B., Goldiamond, I., and Azrin,

N. H. Instatement of stuttering in normally fluent individuals through operant procedures. *Science*, 1959, *130*, 979-981.

Frank, J. D. *Persuasion and healing.* Baltimore: Johns Hopkins Press, 1961.

Geppert, T. V. Management of nocturnal enuresis by conditioned response. *J. Amer. med. Ass.*, 1953, *152*, 381-383.

Goffman, E. *Asylums.* New York: Anchor Books, 1961.

Goldstein, A. P. *Therapist-patient expectancies in psychotherapy.* New York: Pergamon, 1962.

Hilgard, E. R. *Introduction to psychology* (3rd ed.). New York: Harcourt, 1962.

Hollingshead, A. B. and Redlich, F. C. *Social class and mental illness.* New York: Wiley, 1958.

Hollingworth, H. L. *Abnormal psychology.* New York: Ronald, 1930.

Jersild, A. T., and Holmes, Frances B. Methods of overcoming children's fears. *J. Psychol.*, 1935, *1*, 75-104.

Kanfer, F. H., and Marston, A. R. Human reinforcement: vicarious and direct. *J. exp. Psychol.*, 1963, *65*, 292-296.

Kelly, G. A. *The psychology of personal constructs.* New York: Norton, 1955. 2 vols.

Kendler, H. K. *Basic psychology.* New York: Appleton, 1962.

Kety, S. S. Recent biochemical theories of schizophrenia. In D. D. Jackson (Ed.), *The etiology of schizophrenia.* New York: Basic Books, 1960.

Lane, H. Operant control of vocalizing in the chicken. *J. exp. Anal. Behav.*, 1961, *4*, 171-177.

Lazarus, A. A. The elimination of children's phobias by deconditioning. *Med. Proc. S. Afr.*, 1959, *5*, 261-265. (In Eysenck, 1960a)

Lehrman, N. S. Do our hospitals help make acute schizophrenia chronic? *Dis. nerv. Syst.*, 1961, *22*, 489-493.

McReynolds, P., Acker, Mary, and Daily, J. On the effects of perceptual enhancement on certain schizophrenic symptoms. *Res. Rept. V A Palo Alto*, 1959, No. 1.

Mees, H. How to create a monster. Unpublished manuscript, 1964.

Miller, N. E., and Dollard, J. *Social learning and imitation.* New Haven: Yale University Press, 1941.

Molliver, M. E. Operant control of vocal behavior in the cat. *J. exp. Anal. Behav.*, 1963, *6*, 197-202.

Morgan, C. T. *Introduction to psychology.* (2nd ed.) New York: McGraw-Hill, 1961.

Morgan, J. J. B., and Witmer, Frances J. The treatment of enuresis by the conditioned reaction technique. *J. genet. Psychol.*, 1939, *55*, 59-65.

Moss, F. A. Note on building likes and dislikes in children. *J. exp. Psychol.*, 1924, *7*, 475-478.

Mowrer, O. H., and Mowrer, Willie M. Enuresis: a method for its study and treatment. *Amer. J. Orthopsychiat.*, 1938, *8*, 436-459.

Munn, N. L. *Psychology.* (4th ed.) New York: Houghton Mifflin, 1961.

Phillips, E. L. *Psychotherapy: a modern theory and practice.* Englewood Cliffs, N.J.: Prentice-Hall, 1956.

Phillips, L. Case history data and prognosis in schizophrenia. *J. nerv. ment. Dis.*, 1953, *117*, 515-525.

Rheingold, Harriet L., Gerwitz, J. L., and Ross, Helen W. Social conditioning of vocalizations in the infant. *J. comp. physiol. Psychol.*, 1959, *52*, 68-73.

Salzinger, K., and Pisoni, Stephanie. Reinforcement of affect responses of schizophrenics during the clinical interview. *J. abnorm. soc. Psychol.*, 1958, *57*, 84-90.

Salzinger, K., and Pisoni, Stephanie. Some parameters of the conditioning of verbal affect responses in schizophrenic subjects. *J. abnorm. soc. Psychol.*, 1961, *63*, 511-516.

Salzinger, K., and Waller, M. B. The operant control of vocalization in the dog. *J. exp. Anal. Behav.*, 1962, *5*, 383-389.

Sarbin, T. R. Anxiety: the reification of a metaphor. Paper presented to West. Psychiat. Assoc., San Francisco, Sept. 1963.

Scott, W. A. Research definitions of mental health and mental illness. *Psychol. Bull.*, 1958, *55*, 29-45.

Skinner, B. F. Operant behavior. *Amer. Psychologist*, 1963, *18*, 503-515.

Sommer, R., Witney, Gwynneth, and Osmond, H. Teaching common associations to schizophrenics. *J. abnorm. soc. Psychol.*, 1962, *65*, 58-61.

Ullmann, L. P., and Giovannoni, Jeanne M. The development of a self-report measure of the process-reactive continuum. *J. nerv. ment. Dis.*, 1964, *138*, 38-42.

Ullmann, L. P., Krasner, L., and Edinger, R. L. Verbal conditioning of common associations in long-term schizophrenic patients. *Behav. Res. Ther.*, 1964, *2*, 15-18.

Ullmann, L. P., Krasner, L., and Gelfand, Donna M. Changed content within a reinforced response class. *Psychol. Rep.*, 1963, *12*, 819-829.

Watson, J. B., and Rayner, Rosalie. Conditioned emotional reactions. *J. exp. Psychol.*, 1920, *3*, 1-14. (In Eysenck, 1960a).

Weiss, R., Krasner, L., and Ullmann, L. P. Responsivity of psychiatric patients to verbal conditioning: "success" and "failure" conditions and patterns of reinforced trials. *Psychol. Rep.*, 1963, *12*, 423-426.

Wolpe, J. Reciprocal inhibition as the main basis of psychotherapeutic effects. *AMA Arch. Neurol. Psychiat.*, 1954, *72*, 205-226. (In Eysenck, 1960a)

Wolpe, J. *Psychotherapy by reciprocal inhibition.* Stanford, Calif.: Stanford University Press, 1958.

Behavioral Theories:

ETIOLOGY AND DEVELOPMENT

Behaviorists are concerned minimally with when and what is learned. The specific events which may be associated with the development of pathological behavior interest them little; what they have to say on this score usually is a rewording of the speculations of the intrapsychic theorists. Their distinction lies in proposing a limited number of rigorously derived principles which can account for a wide variety of learned pathological behavior patterns. Behaviorists are wary of the excessive number of empirically unanchored concepts included in intrapsychic theory, and propose that all behavior—normal or pathological— can be reduced to a few objective principles and concepts. Their focus on the process of learning in behavioral pathology, rather than on the content of what is learned, has added a precision and clarity to the study of psychopathology that has been sorely lacking.

The excerpts reprinted here from papers by John Dollard and Neal Miller and by Albert Bandura and Richard Walters illustrate how these basic learning principles can be applied in the analysis of pathological behavior.

How Symptoms Are Learned

JOHN DOLLARD and NEAL E. MILLER

PHOBIAS

In a phobia acquired under traumatic conditions of combat the relevant events are recent and well known. Such cases provide one of the simplest and most convincing illustrations of the learning of a symptom.

The essential points are illustrated by the case of a pilot who was interviewed by one of the authors. This officer had not shown any abnormal fear of airplanes before being sent on a particularly difficult mission to bomb distant and well-defended oil

From *Personality and Psychotherapy* by John Dollard and Neal E. Miller, copyright 1950, used by permission of McGraw-Hill Book Company and the authors.

refineries. His squadron was under heavy attack on the way to the target. In the confusion of flying exceedingly low over the target against strong defensive fire, a few of the preceding planes made a wrong turn and dropped their bombs on the section that had been assigned to the pilot's formation. Since not enough bombs were dropped to destroy the installations, the pilot's formation had to follow them to complete the job. As they came in above the rooftops, bombs and oil tanks were exploding. The pilot's plane was tossed violently about and damaged while nearby planes disappeared in a wall of fire. Since this pilot's damaged plane could not regain altitude, he had to fly back alone at reduced speed and was subject to repeated violent fighter attack which killed several crew members and repeatedly threatened to destroy them all. When they finally reached the Mediterranean, they were low on gas and had to ditch the airplane in the open sea. The survivors drifted on a life raft and eventually were rescued.

Many times during this mission the pilot was exposed to intensely fear-provoking stimuli such as violent explosions and the sight of other planes going down and comrades being killed. It is known that intense fear-provoking stimuli of this kind act to reinforce fear as a response to other cues present at the same time.* In this case the other cues were those from the airplane, its sight and sound, and thoughts about flying. We would therefore expect the strong drive of intense fear to be learned as a response to all of these cues.

When a strong fear has been learned as a response to a given set of cues, it tends to generalize to other similar ones (Miller, 1950). Thus one would expect the fear of this airplane and of thoughts about flying it to generalize to the similar sight and sound of other airplanes and thoughts about flying in them. This is exactly what happened; the pilot felt strongly frightened whenever he approached, looked at, or even thought about flying in any airplane.

Because he had already learned to avoid objects that he feared, he had a strong tendency to look away and walk away from all airplanes. Whenever he did this, he removed the cues eliciting the fear and hence felt much less frightened. A reduction in any strong drive such as fear serves to reinforce the immediately preceding responses. Therefore we would expect any response that produced successful avoidance to be learned as a strong habit. This is what occurred; the pilot developed a strong phobia of airplanes and everything connected with them.

---

*For a similar analysis of other combat cases, see Dollard (1945).

Similarly, he felt anxious when thinking or talking about airplanes and less anxious when he stopped thinking or talking about them. The reduction in anxiety reinforced the stopping of thinking or of talking about airplanes; he became reluctant to think about or discuss his experience.

To summarize, under traumatic conditions of combat the intense drive of fear was learned as a response to the airplane and everything connected with it. The fear generalized from the cues of this airplane to the similar ones of other airplanes. This intense fear motivated responses of avoiding airplanes, and whenever any one of these responses was successful, it was reinforced by a reduction in the strength of the fear.

When all of the circumstances are understood, as in this case, there is no mystery about the phobia. In fact, such things as the avoidance of touching hot stoves or stepping in front of speeding cars usually are not called "phobias" because the conditions reinforcing the avoidance are understood. Our contention is that the laws of learning are exactly the same, although the conditions are often different and much more obscure, especially when the fear is elicited by the internal cues of thoughts or drives.

Fear aroused by drive to perform a punished response. The way fear can be elicited by the temptation to perform a forbidden act is illustrated in the case of a four-year-old boy who showed a sudden and prolonged flare-up of extreme resistance to going to bed. Previously the little boy had only shown the normal reluctance. Suddenly this became greatly intensified. He protested at having to leave his toys, asked for extra bedtime stories, came down repeatedly for drinks of water, was found sitting at the head of the stairs, expressed various fears of the bedroom that were hard for the parents to understand, and had to be put back to bed as many as fifteen or twenty times in a single night.

The parents realized that their

child was seriously disturbed but could not figure out why; they were baffled and annoyed. At first they thought that the main interest of the child, who was an only child, was staying up with adults. As they took increasingly firm measures to keep him out of the living room so that they could lead a semblance of a normal social life, they found him sleeping in strange and uncomfortable places such as the threshold of the entrance to the bedroom, in the hall, and even on the stairs. It began to appear that his real motivation was to avoid his bed. Occasionally he would go to sleep wearing two pairs of pants in spite of the fact that it was the middle of the summer in a hot Midwestern city.

The parents tried everything they could think of but nothing seemed to help. Finally they took him to a clinic. There the following facts were gradually pieced together. The mother had had a much younger brother who was severely punished for masturbation during his infancy and so she had resolved that she was never going to treat her own children like that. She began by giving this child complete freedom in this respect and then gradually made him understand that he could masturbate only when he was alone or in his own house without strangers being present. The trouble about going to bed began shortly after a new maid was hired. The mother remembered that the afternoon before the trouble started the little boy had reported to her that the maid had said he was nasty and had slapped him "like she slaps her own little boys." Because the maid seemed so gentle and affectionate the mother had doubted this, and in the face of these doubts the little boy had guessed that he had imagined it. Later the maid was observed to tell the little boy that he was nasty when she found him fingering his penis and was privately told to ignore this kind of behavior. The symptom had faded away somewhat during the week the maid was absent to take care of her sick mother

and flared up again when the maid returned.

On the advice of the psychiatrist at the clinic, the mother made it perfectly clear to the child that the maid was not to punish him for masturbating; she dramatized this by making the maid apologize to him and say that she was wrong in calling him nasty. After this the extreme resistance to going to bed suddenly disappeared, with only a few minor recurrences that were easily met by further reassurance. There was also a marked improvement in the child's cooperativeness and happy, independent spontaneity.

In this case it seems fairly evident that punishment and disapproval from the maid had attached fear to the response of masturbation. The child seems to have been more strongly tempted to masturbate when he was alone in bed. Thus the fear was aroused in bed. (It is also possible that some of the punishments were administered in bed, but unfortunately we have no evidence on this point.) Whenever the child approached the bed or was told to go to bed, his fear was increased; any response that took him away from bed was reinforced by a reduction in the strength of this fear. He learned a variety of such responses. Putting on the two pairs of pants probably also tended to reduce the fear of masturbating in bed, not by physical escape but by covering up the penis. When the fear of masturbation was reduced, the motivation to perform all of these responses (*i.e.*, symptoms) was removed. Freedom from this source of anxiety and conflict also improved the lad's general mood.

Origin of response. When the fear-provoking stimulus is clearly circumscribed (like a hot radiator), the avoidance response that reduces the fear often occurs immediately with relatively little trial and error. Apparently it is either an innate response or is learned early in life and quickly generalized to new situations containing the similar element of a localized fear-provoking stimulus. In cases in which direct avoidance is physically or socially difficult (like dealing with the school bully), the individual may show considerable trial and error, reasoning and planning. Once the responses producing successful avoidance are elicited by any one of these means, they are reinforced by the reduction in the strength of fear and quickly learned as strong habits.

Origin of fear. In phobias, the origin of the responses of avoidance and the way they produce the reinforcing reduction in fear is usually quite clear. The origin of the fear is often obscure, stemming from the childhood conflicts about sex and aggression that were described in the preceding chapter. Further research is needed to enable us to describe in terms of rigorous behavior principles and social conditions all the detailed steps intervening between infancy and adulthood.

How fear is transferred to new cues. Theoretically one would expect the strong fears involved in phobias to transfer to new cues in a number of different ways:

1. *Primary stimulus generalization.* When a person learns to fear one situation, he should also tend to fear other similar ones. Stimuli more similar to the original traumatic ones should elicit stronger generalized fear. This is called a *gradient of generalization*.

2. *Higher-order conditioning.* After strong fear is learned as a response to certain cues, they will serve as learned (*i.e.*, secondary) reinforcing agents so that any cues that consistently precede them will acquire the ability to elicit fear (Pavlov, 1927).

3. *Secondary, or response-mediated, generalization.* When the fear is attached to response-produced cues, any new stimulus that becomes able to elicit the response producing these cues will arouse the fear they elicit. For example, a young man may have fear attached to the cues produced by the first incipient responses of sexual excitement. Then if a previously indifferent girl is labeled "sexy," she may arouse incipient responses of sexual excitement which in turn elicit fear.

When a response produces the cues eliciting the fear, any increase in the drive motivating that response will be expected to cause it to generalize to a greater variety of stimulus situations. In other words, when the young man's sex urge increases, he will be expected to find a wider variety of situations sexually exciting and, hence, frightening. Conversely, when his sexual motivation is low, only the most provocative situations will be exciting and, hence, frightening. In short, the variety of situations feared will be expected to vary with the strength of the drive motivating the response mediating the fear.

Extinction of phobias. If a response to a given cue continues to be repeated without reinforcement, it gets progressively weaker. This is called *extinction*. It will be remembered that such experimental evidence as we have seems to indicate that the internal "response" of fear follows the same laws in this respect also and is subject to extinction. In the case of a strong fear, however, this extinction may proceed so slowly that it is scarcely noticeable within 200 trials. In this case, if only a small sample of behavior were observed, one might easily be led to the false conclusion that no extinction was occurring.

In some cases the extinction of phobias can be noticed. For instance, the pilot in the first example was somewhat less afraid of airplanes several months after his traumatic experience. Similarly, a young man with a moderately strong fear of high places gradually lost his fear when he was strongly motivated to participate in mountain climbing and gradually exposed himself to a series of increasingly steep heights.

In other cases, the fears involved in phobias seem to be enormously resistant to extinction. It will be remembered that the following variables are known to increase resistance to extinction: a stronger drive of pain or fear involved in the original learning; a larger number of reinforced learning trials; intermittent, or so-called partial, reinforcement; the generalization of reinforcement from other similar situations; the similarity of the phobic situation to the original traumatic one; the variability of the cues in the stimulus situation; and, as will be seen, the subject's memory for the original circumstances under which the fear was learned. Phobias also tend to be preserved because subjects usually manage to avoid the phobic situation and so do not receive many extinction trials.

As long as the subject can avoid the cues that elicit fear or that evoke the internal cue-producing responses eliciting fear, he will be expected to experience no fear. Thus the pilot in the first example was not afraid as long as he could stay completely away from airplanes, and the little boy in the second example was reasonably unafraid when he was safely away from the bed. If the social conditions allow successful avoidance of the fear-provoking situations, all that will be noticed is a blank area in the person's life. But as soon as he is forced to go into the phobic situation, strong fear will appear.

To summarize, in phobias the responses of avoidance and their reinforcement by a reduction in the strength of the fear is almost always quite clear. The origin of the drive of fear may be obvious or obscure; it often traces back to childhood conflicts about sex and aggression. Fear can be exceedingly resistant to extinction. The more exact determination of the factors that affect this resistance is a problem with important therapeutic implications.

COMPULSIONS

It is well known that if a compulsive response, for example excessive hand washing, is interrupted by a command or physical restraint, the subject experiences a marked increase in anxiety; he reports that he just feels awful. As soon as the compulsion is resumed, the anxiety disappears (Fenichel, 1945, pp. 306-307; White, 1948, p. 277). Thus it seems clear that the compulsion is reinforced in exactly the same way as the avoidance response in the phobia and the responses of turning the wheel, pressing the bar, or pulling of the handle in the experiments described in an earlier chapter. In fact, a phobia of dirt, which leads the subject to remove visible dirt by washing, may shade over by imperceptible degrees into hand washing where the subject fears dirt even when the hands seem clean, or where he does not know what he fears.

While the existence of the fear, guilt, or other drive motivating compulsive responses usually becomes obvious if the patient is forced to stop performing the compulsive response, the source of this drive is often quite obscure. Frequently a hand-washing compulsion must be traced back to childhood conflicts in which cleanliness training produces an abnormal fear of dirt or sex training results in a strong fear of venereal disease.

The responses involved in compulsions may be the result of more or less random trial and error but often are ones that have already been learned in other more or less similar situations. For example, the mother who arouses anxiety in the child by criticising him for dirty hands teaches him to wash his hands when they are dirty.

Similarly, the anxiety-reducing effects of a particular act, such as hand washing, are often due to social training. Then the act of washing the hands may have a direct reassuring effect because it has been so frequently associated during childhood with escape from criticism for having dirty hands. Stated more exactly, the cues produced by the act may elicit responses that inhibit fear. In other cases the effect may be more indirect; the function of the act may be to elicit thoughts that are incompatible with the ones eliciting the fear. For example, the thought "I have washed my hands so they must be clean" will be incompatible with the one "Perhaps my hands are contaminated."

In other instances the compulsive act may have an anxiety-reducing effect because it serves as a distraction. Keeping the hands busy with an innocent response may help to keep them out of anxiety-provoking mischief.

Usually the compulsive act produces only a temporary reduction in the anxiety. After a relatively short time, the anxiety starts to increase again so that the patient is motivated to repeat the compulsive act.

In conclusion, the drive-increasing effect of interfering with compulsions and the drive-reducing effect of performing them is usually clear-cut. The origin of the fear (or other drive) and the reason why a particular compulsive act reduces it is often not obvious and must be tracked down or inferred.

HYSTERICAL SYMPTOMS

Our analysis of how hysterical symptoms are learned will start with a case of war neurosis where the causation is relatively recent and clear. This is case 12 reported by Grinker and Spiegel (1945b, pp. 28-29). The patient had been directing the firing of an artillery platoon under great danger and with heavy responsibilities. After the acute phase of battle, he was lying on the ground exhausted when three shells landed nearby and exploded, blowing him off the ground each time. He was somewhat shaken up but otherwise fit. Half an hour later he found that he could not remove his right hand from his trouser pocket, having almost complete paralysis. He did not report sick and stayed with his company regaining some strength in his arm but still suffering partial paralysis. Then he was sent to the hospital, where he was calm and cooperative and had no anxiety, tremor, or terror dreams.

His condition was not organic

(*i.e.*, it must have been learned) because under pentothal narcosis he was able to move his arm in all directions with ease. With reeducation and a short series of therapeutic interviews the condition cleared up. When it became obvious, however, that he was fit to return to his unit, he developed frank anxiety and tremor in both arms. The anxiety now appeared directly in relation to his battle experience and had to be dealt with as a separate problem.

Reinforcement vs. adaptiveness. In this case it is obvious that the symptom of a paralyzed arm served a certain adaptive function in that it kept the soldier out of combat. More general evidence that escape from combat is involved in reinforcing the symptoms of war neurosis is given by the fact that they vary with the requirements of the combat task. Thus aviators are likely to turn up with disturbances in depth perception or night vision, symptoms that are peculiarly suited to interfere with flying, while paratroopers are likely to have paralyzed legs (Grinker and Spiegel, 1945a, pp. 103-104).

For the more rigorous type of theory that we are trying to construct, however, merely pointing out the adaptiveness of the symptom is not enough; the reinforcement should be described more exactly. In the case of the soldier with the paralyzed arm, the eventual hospitalization and escape from combat could not have been the original reinforcement because it occurred only after the symptom was firmly established. The original reinforcement must have occurred while the symptom was being learned. Furthermore, we know that, in order to be effective in strengthening a response, reinforcement must occur soon after it.

In this case the drive is fear and the origin of the fear in combat is quite clear. Since the fear was not experienced as long as the symptom persisted but reappeared as soon as the symptom was interrupted, it is apparent that the symptom reduced the fear. But a reduction in the strength of fear is known to act as a reinforcement. Therefore, the symptom of partial paralysis seems to have been reinforced by the immediate reduction that it produced in the strength of fear.

The symptom of paralysis produced this reduction in fear because the patient knew that it would prevent his return to combat. As soon as the patient noticed that it was difficult to move his hand, he probably said to himself something like "They won't let me fight with a paralyzed hand," and this thought produced an immediate reduction in fear. Though the fear reduction probably was mediated by a thought, its reinforcing effect on the symptoms was direct and automatic. In other words, the patient did not say to himself anything like "Since a paralyzed hand will keep me out of combat, I should try to have a paralyzed hand." In fact, when such a patient becomes convinced of the causal relationship between the escape from fear and the symptom, a strong increase in guilt counteracts any reduction in fear. The reinforcement is removed and there is strong motivation to abandon the symptom.

Malingering. Now we can see how the hysterical symptom differs from malingering. In malingering, the guilt attached to thoughts of performing a response in order to escape from a responsibility, such as combat, is not as strong as the fear of the responsibility. Therefore the subject is able to plan to perform a response in order to escape. In hysteria, the response is made directly to the drive, such as fear; in malingering, it is made to the verbal cues of the plan. Therefore we would expect hysterical symptoms to vary with the drive and malingered ones to vary with the plan. Perhaps this is why, as Grinker and Spiegel (1945b, pp. 47, 95) report, hysterical symptoms are relieved by drugs such as pentothal (which according to us operate by reducing the drive of fear) while malingered ones are unaffected. It can also be seen that only responses that are under verbal (*i.e.,* voluntary) control can be involved in malingering, while any response that can occur may be reinforced as an hysterical symptom. In fact, the more plausible the response seems as an involuntary organic defect, the less likely it is to arouse guilt.

Origin of response. Phobias involve the exceedingly natural response of avoidance, and compulsions usually involve common responses. Often the responses involved in hysterical symptoms are much more unusual. Thus there is more of a problem concerning how the response occurs and is available for the initial reinforcement. Often symptoms have an organic basis at first and then persist after the organic basis has been cured (Grinker and Spiegel, 1945a, pp. 111-112). This seems to be a way of getting the response to occur so that it can be reinforced. Aviators' symptoms resemble diseases that often occur in fliers—pseudo air emboli, air sickness, and so forth (Grinker and Spiegel, 1945a, p. 57). Many symptoms appear to be responses that are relatively normal to the drive of strong fear. In spite of these suggestive facts, the factors determining exactly which symptoms will occur are still somewhat of a mystery. For example, does allowing children to escape from school for certain kinds of pains or mild illnesses predispose them to the use of pseudo illnesses to escape from difficulties in later life?

To summarize, in hysteria the reinforcement, or primary gain from the symptom, is often relatively clear; the drives involved may be unclear at first, and the factors determining the occurrence of a particular response may be quite obscure.

References

Dollard, John, March 9, 1945. Exploration on morale factors among combat air crewmen—memorandum to research branch, information and education division. *Psychol. Service Center J.* In press, 1950.

Fenichel, O., 1945. "The Psychoanalytic Theory of Neuroses." Norton, New York.

Grinker, R. R., and Spiegel, J. P., 1945a. "Men Under Stress." Blakiston, New York.

Grinker, R. R., and Spiegel, J. P., 1945b. "War Neurosis." Blakiston, New York.

Miller, N. E., 1950. Learnable drives and rewards. In S. Stevens (ed.), "Handbook of Experimental Psychology." Wiley,

New York (in press).

Pavlov, I. P., 1927. "Conditioned Reflexes," trans. by G. V. Anrep. Oxford, London.

White, R. W., 1948. "The Abnormal Personality." Ronald, New York.

Social Learning of Dependence Behavior

ALBERT BANDURA and RICHARD H. WALTERS

In the psychological literature such responses as seeking proximity and physical contact, help, attention, reassurance, and approval have been categorized as dependent (Beller, 1955). Since the human infant is almost totally helpless and remains relatively incapable of caring for himself for a number of years, dependent responses receive a considerable amount of positive reinforcement in most societies (Whiting and Child, 1953). Although independence training in North America is usually initiated in early childhood, this training is primarily focused on the mastery of developmental tasks. For example, the child is taught to clothe, feed, and occupy himself, and later on to master certain instrumental social and occupational skills that will permit him in adulthood to maintain an independent socio-vocational adjustment.

While there are very marked changes in *task-oriented* dependent responses from infancy to adulthood, *person-oriented* dependency is expected and reinforced throughout all stages of development. Some changes in the form of person-oriented dependency occur, but these are largely attributable to the acquisition of instrumental skills. On the other hand, there are major changes in the objects to which this kind of dependency is expressed. Seeking proximity

and physical contact, for example, is not merely permitted but actually expected at all stages of an individual's life, and particularly during adolescent and adult years as he increasingly engages in heterosexual behavior. Eventually, dependent responses of this kind become focused primarily on a single object, the marriage partner, although in attenuated forms they may still be expressed toward other persons. Indeed, it is culturally expected that within the marriage partnership husband and wife will engage in physical manifestations of dependency that do not differ greatly from those that occur in the parent-child relationship.

Other forms of person-oriented dependency—for example, the seeking of approval and help—are expected to be shown toward a wide variety of persons, such as friends, colleagues, and members of one's reference groups.

Failure to develop task-oriented independent responses is usually attributed to a lack of such factors as motivation, initiative, or achievement drive, to limitations of capacity, social resources, or opportunity, or to just plain laziness, but is rarely, in and of itself, regarded as indicative of psychopathology. Failure to develop and maintain appropriate person-oriented dependency is, in contrast, one of the main criteria for identifying certain forms of behavior disorder. It should be noted that overdeveloped person-oriented dependency does not usually constitute, nor become labeled as, a serious form of deviation. In fact, overdependent individuals are usually regarded as self-indulgent, egocentric, or "spoiled," but not as emotionally disturbed. This perhaps accounts for the paucity of studies of overdependency in the clinical literature. By contrast, deficits in person-oriented dependency have received a great deal of attention, for example, in studies of autism, of the effects of prolonged institutionalization, and of children who have been deprived of a normal family life.

Certain classes of patients, such as psychopaths, are usually regarded as incapable of forming person-oriented dependent relationships; on the other hand, they are also described as possessing highly developed manipulatory skills designed to secure person-oriented dependency gratifications. In fact, in most cases, their deviant behavior is characterized not by an absence of such dependency, but by the transience of the dependency relationships into which they enter. Such failures to maintain appropriate dependency attachments have been of considerable concern to workers in the mental health field.

DEFINITION OF DEPENDENCY

Dependency may be defined as a class of responses that are capable of eliciting positive attending and ministering responses from others. Since dependency responses are prosocial in nature, the presence of intent can perhaps be more readily established than in the case of aggression. These responses, however, do not inevitably elicit positive reactions from others, particularly when they are of high frequency or inappropriately timed. Under these circumstances, the agent may wittingly or unwittingly feign states of disability, lack of capacity, or illness in order to ensure positive rather than negative counter-responses. If the agent does not actively seek attention or care, but simply presents himself as relatively helpless or suffering, the object of dependency

may appear not to be the initiator of the interaction sequence, and the problem of intent then arises.

The problem of intent also occurs in the case of high magnitude responses. For example, a young child kicks his mother's leg, when he has failed to obtain a desired toy that is placed beyond his reach, and the mother has not attended to his verbal requests for assistance. If the kick is mild, there is a good chance that the child's response will be regarded as dependent; if the kick is strongly administered, it is more likely that the response will be labeled "aggressive." The covert assumption, of course, is that a hard kick is *intended* to hurt. But in the case cited, it may be argued that the hard, as well as the mild, kick is intended to procure the mother's attention and so can be categorized as dependent. The intentionality criterion can thus lead to categorization of a single response sequence as both dependent and aggressive. Indeed, negative attention-seeking behavior provides a good example of a response pattern the categorization of which consistently baffles research workers (Bandura and Walters, 1959; Sears, Whiting, Nowlis, and Sears, 1953).

POSITIVE TRAINING IN DEPENDENCY

There have been relatively few observational and interview studies of direct training in dependency and still fewer experimental investigations; research into children's dependency has instead been focused on identifying changes in dependency objects and on the development of independence, on the assumption that independence emerges from dependency. Moreover, greater attention has been given to generalized parental variables such as acceptance, affection, child-centeredness, and indulgence, than to specific aspects of dependency training.

It has generally been assumed that adult nurturance is a critical factor in the establishing of dependency in children. Nurturance involves positive reinforcement of dependency, the active eliciting of dependency responses, and the conditioning of positive emotional responses to the nurturant adult. The occurrence of nurturant behavior, itself complex, has usually been inferred from such parent characteristics as affectional demonstrativeness and warmth that may, but need not, involve all three facets of nurturance and certainly involve many other facets of parent behavior.

Positive relationships between parental demonstrativeness and warmth and the dependency of children have emerged from a number of field studies. Sears, Maccoby, and Levin (1957) found that mothers who were affectionately demonstrative responded positively to the children's dependent behavior and described them as high in dependency. Bandura and Walters (1959) reported that mothers of nonaggressive adolescent boys who were relatively high in dependency showed more warmth than mothers of relatively nondependent aggressive boys; the fathers of the high-dependent boys were both warmer and more affectionately demonstrative than the fathers of the low-dependent group. Moreover, a correlational analysis of data from families of aggressive and inhibited children indicated that parents who were warm, affectionate, rewarded dependency, and had spent a good deal of time in caring for their sons had children who tended to display a high degree of dependency behavior (Bandura, 1960).

Rheingold (1956) carried out an experimental study of "mothering" in which she performed caretaking acts toward institutionalized children for a period of eight weeks. A control group of children remained in the usual hospital routine. An assessment of the children's social behavior at the end of the eight-week period indicated that the infants who had received the nurturant care of the experimenter were more socially responsive both to the experimenter and to an examiner than were the control

children. Clinical case material suggests that an extreme degree of "mothering" may create very strong dependency habits in children. For example, Levy (1943) found that highly indulgent mothers who were extremely solicitous in caring for their children's needs and were constantly rewarding dependency responses had highly dependent children.

Additional indirect evidence that maternal permissiveness for, and reward of, dependency increases children's dependency behavior was obtained by Heathers (1953). Six- to twelve-year-old children were blindfolded and then requested to walk along a narrow unstable plank, which was balanced on springs and raised eight inches from the floor. As the child stood on the starting end of the plank, the experimenter touched the back of the child's hand and waited for him to accept or reject the implied offer of help. Parent-training measures, in the form of ratings previously secured by means of the Fels Parent Behavior Scales (Baldwin, Kalhorn, and Breeze, 1945), were available to the experimenter and were related to the performance of the children. The analysis showed that children who accepted the experimenter's hand on the initial trial of the Walk-the-Plank Test tended to have child-centered parents who encouraged their children to lean on others rather than to take care of themselves and who held their children back from developing age-appropriate skills.

Unlike aggression and sex, dependency is generally regarded as a prosocial form of behavior. Consequently, parents are usually reluctant to acknowledge any failure to reward, or any punishment of, their children's dependency. It is therefore not surprising that field studies in which parental handling of dependency has been directly investigated have generally failed to reveal any strong relationships between the parent behavior and the dependency responses of children. In Bandura's (1960) study, however, thematic interview material secured from aggressive and inhibited boys revealed that the former group of boys, who displayed a great deal of dependency behavior, depicted parents as providing a considerable amount of intermittent reward for their son's dependency responses.

The reward of dependency responses has rarely been used as an antecedent variable within experimental studies. Nelsen (1960) investigated the effects of both reward and punishment of dependency on the incidence of children's dependent responses in a subsequent social-interaction situation. During training half the children were shown approval for dependency while the remaining children received mild verbal rebukes for acting in a dependent manner. Pretest-to-posttest changes indicated that reward for dependency resulted in an increase in dependency responses toward the rewarding agent, while punishment for dependency resulted in a decrease of such responses. The effects of reward were more marked for girls than for boys.

Cairns (1962) reported that prior reward for dependency facilitated children's learning when correct responses were reinforced by verbal approval. Grade-school children were first shown some toys in a cabinet and were told that they could play with a new toy each time a bell rang. For two groups of children the doors of the cabinet were closed, and the toys were therefore accessible only through the help of the experimenter. The children in one of these groups were rewarded, through the experimenter's compliance, for asking help or seeking attention in response to the signal that another toy might be taken from the cupboard; similar behavior from the children in the other group was consistently ignored. The children in a third group were given free access to the toys and experienced rewarding responses from the experimenter that were not contingent upon their exhibiting dependency behavior. Following the experimental treatments, all children were set a discrimination task by a second experimenter, who said "Good" each time a child made a correct response. Children who had been previously reinforced for dependent responses learned more rapidly than children in either of the other two groups. Cairns' results suggest that children in whom dependency habits are strongly developed are more responsive to social reinforcers. Support for this interpretation is provided by Ferguson (1961), who used Beller's (1955) scale to select high-dependent and low-dependent children and then compared their performance on a task similar to that used in Cairns' study. The results indicated that high-dependent children, when rewarded by approval, learned more rapidly than low-dependent children.

Parents who encourage and reward dependency also serve as nurturant models for their children. Consequently, parental reward of dependency should be one antecedent of strongly developed affiliative patterns in children. This joint reinforcement and modeling effect appears to be reflected in the finding of Hartup and Kéller (1960) that nursery-school children who sought help and affection relatively often tended also to give frequent attentive, affectionate, protective, and reassuring responses in their interactions with their peers.

PUNISHMENT AND INHIBITION OF DEPENDENCY

Warmth, affectional demonstrativeness, and "mothering" have been selected for study as possible antecedents of the development of dependency habits; similarly, rejection, another nonspecific parent characteristic, has been made the focus of attention in studies of the negative conditioning of dependency. One important component of severe rejection is probably the punishment of dependency behavior; however, if rejection is not extreme, both reward and punishment may occur, and the effects of rejection will then depend on the extent to which one or other of these types of parental responses predominate.

The effects of punishment on dependency are inevitably modified by the effects of the rewards that are dispensed for dependency from time to time, particularly during the child's early years, in almost every family situation. Thus dependency training contrasts strongly with sex training, during which rewards are rarely, if ever, dispensed, and with aggression training, which in most homes involves only intermittent, highly selective, and relatively infrequent dispensing of rewards. Moreover, especially in early childhood, dependency behavior cannot be relinquished as readily as sexual or aggressive behavior, since a child's immediate needs must receive some attention from even reluctant adults. Consequently, initial discouragement of dependency is likely to intensify a child's efforts to obtain dependency rewards. Indeed, Sears, Maccoby, and Levin (1957) found rejection to have little relationship to dependency if there was, at other times, little reward for dependency, but to have a positive relationship to dependency if the mother had also rewarded this kind of behavior.

In the case of the more severe forms of rejection, one would expect inhibition of dependency behavior, an outcome that is reflected in the finding of Bandura and Walters (1959) that aggressive boys who had experienced a good deal of parental rejection showed much less dependent behavior than more accepted nonaggressive boys. In this study parents who expressed rejection of their children were found to have punished dependency to a greater extent than those who were more accepting; moreover, ratings of the boys' dependency made from interviews with the boys were negatively correlated with ratings of paternal rejection made from father interviews. Finally, boys who felt rejected by their parents showed a low incidence of dependency responses toward parents, teachers, and peers.

When rejection involves primarily the withholding of positive reinforcers, rather than the presentation of negative reinforcers, its effect may be to intensify the dependency toward the frustrating agent. Hartup (1958), in an experimental study of nurturance withdrawal, found that children who had experienced delay of reward for dependency exhibited more dependent behavior than children whose dependency had been consistently rewarded. Similarly, Gewirtz (1954) demonstrated that children displayed more attention-seeking behavior in the presence of a nonresponsive adult than in the presence of an adult who centered his attention on the child. Withholding of positive reinforcers appears to produce more sustained increases in dependency behavior in children whose past social-learning experiences have made them highly dependent than in children in whom dependency habits are weakly established (Baer, 1962; Beller and Haeberle, 1961a, 1961b). Thus, the occurrence of a dependent response to frustration is more likely if dependent responses are dominant in children's response hierarchies.

In the study by Nelsen (1960) children who were negatively reinforced for dependency showed a subsequent decrease in dependency responses; in this case the effect was more pronounced for boys. An analysis of patient-therapist interaction sequences by Winder, Ahmad, Bandura, and Rau (1962) indicated that whereas positive reinforcement of dependency responses greatly increased the extent to which these were emitted in therapy sessions, negative reinforcement resulted in a marked decrease in their frequency. Thus, even with adults, relatively consistent punishment of dependency appears to have an inhibitory effect.

When active punishment is combined with reward, its effects on dependency behavior may under some circumstances be the same as when rewards are intermittently withheld. Fisher (1955) compared the social responses of two groups of puppies. One of these was consistently petted and fondled by the experimenter for approach responses, while the second group of puppies was administered the same kind of reward treatment with the addition of training sessions in which the puppies were handled roughly and on occasions electrically shocked for approach responses. Tests of dependency behavior conducted toward the end of, and following, thirteen weeks' training indicated that the puppies which had received both reward and punishment exhibited greater dependency behavior in the form of remaining close to a human than did the puppies in the reward-only group.

While the withholding of rewards for dependency seems to produce an increase in dependency behavior, active punishment appears to reduce its incidence unless there is relatively frequent concurrent reward. Consequently, since withholding of reward is generally regarded as a less severe disciplinary technique than punishment, it is understandable that Sears, Whiting, Nowlis, and Sears (1953) found some support for the hypothesis that there is a curvilinear relationship between the complex variable of maternal frustration-and-punishment of dependency and the incidence of dependency in preschool children.

The correlational data from Bandura's (1960) investigation into the child-training antecedents of aggressive and inhibited behavior indicated that punishment for dependency behavior decreased its directness, but that significant relationships between punitiveness for dependency and its frequency were largely absent. The only exceptions were found in the case of the aggressive boys, for whom maternal punishment for dependency seemed to have the effect of *increasing* dependency responses to

adults. This outcome was also reflected in the boys' thematic interview responses, which strongly suggested that differential reinforcement histories had led the aggressive and inhibited boys to respond to dependency frustration in quite different ways.

In the first place, the mothers of aggressive boys tended to ignore mild forms of dependency behavior, whereas more intense forms secured their attention. If more vigorous responses are thus differentially reinforced, one would expect these responses, which might well be labeled as aggressive, to become strongly established. Rewarding of responses of this kind in order temporarily to terminate their occurrence could be one means of establishing troublesome behavior. Indeed, teachers were beginning to complain that the dependency behavior of the aggressive boys had become burdensome.

In the case of the inhibited boys, nonaggressive withdrawal reactions occupied a dominant position in the hierarchy of responses elicited by situations in which dependency was frustrated. When the mother punished dependency, inhibited boys depicted the frustrated child as giving up the goal of gaining the mother's nurturance and attention and making dependency responses to other persons. In addition, they reported more withdrawal behavior following frustration of dependency by peers; since there was no indication that they had been greatly punished by peers for exhibiting dependency behavior, it is reasonable to conclude that the withdrawal response had generalized from the home situation to peer interactions.

There was one notable difference between the findings of Bandura's investigation and the authors' earlier study of aggressive adolescent boys (Bandura and Walters, 1959). In contrast to the adolescents, who showed relatively little dependency behavior and a marked inhibition of dependency responses, Bandura's aggressive preadolescent boys exhibited a great deal of dependency behavior toward their parents, teachers, and peers. This difference seems in part to reflect a developmental process, and in part the influence of differential reinforcement histories. In the first place, preadolescents are necessarily more dependent than adolescents; in fact, a number of the parents of the aggressive adolescents had commented on the strength of their sons' dependency behavior during preadolescent years. When the preadolescents expressed dependency, they tended to do so in forms that elicited mild punishment from others, and such forms of dependency had apparently also predominated in the earlier histories of the delinquent adolescents. With increasing age, the aggressive preadolescents would be expected to show a marked decrease in dependency behavior, assuming that their dependency responses continued to be ignored and to elicit punishment.

Moreover, once boys begin to exhibit serious anti-social behavior, as many of the delinquent adolescents had already done, they tend to be openly rejected by parents, teachers, and the majority of peers, and this consequence inevitably promotes dependency inhibition. In addition, there were some differences between the two groups of families, for example, a difference in socioeconomic status, which could have influenced parents' child-training practices and consequently further increased the difference between the two groups of boys in their readiness to express dependency behavior.

Investigations into the effects of maternal privation have shown that institutionalized and other maternally deprived children are socially nonresponsive and nondependent (Bowlby, 1952; Freud and Burlingham, 1944; Gewirtz, 1961; Goldfarb, 1943; Lowrey, 1940; Spitz, 1945; Yarrow, 1961). However, they have also incidentally noted the occurrence of frequent, direct, and intense dependency responses in some children presumably deprived of maternal care. This differential effect would be expected if the children under investigation had experienced differential amounts of reward, nonreward, and punishment for dependency behavior.

References

Baer, D. M. A technique of social reinforcement for the study of child behavior: Behavior avoiding reinforcement withdrawal. *Child Develpm.*, 1962, *33*, 847-858.

Baldwin, A. L., Kalhorn, Joan, and Breeze, Fay H. Patterns of parent behavior. *Psychol. Monogr.*, 1945, *58*, No. 3 (Whole No. 268).

Bandura, A. Relationship of family patterns to child behavior disorders. Progress Report, U.S.P.H. Research Grant M-1734. Stanford Univer., 1960.

Bandura, A., and Walters, R. H. *Adolescent aggression.* New York: Ronald, 1959.

Beller, E. K. Dependency and independence in young children. *J. genet. Psychol.*, 1955, *87*, 25-35.

Beller, E. K., and Haeberle, Ann W. Dependency and the frustration-aggression hypothesis. Unpublished manuscript, Child Develpm. Center, New York City, 1961 (a).

Beller, E. K., and Haeberle, Ann W. Dependency and the frustration-aggression hypothesis: II. Paper read at the Annual Meeting of the Eastern Psychol. Assoc., Philadelphia, 1961 (b).

Bowlby, J. *Maternal care and mental health.* Geneva: World Health Organization, 1952 (WHO Monogr. Series, No. 2).

Cairns, R. B. Antecedents of social reinforcer effectiveness. Unpublished manuscript, Indiana Univer., 1962.

Ferguson, P. E. The influence of isolation, anxiety, and dependency on reinforcer effectiveness. Unpublished M.A. thesis, Univ. of Toronto, 1961.

Fisher, A. E. The effects of differential early treatment on the social and exploratory behavior of puppies. Unpublished doctoral dissertation, Penn. State Univer., 1955.

Freud, Anna, and Burlingam, Dorothy T. *Infants without families.* New York: International Universities, 1944.

Gewirtz, J. L. Three determinants of attention seeking in young children. *Monogr. Soc. Res. Child Develpm.*, 1954, *19*, No. 2 (Serial No. 59).

Gewirtz, J. L. A learning analysis of the effects of normal stimulation, privation, and deprivation on the acquisition of social motivation and attachment. In B. M. Foss (Ed.). *Determinants of infant behavior.* New York: Wiley, 1961, pp. 213-283.

Goldfarb, W. Infant rearing and problem behavior. *Amer. J. Orthopsychiat.*, 1943, *13*, 249-265.

Hartup, W. W. Nurturance and nurturance-withdrawal in relation to the dependency behavior of preschool children. *Child Develpm.*, 1958, *29*, 191-201.

Hartup, W. W., and Keller, E. D. Nurturance in preschool children and its relation to dependency. *Child Develpm.*, 1960, *31*, 681-689.

Heathers, G. Emotional dependence and independence in a physical threat situation. *Child Develpm.*, 1953, *24*, 169-179.

Levy, D. M. *Maternal overprotection.* New York: Columbia Univer. Press, 1943.

Lowrey, L. G. Personality distortion and early institutional care. *Amer. J. Orthopsychiat.*, 1940, *10*, 576-586.

Nelsen, E. A. The effects of reward and punishment of dependency on subsequent dependency. Unpublished manuscript, Stanford Univer., 1960.

Rheingold, Harriet L. The modification of social responsiveness in institutional babies. *Monogr. Soc. Res. Child Develpm.*, 1956, *21*, No. 2 (Serial No. 63).

Sears, R. R., Maccoby, Eleanor E., and Levin, H. *Patterns of child rearing.* New York: Harper, 1957.

Sears, R. R. Whiting, J. W. M., Nowlis, V., and Sears, Pauline S. Some child-rearing antecedents of aggression and dependency in young children. *Genet. Psychol. Monagr.*, 1953, *47*, 135-234.

Spitz, R. A. Hospitalism: An inquiry into the genesis of psychiatric conditions in early childhood. *Psychoanal. Study Child*, 1945, *1*, 53-74.

Whiting, J. W. M., and Child, I. L. *Child training and personality.* New Haven: Yale Univer. Press, 1953.

Winder, C. L., Ahmad, Farrukh Z., Bandura, A., and Rau, Lucy C. Dependency of patients, psychotherapists' responses, and aspects of psychotherapy. *J. consult. Psychol.*, 1962, *26*, 129-134.

Yarrow, L. J. Maternal deprivation: Toward an empirical and conceptual reevaluation. *Psychol. Bull.*, 1961, *58*, 459-490.

Behavioral Theories:

PATHOLOGICAL PATTERNS

Pathology is defined by most behaviorists as socially maladaptive or deficient behavior. Since the varieties of such behavior are infinite, these theorists feel that the traditional classification system adopted by the psychiatric profession is a figment of Kraepelin's imagination. As evidence for this view they point to the fact that classification schemes are constantly revised and rarely hold up under research analysis. To them, whatever regularities are found can be accounted for by similarities in cultural patterns of conditioning.

Joseph Wolpe, a major figure in behavioral therapy, describes his analysis of a number of traditional neurotic disorders in the excerpt printed here. Although he accepts the traditional schema of syndromes, it is evident that he reconstructs these disorders in terms consistent with behavioral theory. A more adventuresome and detailed reformulation of the traditional approach to classification is undertaken in the paper by Frederick Kanfer and George Saslow.

Etiology of Human Neuroses

JOSEPH WOLPE

THE CAUSAL RELATIONS OF PERVASIVE ("FREE-FLOATING") ANXIETY

Under certain circumstances it is not only to well-defined stimulus configurations that anxiety responses are conditioned, but also to more or less omnipresent properties of the environment, of which extreme examples would be light, light and shade contrasts, amorphous noise, spatiality, and the passage of time. Since each of these enters into most, if not

all, possible experience, it is to be expected that if any of them becomes connected to anxiety responses the patient will be persistently, and apparently causelessly anxious. He will be suffering from what is erroneously called "free-floating" anxiety, and for which a more suitable label would be *pervasive anxiety*.

It must be unequivocally stated, in case it is not quite self-evident, that there is no sharp dividing line between specific anxiety-evoking stimuli and stimuli to pervasive anxiety. The pervasiveness of the latter is a function of the pervasiveness of the stimulus element conditioned; and there are degrees of pervasiveness ranging from the absolute omni-

From *Psychotherapy by Reciprocal Inhibition* by Joseph Wolpe, pages 83-94, copyright 1958 by the Board of Trustees of the Leland Stanford Junior University. With the permission of the publishers, Stanford University Press.

presence of time itself through very common elements like room walls to rarely encountered configurations like hunchbacks.

What reason is there for believing that pervasive anxiety has definable stimulus sources?

Questioning of patients with pervasive anxiety usually reveals that definable aspects of the environment are especially related to this anxiety. For example, one patient reported increased anxiety in the presence of any very large object; another an uncomfortable intrusiveness of all sharp contrasts in his visual field—even the printed words on a page, and particularly contrasts in the periphery of the field. A third felt overwhelmed by physical space. Frequently, patients with pervasive anxiety observe that noise causes a rise in the level of their anxiety. In some cases the noise need not be loud, and in some even music is disturbing.

Although pervasive anxiety is usually felt less when the patient lies down and closes his eyes, it does not disappear. To some extent this may be explained on the basis of perseveration due to prolonged reverberation of the effects of the stimulus in the nervous system. But this does not account for the fact that usually *some* anxiety is already felt at the moment of waking. An obvious explanation is that anxiety evocable by stimuli that enter into the very structure of experience is likely to be produced by the first contents of the awakening subject's imagination. Anxiety increases when the outside world makes its impact; and it is consonant with this that, very commonly, the level of pervasive anxiety gradually rises as the day goes on.

This diurnal rise in level is less likely to occur when the general level of pervasive anxiety is low; for then there is a greater likelihood of the arousal, during a normal day's experience, of other emotions which may be physiologically antagonistic to anxiety, so that the anxiety will be inhibited and its habit strength each time slightly diminished. On the other hand, invariably (in my experience) the patient with pervasive anxiety also has unadaptive anxiety reactions to specific stimuli, and if he should encounter and react to any one of the latter during that day, the level of pervasive anxiety will promptly rise. In the normal course of events it is to be expected that level of pervasive anxiety will fluctuate because of "chance" occurrences which strengthen or weaken its habit strength.

Sometimes, when a patient is fortunate enough not to meet with any specific disturbing stimuli over an extended period, his pervasive anxiety may practically cease, but subsequent response to a relevant specific anxiety-evoking stimulus will condition it lastingly again. This reconditioning was beautifully demonstrated in one of my patients, who, in addition to pervasive anxiety, had a number of severe phobias on the general theme of illness. The pervasive anxiety responded extremely well to La Verne's carbon dioxide–oxygen inhalation therapy. The patient stopped coming for treatment until several months later when the pervasive anxiety was reinduced after he had witnessed an epileptic fit in the street. The pervasive anxiety was again speedily removed by carbon dioxide–oxygen and the patient again stopped treatment after a few more interviews. The essence of this sequence was repeated about ten times before the patient finally allowed desensitization to the phobic stimuli to be completed.

The question naturally arises: What factors determine whether or not pervasive anxiety will be part of a patient's neurosis? At the moment two possible factors may be suggested on the basis of clinical impressions. One seems to be the intensity of anxiety evocation at the time of the induction of the neurosis. It is hypothesized that the more intense the anxiety the more stimulus aspects are likely to acquire *some* measure of anxiety conditioning. Indirect support for this hypothesis comes from the observation that, on the whole, it is the patient who reacts more severely to specific stimuli who is also likely to suffer from pervasive anxiety.

The second possible factor is a lack of clearly defined environmental stimuli at the time of neurosis induction. For example, one patient's pervasive anxiety began after a night in a hotel during which he had attempted intercourse with a woman to whom he felt both sexual attraction and strong revulsion. He had felt a powerful and strange, predominantly nonsexual excitation, and ejaculation had occurred very prematurely without pleasure. The light had been switched off, and *only the dark outlines of objects could be seen.* After this, so great was his feeling of revulsion to the woman that he spent the remainder of the night on the carpet. This experience left him, as he subsequently found, with an anxiety toward a wide range of sexual objects, along with much pervasive anxiety, characterized by a special intrusiveness of all heavy dark objects.

THE CAUSAL PROCESS
IN HYSTERIA

Hysterical reactions are clearly distinguishable from the rather diffuse discharges of the autonomic nervous system that characterize anxiety reactions. In most instances hysterical reactions do not find expression in the autonomic nervous system at all, but in the sensory system, the motor system, or groups of functional units involved in the production of imagery or of consciousness in general. Thus, they may take the form of anesthesias, paresthesias, hyperesthesias, or disturbances of vision or hearing; of paralyses, pareses, tics, tremors, disturbances of balance, contractures or fits; of amnesias, fugues, or "multiple personality" phenomena. Occasionally, hysterical reactions do appear to involve functions within the domain of the autonomic nervous system—in the form of vomiting (or nausea) or enuresis, but it is note-

worthy that each of the two functions involved is to some extent within voluntary control.

Anxiety frequently accompanies hysterical reactions and then they occur side by side as two distinct forms of *primary* neurotic response. This state of affairs must be sharply distinguished from that in which sensory or motor phenomena are secondary effects of the normal components of anxiety, and as such do not qualify as hysterical. For example, a headache due to tension of the temporal muscles, backache due to tension of the longitudinal spinal muscles, or paresthesia due to hyperventilation are not to be regarded as hysterical.

It is necessary also to differentiate hysterical from obsessional reactions. Hysterical reactions are at a relatively low level of organization, affecting well-defined sensory areas and specific motor units, and causing changes in the general character of consciousness or the exclusion from consciousness of "blocks" of experience limited in terms of a time span or some other broad category. The details of the reactions tend to be fixed and unchanging. Obsessional reactions consist by contrast of highly organized movements or of elaborate and complex thinking, in either of which there is a great variety in the individual instances of expression of a specific constant theme.

Like other neurotic reactions, hysterical reactions are acquired by learning. It is intriguing to note that Freud's very early observations on hysterical subjects could easily have led him to this conclusion had he not been sidetracked by a spurious deduction from observations on therapeutic effects. In a paper published in 1893, speaking of the relation of the symptoms of hysteria to the patients' reactions at the time of the precipitating stress, he states:

The connection is often so clear that it is quite evident how the exciting event has happened to produce just this and no other manifestation; the phenomenon is determined in a perfectly clear manner by the cause; to take the most ordinary example, a painful effect, which was originally excited while eating, but was suppressed, produces nausea and vomiting, and this continues for months, as hysterical vomiting. A child who is very ill at last falls asleep, and its mother tries her utmost to keep quiet and not to wake it; but just in consequence of this resolution (hysterical counterwill) she makes a clucking noise with her tongue. On another occasion when she wishes to keep absolutely quiet this happens again, and so a tic in the form of tongue-clicking develops which for a number of years accompanies every excitement. . . . A highly intelligent man assists while his brother's ankylosed hip is straightened under an anesthetic. At the instant when the joint gives way with a crack, he feels a violent pain in his own hip joint which lasts almost a year. . . . [pp. 25-26]

The attack then arises spontaneously as memories commonly do; but they may also be provoked, just as any memory may be aroused according to the laws of association. Provocation of an attack occurs either by stimulation of a hysterogenic zone or by a new experience resembling the pathogenic experience. We hope to be able to show that no essential difference exists between the two conditions, apparently so distinct; and in both cases a hyperaesthetic memory has been stirred. [p. 40]

Apart from the reference to the possibility of attacks arising "spontaneously" (which Freud later explicitly repudiated) we have here an account of the formation by learning of stimulus-response connections. That Freud did not *see* this was mainly because, having observed patients cured when they recalled and narrated the story of the precipitating experience, he concluded that the symptoms were due to the imprisonment of emotionally disturbing memories. He states ". . . we are of opinion that the psychical trauma, or the memory of it acts as a kind of foreign body constituting an effective agent in the present, even long after it has penetrated. . . ." There can be little doubt that this statement would not have been made, and the mind-structure theory that is psychoanalytic theory would not have been born, if Freud could have known that memories do not exist in the form of thoughts or images in some kind of repository within us, but depend on the establishment, through the learning process, of specific neural interconnections that give *a potentiality* of evocation of particular thoughts

and images when and only when certain stimulus conditions, external or internal, are present.

When a clear history of the onset of hysterical symptoms is obtained, it is usually found, as illustrated in Freud's cases quoted above, that the hysterical reaction displays a repetition of features that were present in response to the initiating disturbing experience. The stimulus to the reaction varies. Sometimes it is a fairly specific sensory stimulation. For example, a 33-year-old woman had as a hysterical reaction an intolerable sensation of "gooseflesh" in her calves in response to any rectal sensation such as a desire to defecate, ever since, three years previously, a surgeon had unceremoniously performed a rectal examination upon her, while, drowsy from premedication with morphia, she was awaiting the administration of an anesthetic for an abdominal operation.

In other cases it appears that the hysterical reaction is aroused by ubiquitous stimuli, being then the hysterical equivalent of pervasive ("free-floating") anxiety. An example of this is wryneck that is present throughout the working day and relaxes the moment the patient falls asleep. In yet others anxiety appears to *mediate* the hysterical reaction. The hysteria of one of my patients had both a pervasive component and an anxiety-mediated component. This was a 58-year-old woman who 18 months earlier had encountered a deadly snake in a copse. She had been terrified and momentarily paralyzed; her ears were filled with the sound of waves and she had been unable to speak for two hours. The sound of waves had never left her, and any considerable anxiety such as might arise from tension in her home would intensify this sound and then lead to vertigo, loss of balance, and a feeling of great weakness in all her limbs, so that she sometimes fell.

The central feature of hysterical reactions is the conditioning, in situations of stress, of neurotic reactions other than anxiety, although anxiety is often also conditioned as well. It is necessary to ask what determines this. There are two possible answers. One is that these reactions are conditioned when they happen to be evoked in addition to anxiety. The other is that although such reactions may be evoked by stress in all subjects, they become the neurotic responses conditioned only in those in whom some special factor is present that gives preference to nonanxiety conditioning. Since, in fact, the immediate response to neurotigenic stimulation always seems to implicate all response systems, the latter possibility is the more likely to be relevant. And there is evidence that it is people with distinct personality features who usually develop hysterical reactions.

Jung (1923) long ago observed that hysterics tend to exhibit extravert character traits while other neurotic subjects tend to be introverted. In this partition of personalities he was followed by other writers who, while differing in many ways, agreed, as Eysenck (1947, p. 58) concluded from a survey, in the following particulars: (a) the introvert has a more subjective, the extravert a more objective outlook; (b) the introvert shows a higher degree of cerebral activity, the extravert a higher degree of behavioral activity; (c) the introvert shows a tendency to self-control (inhibition), the extravert a tendency to lack of such control. Eysenck (1955b) has pointed out on the basis of experiments performed by Franks (1956) and himself (1955a) that extraverted subjects besides learning more poorly also generate reactive inhibition more readily than introverts do. He postulates (1955b, p. 35) that subjects in whom reactive inhibition is generated quickly and dissipated slowly "are predisposed thereby to develop extraverted patterns of behaviour and to develop hysterico-psychopathic disorders in cases of neurotic breakdown." Clearly what his facts actually demonstrate is that the hysterical type of breakdown is particularly likely in subjects in whom reactive inhibition

has the feature stated. The *causal* role of reactive inhibition is not shown, nor is a possible mechanism suggested.

A possibility is this: that in addition to their easily generated and persistent reactive inhibition (and perhaps in some indirect way bound up with it) extraverted people have one or both of the following characteristics: (a) when exposed to anxiety-arousing stimuli they respond with relatively low degrees of anxiety so that other responses are unusually prominent; (b) when anxiety and other responses are simultaneously evoked in them, contiguous stimuli become conditioned to the other responses rather than to the anxiety—by contrast with introverts.

This hypothesis lends itself readily to direct experimentation. In the meantime a survey from my records of the 22 patients with hysterical symptoms has yielded some suggestive evidence. Nine of them (41 per cent) had initial Willoughby scores below 30. This is in striking contrast to 273 nonhysterical neurotic patients, in only 50 (18 per cent) of whom were the initial scores below this level. The Kolmogorov-Smirnov test shows the difference to be significant at the .05 level. It is interesting to note that insofar as this supports our hypothesis it accords with the time-worn conception of the hysterical patient with little or no anxiety—*la belle indifférence*. It is relevant to the same point that the hysterical patients with low Willoughby scores all benefited by procedures that varied greatly but did not obviously affect anxious sensitivity. By contrast, in the 13 patients whose hysterical reactions were accompanied by much anxiety there was a direct correlation between diminution of anxious sensitivity and decreased strength of hysterical reactions except in two cases where this consisted purely of amnesia, which was unaffected. (In one of these the events of the forgotten period were later retrieved under hypnosis, in the other they remained forgotten. It seemed to make no difference either way to the patient's recovery.)

Summarizing the above facts, it may be said that hysterical reactions may either accompany anxiety or occur on their own. In the former case their treatment is the treatment of anxiety, in the latter it is different in a way that will be discussed in the chapter on treatment. It is supposed that anxiety is a feature when hysteria occurs in subjects relatively far from the extraverted extreme of Eysenck's introversion-extraversion dimension, just because the hypothetical preferential conditioning of responses other than anxiety to neurotigenic stimuli is less marked in these people. This supposition needs to be tested.

Meanwhile it may be noted that there is experimental evidence of a competitive relationship in certain contexts between autonomic and motor responses. Mowrer and Viek (1948), using two groups of rats, placed each animal after a period of starvation on the electrifiable floor of a rectangular cage and offered him food on a stick for ten seconds. Whether the animal ate or not, shock was applied ten seconds later. In the case of one group of ten rats, jumping into the air resulted in the experimenter switching off the shock (shock-controllable group). Each animal in this group had an experimental "twin" to which the shock was applied for the same length of time as it had taken its counterpart to jump into the air (shock-uncontrollable group). One trial a day was given to each animal. The animals in each group whose eating responses during the ten seconds were inhibited (by conditioned anxiety responses resulting from the shocks) were charted each day, and it was found that in the shock-controllable group the number of eating inhibitions was never high and declined to zero, whereas in the shock-uncontrollable group the number rose to a high level and remained there. Apparently, the constant evocation of jumping in the former group resulted in gradual development of

conditioned inhibition of anxiety. By contrast with this, in the typical Cornell technique for producing exprimental neuroses (p. 43) a very localized musculoskeletal conditioned response comes to be increasingly dominated by autonomic anxiety responses. This whole matter has been discussed in more detail elsewhere (Wolpe, 1953a).

OBSESSIONAL BEHAVIOR

Sometimes, besides the autonomic discharges characteristic of anxiety, ideational, motor, and sensory reponses are prominent in a neurosis. If simple and invariate in character, they are labeled *hysterical*. The term *obsessional* is applied to behavior that is more complex and variable in detail, consisting of well-defined and often elaborate thought sequences or relatively intricate acts which, though they may differ in outward form from one occasion to the next, lead or tend to lead to the same kind of result. The term is applicable even to those cases characterized by an obstinate impulse to behavior that rarely or never becomes manifest. Examples of obsessions predominantly of thought are a woman's insistent idea that she might throw her child from the balcony of her apartment, or a man's need to have one of a restricted class of "pleasant" thoughts in his mind before he can make any well-defined movement such as entering a doorway or sitting down. Exhibitionism and compulsive handwashing are characteristic examples of predominantly motor obsessional behavior.

Sometimes the word *compulsive* has been preferred to obsessional for those cases in which motor activity predominates. However, as most cases display both elements, there is little practical value in the distinction. Furthermore, the term compulsive is open to the objection that *all* behavior is compulsive in a sense, for causal determinism implies that the response that occurs is always the only one that could have occurred in the circumstances. The feature of any example of obsessional behavior is not its inevitability but its *intrusiveness*. Its elicitation or the impulse toward it is an encumbrance and an embarrassment to the patient.

If hysterical and obsessional reactions involve similar elements, we may expect that borderline cases will be found. An example of this is a 47-year-old male nurse employed in an industrial first-aid room who for 17 years had an uncontrollable impulse to mimic any rhythmic movements performed before him, e.g., waving of arms or dancing, and to obey any command no matter from whom. In this was combined the basic simplicity of hysteria and the situationally determined variability of obsessional behavior.

It may be stated almost as dogma that the strength and frequency of evocation of obsessional behavior is directly related to the amount of anxiety being evoked in the patient. Pollitt (1957) in a study of 150 obsessional cases noted that obsessional symptoms became more severe and prominent "when anxiety and tension increased for whatever causes." However, it is not always that the source of the anxiety is irrelevant. Sometimes the obsessional behavior is evident only when anxiety arises from specific, usually neurotic sources. For example, an exhibitionist experienced impulses to expose himself when he felt inadequate and inferior among his friends but not when he was anxious about the results of a law examination.

Anxiety-Elevating Obsessions. Two types of obsessional behavior are clearly distinguishable in clinical practice. One type appears to be part and parcel of the immediate response to anxiety-evoking stimulation and has secondary effects entirely in the direction of increasing anxiety. When a motor mechanic of 45 had neurotic anxiety exceeding a certain fairly low level, he would have a terrifying though always controllable impulse to strike people. From the first moment of awareness of the impulse he would

feel increased anxiety, and if at the time he was with an associate or even among strangers—for example, in a bus—he would thrust his hands firmly into his pockets "to keep them out of trouble." In the history of such patients one finds that behavior similar to that constituting the obsession was present during an earlier situation in which conditioning of anxiety took place. In 1942 this motor mechanic, on military service, had been sentenced to 30 days' imprisonment in circumstances which he had with some justice felt to be grossly unfair. Then, as he had resisted the military police rather violently in protest, he was taken to a psychiatrist who said there was nothing wrong with him and that the sentence should be carried out. At this his feeling of helpless rage had further increased and he was taken out by force. Then for the first time he had had "this queer feeling" in his abdomen and had struck a military policeman who tried to compel him to work. Horror at the implications of this act intensified his disturbed state. The obsession to strike people made its first appearance in 1953, eleven years later. He had been imprisoned overnight (for the first time since 1942) because, arriving home one night to find his house crowded with his wife's relatives, he had shouted and been violent until his wife had called the police. After emerging from jail, burning with a sense of injustice much like that experienced during his imprisonment in the army, he had felt the impulse to strike a stranger who was giving him a lift in an automobile, and then again, much more strongly, a few days later toward his wife at their first meeting since his night in jail. This time he had gone into a state of panic, and since then, for a period of five months, the obsession had recurred very frequently and in an increasing range of conditions, e.g., at work he would often have a fear-laden desire to hit fellow workmen with any tool he happened to be holding. (There was subsequently a secondary conditioning of anxiety to the *sight* of tools, including knives and forks.)

Anxiety-Reducing Obsessions. The second type of obsessional behavior occurs as a *reaction* to anxiety, and its performance *diminishes* anxiety to some extent, for at least a short time. It occurs in many forms—tidying, handwashing, eating, buying—activities which are of course "normal" when prompted by usual motivations and not by anxiety; rituals like touching poles, perversions like exhibitionism, and various thinking activities. In some of these cases secondary heightening of anxiety occurs as a response to some aspect of the obsessional behavior. For example, in a case of obsessional eating, the anxiety was at first reduced by the eating, and then its level would rise in response to the idea of getting fat.

Obsessional behavior of this kind owes its existence to the previous conditioning of anxiety-relieving responses. This has been strikingly demonstrated in a recent experiment by Fonberg (1956). This writer conditioned each of several dogs to perform a definite movement in response to several auditory and visual stimuli using food reinforcement. When these instrumental conditioned responses had been firmly established, she proceeded to elaborate defensive instrumental conditioned responses, employing stimuli and responses distinct from those of the alimentary training. The noxious stimulus used was either an electric shock to the right foreleg or a strong air puff to the ear. As a result of this conditioning, upon presentation of the conditioned stimulus an animal would be able to avert the noxious stimulus—for example, by lifting a particular foreleg. The dogs were then made neurotic by conditioning an excitatory alimentary response to a strong tone of 50 cycles and an inhibitory response to a very weak tone of the same frequency, and then bringing the two differentiated tones nearer and nearer to each other from session to session either by progressive strengthening of the inhibitory tone or by both strengthening the inhibitory and weakening the excitatory. In all animals, as soon as neurotic behavior appeared it was accompanied by the previously elaborated defensive motor reaction. Besides this deliberately conditioned reaction, "shaking off" movements were observed in those dogs in whom the noxious stimulation had originally been air puffed into the ear. The more intense the general disturbance the more intense and frequent were the defensive movements. The alimentary conditioned reflexes disappeared completely. With the disappearance of general disturbed symptoms, the defensive movements subsided, reappearing with any new outburst of behavioral disturbance.

It appears clear from these observations that in elaborating the conditioned defensive reaction to the auditory stimulus, anxiety-response-produced stimuli were also conditioned to evoke the defensive reaction, and this reaction was consequently evocable *whenever* the animal had anxiety responses, no matter what the origin of these may have been.

Similarly, in the history of patients displaying this kind of obsessional behavior, it is found that at an earlier period, some important real threat was consistently removed by a single well-defined type of behavior, and this behavior later appears as a response to *any* similar anxiety. The behavior must owe its strength to its association with exceptionally strong reinforcement-favoring conditions— either very massive or very numerous anxiety-drive reductions or both. Its development is also, no doubt, greatly favored when from the outset no other significant anxiety-relieving activity has occurred to compete with it. Its maintenance depends upon the reduction of anxiety it is able to effect at each performance.

One patient was the youngest daughter of a man who despised females and would not forgive his wife for failing to bear him a son. She was very clever at school, and found that intellectual achievement, and that alone, could for brief periods abate her father's blatant hostility and therefore her own anxiety. Consequently, "thinking things out" became her automatic response to *any* anxiety. Since there are many objective fears for which careful thought is useful, there were no serious consequences for years. But when a series of experiences in early adult life led to a severe anxiety state in her, she automatically resorted to her characteristic "problem-solving" behavior. Because the anxiety responses now arose from such sources as imaginary social disapproval, and could not be removed by the solution of a well-defined problem, she began to set herself complex problems in which she usually had to decide whether given behavior was morally "good" or "bad." Partial and brief alleviation of anxiety followed both the formulation of a "suitable" problem and the solution thereof, while prolonged failure to solve a problem increased anxiety sometimes to terror. Although the anxiety soon returned in full force, its temporary decrements at the most appropriate times for reinforcement maintained the problem-finding and problem-solving obsessions, and could well have continued to do so indefinitely.

In other cases obsessional behavior is less episodically determined because everyday circumstances contain aspects of the special situation in which the obsessional mode of behavior alone brought relief from severe anxiety. A history of more than 100 undetected thefts of money by a 17-year-old university student began at the age of 5 when his mother joined the army and left him in the care of an elder sister who beat him severely or tied him to a tree for a few hours if he was slightly dirty or did anything "wrong." He feared and hated her and retaliated by stealing money from her. He was never caught and the possession of the stolen gains gave him a feeling of "munificence and security." The kleptomania continued all through the early home life and school life and was clearly connected with the chronic presence of punishment-empowered authority in the shape of parents or teachers.

It is not surprising, if obsessional behavior is so consistently followed by reduction of anxiety drive, that it is apt to become conditioned to other stimuli too, especially any that happen to be present on repeated occasions. Thus, after therapy had rendered the young woman with the problem-solving obsession mentioned above practically free from neurotic anxieties, mild problem-solving activity was still occasionally aroused by a trifling question, such as "Is it cloudy enough to rain?" The conditioned stimulus was apparently the mere awareness of doubt. Similarly an exhibitionist whose exhibiting had almost entirely disappeared with the overcoming of his anxious sensitivities, still had some measure of the impulse when he saw a girl dressed in a school ("gym") uniform, because he had in the past exhibited to schoolgirls particularly frequently and with special relish. Of course, in this instance sex-drive reduction may have played as important a role in the reinforcement as anxiety-drive reduction.

AMNESIA AND "REPRESSION"

The amnesias that are usually encountered in the course of neurotic states can be conveniently divided into two classes, according to the emotional importance of the incidents forgotten. Patients who are in a chronic state of emotional disturbance frequently fail to register many trifling events that go on around them. For example, a patient may go into a room and conduct a brief conversation with his wife and an hour later have no recollection whatever that he went into that room at all. Here we seem to have a simple case of deficient registration of impressions (retrograde amnesia). Apparently, the patient's attention is so much taken up by his unpleasant anxious feelings that very little is left to be devoted to what goes on around him.

The forgetting of the contents of highly emotionally charged experiences has been given foremost importance by Freud and his followers as the cause of neurosis. It seems, however, that forgetting of this character is rather unusual, and when it does occur it appears to be merely one more of the conditionable occurrences in the neurotigenic situation. It does not appear that the repression as such plays any part in the maintenance of neurosis. It is quite possible for the patient to recover emotionally although the forgotten incidents remain entirely forgotten.

References

Eysenck, H. J. (1947) Dimensions of Personality. London, Routledge.

———. (1955a) A dynamic theory of anxiety and hysteria. *J. Ment. Sci.* 101: 28.

———. (1955b) Cortical inhibition, figural after-effect and theory of personality. *J. Abnorm. Soc. Psychol.* 51: 94.

Fonberg, E. (1956) On the manifestation of conditioned defensive reactions in stress. *Bull. Soc. Sci. Lettr. Lodz. Class III. Sci. Math. Natur.* 7: 1.

Franks, C. M. (1956) Conditioning and personality: A study of normal and neurotic subjects. *J. Abnorm. Soc. Psychol.* 52: 143.

Freud, S. (1893) On the psychical mechanism of hysterical phenomena. In Collected Works of Freud, Vol. I. London, Hogarth Press, 1949.

Jung, C. G. (1923) Psychological Types. New York, Harcourt, Brace.

Mowrer, O. H., and Viek, P. (1948) Experimental analogue of fear from a sense of helplessness. *J. Abnorm. Soc. Psychol.* 43: 193.

Pollitt, J. (1957) Natural history of obsessional states: A study of 150 cases. *Brit. Med. J.* 1: 194.

Wolpe, J. (1953a) Learning theory and "abnormal fixations." *Psychol. Rev.* 60: 111.

Behavioral Analysis: An Alternative to Diagnostic Classification

FREDERICK H. KANFER and GEORGE SASLOW

During the past decade attacks on conventional psychiatric diagnosis have been so widespread that many clinicians now use diagnostic labels sparingly and apologetically. The continued adherence to the nosological terms of the traditional classificatory scheme suggests some utility of the present categorization of behavior disorders, despite its apparently low reliability[1, 21]; its limited prognostic value[7, 26]; and its multiple feebly related assumptive supports. In a recent study of this problem, the symptom patterns of carefully diagnosed paranoid schizophrenics were compared. Katz et al[12] found considerable divergence among patients with the same diagnosis and concluded that "diagnostic systems which are more circumscribed in their intent, for example, based on manifest behavior alone, rather than systems which attempt to comprehend etiology, symptom patterns and prognosis, may be more directly applicable to current problems in psychiatric research" (p 202).

We propose here to examine some sources of dissatisfaction with the present approach to diagnosis, to describe a framework for a behavioral analysis of individual patients which implies both suggestions for treatment and outcome criteria for the single case, and to indicate the conditions for collecting the data for such an analysis.

From the *Archives of General Psychiatry 12*: 529-538, June 1965, copyright 1965 by the American Medical Association, by permission of the publisher and the authors.

PROBLEMS IN CURRENT DIAGNOSTIC SYSTEMS

Numerous criticisms deal with the internal consistency, the explicitness, the precision, and the reliability of psychiatric classifications. It seems to us that the more important fault lies in our lack of sufficient knowledge to categorize behavior along those pertinent dimensions which permit prediction of responses to social stresses, life crises, or psychiatric treatment. This limitation obviates anything but a crude and tentative approximation to a taxonomy of effective individual behaviors.

Zigler and Phillips,[28] in discussing the requirement for an adequate system of classification, suggest that an etiologically-oriented closed system of diagnosis is premature. Instead, they believe that an empirical attack is needed, using "symptoms broadly defined as meaningful and discernible behaviors, as the basis of the classificatory system" (p 616). But symptoms as a class of responses are defined after all only by their nuisance value to the patient's social environment or to himself as a social being. They are also notoriously unreliable in predicting the patient's particular etiological history or his response to treatment. An alternate approach lies in an attempt to identify classes of dependent variables in human behavior which would allow inferences about the particular controlling factors, the social stimuli, the physiological stimuli, and the reinforcing stimuli, of which they are a function. In the present early stage of the art of psychological prognostication, it appears most reasonable to develop a program of analysis which is closely related to subsequent treatment. A classification scheme which implies a program of behavioral change is one which has not only utility but the potential for experimental validation.

The task of assessment and prognosis can therefore be reduced to efforts which answer the following three questions: (a) which specific behavior patterns require change in their frequency of occurrence, their intensity, their duration or in the conditions under which they occur, (b) what are the best practical means which can produce the desired changes in this individual (manipulation of the environment, of the behavior, or the self-attitudes of the patient), and (c) what factors are currently maintaining it and what are the conditions under which this behavior was acquired. The investigation of the history of the problematic behavior is mainly of academic interest, except as it contributes information about the probable efficacy of a specific treatment method.

Expectations of Current Diagnostic Systems. In traditional medicine, a diagnostic statement about a patient has often been viewed as an essential prerequisite to treatment because a diagnosis suggests that the physician has some knowledge of the origin and future course of the illness. Further, in medicine diagnosis frequently brings together the accumulated knowledge about the pathological process which leads to the manifestation of the symptoms, and the experiences which others have had in the past in treating patients with such a disease process. Modern medicine recognizes that any particular disease need not have a single cause or even a small number of antecedent conditions. Nevertheless, the diagnostic label attempts to define at least the necessary conditions which are most relevant in considering a treatment program. Some diagnostic classification system is also invaluable as a basis for many social decisions involving entire populations. For example, planning for treatment facilities, research efforts and educational programs take into account the distribution frequencies of specified syndromes in the general population.

Ledley and Lusted[14] give an excellent conception of the traditional model in medicine by their analysis of the reasoning underlying it. The authors differentiate between a disease complex and a symptom complex.

While the former describes known pathological processes and their correlated signs, the latter represents particular signs present in a particular patient. The bridge between disease and symptom complexes is provided by available medical knowledge and the final diagnosis is tantamount to labeling the disease complex. However, the current gaps in medical knowledge necessitate the use of probability statements when relating disease to symptoms, admitting that there is some possibility for error in the diagnosis. Once the diagnosis is established, decisions about treatment still depend on many other factors including social, moral, and economic conditions. Ledley and Lusted[14] thus separate the clinical diagnosis into a two-step process. A statistical procedure is suggested to facilitate the primary or diagnostic labeling process. However, the choice of treatment depends not only on the diagnosis proper. Treatment decisions are also influenced by the moral, ethical, social, and economic conditions of the individual patient, his family and the society in which he lives. The proper assignment of the weight to be given to each of these values must in the last analysis be left to the physician's judgment (Ledley and Lusted[14]).

The Ledley and Lusted model presumes available methods for the observation of relevant behavior (the symptom complex), and some scientific knowledge relating it to known antecedents or correlates (the disease process). Contemporary theories of behavior pathology do not yet provide adequate guidelines for the observer to suggest what is to be observed. In fact, Szasz[25] has expressed the view that the medical model may be totally inadequate because psychiatry should be concerned with problems of living and not with diseases of the brain or other biological organs. Szasz[25] argues that "mental illness is a myth, whose function it is to disguise and thus render more potable the bitter pill of moral conflict in human relations" (p 118).

The attack against use of the medical model in psychiatry comes from many quarters. Scheflen[23] describes a model of somatic psychiatry which is very similar to the traditional medical model of disease. A pathological process results in onset of an illness; the symptoms are correlated with a pathological state and represent our evidence of "mental disease." Treatment consists of removal of the pathogen, and the state of health is restored. Scheflen suggests that this traditional medical model is used in psychiatry not on the basis of its adequacy but because of its emotional appeal.

The limitations of the somatic model have been discussed even in some areas of medicine for which the model seems most appropriate. For example, in the nomenclature for diagnosis of disease of the heart and blood vessels, the criteria committee of the New York Heart Association[17] suggests the use of multiple criteria for cardiovascular diseases, including a statement of the patient's functional capacity. The committee suggests that the functional capacity be "... estimated by appraising the patient's ability to perform physical activity" (p 80), and decided largely by inference from his history. Further,[17] "... (it) should not be influenced by the character of the structural lesion or by an opinion as to treatment or prognosis" (p 81). This approach makes it clear that a comprehensive assessment of a patient, regardless of the physical disease which he suffers, must also take into account his social effectiveness and the particular ways in which physiological, anatomical, and psychological factors interact to produce a particular behavior pattern in an individual patient.

Multiple Diagnosis. A widely used practical solution and circumvention of the difficulty inherent in the application of the medical model to psychiatric diagnosis is offered by Noyes and Kolb.[18] They suggest that the clinician construct a diagnostic formulation consisting of three parts: (1) A *genetic* diagnosis incorporating the constitutional, somatic, and historical-traumatic factors representing the primary sources or determinants of the mental illness; (2) A *dynamic* diagnosis which describes the mechanisms and techniques unconsciously used by the individual to manage anxiety, enhance self-esteem, ie, that traces the psychopathological processes; and (3) A *clinical* diagnosis which conveys useful connotations concerning the reaction syndrome, the probable course of the disorder, and the methods of treatment which will most probably prove beneficial. Noyes' and Kolb's multiple criteria[18] can be arranged along three simpler dimensions of diagnosis which may have some practical value to the clinician: (1) etiological, (2) behavioral, and (3) predictive. The kind of information which is conveyed by each type of diagnostic label is somewhat different and specifically adapted to the purpose for which the diagnosis is used. The triple-label approach attempts to counter the criticism aimed at use of any single classificatory system. Confusion in a single system is due in part to the fact that a diagnostic formulation intended to describe current behavior, for example, may be found useless in an attempt to predict the response to specific treatment, or to postdict the patient's personal history and development, or to permit collection of frequency data on hospital populations.

Classification by Etiology. The Kraepelinian system and portions of the 1952 APA classification emphasize etiological factors. They share the assumption that common etiological factors lead to similar symptoms and respond to similar treatment. This dimension of diagnosis is considerably more fruitful when dealing with behavior disorders which are mainly under control of some biological condition. When a patient is known to suffer from excessive intake of alcohol his hallucinatory behavior, lack of motor coordination, poor judgment, and other behavioral evidence disorganization can often be related directly to some antecedent condition such as the toxic effect of alcohol on the central nervous system, liver, etc. For these cases,

classification by etiology also has some implications for prognosis and treatment. Acute hallucinations and other disorganized behavior due to alcohol usually clear up when the alcohol level in the blood stream falls. Similar examples can be drawn from any class of behavior disorders in which a change in behavior is associated primarily or exclusively with a single, *particular* antecedent factor. Under these conditions this factor can be called a pathogen and the situation closely approximates the condition described by the traditional medical model.

Utilization of this dimension as a basis for psychiatric diagnosis, however, has many problems apart from the rarity with which a specified condition can be shown to have a direct "causal" relationship to a pathogen. Among the current areas of ignorance in the fields of psychology and psychiatry, the etiology of most common disturbances probably takes first place. No specific family environment, no dramatic traumatic experience, or known constitutional abnormality has yet been found which results in the same pattern of disordered behavior. While current research efforts have aimed at investigating family patterns of schizophrenic patients, and several studies suggest a relationship between the mother's behavior and a schizophrenic process in the child,[10] it is not at all clear why the presence of these same factors in other families fails to yield a similar incidence of schizophrenia. Further, patients may exhibit behavior diagnosed as schizophrenic when there is no evidence of the postulated mother-child relationship.

In a recent paper Meehl[16] postulates schizophrenia as a neurological disease, with learned content and a dispositional basis. With this array of interactive etiological factors, it is clear that the etiological dimension for classification would at best result in an extremely cumbersome system, at worst in a useless one.

Classification by Symptoms. A clinical diagnosis often is a summarizing statement about the way in which a person behaves. On the assumption that a variety of behaviors are correlated and consistent in any given individual, it becomes more economical to assign the individual to a class of persons than to list and categorize all of his behaviors. The utility of such a system rests heavily on the availability of empirical evidence concerning correlations among various behaviors (response-response relationships), and the further assumption that the frequency of occurrence of such behaviors is relatively independent of specific stimulus conditions and of specific reinforcement. There are two major limitations to such a system. The first is that diagnosis by symptoms, as we have indicated in an earlier section, is often misleading because it implies common etiological factors. Freedman[7] gives an excellent illustration of the differences both in probable antecedent factors and subsequent treatment response among three cases diagnosed as schizophrenics. Freedman's patients were diagnosed by at least two psychiatrists, and one would expect that the traditional approach should result in whatever treatment of schizophrenia is practiced in the locale where the patients are seen. The first patient eventually gave increasing evidence of an endocrinopathy, and when this was recognized and treated, the psychotic symptoms went into remission. The second case had a definite history of seizures and appropriate anticonvulsant medication was effective in relieving his symptoms. In the third case, treatment directed at an uncovering analysis of the patient's adaptive techniques resulted in considerable improvement in the patient's behavior and subsequent relief from psychotic episodes. Freedman[7] suggests that schizophrenia is not a disease entity in the sense that it has a unique etiology, pathogenesis, etc., but that it represents the evocation of a final common pathway in the same sense as do headache, epilepsy, sore throat, or indeed any other symptom complex. It is further suggested that the term "schizophrenia has outlived its usefulness and should be discarded" (p 5). Opler[19, 20] has further shown the importance of cultural factors in the divergence of symptoms observed in patients collectively labeled as schizophrenic.

Descriptive classification is not always this deceptive, however. Assessment of intellectual performance sometimes results in a diagnostic statement which has predictive value for the patient's behavior in school or on a job. To date, there seem to be very few general statements about individual characteristics, which have as much predictive utility as the IQ.

A second limitation is that the current approach to diagnosis by symptoms tends to center on a group of behaviors which is often irrelevant with regard to the patient's total life pattern. These behaviors may be of interest only because they are popularly associated with deviancy and disorder. For example, occasional mild delusions interfere little or not at all with the social or occupational effectiveness of many ambulatory patients. Nevertheless, admission of their occurrence is often sufficient for a diagnosis of psychosis. Refinement of such an approach beyond current usage appears possible, as shown for example by Lorr et al[15] but this does not remove the above limitations.

Utilization of a symptom-descriptive approach frequently focuses attention on by-products of larger behavior patterns, and results in attempted treatment of behaviors (symptoms) which may be simple consequences of other important aspects of the patient's life. Emphasis on the patient's subjective complaints, moods and feelings tends to encourage use of a syndrome-oriented classification. It also results frequently in efforts to change the feelings, anxieties, and moods (or at least the patient's report about them), rather than to investigate the life conditions, interpersonal reactions, and environmental factors which produce and maintain these habitual response patterns.

Classification by Prognosis. To

date, the least effort has been devoted to construction of a classification system which assigns patients to the same category on the basis of their similar response to specific treatments. The proper question raised for such a classification system consists of the manner in which a patient will react to treatments, regardless of his current behavior, or his past history. The numerous studies attempting to establish prognostic signs from projective personality tests or somatic tests represent efforts to categorize the patients on this dimension.

Windle[26] has called attention to the low degree of predictability afforded by personality (projective) test scores, and has pointed out the difficulties encountered in evaluating research in this area due to the inadequate description of the population sampled and of the improvement criteria. In a later review Fulkerson and Barry[8] came to the similar conclusion that psychological test performance is a poor predictor of outcome in mental illness. They suggest that demographic variables such as severity, duration, acuteness of onset, degree of precipitating stress, etc., appear to have stronger relationships to outcome than test data. The lack of reliable relationships between diagnostic categories, test data, demographic variables or other measures taken on the patient on the one hand, and duration of illness, response to specific treatment, or degree of recovery, on the other hand, precludes the construction of a simple empiric framework for a diagnostic-prognostic classification system based only on an array of symptoms.

None of the currently used dimensions for diagnosis is directly related to methods of modification of a patient's behavior, attitudes, response patterns, and interpersonal actions. Since the etiological model clearly stresses causative factors, it is much more compatible with a personality theory which strongly emphasizes genetic-developmental factors. The classification by symptoms facilitates social-administrative decisions about

patients by providing some basis for judging the degree of deviation from social and ethical norms. Such a classification is compatible with a personality theory founded on the normal curve hypothesis and concerned with characterization by comparison with a fictitious average. The prognostic-predictive approach appears to have the most direct practical applicability. If continued research were to support certain early findings, it would be indeed comforting to be able to predict outcome of mental illness from a patient's premorbid social competence score,[28] or from the patient's score on an ego-strength scale,[4] or from many of the other signs and single variables which have been shown to have some predictive powers. It is unfortunate that these powers are frequently dissipated in cross validation. As Fulkerson and Barry have indicated[8] single predictors have not yet shown much success.

A FUNCTIONAL (BEHAVIORAL-ANALYTIC) APPROACH

The growing literature on behavior modification procedures derived from learning theory[3, 6, 11, 13, 27] suggests that an effective diagnostic procedure would be one in which the eventual therapeutic methods can be directly related to the information obtained from a continuing assessment of the patient's current behaviors and their controlling stimuli. Ferster[6] has said "... a functional analysis of behavior has the advantage that it specifies the causes of behavior in the form of explicit environmental events which can be objectively identified and which are potentially manipulable" (p 3). Such a diagnostic undertaking makes the assumption that a description of the problematic behavior, its controlling factors, and the means by which it can be changed are the most appropriate "explanations." It further makes the assumption that a diagnostic evaluation is never complete. It implies that additional information about the circumstances of the patient's life pattern, relationships among his behaviors, and controlling stimuli in his social milieu and his private experience is obtained continuously until it proves sufficient to effect a noticeable change in the patient's behavior, thus resolving "the problem." In a functional approach it is necessary to continue evaluation of the patient's life pattern and its controlling factors, concurrent with attempted manipulation of these variables by reinforcement, direct intervention, or other means until the resultant change in the patient's behavior permits restoration of more efficient life experiences.

The present approach shares with some psychological theories the assumption that psychotherapy is *not* an effort aimed at removal of intrapsychic conflicts, nor at a change in the personality structure by therapeutic interactions of intense nonverbal nature, (eg, transference, self-actualization, etc.). We adopt the assumption instead that the job of psychological treatment involves the utilization of a variety of methods to devise a program which controls the patient's environment, his behavior, and the consequences of his behavior in such a way that the presenting problem is resolved. We hypothesize that the essential ingredients of a psychotherapeutic endeavor usually involve two separate stages: (1) a change in the perceptual discriminations of a patient, ie, in his approach to perceiving, classifying, and organizing sensory events, including perception of himself, and (2) changes in the response patterns which he has established in relation to social objects and to himself over the years.[11] In addition, the clinician's task may involve direct intervention in the patient's environmental circumstances, modification of the behavior of other people significant in his life, and control of reinforcing stimuli which are available either through self-administration, or by contingency upon the behavior of others. These latter procedures complement the verbal interac-

tions of traditional psychotherapy. They require that the clinician, at the invitation of the patient or his family, participate more fully in planning the total life pattern of the patient outside the clinician's office.

It is necessary to indicate what the theoretical view here presented does *not* espouse in order to understand the differences from other procedures. It does *not* rest upon the assumption that (a) insight is a sine qua non of psychotherapy, (b) changes in thoughts or ideas inevitably lead to ultimate changes in actions, (c) verbal therapeutic sessions serve as replications of and equivalents for actual life situations, and (d) a symptom can be removed only by uprooting its cause or origin. In the absence of these assumptions it becomes unnecessary to conceptualize behavior disorder in etiological terms, in psychodynamic terms, or in terms of a specifiable disease process. While psychotherapy by verbal means may be sufficient in some instances, the combination of behavior modification in life situations as well as in verbal interactions serves to extend the armamentarium of the therapist. Therefore verbal psychotherapy is seen as an *adjunct* in the implementation of therapeutic behavior changes in the patient's total life pattern, not as an end in itself, nor as the sole vehicle for increasing psychological effectiveness.

In embracing this view of behavior modification, there is a further commitment to a constant interplay between assessment and therapeutic strategies. An initial diagnostic formulation seeks to ascertain the major variables which can be directly controlled or modified during treatment. During successive treatment stages additional information is collected about the patient's behavior repertoire, his reinforcement history, the pertinent controlling stimuli in his social and physical environment, and the sociological limitations within which both patient and therapist have to operate. Therefore, the initial formulation will constantly be enlarged or changed, resulting either in confirmation of the previous therapeutic strategy or in its change.

A Guide to a Functional Analysis of Individual Behavior. In order to help the clinician in the collection and organization of information for a behavioral analysis, we have constructed an outline which aims to provide a working model of the patient's behavior at a relatively low level of abstraction. A series of questions are so organized as to yield immediate implications for treatment. This outline has been found useful both in clinical practice and in teaching. Following is a brief summary of the categories in the outline.

1. Analysis of a Problem Situation: *The patient's major complaints are categorized into classes of behavioral excesses and deficits. For each excess or deficit the dimensions of frequency, intensity, duration, appropriateness of form, and stimulus conditions are described. In content, the response classes represent the major targets of the therapeutic intervention. As an additional indispensable feature, the behavioral assets of the patient are listed for utilization in a therapy program.

2. Clarification of the Problem Situation: Here we consider the people and circumstances which tend to maintain the problem behaviors, and the consequences of these behaviors to the patient and to others in his environment. Attention is given also to the consequences of changes in these behaviors which may result from psychiatric intervention.

3. Motivational Analysis: Since reinforcing stimuli are idiosyncratic and depend for their effect on a number of unique parameters for each person, a hierarchy of particular persons, events, and objects which serve as reinforcers is established for each patient. Included in this hierarchy are those reinforcing events which facilitate approach behaviors as well as those which, because of

their aversiveness, prompt avoidance responses. This information has as its purpose to lay plans for utilization of various reinforcers in prescription of a specific behavior therapy program for the patient, and to permit utilization of appropriate reinforcing behaviors by the therapist and significant others in the patient's social environment.

4. Developmental Analysis: Questions are asked about the patient's biological equipment, his sociocultural experiences, and his characteristic behavioral development. They are phrased in such a way as (a) to evoke descriptions of his habitual behavior at various chronological stages of his life, (b) to relate specific new stimulus conditions to noticeable changes from his habitual behavior, and (c) to relate such altered behavior and other residuals of biological and sociocultural events to the present problem.

5. Analysis of Self-Control: This section examines both the methods and the degree of self-control exercised by the patient in his daily life. Persons, events, or institutions which have successfully reinforced self-controlling behaviors are considered. The deficits or excesses of self-control are evaluated in relation to their importance as therapeutic targets and to their utilization in a therapeutic program.

6. Analysis of Social Relationships: Examination of the patient's social network is carried out to evaluate the significance of people in the patient's environment who have some influence over the problematic behaviors, or who in turn are influenced by the patient for his own satisfactions. These interpersonal relationships are reviewed in order to plan the potential participation of significant others in a treatment program, based on the principles of behavior modification. The review also helps the therapist to consider the range of actual social relationships in which the patient needs to function.

7. Analysis of the Social-Cultural-Physical Environment: In this section we add to the preceding analysis of the patient's behavior as an individual, consideration of the norms in his natural environment. Agreements and discrepancies between the patient's idiosyncratic life patterns and the norms in his environment are defined so that the importance of these factors can be decided in formulating treatment goals which allow as explicitly for the patient's needs as for the pressures of his social environment.

The preceding outline has as its purpose to achieve definition of a patient's problem in a manner which suggests specific treatment operations, or that none are feasible, and specific behaviors as targets for modification. Therefore, the formulation is *action oriented*. It can be used

---

* For each patient a detailed analysis is required. For example, a list of behavioral excesses may include specific aggressive acts, hallucinatory behaviors, crying, submission to others in social situations, etc. It is recognized that some behaviors can be viewed as excesses or deficits depending on the vantage point from which the imbalance is observed. For instance, excessive withdrawal and deficient social responsiveness, or excessive social autonomy (nonconformity) and deficient self-inhibitory behavior may be complementary. The particular view taken is of consequence because of its impact on a treatment plan. Regarding certain behavior as excessively aggressive, to be reduced by constraints, clearly differs from regarding the same behavior as a deficit in self-control, subject to increase by training and treatment.

as a guide for the initial collection of information, as a device for organizing available data, or as a design for treatment.

The formulation of a treatment plan follows from this type of analysis because knowledge of the reinforcing conditions suggests the motivational controls at the disposal of the clinician for the modification of the patient's behavior. The analysis of specific problem behaviors also provides a series of goals for psychotherapy or other treatment, and for the evaluation of treatment progress. Knowledge of the patient's biological, social, and cultural conditions should help to determine what resources can be used, and what limitations must be considered in a treatment plan.

The various categories attempt to call attention to important variables affecting the patient's *current* behavior. Therefore, they aim to elicit descriptions of low-level abstraction. Answers to these specific questions are best phrased by describing classes of events reported by the patient, observed by others, or by critical incidents described by an informant. The analysis does not exclude description of the patient's habitual verbal-symbolic behaviors. However, in using verbal behaviors as the basis for this analysis, one should be cautious not to "explain" verbal processes in terms of postulated internal mechanisms without adequate supportive evidence, nor should inference be made about nonobserved processes or events without corroborative evidence. The analysis includes many items which are not known or not applicable for a given patient. Lack of information on some items does not necessarily indicate incompleteness of the analysis. These lacks must be noted nevertheless because they often contribute to the better understanding of what the patient needs to learn to become an autonomous person. Just as important is an inventory of his existing socially effective behavioral repertoire which can be put in the service of any treatment procedure.

This analysis is consistent with our earlier formulations of the principles of comprehensive medicine[9, 22] which emphasized the joint operation of biological, social, and psychological factors in psychiatric disorders. The language and orientation of the proposed approach are rooted in contemporary learning theory. The conceptual framework is consonant with the view that the course of psychiatric disorders can be modified by systematic application of scientific principles from the fields of psychology and medicine to the patient's habitual mode of living.

This approach is not a substitute for assignment of the patient to traditional diagnostic categories. Such labeling may be desirable for statistical, administrative, or research purposes. But the current analysis is intended to replace other diagnostic formulations purporting to serve as a basis for making decisions about specific therapeutic interventions.

METHODS OF DATA COLLECTION FOR A FUNCTIONAL ANALYSIS

Traditional diagnostic approaches have utilized as the main sources of information the patient's verbal report, his nonverbal behavior during an interview, and his performance on psychological tests. These observations are sufficient if one regards behavior problems only as a property of the patient's particular pattern of associations or his personality structure. A mental disorder would be expected to reveal itself by stylistic characteristics in the patient's behavior repertoire. However, if one views behavior disorders as sets of response patterns which are learned under particular conditions and maintained by definable environmental and internal stimuli, an assessment of the patient's behavior output is insufficient unless it also describes the conditions under which it occurs. This view requires an expansion of the clinician's sources of observations to include the stimulation fields in which the patient lives, and the variations of patient behavior as a function of exposure to these various stimulational variables. Therefore, the resourceful clinician need not limit himself to test findings, interview observations in the clinician's office, or referral histories alone in the formulation of the specific case. Nor need he regard himself as hopelessly handicapped when the patient has little observational or communicative skill in verbally reconstructing his life experiences for the clinician. Regardless of the patient's communicative skills the data must consist of a description of the patient's behavior *in relationship* to varying environmental conditions.

A behavioral analysis excludes no data relating to a patient's past or present experiences as irrelevant. However, the relative merit of any information (as, eg, growing up in a broken home or having had homosexual experiences) lies in its relation to the independent variables which can be identified as controlling the current problematic behavior. The observation that a patient has hallucinated on occasions may be important only if it has bearing on his present problem. If looked upon in isolation, a report about hallucinations may be misleading, resulting in emphasis on classification rather than treatment.

In the *psychiatric interview* a behavioral-analytic approach opposes acceptance of the content of the verbal self-report as equivalent to actual events or experiences. However, verbal reports provide information concerning the patient's verbal construction of his environment and of his person, his recall of past experiences, and his fantasies about them. While these self-descriptions do not represent data about events which actually occur internally, they do represent current behaviors of the patient and indicate the verbal chains and repertoires which the patient has built up. Therefore, the verbal behavior may be useful for description of a patient's thinking processes. To make the most of such an approach, variations on traditional interview procedures may

be obtained by such techniques as role playing, discussion, and interpretation of current life events, or controlled free association. Since there is little experimental evidence of specific relationships between the patient's verbal statements and his nonverbal behavorial acts, the verbal report alone remains insufficient for a complete analysis and for prediction of his daily behavior. Further, it is well known that a person responds to environmental conditions and to internal cues which he cannot describe adequately. Therefore, any verbal report may miss or mask the most important aspects of a behavioral analysis, ie, the description of the relationship between antecedent conditions and subsequent behavior.

In addition to the use of the clinician's own person as a controlled stimulus object in interview situations, *observations of interaction with significant others* can be used for the analysis of variations in frequency of various behaviors as a function of the person with whom the patient interacts. For example, use of prescribed standard roles for nurses and attendants, utilization of members of the patient's family or his friends, may be made to obtain data relevant to the patient's habitual interpersonal response pattern. Such observations are especially useful if in a later interview the patient is asked to describe and discuss the observed sessions. Confrontations with tape recordings for comparisons between the patient's report and the actual session as witnessed by the observer may provide information about the patient's perception of himself and others as well as his habitual behavior toward peers, authority figures, and other significant people in his life.

Except in working with children or family units, insufficient use has been made of material obtained from *other informants* in interviews about the patient. These reports can aid the observer to recognize behavioral domains in which the patient's report deviates from or agrees with the descriptions provided by others. Such information is also useful for contrasting the patient's reports about his presumptive effects on another person with the stated effects by that person. If a patient's interpersonal problems extend to areas in which social contacts are not clearly defined, contributions by informants other than the patient are essential.

It must be noted that verbal reports by other informants may be no more congruent with actual events than the patient's own reports and need to be equally related to the informant's own credibility. If such crucial figures as parents, spouses, employers can be so interviewed, they also provide the clinician with some information about those people with whom the patient must interact repeatedly and with whom interpersonal problems may have developed.

Some observation of the patient's daily *work behavior* represents an excellent source of information, if it can be made available. Observation of the patient by the clinician or his staff may be preferable to descriptions by peers or supervisors. Work observations are especially important for patients whose complaints include difficulties in their daily work activity or who describe work situations as contributing factors to their problem. While freer use of this technique may be hampered by cultural attitudes toward psychiatric treatment in the marginally adjusted, such observations may be freely accessible in hospital situations or in sheltered work situations. With use of behavior rating scales or other simple measurement devices, brief samples of patient behaviors in work situations can be obtained by minimally trained observers.

The patient himself may be asked to provide samples of his own behavior by using tape recorders for the recording of segments of interactions in his family, at work, or in other situations during his everyday life. A television monitoring system for the patient's behavior is an excellent technique from a theoretical viewpoint but it is extremely cumbersome

and expensive. Use of recordings for diagnostic and therapeutic purposes has been reported by some investigators.[2, 5, 24] Playback of the recordings and a recording of the patient's reactions to the playback can be used further in interviews to clarify the patient's behavior toward others and his reaction to himself as a social stimulus.

Psychological tests represent problems to be solved under specified interactional conditions. Between the highly standardized intelligence tests and the unstructured and ambiguous projective tests lies a dimension of structure along which more and more responsibility for providing appropriate responses falls on the patient. By comparison with interview procedures, most psychological tests provide a relatively greater standardization of stimulus conditions. But, in addition to the specific answers given on intelligence tests or on projective tests these tests also provide a behavioral sample of the patient's reaction to a problem situation in a relatively stressful interpersonal setting. Therefore, psychological tests can provide not only quantitative scores but they can also be treated as a miniature life experience, yielding information about the patient's interpersonal behavior and variations in his behavior as a function of the nature of the stimulus conditions.

In this section we have mentioned only some of the numerous life situations which can be evaluated in order to provide information about the patient. Criteria for their use lies in economy, accessibility to the clinician, and relevance to the patient's problem. While it is more convenient to gather data from a patient in an office, it may be necessary for the clinician to have first-hand information about the actual conditions under which the patient lives and works. Such familiarity may be obtained either by utilization of informants or by the clinician's entry into the home, the job situation, or the social environment in which the patient lives. Under all these conditions the clinician is effective only if it is possible for him to maintain a nonparticipating, objective, and observational role with no untoward consequences for the patient or the treatment relationship.

The methods of data collecting for a functional analysis described here differ from traditional psychiatric approaches only in that they require inclusion of the physical and social stimulus field in which the patient actually operates. Only a full appraisal of the patient's living and working conditions and his way of life allow a description of the actual problems which the patient faces and the specification of steps to be taken for altering the problematic situation.

SUMMARY

Current psychiatric classification falls short of providing a satisfactory basis for the understanding and treatment of maladaptive behavior. Diagnostic schemas now in use are based on etiology, symptom description, or prognosis. While each of these approaches has a limited utility, no unified schema is available which permits prediction of response to treatment or future course of the disorder from the assignment of the patient to a specific category.

This paper suggests a behavior-analytic approach which is based on contemporary learning theory, as an alternative to assignment of the patient to a conventional diagnostic category. It includes the summary of an outline which can serve as a guide for the collection of information and formulation of the problem, including the biological, social, and behavioral conditions which are determining the patient's behavior. The outline aims toward integration of information about a patient for formulation of an action plan which would modify the patient's problematic behavior. Emphasis is given to the particular variables affecting the *individual* patient rather than determination of the similarity of the patient's history

or his symptoms to known pathological groups.

The last section of the paper deals with methods useful for collection of information necessary to complete such a behavior analysis.

This paper was written in conjunction with Research grant MH 06921-03 from the National Institutes of Mental Health, United States Public Health Service.

References

1. Ash, P. Reliability of Psychiatric Diagnosis, J Abnorm Soc Psychol 44:272-277, 1949.
2. Bach, G. In Alexander, S. Fight Promoter for Battle of Sexes, Life 54:102-108 (May 17) 1963.
3. Bandura, A. Psychotherapy as Learning Process, Psychol Bull 58:143-159, 1961.
4. Barron, F.: Ego-Strength Scale Which Predicts Response to Psychotherapy, J Consult Psychol 17:235-241, 1953.
5. Cameron, D. E., et al. Automation of Psychotherapy, Compr Psychiat 5:1-14, 1964.
6. Ferster, C. B. Classification of Behavioral Pathology in Ullman, L. P. and Krasner, L. (eds.). Behavior Modification Research, New York: Holt, Rinehart & Winston, 1965.
7. Freedman, D. A. Various Etiologies of Schizophrenic Syndrome, Dis Nerv Syst 19:1-6, 1958.
8. Fulkerson, S. E., and Barry, J. R. Methodology and Research on Prognostic Use of Psychological Tests, Psychol Bull 58:177-204, 1961.
9. Guze, S. B., Matarazzo, J. D., and Saslow, G. Formulation of Principles of Comprehensive Medicine With Special Reference to Learning Theory, J Clin Psychol 9:127-136, 1953.
10. Jackson, D. D. A. Etiology of Schizophrenia, New York: Basic Books Inc., 1960.
11. Kanfer, F. H. Comments on Learning in Psychotherapy, Psychol Rep 9:681-699, 1961.
12. Katz, M. M., Cole, J. O., and Lowery, H. A. Nonspecificity of Diagnosis of Paranoid Schizophrenia, Arch Gen Psychiat 11:197-202, 1964.
13. Krasner, L. "Therapist as Social Reinforcement Machine," in Strupp, H., and Luborsky, L. (eds). Research in Psychotherapy, Washington, D.C. American Psychological Association, 1962.
14. Ledley, R. S., and Lusted, L. B. Reasoning Foundations of Medical Diagnosis, Science 130:9-21, 1959.
15. Lorr, M., Klett, C. J., and McNair, D. M. Syndromes of Psychosis, New York: Macmillan Co., 1963.
16. Meehl, P. E. Schizotaxia, Schizotypy, Schizophrenia, Amer Psychol 17:827-838, 1962.

17. New York Heart Association. Nomenclature and Criteria for Diagnosis of Diseases of the Heart and Blood Vessels, New York: New York Heart Association, 1953.

18. Noyes, A. P., and Kolb, L. C. Modern Clinical Psychiatry, Philadelphia: W. B. Saunders & Co., 1963.

19. Opler, M. K. Schizophrenia and Culture, Sci Amer 197:103-112, 1957.

20. Opler, M. K. Need for New Diagnostic Categories in Psychiatry, J Nat Med Assoc 55:133-137, 1963.

21. Rotter, J. B. Social Learning and Clinical Psychology, New York: Prentice Hall, 1954.

22. Saslow, G. On Concept of Comprehensive Medicine, Bull Menninger Clin 16:57-65, 1952.

23. Scheflen, A. E. Analysis of Thought Model Which Persists in Psychiatry, Psychosom Med 20:235-241, 1958.

24. Slack, C. W. Experimenter-Subject Psychotherapy—A New Method of Introducing Intensive Office Treatment for Unreachable Cases, Ment Hyg 44:238-256, 1960.

25. Szasz, T. S. Myth of Mental Illness, Amer Psychol 15:113-118, 1960.

26. Windle, C. Psychological Tests in Psychopathological Prognosis, Psychol Bull 49:451-482, 1952.

27. Wolpe, J. Psychotherapy in Reciprocal Inhibition, Stanford, Calif: Stanford University Press, 1958.

28. Zigler, E., and Phillips, L. Psychiatric Diagnosis: Critique, J Abnorm Soc Psychol 63:607-618, 1961.

Behavioral Theories:

THERAPY

Behavioral therapy consists of the direct application of experimentally derived principles of learning to the treatment of pathological disorders. The therapist does not seek to remove the "underlying" causes of psychopathology, nor does he give the patient free rein to explore his attitudes and feelings. Instead, he arranges a program of conditioning and extinction in which the behavior patterns he wishes to alter are specified, the environmental elements which have reinforced the maladaptive behavior are eliminated, and a series of new reinforcements are instituted in order to condition new adaptive behaviors.

The British psychologist Hans Eysenck has been in the forefront as an exponent of behavioral therapy. In the paper presented here, he offers an illuminating commentary on the logic and rationale of the entire behavioral movement. Charles Ferster's article brilliantly outlines the procedural steps involved in the extinction of pathological behavior patterns.

Learning Theory and Behaviour Therapy*

H. J. EYSENCK

It would probably be true to say that the present position in the psychiatric treatment of neurotic disorders is characterized by the following features. (1) With the exception of electroshock, the only method of treatment at all widely used is psychotherapy. (2) In practically all its manifestations, psychotherapy is based on Freudian theories. (3) With the exception of intelligence testing, psychological contributions consist almost entirely in the administration and interpretation of projective tests, usually along psychoanalytic lines. I have argued in the past and quoted numerous experiments in support of these arguments, that there is little evidence for the practical efficacy of psychotherapy,† whether strictly Freudian or "eclectic"[7, 8]; that Freud-

From *J. Mental Science* 105: 61-75, 1959, by permission of the Royal Medico-Psychological Association and the author.

* This paper was delivered on 3 July 1958 to a meeting of the R.M.P.A., and its style inevitably bears traces of the fact that it was originally prepared for verbal presentation. It was followed by another paper, delivered by Mr. Gwynne Jones, giving concrete examples of the application of behaviour therapy from our own experience. Some of these are discussed in his article published in this Journal,[1] and it is suggested that readers interested in the theories here advanced may like to consult this article in order to obtain some notion of the practical methods emanating from these theories. A more detailed discussion of many theoretical points that arise may be found in *Dynamics of Anxiety and Hysteria*,[2] as well as several of my previous books.[3, 4, 5]

† When I first suggested that the literature did not contain any kind of unequivocal proof of the efficacy of psychotherapeutic treatment, this conclusion was widely criticized. Since then however, Dr. Weinstock, Chairman of the Fact-Finding Committee of the Amer. Psychoanalyt. Assoc., has

ian theories are outside the realm of science because of their failure to be consistent, or to generate testable deductions[9]; and that projective tests are so unreliable and lacking in validity that their use, except in research, cannot be defended.[10]§ I shall not here argue these points again; the evidence on which these views are based is quite strong and is growing in strength every year. I shall, instead, try to make a somewhat more constructive contribution by discussing an alternative theory of neurosis, an alternative method of treatment and an alternative way of using the knowledge and competence of psychologists in the attempted curing of neurotic disorders. It need hardly be emphasized that the brief time at my disposal will make it inevitable that what I have to say will sound much more dogmatic than I would like it to be; I have to ask your indulgence in this respect, and request you to bear in mind all the obvious qualifying clauses which, if included in this paper, would swell it to three times its present size.

Few psychiatrists are likely to deny that all behaviour ultimately rests on an inherited basis, but even fewer would be prepared to assert that environmental influences played no part in the genesis and modification of behaviour. Once we are agreed that learning and conditioning are instrumental in determining the different kinds of reaction we may make to environmental stimulation, we will find it very difficult to deny that neurotic reactions, like all others, are *learned* reactions and must obey the laws of learning. Thus, I would like to make my first claim by

saying that modern learning theory,[11] and the experimental studies of learning and conditioning carried out by psychologists in their laboratories[12] are extremely relevant to the problems raised by neurotic disorders.[13] If the laws which have been formulated are, not necessarily true, but at least partially correct, then it must follow that we can make deductions from them to cover the type of behaviour represented by neurotic patients, construct a model which will duplicate the important and relevant features of the patient and suggest new and possibly helpful methods of treatment along lines laid down by learning theory. Whether these methods are in fact an improvement over existing methods is, of course, an empirical problem; a few facts are available in this connection and will be mentioned later. It is unfortunate that insistence on empirical proof has not always accompanied the production of theories in the psychiatric field—much needless work, and many heartbreaking failures, could have been avoided if the simple medical practice of clinical trials with proper controls had always been followed in the consideration of such claims.

How, then, does modern learning theory look upon neurosis? In the first place, it would claim that neurotic symptoms are *learned patterns of behaviour* which for some reason or other are *unadaptive*. The paradigm of neurotic symptom formation would be Watson's famous experiment with little Albert, an eleven months old boy who was fond of animals.[14] By a simple process of classical Pavlovian conditioning, Watson created a phobia for white rats in this boy by standing behind him and making a very loud noise by banging an iron bar with a hammer whenever Albert reached for the animal. The rat was the conditioned stimulus in the experiment, the loud fear-producing noise was the unconditioned stimulus. As predicted, the unconditioned response (fear) became conditioned to the C.S. (the rat), and Albert developed a phobia for white rats, and in-

explicitly stated in a lecture delivered at the Maudsley Hospital that his Association made *no claims of therapeutic usefulness for psychoanalytic methods* and in this country Glover[6] has equally explicitly disavowed such claims. On this point, therefore, leading psychoanalysts appear to share my views to a considerable extent.

§ This fact is also beginning to be more widely realized, and it is symptomatic that such well-known departments as that belonging to the New York Psychiatric Hospital, have followed the lead of the Institute of Psychiatry and discontinued the routine use of projective techniques like the Rorschach.

deed for all furry animals. This latter feature of the conditioning process is of course familiar to all students as the generalization gradient[12]; an animal or a person conditioned to one stimulus also responds, although less and less strongly, to other stimuli further and further removed from the original one along some continuum.

The fear of the rat thus conditioned is unadaptive (because white rats are not in fact dangerous) and hence is considered to be a neurotic symptom; a similarly conditioned fear of snakes would be regarded as adaptive, and hence not as neurotic. Yet the mechanism of acquisition is identical in both cases. This suggests that chance and environmental hazards are likely to play an important part in the acquisition of neurotic responses. If a rat happens to be present when the child hears a loud noise, a phobia results; when it is a snake that is present, a useful habit is built up!

The second claim which modern learning theory would make is this. People and animals differ in the speed and firmness with which conditioned responses are built up.[15] Those in whom they are built up particularly quickly and strongly are more likely to develop phobias and other anxiety and fear reactions than are people who are relatively difficult to condition.[2] Watson was lucky in his choice of subject; others have banged away with hammers on metal bars in an attempt to condition infants, but not always with the same success. Individual differences must be taken into account in considering the consequences of any course of attempted conditioning. Nor is the degree of conditionability the only kind of individual variability with which we are concerned. Learning theory tells us that the amount of reinforcement following any action determines in part the amount of conditioning that takes place.[16] Thus the louder the noise, the greater the fright of the infant, and the greater the fright, the stronger the phobia. But different children

have different types of autonomic system, and the same amount of noise produces quite unequal amounts of autonomic upheaval in different children. Consequently, autonomic reactivity must also be considered; the more labile or reactive the child, the more likely he is to produce strongly conditioned fear reactions, anxieties and phobias. The individual differences in autonomic reactivity and in conditionability have been conceptualized as giving rise to two dimensions of personality, namely neuroticism and introversion respectively.[5] The more autonomically reactive, the more prone will the individual be to neurotic disorders. The more easily he forms conditioned responses, the more introverted will his behaviour be. Combine introversion and neuroticism, and you get the dysthymic individual, the person almost predestined to suffer from anxieties, conditioned fears and phobias, compulsions and obsessions, reactive depressions and so forth.

But this is only part of the story. Many conditioned responses are unadaptive, and consequently may embarrass the individual and even drive him into a mental hospital if sufficiently intense. Yet other conditioned responses are obviously necessary and desirable; indeed, many of them are indispensable for survival. It has been argued very strongly that the whole process of socialization is built up on the principle of conditioning[17]; the overt display of aggressive and sexual tendencies is severely punished in the child, thus producing conditioned fear and pain responses (anxiety) to situations in which the individual is likely to display such tendencies. He consequently refrains from acting in the forbidden manner, not because of some conscious calculus of hedonic pleasure which attempts to equate the immediate pleasure to be gained from indulgence with the remote probability of later punishment, but because only by not indulging, and by physically removing himself can he relieve the very painful conditioned anxiety responses to the whole situation. Anxiety thus acts as a mediating drive, a drive which may be exceedingly powerful by virtue of its combination of central, autonomic, skeletal, and hormonal reactions. This mediating role of anxiety, and its capacity to function as an acquired drive, have been subjected to many well conceived experimental studies, and the consensus of opinion appears to leave little doubt about the great value and predictive capacity of this conception.[18]

Let us now consider an individual who is deficient in his capacity to form quick and strong conditioned responses. He will be all the less likely to be subject to phobias and other anxieties, but he will also be less likely to form useful conditioned responses, or to become a thoroughly socialized individual. When this lack of socialization is combined with strong autonomic drive reactions (high neuroticism), such an individual is likely to show the neurotic symptomatology of the psychopath or the hysteric, and indeed, in our experimental work we have found that, as predicted, dysthymic patients, and normal introverts, are characterized by the quick and strong formation of conditioned responses, while psychopaths and normal extraverts are characterized by the weak and slow formation of conditioned responses.[19, 20, 2] Thus the deviation from the average in either direction may prove disastrous—too strong conditioning easily leads to dysthymic reactions, too weak conditioning easily leads to psychopathic and hysterical reactions. The logic of this whole approach leads me to postulate two great classes of neurotic symptoms which between them exhaust in principle all the possible abnormal reactions with which you are all familiar. On the one hand we have *surplus conditioned reactions*, i.e. reactions acquired along the lines I have adumbrated, and where the reaction is unadaptive, even though originally it may have been well suited to circumstances. On the other hand we have *deficient conditioned reactions*, i.e. reactions normally acquired by most individuals in society which are adaptive, but which because of defective conditioning powers have not been acquired by a particular person. It is necessary to emphasize that surplus conditioned reactions and deficient conditioned reactions are due to an interplay between such individual factors as conditionability and autonomic lability, on the one hand, and environmental conditions on the other. There will be no socialization for an individual who cannot form conditioned responses at all, but conversely, there will be no socialization for a person growing up on a desert island, however powerful his conditioning mechanism may happen to be. In this paper I have no time to deal with differences in the conditioning forces of the environment, and their relation to such factors as social class, but they should certainly not be forgotten.

Many other testable deductions, apart from the differential conditionability of dysthymics and hysterics, follow from such a formulation. Some of these deductions can be tested in the laboratory, and examples have been given in my book, *Dynamics of Anxiety and Hysteria*.[2] But others can be tested clinically, and for the sake of an example I shall give just one of these. I have shown how psychopathic reactions originate because of the inability of the psychopath, due to his low level of conditionability, to acquire the proper socialized responses. But this failure is not absolute; he conditions much less quickly and strongly than others, but he does condition. Thus, where the normal person may need 50 pairings of the conditioned and the unconditioned stimulus and where the dysthymic may need 10, the psychopath may require 100. But presumably in due course the 100 pairings will be forthcoming, although probably much later in life than the 10 of the dysthymic, or the 50 of the normal person, and then he will finally achieve a reasonable level of socialization. If this chain of reasoning is correct, it would lead us to expect that the diagnosis "psychopath" would by and large be confined to relatively young people, say under thirty years of age; after thirty the course of life should have brought forth the required 100 pairings and thus produced the needed amount of socialization. As far as I can ascertain, clinical psychiatric opinion is in agreement with this prediction.

How does our theory compare with the psychoanalytic one? In the formation of neurotic symptoms, Freud emphasizes the traumatic nature of the events leading up to the neurosis, as well as their roots in early childhood. Learning theory can accommodate with equal ease traumatic single-trial learning, for which there is good experimental evidence,[21] but it can also deal with repeated sub-traumatic pain and fear responses which build up the conditioned reaction rather more gradually.[22] As regards the importance of childhood, the Freudian stress appears to be rather misplaced in allocating the origins of *all* neurosis to this period. It is possible that many neurotic symptoms find their origin in this period, but there is no reason at all to assume that neurotic symptoms cannot equally easily be generated at a later period provided conditions are arranged so as to favour their emergence.

The point, however, on which the theory here advocated breaks decisively with psychoanalytic thought of any description is in this. Freudian theory regards neurotic symptoms as adaptive mechanisms which are evidence of repression; they are "the visible upshot of unconscious causes."[23] Learning theory does not postulate any such "unconscious causes," but regards neurotic symptoms as simple learned habits; there is no neurosis underlying the symptom, but merely the symptom itself. *Get rid of the symptom and you have eliminated the neurosis.* This notion of purely symptomatic treatment is so alien to psychoanalysis that it may be considered the crucial part of the theory here proposed. I would like to explore its implications a little further later on.

From the point of view of learning theory, treatment is in essence a very simple process. In the case of surplus conditioned responses, treatment should consist in the extinction of these responses; in the case of deficient conditioned responses, treatment should consist in the building up of the missing stimulus-response connections. Yet this apparent simplicity should not mislead us into thinking that the treatment of neurotic disorders offers no further problems. It is often found in scientific research that the solution of the problems posed by applied science is as complex and difficult as is the solution of the problems posed by pure science; even after Faraday and Maxwell had successfully laid the foundations of modern theories of electricity it needed fifty years and the genius of Edison to make possible the actual application of these advances to the solution of practical problems. Similarly here: a solution in principle, even if correct, still needs much concentrated and highpowered research in the field of application before it can be used practically in the fields of cure, amelioration, and prophylaxis.

What are the methods of cure suggested by learning theory? I shall give two brief examples only, to illustrate certain principles; others have been given by G. Jones.[1] One method of extinguishing the neurotic response X to a given stimulus S is to condition another response R to S, provided that R and X are mutually incompatible. This method, called "reciprocal inhibition" by Wolpe,[24] harks back to Sherrington[25] of course, and may be illustrated by returning to our rat-phobic little boy. Essentially, what Watson had done was to condition a strong sympathetic reaction to the sight of the rat. If we could now succeed in establishing a strong parasympathetic reaction to the sight of the rat, this might succeed in overcoming and eliminating the sympathetic response. The practical difficulty arises that, to begin with at least, the already established conditioned response is of necessity stronger than the to-be-conditioned parasympathetic response. To overcome this difficulty, we make use of the concept of stimulus gradient already mentioned. The rat close by produces a strong conditioned fear reaction; the rat way out in the distance produces a much weaker reaction. If we now feed the infant chocolate while the rat is being introduced in the far distance the strong parasympathetic response produced by the chocolate-munching extinguishes the weak sympathetic response produced by the rat. As the conditioned parasympathetic response grows in strength, so we can bring the rat nearer and nearer, until finally even close proximity does not produce sympathetic reactions. The sympathetic reaction has been extinguished; the phobia has been cured. This is in fact the method which was used experimentally to get rid of the experimentally induced fear,[26] and it has been used successfully by several workers in the field of child psychiatry. More recently Herzberg[27] in his system of active psychotherapy, and more particularly, Wolpe[24] in his psychotherapy by reciprocal inhibition, have shown that these principles can be applied with equal success to the severe neuroses of adult men and women —substituting other methods, of course, for the chocolate-munching, which is more effective with children than with adults.

As an example of the cure of deficient conditioned responses, let me merely mention *enuresis nocturna*, where clearly the usual conditioned response of waking to the conditioned stimulus of bladder extension has not been properly built up. A simple course of training, in which a bell rings loudly whenever the child begins to urinate, thus activating an electric circuit embedded in his bedclothes, soon establishes the previously missing connection, and the

extremely impressive list of successes achieved with this method, as compared with the very modest success of psychotherapeutic methods, speaks strongly for the correctness of the theoretical point of view which gave rise to this conception.[28]

We thus have here, I would suggest, an alternative theory to the Freudian, a theory which claims to account for the facts at least as satisfactorily as does psychoanalysis, and which in addition puts forward quite specific suggestions about methods of treatment. I have called these methods "behaviour therapy" to contrast them with methods of psychotherapy.* This contrast of terms is meant to indicate two things. According to psychoanalytic doctrine, there is a psychological complex, situated in the unconscious mind, underlying all the manifest symptoms of neurotic disorder. Hence the necessity of therapy for the psyche. According to learning theory, we are dealing with unadaptive behaviour conditioned to certain classes of stimuli; no reference is made to any underlying disorders or complexes in the psyche. Following on this analysis, it is not surprising that psychoanalysts show a preoccupation with psychological methods involving mainly *speech*, while behaviour therapy concentrates on actual *behaviour*

---

* The growth of the theoretical concepts and practical methods of treatment subsumed in the term "behaviour therapy" owes much to a large number of people. Apart from Pavlov and Hull, who originated the main tenets of modern learning theory, most credit is probably due to Watson, who was among the first to see the usefulness of the conditioned paradigm for the explanation of neurotic disorders; to Miller and Mowrer, who have done so much to bring together learning theory and abnormal human behaviour; to Spence, whose important contributions include the detailed analysis of the relation between anxiety and learning; and to Wolpe, who was the first to apply explicitly some of the laws of learning theory to the large-scale treatment of severe neurotics. If there is any novelty in my own treatment of these issues it lies primarily: (1) in the pulling together of numerous original contributions into a general theory and (2) in the introduction into this system of the concepts of neuroticism and extraversion-introversion as essential parameters in the description and prediction of behaviour. I would like to emphasize, however, that this contribution could not have been made had the ground work not been well and truly laid by the writers quoted above and by many more, only some of whom are quoted in the bibliography.

as most likely to lead to the extinction of the unadaptive conditioned responses. The two terms express rather concisely the opposing viewpoints of the two schools. Below, in summary form, is a tabulation of the most important differences between psychotherapy and behaviour therapy.

that even if in some cases the therapies suggested might be successful, yet in the great majority of cases psychoanalysis would be the only method to produce lasting cures. Let me deal with these points one by one.

There is no doubt that conditioning treatment of alcoholism has

Table 1

Psychotherapy	Behaviour therapy
1. Based on inconsistent theory never properly formulated in postulate form.	Based on consistent, properly formulated theory leading to testable deductions.
2. Derived from clinical observations made without necessary control observations or experiments.	Derived from experimental studies specifically designed to test basic theory and deductions made therefrom.
3. Considers symptoms the visible upshot of unconscious causes (" complexes ").	Considers symptoms as unadaptive conditioned responses.
4. Regards symptoms as evidence of *repression*.	Regards symptoms as evidence of faulty learning.
5. Believes that symptomatology is determined by defence mechanisms.	Believes that symptomatology is determined by individual differences in conditionability and autonomic lability, as well as accidental environmental circumstances.
6. All treatment of neurotic disorders must be *historically* based.	All treatment of neurotic disorders is concerned with habits existing at *present*; their historical development is largely irrelevant.
7. Cures are achieved by handling the underlying (unconscious) dynamics, not by treating the symptom itself.	Cures are achieved by treating the symptom itself, i.e. by extinguishing unadaptive C.Rs and establishing desirable C.Rs.
8. Interpretation of symptoms, dreams, acts, etc. is an important element of treatment.	Interpretation, even if not completely subjective and erroneous, is irrelevant.
9. Symptomatic treatment leads to the elaboration of new symptoms.	Symptomatic treatment leads to permanent recovery provided autonomic as well as skeletal surplus C.Rs are extinguished.
10. Transference relations are essential for cures of neurotic disorders.	Personal relations are not essential for cures of neurotic disorder, although they may be useful in certain circumstances.

What kind of answer would we expect from the Freudians? I think their main points would be these. They would claim, in the first place, that conditioning therapy has frequently been tried, but with very poor results; aversion therapies of alcoholism are often mentioned in this connection. They would go on to say that even where symptomatic treatments of this kind are apparently successful, as in enuresis, the symptom is likely to return, or be supplanted by some other symptom, or by an increase in anxiety. Finally, they would claim

often been tried, and that it has often failed. I have no wish to take refuge in a *tu quoque* argument by pointing out that alcoholism has been particularly difficult to treat by any method whatever, and that psychoanalytic methods also have been largely unsuccessful. I would rather point out that learning theory is an exact science, which has elaborated quite definite rules about the establishment of conditioned reflexes; it is only when these rules are properly applied by psychologists with knowledge and experience in this field that the question of success or failure arises. Thus it is quite elementary knowledge that the conditioned stimulus must precede the unconditioned stimulus if conditioning is to take place; backward conditioning, if it occurs at all, is at best very weak. Yet some workers in the field of alcoholism have used a method in which the unconditioned stimulus regularly preceded the conditioned stimulus; under these conditions learning theory would in fact predict the complete failure of the experiment actually reported! Again, the time relation between the application of the conditioned stimulus and the unconditioned stimulus is a very important one; it is controlled to very fine limits of hundredths of a sec in psychological experimentation and it has been universally reported that conditioning in which any but the optimal time relation is chosen is relatively ineffective. Taking eye-blink conditioning as an example: it is found that a time interval of about $\frac{1}{2}$ sec is optimal and that with intervals of $2\frac{1}{2}$ sec no conditioning at all takes place.[29, 30] No attention seems to have been paid to these points by most workers on alcoholism, who apply the conditioned and unconditioned stimuli in such a vague way that it is often impossible to find out what the actual time relations were. This lack of rigour makes it quite impossible to adduce these so-called experiments as evidence either in favour or against conditioning therapy.[31]

How about the return of symptoms? I have made a thorough search of the literature dealing with behaviour therapy with this particular point in view. Many psychoanalytically trained therapists using these methods have been specially on the outlook for the return of symptoms, or the emergence of alternative ones; yet neither they nor any of the other practitioners have found anything of this kind to happen except in the most rare and unusual cases.[17] Enuresis, once cured by conditioning therapy, remains cured as a general rule; relapses occur, as indeed one

would expect in terms of learning theory under certain circumstances, but they quickly yield to repeat treatment. So certain of success are the commercial operators of this method that they work on a "money back if unsuccessful" policy; their financial solvency is an adequate answer to the psychoanalytic claim. Nor would it be true that alternative symptoms emerge; quite the contrary happens. The disappearance of the very annoying symptom promotes peace in the home, allays anxieties, and leads to an all-round improvement in character and behaviour. Similar results are reported in the case of major applications of behaviour therapy to adults suffering from severe neurotic disorders; abolition of the symptom does not leave behind some mysterious complex seeking outlet in alternative symptoms.[17] Once the symptom is removed, the patient is cured; when there are multiple symptoms, as there usually are, removal of one symptom facilitates removal of the others, and removal of all the symptoms completes the cure.[24]

There is one apparent exception to this rule which should be carefully noted because it may be responsible for some of the beliefs so widely held. Surplus conditioned reactions may themselves be divided into two kinds, autonomic and motor. Anxiety reactions are typical of the autonomic type of surplus conditioned reactions, whereas tics, compulsive movements, etc. are typical of motor conditioned reactions. What has been said about the complete disappearance of the symptom producing a complete disappearance of the neurosis is true only as far as the autonomic conditioned reactions are concerned. Motor reactions are frequently activated by their drive reducing properties *vis a vis* the historically earlier conditioned autonomic responses[17]; the extinction of the motor response without the simultaneous extinction of the conditioned autonomic response would only be a very partial cure and could not be recommended as being sufficient. As pointed out at the end of the previous paragraph, "removal of *all* the symptoms completes the cure," and clearly removal of the motor conditioned response by itself, without the removal of the autonomic conditioned response is only a very partial kind of treatment. Behaviour therapy requires the extinction of all non-adaptive conditioned responses complained of by the patient, or causally related to these symptoms.

But how frequently does this type of treatment result in cures? Again I have made a thorough search of the literature, with the following outcome. GP treatment, not making use of psychotherapy in any of its usual forms, results in a recovery of about two seriously ill neurotics out of three.[32] Eclectic psychotherapy results in a recovery of about two seriously ill neurotics out of three.[7] Psychotherapy by means of psychoanalysis fares slightly worse, but results are at a comparable level.[8] Results of behaviour therapy of seriously ill neurotics, as reported by Wolpe, are distinctly superior to this, over 90 per cent recovering.[24] This difference is highly significant statistically and it should be borne in mind that the number of sessions required by behaviour therapy is distinctly smaller than that required by psychotherapy, whether eclectic or psychoanalytic. (Wolpe reports an average of about 30 sittings for his cases.)

These results are encouraging, but of course, they must not be taken too seriously. Actuarial comparisons of this kind suffer severely from the difficulty of equating the seriousness of disorders treated by different practitioners, the equally obvious difficulty of arriving at an agreed scale for the measurement of "recovery," and the impossibility of excluding the myriad chance factors which may affect gross behaviour changes of the kind we are here considering. I would not like to be understood as saying that behaviour therapy has been *proved* superior to psychotherapy; nothing could be further from my intention. What I am claiming is simply that as far as they go—which is not very far—

available *data* do not support in any sense the Freudian belief that behaviour therapy is doomed to failure, and that only psychoanalysis or some kindred type of treatment is adequate to relieve neurotic disorders. This Freudian belief is precisely this—a belief; it has no empirical or rational foundation. I have no wish to set up a counter-belief, equally unsupported, to the effect that psychotherapy is doomed to failure and that only behaviour therapy is adequate to relieve neurotic disorders. What I would like to suggest is simply that a good case can be made out, both on the theoretical and the empirical level, for the proposition that behaviour therapy is an effective, relatively quick, and probably lasting method of cure of some neurotic disorders. This case is so strong that clinical trials would appear to be in order now to establish the relative value of this method as compared with other available methods, such as psychoanalysis, or electroshock treatment. Even more important, I think the evidence would justify psychiatrists in experimenting with the method, or rather set of methods, involved, in order to come to some preliminary estimate of their efficiency. I have noted with some surprise that many psychotherapists have refused to use such methods as conditioning therapy in enuresis, not on empirical grounds, but on *a priori* grounds, claiming that such mechanical methods simply could not work, and disregarding the large body of evidence available. Even in long established sciences *a priori* considerations carry little weight; in such a young discipline as psychology they are quite out of place. Only actual use can show the value of one method of treatment as opposed to another.

There is one point I would like to emphasize. Freud developed his psychological theories on the basis of his study of neurotic disorders and their treatment. Behaviour therapy, on the contrary, began with the thorough experimental study of the laws of learning and conditioning in normal people and in animals; these well-established principles were then applied to neurotic disorders. It seems to me that this latter method is in principle superior to the former; scientific advance has nearly always taken the form of making fundamental discoveries and then applying these in practice, and I can see no valid reason why this process should be inverted in connection with neurosis. It may be objected that learning theorists are not always in agreement with each other[11] and that it is difficult to apply principles about which there is still so much argument. This is only very partially true; those points about which argument rages are usually of academic interest rather than of practical importance. Thus, reinforcement theorists and contiguity theorists have strong differences of view about the necessity of reinforcement during learning and different reinforcement theorists have different theories about the nature of reinforcement. Yet there would be general agreement in any particular case about the optimum methods of achieving a quick rate of conditioning, or extinction; these are questions of fact and it is only with the interpretation of some of these facts that disagreements arise. Even when the disputes about the corpuscular or wavular nature of light were at their height, there was sufficient common ground between contestants regarding the facts of the case to make possible the practical application of available knowledge; the same is true of learning theory. The 10 per cent which is in dispute should not blind us to the 90 per cent which is not—disagreements and disputes naturally attract more attention, but agreements on facts and principles are actually much more common. Greater familiarity with the large and rapidly growing literature will quickly substantiate this statement.[12]

It is sometimes said that the model offered here differs from the psychoanalytic model only in the terminology used and that in fact the two models are very similar. Such a statement would be both true and untrue. There undoubtedly are certain simi-

larities, as Mowrer[17] and Miller and Dollard[33] have been at pains to point out. The motivating role of anxiety in the Freudian system is obviously very similar in conception to the drive-producing conditioned autonomic responses of learning theory, and the relief from anxiety produced by hysterical and obsessional symptoms in Freudian terminology is very similar to the conditioned drive-reducing properties of motor movements. Similarly, a case could be made out in favour of regarding the undersocialized, non-conditionable psychopathic individual as being Id-dominated, and the dysthymic, over-conditionable individual as being Super-Ego dominated. Many other similarities will occur to the reader in going through these pages and indeed the writer would be the first to acknowledge the tremendous service that Freud has done in elucidating for the first time some of these dynamic relationships and in particular in stressing the motivating role of anxiety.

Nevertheless, there are two main reasons for not regarding the present formulation as simply an alternative differing from the psychoanalytic one only in the terminology used. In the first place, the formulation here given differs from the Freudian in several essential features, as can be seen most clearly by studying Table 1. Perhaps these differences are most apparent with respect to the deductions made from the two theories as to treatment. Psychoanalytic theory distrusts purely symptomatic treatment and insists on the removal of the underlying complexes. Behaviour theory on the other hand stresses the purely symptomatological side of treatment and is unconvinced of the very existence of "complexes." It might, of course, be suggested that there is some similarity between the Freudian "complex" and the "conditioned surplus autonomic reaction" posited by behaviour theory. That there is some similarity cannot be denied, but no one familiar with psychoanalytic writings would agree that the Freudian complex was not in essence a very different conception from the conditioned autonomic response, both from the point of view of its origins, as well as from the point of view of the appropriate method of extinction.

This brings me to the second great difference between the two models. What the Freudian model lacks above all, is an intelligible objectively testable *modus operandi* which can be experimentally studied in the laboratory, which can be precisely quantified and which can then be subjected to the formulation of strict scientific laws. The stress on such a mechanism, namely that of conditioning, is the most noteworthy feature of the model here advocated. It is entirely due to the great body of research which has been done in connection with the elaboration of laws of modern learning theory, that we are enabled to make fairly precise deductions resulting in different methods of treatment for patients suffering from neurotic disorders and it is with respect to this feature of the model that the relevant case histories and accounts of treatment should be read.[34, 35, 36]

It has sometimes been suggested that the criticisms which I have levelled against the psychotherapeutic schools because of their failure to provide adequate control groups to validate their claims regarding the curative properties of their methods, could justifiably be levelled against the accounts given by those who have used behaviour therapy and reported upon the effects achieved. Such a criticism would not be justified for two reasons. In the first place, the cases quoted are *illustrative of methods*, not *proofs of psychotherapeutic efficacy*; the only case in which claims regarding relative efficacy have been made contains a statistical comparison with the effects of psychoanalytic treatment of similar cases.[24] In the second place, the concept of "control" in scientific experiments is somewhat more than simply the provision of a control *group*; the control in an experiment may be *internal*. As an example, consider the experiment re-

ported by Yates[36] on the extinction of 4 tics in a female patient by means of a rather novel and unusual method, namely that of repeated voluntary repetition of the tic by massed practice. Precise predictions were made as to the effects that should follow and these predictions were studied by using the fate of some of the tics as compared to the fate of other tics submitted to dissimilar treatment. Thus, practice for 2 tics might be discontinued for a fortnight, while practice on the other two would go on. By showing that the predictions made could thus be verified and the *rate of extinction* of the tics varied at will— in accordance with the experimental manipulation for such variables as massing of practice—a degree of control was achieved far superior to the simple assessment of significance produced in the comparison of two random groups submitted to different treatments. It is by its insistence on such experimental precision and the incorporation of experimental tests of the hypotheses employed, even during the treatment, that behaviour theory differs from psychotherapy.

There is one further method of pointing up the differences between the two theories and of deciding between them; I mention this matter with some hesitation because to many psychiatrists it seems almost sacrilegious to use animal experimentation in the consideration of human neurosis. However, Fenichel himself,[37] p. 19 has quoted "experimental neuroses" as support for the Freudian conception of neurotic disorders and it is with respect to these experiments that the contrast between the psychoanalytic and our own model may be worked out most explicitly. Fenichel maintains that the model of psychoneurosis "is represented by the artificial neuroses that have been inflicted upon animals by experimental psychologists. Some stimulus which had represented pleasant instinctual experiences or which has served as a signal that some action would now procure gratification is suddenly connected by the experimenter with frustrating or threatening experiences, or the experimenter decreases the difference between stimuli which the animal had been trained to associate with instinct gratification and threat respectively; the animal then gets into a state of irritation which is very similar to that of a traumatic neurosis. He feels contradictory impulses; the conflict makes it impossible for him to give in to the impulses in the accustomed way; the discharge is blocked, and this decrease in discharge works in the same way as an increase in influx: it brings the organism into a state of tension and calls for emergency discharges.

"In psychoneuroses some impulses have been blocked; the consequence is a state of tension and eventually some 'emergency discharges.' These consist partly in unspecific restlessness and its elaborations and partly in much more specific phenomena which represent the distorted involuntary discharges of those very instinctual drives for which a normal discharge has been interdicted. Thus we have in psychoneuroses, first a defense of the ego against an instinct, then a conflict between the instinct striving for discharge and the defensive forces of the ego, then a state of damming up and finally the neurotic symptoms which are distorted discharges as a consequence of the state of damming up—a compromise between the opposing forces. The symptom is the only step in this development that becomes manifest; the conflict, its history, and the significance of the symptoms are unconscious."

Hebb[38] has laid down certain requirements for attempting to demonstrate that experimental neurosis occurs in animals and Broadhurst[39, 40] has examined the literature, and particularly that referred to by Fenichel, from this point of view. Here is his summary. "How does the large body of American work stand up to such an assessment? For the purposes of a recent review,[40] the available literature was examined in the light of Hebb's criteria. Noteworthy among this is the work of the group headed by Lid-

dell,[41] one of the pioneers of conditioning methodology in the United States, who has used principally the sheep as his experimental subject; of Gantt,[42] whose long term study of the dog 'Nick' is well known; and of Masserman,[43] who has done extensive work using cats. This is not the place to enter into the details of this evaluation, which is reported elsewhere,[40] but the overall conclusion which was reached was that there are few instances in all this work of any cases of experimentally induced abnormalities of animal behaviour which meet all of Hebb's criteria. Let us take, for example, the work of Masserman, whose theoretical interpretation of abnormal behaviour need not concern us here except to note that it was the basis upon which he designed his experiments to produce 'conflict' between one drive and another. What he did was this. He trained hungry cats to respond to a sensory signal by opening a food box to obtain food. Then he subjected them to a noxious stimulus, a blast of air, or electric shock, just at the moment of feeding. The resulting changes in behaviour— the animals showed fear of the situation and of the experimenter, and refused to feed further—he identified as experimental neurosis. But the behaviour observed fails to fulfil more than one or two of Hebb's criteria and, moreover, certain deficiencies in the design of his experiments make it impossible to draw any satisfactory conclusions from them. Thus Wolpe[44] repeated part of Masserman's work using the essential control group which Masserman had omitted—that is, he gave the cats the noxious stimulus alone, without any 'conflict' between the fear motivation thus induced, and the hunger which, in Masserman's animals, operated as well— and found that the same behaviour occurred. It hardly needs to be said that a fear response to a threatening stimulus is not abnormal and cannot be regarded as an experimental neurosis."

It is clear from the studies cited that Fenichel is quite wrong in claiming that "experimental neuro-sis" is in any way analogous to the Freudian model of human neurosis. It appears, therefore, that in so far as these studies are relevant at all they can be regarded as demonstrating nothing but simple conditioned fear responses of the kind called for by our theory. It is perhaps worthy of note that the failure of psychoanalysis to use control groups in the human field has extended to their work with ani-mals, as in the case of Masserman quoted above. Fenichel's easy accept-ance of data congruent with his hy-pothesis is paralleled by his failure to mention data contrary to the psy-choanalytic viewpoint. By taking into account all the data it seems more likely that a correct conclusion will be reached.

I would now like to return to some of the points which I raised at the beginning of this paper. I argued then, that the special knowledge and competence of psychologists in mental hospitals was largely wasted because of concentration on and preoccupation with Freudian theories and projective types of test. I would now like to make a more positive suggestion and maintain that by virtue of their training and experience psychologists are (or should be) experts in the fields of conditioning and learning theory, laboratory procedures and re-search design. In suitable cases, surely their help would be invaluable in diagnostic problems, such as ascer-taining a given patient's speed of conditioning, in the theoretical prob-lem of constructing a model of his personality dynamics and in the prac-tical problem of designing a suitable course of behaviour therapy which would take into account all the availa-ble information about the case.* I am

not suggesting that psychologists should themselves necessarily carry out this course of treatment; it would appear relatively immaterial whether the therapy is carried out by one per-son or another, by psychologist or psychiatrist. Both types of procedure have been experimented with and both have shown equally promising results. Indeed, certain aspects of the therapy can obviously be carried out by less senior and experienced person-nel, provided the course of treatment is reviewed periodically by the person in charge. Psychoanalysis lays much stress on what is sometimes called "transference," a devil conjured up only to be sent back to his usual habi-tat with much expenditure of time and energy.[37] Behaviour therapy has no need of this adjunct, nor does it admit that the evidence for its exist-ence is remotely adequate at the pres-ent time. However that may be, re-linquishing the personal relationship supposed to be indispensable for the "transference" relation allows us to use relatively unqualified help in many of the more time-consuming and routine parts of behaviour ther-apy. In certain cases, of course, per-sonal relationships may be required in order to provide a necessary step on the generalization gradient; but this is not always true.†

From a limited experience with this kind of work, carried out by var-ious members of my department, I can with confidence say two things. The direct application of psychologi-cal theories to the practical problem

---

* It will be clear that the function here sketched out for the psychologist demands that he be furnished with the necessary tools of his trade, such as sound-proof rooms, conditioning apparatus and all the other techniques for delivering stimuli and measuring responses on a strictly quantified basis.[45] It is equally clear that such facilities do not exist in the majority of our mental hospitals. Until they do, the handicaps under which the clinical psychologists work at such institutions will be all but insurmountable, and no reasonable

estimate of their potential usefulness can be formed. One might just as well employ an electro-encephalographer and refuse to pay for the ma-chine which he has been trained to use! It would be better to have a few, properly equipped depart-ments than a large number of small, ill-equipped ones as at present. Even in the United States the position is bad; in this country it is worse. A relatively small capital investment would be likely to bear considerable fruit.

† As an example of this we may quote a case reported by Graham White. This concerns a child who became anorexic after the death of her father. The therapist adopted the father's role in a variety of circumstances, ranging in order from play with dolls' teasets to the actual eating situation, and reinforced those reactions which were considered desirable. The theoretical rationale was that the father had become a conditioned stimulus on which eating depended.

of effecting a cure in a particular person, here and now, acts as a very powerful challenge to the psychologist concerned, and makes him more aware than almost anything else of the strengths and weaknesses of the formulations of modern learning theory. And the successful discharge of this self-chosen duty serves more than almost anything else to convince his psychiatric colleagues that psychology can successfully emerge from its academic retreat and take a hand in the day-to-day struggle with the hundred-and-one problems facing the psychiatrist. It seems to me that the tragic fratricidal struggle between psychiatrists and psychologists, which has so exacerbated relations between them in the United States, could easily be avoided here by recognizing the special competence of the psychologist in this particular corner of the field, while acknowledging the necessity of keeping the general medical care of the patient in the hands of the psychiatrist. I believe that most psychiatrists are too well aware of the precarious state of our knowledge in the field of neurotic disorders to do anything but welcome the help which the application of learning theory in the hands of a competent psychologist may be able to bring.

References

1. Jones, H. G. (1958). Neurosis and experimental psychology. *J. Ment. Sci., 104,* 55-62.
2. Eysenck, H. J. (1957). *Dynamics of Anxiety and Hysteria.* Routledge & Kegan Paul, London.
3. Eysenck, H. J. (1947). *Dimensions of Personality.* Routledge & Kegan Paul, London.
4. Eysenck, H. J. (1952). *The Scientific Study of Personality.* Routledge & Kegan Paul, London.
5. Eysenck, H. J. (1953). *The Structure of Human Personality.* Methuen, London.
6. Glover, E. (1955). *The Technique of Psychoanalysis.* Bailliere, London.
7. Eysenck, H. J. (1952). The effects of psychotherapy: an evaluation. *J. Cons. Psychol., 16,* 319-324.
8. Eysenck, H. J. (1960). The effects of psychotherapy. In *Handbook of Abnormal Psychology.* Ed. by H. J. Eysenck. Pitman, London.
9. Eysenck, H. J. (1953). *Uses and Abuses of Psychology.* Pelican, London.
10. Eysenck, H. J. (1958). Personality tests: 1950-1955. In *Recent Progress in Psychiatry.* Ed. by G. W. T. W. Fleming. J. & A. Churchill, London.
11. Hilgard, G. A. (1956). *Theories of Learning.* Appleton-Century, New York.
12. Osgood, C. E. (1953). *Method and Theory in Experimental Psychology.* Oxford Univ. Press, London.
13. Shoben, E. J. (1949). Psychotherapy as a problem in learning theory. *Psychol. Bull., 46,* 366-392.
14. Watson, J. B., and Rayner, R. (1920). Conditioned emotional reaction. *J. Exp. Psychol., 3,* 1-4.
15. Pavlov, I. P. (1927). *Conditioned Reflexes.* Oxford Univ. Press, London.
16. Spence, K. G., Haggard, P. F., and Ross, L. G. (1958). UCS intensity and the associated (habit) strength of the eyelid CR. *J. Exp. Psychol., 95,* 404-411.
17. Mowrer, O. H. (1950). *Learning Theory and Personality Dynamics.* Ronald Press, New York.
18. Miller, V. G. (1951). Learnable drives and rewards. *Handbook of Experimental Psychology.* Ed. by S. S. Spencer. Wiley, New York.
19. Eysenck, H. J. (1954). Zur Theorie der Personlichkeitsmessung. *Z. Diag. Psychol. Personlichkeitsforsch., 2,* 87-101, 171-187.
20. Eysenck, H. J. (1957). Los principios del condicionamiento y la teoria de la personalidad. *Riv. Psicol., 12,* 655-667.
21. Hudson, B. B. (1950). One-trial learning in the domestic rat. *Genet. Psychol. Monogr., 41,* 94-146.
22. Solomon, R. L., Kamin, L. J., and Wynne, L. C. (1953). Traumatic avoidance learning. *J. Abnorm. (Soc.) Psychol., 48,* 291-302.
23. Munroe, R. L. (1955). *Schools of Psychoanalytic Thought.* Dryden Press, New York.
24. Wolpe, J. (1958). *Psychotherapy by Reciprocal Inhibition.* Stanford Univ. Press.
25. Sherrington, C. S. (1926). *The Integrative Action of the Central Nervous System.* Oxford Univ. Press, London.
26. Jersild, A. T., and Holmes, F. B. (1935). Methods of overcoming children's fears. *J. Psychol., 1,* 25-83.
27. Herzberg, A. (1941). Short treatment of neuroses by graduated tasks. *Brit. J. Med. Psychol., 19,* 36-51.
28. Mowrer, O. H., and Morer, W. A. (1938). Enuresis. A method for its study and treatment. *Amer. J. Orthopsychiat., 8,* 436-447.
29. McAllister, W. R. (1953). Eyelid conditioning as a function of the CS-UCS interval. *J. Exp. Psychol., 45,* 412-422.
30. McAllister, W. R. (1953). The effect on eyelid conditioning of shifting the CS-UCS interval. *J. Exp. Psychol., 45,* 423-428.
31. Frank, C. M. (1958). Alcohol, alcoholics and conditioning: a review of the literature and some theoretical considerations. *J. Ment. Sci., 104,* 14-33.

32. Denker, P. G. (1946). Results of treatment of psychoneuroses by the general practitioner. A follow-up study of 500 cases. *N.Y. State J. Med.*, 46, 2164-2166.

33. Dollard, J., and Miller, V. G. (1950). *Personality and Psychotherapy*. McGraw-Hill, New York.

34. Jones, H. G. (1956). The application of conditioning and learning techniques to the treatment of a psychiatric patient. *J. Abnorm. (Soc.) Psychol.*, 52, 414-420.

35. Meyer, V. (1957). The treatment of two phobic patients on the basis of learning principles. *J. Abnorm. (Soc.) Psychol.*, 55, 261-266.

36. Yates, A. (1958). The application of learning theory to the treatment of tics. *J. Abnorm. (Soc.) Psychol.*, 56, 175-182.

37. Fenichel, O. (1945). *The Psychoanalytic Theory of Neurosis*. Kegan Paul, London.

38. Hebb, D. O. (1947). Spontaneous neurosis in chimpanzees: theoretical relations with clinical and experimental phenomena. *Psychosom. Med.*, 9, 3-16.

39. Broadhurst, P. L. (1958). The contribution of animal psychology to the concept of psychological normality-abnormality.

40. Broadhurst, P. L. (1960). Abnormal animal behaviour. In *Handbook of Abnormal Psychology*. Ed. by H. J. Eysenck. Pitman, London.

41. Anderson, O. P., and Parmenter, A. (1941). A long-term study of the experimental neurosis in the sheep and dog. *Psychosom. Med. Monogr.*, 2, Nos. 3 and 4, 1-150.

42. Gantt, W. H. (1944). Experimental basis for neurotic behaviour. *Psychosom. Med. Monogr.*, 3, 1-211.

43. Masserman, J. K. (1943). *Behavior and Neurosis*. Univ. Press, Chicago.

44. Wolpe, J. (1952). Experimental neurosis as learned behaviour. *Brit. J. Psychol.*, 43, 243-268.

45. Eysenck, H. J. (1955). *Psychology and the Foundation of Psychiatry*. H. K. Lewis, London.

46. Estes, W. K. *et al* (1954). *Modern Learning Theory*. Appleton-Century, New York.

47. Hilgard, E. A., and Marquis, D. G. (1940). *Conditioning and Learning*. Appleton-Century, New York.

Reinforcement and Punishment in the Control of Human Behavior by Social Agencies

C. B. FERSTER

Clinical psychiatry and psychology depend on fundamental experimental analyses of behavior just as other fields of medicine depend on the basic sciences of physiology, biochemistry, and pharmacology. The slow development of basic natural-scientific analyses of behavior has resulted in clinical practices developed by rule of thumb or in terms of special theories unrelated to a fundamental or systematic behavioral analysis. Behavioral experimentation with animals has been a continuous, although small contribution, to clinical theory and practice. The work of Pavlov on the conditioned reflex has provided the main source for much of the extensions to clinical problems. John B.

Watson and his students first applied the conditioned reflex to the experimental development, elimination, and generalization of phobic reactions in children.[8] Later, N. E. Miller, J. Dollard, and O. H. Mowrer and others extended the conditioned reflex to a wider range of human performances and clinical problems.[2, 5, 6] The work of B. F. Skinner has given further impetus to applications to problems of psychiatric rehabilitation and therapy by an experimental analysis of "operant" behavior: the behavior of organisms which exists because of its effect on the environment in contrast with the reflex behavior analyzed by Pavlov.[1, 7] Using the framework of Skinner's theoretical and experimental analysis, this paper outlines a program to change the behavior of psychiatric patients or generate new be-

From *Psychiat. Research Reports 10*: 101-118, 1958, by permission of the American Psychiatric Association and the author.

havior by manipulating the actual environmental events maintaining a performance. The manipulatable events in the present and past environment of an organism are used to analyze the current performance in terms of the general processes already dealt with experimentally in animals and humans. The role of positive reinforcement and its corollaries in determining behavior is emphasized over aversive control.

THE NATURE OF THE SOCIAL AGENCY

Most of the behavior of organisms exists because of its effect on the environment (operant reinforcement). The paradigm is: An event following a given instance of behavior subsequently increases the frequency of occurrence of that behavior. The verbal response "good morning" is maintained because it produces a reply from most audiences. In the absence of a reply, the response would disappear. Not all events have this property, and those that do are called reinforcements. Most human behavior is social because it has its effect on other organisms, which in turn arrange the reinforcements; this is in contrast to the physical environment, which reinforces directly. The same reinforcement paradigm may be extended to larger groups of people, such as social institutions and agencies; less well-defined groups involved in social practices, codes of conduct, etc.; small groups, such as the milieu in a certain factory, or neighborhood "gang" of children. These social practices ultimately refer to a set of reinforcements and punishments which the people who constitute the social agency or social practice apply to the behavior of an individual. The social situation is unique only in so far as other organisms mediate the reinforcements, punishments, or other important environmental effects.

A fundamental psychological analysis must deal with the behavior of the individual, and the functional dimensions of social behavior appear only when they are expressed in terms of the consequences that the members of a group of people arrange for an individual. Social approval, for example, refers to a high disposition to supply favorable consequences to a wide range of specific behaviors of the individual; and conversely, a low disposition to arrange punishments. Similarly, an individual with "social prestige" is one whose repertoire is reinforcing to members of a group, and will maintain the behavior of listening, reading, seeking close contact, and supplying reinforcements designed to maximize further performances.

Other social institutions such as law, government, religious agencies, and the family arrange very specific consequences which are somewhat easier to specify. The law and government, for example, have effects on the individual, largely by punishing specified forms of behavior by fines and incarceration. The religious agencies have some of their effects on the behaviors of the individual by similar processes. The punishments of hell and the rewards of heaven, as well as the more usual contingencies involved in the approval and disapproval by the membership of the religious agency, are used to maintain or suppress various behaviors.

THE LARGE ORDER OF MAGNITUDE OF SOCIAL CONTROL

The importance of social behavior in human affairs is heightened by the fact that the majority of human reinforcements are mediated by another individual. Many of the reinforcements deriving their effect from groups of people have a larger order of magnitude of effect than reinforcements supplied only by a single individual or the physical environment. The heightened control by social reinforcement comes about because:

1. Some reinforcements are possible only when a performance is carried out in connection with other individuals. The appeal of the parade

and uniform comes primarily from the prestige which the individual can share only by being a member of a group which in turn is important to the community. The process referred to here is similar to *identification* in dynamic psychology. Other examples in which the individual can have an effect in the community only when he behaves in concert with other individuals include the "gang," the revival meeting, and the cooperative action of three men lifting an object too heavy for any one of them.

2. Large numbers of individuals can potentially arrange reinforcements and punishments contingent on the behavior of the individual. The potential of an audience in rewarding or punishing depends in turn on the relevance of the reinforcements and punishments for the behavioral repertoire of the individual. The larger the number of individuals who can potentially reward, punish, or discontinue reinforcing behavior, the greater the effect is likely to be. Also, as the social agency involves more persons, there is less chance that an individual can avoid the punishment by escaping to another social group or to another environment for the reinforcements to maintain his existing repertoire. The control on the speaker by a relevant and effective audience illustrates this property of social reinforcements. When the audience has only a few members, the speaker may react to punishment or nonreinforcement by turning to other audiences. As the size of the audience increases, however, the effect of the contingencies they arrange on the behavior of the speaker becomes more and more inevitable. The control achieved in brain washing illustrates the large order of magnitude of effect from controlling all of the audiences affecting an individual. Similarly, a group practice or a set of cultural mores has a large order of magnitude of control because the larger number of individuals who will arrange the reinforcements and punishments which constitute the social practice make this almost inevitable.

CHARACTERIZATION OF THE BEHAVIOR OF THE PSYCHIATRIC PATIENT IN TERMS OF A FUNCTIONAL ANALYSIS

Many psychiatric patients or potentially psychiatric patients may be characterized as having repertoires whose performances are not producing the reinforcements of the world: because too much behavior is being punished; because nearly all of the individual's behavior is maintained by avoiding aversive consequences rather than producing positive effects; or a combination of all of these. A potential reinforcing environment exists for every individual, however, if he will only emit the required performances on the proper occasions. One has merely to paint the picture, write the symphony, produce the machine, tell the funny story, give affection artfully, and the world will respond in kind with prestige, money, social response, and love. Conversely, a repertoire which will make contact with the reinforcements of the world will be subsequently maintained because of the effect of the reinforcement on the performance. The problem is social because most of the reinforcements are mediated by other individuals.

A deficient behavioral repertoire may arise because:

1. **Inadequate Reinforcement History.** Under this category belong individuals who are not making contact with important parts of their environment simply because their history did not include a set of experiences (educational) which could develop these performances during the normal maturation of the individual. Especially in the area of everyday social contacts, considerable skill is necessary for producing social reinforcements, and the absence of this skill either results in an individual without a social repertoire or one who achieves affects on his social environment by indirect means, as, for example, using aversive stimulation to gain attention. It is possible that this latter behavior would disappear if the individual had a repertoire which

would be effective in producing positive reinforcements. The existence of weak, positively reinforced repertoires, particularly in the field of ordinary social contacts, could result in "unsocial behavior" designed to affect the behavior of others by generating aversive conditions which are strong enough to produce avoidance, escape, and punishment. The reinforcing effect of these "anti-social" reactions might be large only in respect to the weak, positively reinforced repertoire.

2. Schedule of Reinforcement. The schedule of reinforcement of a given performance might also produce a weakened disposition to engage in this performance so that the normal reinforcements do not occur. This kind of absence of behavior would be produced particularly in situations where large amounts of work are required for reinforcements, as, for example, in the case of the writer, housewife, student, or salesman, where reinforcement depends on a fixed amount of work. The individual's repertoire contains the required performances, but the existing schedule of reinforcement is such as to weaken the repertoire and thereby prevent its occurrence even though the correct form of the behavior would be available if the schedules of reinforcement were more optimal.

3. Punishment May Distort a Performance Which Otherwise Would Be Reinforced. The absence of adequate repertoires in the individual could result from the distortion of the form of the behavior so that the performance does not have its customary effect. Excessive punishment may also generate avoidance behavior which is strong enough to be prepotent over the currently positively reinforced repertoires of the individual.

TECHNIQUES AVAILABLE TO THE THERAPIST

The basic principles governing the development and maintenance of behavior are relevant to the task of generating new performances in an individual whose existing repertoire is not making contact with the reinforcements potentially available to him. The same principles are also relevant to the problem of generating adequate repertoires which will escape punishment.

Some of the reasons for a currently inadequate behavioral repertoire may be found in the history of the organism, perhaps even in the early infancy. In many cases, however, the behavioral history of an individual is inaccessible. To the extent, however, that a current environment exists which can potentially maintain performances in all of the important segments in the individual's life by positive reinforcement, the history of the individual is relevant only in so far as it is useful in assessing the current repertoire of the individual. A functional program of therapy relying on the manipulatable factors in the patient's environment may have important therapeutic effects, without reference to speculative accounts of the patient's history, the current verbal reports of his feelings, and attitudes. Little more is to be desired if a patient is content with his lot, works productively in a job, achieves affection and respect from his fellows, has an adequate sexual and home life, enjoys food and drink in moderation, and has diversions and adequate social relations.

If the therapist is ultimately to be successful, he must alter the relationship between the patient's performance in a wide variety of social situations and the reinforcement and punishment which will result. The therapist initially has the prestige of his profession and social position and the potential reinforcing effect involved in transference. These properties of the therapist, initially at least, give him the ability to change the patient's performance in at least some situations outside of the room in which the therapy is conducted. Ultimately, the reinforcement of these performances in the patient's environment will maintain the continued attention of the patient to the therapist's advice.

THE PROCESSES BY WHICH SOCIAL AGENCIES AFFECT THE BEHAVIOR OF THE INDIVIDUAL

The major processes of behavior provide the technology for generating and eliminating behavior in the individual and are basic to the analysis of social effects. In the final analysis, the agency can have an effect on the individual only by arranging some environmental event contingent on the behavior of the individual. The social situation differs from the nonsocial one by the mediation of another organism in the delivery of the reward, punishment, or other consequence. It must be assumed, in the absence of contrary evidence, that the processes and laws operating in social situations are the same ones which are the basis for all behavioral processes.

Reinforcement. Reinforcement is the most important process by which behavior is generated and maintained. Most of an organism's behavior exists because of the effect on the environment, perhaps with the exception of the psychotic whose repertoire reflects the absence of behavior maintained with positive reinforcement. Reinforcement differs from the colloquial reward in its specificity; it is the immediate environmental consequences of a specific performance. The major effect of reinforcement needs to be distinguished from the classical or Pavlovian-type conditioning where the conditioned response is some elicited reflex, usually autonomic. The increase in the frequency of occurrence of the performance that is reinforced is the property of reinforcement that permits the tremendous variety and subtlety that occurs in the field of "voluntary" behavior as opposed to reflex and autonomic behavior.

Most reinforcements of everyday life are social rather than involving immediately important biological conditions. These social-maintaining events operate as reinforcements because they are in a chain of events leading ultimately to a more basic consequence. Money provides an ex-

ample of a conditioned reinforcer—*par excellence*—which derives its effect because its possession is a condition under which other performances will produce basic environmental effects. The important social consequences of money occur because the reinforcing properties of money nearly always depend immediately or ultimately upon the behavior of other individuals. Similarly, a smile can reinforce behavior because an individual who is smiling is more likely to supply subsequent reinforcements than one who is not.

As with money, many reinforcements in human behavior can be effective in the absence of any specific deprivation, unlike most reinforcements demonstrated in animal experiments. These "generalized" reinforcements maintain much of human behavior, and have large order of magnitudes of effect because their reinforcing power comes from a variety of reinforcements and deprivations and does not depend upon a current level of deprivation. This is especially true of nearly all reinforcements mediated by other organisms, because the mediation by another organism, in general, permits the application of a wider range of reinforcements. Other examples of generalized reinforcers include paying attention, affection, saying "right," or "correct," smiling, etc. These are important reinforcements because they are the usual conditions under which another organism will reinforce a behavior of an individual.

The Development of Complex Forms of Behavior: "Shaping." A major corollary of reinforcement is a procedure by which a reinforcing agency can produce progressively complex forms of behavior by small increments from a preceding simpler form. A commonly used animal-demonstration experiment illustrates the process. If we wish to teach a pigeon to peck at a small disc on the wall of his chamber, we first establish a reinforcer by presenting grain to the bird whenever the grain hopper is illuminated. The bird soon comes to approach the hopper only when it is illuminated, and it is then possible to use the lighted hopper as a reinforcement. The bird faces in the direction of the small disc, is reinforced, and the effect is an immediate increase in the tendency to face the disc. Reinforcement is then withheld until the bird nods slightly in the direction of the disc, and the reinforcement of this slightly more complex form increases its frequency. When the bird is nodding in the direction of the disc, the variation in the magnitude of the nod is noted and the reinforcement is shifted in the direction of those nods bringing the bird's head closer to the disc. By continuing the process, the pigeon can soon be made to strike the disc.

The same process occurs in the development of human behavior, particularly in the formative years. The process by which complex forms are generated is relevant to the therapy situation whenever a patient is lacking parts of the complex repertoire necessary to achieve reinforcement from the complicated social environment. Simply telling a patient what kind of performance is necessary for reinforcement will seldom generate the required complex performance. The situation is analogous to the golfer who would like to drive the ball 250 yards. The necessary performance must be acquired in small steps, beginning with an existing repertoire and approximating the final performance with intermediate, temporary reinforcements.

The therapist is in a position to "shape" behavior in a patient by beginning with a performance already in his repertoire and exposing him to selected portions of his environment designed to generate the new, more complex form. The therapist can select an environment accessible to the patient in which a reinforcing agent is operating which will reinforce with a high degree of probability a variation in the patient's performance in the direction of the desired, more complicated form.

For example, consider the hypothetical case of an individual who has never acquired the performances necessary for facile enough social contact. The patient's current repertoire contains enough verbal behavior to permit him to talk to the therapist. A first step in this hypothetical case might be to send the patient to a college campus one morning and have him say "Good morning" to several people he passes. The environment of the campus is chosen to almost guarantee the reinforcement of this response. This kind of exercise would also illustrate to the patient general verbal processes in human behavior where it is possible to command a verbal response from an audience. In a similar vein, the complexity of the verbal repertoire of the individual could be increased further. Commands, such as "Could you please tell me the time," also produce almost inevitable responses in most situations; and if the rate of development of the new behavior is made small enough from the preceding forms which the patient is emitting successfully, there would be no difficulty from nonreinforcement because of inaudible remarks, mumbling, or other distortion of the behavior which would prevent the reinforcement.

Group therapy or psychodrama could also be adapted to the task of generating new performances as an intermediate step to be used between "office therapy" and exercises using outside environments accessible to the patient. Patients could use each other, under the direction of a therapist, to develop skills necessary in normal social practice. The therapist would set tasks for each patient carefully graded so as to be within the range of the existing behavioral repertoire. Groups of patients would provide an environment potentially capable of supporting at least some kinds of performances, and the exercises would be designed to take advantage of these reinforcements which are possible within the hospital environment. Exercises could be designed, for example, to illustrate and develop behaviors which makes it possible to command behavior from another individual: the effect of saying "please," kinds of performances which will engender conversation, cooperation in projects, techniques for achieving nonsocial reinforcements as in reading, and developing productive skills as in occupational therapy. Many of these goals are already present in many hospital situations. What is required is a program of administration which will maintain motivation during the development of the complex repertoire and establish the behavior firmly enough to provide a basis to go on to a next, more complex form.

Another example on a slightly more complex level might be the behavior of a shy boy or girl having difficulty in social and sexual relations with the opposite sex. The first task is to specify the necessary performances for achieving the potential social reinforcements. A practical program requires the development of a repertoire capable of getting a date and carrying it through adequately. The practical program would include the development of auxiliary skills such as dancing, skating, card-playing, and various sports which would provide performances predominately nonsocial which could be carried out in the company of the opposite sex and provide opportunities for the reinforcements of other kinds of behavior. As in the previous example, it would be necessary to begin with the existing repertoire and develop a situation in which the audience composed of the opposite sex can reinforce the appropriate behavior whenever it occurs. The situation is a potentially difficult one because any nonreinforcement will have large effects on an initially weak verbal repertoire. A series of exercises could be constructed beginning, for example, with a situation in which little is required verbally, such as playing cards, and the emission of only those responses whose reinforcements are guaranteed, such as a command, reading, trite sayings, etc. The development of a repertoire leading to sexual activity would begin with performances de-

signed to extend physical contact; for example, shaking hands, help over minor obstacles, congratulatory pat on the shoulder, etc.

To the extent that enough major performances in enough important areas can be generated, the fundamental historical reason behind the original disinclination to associate with the opposite sex, or avoid contact with the opposite sex, is no longer essential to the correction of the situation. So long as the individual is spending the time with the opposite sex, enjoying adequate sexuo-social relations, and engaged in normal social give-and-take, the historical factors are no longer relevant.

Intermittent Reinforcement. Social reinforcements are intermittent because the reinforcements mediated by another organism are less reliable than those produced by the physical environment. This arises because the social reinforcement depends upon behavioral processes in the reinforcer which are not always under good control by the reinforcee. For example, if one is asked to look outside and report whether it is raining, many factors in the repertoire of the listener could interfere with the successful completion of the report: the listener is afraid of height, some more urgent audience catches the attention of the listener, the listener happened not to be attentive at the moment the request is made, the listener's eye glasses are off at the moment, etc. In contrast, the effects of most behavior on the physical environment is almost inevitable.

The nature of the intermittency has a great influence on the disposition to engage in a given behavior. It is possible to produce an almost complete cessation of some behavior which the individual has emitted literally thousands of times by alteration of the schedule of reinforcement. Similarly, identical frequencies of reinforcements on different reinforcement schedules produce widely differing dispositions to engage in the behavior.

The history by which the individual is exposed to many schedules is also of great importance. Certain schedules of reinforcement will sustain behavior normally if approached in gradual steps but will produce complete cessation (abulia) if the individual is exposed to the final schedule at once. In the most prevalent schedule of reinforcement found in human affairs (ratio reinforcement), the reinforcement occurs as a function of a certain number of instances of a performance. One of the major properties of this schedule of reinforcement is a decline in the disposition to emit the behavior when the amount of work for reinforcement becomes too large. This lessened disposition occurs particularly as inability to begin work just after a reinforcement. The disinclination of the novelist to begin a new novel just after completing one is a pure example of this effect. There is some suggestion that there are inductive effects among the various repertoires of the individual.

An optimal schedule of reinforcement in one area will help sustain a performance under a less optimal schedule of reinforcement in another area; and, conversely, reinforcement on unoptimal schedules of reinforcement may have the opposite effect of weakening a repertoire whose reinforcement schedule is more optimal. These "ratio" or piecework schedules of reinforcement are contrasted with another major schedule class where the reinforcement of a response becomes more likely with passage of time since the previous reinforcement. These schedules are less prevalent in human affairs than ratio schedules, and tend to produce a level of performance more appropriate to the frequency of reinforcement regardless of the history of the individual. Examples of this latter class of schedules of reinforcement include looking in the mailbox when the mail delivery occurs somewhat unpredictably (variable-interval reinforcement), and looking into the pot on the stove as the water is being boiled.

Optimum parameters of a schedule of reinforcement may also result

in very large amounts of behavior and a strong disposition to engage in the reinforced behavior. The behavior of the gambler is an excellent example where an explicit program of reinforcement (technically classified variable-ratio) generates a strong disposition to gamble, even though the individual operates at a loss over a longer period of time. Here the heightened disposition to gamble arising from the optimal variable-ratio schedule of reinforcements (even the loser wins frequently) overrides the overall low net reinforcement.

Applications to therapy. To the extent that a patient's difficulties result from inadequate or unoptimal reinforcement of important repertories, there is little in the immediate therapy situation which can change his performance. The salesman, for example, whose ratio of "selling" to sales becomes too high and suffers from irritability, moodiness, and the disinclination to work, needs more sales for "less selling" before his situation can improve. Arthur Miller's play "Death of a Salesman" provides an excellent example of the deterioration in a performance that can come about under a "piecework" schedule of reinforcement.

It is possible that the general condition of an individual whose behavior is weak because of too much behavior emitted with too little reinforcement resembles conditions arising from aversive control. This may be especially true when the "strained" repertoire is supplemented by aversive conditions such as threats which can be avoided only by emitting more of the "strained" behavior. For example, the factory worker on a piece work pay schedule may be threatened, lose his job, or be fined when he stops working even though his rate of pay is proportional to the amount of work he does. Secondary factors may also influence the way in which a given repertoire is maintained on a schedule of reinforcement. Physical exhaustion, poor health, and inductive effects from other repertoires may produce strain under a schedule of reinforcement which under other conditions might have been satisfactory.

Early exposure to intermittent reinforcement. Many behavioral repertoires are weak because of an accidental history which supplied an inadequate reinforcement at an early stage. This could come about especially when punishment produces forms of behavior which go unreinforced because they are distorted. An optimal schedule of reinforcement of a repertoire is essential at an early stage of development if a strong disposition to engage in the performance is to be maintained later under less optimal schedules. The genesis of avid gamblers illustrates the importance of the schedule of reinforcement during the initial acquisition of the repertoire. Professional gamblers, for example, will arrange a high frequency of reinforcement for the beginner in order to provide conditions under which the beginner will continue to gamble later when the schedule of reinforcement is less adequate. Similarly, at least a part of the difference between the person who continues to gamble, and those who failed to continue after a brief exposure, lies in the initial "luck." The fisherman is on the same schedule of reinforcement as the gambler, and the result is the same. The avid interest of the fishing devotee is extreme compared with others and probably represents the result of an optimal schedule of reinforcement during the initial fishing experiences.

The community maximizes the frequency of reinforcement during the educational phase of an individual by providing reinforcements for rough approximations to the ultimately effective forms. For example, a young child emitting the response "wawer" is likely to be reinforced by a glass of water, while the same response at a later stage of development will be unreinforced, or even punished. Thus, in the early stages of development of the repertoire a higher frequency of reinforcement is more easily achieved than later, when the community demands a more differentiated and closely specified form of behavior and environmental control. Whether newly developing behavior will persist depends upon whether the initial frequency and manner of reinforcement will sustain the performance as it comes under the control of the relevant stimuli, as the form of the behavior becomes more and more differentiated, and as the audience selectively reinforces more effective forms. Whenever a repertoire becomes weakened because of accidental non-reinforcement during the early development of the repertoire it becomes more difficult to reinstate the repertoire because the form of the behavior must now be more exact and under more precise environmental control than during the early stages of development.

Compare, for example, the successful and unsuccessful adult in his sexuo-social relations with the opposite sex. Very highly differentiated behavior under close stimulus control is required. Once an individual matures beyond a given age without developing the performances in respect to the opposite sex which will be reinforced, it becomes more difficult to acquire effective performances. The situation is comparable to the difficulties of the algebra student who tries to learn factoring without being facile in algebraic multiplication and division.

In cases where the individual's repertoire is inadequate because of an unoptimal schedule of reinforcement, it should be possible to do therapy by directing the individual to situations where some approximation to the effective form of the behavior will be reinforced. Only after the repertoire is acquired in a form that is maximally effective in achieving reinforcement, would the individual be directed into situations where progressively more nonreinforcement could occur.

Superstitious Reinforcement. A reinforcing event will increase the disposition to engage in the behavior reinforced even though the reinforcement is spurious or accidental. As in the case of the gambler, the chance history of reinforcement is important in determining whether accidental or spurious reinforcements will sustain the behavior. Once there is some tendency to emit the behavior as the result of some accidental reinforcements, the resulting tendency to continue behaving increases the likelihood that the behavior will be in progress subsequently when another reinforcement occurs. These superstitious performances are most likely to occur under high motivation, as for example the gambler addressing the dice "come seven" or the "posturing" of the bowler. These spurious reinforcements are probably even more effective in the field of aversive control. If the aversively maintained behavior is conditioned strongly enough, the behavior may never extinguish because the avoidance behavior prevents the occurrence of the conditioned aversive stimuli which now would no longer be followed by the aversive event.

Here again the therapist is in a position to select special situations in the patient's environment where the positive reinforcement occurs even though the superstitious behavior is withheld; or in those cases where the superstition is maintained by "avoiding" an aversive event, the behavior is withheld in a situation where the primary aversive event will not occur. Some preliminary experiments in the latter case by English workers have shown large effectiveness of this manner of therapy in dealing with phobic behavior in selected individuals.[1]

Stimulus Control of Behavior. The reinforcement or punishment of a verbal or nonverbal response depends upon the nature of the audience. Not all performances of an individual are reinforced on all occasions, and the situation characteristically present when a given kind of behavior is reinforced comes to control the likelihood that the performance will occur. Nearly all of the behavior of the normal adult comes under very close stimulus control of the various audiences to which he is exposed. De-

tails of speech as subtle as vocabulary and intonation change with different audiences. The thematic material of a conversation varies widely depending upon the audience, from shop talk to a co-worker to the "baby-talk" maximally effective in producing a reaction from an infant. Poor development of stimulus control will result in a lower net frequency of reinforcement. The nonreinforcement of behavior that occurs during the development of stimulus control is tantamount to intermittent reinforcement until the stimulus control develops. To the extent that performances are reinforced only on specific occasions and by particular audiences, a failure of stimulus control results in an increase in the proportion of an individual's behavior which goes unreinforced.

The normal maturation of an individual into childhood and adulthood illustrates the interrelation between intermittent reinforcement and stimulus control. We reinforce almost any form of behavior in infants and very young children so long as there is a remote resemblance to the required performance. As the child grows older, however, the reinforcement is continually shifted in the direction of forms which approximate the normal cultural practices. Many members of the community will reinforce the behavior of the young child even though it has little importance for the listener. As the child develops through school-age, however, the audience becomes more selective and now properly differentiated forms of behavior will go unreinforced if they are not reinforcing for the listener. Hence, a further possibility of nonreinforcement arises whenever a performance is inappropriate for a given audience. The better an individual's performances are controlled by the environment, therefore, the more optimal will be the schedule of positive reinforcement. Inadequate stimulus and audience control of behavior could be one of the conditions under which an inadequate repertoire would develop because of performances occurring where they will not be reinforced and not occurring when they will be reinforced.

Just as accidental reinforcements may generate forms of behavior which is superstitious in the sense that the behavior is not a necessary condition for the occurrence of the reinforcement, it is possible for irrelevant aspects of a situation to acquire stimulus control of a performance. Every occasion on which a reinforcement occurs has multiple dimensions, and the aspects which come to control are somewhat undetermined until there are differential consequences in terms of the various elements. For example, an individual has a history in which many of the people who have given good advice have worn double-breasted suits, bow-ties, and spoken with a cosmopolitan accent. There will, therefore, be a heightened disposition to follow advice from persons exhibiting these characteristics until enough individuals have been encountered who shared some of these properties but have given bad advice. In a similar manner, an audience resembling a parent may increase the likelihood of occurrence of performances previously reinforced by a parent, even though that audience is not a potential reinforcer. This kind of inadequate stimulus control may simply be an accident of the historical conditions under which past reinforcements have occurred in situations which have multiple dimensions, some of which are irrelevant. More adequate stimulus control can develop only by exposure to the irrelevant aspect of the situation and the corresponding nonreinforcement. General motivational factors may also heighten the control by irrelevant aspects of a situation or audience. The man lost on the desert without water is more likely to mistake irrelevant stimuli for water.

It should be possible to sharpen the stimulus control of behavior by alternately exposing the individual to situations containing the various elements separately and allowing the resulting reinforcement and nonrein-

forcement to strengthen the tendency to emit the performance on the relevant occasions and weaken the disposition to emit the behavior when the irrelevant aspects are present.

It may be possible to design exercises using the principles governing the development of stimulus control of behavior to increase the sharpness of the stimulus control of a patient's behavior. What is required is to teach the patient to attend to the differential effects his performances have on the environment. The earlier example of the patient learning to say "Good morning" provides an example of the type of exercise that may be possible. After the patient is saying "Good morning" successfully in situations where the reinforcement is all but inevitable, the therapist points up situations where the likelihood of a verbal response of this kind being reinforced is near zero and explains the relevant factors responsible. For example, the patient is instructed to say "Good morning" to a man running to catch a train or to workers entering a factory a few minutes after the official starting time. Further exercises would include alternating between the situations where "Good morning" will be reinforced and those in which "Good morning" will go unreinforced. The complexity of the exercises could be gradually increased as more and more complex forms were available as a result of the "shaping" from the earlier exercises. Eventually exercises would be carried out in which the thematic material of a conversation would be manipulated in respect to the interest of the audience.

Aversive Control. In social situations most control by aversive stimuli involves the removal or discontinuation of positive reinforcement rather than some kind of primary aversive stimulation. The usual social punishments are (1) *disapproval*: a state of affairs where the reinforcer is not likely to continue reinforcements for specific performances; (2) *fines*: a loss of money or privilege effectively reduces the amount of various kinds of behavior that can be reinforced; (3) *criticism*: an indication of specific performances which will not be reinforced, or which will bring about nonreinforcement in other spheres, and (4) *incarceration*: the extreme case where large portions of the repertoire of the individual can no longer produce their characteristic reinforcement.

While the discontinuation of positive reinforcement can be used as a punishment, it is important to distinguish between the effect of nonreinforcement *per se* and its use as a punishment. As noted earlier, the nonreinforcement of a performance on one occasion and its consistent reinforcement on a second occasion is the main process by which environmental control of behavior takes place. The decline of frequency of occurrence of a performance as a function of nonreinforcement has very different properties from punishment by the discontinuation of reinforcement. In the latter case, the punishment is carried out by presenting a stimulus which is already correlated with a low probability of response because of previous nonreinforcement. Its aversive effect probably derives from the over-all importance in the repertoire of the individual of the behavior being blocked. The simple discontinuation of positive reinforcement shares some of the properties of an aversive stimulus, particularly during the transient phase while the frequency of the nonreinforced performance is still falling. Once the stimulus control is established, however, the resulting low disposition to engage in the extinguished behavior allows concurrent repertoires to take over. The salient feature of punishment is that an aversive stimulus is applied to some performance which is maintained by a positive reinforcement; thus the original source of strength of the performance is still present and the performance can reappear in some strength when the punishment is discontinued. This is to be contrasted with simple extinction or nonreinforcement where the maintaining event for the behavior is discontinued and the performance no longer occurs simply because it no longer has its characteristic effect on the environment.

A second major effect of an aversive stimulus is the disruption of substantial segments of the repertoire of the individual by the situation characteristically preceding the aversive event. The pre-aversive situation (anxiety) has an emotional effect in the sense that it produces a state of affairs where there is a disruption of parts of the individual's repertoire not directly related to the aversive event. For example, the student just before the crucial examination, the patient in the dentist's waiting room, the child just before the parent discovers the broken ash tray, and the soldier just before the battle will all show considerable disruption of the normal repertoire; marked changes in the frequency of occurrence of all of the performances which might normally occur under these situations without the aversive event.

The third function of the aversive stimulus is in maintaining behavior because it terminates or postpones (escapes or avoids) the aversive event. The examples of these kinds of reinforcements in a normal repertoire include opening or closing a window to alter an extreme in temperature; buying fuel in advance of cold weather, or making an apology to reduce the threat of punishment.

The clinical effects of excess of punishment have been fairly widely recognized and analyzed, and much of current therapy is analyzed as eliminating the aversive effects of situations which no longer are associated with punishment.

The disruptive effects of aversive control will interfere with the development of the precise forms of behavior being generated by positive reinforcement. This would be particularly true in the area of social contact such as sexual behavior where punishment is widely applied, and where complex and precise forms of behavior are required. A practical program would be designed to develop forms of behavior which would avoid punishment as well as maximize reinforcement. Situations which would disrupt positively maintained repertoires because of a history of punishment would have to be approached in small steps so that the strength of the positively maintained behavior is large in respect to the disruptive effect and the aversive history.

Another corollary of aversive control is its prepotency over positively reinforced behavior. The use of aversive control generates immediate escape and avoidance behavior, and the wide use of punishment and aversive stimulation as a technique of control probably stems from the immediate effects which this kind of stimulation achieves as opposed to the slower development of behavior by a positive reinforcement. When an aversive condition is set up in order to generate some performance which must ultimately be maintained by positive reinforcement (for example, nagging), the control often backfires when the individual terminates the nagging by counter aversive control rather than emitting the performance which will reinforce the "nagger" and terminate the nagging. It is possible that some psychiatric patients have repertoires almost entirely composed of immediate reactions to threats and punishments which are entirely prepotent over positively reinforced repertoires. To the extent that this is true, the development of strong positively reinforced repertoires would provide an avenue of therapy.

SUMMARY

The present analysis of the psychiatric patient characterizes him in terms of the reinforcements immediately available in his environment, or potentially available if changes can be brought about in his repertoire. The general plan is to bring to bear toward the rehabilitation of the patient whatever techniques are available for generating new behavior and eliminating existing performances. Potential reinforcements for almost any kind of behavioral repertoire exist in some environment. By selectively directing the patient into currently accessible reinforcing environments, it may be possible to build almost any kind of repertoire by proceeding in small steps from a performance that is currently maintained in one part of the patient's environment to a slightly more complex performance which could be reinforced in another situation accessible to the patient. All the known principles by which behavior is generated, differentiated, brought under stimulus control, and eliminated would be used. The major processes appealed to were: (1) Reinforcement; those environmental events which produce an increase in the frequency of occurrence of a specific performance they follow. (2) Differentiation of complex forms; a major corollary of reinforcement which makes it possible to begin with a performance which is currently reinforced and then gradually increase the complexity of the performance by reinforcing progressively more complex forms. (3) the long-term maintenance of a performance by manipulating the occurrence of instances of nonreinforcement of the performance. (4) The stimulus control of behavior; deliberate nonreinforcement of the performance on one occasion coupled with reinforcement of that same performance on another occasion in order to sharpen the environmental or stimulus control of the performance. (5) Elimination of behavior by choosing an environment in which the behavior can occur without punishment or reinforcement, whichever is relevant.

It is possible that many of the symptoms which bring the patient to therapy are largely a by-product of inadequate positively reinforced repertoires; that the disposition to engage in the psychotic, neurotic, and pathological behaviors may seem strong when compared to weak existing repertoires but would disappear as soon as alternative effective ways of dealing with some accessible environment is generated.

The examples of exercises designed to generate positively reinforced repertoires and eliminate debilitating performances are intended only as suggestive. A satisfactory protocol for generating new performances can come about only from experience in an experimental program with patients carried out by persons with sufficient clinical skill.

The present analysis emphasizes the manipulatable aspects of environments potentially available to the patient. The behavior of the patient is treated directly as the subject matter of therapy rather than as a symptom of inner cause. Just as the current behavior of an individual developed as a result of the past exposure to some environment, the current repertoire should be amenable to a similar process in the current environment. To the extent that behavioral processes are reversible, it should be possible to change any performance by manipulating the relevant factor within the context of the same process in which it was originally generated.

References

1. Ferster, C. B., and Skinner, B. F. 1957. Schedules of Reinforcement. Appleton-Century-Crofts, N. Y.
2. Hull, C. L. 1953. Principles of Behavior. Appleton-Century-Crofts, N. Y.
3. Lindsley, O. R. 1956. Operant conditioning methods applied to research in chronic schizophrenia. Psychiat. Res. Repts., 5: 118-139.
4. Meyer, V. 1953. The treatment of two phobic patients on the basis of learning principles. J. Abnorm. Soc. Psychol., 55: 261-266.
5. Miller, N. E., and Dollard, S. 1950. Personality and psychotherapy. McGraw-Hill Book Co., Inc., N. Y.
6. Mowrer, O. H. A stimulus response analysis of anxiety and its role as a reinforcing agent. Psychol. Rev., 46:553-566.
7. Skinner, B. F. 1953. Science and Human Behavior. The Macmillan Co., N.Y.
8. Watson, J. B., and Rayner, R. Conditioned emotional reactions. J. Exp. Psychol., 3:1-14.

Behavioral Theories:

CRITICAL EVALUATION

Behavioral theorists of psychopathology borrow their concepts from experimental learning research; consequently, one would expect their work to be subject to little scientific faulting. The failure to live up to this expectation, according to some critics, points up the difficulty of transferring concepts from one field to another. Borrowing the rigorously derived concepts of laboratory research may be no more than a specious ennoblement of one's meagre accomplishments, a cloak of falsely appropriated prestige which duly impresses the naïve.

David Rapaport's review of Dollard and Miller's work suggests that their scientific sounding terminology is no more than a set of flimsy analogies of psychoanalytic theory, offering no new explanatory powers or insights; old wine in new bottles is still old wine, wine best left in its old container. Breger and McGaugh's penetrating critique of the logical and empirical foundations of the behavioral approach raises the question of whether the laboratory based concepts borrowed from the prestigious field of learning are genuinely useful in psychopathology or whether they are merely bandied about in an allegorical and superficial manner. They note further that the "basic" laws of learning are not so basic after all; much dissent exists among learning theorists as to which concepts and laws are "basic." They ask whether laws of learning should be applied to highly complex clinical processes when the existence of these laws in simple situations remains a matter of dispute.

A Critique of Dollard and Miller's "Personality and Psychotherapy"

DAVID RAPAPORT

This is a difficult volume [Dollard and Miller's *Personality and Psychotherapy*, 1950] to review, because it is hard to pin down its arguments. This for several reasons. First,

From *Amer. J. Orthopsychiat.* 23: 204-208, 1953, by David Rapaport. Copyright, the American Orthopsychiatric Association, Inc. Reproduced by permission.

it professes to be a collection of hypotheses and to use clinical material only to illustrate, and not to prove anything. Second, it is disarming in its admission of our general ignorance and of the need for further knowledge before a definitive theoretical structure can be built. Third, it is ambiguous in its alternating enthusiasm for and rejection of psychoanalytic premises, concepts and theories. Its ground in this respect is shifting and therefore difficult to come to grips with. Last but not least, it has been reviewed before by both psychologists and psychiatrists who, unlimited by familiarity either with learning theory or with psychotherapy, hailed it with the starry-eyed enthusiasm of wishful thinking.

There is one fixed point around which this book pivots, and this is learning theory. There is also a somewhat less fixed point, namely, the use of learning theory in order to explain phenomena of neurosis and therapy. These two points will be taken here as points of departure.

Dollard and Miller suggest that the concepts of drive, cue, response, and reward (reinforcement) are "exceedingly important" for the understanding of all levels of acquired behavior. These concepts readily indicate that this theory of acquired behavior is a learning theory and, more particularly, one of the conditioned-response vintage. The authors guardedly dwell on the question whether these concepts are "essential" or just "important" for the understanding of acquired behavior (pp. 25-26). Nevertheless, their actual argument seems to assume that all behavior can be understood in terms of motivating drives, which elicit responses when the proper cues are present, and that cues and responses are linked to the drive and to each other by the success of the response, which both establishes and reinforces these links.

This theory sounds much like the psychoanalytic theory. At the same time, it appeals much more to "common sense" than the psychoanalytic theory. It is therefore tempting to demonstrate the shortcomings of this theory as a learning theory, and to show up its inadequacy in coping with the phenomena for which psychoanalytic theory was developed. This is, however, neither our task here, nor possible in a brief review. Instead, it should suffice to say that

Dollard and Miller may leave their readers with an erroneous impression. They propound this theory of learning as if to say that those aspects of it which they present are well established, though other aspects of it may be still open to question. This is, however, not the case. The battle of cognitive vs. stimulus-response theories of learning is still on. Not long ago Tolman (1949) summarized his studies in an article entitled "There Is More Than One Kind of Learning"; he found that there are eight different kinds. Only recently the neuropsychologist Hebb (1949) has put forth evidence to show that neither the Gestalt nor the conditioned-response theories of learning do justice to many fundamental observations concerning learning, and particularly to the observation that early learning in infancy is qualitatively different in character from late learning. None of the learning theories have as yet integrated Piaget's (1952) genetic observations concerning learning. Last but not least, the most recent review of the theories of learning by Hilgard (1948) shows clearly that the many competing theories of learning have so far failed to come to grips with its core problems. Surely, Dollard and Miller are entitled to prefer one theory of learning over all the others. They are certainly entitled to apply the theory of their choosing to the problems of neurosis and psychotherapy. One would wish only that they had made it clear that they were applying the *theory they prefer*, that they had made plain to the psychiatrist, social worker, etc., not versed in learning theory, that the concepts they apply to psychotherapy and neurosis are—to say the least —far from being universally accepted. It would have been desirable if they too, like Kendler (1951)—one of the adherents of this type of learning theory—would have spoken out candidly: "In spite of its relative sophistication, S-R reinforcement theory is still basically a primitive formulation. It would be unwise for S-R psychologists to try to 'sell it' for anything more than that" (p. 372). One would also wish the authors had brought to the attention of all who are not versed in the theories of learning that the problems of learning are just as complicated and just as unsolved as the problems of neurosis and psychotherapy. It is certainly to Dollard and Miller's credit that they even attempted to bring the problem of neurosis and the problem of learning to bear on each other. They vitiate their merit, however, by giving the impression that "normal learning" is already understood and that therefore its "laws" can now be applied to "pathological learning." It should be said in their defense, however, that they also stress that much can be learned about learning from patients; patients may oblige us where normals do not have the motivation to let us learn from them.

Dollard and Miller are emphatic that their use of clinical material should not be construed as proof or evidence for their hypotheses but only as concrete illustration of principles (p. 16). Thus we are given a series of principles of learning and a series of illustrations for them from everyday life as well as from clinical experience. Some of the examples of clinical phenomena are labeled with customary psychiatric or psychoanalytic terms, others with new terms. Surely, this again is a justified endeavor. It is in accord with the commonly accepted scientific procedure of taking concepts which apply to some phenomena and applying them to phenomena in a different realm of observation. The question which always arises in such endeavors is whether this new set of concepts is more parsimonious than the one used heretofore to describe, to explain and to predict in this realm. Dollard and Miller in general do not attempt to offer any proof that their concepts and theory are preferable to those of psychoanalysis. All they do is express their hope that they are bringing a better conceptual system into the field of neurosis and psychotherapy than the one used heretofore, slip in a few pejorative assertions concerning some common Freudian concepts, and praise their own concepts as superior to the Freudian. They could have argued explicitly and not merely by implication that their theory which was tested in animal and human experiment should also be "more scientific" in the field of neurosis and psychotherapy than the prevailing, experimentally untested theories. Their implicit argument disregards the fact that their theory was developed to account for a very limited range of animal behavior and an even more limited range of human behavior. It is therefore necessary to stress explicitly that no proof is offered by the authors that the conceptual system of psychoanalysis at large is any better or worse for prediction of phenomena of neurosis and psychotherapy than the conceptual system they champion and attempt to illustrate in this volume. There is an old proverb which says, "When the angels came down to earth, they too did eat." When Miller and Dollard came down from the experimental laboratory to clinical material, their treatment of phenomena and their use of concepts is certainly no more rigorous than the psychiatrists' and psychoanalysts' treatment of phenomena and use of concepts. Indeed one may ask whether theirs has as much consistency and rigor as the latter.

It would be unfair to Dollard and Miller to apply to their study the yardstick of Freudian theory, even if they do occasionally claim acceptance of this theory. Yet it seems important to point out one relationship between psychoanalysis and their theory. From the beginning one of the outstanding characteristics of psychoanalytic theory has been its distinction between, on the one hand, the *primary processes* which are motivated by basic drives and which in their operation display the so-called Freudian mechanisms (condensation, displacement, symbolization, etc.) and, on the other hand, the *secondary processes* which follow the rules of logic and reality-testing. In the course of the development of psychoanalytic theory this distinction developed into the distinction between the ego and the id. The fluid transition between these two types of processes, their interaction in adjustment, creativity, and neurosis, etc., was brought into the framework of psychoanalytic theory. It is one of the merits of Dollard and Miller's theory, as it is of Mowrer's recent theory, that by the distinction between innate and learned drives they attempt to do some justice to the distinction between early and late learning, between primary processes and secondary processes. (Earlier learning theories disregarded this distinction entirely.) This merit is, however, vitiated by the fact that, according to their theories, both innate and learned drives operate by the same reward-reinforcement mechanism. The complexity of clinical phenomena which led to the development of psychoanalytic ego-psychology and which also led to Allport's recognition of functional autonomy within the framework of his ego psychology, the phenomena which made it necessary for all ego psychologies to assume that the ego has constitutional foundations of its own, are not even envisaged by these learning theories. Dollard and Miller's "acquired secondary drives" and their single reliance on the reward mechanism of learning cannot come to grips with these complexities, not even if the concept of reward is formulated so broadly as to include social rewards. It is characteristic for Dollard and Miller's presentation that phenomena of concern to psychoanalytic ego-psychology are as a rule dealt with tangentially and without apparent awareness of the existence of psychoanalytic ego-psychology. This holds for defenses, which are treated only in the sense of "resistance" (pp. 265ff), synthetic functions, differentiation functions, as well as "higher mental processes." It appears that Dollard and Miller's understanding of psychoanalysis is in most— if not in all—respects as of 1922, that is, of a date preceding Freud's *The Ego and the Id* and *The Problem of Anxiety*, as well as Anna Freud's *The Ego and the Mechanisms of Defense*. In this sense these authors are proponents of a peculiar psychoanalytic orthodoxy, which should be as unsatisfactory to any Neo-Freudian psychoanalyst or psychiatrist as it is to the psychoanalyst aware of the development in psychoanalytic ego-psychology. The contributions of Horney to our understanding of defenses, of Sullivan to our understanding of the self, of Fromm to our understanding of social and cultural factors, have as little place in the framework of this theory as anything Freud had to say after 1923, and as any of Anna Freud's, Hartmann's, Kris's, E. H. Erikson's, Redl's, and Bettelheim's contributions.

While we are all eager to reach a state where our theories will be borne out not only by clinical experience but verified also by experiment, we have to acknowledge the fact that the reason that our theories are no better than they are is not simply because we are not clever enough to develop rigorous operational concepts, but because our subject matter is complex and we are yet at the beginning of its exploration. Under such handicaps, not even scientists equipped with the methodology of operationalism and with experimental know-how, as Dollard and Miller certainly are, can develop a neat and simple theory for us. Indeed the more they try to make it neat and pat, the more cavalier they become in their disregard of clinical fact.

Finally, I can't help remarking that in an attempt as ambitious as this we could expect somewhat more clinical sophistication than is evident. A single example of the unfortunate combination of lack of clinical understanding with a mechanical application of an inapt theory, so characteristic of this volume, follows.

"Example of the problem of masturbation. Masturbation presents a special problem to the therapist because it is a response that frequently occurs and produces a marked reduction in drive but is not the socially

most desirable form of sexual adaptation. It is an inferior form of adaptation because it *removes one of the strong rewards from marriage** which seems to provide the best all-around basis for personal adjustment.

"If the patient has too much fear to try any heterosexual responses, masturbation may be good as the first step toward the goal of normal sexual behavior. When the patient first tries masturbation, the orgasm produced in this way will reward the general attempt to try sexual behavior, help to define the goal, and *give the patient a good chance to discover and extinguish some of his fears of sex.** We will expect this extinction to generalize and tend to weaken the fear motivating the inhibition of heterosexual behavior. On the other hand if the therapist shows any signs of *disapproval** at this stage, he will strengthen the patient's fear, and this fear will tend to generalize to all forms of sexual behavior.

"If the therapist *allows** masturbation to become established as more than a transitional habit, it will become so strongly reinforced that it may be hard to abandon. Furthermore it will tend to keep the sex drive so low that the heterosexual responses never can become stronger than their inhibitions. Finally, the patient may be having undesirable phantasies during masturbation. *Associating the strong sexual reward of the orgasm with the cues involved in these phantasies may increase his appetite for childish, perverse, or extramarital sex outlets.**

"This theoretical analysis yields several practical suggestions. If pos-

sible, it is better for the patient to move directly toward a heterosexual marital adjustment. If the patient's inhibitions are too strong for this to be possible, it may be necessary for the therapist to be *permissive** toward masturbation at first. After masturbation is started, it may be desirable for the therapist to try to *exert some control over the accompanying phantasies and direct them toward the heterosexual marital goal.* Finally, after the patient's inhibitions have been weakened enough so that he will be able to try better responses, it may be necessary *to discourage masturbation by pointing out the ways in which it is an inferior response"** (pp. 386-387).

I have to leave it to the reader to judge in what sense this example is consistent with the authors' initial statement: "We have concentrated our analysis on the one type of therapeutic practice with which we are familiar—namely Freudian. Even here, we have attempted to analyze only those features of theory and practice that we understood best" (p. viii).

References

Hebb, D. O. *Organization of behavior: A neuropsychological theory.* New York: Wiley, 1949.

Hilgard, E. R. *Theories of learning.* New York: Appleton-Century-Crofts, 1948.

Kendler, H. H. Reflections and confessions of a reinforcement theorist. *Psychol. Rev.,* 1951, *58,* 368-374.

Piaget, J. *Play, dreams and imitation in childhood.* New York: Norton, 1952.

Tolman, E. There is more than one kind of learning. *Psychol. Rev.,* 1949, *56,* 144-156.

---

* Italics mine—D. R.

Critique and Reformulation of "Learning-Theory" Approaches to Psychotherapy and Neurosis

LOUIS BREGER and JAMES L. McGAUGH

A careful look at the heterogeneous problems that are brought to psychotherapy points up the urgent need for new and varied theories and techniques. While some new methods have been developed in recent years, the field is still characterized by "schools" —groups who adhere to a particular set of ideas and techniques to the exclusion of others. Thus, there are dogmatic psychoanalysts, Adlerians, Rogerians, and, most recently, dogmatic behaviorists.

It is unfortunate that the techniques used by the behavior-therapy group (Bandura, 1961; Eysenck, 1960; Grossberg, 1964; Wolpe 1958) have so quickly become encapsulated in a dogmatic "school," but this seems to be the case. Before examining the theory and practice of behavior therapy, let us first distinguish three different positions, all of which are associated with the behaviorism or "learning-theory" label. These are: (a) Dollard and Miller (1950) as represented in their book, (b) the Wolpe-Eysenck position as represented in Wolpe's work (1958; Wolpe, Salter, & Reyna, 1964) and in the volume edited by Eysenck (1960), and (c) the Skinnerian position as seen in Krasner (1961) and the work that appears in the *Journal of the Experimental Analysis of Behavior*.

Dollard and Miller present an attempt to translate psychoanalytic concepts into the terminology of Hullian learning theory. While many recent behavior therapists reject Dollard and Miller because of their identification with psychoanalysis and their failure to provide techniques distinct from psychoanalytic therapy, the Dollard-Miller explanation of neurotic symp-

toms in terms of conditioning and secondary anxiety drive is utilized extensively by Wolpe and his followers. Wolpe's position seems to be a combination of early Hullian learning theory and various active therapy techniques. He relies heavily on the idea of reciprocal inhibition, which is best exemplified by the technique of counter-conditioning. In line with this Hullian background, Wolpe, Eysenck, and others in this group use explanations based on Pavlovian conditioning. They define neurosis as "persistent unadaptive habits that have been conditioned (that is, learned) [Wolpe et al., 1964, p. 96]," and their explanation of neurosis stresses the persistence of "maladaptive habits" which are anxiety reducing.

The Skinnerian group (see Bachrach in Wolpe et al., 1964) have no special theory of neurosis; in fact, following Skinner, they tend to disavow the necessity of theory. Their approach rests heavily on *techniques* of operant conditioning, on the use of "reinforcement" to control and shape behavior, and on the related notion that "symptoms," like all other "behaviors," are maintained by their effects.

Our discussion will be directed to the Wolpe-Eysenck group and the Skinnerians, keeping in mind that some of the points we will raise are not equally applicable to both. Insofar as the Skinnerians disavow a theory of neurosis, for example, they are not open to criticism in this area.

It is our opinion that the current arguments supporting a learning-theory approach to psychotherapy and neurosis are deficient on a number of grounds. First, we question whether the broad claims they make rest on a foundation of accurate and complete description of the basic data of neuro-

From *Psychol. Bull. 63*: 338-358, 1965, by permission of the American Psychological Association and the authors.

sis and psychotherapy. The process of selecting among the data for those examples fitting the theory and techniques while ignoring a large amount of relevant data seriously undermines the strength and generality of the position. Second, claims for the efficacy of methods should be based on adequately controlled and accurately described evidence. And, finally, when overall claims for the superiority of behavioral therapies are based on alleged similarity to laboratory experiments and alleged derivation from "well-established laws of learning," the relevance of the laboratory experimental findings for psychotherapy data should be justified and the laws of learning should be shown to be both relevant and valid.

In what follows we will consider these issues in detail, beginning with the frequently voiced claim that behavior therapy rests on a solid "scientific" base. Next, we will examine the nature and adequacy of the learning-theory principles which they advocate. We will point out how their learning theory is unable to account for the evidence from laboratory studies of learning. That is to say, the laws or principles of conditioning and reinforcement which form the basis of their learning theory are insufficient explanations for the findings from laboratory experiments, let alone the complex learning phenomena that are encountered in psychotherapy. Then we will discuss how the inadequate conception of learning phenomena in terms of conditioned responses is paralleled by an equally inadequate conception of neurosis in terms of discrete symptoms. Within learning theory, conceptions of habit and response have been shown to be inadequate and are giving away to conceptions emphasizing "strategies," "plans," "programs," "schemata," or other complex central mediators. A central point of this paper is that conceptions of habit and response are also inadequate to account for neuroses and the learning that goes on in psychotherapy and must here too be replaced with conceptions analogous to strategies. Next we will turn our attention to an evaluation of the claims of success put forth by the proponents of behavior therapy. Regardless of the adequacy of their theory, the claims that the methods work are deserving of careful scrutiny. Here we shall raise a number of questions centering around the issue of adequate controls. Finally, we shall attempt a reformulation in terms of more recent developments within learning, emphasizing the role of central processes.

SCIENCE ISSUE

Claims of scientific respectability are made with great frequency by the behavior therapists. Terms such as laboratory based, experimental, behavioral, systematic, and control are continually used to support their position. The validity of a theory or method must rest on empirical evidence, however. Thus, their use of scientific sounding terminology does not make their approach scientific, but rather seems to obscure an examination of the evidence on which their claims are based.

Let us examine some of this evidence. Bandura (1961) provides the following account of a typical behavior-therapy method (Wolpe's counterconditioning):

On the basis of historical information, interview data, and psychological test responses, the therapist constructs an anxiety hierarchy, a ranked list of stimuli to which the patient reacts with anxiety. In the case of desensitization based on relaxation, the patient is hypnotized, and is given relaxation suggestions. He is then asked to imagine a scene representing the weakest item on the anxiety hierarchy and, if the relaxation is unimpaired, this is followed by having the patient imagine the next item on the list, and so on. Thus, the anxiety cues are gradually increased from session to session until the last phobic stimulus can be presented without impairing the relaxed state. Through this procedure, relaxation responses eventually come to be attached to the anxiety evoking stimuli [p. 144].

Without going into great detail, it should be clear from this example that the use of the terms stimulus and response are only remotely allegorical to the traditional use of these terms in psychology. The "imagination of a scene" is hardly an objectively defined stimulus, nor is something as general as "relaxation" a specifiable or clearly observable response. What the example shows is that counterconditioning is no more objective, no more controlled, and no more scientific than classical psychoanalysis, hypnotherapy, or treatment with tranquilizers. The claim to scientific respectability rests on the misleading use of terms such as stimulus, response, and conditioning, which have become associated with some of the methods of science because of their place in experimental psychology. But this implied association rests on the use of the same *words* and not on the use of the same *methods*.

We should stress that our quarrel is not with the techniques themselves but with the attempt to tie these techniques to principles and concepts from the field of learning. The techniques go back at least as far as Bagby (1928), indicating their independence from "modern learning theory." Although techniques such as these have received little attention in recent years (except from the behavior therapists) they are certainly worth further consideration as potentially useful techniques.*

The use of the term conditioning brings us to a second point, that the claims to scientific respectability rest heavily on the attempts of these writers to associate their work with the prestigious field of learning. They speak of something called modern learning theory, implying that psychologists in the area of learning have generally agreed upon a large number of basic principles and laws which can be taken as the foundation

---

* Another early application of behavioral techniques has recently been brought to our attention: Stevenson Smith's use of the Guthrie approach to learning in his work at the children's clinic at the University of Washington. Guthrie's interpretation of reinforcement avoids the pitfalls we discuss shortly, and contemporary behaviorists might learn something from a review of his work (see Guthrie, 1935).

for a "scientific" approach to psychotherapy. For example, Eysenck (1960) states:

Behavior therapy . . . began with the thorough experimental study of the laws of learning and conditioning in normal people and in animals; these well-established principles were then applied to neurotic disorders. . . . It may be objected that learning theorists are not always in agreement with each other and that it is difficult to apply principles about which there is still so much argument. This is only very partially true; those points about which argument rages are usually of academic interest rather than of practical importance. . . . The 10% which is in dispute should not blind us to the 90% which is not—disagreements and disputes naturally attract more attention, but agreements on facts and principles are actually much more common. Greater familiarity with the large and rapidly growing literature will quickly substantiate this statement [pp. 14-15].

As we shall show in the next section, this assertion is untenable. "Greater familiarity with the large and rapidly growing literature" shows that the very core of "modern learning theory," as Eysenck describes it, has been seriously questioned or abandoned in favor of alternative conceptualizations. For example, the notion that the discrete response provides an adequate unit of analysis or that reinforcement can be widely used as an explanation of both learning and performance, or that mediational processes can be ignored are being or have been rejected. Eysenck's picture of the field as one with 90% agreement about basic principles is quite simply untrue. The references that Eysenck himself give for this statement (Hilgard, 1956; Osgood, 1953) do not support the claim. Hilgard presented many theories, not one "modern learning theory," some of which (Gestalt, Tolman, Lewin) might just as easily be said to be in 90% disagreement with behavioristic conditioning approaches. In the same vein, Osgood's text was one of the first to give heavy emphasis to the role of mediation, in an attempt to compensate for the inadequacies of a simple conditioning or one-stage S-R approach. Eysenck seems largely unaware of the very problems within the field of learning which necessitated the introduction of mediational concepts, even by S-R theorists such as Osgood.

These inadequacies center, in part, around the problem of generalization. The problem of generalizing from the level of conditioning to the level of complex human behavior has been recognized for a long time (Lewin, 1951; Tolman, 1933). It is a problem that is crucial in simple laboratory phenomena such as maze learning where it has resulted in the introduction of a variety of mediational concepts, and it is certainly a problem when complex human behavior is being dealt with. For example, Dollard and Miller (1950) began their book with an attempt to explain neurosis with simple conditioning principles. A careful reading of the book reveals, however, that as the behavior to be explained became more and more complex, their explanations relied more and more on mediational concepts, including language. The necessity for these mediators arises from the inadequacy of a simple *peripheral* S-R model to account for the generality of learning, the equivalence of responses, and the adaptive application of behavior in novel situations. We shall return to these points shortly; here we just wish to emphasize that the field of learning is not "one big happy family" whose problems have been solved by the widespread acceptance of a simple conditioning model. The claim to scientific respectability by reference back to established laws of learning is, thus, illusory.

LEARNING AND LEARNING THEORIES

We have already noted the differences between the Wolpe-Eysenck and the Skinnerian approaches; let us now examine the similarities. Three things stand out: the focus on the overt response, the reliance on a conditioning model, and the notion of reinforcement. First, there is the belief that the response, consisting of some discrete aspect of overt behavior, is the most meaningful unit of human behavior. While this should ideally refer to a specific contraction of muscles or secretion of glands, with the possible exception of Guthrie (1935), traditional S-R theorists have tended to define response in terms of an effect on the environment rather than as a specific movement of the organism. The problems raised by the use of the response as a basic unit, both in traditional learning phenomena and in the areas of neuroses and psychotherapy will be discussed in the section entitled What is Learned? A second common assumption is that the concepts taken from conditioning, either as described by Pavlov or the operant conditioning of Skinner, can be used as explanatory principles. The assumption in question here is that conditioning phenomena are the simplest kinds of learning and that all other behavior can be explained in terms of these "simple" principles. We shall deal with the problems that arise from this source in a second section. The third assumption is that rewards play an essential role in all learning phenomena. We shall consider the problems that stem from this assumption in a third section.

WHAT IS LEARNED?

Since its inception in the early twentieth century, behaviorism has taken overt stimuli and responses as its core units of analysis. Learning, as the behaviorist views it, is defined as the tendency to make a *particular response* in the presence of a *particular stimulus*; what is learned is a discrete response. Almost from its inception, however, this view has been plagued by a number of problems.

First, findings from studies of perception, particularly the fact of perceptual constancy, provide embarrassment for a peripheral S-R theory. Perceptual constancy findings show, for example, that the stimulus is much more than peripheral receptor stimulation. For example, once we have learned a song in a particular key (i.e., particular stimulus elements), we can readily recognize it or sing it in other keys. We are amazingly accurate in recognizing objects and events as being "the same" or equivalent, even though the particular stimulation they provide varies considerably on different occasions (Gibson, 1950). Although the bases of perceptual constancies (size, shapes, brightness, etc.) are not yet well understood, the facts of perceptual constancy—invariance in percept with variation in perceptual stimulation—are not in question. The related phenomenon of transposition has received considerable attention in animal experimentation. Animals, infra-human as well as human, respond to relations among stimuli (Köhler, 1929). For a number of years, transposition was not considered to pose a serious problem for a peripheral S-R theory since it was thought that it could be adequately handled by principles of conditioning and stimulus generalization (Spence, 1937). This view has not been supported by later experiments, however (Lawrence & DeRivera, 1954; Riley, 1958). It now appears more likely that stimulus generalization is but a special case of the more general complex phenomenon of stimulus equivalence. The absolute theory of transposition was important and instructive because it revealed in clear relief the nature and limitations of a peripheral S-R approach to behavior. The effective stimulus is clearly more "central" than receptor excitation. The chapters on learning in the recent Koch series make it clear that workers in this area have seen the need for coming to terms with the facts of perception (Guttman, 1963; Lawrence, 1963; Leeper, 1963; Postman, 1963).

Second, the facts of response equivalence or response transfer posed the same kind of problem for a peripheral S-R view. A learned response does not consist merely of a stereotyped pattern of muscular contraction or glandular secretion. Even within the S-R tradition (e.g., Hull, Skinner) there has been a tendency to define responses in terms of environmental achievements. Anyone who has trained animals has recognized that animals can achieve the same general response, that is, make the same environmental change, in a variety of different ways once the response is learned. "What is learned," then, is not a mechanical sequence of responses but rather, *what needs to be done in order to achieve some final event*. This notion is not new; Tolman stressed it as early as 1932 when he wrote of "purposive behavior," and it has been strongly supported by a variety of experimental findings (e.g., Beach, Hebb, Morgan, & Nissen, 1960; Ritchie, Aeschliman, & Peirce, 1950). As this work shows, animals somehow seem to be able to bypass the execution of specific responses in reaching an environmental achievement. They can learn to go to particular places in the environment in spite of the fact that to do so requires them to make different responses from trial to trial. The learning of relatively specific responses to specific stimuli appears to be a special case which might be called stereotyped learning (canalization) rather than a basic prototype on the basis of which all other learning may be explained.

It should be noted further that even the stereotyped learning that forms the basic model of S-R conditioning does not hold up under closer scrutiny. First, once a subject has learned a stereotyped movement or response, he is still capable of achieving a goal in other ways when the situation requires it. Thus, while we have all learned to write our names with a particular hand in a relatively stereotyped fashion, we can switch to the other hand, or even write our name with a pencil gripped in our teeth if we have to, in spite of the fact that we may not have made this specific response in this way before. Second, even a response that is grossly defined as constant, stable, or stereotyped does not appear as such a stereotyped pattern of muscular contractions when it is closely observed.* These findings in the area of response transfer indicate that a response seems to be highly variable and equipotential. This notion is, of course, quite old in the history of psychology, and it has been stressed repeatedly by numerous investigators including Lashley (see Beach et al., 1960), Osgood (1953), Tolman (1932), and Woodworth (1958).

The facts of both response transfer and stimulus equivalence seem much more adequately handled if we assume that what is learned is a *strategy* (alternatively called cognitive maps, programs, plans, schemata, hypotheses, e.g., Krechevsky, 1932) for obtaining environmental achievements. When we take this view, habits, in the traditional behaviorist sense, become a later stage of response learning rather than a basic explanation (building block) for later, more complex learning.

Perhaps this whole problem can be clarified if we look at a specific example such as language learning. As Chomsky (1959) has demonstrated in his excellent critique of Skinner's *Verbal Behavior* (1957), the basic facts of language learning and usage simply cannot be handled within an S-R approach. It seems clear that an adequate view of language must account for the fact that humans, at a rather early age, internalize a complex set of rules (grammar) which enable them to both recognize and generate meaningful sentences involving patterns of words that they may never have used before. Thus, in language learning, what is learned are not only sets of responses (words and sentences) but, in addition, some form of internal strategies or plans (grammar). We learn a grammar which enables us to generate a variety of English sentences. We do not merely learn specific English sentence habits. How this grammar or set of strategies is acquired, retained, and used in language comprehension and generation is a matter for serious

research effort; but, it is clear that attempts to understand language learning on the basis of analogies from bar-pressing experiments are doomed before they start. To anticipate, we will argue shortly that if we are to make an attempt to understand the phenomena of neurosis, using analogies from the area of learning, it will be much more appropriate to take these analogies from the area of psycholinguistics and language learning rather than, as has typically been done, from studies of classical and operant conditioning. That is, the focus will have to be on response transfer, equipotentiality, and the learning of plans and strategies rather than on stereotyped response learning or habituation.

USE OF A CONDITIONING MODEL

As we indicated earlier, when writers in the behaviorist tradition say "learning theory," they probably mean a conditioning theory; most of the interpretations of clinical phenomena are reinterpretations in terms of the principles of conditioning. Thus, a phobic symptom is viewed as a conditioned response, maintained by the reinforcement of a secondary fear drive or by a Skinnerian as a single operant maintained by reinforcement. Two types of conditioning are involved in these explanations by reduction. The first is Pavlovian or classical conditioning, frequently used in conjunction with later Hullian concepts such as secondary drive; the second is operant conditioning of the kind proposed by Skinner. The use of both of these models to explain more complex phenomena such as transposition, response transfer, problem solving, language learning, or neurosis and psychotherapy poses a number of difficulties.

The basic assumption that underlies the use of either kind of conditioning as an explanation for more complex phenomena is that basic laws of behavior have been established in the highly controlled

---

* G. Hoyle, personal communication, 1963.

laboratory situation and may thus be applied to behavior of a more complex variety. When we look at the way conditioning principles are applied in the explanation of more complex phenomena, we see that only a rather flimsy analogy bridges the gap between such laboratory defined terms as stimulus, response, and reinforcement and their referents in the case of complex behavior. Thus, while a stimulus may be defined as an electric shock or a light of a certain intensity in a classical conditioning experiment, Bandura (1961) speaks of the "imagination of a scene"; or, while a response may consist of salivation or a barpress in a conditioning experiment, behavior therapists speak of anxiety as a response. As Chomsky (1959) puts it, with regard to this same problem in the area of language:

He (Skinner in *Verbal Behavior*) utilizes the experimental results as evidence for the scientific character of his system of behavior, and analogic guesses (formulated in terms of a metaphoric extension of the technical vocabulary of the laboratory) as evidence for its scope. This creates the illusion of a rigorous scientific theory with a very broad scope, although in fact the terms used in the description of real-life and of laboratory behavior may be mere homonyms, with at most a vague similarity of meaning [p. 30].

A second and related problem stems from the fact that the behavior-therapy workers accept the findings of conditioning experiments as basic principles or laws of learning. Unfortunately, there is now good reason to believe that classical conditioning is no more simple or basic than other forms of learning. Rather, it seems to be a form of learning that is in itself in need of explanation in terms of more general principles. For example, a popular but naive view of conditioning is that of stimulus substitution—the view that conditioning consists merely of the substitution of a conditioned stimulus for an unconditioned stimulus. Close examination of conditioning experiments reveals that this is not the case, however, for the conditioned response is typically *unlike* the uncon-

ditioned response (Zener, 1937). Apparently, in conditioning, a new response is learned. Most of the major learning theorists have taken this fact into account in abandoning the notion of conditioning as mere stimulus substitution.

More than this, the most important theoretical developments using essentially Pavlovian conditioning principles have not even stressed overt behavior (Osgood, 1953). Hull and the neo-Hullians, for example, have relied quite heavily on Tolman's (1932) distinction between learning and performance, performance being what is observed while learning (conditioning) is but one essential ingredient contributing to any instance of observed performance. The most important, and perhaps the most sophisticated, developments in Hullian and neo-Hullian theory concern the attempts to explain complicated goal-directed behavior in terms of the conditioning of fractional responses. Unobserved, fractional responses (already we see the drift away from the overt behavior criteria of response) are assumed to serve a mediating role in behavior. Once a fractional response is conditioned in a particular situation, it is assumed to occur to the stimuli in that situation when those stimuli recur. The stimulus consequences of the fractional response referred to as the r_g are assumed to serve as guides to behavior either by serving as a cue or by activating responses or by serving to reinforce other responses by secondary reinforcement. The latter-day proponents of a conditioning point of view (Bugelski, 1956; Osgood, 1953) have come to rely more and more heavily on concepts like the fractional response to bridge the gap between stimulus and overt behavior and to account for the facts of response transfer, environmental achievements, and equipotentiality. What this indicates is that a simple conditioning paradigm which rests solely on observable stimuli and responses has proved inadequate even to the task of encompassing simple conditioning and maze-learning phenomena, and the workers within this tradition have come to rely more and more heavily on mediational (central, cognitive, etc.) concepts, although they still attempt to clothe these concepts in traditional conditioning garb. To add to the problem, a number of recent papers (Deutsch, 1956; Gonzales & Diamond, 1960) have indicated that the r_g interpretations of complex behavior are neither simple nor adequate.

When we look again at the way conditioning principles have been applied to clinical phenomena, we see an amazing unawareness of these problems that have been so salient to experimental and animal psychologists working with conditioning.

While the above discussion has been oriented primarily to classical conditioning, the general argument would apply equally well to those attempts to make the principles of learning derived from operant conditioning the basis of an explanation of neurosis and psychotherapy (as in Krasner, 1961). The Skinnerians have been particularly oblivious to the wide variety of problems that are entailed when one attempts to apply concepts and findings from laboratory learning experiments to other, and particularly more complex, phenomena. While we will deal more directly with their point of view shortly, a few comments might be in order now concerning their use of the operant-conditioning paradigm as a basis for the handling of more complex data. When Skinnerians speak of laws of learning, they have reference to the curves representing rate of responding of rats pressing bars (Skinner, 1938), and pigeons pecking (Ferster & Skinner, 1957) which are, in fact, a function of certain highly controlled contingencies such as the schedule of reinforcement, the amount of deprivation, the experimental situation itself (there is very little else to do in a Skinner box), and the species of animals involved. These experiments are of some interest,

both as exercises in animal training under highly restricted conditions, and for what light they may shed on the more general question of partial reinforcement. It is dubious that these findings constitute laws of learning that can be applied across species (see Breland & Breland, 1961) or even to situations that differ in any significant way from the Skinner box.

USE OF REINFORCEMENT

Advocates of the application of learning theory to clinical phenomena have relied heavily on the "law of effect" as perhaps their foremost established principle of learning. We shall attempt to point out that a good deal of evidence from experimental animal studies argues strongly that, at the most, the law of effect is a weak law of performance.

Essentially, the controversy can be reduced to the question of whether or not reward is necessary for learning. The initial source of evidence indicating that it was not came from the findings of latent learning studies (Blodgett, 1929; Tolman & Honzik, 1930) in which it was found, for example, that rats who were allowed to explore a maze without reward made fewer errors when learning the maze than controls who had no opportunity for exploration. Thus, these early latent learning studies, as well as a variety of more recent ones (Thistlethwaite, 1951) indicate that learning can take place without reward but may not be revealed until a reward situation makes it appropriate to do so (or to put it another way, the reward elicits the performance but plays little role during learning). Other sources which point to learning without reward come from studies of perceptual learning (Hebb, 1949), imitation (Herbert & Harsh, 1944), language learning (Chomsky, 1959), and imprinting (Moltz, 1960).

Defenders of the point of view

that reinforcement is necessary for learning have attempted to handle results such as these in a variety of ways. One has been by appealing to the concept of secondary reinforcement (e.g., a maze has secondary reinforcing properties which account for the learning during exploration). When this sort of thing is done, even with respect to experiments where attempts were made to minimize secondary reinforcements (Thistlethwaite, 1951), it seems clear that this particular notion of reinforcement has become incapable of disproof. Another way of handling these potentially embarrassing results has been by the invention of a new set of drives (curiosity drive, exploratory drive, etc.) but this too has a post hoc flavor to it, and one wonders what kind of explanation is achieved by postulating an "exploratory drive" to account for the fact that animals and humans engage in exploration. In fact, the assumption that exploration reduces an exploratory drive makes it difficult to explain why a rat's tendency to enter an alley of a maze *decreases* after he has explored the alley (Watson, 1961). Finally, there are those (particularly the Skinnerians) who tend to define reinforcement so broadly that neither the findings from latent learning nor any other source can prove embarrassing, since whenever learning has taken place this "proves" that there has been reinforcement. To better understand this problem, however, we had best look for a moment at the general problem of defining reinforcement in a meaningful way.

Obviously, if the view that reinforcement is necessary for learning is to have any meaning, what constitutes a reinforcement must be defined independently from the learning situation itself. There has been a great deal of difficulty in getting around a circular definition of the law of effect, and it might be worthwhile to examine some of the attempts that have been made in the past.

One of the best known was the attempt to relate the reinforcing properties of stimuli to their drive-reducing characteristics (Hull, 1951). The drive-reduction model has had to be abandoned, however, because of evidence from a variety of areas including latent learning, sensory preconditioning (Brogden, 1939), and novelty and curiosity (Berlyne, 1960). Other evidence such as that of Olds and Milner (1954) on the effect of direct brain stimulation have strengthened the conviction that the drive-reduction interpretation of reinforcement is inadequate; and, in fact, original adherents of this view have begun to abandon it (e.g., Miller, 1959).

The other most frequent solution to the circularity problem has been by way of the "empirical law of effect," an approach typified by Skinner's definition of reinforcement as any stimulus that can be demonstrated to produce a change in response strength. Skinner argues that this is not circular since some stimuli are found to produce changes and others are not, and they can subsequently be classified on that basis. This seems to be a reasonable position if it is adhered to; that is, if care is taken to define reinforcement in terms of class membership *independently* of the observations that show that learning has taken place. When we examine the actual use of the term reinforcement by Skinner (see especially *Verbal Behavior*, 1957) and by other Skinnerians (Lundin, 1961), we find that care is only taken in this regard within the context of animal experiments, but that when the jumps are made to other phenomena, such as language and psychotherapy, care is usually *not* taken to define reinforcement independently from learning as indicated by response strength. This leads to a state of affairs where any observed change in behavior is said to occur *because of* reinforcement, when, in fact, the change in behavior is itself the only indicator of what the reinforcement has been. Chomsky (1959) reviews the use of the concept of reinforcement by Skinner with regard to language and reaches the following conclusion:

From this sample, it can be seen that the notion of reinforcement has totally lost whatever objective meaning it may ever have had. Running through these examples, we see that a person can be reinforced though he emits no response at all, and the reinforcing "stimulus" need not impinge on the reinforced person or need not even exist (it is sufficient that it be imagined or hoped for). When we read that a person plays what music he likes (165), says what he likes (165), thinks what he likes (438-9), reads what books he likes (163), etc., *because* he finds it reinforcing to do so, or that we write books or inform others of facts *because* we are reinforced by what we hope will be the ultimate behavior of reader or listener, we can only conclude that the term "reinforcement" has a purely ritual function. The phrase "X is reinforced by Y (stimulus, state of affairs, event, etc.)" is being used as a cover term for "X wants Y," "X likes Y," "X wishes that Y were the case," etc. Invoking the term "reinforcement" has no explanatory force, and any idea that this paraphrase introduces any new clarity or objectivity into the description of wishing, liking, etc., is a serious delusion [pp. 37-38].

This problem is exemplified in the area of psychotherapy by the attempts to use the studies of verbal conditioning (Krasner, 1958) as analogues to psychotherapy. First we should note that if these studies are taken at face value (i.e., if subjects are conditioned to increase the emission of certain responses because of reinforcement, without their awareness of this fact) it appears that a simple conditioning model is inadequate since subjects are presumably responding in terms of a class of responses (e.g., plural nouns, etc.) rather than in terms of a specific response (e.g., bar press), such classes implying response transfer and mediation. Second, and more to the point, a number of recent investigators (Eriksen, 1962) have begun to question whether verbal conditioning does occur without the subject's awareness. If it does not, the whole phenomenon begins to look like nothing more than a rather inefficient way to get subjects to figure out what the experimenter wants them to do (telling them directly to emit plural nouns would probably be much more efficient) after which they can decide whether they want to do it or not. In any case, there seems to be enough question about what goes on in verbal conditioning itself to indicate that it cannot be utilized as a more basic explanation for complex phenomena such as psychotherapy. Psychotherapists of many persuasions would agree that rewards of some kind are important in work with patients. Thus, the view that the psychotherapist is a "reinforcement machine" is trivial. The difficult problems are in specifying just what therapist activities are rewarding, in what ways, to what sorts of patients, and with what effects.

The above discussion should make clear that the use of the concept of reinforcement is only of explanatory usefulness when it is specified in some delimited fashion. As an empirical law of performance almost everyone in and out of psychology would accept it, including Lewin, Freud, Tolman, and others outside the traditional S-R movement. But this amounts to saying nothing more than that some events, when presented, tend to increase the probability of responses that they have followed. The hard job, but the only one that will lead to any meaningful use of the concept of reinforcement, is specifying what the various events called reinforcers have in common. Some have argued that since this is such a difficult task, we should restrict ourselves to listing and cataloging so-called reinforcers. But this is nearly impossible, in a general way, because reinforcers differ from individual to individual, from species to species, from situation to situation, and from time to time (the saying "one man's meat is another man's poison" is trite but true). Meaningful analysis must stem from a comprehensive study of the particular learning phenomena in question, whether it is language learning, the development of perceptual and perceptual-motor skills (Fitts, 1964; Hebb, 1949), the acquisition of particular species behavior patterns during critical periods of development (Scott, 1962), the learning of a neurosis, or the learning that takes place during psychotherapy. Experience with all of these phenomena has revealed that different kinds of events seem to be involved and that these can only be understood in the context of the phenomena in question. Lumping all these events together under the single term reinforcement serves to muddle rather than to clarify understanding.

The staunch reinforcement adherent might respond that all these complicated arguments may be true but we can ignore them, since all we are really interested in is predicting what the organism will do, and we can do this when we know the organism's reinforcement history. The answer to this is that the experimental literature does not support such a claim; rather, it shows that, in many instances, performance *cannot* be predicted on the basis of a knowledge of the history of reinforcement.

Latent learning studies indicate this quite clearly. Perhaps of more interest are the findings of discrimination-reversal learning studies (Goodwin & Lawrence, 1955; Mackintosh, 1963). Here we find that subjects that have been trained on a series of discrimination reversals learn to select the correct stimulus with very few errors even though they may have been rewarded *much more frequently and more recently for responding to another stimulus*. Similarly, in the double drive discrimination studies (Thistlethwaite, 1951) animals chose alleys leading to food when they were hungry and water when they were thirsty, even though they have been rewarded equally frequently on the alleys on previous trials. In other words, "what is learned" was not equivalent with "reinforcement history." The law of effect is not disproved by these studies; it is merely shown to be irrelevant.

To summarize: The "law of effect," or reinforcement, conceived as a *"law of learning,"* occupies a very dubious status. Like the principles of conditioning, it appears to be an unlikely candidate as an explanatory principle of learning. As a strong law of learning it has already been rejected by many of the theorists who previously relied on it. As an empirical "law of *performance*" it is noncontroversial, but usually so generally stated as to be of little explanatory value.

CONCEPTION OF NEUROSIS

In this section we will explicate the conception of neurosis that forms the basis of the behavior-therapy approach (particularly of the Wolpe-Eysenck group) and attempt to demonstrate its inadequacies both in terms of learning theory and as a way of accounting for the observed facts of neurosis. Our argument in the first instance will be that the conception of neurosis in terms of symptoms and anxiety parallels the general conception of learning in terms of overt responses, conditioning, and secondary drives, and suffers from the same inadequacies that we have outlined in preceding section. With regard to the facts of neurosis, we will argue that the behavior-therapy position is inadequate at a descriptive level as well as being conceptually incorrect. It should be pointed out again that we are discussing the explanation or theory of neurosis here and not the techniques used by the behavior therapists. The strict Skinnerian may excuse himself at this point if he adheres to a "no-theory" position and is only concerned with the effects of environmental manipulation. Furthermore, certain techniques themselves may be useful and have some of the effects attributed to them regardless of the theory.

In its essence, the conception of neurosis put forth by the behavior therapists is that neuroses are conditioned responses or habits (including conditioned anxiety) and *nothing else*, though it should be noted that they do not adhere to this argument when they describe the success of their methods. Wolpe, for example, while ostensibly treating overt symptoms, describes his patients as becoming more productive, having improved adjustment and pleasure in sex, improved interpersonal relationships, and so forth. The argument that removal of a troublesome symptom somehow "generalizes" to all of these other areas begs the question. Their conception is typically put forth as an alternative to a psychodynamic viewpoint, which they characterize as resting on a distinction between symptoms and underlying causes (unconscious conflicts, impulses, defenses, etc.). They stress the point that inferences about underlying factors of this sort are unnecessary and misleading and that a more parsimonious explanation treats symptoms (which are typically equated with behavior or that which can be objectively observed) as the neurosis per se. They argue that by equating neurosis with symptoms, and symptoms, in turn, with habits (conditioned responses), they are able to bring "modern learning theory" with its "well-established laws" to bear on the understanding and treatment of neurosis.

As we have labored to show in the preceding section, the well-established laws of learning to which they refer have considerable difficulty within the area of simple animal behavior. More specifically, it seems clear that a wide variety of behaviors (from maze learning to more complex forms) cannot be adequately dealt with when the overt response and conditioned habit are the units of analysis. Furthermore, their learning position leads the behavior therapists into postulating an isomorphic relationship between antecedent learning and present behavior in which observed differences are accounted for in terms of principles of generalization. This is a key issue, and we shall explore it a little further at this time.

Much of the behaviorist conception of neurosis rests on a rejection of the distinction between symptoms and underlying causes (Eysenck, 1960) as typified by Yates' (1958) argument against "symptom substitution." By focusing attention on overt symptoms and banishing all underlying causes, however, the behavior therapists are faced with the same problem that has long confronted behaviorism; namely, the difficulty of explaining how *generality* of behavior results from specific learning experiences. The problem of *generality* (i.e., as exemplified by the facts of transposition and response transfer) has, in fact, brought about the downfall of peripheral S-R learning, of the conditioned habit as a basic unit, and tangentially, is leading to the dethroning of the law of effect. With regard to neurosis, this view has led the behavior therapists into the position where they must posit a specific learning experience for each symptom of a neurosis. They have partly avoided this problem by focusing their attention on those neuroses that can be described in terms of specific symptoms (bedwetting, if this is a neurosis, tics, specific phobias, etc.) and have tended to ignore those conditions which do not fit their model, such as neurotic depressions, general unhappiness, obsessional disorders, and the kinds of persistent interpersonal entanglements that characterize so many neurotics. This leaves them free to explain the specific symptom in terms of a specific learning experience, as, for example, when a fear of going outdoors is explained in terms of some previous experience in which the stimulus (outdoors) has been associated with (conditioned to) something unpleasant or painful and has now, through generalization, spread to any response of going outdoors. As our previous analysis should make clear, however, even a simple conceptualization such as this, in terms of stimuli, responses, and conditioning is extremely cumbersome and begs the important questions. Within an S-R framework, in which generalization occurs along the dimension of physical stimulus similarity, it is difficult, if not impossible, to show how a previous experience such as being frightened in the country as a child could generalize to the "stimulus" outdoors without a great deal of *mediation* in which the concept of "outdoors" carried most of the burden of generalization. As we have pointed out, most workers in the field of learning recognize this and rely heavily on mediational concepts in their explanations of complex behavior. Dollard and Miller (1950), for example, return again and again to mediational explanations once they move beyond the "combat neuroses" which lend themselves more readily to a simple isomorphic explanation.

A second important facet of the behaviorist conception of neurosis is the use of the concept of anxiety as a secondary drive. Here, Wolpe and Eysenck and some others seem to follow the explanatory model laid down by Dollard and Miller. Anxiety is viewed as the main motivating force for symptoms and, in general, occupies a central place in their thinking. Briefly, it is worth pointing out that the concept of drive reduction, the distinction between primary drives and secondary drives, as well as the early thinking about the uniquely persistent qualities of fear-motivated behavior have had serious difficulty within learning theory (Watson, 1961; Solomon, 1964). The use of these concepts to explain clinical phenomena thus rests on an exceedingly shaky foundation.

Let us turn our attention now to the phenomena of neuroses. We shall try to point out that underlying the dispute over symptoms versus underlying causes is a real difference in definition that arises at the descriptive level, which, in a sense, antedates disagreements at the level of theory and explanation.

To keep the presentation simple, we will adopt the terms psychodynamic to refer to all those theorists and therapists, following Freud, whose view of neurosis and its treatment deals with motives (conscious and unconscious), conflict, etc. This covers a wide variety of workers, in addition to the more or less traditional followers of Freud, including Sullivan and his adherents (Fromm-Reichman, 1950), other neo-Freudians, and that broad group of psychiatrists and clinical psychologists who have been strongly influenced by the Freudian and neo-Freudian viewpoints even though they may not claim allegiance to any of the formal schools.

The point we wish to make here is that disagreement between the behaviorist and psychodynamic viewpoints seems to rest on a very real difference at the purely descriptive or observational level. The behaviorist looks at a neurotic and sees specific symptoms and anxiety. The psychodynamicist looks at the same individual and sees a complex intra- and interpersonal mode of functioning which may or may not contain certain observable fears* or certain behavioral symptoms such as compulsive motor acts. When the psychodynamicist describes a neurosis, his referent is a cohering component of the individual's functioning, including his characteristic ways of interacting with other people (e.g., sweet and self-effacing on the surface but hostile in covert ways), his characteristic modes of thinking and perceiving (e.g., the hysteric who never "remembers" anything unpleasant, the obsessive whose memories are overelaborated and circumstantial, etc.), characteristic modes of fantasy and dreaming, a variety of secondary gain features, and the like. Specific or isolatable symptoms may sometimes be a part of such an integrated neurotic pattern, but, even viewed descriptively, they in no sense constitute the neurosis per se.

So far, we have considered the behavior therapists' position at face value. In actuality, a good case can be made that they *behave* in a way which is quite inconsistent with their own

---

* The term anxiety is frequently used as a theoretical inference, i.e., a patient deals with personal material in an overly intellectual fashion, and this is described as a defense mechanism—intellectualization—whose purpose is to ward off anxiety.

position. A specific example, taken from one of Wolpe's own case descriptions, will illustrate this point, and, at the same time, show what the psychodynamicist sees when he looks at a neurotic. Wolpe (1960) presents the following case:

Case 5—An attractive woman of 28 came for treatment because she was in acute distress as a result of her lovers' casual treatment of her. Every one of very numerous love affairs had followed a similar pattern—first she would attract the man, then she would offer herself on a platter. He would soon treat her with contempt and after a time leave her. In general she lacked assurance, was very dependent, and was practically never free from feelings of tension and anxiety.

What is described here is a complex pattern of interpersonal relationships, psychological strategies and misunderstandings (such as the way she became involved with men, the way she communicated her availability to them, her dependency, etc.), expectations that she had (presumably that men would not react with contempt to her generosity, that being dependent might lead to being taken care of, etc.), and thoughts and feelings about herself (lack of assurance, acute distress, etc.). Many of the statements about her (e.g., the description of the course of her love affairs) are abbreviations for very complex and involved processes involving two people interacting over a period of time. It is this, the psychodynamicist would argue, that *is* the neurosis. The tension and anxiety may be a part of it in this particular case (though there might be other cases in which there is no complaint of anxiety but, rather, its reverse—seeming inability to "feel" anything) —but it is secondary and can be understood only in relation to the other aspects of the patient's functioning. Wolpe's case histories are classic testaments to the fact that he cannot, and does not, apply the symptom approach when working with actual data. As a further example, consider the argument against a symptom-substitution point of view (Yates, 1958) in which it is implied

that anything other than symptoms is some sort of metaphysical inference. While it may be true that theories such as psychoanalysis deal with a number of inferential and higher-order constructs in their attempts to integrate the complex mass of data that constitutes a neurosis, it is also true that much more than symptoms exist at the level of observation. Secondary-gain features of a neurosis, in which it is apparent that a variety of goals may be served by a set of interchangeable symptoms are the rule in most neurotic individuals. We are not defending the view (attributed to psychoanalysis by Yates) that if one symptom is removed another pops up to take its place; rather, we are arguing that the empirical phenomena of neurosis does not fit the symptom or response theory, but is much more compatible with a theory built around central mediators. Whether unconscious conflicts and defense mechanisms are adequate ways of conceptualizing the problem is an entirely separate question. What is clear is that a view stressing central mediators in which specific responses are seen as equipotential means of reaching certain goals is necessary to encompass the data of neurosis just as it has proven necessary to encompass the phenomena of animal learning.

To sum up, it would seem that the behaviorists have reached a position where an inadequate conceptual framework forces them to adopt an inadequate and superficial view of the very data that they are concerned with. They are then forced to slip many of the key facts in the back door, so to speak, for example, when all sorts of fantasy, imaginary, and thought processes are blithely called responses. This process is, of course, parallel to what has gone on within S-R learning theory where all sorts of central and mediational processes have been cumbersomely handled with S-R terminology (e.g., Deutsch, 1956). Thus, we have a situation where the behavior therapists argue strongly against a dynamic interpretation of neurosis at some points and at other points behave as if they had adopted such a point of view. This inconsistency should be kept in mind in reading the next section in which we evaluate the claims of success put forth by the behaviorist group. Insofar as there is disagreement as to what constitutes the descriptive facts of neurosis, it makes little sense to compare the effectiveness of different methods. However, since the behaviorist group adopts very broad (or psychodynamic, if you will) criteria for improvement, and since their *techniques* may have some effectiveness, in spite of theoretical and conceptual inadequacies, it is crucial that we look carefully at the empirical results that they lay claim to.

CLAIMS OF SUCCESS

While much of the writing of the behavior therapists consists of arguments and appeals to principles of science and learning, the claims that are made for the success of the methods seem open to empirical analysis. No doubt a great deal of the appeal of behavior therapy lies right here. Here seem to be methods whose application can be clearly described (unlike such messy psychodynamic methods as "handling countertransference" or "interpreting resistance"), whose course is relatively short, and which seem to achieve a large number of practical results in the form of removal of symptoms. Wolpe (1960), for example, presents the following data: of 122 cases treated with behavioral techniques, 44% were "apparently cured," 46% were "much improved," 7% were "slightly or moderately improved," and 3% were "unimproved." Combining categories, he claims 90% "apparently cured or much improved," and 10% "improvement moderate, slight or nil." (Criteria of improvement consists of "symptomatic improvement, increased productiveness, improved adjustment and pleasure in sex, improved interpersonal relationships and ability to handle ordinary

psychological conflicts and reasonable reality stresses.")

He compares this with data from the Berlin Psychoanalytic Institute (Knight, 1941) which shows 62—40.5% in the first category and 38—59.5% in the second. Wolpe concludes, as have others (Bandura, 1961; Eysenck, 1960; Lazarus, 1963), that this demonstrates the superiority of the behavior therapy methods. The fact that the psychoanalytic method showed as much as 62% improvement is explained as being due to whatever accidental "reciprocal inhibition" occurred during the therapy. (There is, however, no analysis or description of how this might have happened.) The behavioral methods achieve superior results presumably because of the more explicit application of these techniques.

It is fair to say that if these results can be substantiated they present a very strong argument in favor of behavioral *techniques*—even granting the theoretical and empirical inconsistencies we have discussed. However, we must ask if these claims are any better substantiated than those made by the practitioners of other methods of psychotherapy. Insofar as claims such as Wolpe's are based on uncontrolled case histories, they may reflect the enthusiasm of the practitioner as much as the effect of the method. History shows that new methods of therapy (ECS, tranquilizing drugs, as well as various schools of psychotherapy) have been oversold by their original proponents. Thus, a careful look at what lies behind the claims of the behavior-therapy group is in order.

The following does not purport to be a comprehensive review of the behavior-therapy literature. Rather, it is based on a survey of all the studies reported in the two reviews that have appeared (Bandura, 1961; Grossberg, 1964). The most striking thing about this large body of studies is that they are almost all case studies. A careful reading of the original sources reveals that only one study (Lang & Lazovik, 1963) is a controlled experiment, and here the subjects were not neurotics but normal college students. Thus, most of the claims (including those of Wolpe which have been widely quoted) must be regarded as no better substantiated than those of any other enthusiastic school of psychotherapy whose practitioners claim that their patients get better. Behavior therapy has appeared to differ on this score because of its identification with experimental psychology and with "well-established laws of learning." We have already dealt with this issue, so let us now turn to some problems in evaluating psychotherapy as a technique.

The problems here are essentially those of control, and they may be broken down into three areas: (a) sampling biases, (b) observer bias, and (c) problems of experimental control. While research in psychotherapy presents particular difficulties in controlling "experimental input," more sophisticated workers (Frank, 1959) have attempted to deal with at least the sampling and observer problems. It thus comes as somewhat of a surprise that the behavior-therapy workers, despite their identification with experimental psychology, base their claims on evidence which is almost totally lacking in any form of control. Let us examine these issues in greater detail.

Sampling biases. Obviously a claim such as Wolpe's of 90% success has meaning only when we know the population from which the sample of patients was drawn and the way in which they were selected. Ideally, a comparison of treatment techniques would involve the random assignment of patient from a common population pool to alternative treatments. Since, in practice, this is rarely feasible, it is essential for anyone making comparisons of different treatment methods to, at the very least, examine the comparability of the populations *and* of the methods used in selecting from these populations. Neither Wolpe's data nor that of Lazarus (1963) con-

tains this evidence. Wolpe reports, for example, that:

Both series (70 patients reported on in 1952 and 52 patients reported on in 1954 on which the 90% figure is based) include only patients whose treatment has ceased after they have been afforded a reasonable opportunity for the application of the available methods; i.e., they have had as a minimum both a course of instruction on the changing of behavior in the life situation and a proper initiation of a course of relaxation-desensitization. This minimum takes up to about 15 interviews, including anamestic interviews and *no patient who has had 15 or more interviews has been omitted from the series* [emphasis added].

We may conclude from this that some patients (how many we do not know) having up to 14 interviews have been excluded from the sample—a procedure highly favorable to the success of the method but which violates the simplest canons of sampling. Wolpe's final sample of 122 consists of those patients most likely to show improvement, since both they and he were satisfied enough with the first 14 (or less) interviews to warrant proceeding further. Those patients least likely to improve are those most likely to drop out early (14 sessions or less) and not be included in the computation of success rate. The fact that a large number of poor-prognosis patients would very likely be eliminated during these early sessions is supported by a variety of research findings (Strickland & Crowne, 1963), which show that most dropping-out of untreatable or unsuccessful cases occurs during the first 10 sessions. This serious sampling bias would be expected to spuriously inflate the percent showing improvement.

When we add this to whatever unknown factors operate to delimit the original population (presumably there is some self-selection of patients who seek out this form of treatment), it becomes apparent that little confidence can be given to the reports of success.

Observer bias. Psychologists have long been aware that human beings are fallible observers, particularly when they have predispositions or vested interests to protect. In controlled studies, we try to protect judges from their own biases by not acquainting them with the hypotheses, or with the nature of the groups they are judging, or by using blind and double-blind designs. This problem is particularly acute with regard to psychotherapy because both therapist and patient have investments of time, involvement, competence, and reputation to protect. For these reasons, workers in the area have become extremely skeptical of claims put forth for any method which rests on the uncontrolled observation of the person administering the treatment. At a minimum we expect some sort of external evidence. Beyond this minimum we hope for an independent judge who can compare differentially treated groups without knowing which is which.

In addition, there is the problem of the patient's freedom to report effects which may be seriously curtailed when all his reports go directly to the person who has treated him. It seems reasonable to assume that some patients are prevented from expressing dissatisfaction with treatment when they must report directly to the therapist, either because they do not want to hurt his feelings, or are afraid, or are just saying what they think is being demanded of them, or are being polite, or for some other reason. Again, it would be highly appropriate to provide the patients with the opportunity of reporting results in a situation as free from such pressure as possible.

Examination of the 26 studies reviewed by Bandura reveals a surprising lack of concern with these problems. Of the 26 studies sampled, only 12 report evaluation of results by persons other than the treating therapist; four of these use ratings of the hospital staff (who may be acquainted with the treatment), four use mothers or parents reporting on their children to the treating therapist, one is a wife reporting on her husband to the therapist, and three use a second

observer. Obviously, whatever factors enter in to cause observer and reporter biases are allowed full reign in most of these cases. While we cannot conclude from this that the reported results are *due to* observer and reporter biases (as is clearly indicated with the sampling biases), it is impossible to rule them out. Furthermore, a great deal of evidence from many areas of psychology leads us to be very skeptical of claims in which biases of this sort go uncontrolled.

Experimental control. While control of sampling and observer effects are basic to a wide variety of research activities, including field and clinical research, more exacting control over experimental conditions has long been the sine qua non of the laboratory methods of experimental psychology. The power of the experimental method stems, in part, from keeping careful control over all but a few conditions, which are experimentally varied, with the subsequent effects of these variations being observed. Since psychotherapy is not a controlled experiment, it is probably unfair to expect this type of control. However, there are more and less accurate descriptions of what goes on during any form of therapy, and we can demand as accurate a description as possible in lieu of experimental control. Thus, while we are led to believe that methods, such as counterconditioning, extinction of maladaptive responses, methods of reward, and the like, are applied in a manner analogous to their laboratory counterparts—examination of what is *actually done* reveals that the application of the learning techniques is embedded in a wide variety of activities (including many of the traditional therapy and interview techniques) which make any attribution of effect to the specific learning techniques impossible. Let us consider a few examples. From Wolpe (1960):

Case 4—The patient had 65 therapeutic interviews, unevenly distributed over 27 months. The greater part of the time was devoted to discussions of how to gain control of her interpersonal relationships and stand up for herself. She had considerable difficulty with this at first, even though it had early become emotionally important to her to please the therapist. But she gradually mastered the assertive behavior required of her, overcame her anxieties and became exceedingly self-reliant in all interpersonal dealings, including those with her mother-in-law.

From Lazarus and Rachman (1957) on systematic desensitization:

Case 1—The patient was instructed in the use of assertive responses and deep (non-hypnotic) relaxation. The first anxiety hierarchy dealt with was that of dull weather. Starting from "a bright sunny day" it was possible for the subject to visualize "damp overcast weather" without anxiety after 21 desensitization sessions, and 10 days after the completion of this hierarchy, she was able to report that, "the weather is much better, it doesn't even bother me to look at the weather when I wake up in the morning" (previously depressing). . . . During the course of therapy, part of the reason for the development of the anxiety state in this patient was unearthed. When she was 17 years old she had become involved in a love affair with a married man 12 years her senior. This affair had been conducted in an extremely discreet manner for 4 years, during which time she had suffered from recurrent guilt feelings and shame—so much so, that on one occasion she had attempted suicide by throwing herself into a river. It was her custom to meet her lover after work *in the late afternoon*. The dull weather can be accounted for, as this affair took place in London.

From Rachman (1959):

Interview No. 12. The patient having received a jolt in her love relationship, this session was restricted to a sort of nondirective, cathartic discussion. No desensitizing was undertaken because of A.G.'s depressed mood and obvious desire to "just talk."

These excerpts have been presented because they seem representative of the practices of the behavioral therapists. As can be seen, the number and variety of activities that go on during these treatment sessions is great, including, in these few examples, discussions, explanations of techniques and principles, explanations of the unadaptiveness of anxiety and symptoms, hypnosis of various sorts, relaxation practice and training with and without hypnosis, "nondirective cathartic discussions," "obtain-

ing an understanding of the patient's personality and background," and the "unearthing" of a 17-year-old memory of an illicit affair. The case reports are brief and presented anecdotally so that it is really impossible to know what else went on in addition to those things described. What should be abundantly clear from these examples is that there is no attempt to restrict what goes on to learning techniques. Since it seems clear that a great variety of things do go on, any attribution of behavior change to specific learning techniques is entirely unwarranted.

In summary, there are several important issues that must be differentiated. First, a review of both learning theory and of the empirical results of behavior therapy demonstrates that they can claim no special scientific status· for their work on either ground. Second, there are important differences of opinion concerning the type of patient likely to be affected by behavior therapy. Grossberg (1964), for example, states that: "Behavior therapies have been most successful when applied to neurotic disorders with specific behavioral manifestations [p. 81]." He goes on to point out that the results with alcoholism and sexual disorders have been disappointing and that the best results are achieved with phobias and enuresis. He later states that "desensitization only alleviates those phobias that are being treated, but other coexisting phobias remain at high strength, indicating a specific treatment effect [p. 83]." Wolpe et al. (1964), on the other hand, argue that: "The conditioning therapist differs from his colleagues in that he *seeks out* the precise stimuli to anxiety, and finds himself able to break down almost every neurosis into what are essentially *phobic systems* [p. 11]." The best controlled study (Lang & Lazovik, 1963) indicates that "desensitization is very effective in reducing the intense fear of snakes held by normal subjects, though it can be questioned whether this is a phobia in the clinical sense."

Thus, there seems to be some evidence that these *techniques* (as techniques and not as learning theory) are effective with certain conditions.* We feel that this bears stressing because psychotherapy has come to be narrowly defined in terms of dynamic, evocative, and nondirective methods, placing unnecessary limitations on the kind of patient suitable for psychotherapy. First, we must note that behavior techniques are not new (as Murray, 1964, points out in a recent article). Freud and Breuer used similar techniques prior to the development of psychoanalysis, Bagby described a number of these methods in 1928, and therapy based on techniques designed to eliminate undesirable responses was used for many years by Stevenson Smith at the University of Washington Clinic. While most of these techniques have been superseded by the various forms of dynamic psychotherapy, recent work (Frank, 1961) suggests that the time may be ripe for taking a fresh look at a variety of methods such as hypnosis, suggestion, relaxation, and other approaches of a more *structured nature* in which the therapist takes a *more active role*. Needless to say, this fresh look would best proceed unencumbered by an inadequate learning theory and with some minimal concern for control. As an example of a nondynamic approach to patient management, we refer to the work of Fairweather (1964) and his colleagues.

REFORMULATION

Up to this point our analysis has been primarily critical. We have tried to show that many of the so-called principles of learning employed by

* Just how many neurotics fit the phobia and/or specific symptom model is a complicated question, the answer to which depends in part on what one's own point of view leads one to look for. For example, an informal census of the first 81 admissions to the University of Oregon Psychology Clinic in 1964 revealed only 2 patients who could be so classified.

workers with a behaviorist orientation are inadequate and are not likely to provide useful explanations for clinical phenomena. In this section we will examine the potential value of ideas from different learning conceptions. Before proceeding, however, we would like to discuss briefly the issue of the application of "laws," principles, and findings from one area (such as animal experimentation) to another (such as neurosis and psychotherapy). The behaviorists have traditionally assumed that principles established under highly controlled conditions, usually with animal subjects, form a scientific foundation for a psychology of learning. Yet when they come to apply these principles to human learning situations, the transition is typically bridged by rather flimsy analogies which ignore crucial differences between the situations, the species, etc. Recently, Underwood (1964) has made the following comments concerning this problem:

Learning theories as developed in the animal-learning laboratory, have never seemed . . . to have relevance to the behavior of a subject in learning a list of paired associates. The emphasis upon the role of a pellet of food or a sip of water in the white rat's acquiring a response somehow never seemed to make contact with the human S learning to say VXK when the stimulus DOF was presented [p. 74].

We would add that the relevance is at least equally obscure in applications of traditional S-R reinforcement theory to clinical phenomena.

We do *not* wish, however, to damn any and all attempts to conceptualize clinical phenomena in terms of principles of learning developed outside the clinic. On the contrary, recent work in learning may suggest certain theoretical models which may prove useful in conceptualizing the learning processes involved in psychotherapy and the development of neuroses. Whether these notions can form the basis for a useful learning conceptualization of clinical phenomena will depend upon the ingenuity with which they are subsequently developed and upon their adequacy in encompassing the facts of neurosis and psychotherapy. Further, we would like to stress that their association with experimental work in the field of learning does not give them any a priori scientific status. Their status as explanatory principles in the clinical area must be empirically established within that area. In what follows, then, we will outline some ideas about learning and make some suggestions concerning their relevance to clinical problems.

Our view of learning centers around the concepts of information storage and retrieval. Learning is viewed as the process by which information about the environment is acquired, stored, and categorized. This cognitive view is, of course, quite contrary to the view that learning consists of the acquisition of specific responses; responses, according to our view, are mediated by the nature of the stored information, which may consist of facts or of strategies or programs analogous to the grammar that is acquired in the learning of a language. Thus, "what is learned" may be a system for generating responses as a consequence of the specific information that is stored. This general point of view has been emphasized by Lashley (see Beach et al., 1960), by Miller, Galenter, and Pribram (1960), in the form of the TOTE hypothesis, and by a number of workers in the cognitive learning tradition (Tolman, 1951; Woodworth, 1958). Recently it has even been suggested as a necessary formulation for dealing with that eminently S-R area, motor skills (Adams, 1964; Fitts, 1964).

This conception of learning may be useful in the clinical area in two ways: one, in formulating a theoretical explanation for the acquisition or development of neurosis, symptoms, behavior pathology, and the like, and, two, in conceptualizing psychotherapy as a learning process, and suggesting new methods stemming from this learning model.

A conceptualization of the problem of neurosis in terms of informa-tion storage and retrieval is based on the fundamental idea that what is learned in a neurosis is a set of central strategies (or a program) which guide the individual's adaptation to his environment. Neuroses are not symptoms (responses) but are strategies of a particular kind which lead to certain observable (tics, compulsive acts, etc.) and certain other less observable, phenomena (fears, feelings of depression, etc.). The whole problem of symptom substitution is thus seen as an instance of response substitution or response equipotentiality, concepts which are supported by abundant laboratory evidence.

Similarly, the problem of a learning conceptualization of unconscious phenomena may be reopened. Traditional S-R approaches have equated the unconscious with some kind of avoidance of a verbalization response. From our point of view, there is no reason to assume that people can give accurate descriptions of the central strategies mediating much of their behavior any more than a child can give a description of the grammatical rules which govern the understanding and production of his language. As a matter of fact, consciousness may very well be a special or extraordinary case—the rule being "unawareness" of the mediating strategies—which is in need of special explanation, rather than the reverse. This view avoids the cumbersome necessity of having to postulate specific fear experiences or the persistence of anxiety-motivated behavior, as has typically been done by S-R theorists with regard to unconscious phenomena. It also avoids equating the unconscious with the neurotic, which is a virtue since there is so much that goes on within "normal" individuals that they are unaware of. It further avoids the trap of attributing especially persistent and maladaptive consequences to painful experiences. As Solomon (1964) points out, the existing evidence does not support the view that punishment and pain lead unequivocally to anxiety and maladaptive consequences.

The view of learning we have outlined does not supply a set of ready-made answers to clinical problems that can be applied from the laboratory, but it indicates what sort of questions will have to be answered to achieve a meaningful learning conceptualization of neurosis and symptoms. Questions such as "What are the conditions under which strategies are acquired or developed?" stress the fact that these conditions may be quite different from the final observed behavior. That is to say, a particular symptom is not necessarily acquired because of some learning experience in which its stimulus components were associated with pain or fear-producing stimuli. Rather, a symptom may function as an equipotential response, mediated by a central strategy acquired under different circumstances. As an example, consider Harlow's (1958, 1962) monkeys who developed a number of symptoms, the most striking being sexual impotence (a much better animal analogue of human neurosis than those typically cited as experimental neuroses [Liddell, 1944]). Their longitudinal record, or "learning history," indicates that the development of this abnormal "affectional system," as Harlow terms it, is dependent on a variety of nonisomorphic experiences, including the lack of a mother-infant relationship and the lack of a variety of peer-play experiences.

These brief examples are only meant to give a flavor of where a learning conception of neurosis which stresses the acquisition of strategies will lead. A chief advantage of this view is that it has *generality* built in at the core, rather than imported secondarily, as is the case with S-R concepts of stimulus and response generalization.

Let us now turn our attention to the very difficult problem of applying learning concepts to psychotherapy. Basically, we would argue that the development of methods and techniques is largely ⁻a function of the empirical skill and ingenuity of the individual-craftsman-therapist. Even a carefully worked-out and well-established set of learning principles (which we do not have at this time) would not necessarily tell us how to modify acquired strategies in the individual case—just as the generally agreed-upon idea that rewards affect performance does not tell us what will be an effective reward in any specific instance.

Bearing these cautions in mind, we might still address ourselves to the question of what applications are suggested by the learning approach we have presented. As a first suggestion, we might consider the analogy of learning a new language. Here we see a process that parallels psychotherapy insofar as it involves modifying or developing a new set of strategies of a pervasive nature. A careful study of the most effective techniques for the learning of a new language might yield some interesting suggestions for psychotherapy. Learning a new language involves the development of a new set of strategies for responding —new syntax as well as new vocabulary. Language learning *may or may not* be facilitated by an intensive attempt to make the individual *aware* of the strategies used, as is done in traditional language instruction which teaches old-fashioned grammar, and as is done, analogously, in those psychotherapies which stress insight. Alternatively, language learning sometimes seems most rapid when the individual is immersed in surroundings (such as foreign country) where he hears nothing but the new language and where his old strategies and responses are totally ineffective.

Using this as a model for psychotherapy, we might suggest something like the following process: First, a careful study should be done to delineate the "neurotic language," both its vocabulary and its grammar, of the individual. Then a situation might be constructed (e.g., a group therapy situation) in which the individual's existing neurotic language is not understood and in which the individual must develop a new "language," a new set of central strategies, in order to be understood. The detailed working out of such a procedure might very well utilize a number of the techniques that have been found effective in existing therapies, both group and individual, and in addition draw on some new techniques from the fields of psycholinguistics and language learning.

These are, of course, but initial fragmentary guesses, and they may be wrong ones. But we believe that the conceptions on which these guesses are based are sufficiently supported by recent learning research to warrant serious attention. Although this reconceptualization may not lead immediately to the development of effective psychotherapeutic techniques, it may at least provide a first step in that direction.

References

Adams, J. A. Motor skills. In P. R. Farnsworth (Ed.), *Annual Review of Psychology*, 1964, *15*, 181-202.

Bagby, E. *The psychology of personality.* New York: Holt, 1928.

Bandura, A. Psychotherapy as a learning process. *Psychological Bulletin*, 1961, *58*, 143-159.

Beach, F. A., Hebb, D. O., Morgan, C. T., and Nissen, H. *The neuropsychology of Lashley.* New York: McGraw-Hill, 1960.

Berlyne, D. E. *Conflict, arousal, and curiosity.* New York: McGraw-Hill, 1960.

Blodgett, H. C. The effect of introduction of reward upon the maze performance of rats. *University of California Publications in Psychology*, 1929, *4*, 113-134.

Breland, K., and Breland, M. The misbehavior of organisms. *American Psychologist*, 1961, *16*, 681-684.

Brogden, W. J. Sensory preconditioning. *Journal of Experimental Psychology*, 1939, *25*, 323-332.

Bugelski, B. R. *The psychology of learning.* New York: Holt, 1956.

Chomsky, N. Review of B. F. Skinner, *Verbal behavior. Language*, 1959, *35*, 26-58.

Deutsch, J. A. The inadequacy of Hullian derivations of reasoning and latent learning. *Psychological Review*, 1956, *63*, 389-399.

Dollard, J., and Miller, N. E. *Personality and psychotherapy.* New York: McGraw-Hill, 1950.

Eriksen, C. W. (Ed.) *Behavior and awareness.* Durham, N. C.: Duke Univer. Press, 1962.

Eysenck, H. J. (Ed.) *Behaviour therapy and the neuroses.* New York: Pergamon Press, 1960.

Fairweather, G. W. *Social psychology in treating mental illness: An experimental approach.* New York: Wiley, 1964.

Ferster, C. B., and Skinner, B. F. *Schedules of reinforcement.* New York: Appleton-Century-Crofts, 1957.

Fitts, P. M. Perceptual-motor skill learning. In A. W. Melton (Ed.), *Categories of human learning.* New York: Academic Press, 1964. Pp. 244-285.

Frank, J. D. Problems of controls in psychotherapy as exemplified by the psychotherapy research project of the Phipps Psychiatric Clinic. In E. A. Rubenstein and M. B. Parloff (Eds.), *Research in psychotherapy.* Washington, D. C.: American Psychological Association, 1959.

Frank, J. D. *Persuasion and healing: A comparative study of psychotherapy.* Baltimore: Johns Hopkins Press, 1961.

Fromm-Reichmann, Frieda. *Principles of intensive psychotherapy.* Chicago: Univer. Chicago Press, 1950.

Gibson, J. J. *The perception of the visual world.* Boston: Houghton Mifflin, 1950.

Gonzales, R. C., and Diamond, L. A test of Spence's theory of incentive motivation. *American Journal of Psychology*, 1960, *73*, 396-403.

Goodwin, W. R., and Lawrence, D. H. The functional independence of two discrimination habits associated with a constant stimulus situation. *Journal of Comparative and Physiological Psychology*, 1955, *48*, 437-443.

Grossberg, J. M. Behavior therapy: A review. *Psychological Bulletin*, 1964, *62*, 73-88.

Guthrie, E. R. *The psychology of learning.* New York: Harper, 1935.

Guttman, N. Laws of behavior and facts of perception. In S. Koch (Ed.), *Psychology: A study of a science.* Vol. 5. New York: McGraw-Hill, 1963. Pp. 114-179.

Harlow, H. F. The nature of love. *American Psychologist*, 1958, *13*, 673-685.

Harlow, H. F. The heterosexual affectional system in monkeys. *American Psychologist*, 1962, *17*, 1-9.

Hebb, D. O. *The organization of behavior: A neurophysiological theory.* New York: Wiley, 1949.

Herbert, M. J., and Harsh, C. M. Observational learning by cats. *Journal of Comparative Psychology*, 1944, *37*, 81-95.

Hilgard, E. R. *Theories of learning.* New York: Appleton-Century-Crofts, 1956.

Hull, C. L. *Essentials of behavior.* New Haven: Yale Univer. Press, 1951.

Knight, R. P. Evaluation of the results of psychoanalytic therapy. *American Journal of Psychiatry*, 1941, *98*, 434.

Kohler, W. *Gestalt psychology.* New York: Liveright, 1929.

Krasner, L. Studies of the conditioning of verbal behavior. *Psychological Bulletin*, 1958, *55*, 148-170.

Krasner, L. The therapist as a social reinforcement machine. In H. H. Strupp (Ed.), *Second research conference on psychotherapy.* Chapel Hill, N. C.: American Psychological Association, 1961.

Krechevsky, I. The genesis of "hypotheses" in rats. *University of California Publications in Psychology*, 1932, *6*, 45-64.

Lang, P. J., and Lazovik, A. D. Experimental desensitization of a phobia. *Journal of Abnormal and Social Psychology*, 1963, *66*, 519-525.

Lawrence, D. H. The nature of a stimulus: Some relationships between learning and perception. In S. Koch (Ed.), *Psychology: A study of a science.* Vol. 5. New York: McGraw-Hill, 1963. Pp. 179-212.

Lawrence, D. H., and DeRivera, J. Evidence for relational transposition. *Journal of Comparative and Physiological Psychology*, 1954, *47*, 465-471.

Lazarus, A. A. The results of behaviour therapy in 126 cases of severe neurosis. *Behaviour Research and Therapy*, 1963, *1*, 69-80.

Lazarus, A. A., and Rachman, S. The use of systematic desensitization in psychotherapy. *South African Medical Journal*, 1957, *32*, 934-937.

Leeper, R. L. Learning and the fields of perception, motivation, and personality. In S. Koch (Ed.), *Psychology: A study of a science.* Vol. 5. New York: McGraw-Hill, 1963. Pp. 365-487.

Lewin, K. *Field theory in social science.* New York: Harper, 1951. Ch. 4, pp. 60-86.

Liddell, H. S. Conditioned reflex method and experimental neurosis. In J. McV. Hunt (Ed.), *Personality and the behavior disorders.* New York: Ronald Press, 1944. Ch. 12.

Lundin, R. W. *Personality: An experimental approach.* New York: MacMillan, 1961.

Mackintosh, N. J. Extinction of a discrimination habit as a function of overtraining. *Journal of Comparative and Physiological Psychology*, 1963, *56*, 842-847.

Miller, G. A., Galanter, E. H., and Pribram, K. H. *Plans and the structure of behavior.* New York: Holt, Rinehart, & Winston, 1960.

Miller, N. E. Liberalization of basic S-R concepts: Extension to conflict behavior, motivation, and social learning. In S. Koch (Ed.), *Psychology: A study of a science.* Vol. 2. New York: McGraw-Hill, 1959. Pp. 196-292.

Moltz, H. Imprinting, empirical basis, and theoretical significance. *Psychological Bulletin*, 1960, *57*, 291-314.

Murray, E. J. Sociotropic learning approach to psychotherapy. In P. Worchel and D. Byrne (Eds.), *Personality change.* New York: Wiley, 1964. Pp. 249-288.

Olds, J., and Milner, P. Positive reinforcement produced by electrical stimulation of septal area and other regions of rat brain. *Journal of Comparative and Physiological Psychology*, 1954, *47*, 419-427.

Osgood, C. E. *Method and theory in experimental psychology.* New York: Oxford Univer. Press, 1953.

Postman, L. Perception and learning. In S. Koch (Ed.), *Psychology: A study of a science.* Vol. 5. New York: McGraw-Hill, 1963. Pp. 30-113.

Rachman, S. The treatment of anxiety and phobic reactions by systematic desensitization psychotherapy. *Journal of Abnormal and Social Psychology*, 1959, *58*, 259-263.

Riley, D. A. The nature of the effective stimulus in animal discrimination learning: Transposition reconsidered. *Psychological Review*, 1958, *65*, 1-7.

Ritchie, B. F., Aeschliman, B., and Peirce, P. Studies in spatial learning. VIII. Place performance and the acquisition of place dispositions. *Journal of Comparative and Physiological Psychology*, 1950, *43*, 73-85.

Rotter, J. B. *Social learning and clinical psychology.* New York: Prentice-Hall, 1954.

Scott, J. P. Critical periods in behavioral development. *Science*, 1962, *138*, 949-958.

Skinner, B. F. *The behavior of organisms: An experimental analysis.* New York: Appleton-Century-Crofts, 1938.

Skinner, B. F. *Verbal behavior.* New York: Appleton-Century-Crofts, 1957.

Solomon, R. L. Punishment. *American Psychologist*, 1964, *19*, 239-253.

Spence, K. W. The differential response in animals to stimuli varying within a single dimension. *Psychological Review*, 1937, *44*, 430-440.

Strickland, Bonnie R., and Crowne, D. P. The need for approval and the premature termination of psychotherapy. *Journal of Consulting Psychology*, 1963, *27*, 95-101.

Thistlethwaite, D. A critical review of latent learning and related experiments. *Psychological Bulletin*, 1951, *48*, 97-129.

Tolman, E. C. *Purposive behavior in animals and men.* New York: Appleton-Century, 1932.

Tolman, E. C. Sign gestalt or conditioned reflex? *Psychological Review*, 1933, *40*, 391-411.

Tolman, E. C. *Collected papers in psychology.* Berkeley: Univer. California Press, 1951.

Tolman, E. C., and Honzik, C. H. Introduction and removal of reward and maze performance in rats. *University of California Publications in Psychology*, 1930, *4*, 257-275.

Underwood, B. J. The representativeness of rote verbal learning. In A. W. Melton (Ed.), *Categories of human learning.* New York: Academic Press, 1964. Pp. 47-78.

Watson, A. J. The place of reinforcement in the explanation of behavior. In W. H. Thorpe and O. L. Zangwill, *Current problems in animal behavior.* Cambridge: Cambridge Univer. Press, 1961.

Wolpe, J. *Psychotherapy by reciprocal inhibition.* Palo Alto: Stanford Univer. Press, 1958.

Wolpe, J. Reciprocal inhibition as the main basis of psychotherapeutic effects. In H. J. Eysenck (Ed.), *Behaviour therapy and the neuroses.* New York: Pergamon Press, 1960. Pp. 88-113.

Wolpe, J., Salter, A., and Reyna, L. J. (Eds.) *The conditioning therapies.* New York: Holt, Rinehart, & Winston, 1964.

Woodworth, R. S. *Dynamics of behavior.* New York: Holt, 1958.

Yates, A. J. Symptoms and symptom substitution. *Psychological Review,* 1958, *65,* 371-374.

Zener, K. The significance of behavior accompanying conditioned salivary secretion for theories of the conditioned response. *American Journal of Psychology,* 1937, *50,* 384-403.